Law, Governance and Technology Series

Volume 39

The *Law-Governance and Technology Series* is intended to attract manuscripts arising from an interdisciplinary approach in law, artificial intelligence and information technologies. The idea is to bridge the gap between research in IT law and IT applications for lawyers developing a unifying techno-legal perspective. The series will welcome proposals that have a fairly specific focus on problems or projects that will lead to innovative research charting the course for new interdisciplinary developments in law, legal theory, and law and society research as well as in computer technologies, artificial intelligence and cognitive sciences. In broad strokes, manuscripts for this series may be mainly located in the fields of the Internet law (data protection, intellectual property, Internet rights, etc.), Computational models of the legal contents and legal reasoning, Legal Information Retrieval, Electronic Data Discovery, CollaborativeTools (e.g. Online Dispute Resolution platforms), Metadata and XML Technologies (for Semantic Web Services), Technologies in Courtrooms and Judicial Offices (E-Court), Technologies for Governments and Administrations (E-Government), Legal Multimedia, and Legal Electronic Institutions (Multi-Agent Systems and Artificial Societies).

More information about this series at http://www.springer.com/series/8808

Maria Angela Biasiotti •
Jeanne Pia Mifsud Bonnici • Joe Cannataci •
Fabrizio Turchi
Editors

Handling and Exchanging Electronic Evidence Across Europe

Springer

Editors
Maria Angela Biasiotti
ITTIG-Institute of Legal Information Theory and Techniques
CNR-National Research Council of Italy
Florence, Italy

Jeanne Pia Mifsud Bonnici
RUG-University of Groningen
Groningen, The Netherlands

Joe Cannataci
RUG-University of Groningen
Groningen, The Netherlands

Fabrizio Turchi
ITTIG-Institute of Legal Information Theory and Techniques
CNR-National Research Council of Italy
Florence, Italy

ISSN 2352-1902 ISSN 2352-1910 (electronic)
Law, Governance and Technology Series
ISBN 978-3-030-09094-4 ISBN 978-3-319-74872-6 (eBook)
https://doi.org/10.1007/978-3-319-74872-6

Printed on acid-free paper

This Springer imprint is published by the registered company Springer International Publishing AG part of Springer Nature.
The registered company address is: Gewerbestrasse 11, 6330 Cham, Switzerland

Contents

Part I
Setting the Scene

Chapter 1
Introduction: Opportunities and Challenges for Electronic Evidence

Maria Angela Biasiotti, Joseph A. Cannataci, Jeanne Pia Mifsud Bonnici, and Fabrizio Turchi

Abstract Beyond the different and varied rules that each Member State adopts regarding the admissibility and development of evidence, including digital evidence, elements that in any case must be guaranteed are its relevance and its authenticity with respect to the case being examined. However, these requirements are far from easy to achieve, taking into account some peculiar characteristics of digital evidence, for example, its fragility (easily alterable, damageable and destructible) and its immateriality, namely, the difficulty in associating particular evidence to a physical object: Often it is confused with the device that contains it and therefore closely linked to the concepts of changeability and volatility. This means that the lifecycle of digital evidence must always be accompanied by documentation, always kept up to date, constituting the so-called chain of custody, i.e., the document that describes in detail what happens to digital evidence from the moment in which it was identified as evidence until its presentation before the judge in the trial phase, more specifically, the person who took possession of it to preserve its authenticity, when, where and how, and in what manner. The issue of digital evidence is necessarily interdisciplinary in that it affects different areas: the law in its national, European and international forms, digital forensics, computer science, sociology of law and diplomatics. The latter discipline, perhaps the least known among those mentioned, is focused on "studying the forms that official, legally probative or even constitutive documentation has taken over time".

M. A. Biasiotti (✉) · F. Turchi
CNR, Institute of Legal Information Theory and Techniques, Florence, Italy
e-mail: mariangela.biasiotti@ittig.cnr.it; fabrizio.turchi@ittig.cnr.it

J. A. Cannataci · J. P. Mifsud Bonnici
University of Groningen, Security, Technology and e-Privacy (STeP), Groningen, The Netherlands
e-mail: j.a.cannataci@step-rug.nl; g.p.mifsud.bonnici@step-rug.nl

M. A. Biasiotti et al. (eds.), *Handling and Exchanging Electronic Evidence Across Europe*, Law, Governance and Technology Series 39,
https://doi.org/10.1007/978-3-319-74872-6_1

1.1 The Current Scenario

Electronic evidence is any data resulting from the output of an analogue device and/or a digital device of potential [probative] value that are generated, processed, stored or transmitted using any electronic device. Digital evidence is that electronic evidence that is generated or converted to a numerical format.

This definition, proposed by the Evidence project[1] is important because it clarifies the various definitions proposed in recent years and also resolves some of their ambiguities. It takes stock of the concreteness of electronic evidence and demonstrates the profound interdisciplinary character hiding behind this issue.

The definition of electronic evidence introduced above has a broader application than other proposed descriptions, for example, by the Standard Working Group on Digital Evidence[2] or by the International Organisation of Computer Evidence,[3] as it includes both evidence that is born digital, and that which in the course of its life is transformed and then stored or exchanged in electronic form.

In today's modern technological society, every type of investigation potentially has a digital dimension, i.e., a significant part of the relevant information for the case investigated, if not all, can be traced back to and extracted from the digital devices of the parties involved, whether they be victims, suspects or their families.

It is now clear that each of us leaves digital traces everywhere, and these traces can, in the future, be potential evidence in an investigation or a course case.

From a legal point of view, one of the most important results of this phenomenon is that the use of new technologies in the justice sector is emerging in an ever more pervasive and wide-ranging manner, in Europe. After starting the process of computerisation of civil and administrative judicial systems in the various EU Member States, and because of the big push by the European Commission and the Council of Europe towards the computerisation of the justice sector (e.g., the e-Justice program[4] and its portal), the criminal process is also feeling the need to use information technology for the management of procedures and activities connected to investigations and legal proceedings.

In a recent paper in December 2016, the EU Council adopted conclusions to improve the efficiency of criminal justice in cyberspace. Among other things, the document refers to the creation of a secure and trustworthy online portal for the exchange of digital evidence in the context of the imminent entry into force of the European investigation order and mutual legal assistance procedures.

---

[1]The European Evidence project, European Data Informatics Exchange Framework for Courts and Evidence, is a project financed by the European Commission as part of the 7th Framework Programme (Grant Agreement 608185), www.evidenceproject.eu.

[2]"Digital Evidence is any information of probative value that is either stored or transmitted in a digital form".

[3]"Digital evidence is an information stored or transmitted in binary form that may be relied upon in court".

[4]See also e-justice.europa.eu/home.do?action=home&plang=en&init=true.

In fact, digital evidence is assuming strategic importance not only for so-called cybercrimes (as they have been defined in the Budapest Convention of 2001, ratified in Italy by Law 48/2008), but also for common crimes, in which digital traces can represent a significant potential source of evidence for investigators and judicial authorities.

Beyond the different and varied rules that each Member State adopts regarding the admissibility and development of evidence, including digital evidence, elements that in any case must be guaranteed are its relevance and its authenticity[5] with respect to the case being examined. However, these requirements are far from easy to achieve, considering some peculiar characteristics of digital evidence, for example, its fragility (easily alterable, damageable and destructible) and its immateriality, namely the difficulty in associating particular evidence to a physical object: often it is confused with the device that contains it and therefore closely linked to the concepts of changeability and volatility.

This means that the lifecycle of digital evidence must always be accompanied by documentation, always kept up to date, constituting the so-called chain of custody, i.e., the documentation that details how digital evidence was handled from the moment it was identified as evidence until its presentation to judge in the trial phase. More specifically, chain of custody tracks who took possession of evidence to preserve and maintain its authenticity, when, where and how, and in what manner.

The issue of digital evidence is necessarily interdisciplinary in that it affects different areas: the law in its national, European and international forms, digital forensics, computer science, sociology of law and diplomatics. The latter discipline, perhaps the least known among those mentioned, is focused on "studying the forms that official, legally probative or even constitutive documentation has taken over time" (Valenti, 1961).

Concerning the issue of digital evidence, it becomes important where it deals with contemporary records and even digital documents (Duranti, 1998).

Furthermore, dealing with digital evidence means addressing the separate reality that surrounds it. This means basing oneself not only on studies and analyses on a theoretical level but also on the experience of those who routinely work with this particular type of evidence in real life, and also managing the variety of actors involved in various capacities in the lifecycle of electronic evidence. Constant and open dialogue with these actors is crucial in this area, especially given the continued and rapid evolution of technology. Comparing design ideas, operational proposals and practical needs that are waiting to be fulfilled, if done directly by the stakeholders concerned, can only produce a shared and efficient outcome for all parties involved.

The following entities are to be considered among the main stakeholders involved in various ways and with different roles in the domain of electronic evidence:

- Communities involved in the processing and/or exchange of electronic evidence: the Digital Forensics Research Workshop (DFRWS), the Netherlands Forensic

[5]ISO/IEC 27043:2015, Incident investigation principles and processes.

Institute—NFI, the National Institute of Standards and Technology—NIST, academic/scientific community of the INTERPARES project.
- European organisations and agencies: Eurojust, Europol, OLAF—European Anti-Fraud Office.
- International institutions: Interpol, International Criminal Court—ICC and European Council.
- Forensic software companies: Cellebrite, Oxygen Forensics, Magnet Forensics, Microsystemation (MSAB).
- The major Internet service providers and large software companies: Apple, Facebook, Google, Microsoft, Samsung and Yahoo.
- Prosecutors, judges and police forces of various European Union Member States.

There are, then, various European projects connected with subjects complementary to that of digital evidence: LASIE, e-Crime, GIFT, Mapping, SIIP, e-Codex, e-Sens, EA-Fit Tools, and others. Strengthening relations and synergies among the various players is an ambitious challenge, but success would make it possible to address common problems in a systematic and shared manner, developing solutions that can stimulate the future work of policy makers.

1.2 Digital Forensics

The concept of digital evidence is inextricably linked to digital forensics,[6] the discipline that deals with the recognition, preservation, acquisition and analysis of digital information, with the objective of addressing forensic questions relevant to the legal inquiry being carried out.

Digital forensics is definable not only about techniques and tools for the extraction of investigative information in accordance with certain technological standards,[7] but above all focuses on the study of the scientific processes, procedures, technologies and rules to use, develop, adapt or propose to improve the results achievable while at the same time better protecting the integrity of digital evidence.

Recent developments in digital forensics, as a profession and as a scientific discipline, have grown out of efforts by organizations that support criminal justice to address the growing prevalence of crimes committed through the use of new technologies. Consequently, groups of specialists for investigations into cybercrime have been establish on a national level in Europe, the United States and other countries. Furthermore, in some countries specific training programmes on digital forensics were developed, aware that the spread and pervasiveness of digital devices requires that every police officer have solid basic training in dealing with electronic evidence.

[6]Following is a brief and non-exhaustive bibliography on the subject: Carrier (2003, 2006), Casey (2011), Daniel (2012), Henseler (2000), Mason (2012), and Richardson (2009).

[7]ISO/IEC 27037:2012, Guidelines for identification, collection, acquisition, and preservation of digital evidence, ISO/IEC 27042:2015, Guidelines for the analysis and interpretation of digital evidence, etc.

Originally digital forensics concerned a single discipline, currently indicated by the name computer forensics, which mainly focused on the computer as a source of evidence. In the last 20 years, the technological evolution has gradually shifted towards mobile devices, connectivity has assumed a global dimension and the use of increasingly newer and more complex devices and systems is spreading: just consider for example the development of so-called IoT—Internet of Things devices like the Smart Watch, Smart TV, Smart Home, the growing use of cloud storage systems, the use of virtual currencies (like Bitcoin) and the Dark Net. People are therefore moving away from traditional devices towards a completely interconnected world where digital traces left by each person are on the rise, locally recorded on different devices or remotely in the cloud even beyond national borders. This rapid and continuous technological evolution has resulted in the equally rapid development of the sub disciplines of digital forensics, outlined, although not exhaustively, in the following list:

- computer forensics: discipline that includes software tools for the forensic analysis of file systems, operating systems, applications. In particular, there are numerous tools to manage the sources of evidence generated by the use of applications. Some of these include tools for various types of analysis: for digital traces generated by the use of browsers, for chat configuration and log files, configuration files related to cloud storage, email archives, data and configuration files relating to peer-to-peer applications, data and configuration files related to social networks (Facebook, LinkedIn, Twitter, etc.).
- Mobile forensics, for the analysis of mobile devices.
- Network forensics, for the analysis of network traffic.
- Memory forensics, for the analysis of RAM memory and hibernation files.
- Malware forensics, for the analysis of malware.

The need felt by law enforcement in this specific area is to increase confidence through the preparation of rules and procedures established by law, and a set of guarantees associated with the acquisition and analysis of digital evidence. In this regard, it would seem particularly important to render the relatively young field of digital forensics more professional. Digital forensic professionals have expressed an interest in their field of expertise reaching a level of professionalism and recognition similar to that achieved in the field of DNA analysis. However, this requires a review of the potential regulation of digital forensic professions to ensure that operators meet a certain standard. Moreover, as these professionals often rely on automated digital forensic tools for the acquisition and analysis of digital evidence, these tools should ideally be subject to validation procedures to ensure they are fit for the purpose. Finally, there are currently no universal standards applicable to digital forensic laboratories, so it is therefore appropriate to consider the development of an accreditation procedure to ensure that laboratories meet predetermined levels of quality.

Of equal importance in digital forensics appears to be the need to "build bridges" between police forces and other stakeholders, including the private sector and the judiciary. Therefore, the cooperation between all these stakeholders is of particular importance. In the end, the acquisition of technical skills is critical for prosecutors and judges, so they can understand the processes behind the collection and analysis of digital evidence.

Further, it is also necessary to address the issue of the relationship with the companies that produce the tools that are used for the acquisition and analysis of digital evidence. On this front, it is necessary to stimulate dialogue with these producers, leading to the adoption of a standard language that, above all, supports interoperability of the results produced by the various tools and systems.

1.3 Legal Framework in Europe

At the European level, there is still neither a unified legal framework nor shared rules that make it possible to handle digital evidence and its possible exchange in a uniform manner across the Member States.

Currently, evidence is exchanged in transnational contexts from the competent authority of one Member State to the competent authority of another Member State. However, there are no specific rules that systematically and clearly regulate the collection, storage, processing and exchange of electronic evidence.

Among the most urgent needs felt by the various parties involved in the lifecycle of digital evidence, particularly worthy of mention are:

- A uniform European regulation regarding digital evidence, first in terms of acquisition and admissibility.
- A common perception, even regarding the reliability of digital evidence, held by all stakeholders (police, judges, lawyers, forensic specialists, etc.).
- Greater cooperation and greater mutual trust among the forces that fight crime, especially when it involves different countries.
- Common investigation and criminal procedures to counteract or prevent the globalisation of crime.
- Secure and reliable tools that ensure the integrity and authenticity both in the transmission and the reception of the request and the evidence itself.

The lack of common rules is all the more problematic considering evidence and the person committing the crime may be located outside the borders of a particular State, raising issues of territoriality.

To overcome these difficulties, it is necessary to promote and develop international cooperation between judicial and police authorities of the different States, especially considering the differences in legal systems and methods of investigation.

At a European level, there are a limited number of legal instruments that can be directly or indirectly relevant to the collection, storage, processing and exchange of electronic evidence. Most of them have been implemented by the various Member States, but often in different ways, according to their own legal systems and traditions.

Although initiatives have been promoted to overcome legal gaps, including by the European Union and the Council of Europe, there are still many limitations. Given that the specific nature of electronic evidence and the rapid evolution of both technology and of crimes committed using it, it is essential to activate an action plan for creating a single legal framework on a European level for the collection, processing and exchange of electronic evidence.

This European framework should be a compromise between the need to ensure efficient police investigations and respect for the fundamental rights of every citizen, on which the new technologies have a major impact.

1.4 The Volume

The volume collects all the efforts made during the EVIDENCE project to create the knowledge and the necessary awareness on this topic. It is also emblematic of the huge network of stakeholders with whom the Project got in contact with and established a solid relation and connection. Therefore, the volume collects contributions by those who have played a leading role in the project activities, as well as by representatives of the different institutions engaged in the growth of the awareness on this topic from a European and International perspective.

It can be affirmed that almost all the stakeholders involved in the handling and exchanging of electronic evidence have contributed to this Volume. Their perspectives, according the specific roles played, are described and shared with the largest community.

The volume is divided into four parts.

The first part is devoted to provide the context of interest of the Volume and to set the scene of the Electronic Evidence handling and exchange scenario at European and international level. It comprises a brief introduction of the editors of the manuscript where some relevant points are emphasised. This chapter is followed by the contribution by M.A. Biasiotti who sets the scene of the Electronic Evidence Treatment and Exchange in Europe, summarises the actions taken by the European Union concerning the processing and exchange of electronic evidence, and also gives account both of the provisions for Mutual Legal Assistance (MLA) and European Investigation Order (EIO), as well as actions carried out by the Council and the European Commission through working groups, emphasising the important innovative contribution resulting from the on-going initiatives and projects.

The second part hosts contributions of authors offering an international perspective and view of how electronic evidence is treated in those contexts outside European Union, mainly international. In this part A. Seger, briefly reports on the important process in which the Council of Europe is engaged with the Cloud Evidence Group and describes the way the Council of Europe, Cybercrime Convention is currently dealing with the e-evidence and access to data in the cloud, whilst Eoghan Casey et al., present the new frontier of digital forensics by describing the evolution of expressing and exchanging cyber-investigations data and metadata in a standardised form. This part is concluded by F. Cajani, who gives an overview of the matters not yet solved regarding communications, interception systems and electronic data detained on foreign servers, mainly involving Internet Service Providers.

The third part hosts contributions by representatives of the various institutions dealing with the electronic evidence treatment and exchange from a practical point of view in the context of criminal field, with the aim to trace the operational scenario and give the practitioners point of view. The first contribution by S. Berghs et al., from INTERPOL, describes the operational scenario of their institution, specifically focusing on the work related to the treatment and exchange of electronic evidence; the contribution by H. Ilyoung, from International Criminal Court, provides an introduction to the activities and challenges of digital forensics in international criminal investigations, and draws attention to requirements for more international cooperation, awareness improvement, standard establishment and the need for a joint effort at solving technical issues; D. Drewer and J. Ellermann, from EUROPOL, describe how the online environment represents a challenge for privacy and the suppression of crime in the context they work for; finally X. Tracol, from EUROJUST offers argues about the use of MS PowerPoint presentation by prosecutors and attorneys during the criminal trials.

The last part describes the effort and the success results and story of the activities carried out during the EVIDENCE project reporting on the results achieved. S. Avveduto et al., describe the categorisation realised for the electronic evidence domain with a specific perspective in the criminal field; J. Mifsud Bonnici et al., report on the analysis of the legal scenario existing in the EU when dealing with the treatment and exchange of electronic evidence; F. Turchi and M. Epifani present the building up process for creating the first Digital Forensic Tools Catalogue, whilst N. Forgò et al., analyse the specific data protection issues arising with the treatment and exchange of electronic evidence in the EU, D. Mezzana describes the social arena of all actors involved in the electronic evidence chain also considering facilitating factors and obstacle in the process of implementing the change needed to pave the way to the electronic evidence exchange in Europe; F. Turchi and E. Epifani gives details of the proposal and the need to adopt a formal standard language when exchanging electronic evidence and describe benefit of such proposal; and N. Matskanis et al. present the Environment realised to allow the exchange process in Europe by adopting the proposal achieved under the EVIDENCE project. A. Tsvetkova stresses the work needed to manage and render successful a EU funded project where experts from different background and different expertise are put together and must find a way to collaborate and to integrate their knowledge. Finally J. Mifsud Bonnici, J. Cannataci and M.A. Biasiotti present the EVIDENCE Road map to the future realisation of a common legal Framework in Europe dealing with the treatment and exchange of electronic evidence.

1.5 Final Reflections

When we started working on the activities of the EVIDENCE Project, there were few who were sufficiently knowledgeable about the topic to have a good understanding of the nature of the problems with electronic evidence. The approach was to be aware of the different challenges and gaps and try to recommend suitable solutions from interdisciplinary perspective, bringing into the scope of the project a significant number of organisations.

Even actors directly involved in the treatment of electronic evidence by default (public prosecutors, law enforcement agencies (LEAs) and judges) demonstrated significant gaps and challenges in their knowledge and training. The status quo at the beginning of the EVIDENCE project was "I know electronic evidence exists, I know I cannot make it without but I don't know how to deal with it and treat and handle it without compromising it...".

We realised that fragmentation cannot only be found in the legal framework, but is also reflected by the vast number of actors involved. On an international level there are several actors involved, such as Interpol, Eurojust, Europol and its EC3 cybercrime centre and Joint Cybercrime Action Taskforce (J-CAT), CEPOL and ENISA. However, when we look at a national level the number of actors involved in one way or another becomes numerous. Certain public and private actors providing technical solutions and assistance have a direct interest in electronic evidence. These are process actors that make up the supply and demand for technologies and services. Other type of actors are context actors and play an indirect role in electronic evidence in a broader political, social or economic context.

Considering this vast number of actors involved, one of the issues is that these actors are not always in agreement considering the different interests involved and that they do not always coordinate with each other. Other obstacles include mistrust within the judiciary, lack of necessary competences and professionalisation, cultural differences, lack of governance and functional difficulties. Solutions to address these issues include mandatory training and education, certification, building bridges between the private and public sector, raising awareness, validation of digital forensic tools, etc.

The Impact of such an initiative was very big. The added value realised by the results of the Project to its context is emphasised by the many positive reactions and feedback received from the electronic evidence community and from the European Commission as well. Since the beginning of the project, in 2014, in two and a half years we have been able to generate awareness, stimulated the debate, opening/setting up a dialogue and creating specifically a network and community, also merging into the EVIDENCE initiative one the various communities and stakeholders belonging to different disciplines and domains.

It is now clear that it is necessary to establish a common European framework for the processing and exchange of digital evidence to effectively counter crime, which is increasingly international, be it terrorism or cybercrime.

All the actors at a European level, like Eurojust, Europol, the European Commission, the magistrates and the police forces, now seem convinced that it is of vital interest to achieve the exchange of evidence in legal matters. Because the evidence comes in the form of information of a certain type, chain of custody, integrity and authenticity must be ensured, both of the request and of the response that will be given. Once again, the obstacle to be overcome together for the implementation of a digital platform that will enable exchange is and remains the lack of "trust". It all revolves around the ability to develop and deploy operational, political, legal and technological tools that are able to feed and cultivate this simple but fundamental relational concept.

The many meetings with the experts, often behind closed doors, and the many contributions gathered in this volume make us very hopeful.

References

Carrier BD (2003) Defining digital forensic examination and analysis tool using abstraction layers. Int J Digit Evid 1(4):1–12

Carrier BD (2006) A hypothesis-based approach to digital forensic investigations. CERIAS technical report 2006-06. www.cerias.purdue.edu/assets/pdf/bibtex_archive/2006-06.pdf

Casey E (2011) Foundations of digital forensics. In: Casey E (ed) Digital evidence and computer crime, 3rd edn. Academic, Waltham

Daniel L (2012) Digital forensics for legal professionals. Understanding digital evidence from the warrant to the courtroom. Syngress, Amsterdam, p 368

Duranti L (1998) Diplomatics. New uses for an old science. Scarecrow, Lanham, p 186

Henseler J (2000) Computer crime and computer forensics. In: The encyclopedia of forensic science. Academic, London

Mason S (2012) Electronic evidence, 3rd edn. Lexis Nexis Butterworths, London, p 934

Richardson J (ed) (2009) Archbold: criminal pleading, evidence and practice. Sweet & Maxwell, Thomson Reuters, London

Valenti F (1961) Il documento medievale. Nozioni di diplomatica generale e di cronologia, Modena, Società Tipograca Editrice Modenese, p 226

Chapter 2
Present and Future of the Exchange of Electronic Evidence in Europe

Maria Angela Biasiotti

Abstract Crime has become global, and almost all crimes involve electronic evidence. A significant problem has become the exchange of data, across jurisdictions and between the domestic participants in the criminal judicial process. The exchange becomes crucial in counterterrorism operations and when dealing with global crimes. At the same time, a secure and trusted exchange of information and of electronic evidence relating to crimes is an important element in order to promote judicial cooperation in criminal matters, as well as to contribute to an effective and coherent application of EU Mutual Legal Assistance (MLA) and European Investigation Order (EIO) procedures. This paper deals with the electronic evidence exchange in Europe, and more specifically with the new challenges of the implementation of the European Investigation Order Directive, in particular, and some of the results of the work carried out by the European Commission internally and by EU-funded projects. This contribution also proposes recommendations for future activities, and ideas for the follow-up of the results achieved and the policies promoted by the European Commission.

2.1 Introduction

Almost every action performed during a normal day, a phone call, a WhatsApp message, accessing a social network, even a quick errand in the car, generates a digital trail, and each of these trails may in the future be evidence in a court case in support of the innocence or the guilt of one or more persons associated with it.

We live in a digital and digitised world in which electronic evidence is not only evidence that can be used to prove or disprove a so-called "cyber" crime, i.e., a crime committed through the use of a digital or IT device, but also to prove or disprove

M. A. Biasiotti (✉)
CNR, Institute of Legal Information Theory and Techniques, Florence, Italy
e-mail: mariangela.biasiotti@ittig.cnr.it

M. A. Biasiotti et al. (eds.), *Handling and Exchanging Electronic Evidence Across Europe*, Law, Governance and Technology Series 39,
https://doi.org/10.1007/978-3-319-74872-6_2

common crimes. The assumption that for computer crimes the proof is to be found in digital traces, while for ordinary crimes the evidence is to be found among more traditional sources, is no longer valid: investigations of common crimes increasingly rely on searches for digital evidence.

The growing importance of electronic evidence becomes even more significant in view of the fact that crime has now become global. The principle of territorial prosecution clashes with the true scope and the increasingly international dimension of crime. Suffice it to say that terrorists organise their attacks communicating through social networks or "chatting" online using instant messaging systems.

To pursue and prevent crime, the LEAs must therefore adapt to the rapid development of technology, working with electronic evidence generated by these new technologies and using the same digital technologies to acquire and analyse them.

However, the type of evidence that they are dealing with is particular in that it is generated and recognised outside of regulatory contexts, i.e., its affirmation is independent of formal recognition in a specific provision of law, since, as is often the case when combining new technologies and regulations, the laws follow on the heels of the technological phenomenon to "close the gap", and are almost never able to get out in front of it.

There is no uniform legal framework among the various EU countries concerning the collection, storage and exchange of electronic evidence. This situation forces police and judicial authorities to operate in an uncertain environment, and, from time to time, adopt solutions that are inconsistent or confused both from a legal point of view and from the point of view of the technological solutions themselves. In concrete reality these are the points—practically interdependent—to be considered for a future harmonisation:

- The question of admissibility: the evidence obtained, especially electronic evidence, often becomes uncertain in court; there is no clear legal principle to which the judge can refer to determine the admissibility or otherwise of certain evidence, resulting in inconsistent or unbalanced application of the law;
- the rapid evolution of forensic technologies: new technologies can quickly lose their effectiveness in terms of their capacity to extract evidence, as criminal organisations become aware of their existence and take countermeasures to make them technically useless or ineffective.[1] Even the absence of standards or good rules to keep the characteristics of forensic techniques from being revealed during trials makes these measures quickly obsolete and inefficient;
- the globalisation of crime: this requires close cooperation among police forces and judicial authorities of different countries. For this purpose it is essential that evidence obtained in a certain country be shared and accepted in other nations, naturally guaranteeing respect for the fundamental rights of the person. The lack of common legislation and national and international standards makes this objective particularly difficult to achieve.

[1]This is particularly true for international criminal organisations that have access to financial resources that are virtually unlimited.

It is therefore necessary to prepare an action plan to be rendered operational to establish a common European framework for the processing and exchange of electronic evidence. The purpose of this common framework is to improve the efficiency of investigations and prosecutions, while maintaining adequate safeguards to protect fundamental human rights and respecting clear standards of operational conduct.

In the following paragraphs, this paper intends to summarise the actions taken by the European Union concerning the processing and exchange of electronic evidence, giving account both of the provisions for Mutual Legal Assistance (MLA[2]) and European Investigation Order (EIO), as well as actions carried out by the Council and the European Commission through working groups, emphasising the important innovative contribution resulting from the projects. Conclusions will be made considering the suggestions that emerged regarding the need for a common European framework for the processing and exchange of electronic evidence with a particular focus on the roadmap recently proposed to the European Commission by the Evidence project[3] and the ideas for concretely realising the exchange in a real online environment.

2.2 The EU's Action on the Subject of Electronic Evidence: Modernising the Procedures

The objective of creating a comprehensive European regulatory framework for the exchange of electronic evidence originates from the need to strengthen judicial cooperation in criminal matters and refers mainly to existing MLA provisions and the new frontier opened by the directive regarding EIO.[4]

The principle of *mutual assistance* transformed into the broader principle of mutual recognition was specifically designed for the collection and exchange of evidence.

Mutual recognition was first discussed at the Cardiff European Council on 15–16 June 1999 (Del Coco, 2015; Janssens, 2013; Spencer, 2014), in which it was stated that the principle of mutual recognition would have made it possible—based on a relationship of mutual trust and with the intent of "providing mutual assistance"—

[2]"European Convention on Mutual Assistance in Criminal Matters", Strasbourg, 20 April 1959, Article 1 (1). See also: "Council of Europe Convention on Laundering, Search, Seizure and Confiscation of the Proceeds from Crime", Strasbourg, 8 November 1990, ETS No. 141, Article 7 (1); "Council of Europe Convention on the Transfer of Sentenced Persons", Strasbourg, 21 March 1983, ETS No. 112, Article 2 (1); "Second Additional Protocol to the European Convention on Mutual Assistance in Criminal Matters", Strasbourg, 8 November 2001, ETS No. 182, Article 1 (1); "Council of Europe Convention on Cybercrime", Budapest, 23 November 2001, ETS 185, Article 23.

[3]Evidence Project—"European Informatics Data Exchange Framework for Courts and Evidence", www.evidenceproject.eu.

[4]Directive 2014/41/EU.

for the authorities of a Member State to recognise judicial decisions made in other member countries, as if they had been made internally. This principle was then explicitly and officially recognised in the conclusions of the Tampere European Council of 1999,[5] which made it a "cornerstone of the EU's judicial cooperation", subsequently made legislatively definitive in the Lisbon Treaty. There is no doubt that the principle started to have a major impact when, by the end of the nineties, the Amsterdam Treaty set the objective of creating an "area of freedom, security and justice" (Castellaneta, 2009; Siracusano, 2016).

Relative to the movement of evidence, the principle of mutual recognition means that "evidence lawfully gathered by authorities of a Member State is admissible in the courts of other Member States, taking into account the standards that apply there".[6] Conversely, even if developed in another State distinguished by a different court system, the evidence is likely to be accepted and used by the judicial authorities of each of the member countries for making a decision.

The realisation of such an ambitious goal of exchanging evidence is based primarily on mutual trust among EU states. Creating an atmosphere of mutual trust among the various EU countries presupposes that the various judicial cultures share the same democratic evolution pursuing a respect for fundamental human rights. Only if the different legal systems share a reasonably uniform standard of guarantees is it possible to certify the validity and, therefore, the reliability of the evidence given, necessary characteristics for its recognition and implementation in all its authenticity in a different legal system.

A matter of no small importance for the practical application of the principle of mutual recognition—in a European system characterised by profound differences between the various laws, inspired by procedural models that are quite different from each other—is the ability of Member States to create a climate of mutual trust. In practice, admissibility and usability criteria for evidence found outside the country have been and continue to be entrusted to the interpretation of the judges in the States concerned. While being aware of the many difficulties and resistance that hinder the realisation of such an objective of harmonisation, it appears correct, however, to say that only through a shared system of mutual admissibility of evidence can mutual recognition effectively and efficiently improve judicial cooperation, with a view to strengthen the "Area of freedom, security and justice".

However, despite efforts to generate mutual trust, MLA procedures have not proved suitable to the reality of current crimes that are increasingly global and complex, and the efforts to contrast and prevent them necessarily pass through the rapid and efficient transfer of potential electronic evidence. Besides the fact that MLA procedures have a limited scope, one might even advance the hypothesis

---

[5]"Conclusioni del Consiglio europeo di Tampere" (15–16 October 1999), point 33 in www.europarl.europa.eu/summits/tam_it.htm.

[6]"COM (2009) 624: Green Paper on obtaining evidence in criminal matters from one Member State to another and securing its admissibility.

that the reluctance of nations to implement the principle of mutual recognition contributes to the lack of will to fully implement and use them effectively. Yet, in its research, the Vermeulen study group (Vermulen et al., 2010) found that "90% of the Member States are willing to cooperate, even if the investigative measure relates to acts that do not constitute an offence to its national law. In current practice, 60% of Member States still do not apply the requirement of double criminality, even if they are allowed to do so".[7] Regarding investigative measures not expressly covered by legislation, 70% of Member States have stated that they would accept the abandonment of the double criminality requirement as a policy in the future. The study therefore shows a real will to cooperate on the part of Member States that goes beyond existing procedures. So, the principle of mutual recognition is widely recognised and accepted as the appropriate instrument to improve cooperation on the collection of evidence within the EU. However, as demonstrated by the fact that a tool such as the Evidence Warrant has failed and has been repealed,[8] one clearly sees the need to adopt a different approach that moves more towards the harmonisation of instruments and procedures within the EU. In fact, while on the one hand the expansion of the principle of mutual recognition facilitates the MLA procedures, making them faster and simpler, it can also be an obstacle to the development of international cooperation by strictly limiting the offences that may be subject to MLA procedures. And in fact the European Union expressed the need to adopt a new approach based on mutual recognition considering the flexibility of the traditional system of mutual legal assistance. And thus was recently instituted the European Investigation Order (EIO), introduced by Directive 41/2014. It is an innovative tool, developed to be the only tool needed for the acquisition and transfer of evidence relating to cross-border proceedings in the EU context. The EIO is generated in a particular judicial decision issued or validated by a competent authority of a Member State ("the issuing State"), that orders the court of another Member State ("the executing State") to perform one or more specific acts of investigation to acquire evidence or obtain evidence already in the possession of the competent authorities of the executing State (Article 1). By way of example there may be seizures, environmental or telephone interceptions, or direct acquisition of documentation having probative value.

The EIO must be issued by a court or an investigating magistrate, or must be validated by them, prior to transmission to the executing authority (Article 2). The EIO is sent by the issuing authority to the executing authority by any means capable of producing a written record and that allows the executing State to establish authenticity (Article 7).

[7]The requirement of double criminality, cornerstone of the extradition system, implies that extradition cannot be granted if the offence which is the subject of the request is not considered by law as a crime by both legal systems of the states involved in the procedure.

[8]The evidence warrant was repealed by Regulation (EU) 2016/95 of the European Parliament and of the Council on 20 January 2016, regarding the repeal of certain acts in the field of police cooperation and judicial cooperation in criminal matters.

The recognition and execution of the EIO take place without any further formalities. The competent authority of the executing State is required to immediately take all necessary measures, in the same manner that they would be observed if the investigative measure had been ordered by an authority of the issuing State (Article 9). The implementing provisions of the Directive must be adopted by the Member States[9] by 22 May 2017.

On paper the EIO directive takes precedence over all MLA instruments and constitutes a single legal regime for obtaining evidence within the EU that applies to all investigative measures. Still, some critics believe that the adoption of a single legislative act is not actually sufficient (Aulitano, 2016). In fact, the creation of a harmonised and comprehensive cooperation mechanism with general rules not accompanied by mutual recognition mechanisms and appropriate safeguards for fundamental rights could prove ineffective (Camaldo, 2014; De Amicis, 2011). Understandably, the aim of preventing confusion is crucial. However, the adoption of different measures may be appropriate, provided that such measures are taken at the same time to ensure completeness and consistency. So, the concentration and substitution of (almost) all mutual legal assistance instruments with a single legal instrument is not sufficient to achieve the free movement of evidence in the EU until it means creating a practical system with appropriate safeguards.

Unlike the MLA, the EIO is applicable to all investigative measures aimed at obtaining evidence. The fact that the evidence already exists or not is not relevant to the EIO. The only exception relates to joint investigative teams, which remain subject to the previous legal regime. It is important to note that the EIO focuses on mutual recognition of decisions made to obtain evidence while the evidence search warrant was based on the specific type of evidence to be obtained.

The EIO raises questions also in other ways. The protection of personal data is assured by instruments that either offer limited protection or are not sufficiently implemented to be efficient. A further concern is the strengthening of cooperation instruments not accompanied by additional specific procedural guarantees for the accused. The EIO facilitates cooperation by introducing for the first time the principle of availability of investigative measures, giving the opportunity to the authority of country A to request that the authority in country B perform a real investigation and possibly acquire evidence. However, concerns have been raised regarding the practical application of the deadlines set by the directive. Finally, the EIO appears to facilitate the interception of telecommunications, with the technical assistance of another Member State and also legitimate cross-border interception of telecommunications without technical assistance, things that require a comprehensive and far-reaching framework in terms of data protection to ensure that an individual's privacy is respected and data integrity guaranteed.

Ultimately, this legislation has numerous complexities. On the one hand, it is clear that information technologies can offer the ideal platform for the exchange of all documentation submitted during the procedure. On the other hand, the use of the

[9]Including the United Kingdom, excluding Ireland and Denmark.

computer poses concerns of security, confidentiality, proper and reliable identification of the authority of the issuing State and that of execution, and the proceeding judicial authorities. In addition, the directive requires the implementation of national provisions that at this time should be in development and therefore not yet delineated.

2.3 Operational Initiatives of European Institutions

It is important here to emphasise the fact that the European institutions involved in various ways and with various competencies in strengthening judicial cooperation in criminal matters have actually started working in work groups on the possibilities and ways that can be taken to allow for the exchange of evidence at a European level with a view to facilitating the operation and success of the EIO. The European Justice and Home Affairs Council of 9 June 2016 identified some actions in its conclusions for the improvement of criminal justice in Europe:

- the rationalisation of procedures for mutual legal assistance, and, where applicable, of mutual recognition with respect to cyberspace through the use of standardised electronic modules and tools;
- improving cooperation with service providers through the development of a common framework (e.g., use of aligned modules and tools) to request specific categories of data;
- initiating a process of reflection on possible connecting factors for executive competence in cyberspace. Specifically, ministers held a policy debate on the following issues:
  - the possible criteria of executive competence in cyberspace, for example, the criteria according to which the relevant authorities may perform any act of investigation in cyberspace when the existing frameworks are not sufficient, such as in cases where the relevant electronic evidence is hidden or moving quickly between jurisdictions and
  - differentiated processing of specific categories of data in criminal proceedings, for example, the repercussions of a differentiated approach—including data that do not relate to the content (relating to subscribers or traffic) and the content data or between the real-time data and the data stored—on individual national legal frameworks, the type of items that would be relevant for a common approach at an EU level and the measures to be considered (Council of the European Union, 2016).

In this regard the Council asked the Commission to present by June 2017 tangible results regarding the three lines of action. So, precisely about the request to strengthen cooperation with Internet service providers and to streamline procedures for mutual assistance and mutual recognition, the European Commission emphasised the need to develop a secure online portal to allow the exchange of digital evidence by appointing two expert groups: an *Expert group—reliable electronic platform for MLA and EIO requests and the Horizontal Working Party on Cyber Issues and JHA Counsellors.*[10]

The first guidelines that emerge from the work of the former group are mainly focused on features that an online platform for the exchange of electronic evidence must be secure, reliable and easy to manage by the Commission and the Member States.

In this respect, the Commission must decide, dealing with the Member States, on possible ways to adopt an online system for exchanging electronic evidence as soon as possible. The big question seems to concern the nature of the system:

- a centralised system managed by the European Commission to which all Member States will need to connect and link their national databases, or
- a decentralised system in which States interact directly without any intervention of management of requests and transmission by the European Commission, leaving the national databases in their local dimension.

It is clear that the option of centralised management/storage of digital evidence by the European Union necessarily requires that there be a legal basis related to the centralised processing of data and electronic evidence with particular attention to the regulation of personal data protection, the security of data transmission and of the chain of custody of the evidence itself. This solution is more complicated to manage. After settling the question of the nature of the system, still to be resolved and addressed are the characteristics that the system must satisfy, regardless of whether the system is centralised or decentralised. These are the points on the published agenda of the Expert Meeting on Principles and options for an e-evidence exchange platform[11]:

(A) Users
(B) Security needs
(C) Location of saving the requests and the e-evidence
(D) Functions: size and translation

Developing some hypotheses on the possible directions that will be taken based on existing scenarios on the first point (Users), we can easily guess that the objective to be pursued must be a system built to capture the widest possible range of users: all judges and prosecutors, as well as police forces of Member States and other pertinent actors. Even the back office to be used by these actors must be particularly user-friendly.

---

[10]The panel is an advisory body that can be established by the Commission or its services for advice and specialised expertise, consists of members of the public and/or private sector and meets more than once.

[11]"Experts' Meeting on the Setting Up of a Reliable and Secure e-platform for the European Investigation Order on Mutual Legal Assistance (MLA)", in ec.europa.eu/transparency/regexpert/index.cfm?do=groupDetail.groupDetail&groupID=636&NewSearch=1.

Regarding security, the guidelines must guarantee different aspects and meet diverse needs including ensuring that the system has a method of authentication and authorisation that can ensure the reliability of the request and response, i.e., those who receive the request must be able to know that the request is valid; the system should ensure the security of the exchange for both the request and for the transmission of the electronic evidence.

Regarding the third point, the location where the requests for transmission and even electronic evidence itself will be stored will vary depending on which option is chosen, centralised or decentralised. In fact, the choice made will determine how the data are managed given that the data management systems are different from one Member State to another and therefore it is difficult to connect them in a systematic way. Regarding this point may prevail the freedom to directly connect the single archives to the system, or otherwise manage differently the response to requests for transmission. Regarding the specific point of the volume of evidence to be transmitted, the system must allow for the sending of electronic evidence in a manner that is different from traditional methods: for example, the transmission could be facilitated by the sending of a link for download, or through the sending of metadata followed by the sending of only some selected data. From the agenda cited it is clear that the European Commission is considering European project initiatives on topics of interest like the Evidence project and the e-Codex project.[12] Precisely in relation to the option of basing the exchange system on a decentralised approach, the infrastructure realised as part of the e-Codex project could offer an excellent starting point. This approach presupposes that Member States have national solutions for interconnection via e-Codex and that they possess the technical capacity to manage and store large electronic documents. However, not all Member States have implemented the e-Codex infrastructure, which among other things also presupposes the existence of structured national databases. So, to help those Member States that do not yet have the ability to develop a national database within a reasonable time, the system could be designed in a hybrid manner combining centralised and decentralised approaches. We will see how the European Commission will decide to proceed fast enough, given the impending expiry tied to the implementation by Member States of the EIO Directive in May 2017.

The second working group, the one that deals specifically with Cyber Issues, at its last meeting held in Brussels on 20 January 2017 also discussed the subject of the exchange of digital evidence, reiterating that the strengthening of cooperation in criminal matters remains the key factor in the fight against cybercrime and terrorism and that this passes necessarily through increased awareness of the tools, by increasing the mutual trust between Member States and through the availability of systems that allow the secure and reliable exchange of information and digital evidence among police forces and other actors involved in the criminal procedure. This group has stressed the strategic importance of the subject of electronic evidence, to network with the various stakeholders involved, including the priority role of Internet service providers, and to build, together with these, using a shared

[12]www.e-codex.eu.

approach, the regulatory basis and the necessary dialogue to increase the much desired trust.

2.4 European Project Action to Promote the Exchange of Electronic Evidence

The issue of the processing and exchange of electronic evidence in Europe has also directly or indirectly been the subject of study and research by various European projects. Following is summarised the work of some of the most important European projects that have addressed the exchange of electronic evidence from a formal and legal point of view, both to streamline procedures that allow such exchange (e-MLA), and to encourage alternative forms of cooperation to facilitate communication with certain holders of electronic evidence and information to be exchanged. About the EU-funded projects, the choice of the Commission to finance projects that are complementary and with a common radius of action tending towards the strengthening of judicial cooperation and the standardised processing of information in the criminal field turned out to be practical and effective.

2.4.1 European Project Initiatives

2.4.1.1 The Evidence Project

The Evidence project, funded by the European Commission under the 7th Framework Programme, started in March 2013 and ended in October 2016, used a multidisciplinary approach in close collaboration with the various stakeholders to identify, define and evaluate a set of actions that should be undertaken at the EU level and national measures to enable the electronic exchange of evidence between the competent authorities in Europe. These are the points on which the project based its research:

- comparative analysis of existing regulatory systems at the level of EU countries regarding any matter related to the concept of electronic evidence;
- Identification and definition of the necessary legislative changes to be promoted both nationally and at a European level;
- definition of open standards for the exchange of electronic evidence between different countries, preserving the chain of custody requirements and including the aspects of protection of personal and ethical data;
- identification of operational and ethical implications for law enforcement agencies;
- identification of the technical developments necessary to achieve the aforementioned objectives.

Activities under the Evidence project also had the goal of creating a stable network of experts in computer forensics[13] and the main actors (for example, judicial authorities, police forces, etc.) to stimulate a debate and an exchange of ideas during seminars and workshops on the main topics of interest, in a collaborative network environment. To address the issues briefly presented, Evidence sought to provide the European Commission with a roadmap (guidelines, recommendations, operational guidelines, technical standards, etc.) to create a common framework at a European level, which is currently lacking, for the uniform and systematic application of new technologies for the collection, processing and exchange of electronic evidence. This roadmap is based on standard solutions that can help policy makers to facilitate the adoption and/or the introduction of effective legislation concerning the handling and exchange of electronic evidence, also providing, to all the stakeholders, i.e., police forces, judicial authorities and lawyers, a common legal/technological background that enables them to deal with electronic evidence in compliance with common rules and standards. To create a roadmap, the following objectives have been identified:

- definition of a common and shared terminology on the concept of "electronic evidence" and the relevant concepts in the context of its domain (for example, digital forensics, criminal law, criminal procedure, criminal international cooperation);
- identification of rules and criteria used for the processing of electronic evidence in the various member countries and for their exchange;
- identification of criteria and standards to ensure the reliability, integrity and protection of the "chain of custody" of electronic evidence in the various member countries;
- definition of the operational consequences for police forces through:
  - description of the state of the art relative to the collection, storage and exchange of electronic evidence from an operational point of view;
  - proposal of guidelines to incorporate in the common European framework relating to this area;
  - definition of the implications and problems associated with privacy protection;
  - identification and development of technological standards for the collection, processing and exchange of electronic evidence;
  - identification of the actors involved, directly or indirectly, to facilitate and implement the innovations necessary for the exchange of electronic evidence.

Still unresolved is the problem relating to evidence in the possession of Internet service providers and relationships with the growing world of services on mobile devices, based on applications. Indeed, whereas before it was fairly simple to identify the Internet service provider, currently each developer of applications, in theory, can become a service provider, but at the same time not be seen as such

[13]Computer forensics is the science that deals with the preservation, identification and study of all the information that is contained in the computer to highlight the existence of evidence relevant to the fulfilment of investigation activities.

in legal terms. The problem with this type of entities not recognised as service providers lies mainly in the non-applicability of the relevant legal obligations. ISPs, for example, are subject to specific requirements when it comes to providing information to the police authorities, as envisaged by some national laws on data retention.

2.4.1.2 The e-Codex Project

It seems appropriate to discuss the e-Codex project to describe the infrastructure built that could be the means for exchanging electronic evidence in Europe.

e-Codex is a large-scale project in the e-Justice domain to improve access of citizens and businesses to transnational judicial procedures between EU Member States. The project aims to use ICT to improve interoperability of information systems of judicial authorities and supports the implementation of common standards and solutions within the EU. The project involves 25 partners:

- 19 European countries[14];
- 3 candidate countries (Jersey, Norway, Turkey);
- 2 primary associations of legal practitioners (CCBE and CNUE);
- 1 standardisation body (OASIS).

The use of ICT makes the judicial proceedings more transparent, efficient and cost effective, facilitating access to justice for citizens, businesses, administrations, and legal professionals.

The connection of the existing systems allows communication and exchange of data based on the development of common technical standards. To this end, the following blocks have been developed:

- e-Delivery for the transmission of information across borders in a secure and reliable manner;
- e-Signature for the electronic signature of documents and validation of electronic signatures;
- e-Document for the exchange of common documents;
- e-Identity for the identification of persons by means of national identity cards.

Up until now e-Codex has focused on communications regarding requests for judicial assistance. However, evidence could be exchanged via the infrastructure even if this requires a further step, for example, in terms of common formats of the evidence. It should also be noted that several Member States restrict the size of files that they can receive in their national applications. The e-Codex community is adjusting the procedure to align it with the needs underlying the EIO Directive.

[14]Austria, Belgium, Czech Republic, Estonia, France, Germany, Greece, Hungary, Italy, Ireland, Lithuania, Malta, Netherlands, Poland, Portugal, Romania, Spain, Sweden, United Kingdom.

2.4.1.3 The e-MLA Project (Interpol)

The e-MLA project[15] is coordinated by Interpol and has the objective to modernise and streamline formal processes of transmission of requests for MLA in the framework of existing procedures in the European Union and Council of Europe (CoE).

This will increase the effectiveness of judicial cooperation within the framework of applicable treaties on judicial cooperation in criminal matters. The ultimate goal is the creation of a very practical electronic instrument allowing the competent authorities to exchange information related to mutual assistance procedures, in accordance with commitments under existing treaties, national legislation and other initiatives.

The same process of developing an e-MLA platform will be an opportunity for participating countries to discuss good practices in mutual legal assistance in criminal matters. The proposed assessment will be carried out after consultation with experts of the EU/CoE member countries, as well as Eurojust and the European Justice Network.

The project will also enable the development of a consensus on complex legal issues, specifically on the value of electronic evidence and the admissibility before the courts of the requesting States. The project has just started and will produce its results in 2019.

2.4.1.4 The Programme of the Council of Europe: Council of Europe Cybercrime Programme

The Council of Europe, as part of the Working Group on Cybercrime Convention (T-CY), addressed the issue of the exchange of electronic evidence in its most thorny prospect, namely relating to the acquisition of electronic evidence from the cloud, by creating a special working group.[16] Among other things, the working group is looking into jurisdiction and territoriality problems related to the acquisition of evidence from the cloud and therefore the relationship between the police, judicial authorities and Internet service providers (Seger, 2016). Among the practical proposals of the working group is the expressed need to create an online resource that is able to provide the necessary information on the laws applicable to electronic evidence and computer crimes, as well as for the transmission of digital information stored on various devices useful in the context of a criminal trial. Therefore, the

[15]Programme JUST/2015/AG, proposed e-MLA, SEP-10333474.

[16]The Committee on Computer Crimes (T-CY), established in the Council of Europe, in its 12th Plenary Session on 2–3 December 2014 decided to establish a working group (Cloud Evidence Group), giving it the mandate to study what solutions can be taken to ensure criminal justice access to evidence kept in cloud environments, including solutions that can be compatible with the procedures of mutual assistance.

Council of Europe also considers it necessary to guide the resolution of issues towards the creation of an online platform to facilitate and enable rapid exchange of electronic evidence to be used in criminal trials.[17]

2.4.1.5 The UNODC-United Nations Office for Drugs and Crime Project

UNODC has developed the Mutual Legal Assistance Request Writer Tool[18] that provides assistance in the drafting stage of requests for mutual assistance to facilitate and strengthen international cooperation.

The tool requires virtually no prior knowledge or experience to draft requests for mutual legal assistance. It helps to avoid incomplete requests for legal assistance and therefore minimises the risk of delay or refusal. It is easily adaptable to the substantive and procedural law of any country, it allows the user to retrieve key information on treaties and national legislation.

The tool also has a monitoring-management system for incoming and outgoing requests. Step by step, the tool guides those who perform operational activities through the mutual assistance application process, using a series of models differentiated by type of request. Finally, the tool combines all entered data and automatically generates a request in the proper form, complete and effective, ready to be signed.

Access to the tool, which is currently available in English, French, Spanish, Russian, Portuguese, Bosnian, Croatian and Serbian, is reserved for professionals of the justice system.

2.5 Suggestions for the Creation of a Common European Framework for the Exchange of Electronic Evidence

The evidence in criminal matters must be collected, stored and used in criminal proceedings and, eventually exchanged, even across borders, among authorities. As explained above, there is no uniform legal framework in Europe about electronic evidence. While there have been some initiatives to fill the legislative gaps, even by the EU and the Council of Europe, the limitations remain. This creates a series of challenges for police and the judiciary.

Traditional means of international cooperation for the prevention and suppression of crime are no longer sufficient given the special nature of electronic evidence, particularly volatile and subject to being manipulated or altered. The mechanisms agreed to on an international level for the storage and exchange of electronic

[17]For a more complete reconstruction of the position of the Council of Europe on the questions just cited, see the many official documents, in particular the work of the T-CY CLOUD EVIDENCE GROUP, "Criminal Justice Access to Data in the Cloud: Recommendations", 16 September 2016, www.coe.int/cybercrime.

[18]www.unodc.org/mla/en/index.html.

evidence in criminal matters must be reinforced, considering the need to ensure the authenticity and integrity of the evidence to be admissible in the courts of a State other than that in which they were acquired or analysed. There are big differences among the instruments used by the police for the acquisition and analysis of electronic evidence; the practices are different not only from State to State but also within individual countries; the terminology used is inconsistent with respect to the domain of interest; the dialogue with the Internet service providers is still lacking a systematic communication channel, which then needs to be developed and regulated in an organic way; companies that produce software for the acquisition and analysis of electronic evidence in most cases protect their patents and their applications, forced into this by the stringent laws of the niche market in which they act. It is necessary to focus the efforts made so far in a real roadmap showing the way to go, to develop the missing European common framework for the systematic and uniform collection, storage and exchange of electronic evidence.

The roadmap[19] prepared for the Evidence project is largely based on the challenges and critical issues identified in the processing and exchange of electronic evidence in Europe and proposes strategies and actions to be taken at national and European levels to implement a common European framework.

The Evidence project conducted a thorough study on the use and handling of electronic evidence in Europe, to define how the various Member States currently handle the stages of collection, storage, use and exchange of the evidence from multiple perspectives: in legal terms, for compliance with existing standards, from a technological point of view, from the perspective of the police and judicial authorities, that of the market, from the point of view of protection of personal data. During the preparation of the study, it identified a number of critical issues in processing of electronic evidence, understood in its general meaning, like: regulatory gaps, challenges that police must deal with every day because of the rapid evolution of technology, the many forms in which cybercrime evolves and is perpetrated, the high number of entities possibly involved and the corresponding trust that must be established, the issues regarding ethics and protection of personal data. All these complexities were highlighted in the map and for each of them solutions and/or appropriate action to address them have been proposed.

The road map then provides a set of goals whose achievement can be accomplished through a series of actions to be implemented in the short, medium and long term to achieve effective results.

The short-term solutions should be carried out in 2–3 years, medium-term in 3–4 years and finally the long-term in 5–6 years. The result of each of the foreseen time phases will represent the starting point for the next stage, and so in this sense is a prerequisite for the next phase to begin. Another fundamental principle is that none of the proposed actions can, by themselves, solve the problem: the actions or solutions are to be taken together because the benefits are more effective, significantly

[19]The paragraph takes into consideration the roadmap of the Evidence project, submitted to the European Commission in January 2017.

perceived by stakeholders and, above all, to achieve substantial progress in the context of greater international judicial cooperation to combat crime.

The stronger legal framework suggested by the roadmap should address the legislative gap regarding the collection, storage, use and exchange of electronic evidence. Existing legislative frameworks of most of the Member States, as well as the concepts that are regulated, such as the concept of data protection, date back to before the creation of the Internet as we know it today, and do not contemplate the reality of technological developments and the dynamic nature of modern investigations.

The roadmap provides for actions which basically tend to modernise and harmonise legislation and public policies, including international law and treaties, as well as operational guidelines and standards for police forces, adapting them to new technologies. It is necessary to have clear and unambiguous rules on the procedures and methods to be followed in the process of collection, storage and exchange of electronic evidence that ensure the right proportion between the need for protection of privacy and the need for prevention and control of crime. Furthermore, action seems to be necessary regarding the data collected by the private sector and improvement of the dialogue between the sector and the law enforcement/judicial powers, as well as the development and adoption of clear rules as regards the transfer of data and management of electronic evidence.

Investigative measures may have an impact on the fundamental rights of suspects, particularly in a digital environment, where one can easily gather (personal) information using different channels. Consequently, there must be a balance between, on the one hand, the effective application of the law, and on the other, the proper protection of the fundamental rights of the person. Furthermore, the development of a common European framework should also be an opportunity to address specific challenges like cloud computing, the admissibility of data collected by national intelligence agencies, the transfer, exchange, and retention of data and virtual currencies. The challenges identified in this roadmap cannot be addressed without clear policies that reflect the objectives for improving legislation, law enforcement, trust and technical standards.

Law enforcement agencies implement very different solutions from Member State to Member State and sometimes operate even in scenarios where the legal rules are not clear or are not present at all. However, there are number of actions that can be taken within the community of law enforcement and digital forensics. It would be important to work on some issues of great impact in the activity of law enforcement: solutions for shared databases among law enforcement agencies, uniform guidelines for the processing of electronic evidence, upgrading of skills in the field of digital forensics, recognition of competencies of digital forensics labs.

This last aspect regarding the need for "professional development" in the field of digital forensics is a finding of great importance in a survey performed[20] as part of the Evidence project. Efforts in this regard should aim at standardising the

[20]Deliverable D6.2 and Deliverable D6.3 from Interpol, EVIDENCE, "Status quo assessment and analysis of primary challenges and shortcomings" and "Identification of best practices and guidelines to be integrated into a comprehensive European Framework", not public.

field of digital forensics, on the one hand regulating the career of experts who work in the area, by creating, where possible, appropriate professional bodies, such as the Netherlands Register of Court Experts,[21] recently established in the Netherlands, and even creating procedures for the validation and formal recognition or accreditation of laboratories of digital forensics, whether public or private.

2.6 Future Scenarios

In conclusion, the EU has introduced a series of instruments to improve judicial cooperation in criminal matters. In this sense, the principle of mutual recognition has been the main driver of judicial cooperation (Aulitano, 2016). To ensure the acquisition of evidence, the EIO is a significant step forward as it creates a harmonised instrument of rules for the collection and exchange of evidence, including material acquired through digital interceptions. However, this attempt does not yet fully meet the need for harmonisation of the collection and exchange of electronic evidence in criminal investigations. The investigative powers and the rules of criminal procedure of countries with similar legal traditions are still different and vary greatly from one jurisdiction to another. Therefore, it may be that electronic evidence acquired under the rules of legal system X are not suitable to form a reliable basis and are not admissible for use in another country Y. Without a single legal framework at a European level, defining specific rules on procedures and conditions for the collection, processing and exchange of electronic evidence, the Member States will tend to act differently and to decide on a case-by-case approach, relying on an approach more based on personal trust (in the relationships between the individual operators) than "institutional" trust.

However, there are some encouraging aspects that demonstrate an attitude that is all the same "aligned" among Member States concerning the processing and exchange of electronic evidence in the absence of a uniform framework, and maybe even show an implicit desire to converge towards uniform solutions:

- there is a common trend in applying the general principles and rules applicable to traditional evidence concerning the collection, exchange and probative value, even in cases that involve electronic evidence;
- the processing of electronic evidence is mainly a question of national laws and the provisions of criminal procedure;
- even in the absence of harmonisation at the regulatory level, the courts tend to be more prepared to handle and interpret the existing rules to regulate cases that involve electronic evidence;

[21]The Netherlands Register of Court Experts (NRGD), available to the Courts, was created in the Netherlands by a legislative measure in 2009, www.linkedin.com/company/the-netherlands-register-of-court-experts-nrgd-.

- the Convention on Cybercrime remains, at present, the most important point of reference for an international legal framework.

The natural consequence of this last finding is perhaps that the Council of Europe remains the most appropriate forum for a discussion on how to modify and/or supplement the existing legislation at a European level for the regulation of the processing and exchange of electronic evidence.

It is clear that the future effectiveness and success of the MLA procedures and especially of the EIO rely heavily on the realisation of secure and reliable exchange of evidence through the use of new technologies. Therefore, the fundamental need to be tackled in the near future, also in line with recent actions of working groups of the European Commission, is to increase, facilitate and support cooperation in criminal matters by working on specific needs in practice and in reality. Two key elements on which to focus in the coming years:

- foster mutual trust between all parties involved, which also strongly depends on a good level of knowledge and awareness of policies, actions and processes that must be undertaken by all actors involved;
- prepare an instrument, as desired by the Commission and the Council, which allows the exchange of electronic evidence between different Member States' authorities in a secure and reliable environment. Simply put, it is essential to know what must be done, be assured that what has been acquired and analysed as evidence remains so during the transmission from one Member State to another and that the tool that allows for the transmission is secure and reliable.

All parties involved in the exchange must be adequately informed and trained to understand, accept and finally to promote the exchange of electronic evidence. What is needed now is to move from theory to practice and to begin to experience what has been achieved so far with European level projects, actually trying to make the exchange, creating that awareness needed to make concrete, effective and operational strategies put in place until now. It is therefore necessary to start checking whether what was implemented and considered until now "on paper" can really work in real life. In this regard, it seems very useful to develop a "case study" for the exchange of electronic evidence that brings together the fast, secure and reliable infrastructure built by the e-Codex project with what is proposed by the Evidence project on the adoption of a formal language of exchange.

In addition, an awareness campaign on the subject, together with an open dialogue with stakeholders, will allow the assessment and building of a "custom" methodology to extend the exchange of electronic evidence to all Member States.

The European projects to use as starting points exist, the will of European institutions involved is there, the awareness on the part of the Member States of the need to cooperate effectively in criminal matters has greatly developed, the growing need of law enforcement is now crystal clear. All that remains is to start working concretely on the effective exchange of evidence in Europe and to build that virtual environment, whether centralised or decentralised, that will enable a secure and reliable exchange.

In Table 2.1 below the main initiatives or projects that somehow touch upon the Electronic Evidence domain and cross-border judicial cooperation are listed:

Table 2.1 Initiatives/projects related to electronic evidence domain or cross-border judicial cooperation

Project/initiative	Coordinated by	Topic
EVIDENCE	CNR-ITTIG, Institute of Legal Information Theory and Techniques of the National research Council of Italy	Electronic evidence handling and exchange cross-border cooperation
e-EVIDENCE	European Commission Directorate-General for Justice and Consumers	European Investigation Order (EIO), Electronic Evidence exchange, Reference Implementation Portal
EVIDENCE2e-CODEX	CNR-ITTIG, Institute of Legal Information Theory and Techniques of the National Research Council of Italy	Electronic Evidence Exchange, EIO and MLA e-Codex Infrastructure
EXEC	Ministry of Justice of Austria	Exchange European Investigation Orders (EIO) and related e-evidences fully electronically
me-CODEX	Ministry of Justice of North Rhine-Westphalia, Germany	Maintenance of the infrastructure realised by the e-Codex Project
e-CODEX	Ministry of Justice of North Rhine-Westphalia, Germany	Cross-border e-Justice in Europe
e-MLA	INTERPOL	Mutual Legal Assistance Requests Forms
MLA Tool	UNODOC	Mutual Legal Assistance Requests Forms drafting
Cybercrime Programme	Council of Europe	International Cooperation, Cybercrime, Electronic evidence treatment and exchange
ASGARD—Analysis System for Gathered Raw Data	Vicomtech-IK4—Visual Interaction and Communication Technologies	Tool set for the extraction, fusion, exchange and analysis of Big Data including cyber offenses data for forensic investigation
e-CRIME	TRILATERAL RESEARCH & CONSULTING LLP	Economic impacts of cyber crime
GIFT	Netherlands Forensic Institute	Forensic toolbox for CBRN Incidents
e-SENS	Ministry of Justice of North Rhine-Westphalia, Germany	Cross-border Public services, EU digital single market
LASIE	Engineering—Ingegneria Informatica Spa	Forensic tools, data extraction, electronic evidence
SIIP—Speaker Identification Integrated Project	VERINT	Suspect Identification solution based on a novel Speaker Identification (SID) engine and Global Info Sharing Mechanism (GISM)

References

Aulitano S (2016) E-evidence in the European union. In: De Zan T, Aulitano S (eds) EUnited against crime: improving criminal justice in European union cyberspace. IAI Documents, 16–17 November 2016

Camaldo L (2014) La direttiva sull'ordine Europeo di Indagine penale (EIO): un congegno di acquisizione della prova dotato di molteplici potenzialità, ma di non facile attuazione. www.penalecontemporaneo.it

Castellaneta M (2009) Uno scambio di informazioni tra gli Stati per rafforzare la lotta al crimine organizzato. In: Guida al diritto, vol 30, pp 63–66

Council of the European Union (2016) Conclusioni del Consiglio sul miglioramento della giustizia penale nel cibserspazio. www.consilium.europa.eu/it/press/press-releases/2016/06/09-criminal-activities-cyberspace

De Amicis G (2011) Limiti e prospettive del mandato europeo di ricerca della prova. In: Grasso G, Picotti L, Sicurella R. (eds) L'evoluzione del diritto penale nei ettori di interesse europeo alla luce del Trattato di Lisbona, Giuffrè, Milano, p 10

Del Coco R (2015) Ordine Europeo di indagine e poteri sanzionatori del giudice. www.penalecontemporaneo.it

Janssens C (2013) The principle of mutual recognition in EU law. Oxford University Press, Oxford

Seger A (2016) E-evidence and access to data in the cloud. Issues and options under consideration by the cloud evidence group of the cybercrime convention committee. In: Cajani F, Cernuto G et al (eds) Le nuove frontiere della'cquisizione degli elementi di prova nel cyberspace. IISFA, Available only as an ebook on www.amazon.it

Siracusano F (2016) Procedure di cooperazione giudiziaria e garanzie difensive: lungo la strada, a piccoli passi. Archivio Penale 3:14 pp

Spencer JR (2014) Il principio del mutuo riconoscimento. In: Kostoris RE (ed) Manuale di procedura penale europea, 2nd edn. Giuffrè, Milan, p 235

Vermulen G, De Bondt W, Van Damme Y (2010) EU cross-border gathering and use of evidence in criminal matters: towards mutual recognition of investigative measures and free movement of evidence? IRCP series, vol 37. Maklu Publishers, Antwerpen, p 57

Part II
International Perspective

Chapter 3
e-Evidence and Access to Data in the Cloud Results of the Cloud Evidence Group of the Cybercrime Convention Committee

Alexander Seger

Abstract Evidence in relation to any crime is increasingly (only) available in electronic form on computer systems or storage devices and needs to be secured for criminal proceedings. Criminal investigations not relying on electronic evidence are becoming the exception. Access to electronic evidence—in relation to cybercrime and any other type of crime—is thus essential for criminal justice, as well as for ensuring the rule of law. A major problem is that electronic evidence is often not located in the territory of the investigating criminal justice authority but increasingly in foreign, multiple or unknown jurisdictions, that is, somewhere "in the cloud". To address this issue, the Cybercrime Convention Committee of the Council of Europe—representing the Parties to the Budapest Convention on Cybercrime—in December 2014 established a Cloud Evidence Working Group (CEG) which has identified options for common international solutions.

3.1 Background

Millions of attacks against computers and data are recorded each day worldwide. At the same time, only a very small fraction of cybercrime—that is, offences against and by means of computers—is actually prosecuted and adjudicated. Moreover, evidence in relation to any crime is increasingly (only) available in electronic form on computer systems or storage devices and needs to be secured for criminal proceedings. Criminal investigations not relying on electronic evidence are becoming the exception.

Access to electronic evidence—in relation to cybercrime and any other type of crime—is thus essential for criminal justice, as well as for ensuring the rule of law.

A. Seger (✉)
Council of Europe, Cybercrime Convention Committee, Strasbourg, France
e-mail: alexander.seger@coe.int

M. A. Biasiotti et al. (eds.), *Handling and Exchanging Electronic Evidence Across Europe*, Law, Governance and Technology Series 39,
https://doi.org/10.1007/978-3-319-74872-6_3

However, the matter is complex. A major problem is that electronic evidence is often not located in the territory of the investigating criminal justice authority. Data is increasingly stored on, mirrored on, or fragmented or moving between servers "somewhere in the cloud" in possibly multiple or unknown jurisdictions, while criminal justice authorities and their jurisdiction to enforce are normally limited by the principle of territoriality.

Even if data is stored in the territory of an investigating authority and a server or device could be lawfully searched and seized, this will not be sufficient if the natural or legal person in possession or control of the data—that is, the person with the keys to the data—is elsewhere.

To address this question and identify common international solutions, the Cybercrime Convention Committee of the Council of Europe—representing the Parties to the Budapest Convention on Cybercrime—in December 2014 established a Cloud Evidence Working Group (CEG). In November 2016, the plenary of the Committee discussed the recommendations resulting from the work of the CEG. The present paper summarises the key issues and offers an update on the recommendations.

3.2 Key Issues

The CEG has identified the following specific issues:

3.2.1 Subscriber Versus Traffic Versus Content Data

It is necessary to distinguish different subscriber information, traffic data and content data. Subscriber information is most often required in criminal investigations. It is less privacy-sensitive than traffic or content data. At the same time, rules for access to subscriber information not harmonised.

Subscriber information is held by service providers and obtained through production orders. Such orders represent a lesser interference in the rights of individuals than search and seizure.

3.2.2 Mutual Legal Assistance

Mutual legal assistance remains a primary means to obtain electronic evidence for criminal justice purposes. However, MLA needs to be made more efficient.

Often subscriber information or traffic data are needed first to substantiate or address an MLA request.

And often, MLA is not a feasible option to secure volatile evidence in unknown or multiple jurisdictions.

3.2.3 Loss of (Knowledge) of Location

In "loss of location" situations (unknown source of attack, servers in multiple or changing locations, live forensics, etc.) MLA is not feasible and the principle of territoriality is not always applicable. Direct transborder access to data without MLA may be necessary.

However, what conditions and safeguards apply?

Article 32b Budapest Convention offers only limited possibilities. In the absence of international legal framework for lawful transborder access, unilateral solutions are pursued by governments. This leads to a jungle of approaches with risks to rights of individuals and state to state relations.

3.2.4 A Provider Offering a Service in the Territory of a State

Natural or legal persons that are physically in territory of a state are within the enforcement jurisdiction of that state. However, often providers are offering a service in the territory of a state without being represented there. This raises the question of whether a criminal justice authority could issue a production order to such a provider, at least for subscriber information.

3.2.5 Voluntary Disclosure by Private Sector Entities

European countries in 2015 sent more than 130,000 requests—mostly for subscriber information—directly to major US service providers; and these responded positively in about 60% of the cases on average. This is most valuable for criminal justice authorities.

At the same time, this raises concerns. US providers may cooperate voluntarily and thus decide themselves whether or not to cooperate. Their policies and practices are volatile with considerable variations between providers and countries. In short, this practice is unpredictable. At the same time, European providers do not disclose data at all directly to foreign authorities.

A clearer and more stable framework is required.

3.2.6 Emergency Procedures

Often data is needed in emergency situations such as an imminent threat to life. However, few countries have legal provisions and practical procedures in place for mutual legal assistance in emergency cases and to obtain and disclose data without delay.

Major US providers do have policies for emergency situations and sometimes are willing to cooperate upon a direct request from a criminal justice authority abroad. However, the same concerns as above apply. And again, European providers do not disclose data directly to foreign authorities, even in emergency situations.

3.2.7 Data Protection and Other Safeguards

Data protection requirements are normally met if powers to obtain data are defined in domestic criminal procedure law and/or mutual legal assistance (MLA) agreements. However, MLA is not always feasible.

Increasingly, personal data is disclosed "asymmetrically" transborder from criminal justice authorities to service providers and vice-versa.

The legal basis for such transfers and the conditions under which they would be permitted, are often not clear. Greater legal certainty is needed.

3.3 Recommendations

The Cloud Evidence Group—in its final report—recommends five solutions to address these issues and considers that these should be pursued as a package at the same time.

3.3.1 More Efficient Mutual Legal Assistance

In December 2014, the Cybercrime Convention Committee had completed a detailed assessment of the functioning of mutual legal assistance and adopted a set of 24 recommendations. The first 15 should be pursued by Parties to the Budapest Convention at domestic levels. They include allocation of more resources for MLA, streamlining of procedures, or electronic transmissions of requests. These recommendations remain relevant and should be implemented.

Obviously, if States are not prepared to make the MLA process with its built-in safeguards more efficient, more far-reaching solutions will find little acceptance.

This proposal was accepted by the plenary of the Cybercrime Convention Committee in November 2016. The Committee is now carrying out an assessment of follow up given by Parties to these 15 recommendations.

3.3.2 Guidance Note on Article 18 on the Production of Subscriber Information

Article 18 Budapest Convention covers two situations:

- Domestic production orders if a provider is in the territory of a Party even if data is stored in another jurisdiction (Article 18.1.a)
- Domestic production orders for subscriber information if a provider is NOT in the territory of a Party but is offering a service in the territory of the Party (Article 18.1.b)

A common understanding of the Parties on the interpretation of in particular Article 18.1.b could mean that this provision—if implemented in this manner in domestic law—may serve as a legal basis for direct requests to service providers in other jurisdictions.

This recommendation proved rather difficult to reach agreement upon in the Plenary of November 2016. However, following further negotiations, consensus was reached on a revised text of the "Guidance Note on the Production of Subscriber Information" on 28 February 2017. This Note is now considered adopted.

3.3.3 Domestic Regimes for the Disclosure of Subscriber Information

Parties should fully implement Article 18 Budapest Convention on production orders. This includes a lighter regime for the disclosure of subscriber information as opposed to other types of data.

This recommendation was adopted by the Plenary in November 2016.

Obviously, the above Guidance Note should be considered so that data received from providers in other jurisdictions can also be used as evidence in criminal proceedings.

3.3.4 Practical Measures to Improve Cooperation with Providers

Pending longer-term solutions (see solution 5 below), cooperation with providers could be improved, for example, through regular meetings and sharing of experience, online tools through which law enforcement obtains a better understanding of provider policies and providers understand the legal basis for requests from law enforcement, training and other support by providers in capacity building programmes.

This recommendation was adopted by the Plenary of November 2017.

3.3.5 An Additional Protocol to the Budapest Convention on Cybercrime

Such a Protocol may take some time to negotiate and to be implemented by Parties to the Budapest Convention. However, the Cloud Evidence Group considers that it is necessary to invest in such an effort. Elements for consideration include:

(a) Provisions for more efficient MLA

- International production orders or simplified MLA for subscriber information
- Direct cooperation between judicial authorities in MLA
- Joint investigations and joint investigation teams
- Requests in English
- Emergency procedures

(b) Provisions for direct transborder cooperation with providers

- Disclosure of data by LEA to a service provider abroad in specific situations
- Disclosure of subscriber information by service providers to LEA abroad with conditions and safeguards
- Direct preservation requests to providers abroad
- Admissibility of data obtained directly in domestic proceedings
- Emergency procedures

(c) Framework and safeguards for practices of transborder access to data

- Transborder access to data with lawfully obtained credentials
- Transborder access in good faith or in exigent circumstances
- The power of disposal as connecting legal factor

(d) Data protection provisions

The Plenary of the Cybercrime Convention Committee in November 2017 "agreed in principle on the need for an Additional Protocol". The Plenary of June 2017 is expected to come to a formal decision.

3.4 Conclusions and Follow Up

The issue of criminal justice access to electronic evidence in the cloud with the necessary safeguards remains a major challenge. Without access to data and thus evidence, it will be difficult for governments to protect society and individuals against crime and to ensure the rule of law in cyberspace.

In the course of 2017, the recommendations of the Cloud Evidence Group were adopted by the Cybercrime Convention Committee. In September 2017, negotiations on an additional Protocol to the Budapest Convention commenced. The years 2018 and 2019 will show whether more extensive rules can be negotiated and agreed upon in a binding international legal instrument. In all likelihood, this is the most concrete avenue to come to an international agreement on these matters for the next one or two decades.

Chapter 4
The Evolution of Expressing and Exchanging Cyber-Investigation Information in a Standardized Form

Eoghan Casey, Sean Barnum, Ryan Griffith, Jonathan Snyder, Harm van Beek, and Alex Nelson

Abstract The growing number of investigations involving digital traces from various data sources is driving the demand for a standard way to represent and exchange pertinent information. Enabling automated combination and correlation of cyber-investigation information from multiple systems or organizations enables more efficient and comprehensive analysis, reducing the risk of mistakes and missed opportunities. These needs are being met by the evolving open-source, community-developed specification language called CASE, the Cyber-investigation Analysis Standard Expression. CASE leverages the Unified Cyber Ontology (UCO), which abstracts and expresses concepts that are common across multiple domains. This paper introduces CASE and UCO, explaining how they improve upon prior related work. The value of fully-structured data, representing provenance, and action lifecycles are discussed. The guiding principles of CASE and UCO are presented, and illustrative examples of CASE are provided using the default JSON-LD serialization.

E. Casey (✉)
University of Lausanne, School of Criminal Sciences, Lausanne, Switzerland
e-mail: eoghan.casey@unil.ch

S. Barnum
Mitre Corporation, McLean, VA, USA
e-mail: sean.barnum@fireeye.com

R. Griffith · J. Snyder
Department of Defense Cyber Crime Center, Linthicum, MD, USA
e-mail: ryan.griffith@dc3.mil; jonathan.snyder@dc3.mil

H. van Beek
Netherlands Forensic Institute, The Hague, The Netherlands
e-mail: harm.van.beek@nfi.minvenj.nl

A. Nelson
National Institute of Standards and Technology, Gaithersburg, MD, USA
e-mail: alexander.nelson@nist.gov

M. A. Biasiotti et al. (eds.), *Handling and Exchanging Electronic Evidence Across Europe*, Law, Governance and Technology Series 39,
https://doi.org/10.1007/978-3-319-74872-6_4

4.1 Introduction

This paper describes the evolution of a community-developed, standardized specification language for representing and exchanging information in the broadest possible range of domains involved with cyber-investigations, including digital forensics, criminal justice, incident response, and counter terrorism.[1] This initiative was originally called the Digital Forensic Analysis eXpression (DFAX), which has evolved into the Cyber-investigation Analysis Standard Expression (CASE)[2]. To further promote a common structure, CASE aligns with and extends the Unified Cyber Ontology (UCO) construct, which provides a scaffolding for representing all cyber artifacts and associated activities. The UCO stands to abstract artifacts that are not CASE-specific, so that they can be used across other cyber disciplines that can extend the UCO.

4.2 Motivation

A primary motivation for this community-driven initiative is interoperability and interconnection to enable the exchange of cyber-investigation information between tools and organizations. The CASE specification language and underlying UCO are a rational progression from the foundational work on Digital Forensic Analysis eXpression (DFAX), which focused on digital forensic information and provenance context (Casey et al., 2015).

> When investigating a single incident, being able to combine the results from multiple tools that are used to extract information from the digital evidence supports forensic reconstruction, including timeline creation and link analysis. In addition, being able to automate the comparison of similar results from multiple tools facilitates dual-tool verification. When crime spans borders, sharing of information between investigative agencies in multiple jurisdictions is crucial for a successful resolution. A fundamental requirement in digital forensics is to maintain information about evidence provenance as it is exchanged and processed, to help establish authenticity and trustworthiness. Furthermore, without a standardized approach to representing and sharing digital forensic information, investigators in different jurisdictions may never know that they are investigating crimes committed by the same criminal. (Casey et al., 2015)

For example, standardizing how cyber-information is represented addresses the current problem of investigators receiving the same kind of information from different sources in a variety of formats (e.g., call detail records, ISP logs).

The exchange of information in a standardized format helps break down data silos, increasing visibility across disparate data sources as depicted in Fig. 4.1.

Another primary motivation for CASE is to enable more advanced and comprehensive correlation and analysis (Casey et al., 2017). CASE can be used to automate

[1]For more technical details, design decisions, and comprehensive examples, see Casey et al. (2017).

[2]https://sites.google.com/view/casework/

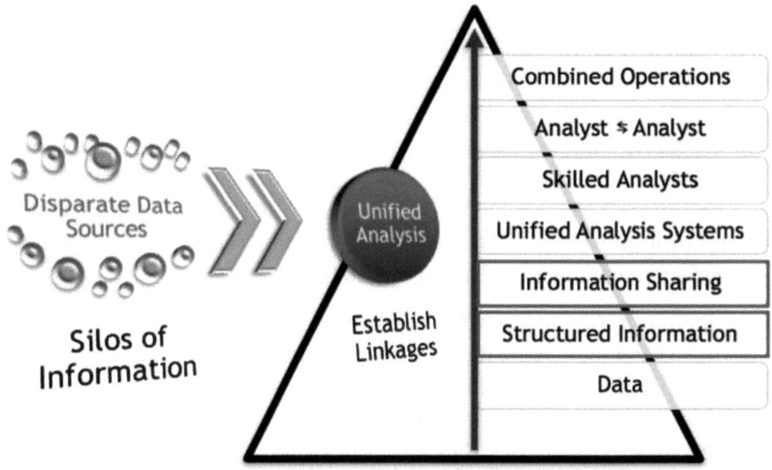

Fig. 4.1 Representing data in a standardized format facilitates information sharing, helping break down data silos, increasing visibility across multiple data sources, and enabling more comprehensive correlation and analysis

the validation, normalization, and combination of data to provide a cohesive and comprehensive analysis platform. In addition to fusing together disparate sources of information, CASE expresses information in a fully structured form that supports a multitude of analysis methods. In addition to searching for specific keywords or characteristics within a single case or across multiple cases, having a structured representation of cyber-investigation information allows pattern searching, graph query, data mining, and other sophisticated analytics (Casey et al., 2017). Improved capabilities to find important items can help solve a case, and more effective approaches to finding repetitions between cases to support crime analysis and can help overcome linkage blindness.[3] Overcoming linkage blindness can find connections between cases involving the same criminal activity or crime pattern across multiple jurisdictions. More generally, observing patterns across cases can improve understanding of crime phenomena and trends, which can help develop strategies to fight certain crimes.

The capabilities, flexibility, and overall scope of CASE goes beyond all prior efforts to represent digital forensic information, including:

- The XML Data Encoding Specification for Intelligence Document and Media Exploitation (DOMEX) was developed by the U.S. government to share certain types of information, including mobile device details (Office of the Director of National Intelligence, 2017). Although some elements in the DOMEX standard

[3]Linkage blindness is a term coined by a criminologist Steve Egger in the context of serial homicides to describe the failure to recognize a pattern that links one crime to another, such as crimes committed by the same offender in different jurisdictions (Egger, 1984).

are used to keep track of provenance, the lack of supporting ontology, the very limited expressivity for characterizing cyber observables, and the inability to capture relationships limit the expressivity and flexibility of this standard.
- CybOX, which has been replaced by STIX Observables as an integrated component of STIX, and concentrates on representing cyber threat intelligence (Barnum, 2014).
- Digital Forensics XML, or DFXML (Garfinkel, 2012), is a schema that is used by several tools to represent file system information (Garfinkel, 2009) and cross-verify extracted metadata (Nelson et al., 2014).

Development of CASE and UCO is coordinated through GitHub (https://github.com/ucoProject) and the CASE-dev Google Group (case-dev@googlegroups.com).

This paper provides a brief history of CASE and the UCO, followed by an overview of the ontology and specification language with illustrative examples for common use cases. Additional JSON examples and supporting documentation are provided on the GitHub site.

4.3 Background

The foundation for this evolving community-driven standard was called DFAX, which included initial work on the UCO, and concentrated on representing and sharing digital forensic information. DFAX utilized Cyber Observable eXpression (CybOX) to represent the purely technical information, such as binary artifacts and sources of matched search patterns (Casey et al., 2015).

In 2016, the independent CybOX was replaced by STIX Observables as an integrated component of the STIX standard, which focuses on cyber threat intelligence (CTI). Because of this CTI focus, STIX Observables do not provide many of the elements needed to represent digital forensic and cyber-investigation information.

Leveraging all of the lessons learned from CybOX and DFAX, this standardization effort evolved into CASE and the UCO to provide an improved data model and underlying ontology. CASE, as a specific profile of the UCO, provides support for cyber-investigations in any context, including criminal, corporate and intelligence.

CASE, and relevant portions, of the UCO, build on the Hansken data model developed and implemented by the Netherlands Forensic Institute (NFI). Building on the success of its precursor XIRAF, Hansken provides a robust platform that supports hundreds of investigations each year. The Hansken data model provides a solid foundation for developing CASE, including traces that are commonly encountered in cyber-investigations, and sufficient flexibility to add new types of traces (van Baar et al., 2014).

Fully structuring data, which is supported by CASE and the UCO, enables a wide range of analysis and correlation techniques. Other ontology-based efforts aimed at analyzing digital evidence have addressed specific issues, and can use CASE as their specification language. For instance, the Ontology for the Representation of Digital Incidents and Investigations (ORD2i) referenced DFAX and the UCO, and provided a proof-of-concept implementation for timeline reconstruction and analysis (Chabot et al., 2015). The Digital Evidence Semantic Ontology (DESO) ontology-based approach was proposed to represent known digital traces and to support triage searches of a digital crime scene for matching characteristics (Brady et al., 2015). The ParFor project also proposed an ontology-based approach to representing activities on computer systems (Turnbull and Randhawab, 2015). The DEMF proposed a framework for representing digital evidence metadata and provenance information (Cosic and Baca, 2015). These efforts demonstrate that the need for a standardized way to represent and share cyber-investigation information is well recognized. Before the UCO, there was limited agreement across the diverse community for such an ontology. CASE and the UCO address this gap with an ontology that can be used as a basis for community consensus and interoperability across tools and organizations.

The CASE specification language is not intended to define how tools or systems arrange data internally, but rather as a common language that applications can export and import to support interoperability and normalization. Developers of systems and applications can translate CASE to their internal implementations. The proposed default JSON serialization is only one form of serialization, and CASE could be represented in XML, Turtle (RDF), protocol buffers, or other serializations.

4.4 UCO Overview

For the cyber-investigation scope of CASE, the types of information that need to be represented in cyber-investigations can be treated as layers of different types of information, with the lowest layer representing raw information, the middle layer representing provenance, and the higher layer representing behavior (Fig. 4.2).

The UCO (see Fig. 4.3) provides an ontology that generalizes how each of these types of information is structured (among many others), and can be useful across multiple domains.

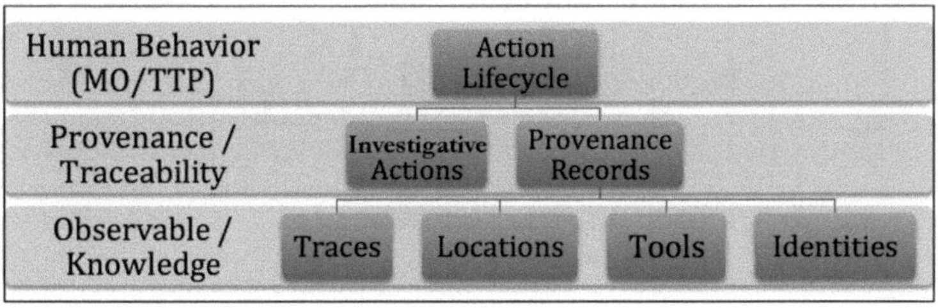

Fig. 4.2 Layers of representing cyber-investigation information

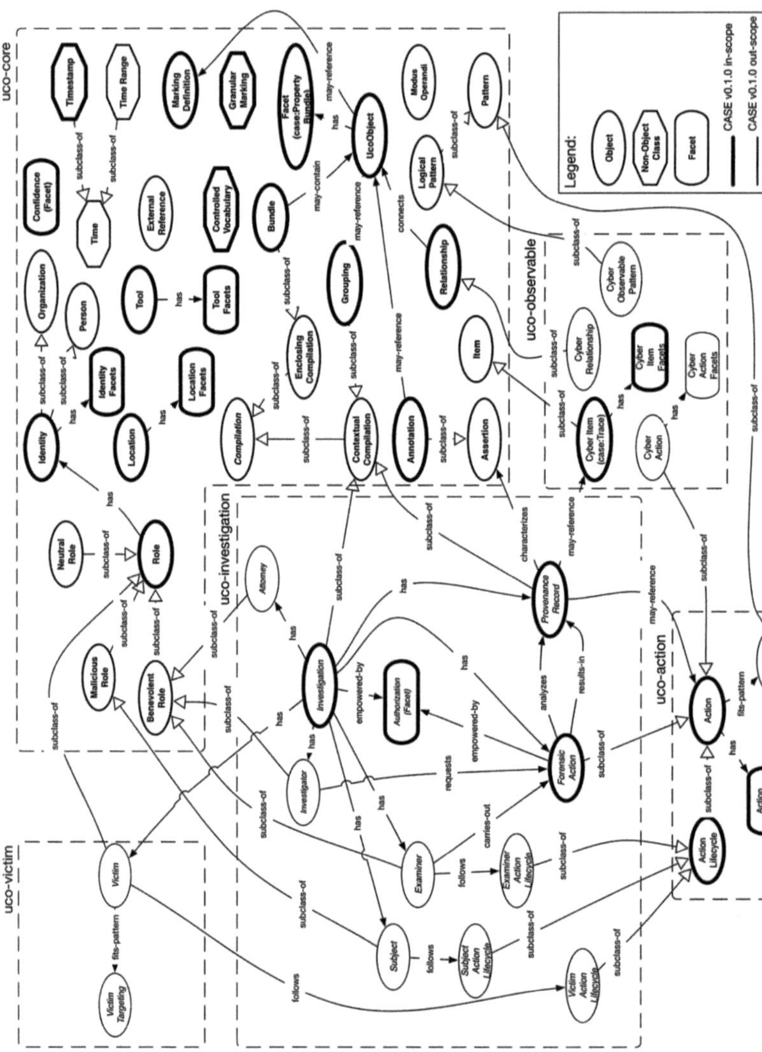

Fig. 4.3 High level depiction of the Unified Cyber Ontology

4.5 CASE Overview

A fundamental aspect of cyber-investigations is the extraction and analysis of traces, where the definition of a trace is any observable modification, including an absence of expected data, resulting from an incident or offense (Casey, 2013). In the context of cyber-investigations, traces are *"silent witnesses that need to be detected, seen, and understood to make reasonable inferences about criminal phenomena, investigation or demonstration for intelligence, investigation and court purposes"* (Margot, 2011). The state of a trace is also important to capture, such as whether an item is allocated or deleted, or even whether an expected trace exists or is missing.

CASE is flexible enough to represent a wide range of traces (corresponding to cyber-items as defined in the UCO) and their associated properties, including disks, devices, and file systems, providing a solid foundation for representing details within cyber-investigations. Figure 4.4 depicts a File object with multiple property bundles. The use of Property Bundles in CASE was inspired by the data model implemented in the Hansken system which uses duck typing[4] (van Beek et al., 2015). Properties include date-time stamps, the contents of a trace, and the hash values (e.g., MD5 and SHA256) of the data, amongst others.

Whereas DFAX utilized XML as its default serialization, in response to community input, CASE/UCO selected JSON-LD as the initial serialization binding (Lanthaler and Gütl, 2012). JSON is powerful and flexible but requires some scaffolding to support validation against an ontology. JSON-LD provides the necessary structure to support full validation of JSON content to its associated ontological specification as shown in *List 1*. The explicit validation enabled by JSON-LD yields assured integrity between the ontology and the serialization, and offers significant automation advantages including built-in API support for a range of languages (Python, Ruby, PHP, Go, C#, Java, etc.) and for lossless transformation between several serialization formats (JSON-LD, RDF-XML, Turtle-RDF, etc.).

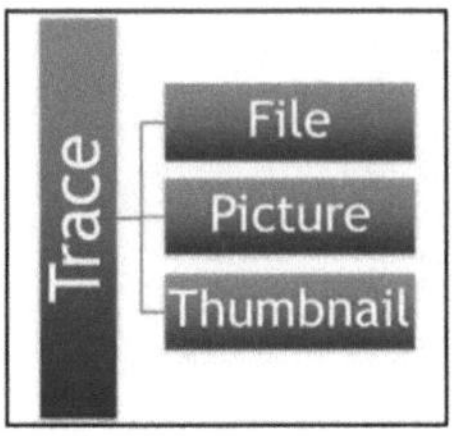

Fig. 4.4 Duck model allows flexible representation of traces using various combinations of property bundles

[4]Duck typing allows data to be defined by its inherent characteristics rather than enforcing strict data typing. CASE objects can be assigned any rational combination of property bundles, such as a file that is an image and a thumbnail. When employing this approach, data types are evaluated with the duck test. Simply stated, if it walks like a duck, swims like a duck, quacks like a duck, and looks like a duck, then it probably is a duck.

```
{
  "@context": {
    "@vocab": "http://case.example.org/core#"
},
  "@graph": [
{
      "@id": "digital_photograph1",
      "@type": "Trace",
      "propertyBundle": [
        {
          "@type": "File",
          "fileSystemType": "EXT4",
          "fileName": "IMG_0123.jpg",
          "filePath": "/sdcard/IMG_0123.jpg",
          "extension": "jpg",
          "sizeInBytes": 35002
        },
        {
          "@type": "ContentData",
          "byteOrder": "BigEndian",
          "magicNumber": "/9j/ww==",
          "mimeType": "image/jpg",
          "sizeInBytes": 35000,
          "dataPayload": "<base 64 encoded data of the file>",
          "hash": [
            {
              "@type": "Hash",
              "hashMethod": "SHA256",
              "hashValue": "6b86b273ff34fce19d6b804eff5a3f5
               747ada4eaa22f1d49c01e52ddb7875b4b"
            }
          ]
        }
        {
          "@type": "RasterPicture",
          "pictureType": "jpg",
          "pictureheight": 12345,
          "picturewidth": 12345,
          "bitsPerPixel": 2
        },
        {
          "@type": "EXIF",
          "exifData": [
            {
              "key": "Make",
              "value": "Canon"
            },
            {
              "key": "Model",
              "value": "PowerShot SX540"
            },
            {
              "key": "Orientation",
              "value": "Horizontal (normal)"
```

```
            },
            {
              "key": "DateTimeDigitized",
              "value": "2010-01-15T17:59:43.25Z"
            }
          ]
}
```


List 1 Example of CASE being used to represent a file. The JSON in this example is JSON-LD, which uses strict, namespaced `@type` values to specify the type for all JSON objects, enabling their explicit traceability back to the specifications for these types in the UCO (see "exif_data.json" on GitHub)

The ongoing community development of CASE is working to expand the specification language to cover other types of information.

4.6 Provenance

For cyber-investigation purposes, to help establish the authenticity and reliability of information, it is important to capture where it originated or was found, as well as how it was handled after it was found. This lineage is collectively referred to as provenance.

Provenance includes collection documentation, chain of custody details, audit logs from forensic acquisition tools, and integrity records, which all help to establish the trustworthiness of cyber-investigation information. Provenance also involves tracking the data source and extraction method for each trace, such as a digital photograph obtained from a smartphone as depicted in Fig. 4.5.

CASE and the UCO provide structures to represent all aspects of provenance in cyber-investigations, including chain-of-custody, case management, and forensic processing. CASE captures provenance information using Provenance Records that can include environmental characteristics such as the details of a crime scene or where the evidence was physically located. In addition, CASE captures information about any Investigative Action associated with each Provenance Record, including who performed each Investigative Action and when it was performed (see Fig. 4.6).

A basic example of a Investigative Action and Provenance Record is provided in *List 2*. In addition to supporting provenance, Investigative Actions can give insight into which tools and methods are effective in particular circumstances. Complete technical representation of the physical location where evidence was obtained and the people associated with the evidence can be covered by existing schemas. Therefore, rather than creating a new representation of such information, it is more effective to leverage an existing schema for such data. CASE and the UCO have been designed to accommodate such re-use. Rather than creating a new geolocation schema, CASE defines an extension point where an existing schema can be used.

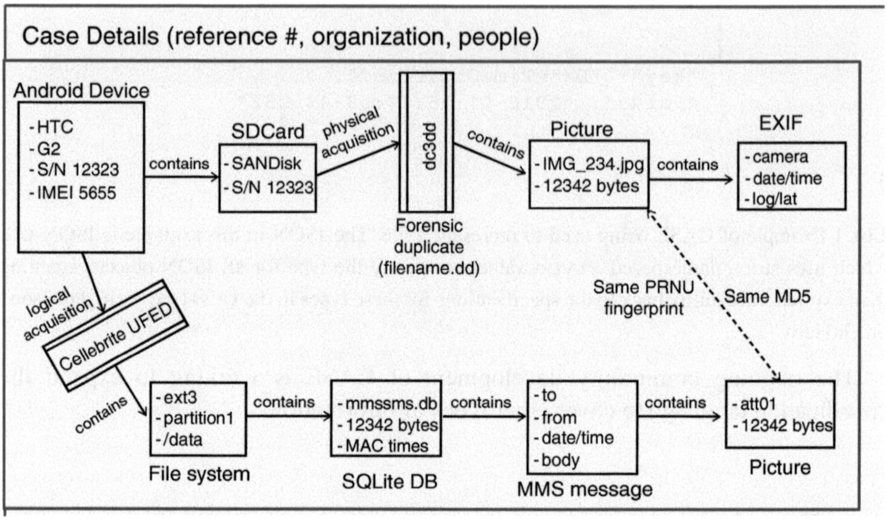

Fig. 4.5 Provenance of a digital photograph extracted from an Android device, with one copy on the SDCard and another in an MMS attachment

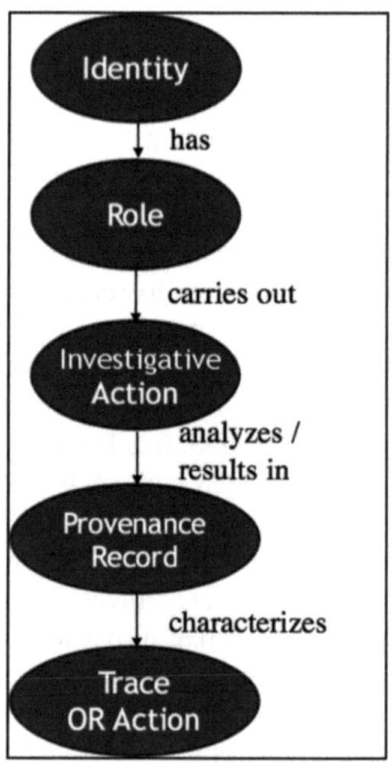

Fig. 4.6 Conceptual depiction of representing provenance

```
{
  "@id": "provenance_record1",
  "@type": "ProvenanceRecord",
  "description": "Android Smartphone",
  "exhibitNumber": " DFL-20170115-001",
  "object": "device1"
},
{
  "@id": "provenance_record2",
  "@type": "ProvenanceRecord",
  "description": "Forensic image of Android Smartphone",
  "exhibitNumber": "DFL-20170115-001-MD",
  "object": "android_image"
},
{
  "@id": "annotation1",
  "@type": "Annotation",
  "description": "Create forensic image of Android device",
  "tags": [
    "forensic"
  ],
  "object": [
    "forensic_action2"
  ]
},
{
  "@id": "investigative_action2",
  "@type": "InvestigativeAction",
  "name": "imaged",
  "startTime": "2017-01-15T17:59:43.25Z",
  "endTime": "2017-01-15T19:59:43.25Z",
  "propertyBundle": [
    {
      "@type": "ActionReferences",
      "performer": "investigator1",
      "instrument": "tool1",
      "object": [
        " provenance_record1"
      ],
      "result": [
        "provenance_record2"
      ],
      "location": "forensic_lab1",
      "environment": "forensic_lab_computer1"
    },
    {
      "@type": "acme:ToolArguments",
      "aquisitionType": "Logical",
      "method": "ADB"
    }
  ]
},
```

List 2 Example of investigative action and provenance records representing using CASE

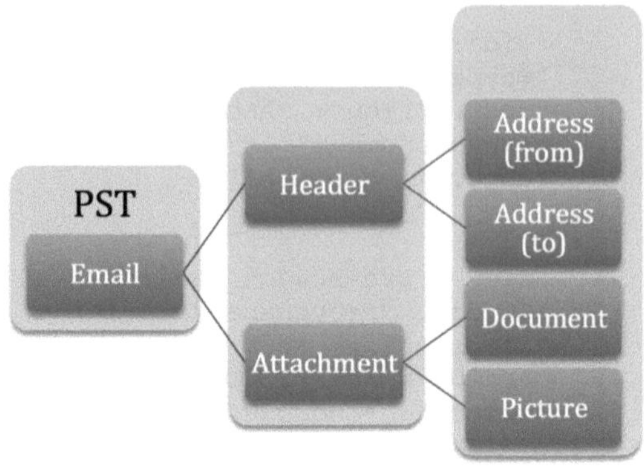

Fig. 4.7 Structured representation of an Outlook PST file that contains an email message with multiple attachments

4.7 Fully-Structured Data in CASE

In addition to representing individual traces, it is important to capture their context and relationship with other traces and entities, for provenance and analysis purposes. CASE represents the linkages between traces using a combination of embedded references for properties that cannot change and relationships for things that can change or are externally asserted. The example in Fig. 4.7 depicts the links between a PST file and the email that it contains, which in turn contains email addresses and attachments.

Being able to represent structure by defining relationships within the data enables search and analysis methods at a higher level of abstraction, including graph querying and pattern matching. For instance, defined relationships between traces as shown in Fig. 4.7 could be utilized to perform a graph search for all email messages with a picture attachment from the subject to the victim (Casey et al., 2015).

4.8 Representing Actions in CASE

CASE and the UCO provide a simple and adaptable way to represent an action or multiple related actions, which can be useful for sharing knowledge and supporting more advanced forensic analysis. In the context of cyber-investigations, CASE can represent actions involving digital traces such as a USB device being inserted into a computer and its associated traces (Casey et al., 2015). CASE can also be used to represent offender and victim actions and their associated traces. This type of abstraction can provide higher-level, human understandable portrayals of activities for more efficient forensic analysis.

Some forensic tools are adding features to support such abstractions for generalized activities of interest that comprise various low-level artifacts. For instance, the tagging feature in Plaso (https://code.google.com/p/plaso/) can group certain combinations of digital artifacts into event categories such as *Application Execu-*

tion, *Document Opened*, and *File Downloaded* that can be queried to return the underlying low-level digital artifacts associated with these events. CASE provides a standardized way to represent these kinds of actions. Furthermore, beyond simply categorizing low-level artifacts, CASE can be used to define relationships between actions and traces, thus enabling more structured searches and refined analysis.

4.9 Action Lifecycle

The Action Lifecycle from the UCO can be adapted within CASE to define phases of a forensic investigation (e.g., documentation, preservation, examination, analysis, presentation) as shown in Table 4.1. This generalized approach can be used to classify each action in a case, which provides context to support further analysis.

In ORD2i, the Extraction, Settlement, Enhancement, and Analysis phases of SADFC (Semantic Analysis of Digital Forensic Cases) can be represented in CASE as an Action Lifecycle. This type of information can be used to address various questions such as how much time was taken by each phase of an investigation, determining which tools are most useful for a given phase, and isolating which results were generated at different phases.

As shown in Table 4.2, the Action Lifecycle can also be used to categorize criminal activities such as a sexual predator's grooming of victims or a network intruder's method of operation (e.g., kill chain phases).

Table 4.1 Forensic processes with different phases can be represented as an Action Lifecycle to categorize actions using CASE

Forensic process #1	Forensic process #2	Forensic process #3	Forensic process #4
		Authorization	
	Planning	Planning	Preparation
Identification	Identification	Notification	
Preservation	Reconnaissance	Search	Incident response
Collection	Transport and storage	Collection	Data collection
Examination		Transport	
Analysis	Analysis	Storage	Data analysis
Presentation	Proof and defense	Examination	Presentation of findings
	Archive storage	Presentation	
		Proof/defense	Incident closure
		Dissemination	

Table 4.2 Forensic processes with different phases can be represented as an Action Lifecycle to categorize actions using CASE

Grooming (sexual assaults)	Kill chain (intrusion)
Victim selection {traces of search history for vulnerable youths}	Reconnaissance {traces of attackers exploring org website}
Establish trust {traces of messages from subject to victim}	Development {traces of targeted malware development}
Desensitization to sexual activity/abuse {traces of pornography from subject to victim}	Delivery {traces of phishing emails}
Maintain secrecy (persuasion/threats) {traces of messages from subject to victim}	Exploitation {traces of malware and compromise}
Arrange meeting {traces of messages from subject to victim}	Configuration {traces of entrenchment}
Conceal evidence {traces of encryption}	Beaconing and C2 {traces of command and control}

4.10 Guiding Principles

This initiative to structure and share cyber-investigation information strives to implement a core set of guiding principles that community consensus has deemed necessary. Using lessons learned from DFAX, CybOX, STIX and Hansken, these principles are as follows:

1. **Expressivity:** To fully support the diversity of use cases in digital forensics, this initiative aims to address all defined use cases rather than focusing on a specific one. This goal involves covering all types of information relevant to digital forensics for various purposes.
2. **Integrate Rather Than Duplicate:** Build on existing standardized representations, rather than create a separate one, to avoid redundancy and duplication of effort.
3. **Flexibility:** Avoid mandatory features to allow users to employ any portions of the standardized representation that are relevant for a given context.
4. **Extensibility:** Support community-driven refinement and evolution of the language by building in extension mechanisms for domain-specific use, for localized use, for user-driven refinements and evolution, and for ease of centralized refinement and evolution.
5. **Automatability:** Intentionally seek to maximize structure and consistency to support machine-processable automation.

4.11 Conclusions and Next Steps

The CASE specification language and underlying UCO support information standardization and interoperability for tools and organizations dealing with cyber-investigations. In addition to sharing cyber-investigation information in a specific case, sharing traces or patterns of particular activities in a standardized format can help others find similar traces and patterns in new cases. Standardized representation of traces can also be useful for application footprinting by recording all traces of a given action (e.g., install, execute, uninstall). For example, the NIST Diskprint project is expanding the National Software Reference Library (NSRL) metadata reference set by recording changes made to a system by an application over its lifecycle (https://www.nist.gov/itl/ssd/cs/diskprints). As a way of communicating these changes, NIST outputs the file metadata in multiple serialized formats. Sharing this kind of software Diskprint information is a powerful means of facilitating digital forensic analysis and tool development.

Codifying and sharing information in a standardized manner enables digital investigators to search for similar patterns in their cases. Finding similar patterns between cases can support reuse of previously effective solutions, such as forensic analysis methods for proving that wiping occurred and possibly recovering remnants of overwritten files, thus reducing duplication of effort and increasing consistency of forensic analysis (Casey, 2013). Furthermore, searching for specific patterns across cases can potentially reveal links between related crimes.

Additional information and resources are available via the CASE website (https://sites.google.com/view/casework/home) and development of CASE and UCO is coordinated through GitHub (https://github.com/ucoProject). Community development is ongoing to expand the types of information that CASE can represent and to provide more comprehensive and refined documentation. In addition, an API/library has been developed to enable tools to "speak" CASE.

Acknowledgements This work has been encouraged and supported by Steven Shirley and William Eber at DoD Cyber Crime Center, Barbara Guttman and Mary Laamanen at the National Institute of Standards and Technology, Erwin van Eijk and Ruud van Baar at Netherlands Forensic Institute, and Greg Back, Eric Katz and Justin Grover at MITRE.

References

Barnum S (2014) Whitepaper: standardizing cyber threat intelligence information with the Structured Threat Information eXpression (STIX), February 20, 2014, Version 1.1, Revision 1. http://stixproject.github.io/getting-started/whitepaper

Brady O, Overill R, Keppens J (2015) DESO: addressing volume and variety in large-scale criminal cases. J Digit Investig 15:72–82

Casey E (2013) Reinforcing the scientific method in digital investigations using a case-based reasoning (CBR) system. PhD Dissertation, University College Dublin

Casey E, Back G, Barnum S (2015) Leveraging CybOX to standardize representation and exchange of digital forensic information. In: Proceedings of the 2nd annual DFRWS EU conference. Digital investigation, vol. 12(1)

Casey E, Barnum S, Griffith R, Snyder J, Beek H, Nelson A (2017) Advancing coordinated cyber-investigations and tool interoperability using a community developed specification language. J Digit Investig 22:14–45

Casey E, Biasiotti MA, Turchi F (2017) Using standardization and ontology to enhance data protection and intelligent analysis of electronic evidence. In: Proceedings of discovery of electronically stored information workshop (DESI VII), ICAIL 2017. Available at https://www.umiacs.umd.edu/~oard/desi7

Chabot Y, Bertaux A, Nicolle C, Kechadi T (2015) An ontology-based approach for the reconstruction and analysis of digital incidents timelines. J Digit Investig 15:83–100. https://doi.org/10.1016/j.diin.2015.07.005

Cosic J, Baca M (2015) Leveraging DEMF to ensure and represent 5ws&1h in digital forensic domain. Int J Comput Sci 13(2):7–10

Egger SA (1984) A working definition of serial murder and the reduction of linkage blindness. J Police Sci Admin 12(3):348–357

Garfinkel SL (2009) Automating disk forensic processing with SleuthKit, XML and Python. In: Proceeding of systematic approaches to digital forensics engineering (IEEE/SADFE 2009), Oakland, CA

Garfinkel SL (2012) Digital forensics XML and the DFXML toolset. J Digit Investig 8:161–174

Lanthaler M, Gütl C (2012) On using JSON-LD to create evolvable RESTful services. In: Proceedings of the 3rd international workshop on RESTful design (WS-REST 2012) at WWW2012, Lyon. ACM, New York, pp 25–32

Margot P (2011) Forensic science on trial - what is the law of the land? Aust J Forensic Sci 43(2–3):89–103

Nelson AJ, Steggall EQ, Long DDE (2014) Cooperative mode: comparative storage metadata verification applied to the Xbox 360. In: Proceedings of the 14th annual DFRWS USA conference. J Digit Investig, vol 11(1)

Office of the Director of National Intelligence (2017) XML data encoding specification for intelligence document and media exploitation. https://www.dni.gov/index.php/about/organization/chief-information-officer/information-security-marking-access?id=1204. Accessed 15 Mar 2017

Turnbull B, Randhawab S (2015) Automated event and social network extraction from digital evidence sources with ontological mapping. J Digit Investig 13:94–106

van Baar RB, van Beek HMA, van Eijk EJ (2014) Digital forensics as a service: a game changer. In: Proceedings of the 1st annual DFRWS EU conference. J Digit Investig, vol 11(S1): S1–S120

van Beek HMA, van Eijk EJ, van Baar RB, Ugen M, Bodde JNC, Siemelink AJ (2015) Digital forensics as a service: game on. J Digit Investig (Special Issue on Big Data and Intelligent Data Analysis) 15:20–38

Chapter 5
"All Along the Watchtower": Matters Not Yet Solved Regarding Communication Interception Systems and Electronic Data Retained on Foreign Servers

Francesco Cajani

Abstract The chapter describes an overview of the current situation in the EU with respect to matters not yet solved regarding communication interception systems and electronic data retention, also based on direct and personal experience of the author who is a public prosecutor. A state of the art on this topic is well described also focusing on some experiences and cases experimented by the Italian authorities when dealing with VOIP Systems and the cross-border acquisition of such information as probative values in the investigation phase. After having summarised the technological landscape with which investigators must deal in their daily activities fighting (not just organised) crime, the author tries to answer to the practical question of what can be done to overcome the legislative gap. Some solutions are given also considering the current scenario taking place in the USA with respect to the same issues and barriers.

5.1 Athens, October 2008

The year was 2008 when Eurojust organised the first "Strategic meeting on cybercrime" in Athens and I had the honour of being invited to represent Italy. For the love that binds me to classical studies, I remembered one of the most significant places of that city—the Agora—where it was still possible to reach the Monument of Eponymous Heroes: here the tables of the laws were displayed so that all Athenian citizens could see them and learn from them. I therefore concluded my heartfelt speech claiming the existence of many laws suitable for regulating the new Internet phenomena, although there were still too many people pretending not to see them, hiding behind a "virtuality of cyberspace" that is nothing more than appearances.

F. Cajani (✉)
Court of Law in Milan, Public Prosecutor's Office Counterterrorism Department, Milan, Italy
e-mail: francesco.cajani@giustizia.it

M. A. Biasiotti et al. (eds.), *Handling and Exchanging Electronic Evidence Across Europe*, Law, Governance and Technology Series 39,
https://doi.org/10.1007/978-3-319-74872-6_5

It has been almost 10 years and only the recent terrible events of terrorism that struck the heart of Europe have ensured that—at last—such laws can no longer go unnoticed!

In the hope that the next steps are not suggested by further innocent victims, the occasion is propitious to sum up—again—the old issue of relationships with Internet service providers to obtain, for any reason relating to criminal proceedings, efficient information in their possession.

5.2 Once Upon a Time There Was the Problem of VoIP Calls and the Interception of Their Communications

It is well known that VoIP (Voice over IP) services commonly refer to communications that, in fact and as can be understood from the literal definition, use the Internet as a vocal communication channel.[1]

Concrete experiences had led legal practitioners to focus particularly on technical problems because as a rule such communication systems have encrypted communication protocols. Furthermore, these profiles could have rendered legal discussions irrelevant, since—in fact—VoIP communication systems, starting from the most popular (i.e., Skype, a company acquired in May 2011 by Microsoft[2]), at that time represented themselves as being technically non-interceptable.[3] Indeed, end-to-end security[4] in transmissions has been present for many years in secure communications technologies.

The fundamental concept (in addition to the mathematical algorithms[5] that make it possible) is the following: do not delegate to any underlying transmission channel the communication of two speakers. Security must therefore be provided by the channel that directly connects the two parties and it must be under their control.

[1]VOIP are all those services that, in fact and as can be understood from the literal definition, use the Internet as a vocal communication channel.

[2]It is worth noting that despite this acquisition, the company Skype Communications SARL in fact continues to maintain policies that are different from those of Microsoft Corp. concerning judicial authorities.

[3]Regarding this matter see MCCULLAGH, "Skype: We can't comply with police wiretap requests", in news.cnet.com (9.6.2008).

[4]The basic concept of end-to-end encryption is creating for each party a secret key (known only by the other party) and a public key that the party "publishes" in directory services to allow others to speak securely with him. That which is encrypted with the public key can only be decrypted with the secret key.

[5]From the point of view of cryptographic algorithms, end-to-end encryption is based on asymmetric cryptographic systems, the first commercially available product being RSA's free version called PGP, an implementation of an RSA system with free code (at the time these algorithms were protected by the US DOD and the author, who developed the program and then made it public, was convicted and sentenced to serious time).

Rereading today the famous Egyptian security service note about Skype[6] it seems that time has truly stopped. While on the one hand some State Authorities have made unsuccessful attempts (as far as is known by the scientific community) to get the encryption code from the company (with procedures and guarantees such that it can only be used in specific cases provided for by the pertinent legal systems[7]), the Italian situation—which was revealed in all its drama following a journalistic investigation in 2009[8]—was later reconstructed by the same reporters.[9]

What we can say with certainty, having had direct knowledge of the matter, is that the Italian Desk at Eurojust, after receiving a request for assistance articulated by the then National Anti-Mafia Prosecutor Pietro Grasso,[10] as well as a similar formal request by the Public Prosecutor of Milan,[11] thanks to the decisive push by Carmen Manfredda (at that time vice Italian representative at Eurojust) in 2009 had achieved the opening of a case at the European level to identify—in concert with all the representatives of the Member States—aspects useful for a positive resolution of the issue, also considering the legal approach on the point already indicated in 2008 precisely during that first "Strategic meeting on cybercrime" mentioned above. The company had initially expressed its willingness, once again, to cooperate[12] ... but then nothing has changed.

That the issue was already of fundamental importance at the time—as already mentioned—was made clear by some events known to the Italian investigators. Among the saddest in Italy surely cannot be forgotten those relating to the kidnapping and subsequent murder of the entrepreneur Roveraro,[13] since it was precisely the use of Skype that had initially resulted in a considerable obstacle for the criminal investigation.

Like other nations, the problem today is with international terrorism since these communications are not, by definition, confined to a single country. So the problem of encryption, in the past mainly an offline problem (e.g., data stored on a HD),

---

[6]Cited by Stecklow et al. (2011): "*The Skype communication system... counts as a safe and encrypted Internet communication system to which most extremist groups have resorted to communicate with each other*".

[7]On this point it is interesting to recall that in June 2011 the US Patent and Trademark Office (USPTO) published the patent application—filed by Microsoft in December 2009—that describes a way to legally intercept VoIP calls, explicitly mentioning Skype as an example.

[8]Mensurati, Tonacci, *I boss si parlano su Skype, impossibile intercettarli*, in www.repubblica.it (14.2.2009).

[9]Mensurati, Tonacci, *Boss e intercettazioni, Skype sotto accusa*, in www.repubblica.it (15.2.2009).

[10]Letter dated 27 February 2009.

[11]Note of the Deputy Prosecutors Ferdinando Pomarici (coordinator of the District Anti-Mafia Directorate) and Armando Spataro (coordinator of the counterterrorism pool).

[12]Mensurati, Tonacci, *Skype collaborerà con la polizia per inseguire i criminali sul VoIP*, in www.repubblica.it (27.2.2009).

[13]On this point see the effective journalistic reconstruction of GRIMALDI, "Due giorni di misteri, poi l'esecuzione", in www.corriere.it (6.4.2008).

today is of fundamental importance in relation to online conversations through instant messaging.

It is also well known that WhatsApp, among the systems most used in the world, right at the beginning of 2016 introduced end-to-end encryption, as other systems like Skype had already done in the past.

Yet feasibility studies, at that time made on behalf of Eurojust by two technical consultants of the Milan Prosecutor's office, confirmed that it is possible—for Skype then and for WhatsApp today—to make a change in the encryption system to allow the presence of a third party (which remains unknown to the other parties). All this, of course, at the request of the judicial authorities by specific decree, in relation to well-predetermined communication flows and only in cases where investigative needs have emerged deserving protection. Therefore, from this point of view as well there are no obstacles regarding the respect of fundamental human rights.

At the same time from a technical point of view there is no problem for the providers that convey the flow of communications[14] since they have long been subject to European technical regulations issued by ETSI (European Telecommunications Standards Institute[15]), which already allow them to redirect this type of traffic to judicial authorities.

After all, it must be considered that Skype tried to enter the business world while wanting to maintain the impenetrability of the content transmitted. However, these two requirements are antithetical to each other, especially now that businesses' awareness of the issue of cybercrime is very high: companies can no longer afford not to know what enters or exits their systems, and so Microsoft had to make available a business version of Skype where the control of the keys remains with the company and not the employee[16]!

5.3 The Interception of @.com Email Accounts

But the problems for Italian investigators do not end here.

In fact, it is also known that, using the most popular email systems offered by well-known American companies, a communication flow is generated between people who often are both located in Italy.

[14]One must remember this fundamental point: the fact that the providers cannot "enter" into the communications between the two parties, especially because in most cases the traffic does not pass through their servers, does not mean that they cannot make it available. In fact, the telecom operators manage the most important information, i.e., the public keys and the cryptographic algorithms in their code. End-to-end encryption provides for the possibility of introducing "escrow keys" in the programming code, even "hidden" and not easily detectable by third parties.

[15]www.etsi.org.

[16]For the constant exchange of views regarding this matter, I'd like to thank Maurizio Bedarida (one of the two technical consultants of the Milan Prosecutor's office indicated in the text of this paragraph).

After almost 10 years from the "first signs of trouble", it is in this context that the catastrophic effects of a theoretical approach occur even today: we refer to the approach briefly defined "no server no law opinion"[17] that privileges the physical location of the interested servers about the applicability of pertinent law (and the resolution of issues regarding conflicts of jurisdiction).

With the paradox that, originally, the servers were situated outside the European Union: and so at that time Google, Yahoo! and Microsoft could easily maintain that, since there were no servers on European territory, national or European laws could not be invoked by the country requesting interception.[18]

Today the situation has changed: Google[19] and Microsoft[20] now have numerous data centres in Europe (just like other US ISPs like Facebook[21] and Apple[22]) and the scenario has also taken on the contours of an ironic joke when, in 2014, it was an American judge's turn to hear an argument against a prohibition of data acquisition (regarding a Microsoft account) because the servers were ... in Ireland![23]

But let us try to put things in order, even regarding this matter, hoping that here as well—as already indicated at a European level since 2008—things can be viewed under what is defined as "no server but law opinion", where what matters is the location of the web service being offered, even for the law. Because, in the face of opposing theoretical approaches, the preliminary investigative value is obvious.

For the Italian telecommunications company it is possible to request—to execute the decision of the judge who has allowed online interception—that email addressed to the intercepted account be redirected to an account specifically created by the Criminal Investigation Department. This allows not only savings in the overall cost of interception operations but also, above all, the possibility of initiating them in reasonably short times[24] (a matter of no small importance when one or more lives are in danger).

---

[17]The origin of this definition should be drawn from the paper shown in the first "Strategic meeting on Cybercrime", organised by Eurojust in Athens on 23–24 October 2008: see Cajani (2009).

[18]It is evident that there are no problems of jurisdiction where the prosecution is able to tell the magistrate for preliminary investigations that the communications needing to be intercepted are taking place between two Italian citizens or in any case between two people within the country's borders, regardless of whether—accidentally—these conversations go through a server located abroad.

[19]www.google.com/about/datacenters/inside/locations/index.html.

[20]www.microsoft.com/en-us/cloud-platform/global-datacenters.

[21]www.facebook.com/LuleaDataCenter.

[22]See LUMB, "Why Apple Is Spending $1.9 Billion to Open Data Centers in Denmark and Ireland", in www.fastcompany.com (23.2.15).

[23]The news practically travelled around the world: see among many LOHR, "Microsoft Protests Order to Disclose Email Stored Abroad", in www.nytimes.com (10.6.2014).

[24]Otherwise it would be necessary to first seek phone records of the number used for the connection to the Internet (to identify the service provider) and then to plan, in consultation with the provider, the deployment of the so-called probes (technically necessary to intercept the useful traffic). Overall these operations can reasonably take up to a whole week!

However, concerning @.com accounts this very simple mechanism becomes impossible. In fact, when the Criminal Investigation Department went to serve Google or Microsoft (both having Italian subsidiaries subject to Italian law based in Milan) with a judge's decree authorising the interception, the typical answer was: "Sorry, our servers are in America … so request the interception with a rogatory letter!".

Only Yahoo! (which also at the time had an Italian subsidiary based in Milan) had a software program called Yahoo! Account Management Tool that allowed for the interception of email accounts in this way, but with some limits[25] (and with some problems, as occurred in a famous investigation in Milan[26]). But this was the case only for a short period,[27] and then Yahoo! adopted the same policies as the other American companies.

[25]More precisely, based on the principle of Net Citizenship, the user could choose which legislation the email account would be subject to when registering for a @yahoo email account. Only in the cases in which the user had chosen Italian legislation would the mentioned software allow the immediate interception where necessary for investigative purposes and authorised by the order of the Criminal Investigation Department.

[26]The case arose from a @yahoo.it account subjected to interception—in the manner permitted by the Yahoo! Account Management Tool—without any result (i.e., the Criminal Investigation Department received nothing on the account that had been set up). After the arrest of the suspect (a phisher from Romania), the same during an interrogation and in the presence of the counsel for the defence gave the prosecutor the access credentials to his account (i.e., the one that had been intercepted without success). It was then discovered to their surprise that instead there were many messages available, received in the period in which the account had been subject to interception. Subsequent investigations of the Guardia di Finanza—Gruppo Pronto Impiego (Italian Fiscal Police) of Milan positively established that the Tool could actually be accessed by many within the various European subsidiaries of Yahoo!, compromising users' privacy (and not only for inquiries of Criminal Investigation units). The documentation was sent to the Italian Data Protection Authority, which confirmed the technical findings and the legal argument of the Prosecutor of Milan. See Ferrarella, *Buco' nei controlli in Rete*. I pm mettono in regola Yahoo", in www.corriere.it (30.10.2008).

[27]Significantly, in 2008, while in Italy it was actually possible to intercept an @yahoo.com email account, in Belgium to the contrary the American company denied any form of cooperation with judicial authorities requesting access to data traffic. This fact was at the origin of the famous "Yahoo! Case" that, after 7 years, finally saw the Belgian Federal Prosecutor's Office victorious in the Court of Cassation. See Roland, *Court of Cassation definitively confirms Yahoo!'s obligation to cooperate with law enforcement agencies* in www.stibbe.com (7.1.2016). Regarding the various policies of American ISPs and the number of requests for data from the Member States of the Council of Europe see the paper of the T-CY Cloud Evidence Group entitled "Criminal justice access to data in the cloud: cooperation with 'foreign' service providers" in www.coe.int/web/cybercrime.

5.4 The Current State of Interceptions: Via Trojans—of VoIP Communications Systems (Including Today's Online Instant Messaging Systems) with Encryption Protocols and of @.com Email Accounts

Having summarised the technological landscape with which investigators must deal in their daily activities fighting (not just organised) crime, the practical question that arises is: what could they done?

Should they wait for the European legislature to intervene regarding matters related to encrypted communications to clarify that the European legislation[28] on electronic communications[29]—with its obligation to make interceptions available to Judicial Authorities[30]—must be deemed applicable to all the companies that offer services to European citizens?

Should they wait for the Council of Europe to be able to establish an Additional Protocol to the Budapest Convention on cybercrime[31] or for the European Union to implement new tools of cooperation[32] to obtain—without rogatory letters—data relating to the communications that pass through @.com accounts?

---

[28]From the European legislation on electronic communications also derives the legislative decree of 1 August 2003, no. 259—Italian Electronic Communications Code.

[29]And precisely: Directive 2002/19/EC of the European Parliament and of the Council, 7 March 2002 regarding access to electronic communications networks and associated resources, and interconnection of the same (Access Directive); Directive 2002/20/EC of the European Parliament and of the Council of 7 March 2002 on the authorisation of electronic communications networks and services (Authorisations Directive); Directive 2002/21/EC of the European Parliament and of the Council of 7 March 2002 establishing a common regulatory framework for electronic communications networks and services (Framework Directive); Directive 2002/22/EC of the European Parliament and of the Council of 7 March 2002 on universal service and users' rights relating to electronic communications networks and services (Universal Service Directive).

[30]In particular see the provisions of Article 6 of Directive no. 20/2002 regarding the obligation to make available the interception of communications, as a condition for issuing ministerial authorisation to the operator concerned to operate in the country. On this point it seems appropriate to recall, once again, how the Ministry of Economic Development—Telecommunications with a notice dated 12 September 2008 had expressed a written opinion, upon special request of the National Anti-Mafia Directorate, according to which Skype connections be included in the provisions of Italian Legislative Decree 259/2003 and therefore subject to the general authorisation referred to in Article 25. It is therefore possible to speak of "operator" in accordance with Article 1 letter u) of Italian Legislative Decree 259/2003, a concept which, moreover, is itself very broad in that it refers not only to "a company that is authorised to provide a public communications network" but even where the same provides "a similar resource".

[31]To this end, in December 2014 was established the T-CY Cloud Evidence Group, in which Italy also participates (www.coe.int/en/web/cybercrime/ceg). Regarding the outcome of the work of the T-CY Cloud Evidence Group, see the paper entitled "Criminal justice access to data in the cloud: Recommendations for consideration by the T-CY" in www.coe.int/web/cybercrime.

[32]See the press release entitled "Fight against criminal activities in cyberspace: Council agrees on practical measures and next steps" in www.consilium.europa.eu (9.6.2016).

Well, in the meantime, given the existence of an easier remedy (albeit more expensive) like that of the trojan, the investigators have chosen their battlefield.

That the issue that we are dealing with has global implications and should not therefore be hastily dismissed as a "mere Italian question" is well known abroad. An example is the analysis that appeared in the New York Times last December: "Because American law has made it nearly impossible to obtain digital evidence through legitimate channels, foreign police are turning to illegitimate ones".[33] An analysis that can be shared, based solely on its premise, since even the United Sections of the Court of Cassation in Italy that recently deliberated on the point[34]—if we had to sum up the basic reasoning—have simply "remembered" the pre-existence of a regulatory framework that on the whole renders legitimate the use of trojans for criminal investigations.

But even before the problems explained to the American people by a professor of the University of Kentucky, the use of trojans has in fact had some problems of effectiveness.

Because, as far as can be revealed here, the state of the art that allows investigators to successfully initiate an interception of these two types of communications using a trojan is possible only when the exact location of the suspect's digital device (desktop or laptop computer, cell phone) is known. This is certainly a first investigative limit, since often—despite the parties being known—it is not possible to know in advance their precise location in the Italian territory.

Having overcome this first limit, in cases where it is possible to physically interact with the suspect's device, as a rule a particular software will be installed on it that, among its functions, is also capable of:

- Intercepting the user's voice before the audio signal is encoded by the encrypted communication protocol (such as, most recently, the flows generated by instant messaging applications like WhatsApp).

[33]Keane Woods, *Dark Clouds Over the Internet* in www.nytimes.com (1.12.2015). Also touched on by Segantini, *Difesa di privacy e sicurezza alla rete serve una governance* in www.corriere.it (23/12/2015).

[34]See the United Sections of the Court of Cassation, sentence 1 July 2016, no. 26889: although limited to one of the many features of the trojan (and, in particular, the possibility to activate the microphone of a mobile phone or a of portable computer also in a private place where the crime under investigation is not committing to intercept all the conversation of the people present in this place), it indicates some more key points that—after 7 years from the first Supreme Court judgment (Section V of the Court of Cassation, sentence 14 October 2009 no. 16556) that had begun to outline the legal regime—allow to state the legitimacy of its use, despite criticism promoted by a lot of people. The sentence concludes for the admissibility of an environmental interception with the trojan when the public prosecutor is investigating an organised crime (according to Article 13 of Law 203/1991 that consents, for this important crime, the environmental interception also in the private place even if the crime under investigation is not committing there). For the other crimes Article 266.4 of Italian Criminal Procedure Code provides the admissibility of such type of interception only if in the private place is committing the crime under investigation, and so is not admissible a trojan able to activate an environmental interception everywhere.

- Intercepting the flow of communications generated on @.com accounts to which the digital device has full access.

Where it is not possible to physically access the place where the device is located, social engineering techniques can be used—specifically authorised by the Public Prosecutor—such as, for example, sending emails containing scripts that will also allow the installation of the necessary software to intercept these communication flows.

In any case, this activity must be preceded by a technical analysis tailored to the individual case and all other relevant information (hardware/software characteristics in relation to the computer system to be intercepted, technical characteristics of the potentially usable Internet connections) available to investigators, also to avoid that the presence of any anti-virus system on a computing device subject to so-called active interception can easily frustrate the successful conclusion of the operation, blocking the continuation of the investigation.

5.5 USA vs. EU

If this is the situation for communication flows, what about the cases—and they are the majority—where it is not remotely conceivable to use a trojan, without even getting into the technical aspect? We once allowed ourselves (Cajani 2010) to deploy an argument that went like this:

[...] Where the Italian Judge states (as indeed even today) that such communication systems (physically located in the United States, at least in relation to the affected servers) are used by Italian citizens, what additional regulatory barriers would remain?

In these cases could not the Italian State reasonably affirm its jurisdiction in the matter, it being only an accident that the communication service used by its citizens, operating on Italian territory, is located in a different place?

I think so.

Well, some time ago the United States ratified the Budapest Convention, which provides - precisely regarding the two matters under discussion - two precise duties of "real time" cooperation (Article 33 regarding the collection of traffic data; Article 34 concerning the interception of content). And so, since Italy has also finally ratified this Convention, these obligations now effectively acquire a bilateral legal significance (pacta sunt servanda).

Now as then it seems obvious, although Article 33 Budapest Convention textually refers only to a "real-time collection", that the "Budapest Convention' spirit of the law" is to provide precise obligations of a "real-time cooperation": this means, in fact, the need that the traffic data—after being collected in real-time—are communicated in real-time to the State that is conducting the investigation. In this legal contest, it is evident that the use of national instrument (instead of a rogatory letter) should be able to ensure a greater speed in achieving this purpose.

Today therefore, after so many years, the matter returns to the Internet service providers and the position of the US Department of Justice, which, having appealed the refusal received by Microsoft to provide the required data, in July was once again unsuccessful.

All with an order of the 2nd US Circuit Court of Appeals in Manhattan, which, however, includes the observation of one of its judges[35] in his separate opinion: "I concur in the result (of the case), but without any illusion that the result should even be regarded as a rational policy outcome, let alone celebrated as a milestone in protecting privacy". In fact, he points out that "the dispute here is not about privacy, but rather about the international reach of American law" and that there is need "for congressional action to revise a badly outdated statute". Adding this significant reflection: "The case looks rather different, however—at least to me, and I would hope to the people and officials of Ireland and the E.U.—if the American government is demanding from an American company emails of an American citizen resident in the U.S., which are accessible at the push of a button in Redmond, Washington, and which are stored on a server in Ireland only because of the American customer's misrepresenting his or her residence for facilitating domestic violations of American law, by exploiting a policy of the American company that exists solely for reasons of convenience and that could be changed, either in general or as applied to the particular customer, at the whim of the American company".[36]

And maybe really, because of this judgement, the US will finally update its laws. Hopefully also to the benefit of the European Union.

One thing is certain: such a Copernican revolution would exponentially increase the chances of identifying the perpetrators of crimes committed online. The problem, moreover, not only concerns the "content data"[37] but also "subscriber information"[38]

[35]Gerard E. Lynch.

[36]See also Henning, *Microsoft Case Shows the Limits of a Data Privacy Law*, in www.nytimes.com (18.7.2016).

[37]"Content data" is not defined in the Convention but refers to the communication content of the communication; i.e., the meaning or purport of the communication, or the message or information being conveyed by the communication (other than traffic data)": thus paragraph 209 of the Explanatory Report to the Budapest Convention on cybercrime.

[38]"For this article, the term "subscriber information" means any information contained in the form of computer data or any other form that is held by a service provider, relating to subscribers of its services other than traffic or content data and by which can be established: a the type of communication service used, the technical provisions taken thereto and the period of service; b the subscriber's identity, postal or geographic address, telephone and other access number, billing and payment information, available on the basis of the service agreement or arrangement; c any other information on the site of the installation of communication equipment, available on the basis of the service agreement or arrangement": thus Article 18.3 Budapest Convention. Paragraph 178 of the Explanatory Report to the Budapest Convention explains that subscriber information may be needed for a criminal investigation "primarily in two specific situations" - "First, subscriber information is needed to identify which services and related technical measures have been used or are being used by a subscriber, such as the type of telephone service used (e.g., mobile), type of other associated services used (e.g., call forwarding, voice-mail, etc.), telephone number or other technical address (e.g., e-mail address)" - "Second, when a technical address

and "traffic data"[39]: and, in fact, while it is true that for the latter two types of data American ISPs have for some time[40] adopted a voluntary disclosure regime, this situation poses many problems still today.[41]

Some, such as greater speed in the mechanisms of exchange of the requested data, surely could well be solved simply by taking a cue from the results of the Evidence project.

But others remain unresolved, requiring an intervention that is legislative in nature rather than technical. First of all is the problem of not being able to execute an order issued by national authorities with respect to a foreign ISP,[42] even where the

---

is known, subscriber information is needed in order to assist in establishing the identity of the person concerned". Paragraph 178 goes on stating that "other subscriber information, such as commercial information about billing and payment records of the subscriber may also be relevant to criminal investigations, especially where the crime under investigation involves computer fraud or other economic crimes". Paragraph 180 of the Explanatory Report clarifies the range of data to be considered as subscriber information: "Subscriber information is not limited to information directly related to the use of the communication service. It also means any information, other than traffic data or content data, by which can be established the user's identity, postal or geographic address, telephone, and other access number, and billing and payment information, which is available on the basis of the agreement or arrangement between the subscriber and the service provider".

[39]" 'traffic data' means any computer data relating to a communication by means of a computer system, generated by a computer system that formed a part in the chain of communication, indicating the communication's origin, destination, route, time, date, size, duration, or type of underlying service": thus Article 1.d Budapest Convention. As already shown in the EU Forum on Cybercrime Discussion Paper for Expert's Meeting on Retention of Traffic Data (6 November 2001): "To investigate and prosecute crimes involving the use of the communications networks, including the Internet, law enforcement authorities frequently use traffic data when they are stored by service providers for billing purposes. As the price charged for a communication is becoming less and less dependent on distance and destination, and service providers move towards flat rate billing, there will no longer be any need to store traffic data for billing purposes. Law enforcement authorities fear that this will reduce potential material for criminal investigations and therefore advocate that service providers keep certain traffic data for at least a minimum period of time so that these data may be used for law enforcement purposes".

[40]In the experience of some Italian investigations, Microsoft was the first to provide—without a rogatory but only with a request from the Italian Public Prosecutor—such data, not only regarding @hotmail.it accounts but also @hotmail.com. At first, Google considered a rogatory to be necessary, but it changed its policy after the Google vs. Vividown case, and now provides all the data required if the request comes with an order from the Italian Public Prosecutor (not only from the Italian Criminal Investigation Department). Nevertheless, if an IP address (logged by the Google electronic systems concerning an e-mail @gmail.com) is not related to an Italian or an European server, currently the company does not maintain to be allowed to communicate it to the Italian Judicial Authority.

[41]See the paper of the T-CY Cloud Evidence Group entitled "Criminal justice access to data in the cloud: cooperation with 'foreign' service providers", cit.

[42]For a hypothesis of criminal sanction regarding the ISP's refuse to communicate the data see Article 46bis (§2) of the Belgian Code of Criminal Procedure, stating: "§1. In investigating the crimes and misdemeanours, the Public Prosecutor may, by means of a motivated decision in writing, if necessary by summoning the cooperation of the operator of an electronic communications network or the provider of an electronic communications service or a police department

latter provides services to citizens in the territory of the nation making the request.[43] On second thought, it is normal—and moreover lying in Article 18.1.b "Budapest Convention' spirit of the law"[44]—that if a company offers its services in a particular country for those services to be subject to that nation's regulations.

Yet, while in Europe there is legislation that strictly regulates manufacturers that produce toys used by our children, paradoxically, this is not the case for mobile and communications applications installed on them (as well as for the data conveyed by the same). Maybe it is truly high time for technology to adapt to the Law.

---

appointed by the King, proceed or order to proceed based on any data in his possession or by means of access to the operator's or service provider's customer files, to: 1° the identification of the subscriber or the regular user of an electronic communications service or the used electronic medium of communication; 2° the identification of the electronic communications services to which a specified person is subscribed or which are regularly used by a specified person. The motivation reflects proportionality, with respect for the privacy and subsidiarity, compared to any other act of inquiry. In case of extremely urgent necessity, any officer of the criminal investigation department may summon to receive these data by means of a motivated decision in writing, after prior verbal authorisation from the Public Prosecutor. The officer of the criminal investigation department shall communicate this motivated decision in writing and the acquired information within 24 h to the Public Prosecutor and motivates the extremely urgent necessity. §2. Any operator of an electronic communications network and any provider of an electronic communications service that may be summoned to communicate the data as referred to in paragraph 1, is to provide the data that were requested to the Public Prosecutor or the officer of the criminal investigation department within a period to be determined by the King, upon proposal from the Minister of Justice and the Minister in charge of Telecommunications. The King defines, upon advice from the Commission for the protection of privacy and upon proposal from the Minister of Justice and the Minister in charge of Telecommunications, the technical conditions for access to the data as referred to in §1, that are available for the Public Prosecutor and for the police department as indicated in the same paragraph. Any person that may become aware of the measure because of being served or that may participate in the same, is bound by secrecy. Any violation of secrecy shall be sanctioned in accordance with Article 458 of the Penal Code. Any refusal to communicate the data shall be sanctioned with a pecuniary penalty of twenty-six Euros up to ten thousand Euros.".

[43]That the issue is still under debate is evidenced by the observations of some countries (Canada, Germany, Japan, Slovakia and USA) contrary to a broad interpretation of Article 18.1.b of the Budapest Convention in view of the adoption of the associated Guidance Note, in the documentation of the T-CY 16th Plenary—item 5: www.coe.int/en/web/cybercrime/t-cy-plenaries. On 1 February 2017 Cloud Evidence Group (together with representatives of Canada, France, Germany, Japan, Liechtenstein, Slovakia and USA) reached agreement on a shared text. So the "Guidance Note on production orders for subscriber information (Article 18 Budapest Convention)", subject to a new written approval process without any further comments were adopted on 28 February 2017: www.coe.int/en/web/cybercrime/-/t-cy-adopts-guidance-note-on-article-18.

[44]"Each Party shall adopt such legislative and other measures as may be necessary to empower its competent authorities to order: a. a person in its territory to submit specified computer data in that person's possession or control, which is stored in a computer system or a computer-data storage medium; and b. a service provider offering its services in the territory of the Party to submit subscriber information relating to such services in that service provider's possession or control": thus Article 18.1 Budapest Convention.

References

Cajani F (2009) Interception of communications: Skype, Google, Yahoo! and Microsoft tools and electronic data retention on foreign servers: a legal perspective from a prosecutor conducting an investigation. Digital Evid Electron Signature Law Rev 6:158 and following

Cajani F (2010) La Convenzione di Budapest nell'insostenibile salto all'indietro del Legislatore italiano, ovvero: quello che le norme non dicono. Ciberspazio e diritto 11:207 and following

Stecklow S, Sonne P, Bradley M (2011) Mideast uses western tools to battle the skype rebellion in online.wsj.com (1.6.2011)

Part III
Institutional/Operational Perspective

Chapter 6
Electronic Evidence: Challenges and Opportunities for Law Enforcement

Sabine Berghs, Geoffrey Stewart Morrison, and Caroline Goemans-Dorny

Abstract This chapter presents a cross-section of law enforcement issues addressed as part of the research conducted by INTERPOL in the framework of the European Informatics Data Exchange Framework for Courts and Evidence (EVIDENCE) project. The aim of the research was to formulate recommendations and best practice based on the status quo and challenges identified regarding the handling of electronic evidence by law enforcement agencies (LEAs).

First, the status quo on the handling of digital evidence by LEAs and the main trends identified for each phase of the electronic evidence lifecycle are set out. Subsequently, the main challenges hampering law enforcement investigations and forensic analyses involving digital evidence are presented. These challenges can be categorised under two main headers, namely challenges caused by technical measures such as encryption and anonymisation tools and those caused by legal lacunae.

Then, building further upon these findings, a set of recommendations are presented to strengthen law enforcement action in the field of digital evidence. This can, first, be done by working towards the professionalisation of digital forensics, as suggested by digital forensics practitioners themselves. Furthermore, as LEAs are not the only actors within the electronic evidence domain, it is also essential to continue enhancing the collaboration between LEAs and other actors, such as the judiciary and policymakers. Lastly, mutual legal assistance (MLA) procedures are no longer considered fit-for-purpose and LEAs continue to increasingly call for initiatives to expedite these often lengthy procedures.

S. Berghs (✉) · C. Goemans-Dorny
INTERPOL, Lyon, France
e-mail: s.berghs@interpol.int; c.goemans@interpol.int

G. S. Morrison
University of Alberta, Department of Linguistics, Edmonton, AB, Canada
e-mail: g.s.morrison@aston.ac.uk

M. A. Biasiotti et al. (eds.), *Handling and Exchanging Electronic Evidence Across Europe*, Law, Governance and Technology Series 39,
https://doi.org/10.1007/978-3-319-74872-6_6

6.1 Introduction

This chapter presents a cross-section of the topics and findings on law enforcement issues addressed as part of the research conducted by the International Criminal Police Organization, INTERPOL, in the framework of the European Informatics Data Exchange Framework for Courts and Evidence (EVIDENCE) project.[1] The aim of the research was to formulate recommendations and best practice based on the status quo and challenges identified regarding the handling of electronic evidence by law enforcement agencies (LEAs). As LEAs play a key role within the "electronic evidence process", their actions may consequently impact the admissibility of such evidence before court. Logically, it was thus opted to focus the research on the full cycle of the electronic evidence process covering the collection, preservation, analysis and exchange of electronic evidence, as well as its presentation before court, from a law enforcement perspective.[2]

For each of the above-mentioned phases, the status quo and main challenges will be presented, as well as the direction practitioners are working towards to mitigate these challenges based on recommendations or best practice. Prior to delving into those findings, the methodology followed will be set out, specifically the main fact-finding methods deployed, including a questionnaire, expert group meeting, semi-structured telephone interviews, as well as regular desktop research and participation in law enforcement conferences.

First, regarding the status quo on the handling of digital evidence by LEAs, the main trends identified throughout each phase of the electronic evidence lifecycle will be set out, followed by the trends regarding collaboration between agencies and on the use of channels for international cooperation. These trends will primarily be based on the results of the questionnaire that INTERPOL circulated to its 190 member countries.

Subsequently, the main challenges hampering law enforcement investigations and forensic analyses involving digital evidence are presented. These challenges can be categorised under two main headers, namely challenges caused by technical measures such as encryption and anonymisation tools and those caused by legal lacunae, such as a lack of international consensus on transborder access to evidence in the cloud and the uncertainties following EU case law on data retention.

Then, building further upon these findings, a set of recommendations are presented to strengthen law enforcement action in the field of digital evidence. This can, first, be done by working towards the professionalisation of digital forensics,

[1]INTERPOL was in charge of the work package on law enforcement issues in the EVIDENCE project. However, the views of the authors in no form or manner represent the views or policies of the Organization.

[2]While legal and data protection issues are also paramount to the handling of electronic evidence by law enforcement, these topics are more comprehensively addressed in the research conducted by the University of Groningen (RUG) and the Leibniz University of Hannover (LUH) within the framework of the EVIDENCE project.

as suggested by digital forensics practitioners themselves. Furthermore, as LEAs are not the only actors within the electronic evidence domain, it is also essential to continue enhancing the collaboration between LEAs and the other actors involved, such as the judiciary and policymakers. Lastly, with the globalisation of serious crime, exacerbated by the widespread use of the Internet, LEAs are more than ever reiterating the need for the modernisation of international cooperation. As current mutual legal assistance (MLA) procedures are no longer considered fit-for-purpose, regional and international organisations are developing initiatives to expedite these otherwise lengthy procedures.

6.2 Methodology

While this research focuses on the law enforcement perspective, it is nevertheless important to bear in mind the wide range of actors involved in the electronic evidence process. These actors each bring their specific expertise to the electronic evidence process and may, thus, be involved in different stages of the process. To obtain a complete overview of the current state of affairs, to determine where the challenges lie and to identify best practices on how the process can be improved, all these actors need to be included in the discussion: from law enforcement officers and digital forensics specialists to legal professionals and members of the judiciary. As INTERPOL is a law enforcement organisation, however, the status quo assessment and analysis of challenges and best practices will concentrate on the role of LEAs whilst addressing the role of other stakeholders from the perspective of their interactions with LEAs or their impact upon the work of LEAs.

6.2.1 Questionnaire

In the framework of the EVIDENCE project, a questionnaire was circulated via INTERPOL's 190 National Central Bureaus (NCBs) as a fact-finding tool. Bearing in mind the diversity of actors, even within law enforcement itself, involved in the electronic evidence process, the questionnaire was divided into three main sections, which could be separately forwarded to the relevant (law enforcement) agencies, units or labs:

- The first section included questions on the legal framework for the collection, analysis, preservation and exchange of electronic evidence, as well as for the presentation of electronic evidence before court. It was decided to start the questionnaire with this section, because it sets the foundation on which law enforcement can conduct their operational activities.
- The second section, consequently, dealt with law enforcement issues and aimed to identify current practices in dealing with digital evidence, as well as challenges and best practices encountered by law enforcement. The answers to this section assisted in the formulation of regulatory and policy recommendations aiming

at facilitating online investigations, as well as investigations involving digital evidence.
- The third section specifically focused on digital forensics to identify the forensic tools generally used and accepted by the digital forensic community, as well as to identify preservation and exchange formats for digital evidence. The answers to this section fed into the work of the technical partners within the EVIDENCE project.[3]

The questionnaire elicited 56 responses from 47 countries. Of those 56 responses, 3 LEAs answered that they were currently not in a position to answer the questionnaire and 2 NCBs confirmed that they had forwarded the questionnaire to a relevant unit, but it had not been returned. These five respondents represent three European countries and two non-European countries. Consequently, there were 51 actual replies to the questionnaire from 42 countries. The respondents span both smaller and larger countries and are geographically distributed:

- 22 countries from Europe accounting for 23 replies;
- 6 countries from Africa accounting for 7 replies;
- 7 countries from the Americas accounting for 10 replies; and
- 7 countries from Asia and the South Pacific accounting for 11 replies.

The 51 replies can be divided in accordance with the three main sections of the questionnaire:

- 46 replies to the legal section;
- 47 replies to the law enforcement section; and
- 44 replies to the digital forensics section.

Overall, that entails that over the three sections of the questionnaire, 137 replies were received.

To enable a comparison between the situation in Europe and the situation beyond Europe, the answers provided by the respondents in Europe will be presented separately from the answers provided by the respondents at a global level without Europe. Both categories represent a fairly equal amount of countries and replies, namely:

- 22 countries from Europe accounting for 23 answers; and
- 20 countries at a global level (without Europe) accounting for 28 answers.

[3]The questionnaire was conceived in such a way that it would also contribute to the fact-finding activities of several consortium partners. To this end, the partners of the University of Groningen (RUG) in The Netherlands, the Institute of Legal Information Theory and Techniques of the National Research Council (CNR-ITTIG) in Florence, Italy, and the Centre of Excellence in Information and Communication Technologies (CETIC) in Liège, Belgium, contributed to the drafting of the questionnaire, particularly the legal and digital forensics sections. The widest possible dissemination of the questionnaires was ensured by making it available in INTERPOL's four working languages: Arabic, English, French, and Spanish.

The EVIDENCE project is an EU funded project and, hence, interested in the identification of European trends. Nevertheless, the emergence of electronic evidence, as well as the use of new technologies for the collection, analysis and exchange of electronic evidence, is a worldwide phenomenon. INTERPOL is an international organisation with 190 member countries and the research, therefore, also focuses on trends identified at a global level. The research does not intend to develop country profiles. The identified trends will, however, be presented in a manner that distinguishes between European trends and global trends (without Europe). Consequently, this enables the authors to draw distinctions or parallels in the trends identified at both levels or to even position European practices within a global setting, thereby benefiting the interpretation of certain results.

Alternatively, a comparison could have been made between Europe and the previously mentioned regions. However, based on the amount of replies received and to obtain the highest possible level of accuracy, it was opted to only compare Europe with the global situation outside of Europe as the amount of answers would allow for a more even-handed comparison. Nevertheless, the answer rate for certain questions may be relatively low and although the greatest possible attention was paid to encouraging and achieving accuracy, the results of this research are not intended to produce a precise quantitative study but rather an indication of trends in the countries surveyed. While emphasising that the results should not be interpreted in a conventional approach to statistical significance, it is worth noting that the response rates have provided a sampling of data from roughly a quarter of the countries in the world, including approximately half of the 50-odd countries, which may be classified as European. Thus, while the figures need to be interpreted with caution, the sample size is large enough to strongly suggest the existence or absence of certain trends.

When describing the results of the questionnaire and referring to the number of respondents who provided an answer to a question, this is often done in rather broad terms, such as 'the majority of European respondents' or 'a third of the respondents at the global level'. It is important to note that such references will always pertain to the amount of answers received to a specific question and not the amount of answers received to the questionnaire.

6.2.2 Expert Group Meeting

In the questionnaire, which was circulated among INTERPOL's 190 member countries, the respondents were asked whether they would be interested in participating in an expert group meeting on electronic evidence. Based on the answers provided and the field of expertise of the respondents, INTERPOL invited several respondents, as well as other experts in the field of electronic evidence, to participate in an expert group meeting on the topic. Thus, on 2 and 3 December 2014, the INTERPOL General Secretariat (IPSG) hosted an Expert Group Meeting on Electronic Evidence with a total of 33 participants. Bearing in mind the wide range of actors involved in the electronic evidence process, law enforcement experts from national cybercrime units and digital forensic labs were invited, as well as cyber forensic investigators from the International Criminal Court (ICC) and a magistrate from the French judiciary.

The agenda of the 2-day meeting was built up around four main topics and aimed to cover the operational framework including the full cycle of the electronic evidence process, as well as its legal framework and established institutional cooperation. Each of the main topics consisted of expert presentations followed by group discussions.

As a follow up to the questionnaire, the expert group meeting enabled a more in-depth discussion on topics already touched upon in the questionnaire, as well as open discussions to uncover practices and challenges not yet addressed. Thus, while the objective of the questionnaire and the expert group meeting was rather similar, namely to uncover current practices and challenges, the latter provided the opportunity to gain a more in-depth understanding of these practices and the challenges with which the participants are confronted. Therefore, the meeting can also be considered a fact-finding activity fitting the qualitative approach adopted within this research.

6.2.3 Semi-structured Telephone Interviews

Furthermore, to complement the first findings of the questionnaire and the expert group meeting, subject matter experts were contacted with the requests to participate in semi-structured telephone interviews. Among the respondents who were available and willing to participate in these interviews were:

- an investigating judge;
- a prosecutor;
- a law enforcement cybercrime investigator; and
- a specialist within a ministerial office.

The respondents were presented with the interview questions prior to the telephone interview and were informed that they would only have to respond to the questions that related to their professional expertise. Many respondents, however, still contacted colleagues within different departments or units who could potentially provide more information on a topic matter and several of them, thus, also sent written replies with this additional information to INTERPOL after the telephone interviews had been completed.

6.2.4 Other Sources of Information

In addition to the data gathered via the questionnaire, the expert group meeting and through INTERPOL's participation in related projects, several meetings and seminars were attended by the INTERPOL team in which the topic of online investigations or electronic evidence were discussed and which turned out to be valuable sources of information for the reports. The 2nd Eurasian Working Group Meeting on Cybercrime for Heads of Units, organised by the INTERPOL Global Complex for Innovation (IGCI) and hosted in Istanbul, Turkey, on 28–30 May 2014 was particularly relevant as the discussion topics included not only challenges encountered during online investigations and best practices identified, but also the struggles encountered with MLA procedures in dealing with modern forms of criminality. Furthermore, the seminar on the Validity and Admissibility of Electronic Evidence in Cybercrime Cases: Child pornography, online fraud, cyberlaundering and other offences, organised by the Academy of European Law (ERA) in Prague, Czech Republic, on 5–6 June 2014 proved to be highly relevant for this research. Also, the 3rd INTERPOL-Europol Cybercrime Conference hosted at the Europol Headquarters in The Hague, The Netherlands, from 30 September to 2 October 2015 addressed topics related to online investigations, capacity building, international cooperation and recent law enforcement operations against cybercrime.[4]

Moreover, further interviews and e-mail exchanges took place with law enforcement officers, both from cybercrime units and digital forensic labs. These exchanges provided an opportunity to request some additional information as a follow-up to the questionnaire and the expert group meeting.

Lastly, the above-mentioned sources of information are also complemented by regular desktop research pertaining to legal instruments, International Organization for Standardisation (ISO) and International Electrotechnical Commission (IEC) standards, academic research papers and literature, open source material and prior studies on the topic of online investigations and electronic evidence.

6.3 Status Quo on the Handling of Digital Evidence by LEAs

This section presents the **current state of affairs** concerning the use of digital evidence by law enforcement agencies, both in Europe and at a global level. Therefore, the research focused on each of the phases of the digital evidence process, commencing with the collection (or acquisition) of digital evidence, followed by the preservation and analysis and concluding with the use of digital evidence before court, as well as its transfer to foreign jurisdictions. Subsequently, the collaboration between the actors responsible for the implementation was addressed by looking at the legal basis and modalities for collaboration, as well as the reasons for collaboration from a law enforcement point of view. Lastly, a brief overview of the channels of international cooperation used by LEAs regarding digital evidence is provided to obtain a better understanding of the purposes for which LEAs turn to both formal and informal cooperation channels.

[4] https://www.europol.europa.eu/latest_news/europol-interpol-cybercrime-conference.

6.3.1 *Status Quo Throughout the Lifecycle of Digital Evidence*

To determine how LEAs implement the existing legal framework surrounding digital evidence in practice, the respondents of the questionnaire were asked about their experiences regarding the different phases of the digital evidence process.

6.3.1.1 Investigative Measures for the Collection and Acquisition of Digital Evidence

The questionnaire included a question to determine which investigative measures LEAs are permitted to take for the identification, collection and acquisition of digital evidence.[5] Based on the replies to this question, it was identified that the investigative measures most often permitted for the identification and collection of digital evidence in the respondents countries are:

- the search and seizure of digital data;
- the search and seizure of hardware;
- the search without seizure of digital data; and
- the search without seizure of hardware.

The investigative measures that are generally also broadly permitted are:

- the order to supply stored content data;
- the order to supply stored traffic data; and
- the order to supply identity or subscriber information.

The investigative measures least often permitted or most often prohibited are:

- remote access;
- transborder access to data;
- covert online investigations; and
- geolocation tracking (in Europe).

Most respondents would find additional investigative measures useful, particularly remote access, transborder access to data and covert online investigations. Incidentally these were the investigative measures least often legally permitted. Only a small minority of countries have specific legal provisions allowing for the acquisition of data from the cloud or for the remote access to transborder data. According to those provisions, remote access is usually only permitted if the data is directly accessible from a suspect's device during a search.[6] In Figs. 6.1 and 6.2 the replies about the investigative measures for the collection and acquisition of digital evidence are shown.

[5]Questionnaire, Law enforcement section, Question 2.

[6]Questionnaire, Law enforcement section, Question 11.

Fig. 6.1 Investigative measures for the collection and acquisition of digital evidence, global without Europe

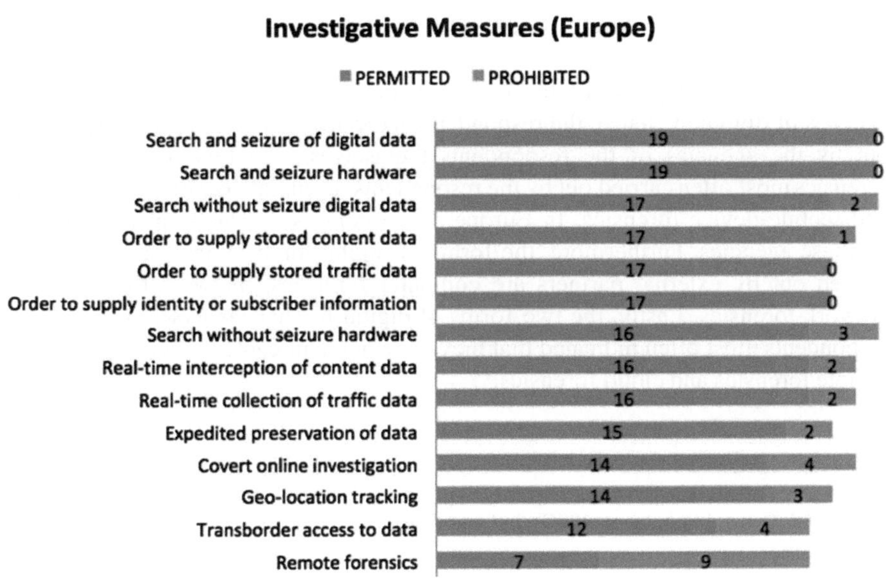

Fig. 6.2 Investigative measures for the collection and acquisition of digital evidence, Europe

6.3.1.2 The Preservation of Digital Evidence

For the implementation of the legal framework of digital evidence regarding the preservation phase of the digital evidence process, it was noted that, at international level, rules on the expedited preservation of data provide a solution for safeguarding digital evidence prior to commencing lengthy MLA procedures.

For the preservation of digital evidence in the field, however, digital forensic examiners may have to conduct live forensics to ensure potential evidence is not lost when switching off a device. Existing SOPs are often not detailed enough for the more complex cases and digital forensic examiners will sometimes make a judgement call on how to proceed. The tools used for live forensics may, additionally, modify the computer system and the digital forensic examiner must be able to explain the potential impacts of such modifications on the digital evidence.[7]

The preservation of digital evidence is, furthermore, strongly linked to the digital evidence management lifecycle and the respondents of the questionnaire mentioned that providing a complete chain of custody was listed as one of the main lessons learned by the respondents.[8]

When it comes to the storage of digital evidence, none of the respondents subcontract the storage of digital evidence to third parties.[9] Conversely, the current or future use of Storage Area Networks (SANs) can be considered one of the main solutions by which LEAs attempt to deal with storage challenges.[10]

6.3.1.3 The Forensic Analysis of Digital Evidence

Regarding the next phase of the digital evidence process, namely the forensic analysis of digital evidence, the respondents indicated that this is primarily carried out by the agencies of the respondents themselves. The two forms of digital forensics most often carried out by the respondents' agencies are computer forensics and mobile device forensics. In Europe, live forensics is usually also performed by these agencies. Furthermore, the forms of digital forensic analyses most often carried out by external partners are computer forensics, malware forensics and network forensics. Lastly, the two forms of digital forensic analyses of which the respondents most often indicated that they were not applicable to their agencies are remote forensics and cloud forensics.[11]

---

[7]Based on the Electronic Evidence Expert Group Meeting held on 2 and 3 December 2014 at the INTERPOL General Secretariat (IPSG), in Lyon, France.

[8]Questionnaire, Law enforcement section, Question 8.

[9]Questionnaire, Law enforcement section, Question 7d.

[10]Questionnaire, Law enforcement section, Question 7d and based on the Electronic Evidence Expert Group Meeting held on 2 and 3 December 2014 at the INTERPOL General Secretariat (IPSG), in Lyon, France.

[11]Questionnaire, Law enforcement section, Question 5.

Concerning the tools used to conduct the forensic analyses, the respondents listed a mix of digital forensic software suites and purpose specific tools, as well as a mix of commercially available tools and tools freely available through open sources. However, only few tools were listed to conduct remote forensics and cloud forensics. Furthermore, in Europe, only very few respondents stated that the analysis of certain devices or applications is not applicable to their agencies. At a global level, the acquisition and analysis of data from satellite navigation systems is not applicable to the agencies of a notably large number of respondents and, thus, few tools were listed for this type of acquisition and analysis.[12]

Most respondents indicated that their agencies have internally developed their own manuals of procedures, guidelines and/or best practices regarding the handling of digital evidence. In addition, ISO standards and guidelines were said to apply, as well as externally developed guidelines, such as those published by the Association of Chief Police Officers (ACPO). In Europe, some respondents also mentioned that their agencies do not follow specific guidelines, but rely on the requirements laid down in their Code of Criminal Procedure. Of the European respondents who indicated that guidelines and best practices are binding in their countries, approximately half stated that there would be no legal consequences to not adhering to those guidelines and best practices. At a global level, most respondents who have binding guidelines and/or best practices in their countries affirmed that there could be legal consequences for non-adherence.[13]

Furthermore, when it comes to the profiles of personnel handling digital evidence, most European respondents explicitly mentioned the requirement of a university degree for certain positions while, at a global level, only half of the respondents referred to a university degree. Alternatively, a training or background in IT is also often sought after and personnel often receive additional training on the software tools used on the job. Overall, the personnel handling digital evidence have a police background, but it is common for LEAs to also employ civilians with technical backgrounds. Regarding the types of personnel profiles for staff handling digital evidence, in Europe, the most common distinction made is between digital evidence first responder (DEFR) and digital evidence specialist (DES). At a global level, a more diverse range of positions was mentioned. The position of cybercrime investigator also reoccurred a few times.[14] In Figs. 6.3 and 6.4 the replies about the types of digital forensic analysis are shown.

[12]Questionnaire, Law enforcement section, Question 5 and Questionnaire, Digital forensics section, Question 1.

[13]Questionnaire, Law enforcement section, Question 4.

[14]Questionnaire, Digital forensics section, Question 2.

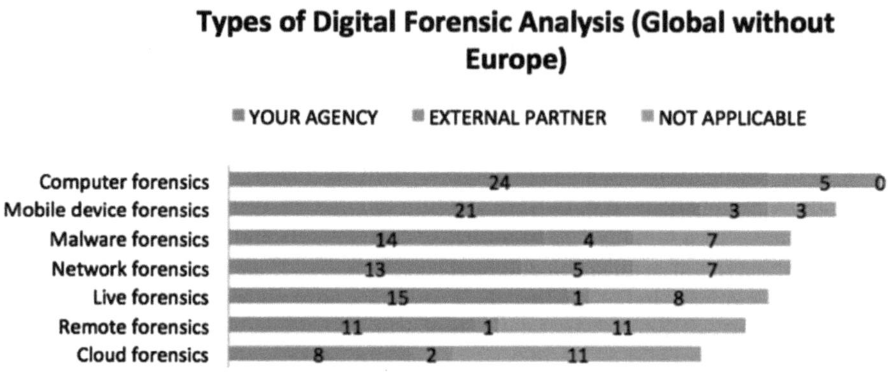

Fig. 6.3 Types of digital forensic analysis, global without Europe

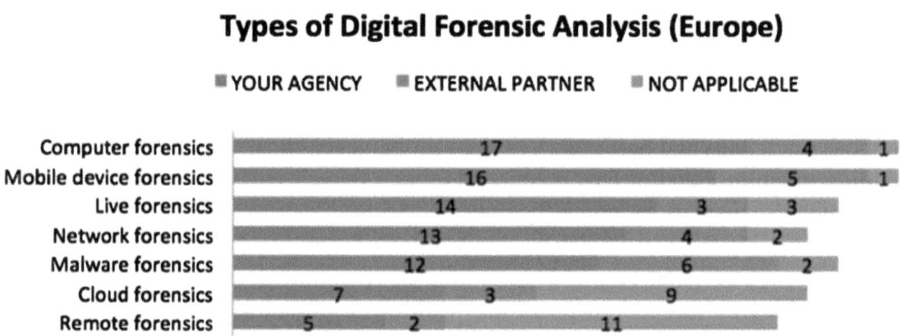

Fig. 6.4 Types of digital forensic analysis, Europe

6.3.1.4 The Presentation of Digital Evidence Before Court

Most respondents affirmed that their agencies can be called upon to provide expertise before court. In Europe, a minority of respondents indicated that the prosecution can also call upon external independent experts. However, this is not common practice. Meanwhile, at the global level, a significant portion of the respondents indicated that external experts could be called in by the prosecution and in some jurisdictions this is regular practice.[15]

The use of specific software or hardware tools is, generally, accepted for the presentation of digital evidence in court. Nevertheless, such tools are not widely used and this is seemingly not perceived as an issue by law enforcement officers who often prefer to present evidence in a clear and simple manner. This may, however, be linked to the fact that judges, prosecutors and juries are reported to

[15]Questionnaire, Law enforcement section, Question 6.

have a low level of technical knowledge and this is perceived as a serious issue by the respondents.[16]

6.3.1.5 The Transfer of Digital Evidence

Most of the European respondents' countries do not have legal rules on the transfer of digital evidence within their country. However, a small majority of the respondents' countries outside of Europe do. In the European countries where there are rules on the transfer of digital evidence within the country, these rules do not differ for different types of evidence while the contrary holds true for about half of the global respondents with such rules. Furthermore, many European countries indicated that the transfer of digital evidence within their countries does not occur digitally. At a global level, the opposite is true and the transfer usually occurs by means of storage media, such as CDs, flash drives and hard drives.[17]

Concerning international transfers of digital evidence, approximately half of the respondents indicated that there are legal rules on the transfer of digital evidence to a requesting country and from a requested country. In the latter case, this even holds true for most respondents at the global level. In Europe, most of countries that have rules on this matter referred to national rules while at a global level the respondents most often mention Mutual Legal Assistance Treaties (MLATs) and Mutual Legal Assistance in Criminal Matters Acts (MLACMAs). None of the European respondents and only a small minority of the global respondents with rules on the matter stated that these rules differ depending on the types of evidence transferred. Moreover, in a small majority of cases the transfer to requesting countries and from requested countries occurs digitally and, primarily, by means of storage media, such as CDs, DVDs and hard disks.[18]

6.3.2 Status Quo on the Collaboration Between Agencies Responsible for Implementation

The agencies primarily responsible for the implementation of the legal framework of digital evidence are, according to the questionnaire, primarily:

- cybercrime units;
- digital forensic labs;
- high-tech crime units; and
- criminal investigation units.

---

[16]Questionnaire, Law enforcement section, Question 7e.

[17]Questionnaire, Legal section, Question 4.

[18]Questionnaire, Legal section, Question 5 and 6.

About half of the European respondents and two thirds of the global respondents who replied to the question pertaining to the legal basis for collaboration, indicated that there are legal rules that determine the body that carries out the forensic analysis of digital evidence.[19] In Europe, there is seemingly an even mix between the countries that have formally regulated collaborations and those that rely on informal collaborations. At the global level, most of the respondents to the question refer to formally regulated collaborations (most often MoUs) while a minority of just a few respondents state that there is no collaboration with external entities. None of the respondents outside of Europe cite informal collaborations.[20]

About a fourth of the global respondents stated that collaborations with external parties do not apply to their agencies. One respondent clarified that for collaborations with external parties, as a minimum, their procedures must be consistent with those expected for admissibility of evidence in a Court of Law.[21]

Most of the respondents indicated that the acquisition and analysis of digital evidence is entirely carried out by their agencies' in-house digital forensics specialists or their in-house digital forensics lab. A minority of respondents indicated that this is only partially the case. Furthermore, a few respondents point out that the acquisition and analysis of digital evidence is entirely conducted by external public digital forensics labs or specialists. In Europe, external private digital forensics labs or specialists were mentioned as well. None of the respondents, outside of Europe, indicated that the acquisition or analysis of digital evidence is entirely carried out by external private digital forensics specialists or labs.[22]

The most common reason for the collaboration with external entities, mentioned by the respondents, is a lack of digital forensic tools in-house. Furthermore, a lack of digital forensics specialisation in-house was also a common reason for collaboration, as well as legal obligations (in Europe) and the lack of a digital forensics lab in-house (outside of Europe[23]).

At the global level, training and knowledge sharing were also given as important reasons for collaboration. One respondent emphasised the need for research and development (R&D) at international level, as R&D is essential to grow capability. However, too many agencies, it was stated, do not have a sharing culture and this is limiting international development of the science.[24] R&D nevertheless requires resources and, despite the great value electronic evidence adds to modern law enforcement, it is a hard sell to gain adequate resources within the myriad of responsibilities that modern agencies retain.

[19]Questionnaire, Legal section, Question 10.

[20]Questionnaire, Law enforcement section, Question 3a and 3b.

[21]Ibidem.

[22]Questionnaire, Law enforcement section, Question 3.

[23]Questionnaire, Law enforcement section, Question 3c.

[24]Ibidem.

6.3.3 *Status Quo on the Use of Channels for International Cooperation*

Regarding informal international cooperation, police to police contact is, according to the respondents, primarily sought in obtaining operational and technical information. According to the respondents of the questionnaire, 24/7 networks are also primarily used in obtaining operational and technical information. In Europe, legal information is also sought through these networks while, outside of Europe, this is also the case for the search and seizure of digital evidence. Only a small number of the respondents' agencies directly contact foreign service providers. Those that do, primarily, do so to obtain technical and operational information, followed by the expedited preservation of data. In Europe, obtaining legal information can also be added to this list.[25]

Furthermore, the European respondents indicated that formal MLA requests are primarily used to obtain the production of stored traffic data and operational information, as well as for the search and seizure of digital evidence and of computer hardware. At a global level, formal MLA requests are primarily used to obtain the exchange of digital evidence and the production of stored traffic data.[26] Law enforcement representatives have, time and again, stated that they are far from satisfied with the current procedures for formal MLA requests and heavily rely on informal police to police cooperation to ensure no valuable time is lost.[27] In Figs. 6.5 and 6.6 the replies about the channels of international cooperation are shown.

6.4 Challenges Hampering Law Enforcement Investigations and Forensic Analyses Involving Digital Evidence

This section provides a status quo assessment and analysis of the primary challenges that law enforcement is confronted with throughout the electronic evidence lifecycle. Therefore, the research first addresses the different legal systems at international level and how the main legal principles and rules of evidence in the most dominant legal systems, i.e. the civil law system and the common law system, may impact international law enforcement cooperation. After setting this backdrop, certain challenges impacting law enforcement investigations are assessed. A comprehensive study was undertaken about the use of encryption and

[25]Questionnaire, Law enforcement section, Question 12.

[26]Ibidem.

[27]As presented during the 2nd Eurasian Working Group Meeting on Cybercrime for Heads of Units, organised by the INTERPOL Global Complex for Innovation (IGCI) and hosted in Istanbul, Turkey, on 28–30 May 2014 and as confirmed by semi-structured telephone interviews conducted in August 2015.

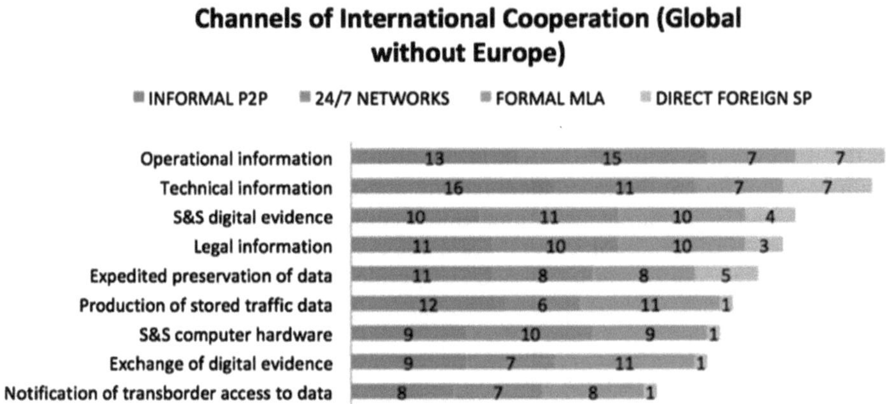

Fig. 6.5 Channels of international cooperation, global without Europe

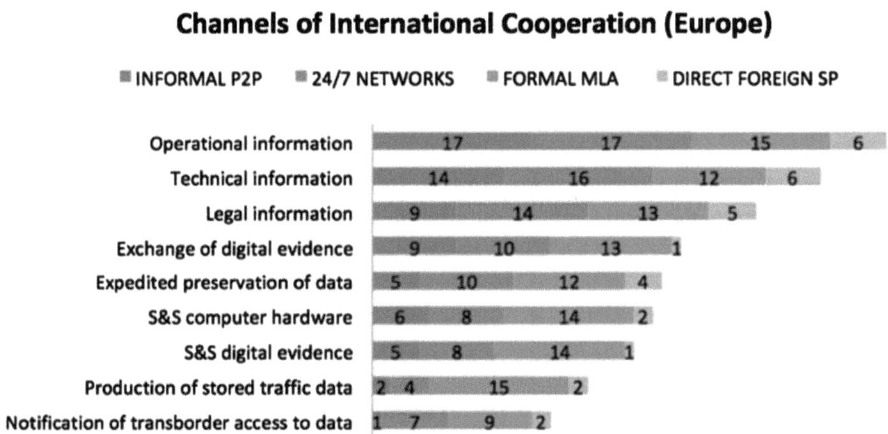

Fig. 6.6 Channels of international cooperation, Europe

anonymisation tools considering the recent and fast-moving developments on the matter that arose shortly after the distribution of the EVIDENCE questionnaire. Finally, the report focuses on recent and more long-standing examples of legal lacunae leaving LEAs to investigate and cooperate within fields of uncertainty.

6.4.1 *Different Legal Systems: A Challenge to International Law Enforcement Cooperation?*

After a comparison of common law and civil law systems, one may conclude that common law systems seem to rely more heavily on exclusionary rules to make unreliable evidence inadmissible while civil law systems, conversely, may be seen as less procedural in that they rely on the principle of freedom of evidence thereby giving more predominance to the probative value of evidence (Ashouri et al. 2014). Nevertheless, common ground can be found for both legal systems, where the principle of freedom of evidence would prevail in both cases over the role played by exclusionary rules. The importance of evidence-sorting rules has been noted to be diminishing in criminal trials (Choo 2015). Indeed, freedom of evidence is slowly becoming an important component in common law, particularly in the English and Welsh legal system. Furthermore, as can be seen in the practice of courts, exclusionary rules such as the best evidence rule and hearsay are progressively evolving to adapt to the evolutions produced by the introduction of digital evidence and to further the interests of justice.

Thus, it appears that the common law and civil law systems are, in practice, showing signs of a gradual move towards assimilation of each other's principles, including the principle of freedom of evidence. Yet, when translating this "practical assimilation" into legal texts, one must pay attention to important aspects that may have serious consequences. For instance, importing the practice of cross-examination into civil law systems could prove to be detrimental to the efficiency of criminal proceedings as civil law traditions are seemingly neither adapted nor equipped to face such procedures.[28] Given the circumstances, however, it appears quite clearly that common law and civil law systems are not incompatible. Indeed, working within a civil law system, for instance, does not preclude from possibly using specific rules of evidence from the common law system. A good illustration of that is how the International Criminal Court successfully managed to combine different features coming from both the common law and civil law system when adopting its rules of evidence.

6.4.2 Encryption and Anonymisation Tools: Hampering Investigations and Digital Forensics

Based on the replies to the questionnaire and the telephone interviews conducted subsequently, it was determined that encryption and anonymisation tools can be listed among the greatest challenges for law enforcement when investigating crime and analysing digital evidence.[29] This warranted a more in-depth study of the encryption debate, going back to the first crypto wars of the 1990s, as well a more comprehensive look at the way online anonymous ecosystems act as a catalyst for serious crime.

[28]Based on semi-structured telephone interviews conducted in August 2015.

[29]Questionnaire, Law enforcement section, Question 7a and semi-structured telephone interviews conducted in August 2015.

6.4.2.1 The Encryption Debate: Moving to Europe

The current debate on encryption, dubbed "the second crypto wars" requires a revisit of the crypto wars of the 1990s. The debate back then pertained to the fact that the US government, with the transition to digital communications, wanted to introduce key escrow solutions to ensure LEAs and intelligence services could continue to benefit from telecommunications interceptions. In addition, the US government did not want foreign adversaries using high-grade encryption hindering their intelligence capabilities, so the discussion also involved the implementation of export controls on encryption that would entail only lower-grade encryption could leave the country (Wilson et al. 2015a,b).

Eventually, the idea to implement key escrow was abandoned after privacy and information security advocates strongly opposed the proposal by emphasising the vulnerabilities it would bring to information systems that malicious third parties could equally exploit. The export controls in the US were, however, implemented and, subsequently led to US tech companies developing products with lower-grade encryption for the international market or, to reduce costs, developing only lower-grade encryption products for both the US and international markets. Under pressure of these companies, placed in a less beneficial position on the international market, the US government finally loosened export controls on encryption. This rang in the end of the crypto wars in the 1990s. The harm was, however, already done and the export-grade encryption of the 1990s is still responsible for vulnerabilities in online services today (Wilson et al. 2015a,b).

After the Snowden revelations, US tech companies, again, suffered on the international market and, reacting to their users' privacy concerns, started implementing encryption-by-default and encryption-by-design in their products (Farivar 2014; Fox-Brewster 2014). This caught the attention of LEAs that, concerned with their capabilities to investigate crime and collect evidence, reintroduced the topic of "backdoors" into the public debate (Comey 2014). Some of the same activists who were involved in the debate during the 1990s, again took up an active role against the proposal stating that nothing had sufficiently changed since the first debate that would warrant the introduction of backdoors today (Abelson et al. 2015). The US government, after appointing a working group into studying potential solutions, finally decided not to implement any legislation enforcing the introduction of backdoors (Obama Administration's Draft Paper on Technical Options for the Encryption Debate 2015; Peterson and Nakashima 2015). The EU, like its stance during the first crypto wars, did not consider backdoors a viable policy option (Essers 2015).

Fast forward 2 years in which a wave of terrorist attacks occurred on European soil, including the Paris attacks in November 2015, the Brussels suicide bombings of March 2016, the Nice truck attack in July 2016 and the Berlin Christmas market attack in December 2016, and the calls to take stronger measures to prevent terrorism are growing louder across Europe. These calls also encompass EU Member State requests to find a solution for the use of encryption to allow for more effective counter-terrorism investigations. In February 2017, the French and German Ministers of Interior sent a joint communication to the European Commission calling for stronger measures in the fight against terrorism. Among these measures, there is a call to study the possibility to define new obligations upon service providers of electronic communications while simultaneously ensuring the reliability and security of systems.[30] While this is not the first time that the French and Germans jointly call for measures against encryption[31]; this time they are placing more pressure on the matter by proposing legislative action to take place by October 2017.[32]

6.4.2.2 Online Anonymous Ecosystems: A Catalyst for Serious Crime

Today, those seeking anonymity for legitimate reasons, as well as those with criminal intent, can turn to a whole online ecosystem of anonymity, including encryption and anonymisation tools, darknets with hidden services and crypto currencies. In fact, UN Special Rapporteur David Kaye recommends the use of such tools in his report on the promotion and protection of the right to freedom of opinion and expression, as they can be considered enablers of these rights in an online environment (Kaye 2015). While the report was lauded by civil liberties groups, it, nevertheless, falls short of proposing directions or reflections towards the beginning of a solution to find a balance between the right to freedom of opinion and expression and citizens' right to security.

The use of these technical means, indeed, provides significant challenges for law enforcement during criminal investigations, particularly about the identification of suspects, as well as for the collection and analysis of potential evidence.[33] In addition, the continuous innovation within this arena requires LEAs to keep up to date through continuous training efforts on the latest innovations on darknets, such as digital wallet formats, bitcoin tumblers and the blockchain (Nylander 2015; Schofield 2015).

[30]Joint communication of the French and German Ministers of Interior to the EU, 20 February 2017, available at http://www.politico.eu/wp-content/uploads/2017/02/2017-02-17-Declaration-FR-DE-II_Officielle.pdf. See also Computer and Communications Industry Association, Is Europe about to weaken encryption, 24 February 2017, available at: https://www.ccianet.org/2017/02/is-europe-about-weaken-encryption.

[31]Tech Crunch, Encryption under fire in Europe as France and Germany call for decrypt law, 24 August 2016, available at https://techcrunch.com/2016/08/24/encryption-under-fire-in-europe-as-france-and-germany-call-for-decrypt-law.

[32]Joint communication of the French and German Ministers of Interior to the EU, 20 February 2017, available at http://www.politico.eu/wp-content/uploads/2017/02/2017-02-17-Declaration-FR-DE-II_Officielle.pdf. See also Computer and Communications Industry Association, Is Europe about to weaken encryption, 24 February 2017, available at https://www.ccianet.org/2017/02/is-europe-about-weaken-encryption.

[33]Questionnaire, Law enforcement section, Question 7a and based on semi-structured telephone interviews conducted in August 2015.

6.4.2.3 Continuing the Debate...

For law enforcement, this requires innovative policing applying a combination of new investigative measures, such as law enforcement remote systems access, with traditional undercover work applied online, as illustrated by some recent cases conducted on the darknet.[34] From the replies to the EVIDENCE questionnaire, remote capabilities and powers to conduct undercover operations online were the measures considered most useful to expand their current options with.[35] The expansion of investigative powers for law enforcement in the context of such a highly political and economically driven discussion, however, requires law enforcement to present the public with a strong evidence-basis to enable a fully informed public debate.

LEAs should, thus, aim to continue furthering their developments on a methodology by which both quantitative and qualitative facts can be collected, compared and presented to the public and policymakers. LEAs should continue to increase transparency and further the development of trustful collaborations with other stakeholders, such as the private sector and academia, to tackle criminal activity in a highly innovative and increasingly anonymous online environment.

Only by further enhancing their bridges with other stakeholders in this debate, such as the public and the private sector, can LEAs discuss common ground to direct the discussion. The Obama Administration Working Group on Encryption recognised this and set forth several principles to further the debate in a constructive manner. The nine principles set out by the Working Group to guide the public debate are, therefore, worth recalling. They emphasise that there should be:

1. no bulk collection as there should be a focus on targeted access;
2. no unilateral government access, thus no "golden keys" for the government, but the involvement of a trusted third party (TTP);
3. technologically-enforced limits rather than reliance on procedural protections;
4. international adoption, recognising that a US solution would be adopted in other countries as well;
5. maximum security and minimum complexity to minimise the ability of malicious third parties exploiting the solution;
6. minimum impact of malicious exploitation, for instance by requiring physical access to a device;
7. minimum negative impact on innovation by ensuring that new types of encryption, such as those implementing "forward secrecy", are not impacted;
8. a no "one size fits all" approach that entails that "providers, not the governments should be responsible for determining how to design any feasible approaches to their communications data"; and

[34]For example see http://www.independent.co.uk/news/world/europe/eric-eoin-marques-28-year-old-architect-s-son-from-dublin-accused-of-being-world-s-biggest-dealer-in-8782756.html and Mullin (2015).

[35]Questionnaire, Law enforcement section, Question 11.

9. an avoidance of undermining trust in security, as the online ecosystem requires participants trust the security of their transactions and communications.[36]

6.4.3 *Legal Lacunae: Hampering International Law Enforcement Cooperation*

Law enforcement capabilities and cooperation in the field of digital evidence are not only challenged by technical innovation, but also by legal frameworks that are increasingly lagging behind technical advancements. In addition, when legislation is implemented that aids LEAs in fulfilling their mandate of tackling crime in an increasingly digital environment, such as data retention legislation, the lack of adequate fundamental rights safeguards may lead to the invalidation of such rules leaving LEAs and other stakeholders to act in a legal grey zone.

6.4.3.1 Data Retention: European Case Law

The 2014 annulment of the EU Data Retention Directive[37] has created a patchwork of legal situations across the EU, as some countries decided to invalidate their national legislation while other countries adapted their legislation to the ruling of the European Court of Justice and several countries did not take any action at all. Even before the annulment of the Directive, LEAs that responded to the EVIDENCE questionnaire criticised the lack of harmonisation regarding data retention periods as inconsistencies between countries hampered criminal investigations.[38]

In December 2016, the challenges surrounding data retention in the EU again culminated when the European Court of Justice had to deal with the references for a preliminary ruling over the joined cases Tele2 Sverige AB v Post-och telestyrelsen and Secretary of State for the Home Department v Tom Watson & Others.[39] The Court rules that Article 15(1) of the e-Privacy Directive, following the Digital Rights judgement, can allow for national legislation on data retention and the access of national authorities thereto. However, Article 15(1) [...] "must be interpreted as

[36]http://apps.washingtonpost.com/g/documents/world/read-the-obama-administrations-draft-paper-on-technical-options-for-the-encryption-debate/1753.

[37]Judgment of the Court (Grand Chamber) of April 2014, High Court of Ireland, Verfassungsgerichtshof v. Ireland, Austria (joined cases C-293/12 and C-594/12), Available from: http://curia.europa.eu/juris/document/document.jsf?text=&docid=150642&pageIndex=0&doclang=EN&mode=req&dir=&occ=first&part=1&cid=332880.

[38]Questionnaire, Law enforcement section, Question 10.

[39]Judgment of the Court (Grand Chamber) of 21 December 2016, Tele2 Sverige AB v Post- och telestyrelsen and Secretary of State for the Home Department v Tom Watson and Others (joined cases C-203/15 and C-698/15), available at: http://eur-lex.europa.eu/legal-content/EN/TXT/PDF/?uri=CELEX:62015CJ0203&from=EN.

precluding national legislation which, for the purpose of fighting crime, provides for general and indiscriminate retention of all traffic and location data of all subscribers and registered users relating to all means of electronic communication[40]". It clearly states that "it is to be ensured that data retention is limited to what is strictly necessary[41]".

The Court recognises that "the effectiveness of the fight against serious crime, in particular organised crime and terrorism, may depend to a great extent on the use of modern investigation techniques," but also states that an "objective of fundamental interest" cannot in itself justify the general and indiscriminate retention of all traffic and location data "considered to be necessary for that fight[42]".

Furthermore, the Court reasoned that national legislation must have an objective evidence basis upon which it is possible "to identify a public whose data is likely to reveal a link, at least an indirect one, with serious criminal offences, and to contribute in one way or another to fighting serious crime or to preventing a serious risk to public security." As an example, the Court refers to geographical criteria as, based on objective evidence, a competent national authority may consider "that there exists, in one or more geographical areas, a high risk of perpetration for or commission of such offences[43]".

In addition, the Court ruled that Article 15(1) "must be interpreted as precluding national legislation governing the protection and security of traffic and location data and, in particular, access of the competent national authorities to the retained data, where the objective pursued by that access, in the context of fighting crime, is not restricted solely to fighting serious crime, where access is not subject to prior review by a court or an independent administrative authority, and where there is no requirement that the data concerned should be retained within the European Union[44]".

While these criteria are sufficiently clear, the rejection of "general and indiscriminate" data retention in favour of targeted and differentiated data retention raises more questions than it provides answers. The need for a stronger evidence basis to justify data retention measures is far from unreasonable, but the way differentiated data retention measures can be implemented in an effective manner may require more guidance. Moreover, the example of geographical criteria provided by the Court, even with a strong evidence basis, may, for instance, still raise concerns about socio-economic discrimination.

The ruling thus only exacerbates existing uncertainties with national laws being annulled or called into question across EU Member States, thereby leaving LEAs to act in a field with even more lacunae than before.

---

[40]Ivi par. 134.

[41]Ivi par. 110.

[42]Ivi par. 103.

[43]Ivi par. 111.

[44]Ivi par. 134.

6.4.3.2 Remote Access to Data in the Cloud

Furthermore, the topic of transborder access to data was addressed, as, here too, LEAs are left to operate in a field of patchwork solutions. Based on the results of the questionnaire, it was determined that a large majority of respondents would find transborder access to data a useful investigative measure. However, only a small minority of countries, at European and global level, have specific legal provisions allowing for remote access to transborder data and the acquisition of data from the cloud.[45] According to those provisions, remote access is usually only permitted if the data is directly accessible from a suspect's device during a search. Nevertheless, in the absence of such provisions, practice and case law in several countries are leaning towards permitting such access if the location of the data cannot be determined. The patchwork solution that ensues creates legal uncertainty regarding transborder searches and requires a solution agreed upon at international level (Council of Europe 2014).

Therefore, this research presented a more in-depth overview of the current state of affairs at international level regarding transborder access, including the challenges it presents for all stakeholders involved. The potential impact upon individuals' fundamental rights because of transborder searches of computers and networks, however, deserves particular attention, as it requires adequate safeguards to be put in place. This latter point, nevertheless creates divergence of opinion between States as they find it difficult to agree upon which safeguards and protections should apply. Thus, the continuation of discussions on the creation of safeguards is crucial to ensure that transborder access of data will only take place in a lawful manner that provides data subjects with sufficient protections.

The Council of Europe has looked into potential solutions to meet LEAs needs for transborder access to data that resulted in several proposed solutions, including a draft Proposal for an Additional Protocol to the Cybercrime Convention on access to electronic evidence. Because of the above-mentioned challenges, and given the highly political context in which such a solution needs to be reached, the transborder group stated that negotiation of the Protocol would not be feasible. Although the arguments in favour of an extension of transborder access will most likely not disappear but rather increase, the transborder group recognised that "in absence of an agreed upon international framework with safeguards, more and more countries will take unilateral action and extend law enforcement powers to remote transborder searches either formally or informally with unclear safeguards" (Council of Europe 2014).

Nevertheless, in November 2016, during the plenary meeting of the Cybercrime Convention Committee (T-CY) at the Council of Europe, recommendations were adopted on criminal justice access to electronic evidence in the cloud "which includes the negotiation of an additional Protocol to the Cybercrime Convention as of the middle of 2017" (Council of Europe 2016). This additional protocol is

[45]Questionnaire, Legal section, Question 7.

set to include provisions for more effective mutual legal assistance; provisions allowing for direct cooperation with service providers in other jurisdictions; a clearer framework and stronger safeguards for existing practices of transborder access to data; and safeguards, including data protection requirements (Council of Europe 2016).

The above concerns, however, were illustrated by the Yahoo and Microsoft cases in which national authorities were trying to force the arm of justice to take a decision on the matter of transborder access and provide clarity for LEAs and prosecution in the absence of any statutory rules.[46] These cases are, furthermore, also illustrative of the different forces at play, be it the EU pushing back against the US tech industry's monopoly impacting law enforcement action or the US tech industry pushing back against its own government impacting their credibility on the international market, in an already highly political debate.

The Snowden revelations, here too, had an impact on the debate. The increasing public opposition against the disproportionate, and often reportedly unlawful, processing of personal data of EU citizens by US companies and US government agencies, such as the NSA, has led European courts to push back against such harmful practices in protection of the fundamental rights of EU citizens, as illustrated by the Safe Harbour ruling.[47] The impact upon LEAs of the rulings of the European Court of Justice concerning data retention and the safe harbour framework cannot be understated, equally so the lack of legislative action at international level pertaining to the topic of transborder access to data. Thus, while the tech industry continues to push boundaries, LEAs are left playing catch up and manoeuvring their way through a highly uncertain and politically sensitive landscape filled with legal lacunae.

6.5 Recommendations to Strengthen Law Enforcement Action in the Field of Digital Evidence

This section focuses on best practices and guidelines, identified from a law enforcement perspective, to be integrated into a comprehensive European Framework. For this, the research provided an assessment on how to continue efforts towards the professionalisation of the relatively young field of digital forensics. As law

[46]In 2007 a Belgian public prosecutor asked Yahoo to release information regarding a subscriber, Yahoo refused to do so and it was the beginning of an ongoing judicial saga, see http://www.stibbe.com/en/news/2016/january/court-of-cassation-definitively-confirms-yahoos-obligation-to-cooperate-with-law-enforcement-agenci Harvard law review (2014) [Online], In re Warrant to Search a Certain Email Account Controlled & Maintained by Microsoft Corp, available at http://harvardlawreview.org/2015/01/in-re-warrant-to-search-a-certain-email-account-controlled-maintained-by-microsoft-corp.

[47]Judgment of the European Court of Justice, 6 October 2015, Case C-362/14, Maximilian Schrems V. Data Protection Commissioner and Digital Rights Ireland Ltd.

enforcement is, however, not the sole actor within the digital evidence domain, the importance of "building bridges" between LEAs and other stakeholders, including the public, policymakers, the private sector and the judiciary cannot be understated. Therefore, the collaboration between LEAs and these other stakeholders is also analysed. Moreover, in an increasingly globalised online environment, the collection and exchange of digital evidence is hampered by outdated and lengthy mutual legal assistance practices no longer adapted today's realities. The need for modernisation efforts in the field of international police and judicial cooperation are, therefore, discussed as well.

6.5.1 The Professionalisation of Digital Forensics

As digital forensics is a relative new field of forensics and has developed differently from other fields of forensics, practitioners themselves notice the different level of professionalism between, for instance digital forensic analysis and DNA analysis. Digital forensic experts have, nevertheless, expressed a wish for their field of expertise to reach a similar level of professionalism and recognition. However, certain practitioners fear that standardisation efforts in this field too early on may hamper innovation. Despite such concerns, there is a consensus that this is only the commencement phase of a lengthy standardisation process.[48]

The "professionalisation of digital forensics", as the experts called it during the Electronic Evidence Expert Group Meeting, requires a reassessment of the potential regulation of digital forensics professions to ensure that practitioners meet a certain standard. These practitioners often rely on certain methods for the acquisition and analysis of digital evidence and these methods also include the use of digital forensic tools, thus these methods and tools should ideally be subject to validation procedures to ensure they are fit-for-purpose. Lastly, there are currently no universal standards specifically applicable to digital forensic labs, thus it is also worth considering the development of an accreditation procedure to ensure digital forensic labs meet certain pre-determined quality levels.

6.5.1.1 Independent Certification of Digital Forensics Professionals

According to experts in the field of digital forensics, digital forensics professionals should at the very least have obtained a bachelor degree in IT. As without a thorough understanding of the basic concepts of IT, it will be extremely difficult for an individual to go beyond the standard application of tools and develop

[48]Based on the Electronic Evidence Expert Group Meeting held on 2 and 3 December 2014 at the INTERPOL General Secretariat (IPSG), in Lyon, France.

creative solutions in more complex cases.[49] Any further form of education in digital forensics could be provided by universities, as there are now increasingly often courses provided on digital forensics (Mason 2012), or by specialised organisations or professional associations. While the latter often deliver highly commended trainings and certifications, there are also commercially driven organisations that do not shy away from awarding individuals with certifications merely based on the attendance of a training course. Certain software companies provide a similar service, which furthermore works in their favour as law enforcement personnel will be tempted to stick with the tools they know and renew costly licenses.[50]

Therefore, it is recommended that an independent certification board be accredited with the certification of digital forensic professionals, in accordance with different levels of expertise, considering academic education, subject related expertise and practical experience that could be attained by means of apprenticeship, as the "soft skills" of digital forensic experts are currently insufficiently considered. Such an independent certification board or organisation should operate at an international or regional level, for instance covering Europe, ensuring a shared standard of expertise for digital forensic experts implemented by nationally accredited bodies.[51]

The independent certification board would equally certify the private sector and independent digital forensics professionals.[52] This would ensure that LEAs who outsource digital forensic tasks maintain a similar, or perhaps higher, level of professional quality. Nevertheless, the reliance on private sector experts or labs requires that mandates are clearly outlined and that systems are in place to ensure a high-level of quality and deontological compliance. The Netherlands Register of Court Experts is, for instance, an example of good practice in this matter.

6.5.1.2 Method Validation

Validation is the process of demonstrating that a method is fit for purpose—that the performance resulting from the combination of equipment and procedures used is good enough to satisfy the needs of the customer. Without empirical demonstration of how well a method performs, the customer cannot know whether the method will actually fulfil their needs.

A method includes all steps and components, which form part of an analytical process including any hardware and software used and any actions taken by a human

[49] As presented by Y. Vandermeer and further discussed at the EVIDENCE Status Quo Workshop in Sofia, Bulgaria.

[50] As presented by Y. Vandermeer and further discussed at the EVIDENCE Status Quo Workshop in Sofia, Bulgaria and confirmed during the semi-structured telephone interviews conducted in August 2015.

[51] As presented by Y. Vandermeer and further discussed at the EVIDENCE Status Quo Workshop in Sofia, Bulgaria.

[52] Ibidem.

as part of that process. The competence of the human must be assessed as part of the validation of the method. There are three types of methods, namely standard, laboratory-developed and non-standard methods. All methods used by a laboratory need to be validated by the laboratory. Even the implementation of a standard method needs to be verified in the particular laboratory and with particular staff.

Method validation requires that the method be applied to test data for which true answers are known, and compares the output of the method with the known truth. This constitutes the accuracy or validity of the method. Another relevant aspect of method validation is the extent to which the results are similar when the method is retested and this constitutes the precision or reliability of the method.

There are, nevertheless, limitations to method validations. An infinite number of validations cannot be conducted, the amount of data available for validation testing may be limited and may not exactly replicate the casework conditions, as the latter may not be fully known. These limitations should be acknowledged in reports.

The performance of a method, however, does not have to be perfect. Perfect performance may be impossible for fundamental reasons, not just because of the limitations of technology. Performance of a method must, however, be good enough to suit the needs of the customer. Normally, the required level of performance needed by the customer should be determined before initiating the validation tests. If the method does not meet these performance levels then it should not be used. In deciding the required performance criteria, risk-benefit should be considered. If the best method available only recovers 1 out of 10 deleted files, this may still be acceptable because of the value of recovering that one file. If the same system, however, recovers nine spurious files for every real deleted file, the risk might outweigh the benefit.[53]

Although individual labs would still need to validate/verify their own implementation of the methods, published validations of tools and methods conducted by reputable organisations may help them to decide which tools and methods could potentially be fit for purpose. Such validation reports also provide a template for the laboratory to follow in conducting their own validations. Online repositories of such validation reports can, thus, be considered as an example of good practice. Furthermore, a potential role for an international law enforcement body could be to host a repository of validation studies contributed by digital forensics laboratories in LEAs in member countries, and hence facilitate sharing of this type of information with digital forensics laboratories in LEAs in other member countries. In order to generate a large number of reports of validations of a large number of digital forensics methods it would be helpful to have centralised agencies delegated and funded to conduct such validation studies.

[53]On method validation, see Forensic Science Regulator, Guidance: Validation, November 2014, available at https://www.gov.uk/government/publications/forensic-science-providers-validation and Forensic Science Regulator, Draft Guidance: Digital Forensics Method Validation, August 2014, available at https://www.gov.uk/government/uploads/system/uploads/attachment_data/file/355996/2014.08.28_FSR_Digital_validation_Draft.pdf.

Bearing in mind that tools have different features that work in a different manner, based on their algorithms or source code, developing a taxonomy of features and a corresponding model of "validation" based on their accuracy and efficiency could provide a solution of greater value to digital forensic practitioners. Such a model could also be considered an example of good practice, as tools could be mapped by feature, as to provide practitioners with a clear overview of tools and the quality or strength of their different features for each version of the tool. By "ranking" these features and highlighting the complementarity and interoperability of tools and their respective features, practitioners can make a more informed decision regarding their needs and the tools that provide the best solution to meet them. Furthermore, it can aid managers to make a case for the allocation of resources towards certain tools over others.[54]

6.5.1.3 Accreditation of Digital Forensics Labs

Digital forensics laboratories may be required to be accredited by their customers or by national legislation. In addition to the UK Forensic Science Regulator's guidance, there are relevant ISO/IEC guidelines such as ISO/IEC 27042:2015 "Guidelines for the analysis and interpretation of digital evidence", but these are guidelines rather than standards. Following best-practice guidelines is recommended and may even be required by a customer, but it is demonstration of conformity with standards that counts for accreditation. A current problem for digital forensic laboratories seeking accreditation is that they must be accredited to ISO/IEC 17025:2005, a standard developed for testing and calibration laboratories whose activities differ somewhat from the activities of a digital forensics laboratory. Some practitioners have expressed that they do not consider ISO/IEC 17025:2005 to be an appropriate standard for forensic evaluation.[55] A potential solution could be to develop new standards that are more applicable to forensic science in general, and/or to convert existing ISO/IEC guidelines on digital forensics into standards. Both are processes that can take considerable time. In some countries national standards could potentially be developed faster, allowing digital forensic laboratories to be accredited for domestic work. Given that digital evidence is often relevant for crimes that are transnational, the latter solution would, however, not be ideal in the long term.

The appointment of an independent Forensic Science Regulator, as seen in the UK, can be considered a form of good practice at national level as the position aids forensic service providers to reach certain quality standards and can, for instance, provide guidance regarding the validation of digital forensic tools. Furthermore, it has been recognised that effective police and judicial cooperation requires broader, international and regional standardisation efforts, therefore the establishment of regional Forensic Science Regulators would be recommended and, in the framework

[54] Ibidem.

[55] Comments were not specifically about digital forensics.

of the EVIDENCE project, a European Forensic Science Regulator in particular (Smithuis and van Ruth 2013).

In conclusion, the professionalisation of digital forensics should be approached not only at national level, but at international and regional level, as well to avoid any duplication of efforts and to enhance the efficiency of cross-border police and judicial cooperation. Any standardisation efforts embarked upon should, nevertheless, refrain from hampering innovation and advances in this relatively young field. Furthermore, the process of professionalisation should involve all stakeholders in the digital evidence domain, from the public to the judiciary, to ensure a balanced approach adapted to the needs of a fair and correct criminal justice system.

6.5.2 *Enhancing Collaboration Between LEAs and Other Actors in the Digital Evidence Domain*

Law enforcement is far from the sole actor within the digital evidence domain and the importance of "building bridges" between LEAs and other stakeholders, including the public, policymakers, the private sector and the judiciary cannot be understated. Enhancing relationships between LEAs and other stakeholders in a trustful manner, however, requires continued efforts from all parties.

6.5.2.1 Collaboration with the Public and Policymakers: Increasing Transparency and Accountability

Keeping of Statistics and Case Examples as Evidence-Basis for Additional Resources

Particularly towards the public, that entrusts LEAs with the powers and resources to fulfil their mandate, LEAs should continue to expand their efforts in increasing transparency and accountability concerning their activities and spending. By providing statistics and documented case examples of law enforcement activities and needs, LEAs can, furthermore, provide the evidence-basis for an informed public debate upon which policymakers can, in turn, base their decisions.

With the economic downturn of the last several years and an increasing wave of budget cuts affecting law enforcement across continents, there is very strong competition for resources within the public sector and even between different law enforcement units (National Audit Office 2015; Syal 2015; Ward 2012). To obtain an understanding of the resources required to conduct digital investigations and digital forensics within LEAs, one, however, first needs to obtain an overview of the current situation within LEAs. Only, by obtaining all the current facts, can LEAs also start to anticipate new developments and future strategies (Bundeskriminalamt 2014).

Furthermore, the tracking of statistics and documenting of case examples can aid LEAs in setting performance indicators as well (Association of Chief Police Officers

(ACPO) 2011). Without an evidence-based strategy and adapted performance indicators upon which to evaluate an agency's work, it is very difficult for an agency to make a strong case for additional resources. Moreover, as LEAs are primarily funded by the taxpayer, a lack of evidence-based figures does not provide the public with the transparency and accountability it deserves regarding the allocation and return on investment of public funds.

Keeping of Statistics and Case Examples as Evidence-Basis for Policy Decisions

The crime prevention and investigation tasks of LEAs can be strongly impacted by societal and economic driving forces influencing policy decisions, court rulings and law reforms. The court rulings and changes to national laws on data retention and the public debate surrounding the use of encryption and anonymisation tools after the Snowden revelations are just two examples. Both topics, however, illustrate that LEAs may sometimes have difficulties regarding the methodology to collect the relevant facts to provide an evidence-basis for their standpoints. They may lack the statistics to back up their arguments or may have difficulties providing documented case examples during public debates.

LEAs continue to recognise the importance of such facts and are continuing efforts to obtain figures, for instance by means of surveys.[56] The European Commission also acknowledged the need for a stronger evidence-basis surrounding the data retention debate and requested EU Member States to provide additional quantitative data, but also qualitative data by means of case examples. The Commission had previously encountered difficulties comparing certain metrics on the topic based on a misinterpretation of certain terms in the template they had provided to Member States (DG Home, European Commission 2013).

Thus, one can suggest that documenting both quantitative and qualitative data to provide an evidence-basis for policy decisions and legal amendments is essential. For many law enforcement officers, prosecutors and investigating judges this may seem like an additional bureaucratic exercise, nevertheless, they recognise that the keeping of statistics is the biggest challenge in trying to explain why LEAs and prosecution need certain measures.[57] Here too, it is recognised that such data can be used as performance indicators, enabling LEAs and the judiciary to potentially develop more efficient working methods. LEAs, for instance, mention that they

[56]For instance, concerning the potential adoption of a data retention law in Norway, a public hearing was organised for which the National Criminal Investigation Service (NCIS) analysed how various types of electronic evidence are acquired and used by the police in Norway. Therefore, NCIS circulated a survey among the police districts in Norway. Also, for an example of a US survey regarding the impact of digital evidence on LEAs, see Emerson (2014).

[57]Based on semi-structured telephone interviews conducted in August 2015.

would like to obtain feedback on the outcome of judicial cases as this can help them improve the services they provide.[58]

As a matter of good practice, LEAs should continue to dedicate efforts to developing methodologies for recording and tracking of case-related statistics, preferably as part of a case management system for ease of use and with little room for misinterpretation. Furthermore, such methodologies must be applied across agencies, and preferably across countries, to enable a comparison and evaluation of these metrics. One could potentially foresee a role for national Forensic Science Regulators on this matter with the coordination of a European Forensic Science Regulator.

In conclusion, the importance of collecting data, both quantitative and qualitative, is essential for LEAs not only to develop better strategies to deal with certain challenges, but also to provide more transparency and accountability towards the public and policymakers. In the end, LEAs are entrusted with their mandate by the public and they are there to serve the public. However, if the public cannot hold an informed debate on certain societal topics, LEAs are also falling short towards the public as they will not be able to make a fully-informed decision. The public and policymakers should be able to weigh the pros and cons of certain policy decisions and make a risk assessment considering a range of different societal interests, in which security should at least not be under represented because of a lack of evidence-based information.

6.5.2.2 Evidence Sourced from Other Actors: Enhancing Trust

LEAs are increasingly confronted with evidence that has been collected and analysed by others stakeholders, particularly private companies, other public sector entities and citizens. LEAs will need to continue developing best practices in recognition of the fact that trustful collaborations with other actors are of essence in this field.

Evidence Emanating from the Private Sector

LEAs collaborate with private sector companies in a variety of different circumstances. Often, LEAs now must turn to these companies to obtain evidence, as large tech companies have more data on individuals at their disposal than governments usually do. Furthermore, these companies may be able to provide digital forensics solutions for which LEAs do not have the specialised tools or expertise. Thus, it is expected that LEAs will increasingly collaborate with the private sector in highly complex cases. Nevertheless, companies also fall victim to crime and LEAs will

[58] Ibidem.

have to closely collaborate with these companies in a trustful manner to investigate these crimes.

With cybercrime on the rise, the private sector is a favoured target because of the high amount of personal data and financial transactions processed within this sector. Nevertheless, it is often mentioned that there is an underreporting of these types of crimes by the private sector because of concerns of reputational damage. Additionally, large companies often employ their own online investigators or digital forensic analysts who, linked to the high salaries paid in this sector, may even be better equipped than LEAs to investigate specific types of crime, such as malware attacks.

LEAs have confirmed that they are seeing a greater willingness of companies to report computer crimes after they have managed to prove their discretion and ability to investigate such crimes in the past, thus by creating trust over time (Office of Legal Education, Executive Office for United States Attorneys 2010). Furthermore, companies are also increasingly sharing threat intelligence with one another through industry associations. As an example of good practice, LEAs can continue to enhance their relationships with the private sector through these industry associations (Office of Legal Education, Executive Office for United States Attorneys 2010). This enables LEAs to reach a greater amount of companies or industry partners dealing with the same issues and they can, in turn, rely on their trusted intermediary, the industry association to represent their best interest. Furthermore, these forms of collaboration enable all parties to collectively discuss setting quality standards across the sector, thereby allowing for more efficient and effective criminal investigations involving digital evidence.[59]

Evidence emanating from the private sector can be provided by large companies or financial institutions employing highly skilled technical personnel and can, thus, be correctly documented and already analysed, requiring little additional work. However, this is not always the case. There is also a whole range of small and medium enterprises that do not have the required skills to acquire and analyse digital evidence, which may lead to certain issues regarding the integrity of potential evidence.

LEAs usually consider evidence emanating from the private sector on a case-by-case basis. In some cases, companies do a great job at securing the evidence, potentially relying on third parties, such as information security companies to preserve the evidence. Nevertheless, sometimes the data provided is too limited and LEAs must go back and make their own analysis. However, it was clarified that this is usually the case, as a full case review will always have to be undertaken. Evidence provided by the private sector is only considered a "trace". An investigator explained that only once the documentation on how and by whom the data were collected and analysed is deemed acceptable, the traces are seized and a statement is taken from the specialist who initially handled the evidence.[60]

[59]Based on semi-structured telephone interviews conducted in August 2015.

[60]Ibidem.

The impact of certain mistakes made during the collection or analysis phase may, however, differ in civil and common law systems. Common law systems may not contain the same principle of freedom of evidence as many civil law systems do and this, thus, entails that digital evidence which was not correctly handled may be deemed inadmissible before court. As a measure to ensure companies and organisations correctly handle digital evidence, the concept of "forensic readiness" was introduced over a decade ago (Rowlingson 2004; Tan 2001). As a matter of good practice private sector entities should aim to reach an adequate level of forensic readiness based on their activities and scale. This can enhance the collaboration between private sector entities and LEAs, as the principle of forensic readiness is aimed at maximising the potential use of digital evidence while simultaneously also minimising the costs of investigations.

Evidence Collected and/or Analysed by Other Public Sector Entities

Evidence deriving from other public sector agencies may not always be sufficient to prosecute a criminal case. As other agencies, such as tax authorities, have different mandates and objectives, they may collect data in accordance with different standards than LEAs. Thus, LEAs recognise that they need to approach third party evidence with a critical eye, as the quality of the evidence provided may not always be sufficient for the needs that may arise in different types of cases. For instance, some cases may be aimed at obtaining restitution and the criminal component may, hence, be of less interest to the initial public authority investigating the case. Often more complicated criminal issues are, therefore, postponed to be dealt with in a separate case at a later date.[61]

Furthermore, privacy advocates have often raised concerns regarding law enforcement access to other public sector databases. The access to non-criminal databases would, at least in Europe, usually be circumscribed by data protection laws and require an official authorisation. LEAs acknowledge that there need to be rules in place that balance the powers their mandates come with. However, they also struggle with the fact that data protection laws may unduly hinder the investigation of certain cases, even when they are granted a judicial authorisation to access certain data key to a criminal investigation.[62]

Since the Snowden revelations, additional concerns have been raised regarding law enforcement use of information gathered by intelligence services. While LEAs fall under stricter legal scrutiny regarding the collection of potential evidence, often subject to judicial authorisation, unease has been expressed with the possibility that information provided by intelligence services may circumvent such procedural safeguards. Law enforcement officers from within the EU have mentioned that infor-

---

[61] Based on semi-structured telephone interviews conducted in August 2015.

[62] As presented by D. Szumilas at the Final Conference of the SMART Project, 4–5 March 2014, in Brussels, Belgium.

mation deriving from intelligence services is marked as such and this classification entails that it may not be used as evidence. Nevertheless, cases have emerged in the past where such data has been used to develop so called "parallel constructions" (Syrmopoulos 2014).

While it is likely that such constructions have taken place in several countries, information on such practices is scarce and there is insufficient information that can provide an evidence-basis to derive any findings from on this matter. From current, but limited, law enforcement officers' feedback, collaboration is more perceived to be a one-way street where LEAs are most often the ones providing intelligence services with information considered relevant for national security purposes. Nevertheless, the potential impact of "intelligence information laundering" practices upon the fundamental rights of individuals is severe enough to conclude that the topic deserves more comprehensive research to identify the way intelligence services and law enforcement exchange information, as well as whether there is a need to review safeguard measures and oversight mechanisms as a form of good practice.

Evidence Collected by Citizens: Participative Policing and Crowdsourcing

LEAs in Europe state that they deal with evidence collected by citizens in the same manner as with evidence emanating from the private sector. The authenticity, integrity and chain of custody of the evidence are ensured by taking a statement from the citizen on how, when and why he or she collected the traces. When possible, a cross-check of the stated actions is performed before conducting an in-depth analysis.[63]

During the 2015 Internet Governance Forum, the issue was raised that with the implementation of certain security measures by design, such as device encryption, a higher level of responsibility is shifted towards the user. Most online users have, however, been reported to practice poor "cyber hygiene" indicating the user may not be sufficiently prepared to take on such responsibility.[64] Thus, as a form of good practice LEAs and other organisations should continue to initiate and contribute to awareness raising campaigns aimed at increasing individuals' understanding of information security, data protection and cybercrime issues.

Furthermore, LEAs are increasingly looking at the development of web portals or apps by which citizens can forward electronic evidence, such as pictures or video recordings. With the rise of citizen journalism and constant technological progress, recording devices are, indeed, increasingly present at the scenes of crime and evidence in digital format has become increasingly present in legal proceedings. Compared to fixed surveillance cameras that experience limitations such as blind

[63] Based on semi-structured telephone interviews conducted in August 2015.

[64] Intervention by P. Curry, Director British Business Federation Authority—BBFA Ltd, at the Internet Governance Forum (IGF) 2015, 9–13 November 2015, Workshop WS141, Law Enforcement in a world where encryption is ubiquitous.

spots, citizens equipped with smartphones and other recording devices can provide multiple perspectives of a site. Unsurprisingly, official authorities reach out at greater frequency to the public for help in gathering potential evidence.

In addition to problems linked to the crowdsourced nature of such evidence, when presented in court such evidence must satisfy the digital specific requirements against counter-claims that it has been falsified or digitally altered. There are contrasting interpretations as to the contribution of such apps in establishing effective synergies between police and the public or rather extending "surveillance powers" to the public (McMillan 2012). This is reminiscent of the need to reconcile the right to security and the right to privacy, often seen as mutually exclusive, whereas public wellbeing relies on the comprehensive respect of both.

Citizens' engagement and evidence crowdsourcing, however, certainly have numerous advantages and the implementation of applications allowing for their contribution, can empower citizens confronted with crime and contribute to the spread of viable information. The development of these apps is illustrative of the efforts LEAs have already undertaken in this area and, as a matter of good practice, the continued development of such engagement efforts with the public should be encouraged.

6.5.2.3 Collaboration with the Judiciary: Strengthening Communication

Finally, as the examined cases and the evidence collected by LEAs is aimed to be brought before court to prosecute wrongdoers, the technical competences of prosecutors and magistrates to understand the digital evidence process are also key. LEAs should aim to further strengthen their communication channels with those in the justice system, as this can contribute to enhancing the understanding of digital evidence within the judiciary, thereby potentially also alleviating LEAs from unnecessarily burdensome analysis requests.

Preventing the Overconsumption of Digital Forensics

Cybercrime units and digital forensic labs have reported to be the victim of the "overconsumption" of digital forensics.[65] Very often in cases, they are provided with all the hard drives, USBs and other digital devices seized, leading to significant backlogs ranging from a few weeks up to 9 months.[66] The main reason for these backlogs is primarily linked to an inadequate number of personnel. A cybercrime

[65]As discussed during the EVIDENCE Workshop hosted by Eurojust in The Hague, the Netherlands.

[66]Based on semi-structured telephone interviews conducted in August 2015; the Electronic Evidence Expert Group Meeting held on 2 and 3 December 2014 at the INTERPOL General Secretariat (IPSG), in Lyon, France; Questionnaire, Law enforcement section, Question 7b; and also see Emerson (2014).

investigator confirmed that often priority is given to quantity which, in turn, however may lead to poor quality.[67] Consequently, so called “triage” approaches are now very popular. However, their application requires a strong communication channel between the investigators and the forensic specialists to update one another on investigation leads and to avoid a simplification of the investigation at the detriment of quality.

As a form of good practice, many agencies now ensure their personnel are trained based on a tiered system of expertise. The lowest tier, encompassing most officers, must be trained in preview and triage techniques. The more complex the task, the higher it moves up the pyramid and the more training is required.[68]

Many forensic software tools provide a preview function or are specifically developed as triage solutions. When resources are scarce, a combination of case intelligence and a triage solution can aid in reducing the number of devices subjected to a full examination (Association of Chief Police Officers (ACPO) 2011). However, it is recommended to conduct a risk assessment prior to performing a partial examination or preview. As an example of good practice, the triage solution for child abuse material of the State Electronic Evidence Branch (SEEB) of the Australian New South Wales (NSW) Police Force can be mentioned. They use random sampling to provide a statistical estimation regarding the quantity and severity of the abuse material on a device. By implementing this solution, the SEEB has reduced the exposure of its staff to child abuse material and its backlogs from 3 months to 24 h (Jones et al. 2012).

For such triage solutions to be effective and lead to quality results, a strong communication channel between LEAs and prosecution services or judiciary are necessary. Thus, by strengthening the communication between LEAs and prosecution services or judiciary, this may lead to both sides reaching a better understanding of what exactly is needed from one another during each phase of a criminal case.

Bringing the Judiciary Up To Speed

Based on the results of the EVIDENCE questionnaire, it could be determined that, from a law enforcement point of view, the technical knowledge of prosecution and judges, as well as defence lawyers to understand and correctly deal with digital evidence was called into question.[69] The principle of the freedom of evidence in civil law systems has been cited to influence this matter. While evidence in Anglo-Saxon countries is very much challenged, courts in some civil law countries seem

[67] Based on semi-structured telephone interviews conducted in August 2015.

[68] Global Action on Cybercrime (GLACY), EU/CoE, Law Enforcement Training Strategy: Project area specific strategies, Draft version 17 April 2014, pp. 8–15, available at https://rm.coe.int/CoERMPublicCommonSearchServices/DisplayDCTMContent?documentId=090000168030287b.

[69] Questionnaire, Law enforcement section, Question 7e.

to place a high level of trust in reports coming from the police.[70] In some countries, even the investigating judge does not know what type of tools LEAs have applied in a case. As an example of potential good practice, one investigating judge mentioned he would prefer to be able to make the decision on which tools are used and whether their use, certainly regarding online investigations, are in compliance with EU law. Ideally, LEAs would present a tool and a judge would decide on the legal definition it falls under and whether a warrant is required to use that tool.[71]

The civil law system often also differs from the common law system regarding cross-examinations of experts which, according to some, could hurt the way some civil law countries proceed, as their LEAs are not prepared for such cross-examinations. Defence lawyers would end up calling the character of law enforcement officers or digital forensics specialists on a case into question and not the handling of the evidence or the merits of the case itself. While such a system would be more beneficial for the defence, it may, in some civil law countries, not necessarily be more beneficial to find the truth.[72]

Furthermore, it remains a challenge for the judiciary to stay “up to date”İ with all the innovations and tools out there, as they do not have the budget, tools or human resources to look into what is on the market while it is, nevertheless, essential for them to know about these developments.[73] The results of the EVIDENCE questionnaire indicate that while prosecutors and magistrates may not be very well versed on technical matters linked to digital evidence, neither are defence lawyers. Their arguments often pertain to procedural mistakes or attribution of an act to the suspect.[74] As an example of good practice, UNODC recognised the need to compile more information on the subject matter and developed a cybercrime repository, which also includes a repository of case law and a repository of lessons learned.[75]

The importance of training for prosecutors and magistrates was also emphasised in response to the questionnaire.[76] As the importance of digital evidence and the reliance upon digital forensics services is only increasing, one could conclude that it is no longer sufficient to only provide training on these topics during continued professional training sessions and that these subject-matters should be made mandatory as part of their vocational training. The latter also holds true for lawyers, regardless of their field of specialisation as digital evidence is now so common place in all fields of law.

As an example of good practice, one can look at Belgium, where a 3-day training course was developed for magistrates several years ago in which specialised police officers clarify how they proceed in the handling of digital evidence throughout its

[70]Based on semi-structured telephone interviews conducted in August 2015.

[71]Ibidem.

[72]Ibidem.

[73]Ibidem.

[74]Questionnaire, Law enforcement section, Question 7e.

[75]UNODC, Cybercrime Repository, available at https://www.unodc.org/cld/v3/cybrepo.

[76]Questionnaire, Law enforcement section, Question 7e.

lifecycle. This training is considered very successful, but only a few magistrates have been trained thus far.

Another example of good practice can be found in The Netherlands, where a pilot project was set up in which the assistance of a forensic professional was provided to criminal courts. As forensic analysis can often be a rather complex and technical subject for judges, the aid of such professionals in, for example, clarifying certain concepts was very much appreciated. Nevertheless, there is a strict delineation to be maintained between the mandates of the judges and the forensic professionals. Additionally, forensic professionals aiding the court are not there to provide interpretations of forensic evidence, but to assist magistrates with more general requests. The results of the project were deemed successful and the project was extended to other courts as well (Hoving 2015; De Rechtspraak 2013).

Moreover, the website of the International Association of Prosecutors (IAP)—Global Prosecutors E-Crime Network (GPEN) provides recourses for prosecutors on cybercrime and the exchange of electronic evidence.[77]

There are, thus, certainly examples of good practice to which different stakeholders within the digital evidence domain can contribute by sharing their knowledge and expertise to all work towards enhancing the understanding of the role of digital evidence throughout the whole criminal justice process, thereby strengthening the criminal justice system itself.

6.5.3 The Modernisation of International Cooperation

In an increasingly globalised online environment, the collection and exchange of digital evidence is hampered by outdated and lengthy mutual legal assistance practices no longer meeting the requirements of law enforcement investigations. The need for modernisation efforts in the field of international police and judicial cooperation were therefore also addressed as part of the research. The challenges for EU cooperation are first assessed by providing an overview of EU regulatory efforts to facilitate the collection and exchange of evidence. Moreover, efforts undertaken to enhance law enforcement cooperation through joint international actions as a form of "MLA avoidance" are discussed and, lastly, potential solutions for expediting current MLA procedures are presented.

[77]As mentioned during the 2nd Eurasian Working Group Meeting on Cybercrime for Heads of Units, organised by the INTERPOL Global Complex for Innovation (IGCI) and hosted in Istanbul, Turkey, on 28–30 May 2014.

6.5.3.1 International Cooperation Within the EU: From Mutual Assistance to Mutual Recognition

The principles of mutual legal assistance that designates the international cooperation process related to the cross-border obtaining of evidence was also addressed as part of the research.

The legal basis of such processes can be treaties, domestic laws or the principle of reciprocity.[78] Informal MLA approaches are also widely used. They take the form of police-to-police cooperation, agency-to-agency communication and consular relations.[79] Some core principles of MLA are that of the sufficiency of elements to request cooperation, the principle of double criminality and frequent reoccurrence of specific grounds for refusing MLA requests. However, MLA proves limited when dealing with new types of offences. The EU has progressively moved from an MLA-based regime to a mutual recognition regime that is based on the idea of trust and equivalence of criminal law systems.[80] This evolution can be observed in the various legal instruments aiming at framing the cooperation on criminal matters within the Union.

The current framework for cooperation for the exchange of evidence in criminal matters within the EU can be found in the European Evidence Warrant (EEW), for the cooperation involving already existing evidence.[81] However, this limited scope of application has proven to not adequately respond to the needs of daily cooperation. Moreover, the introduction of a list of 32 mutually recognised offences that shall not be subject to double criminality constitutes a novelty in cross-border gathering of digital evidence.[82]

Consequently, the European Investigation Order (EIO),[83] to be transposed by the EU Member States by May 2017, aims at introducing a single and comprehensive legal framework for cooperation on criminal matters based on mutual recognition while considering the flexibility of the MLA regime.[84] Although not yet implemented at the time of drafting, the EIO raises questions as to its practical implementation. The EIO facilitates cooperation in introducing the principle of

78On formal MLA, see UNODC, Manual on Mutual Legal Assistance and Extradition (United Nations, New York, 2012), pp. 19–23.

79On informal MLA, see UNODC, Manual on Mutual Legal Assistance and Extradition (United Nations, New York, 2012), pp. 66–68.

80Communication from the Commission of the European Communities, Mutual Recognition of Final Decisions in Criminal Matters, COM(2000) 495 final, Brussels 26 July 2000, p. 4.

81Council Framework Decision 2008/978/JHA of 18 December 2008 on the European evidence warrant for the purpose of obtaining objects, documents and data for use in proceedings in criminal matters [2008] OJ L 350/72, [hereinafter: EEW Decision] Recitals Nr. 2, 3, 6.

82EEW Decision, Article 14(2).

83Directive 2014/41/EU of the European Parliament and of the Council of 3 April 2014 regarding the European Investigation Order in criminal matters, available at http://eur-lex.europa.eu/legal-content/EN/TXT/?uri=celex%3A32014L0041.

84EIO Directive, Recital Nr. 6. See also Ruggeri (2014), p. 9.

availability of investigative measures. However, concerns have been expressed towards the practical application of the deadlines set in the Directive.[85] Finally, the EIO seems to ease the interception of telecommunications with technical assistance from another Member State and legitimises the cross-border interception of telecommunications without technical assistance. Because of the potentially increased use of such intrusive measures in the framework of international cooperation, the safeguards and legal remedies must be effective and consider the specific details of practically exercising legal remedies in the context of international judicial cooperation (Ruggeri 2014).

6.5.3.2 Joint International Actions as MLA Avoidance Tactic

Based on the results of the EVIDENCE questionnaire, MLA requests are considered too slow to still be considered fit-for-purpose for international police and judicial cooperation on crimes involving digital evidence. Therefore, it is no surprise that law enforcement representatives increasingly mention the avoidance of formal MLA procedures by opting for alternatives, such as parallel investigations or JITs.[86]

Parallel Investigations

Based on the results of the questionnaire, there seems to be a fair amount of countries with experience in taking part in parallel investigations and JITs. Overall, those countries that have been involved in such investigations reported a positive experience.[87] Parallel investigations occur when LEAs in different countries agree to separately, but simultaneously, act upon cases impacting both countries, bearing in mind that there needs to be a nexus with the country, such as the suspect or evidence.

Article 19 on Joint Investigations of the UN Convention on Transnational Organised Crime provides that "States Parties shall consider concluding bilateral or multilateral agreements or arrangements whereby, in relation to matters that are the subject of investigations, prosecutions or judicial proceedings in one or more States, the competent authorities concerned may establish joint investigative bodies. In the absence of such agreements or arrangements, joint investigations may be undertaken by agreement on a case-by-case basis. The States Parties involved shall ensure that the sovereignty of the State Party in whose territory such investigation is to take place is fully respected[88]".

---

[85]Based on semi-structured telephone interviews conducted in August 2015.

[86]Questionnaire, Law enforcement section, Question 7c.

[87]Ibidem.

[88]https://www.unodc.org/documents/middleeastandnorthafrica/organised-crime/UNITED_NATIONS_CONVENTION_AGAINST_TRANSNATIONAL_ORGANIZED_CRIME_AND_THE_PROTOCOLS_THERETO.pdf.

Based on a discussion of case examples, it was illustrated that LEAs must be well-prepared and committed when deciding to conduct such joint investigations, as it may hamper relationships between LEAs if things were to go wrong, thereby negatively impacting future opportunities to cooperate. Furthermore, the fact was highlighted that both police-to-police cooperation and MLA have their pros and cons, but neither is ideal when dealing with multi-country investigations for which a third party should ideally take over the coordination. Both Europol and INTERPOL have coordinated such joint investigations in the past and, as an example of good practice, should be encouraged to continue to expand such coordination efforts.[89]

Joint Investigation Teams

A Joint Investigation Team (JIT) can be defined as "an investigation team set up on the basis of an agreement between two or more Member States and/or other parties, for a specific purpose and limited duration".[90] Using JITs rather than traditional forms of international law enforcement and judicial co-operation, such as "mirror" or "parallel" investigation, present several advantages mainly in terms of simplification of procedures. For instance, JITs allow for the possibility to exchange information without needing formal requests.

JITs can be organised between EU Member States, as well as an additional ten countries with which Europol has an operational agreement. The information obtained through MLA requests can be shared among the JIT countries. Thus, if one country in the JIT has an agreement with a third country this applies to all the JIT members in practice. Nevertheless, even within such a framework, international police and legal cooperation takes time and requires more attention because of language, cultural matters and legal differences.[91]

The initiative to set up a JIT often comes from Member States but could also come from Europol or Eurojust. As both institutions have been created to support Member States in their fight against cross-border criminality, they play an important role in JITs. However, while it is not compulsory to involve these organisations in investigations, it can be very useful to do so for the efficiency and the capacity of the JIT, as well as for assisting and advising on obtaining funding. JITs are established by written agreement. To ease the JITs process, the Council of the EU adopted a resolution with several model agreements on setting up a JIT.[92]

---

[89]As discussed during the 2nd Eurasian Working Group Meeting on Cybercrime for Heads of Units, organised by the INTERPOL Global Complex for Innovation (IGCI) and hosted in Istanbul, Turkey, on 28–30 May 2014.

[90]See Council of the European Union (2011), p. 2.

[91]As discussed during the 2nd Eurasian Working Group Meeting on Cybercrime for Heads of Units, organised by the INTERPOL Global Complex for Innovation (IGCI) and hosted in Istanbul, Turkey, on 28–30 May 2014.

[92]Council resolution of 26 February 2010 on a Model Agreement for setting up a Joint Investigation Team (JIT), C 70/01.

As an example of good practice, some countries have documented their lessons learned from past experiences with JITs, for instance, when setting up a JIT it is important to begin the international cooperation as early into the investigation as possible as the procedure will require time. Furthermore, it is suggested to share information with Europol and/or INTERPOL as they can provide added support and expertise based on past experiences.[93]

6.5.3.3 Expediting MLA Procedures

A great number of LEAs have mentioned avoiding formal MLA procedures if alternatives are available and pointed out the need for modernisation, including the digitisation and expediting of MLA requests, as well as the involvement of industry.

"MLA Light" for Subscriber Information

In the actual context of tremendous data flows across State borders, the ability of LEAs to access data stored outside of their jurisdiction or managed by a foreign company becomes increasingly important. For criminal investigations, three types of data may be needed: subscriber information, traffic data and content data (Council of Europe 2015). Most requests for international cooperation in this field, however, pertains to subscriber information.

One of the peculiarities of subscriber information is that while it is often held by service providers "offering its services on the territory", the information is, indeed, often stored in another jurisdiction (Council of Europe 2015). This entails a need for international cooperation. It could even lead to situations where it is not clear to whom a request for subscriber information should be addressed. However, the Cybercrime Convention offers a solution in article 18.1 stating that a Party shall adopt the measures necessary to empower its competent authorities to order a service provider, offering its services in the territory of the Party, to disclose information regarding that service.[94] This was implemented in some countries, for instance, article 46bis of the Belgian Code of Criminal Procedure provides that the public prosecutor can request that the provider or operator of an electronic

[93]As discussed during the 2nd Eurasian Working Group Meeting on Cybercrime for Heads of Units, organised by the INTERPOL Global Complex for Innovation (IGCI) and hosted in Istanbul, Turkey, on 28–30 May 2014.

[94]Council of Europe, Convention no. 185 on Cybercrime signed in Budapest the 23 November 2001, Article 18.1. *"Each Party shall adopt such legislative and other measures as may be necessary to empower its competent authorities to order [...] a service provider offering its services in the territory of the Party to submit subscriber information relating to such services in that service provider's possession or control"*.

communication service provide him the personal and communication data of its subscribers. This provision was, for instance, used in the Belgian Yahoo case.[95]

LEAs have three main channels for accessing data stored abroad: MLA, police cooperation and "goodwill".[96] Moreover, the Council of Europe and the European Union adopted a Mutual Legal Assistance Manual in which the use of administrative assistance (i.e. informal assistance) is promoted, particularly for obtaining basic subscriber information. This procedure's feasibility depends mainly on national legislation, the nature of the relationship between the requesting and requested State and the helpfulness of the officials whom the request is made (Council of the European Union 2013).

A reform of the MLA system seems to be necessary regarding the critical limitation of the existing procedure. Thereupon, the T-CY adopted a set of recommendations. The most relevant recommendation regarding subscriber information is "that Parties should consider allowing—via legal domestic amendments and international agreement—for the expedited disclosure of the identity and physical address of the subscriber of a specific IP address or user account" (Council of Europe 2014).

In March 2017, the T-CY published a guidance note on production orders for subscriber information, based on Article 18 of the Cybercrime Convention, adopted by written procedure following the plenary meeting in November 2016. The T-CY considered such a guidance note relevant, inter alia, because "currently, practices and procedures, as well as conditions and safeguards for access to subscriber information vary considerably among Parties to the Convention (Council of Europe 2017).

In October 2015, The Economist, furthermore, published an article in which an alternative solution to the issue is suggested, namely the establishment of a global clearing-house deal involving LEA requests according to a set of common rules. However, it was recognised that setting up such a supranational body would take years of negotiations and still might fail. Therefore, Brad Smith, Chief Legal Officer at Microsoft, proposes to implement the idea at a smaller scale, including the US and some European countries with other potentially joining at a later stage.[97] This clearly illustrates that not only LEAs and international organisations are working towards finding a solution for these challenges, but that the tech industry is equally interested in finding a less cumbersome and resource intense

[95]In 2007 a Belgian public prosecutor asked Yahoo to release information regarding a subscriber, Yahoo refused to do so and it was the beginning of a judicial saga. See http://www.stibbe.com/en/news/2016/january/court-of-cassation-definitively-confirms-yahoos-obligation-to-cooperate-with-law-enforcement-agenci.

[96]Expression used by the British parliament in the Draft Communications Data Bill Joint Committee, Jurisdictional issues, available at http://www.publications.parliament.uk/pa/jt201213/jtselect/jtdraftcomuni/79/7909.htm.

[97]The Economist, Under my thumb, 10 October 2015, available at http://www.economist.com/news/international/21672204-governments-grapple-law-enforcement-virtual-world-under-my-thumb.

solution. Thus, as a form of good practice, a continued cooperation and discussion involving all stakeholders concerned can only be further encouraged. Finding a solution to the current MLA challenges will, however, only be a subset of larger policy discussions strongly linked to questions regarding public international law and Internet governance.

Digitisation of MLA Procedures

At the European level, successful formal transmission of MLA requests is still a challenge and European States still have difficulties with judicial cooperation. States often ask Eurojust to assist in the transmission of MLA requests when the direct contact between judicial authorities did not initially work. Adequate communication between judicial authorities is a challenge for European States.[98] These challenges amplify when we look at the relationships of the European States with third States. Most third States do not have vast diplomatic networks or have limited financial resources to remedy this absence. Nor can European States sometimes identify the right authority in the requested state to whom they should address. The lack of efficiency of the transmission process of MLA requests to third States is even more problematic as the need to cooperate beyond European frontiers is increasing.

INTERPOL took note of the invoked shortcomings characterising the MLA procedure and decided to come up with the e-MLA initiative. The main objective of the e-MLA initiative is to modernise the MLA formal transmission processes to strengthen the effectiveness of judicial cooperation in and outside of Europe. The first stage of INTERPOL's e-MLA initiative is to study the feasibility of the creation of a practical electronic tool for the transmission of formal MLA requests at the European level. Secondly, the purpose is to engage into the development of the legal and technical frameworks for the transmission of MLA requests in and outside Europe.

Important initiatives have already been taken by various international and regional institutions with the aim of creating guidebooks, forms, discussion fora and capacity building programmes for MLA practitioners. The purpose has been to provide useful support for the drafting of MLA requests to improve the quality of communication and to allow faster and more efficient exchanges, at least at the regional level. For example, the Eurojust National Desks can provide advice on the drafting of MLA requests, explain how to interpret the MLA Convention in light of national provisions and assist in speeding up specific MLA requests. The contacts points of the European Judicial Network (EJN) also play a key role as active intermediaries in facilitating direct contacts within the EU and the EJN website contains an interesting platform of IT tools (Atlas and Compendium) helping practitioners to identify the competent authorities.

---

[98] Eurojust Annual Report 2014, http://www.eurojust.europa.eu/doclibrary/corporate/eurojust%20Annual%20Reports/Annual%20Report%202014/Annual-Report-2014-EN.pdf.

INTERPOL's proposition to create the e-MLA platform is based on its expertise in the field of development of secured networks at the international level. Building on its recognised capacities and experience in information exchange, INTERPOL's intention is to develop technical means for the fast, secure, electronic transmission of extradition and MLA requests. The e-MLA initiative is addressed to states' authorities competent in the field of judicial cooperation in criminal matters, as well as other relevant authorities. These authorities would greatly benefit from more efficient transmissions of formal MLA requests. For now, there is no existing tool for the fast and secure transmission of formal MLA requests in criminal matters at the international level. The existing technical initiatives are either limited to the regional level or do not guarantee the transfer of data in the best conditions of security. e-MLA is innovative as it aims to provide a real secure channel for the formal electronic transmission of MLA requests within a robust data protection framework provided by INTERPOL's Rules on the Processing of Data.[99]

6.6 Conclusions

Following two-and-a-half years of research, involving the analysis of a questionnaire that was circulated to INTERPOL's 190 member countries, an expert group meeting on electronic evidence hosted at the INTERPOL General Secretariat, lengthy interviews and e-mail exchanges with subject matter experts, as well as the participation in the EVIDENCE project's workshops and law enforcement conferences, the facts and findings on law enforcement issues regarding electronic evidence have led to the following recommendations.

First, digital forensics experts expressed a wish for their field of expertise to reach a similar level of professionalism and recognition as other fields of forensics, such as DNA analysis. The "professionalization of digital forensics", as the experts called it, could be worked towards by developing a certification mechanism for digital forensics professionals by an independent certification board to ensure that practitioners meet certain harmonised knowledge thresholds. Furthermore, as these practitioners often rely on certain methods for the acquisition and analysis of digital evidence and these methods also include the use of digital forensic tools, these methods and tools should ideally be subject to validation procedures to ensure they are fit-for-purpose. Lastly, there are currently no universal standards specifically applicable to digital forensic labs, thus it is also worth considering the development of an accreditation procedure to ensure digital forensics labs meet certain predetermined quality levels.

Second, the importance of "building bridges" between LEAs and other stakeholders within the digital evidence domain, including the public, policymakers, the

---

[99] https://www.interpol.int/Media/Files/Legal-material/Reference-Documents/INTERPOL%E2%80%99s-Rules-on-the-Processing-of-Data.

private sector and the judiciary cannot be understated. By enhancing transparency vis-à-vis the public and policymakers, for instance through the keeping of statistics and case examples, LEAs can provide a stronger evidence-basis for additional resources, as well as for informed public debates on policy decisions that may influence law enforcement capabilities. Furthermore, building trustful relationships is even more important now that most digital evidence resides with the public and online service providers. LEAs thus need to move towards more innovative collaboration frameworks, such as crowdsourcing and participative policing. The eventual aim of gathering evidence, however, is to bring evidence before court and prosecute wrongdoers. The technical competences of prosecutors and magistrates are therefore key. Hence, LEAs should aim to further strengthen their communication with the judiciary, as this can contribute to enhancing the understanding of digital evidence within the justice system, thereby potentially also alleviating LEAs from unnecessarily burdensome analysis requests.

Third, LEAs continue to reiterate that the collection and exchange of digital evidence is hampered by outdated and lengthy mutual legal assistance procedures that no longer meet the needs of increasingly complex cross-border investigations. The modernisation of international police and judicial cooperation is therefore one of the three main recommendations of this research. While LEAs are increasingly relying on joint international action as a form of MLA avoidance, one can note that regional and international organisations are developing initiatives to expedite otherwise lengthy MLA procedures. Within the EU, cooperation in this field is moving from mutual assistance to mutual recognition with the implementation of the European Investigation Order coming closer. Furthermore, the Council of Europe, particularly the Cybercrime Convention Committee, is also continuing its longstanding efforts on facilitating transborder access to evidence and the exchange of digital evidence. Lastly, INTERPOL is also acting to expedite MLA procedures through its e-MLA initiative that aims to transfer formal MLA requests through its secure I-24/7 channel.

As a final observation, it should be stressed that the EVIDENCE project research carried out by INTERPOL on law enforcement issues made it possible to identify important challenges and best practices in the field of electronic evidence, which should be the subject of further research. Building on previous EU funded research projects, such as SMART and RESPECT,[100] in which INTERPOL was actively participating as a full partner, the research carried out under the EVIDENCE project also contributed to further develop a growing multi-stakeholder community of LEAs, academics and private sector representatives. The impact of this growing

[100]Scalable Measures for Automated Recognition Technologies; http://www.smartsurveillance.eu/ and Rules, Expectations & Security through Privacy-Enhanced Convenient Technologies, http://respectproject.eu.

community reaches out far beyond the EVIDENCE project and creates synergies with ongoing EU funded projects, such as the ongoing MAPPING project.[101]

The research carried out under the EVIDENCE project would not have been possible without the commitment of this community and we would like to thank everyone who took the time and effort to share their expertise with INTERPOL and the EVIDENCE consortium.

References

Abelson H, Anderson R, Bellovin M, et al (2015) Keys under doormats: Mandating insecurity by requiring government access to all data and communications, 7 July 2015. http://www.crypto.com/papers/Keys_Under_Doormats_FINAL.pdf

Ashouri A, Bowers C, Warden C (2014) The 2013 Salzburg workshop on cyber investigations: an overview of the use of digital evidence in international criminal courts. Digital Evid Electron Signature Law Rev 11:116

Association of Chief Police Officers (ACPO) (2011) Manager's Guide: Good Practice and Advice Guide for Managers of e-Crime Investigations. http://www.4matdata.co.uk/LiteratureRetrieve.aspx?ID=116738&usg=AFQjCNEoltGErOeWVZZiMHf8RqRmalS2RA

Bundeskriminalamt (2014) Cybercrime: Bundeslagebild, p 5. http://www.bka.de/nn_205924/SharedDocs/Downloads/DE/Publikationen/JahresberichteUndLagebilder/Cybercrime/cybercrimeBundeslagebild2014,templateId=raw,property=publicationFile.pdf/cybercrimeBundeslagebild2014.pdf

Choo A (2015) Evidence, (In)efficiency, and freedom of proof: a perspective from England and Wales. Ala Law Rev 66(3):493–505

Comey J (2014) Going dark: are technology, privacy, and public safety on a collision course? Speech delivered at the Brookings Institute, Washington, DC, 16 October 2014. https://www.fbi.gov/news/speeches/going-dark-are-technology-privacy-and-public-safety-on-a-collision-course

Council of Europe (2014) Transborder access to data and jurisdiction: options for further action by the T-CY, 2–3 December 2014

Council of Europe (2014) T-CY assessment report: the mutual legal assistance provisions of the Budapest convention on cybercrime, 3 December 2014, Recommendation 19. https://www.coe.int/t/dghl/cooperation/economiccrime/Source/Cybercrime/TCY/2014/T-CY(2013)17_Assess_report_v50adopted.pdf

Council of Europe (2015) Criminal justice access to data in the cloud: challenges, T-CY cloud Evidence Group, 26 May 2015. http://www.coe.int/t/dghl/cooperation/economiccrime/Source/Cybercrime/TCY/2015/T-CY%282015%2910_CEG%20challenges%20rep_sum_v8.pdf

Council of Europe (2016) Cybercrime: towards a new legal tool on electronic evidence, 16 November 2016. https://www.coe.int/en/web/portal/-/cybercrime-towards-a-new-legal-tool-on-electronic-evidence

Council of Europe (2016) Cybercrime Convention Committee (T-CY), Criminal justice access to electronic evidence in the cloud: recommendations for consideration by the T-CY – Final report of the T-CY Cloud Evidence Group, 16 September 2016, pp 40–46. http://rm.coe.int/CoERMPublicCommonSearchServices/DisplayDCTMContent?documentId=09000016806a495e

[101]Mapping Alternatives for Privacy, Property and Internet Governance, https://mappingtheinternet.eu.

Council of Europe (2017) Cybercrime Convention Committee (T-CY) T-CY Guidance note #10: production orders for subscriber information (Article 18 Budapest Convention), March 2017. http://rm.coe.int/doc/09000016806f943e
Council of the European Union (2011) Joint investigation teams manual, 4 November 2011
Council of the European Union (2013) Mutual legal assistance manual. https://www.coe.int/t/dghl/cooperation/economiccrime/corruption/Publications/CAR/Mutual%20Legal%20Assistance%20Manual_EN.pdf
De Rechtspraak (2013) Forensische ondersteuning helpt strafrechters, 11 April 2013. https://www.rechtspraak.nl/Actualiteiten/Nieuws/Pages/Forensische-ondersteuning-helpt-strafrechters.aspx
DG Home, European Commission (2013) Evidence for necessity of data retention in the EU, March 2013, p 7. http://ec.europa.eu/dgs/home-affairs/pdf/policies/police_cooperation/evidence_en.pdf
Emerson J (2014) Assessing the impact of digital evidence on state and local policing, October 2014. http://www.policechiefmagazine.org/assessing-the-impact-of-digital-evidence-on-state-and-local-policing
Essers L (2015) No encryption back doors, says EU digital commissioner, in Computerworld, 20 May 2015. http://www.computerworld.com/article/2924330/security0/no-encryption-back-doors-says-eu-digital-commissioner.html
Farivar C (2014) Apple expands data encryption under iOS8, making handover to cops mute, 18 September 2014. http://arstechnica.com/apple/2014/09/apple-expands-data-encryption-under-ios-8-making-handover-to-cops-moot
Fox-Brewster T (2014) Whatsapp adds end-to-end encryption using textsecure. The Guardian, 19 November 2014. http://www.theguardian.com/technology/2014/nov/19/whatsapp-messaging-encryption-android-ios
Hoving R (2015) Forensische ondersteuning strafrechters is niet vanzelfsprekend. Ivoren Toga, Boom Juridische uitgevers, 30 June 2015. http://ivorentoga.nl/archieven/3759
Jones B, Pleno S, Wilkinson M (2012) The use of random sampling in investigations involving child abuse material. Digit Investig 9. http://www.sciencedirect.com/science/article/pii/S1742287612000369
Kaye D (2015) Report of the special rapporteur on the promotion and protection of the right to freedom of opinion and expression, David Kaye, A/HRC/29/32, 22 May 2015. http://www.ohchr.org/EN/HRBodies/HRC/RegularSessions/Session29/Documents/A.HRC.29.32_AEV.doc
Mason S (2012) Electronic evidence, 3rd edn, p 75. LexisNexis Buttersworth, London
McMillan G (2012) Now you can be big brother's little helper with facewatch app, in Digital Trends, 27 June 2012. http://www.digitaltrends.com/mobile/now-you-can-be-big-brothers-little-helper-with-facewatch-app
Mullin J (2015) At silk road trial, federal agent explains how he trapped Ulbricht, in ArsTechnica, 15 January 2015. http://arstechnica.com/tech-policy/2015/01/silk-road-trial-federal-agent-explains-how-he-trapped-ulbricht
National Audit Office (2015) Financial sustainability of police forces in England and Wales, 4 June 2015. https://www.nao.org.uk/wp-content/uploads/2015/06/Financial-sustainability-of-police-forces.pdf
Nylander J (2015) Interpol creates digital currency to fight bitcoin crimes. Forbes, 31 August 2015. http://www.forbes.com/sites/jnylander/2015/08/31/interpol-creates-digital-currency-to-fight-bitcoin-crimes
Obama administration's draft paper on technical options for the encryption debate (2015). http://apps.washingtonpost.com/g/documents/world/read-the-obama-administrations-draft-paper-on-technical-options-for-the-encryption-debate/1753
Office of Legal Education, Executive Office for United States Attorneys (2010) Prosecuting computer crimes, p 176. http://www.justice.gov/sites/default/files/criminal-ccips/legacy/2015/01/14/ccmanual.pdf
Peterson A, Nakashima E (2015) Obama administration explored ways to bypass smartphone encryption, in The Washington Post, 24 September 2015. https://www.washingtonpost.com/

world/national-security/obama-administration-ponders-how-to-seek-access-to-encrypted-data/2015/09/23/107a811c-5b22-11e5-b38e-06883aacba64_story.html

Rowlingson R (2004) A ten step process for forensic readiness. Int J Digit Evid 2(3):1–28. http://www.digital4nzics.com/Student%20Library/A%20Ten%20Step%20Process%20for%20Forensic%20Readiness.pdf

Ruggeri S (2014) Introduction to the proposal of a European investigation order: due process concerns and open issues. In Ruggeri S (ed) Transnational evidence and multicultural inquiries in Europe. Springer, Cham

Ruggeri S (2014) Transnational investigations and prosecution of cross-border cases in Europe: guidelines for a model of fair multicultural criminal justice. In Ruggeri S (ed) Transnational evidence and multicultural inquiries in Europe. Springer, Cham

Schofield J (2015) Interpol is training police to fight crime on the darknet. ZDNet, 2 August 2015. http://www.zdnet.com/article/interpol-is-training-police-to-fight-crime-on-the-darknet/#!

Smithuis M, van Ruth E (2013) Forensic science service expertise – not as solid as it seems. The Netherlands Register of Court Experts, pp 6–7. http://english.nrgd.nl/Images/forensic-science-service-expertise-not-at-solid-as-it-seems_tcm98-548990.pdf

Syal R (2015) Home office making police cuts without understanding, report says, in The Guardian, 4 June 2015. http://www.theguardian.com/uk-news/2015/jun/04/home-office-making-police-cuts-without-understanding-report-says

Syrmopoulos J (2014) Parallel construction: how the NSA and police have rigged the legal system. The Free Thought Project, 16 October 2014. http://thefreethoughtproject.com/parallel-construction-law-enforcement-illegally-collected-evidence-criminal-prosecutions/#PmMdZcO0e8FkqdTr.99

Tan J (2001) Forensic readiness, 17 July 2001. http://citeseerx.ist.psu.edu/viewdoc/download?doi=10.1.1.480.6094&rep=rep1&type=pdf

Ward M (2012) What sequestration means to state, local, and tribal law enforcement Police Chief Mag (2012). http://www.policechiefmagazine.org/magazine/index.cfm?fuseaction=display_arch&article_id=2819&issue_id=122012

Wilson A, Kehl D, et al (2015) Lessons from the 1990s crypto wars. Forensic Mag. June 2015. http://www.forensicmag.com/news/2015/06/lessons-1990s-crypto-wars

Wilson A, Kehl D, et al (2015). Doomed to repeat history? Lessons from the crypto wars of the 1990s, pp 2–3. June 2015 https://static.newamerica.org/attachments/3407--125/Lessons%20From%20the%20Crypto%20Wars%20of%20the%201990s.882d6156dc194187a5fa51b14d55234f.pdf

Chapter 7
International Digital Forensic Investigation at the ICC

Ilyoung Hong

Abstract The International Criminal Court ("ICC" or "the Court") investigates and tries individuals charged with crimes of concern to the international community: genocide, war crimes and crimes against humanity. With regard to digital forensic investigations, the ICC has been confronted with various challenges especially derived from the nature of the crimes it handles and the fact that its procedure is distinct from national criminal procedure. This paper provides an introduction to the activities and challenges of digital forensics in international criminal investigations, and draws attention to requirements for more international cooperation, awareness improvement, standard establishment and the need for a joint effort at solving technical issues.

7.1 Introduction

The ICC is a permanent institution that has the power to exercise its jurisdiction over persons for the most serious crimes of international concern. As an international tribunal, the ICC applies unique criminal procedure in its investigations and prosecutions that may differ from the criminal procedure and laws of national jurisdiction. Its investigations are often conducted in fragile and volatile security situations, including amid on-going or post conflict environments. These overall features impact the ICC's investigative activities and sometimes impose severe constraints in the timely evidence preservation and collection. Meanwhile, with the worldwide growth of digital devices and the information technology revolution, digital evidence is becoming increasingly important to the ICC's investigations. However, this trend is also bringing forth diverse challenges and questions. Given the growing role and importance of digital evidence, the level of speed needed to

I. Hong (✉)
International Criminal Court, Office of the Prosecutor, The Hague, The Netherlands
e-mail: ilyoung.k.h@gmail.com

M. A. Biasiotti et al. (eds.), *Handling and Exchanging Electronic Evidence Across Europe*, Law, Governance and Technology Series 39,
https://doi.org/10.1007/978-3-319-74872-6_7

cope with these challenges is becoming an important factor for the productivity of ICC's investigations. However, the most difficult part of solving these challenges is that the Court must rely on leveraging a global solution based on collective commitment and cooperation from external parties to resolve many issues. This chapter explores the features of ICC investigations and the challenges it faces relating to digital evidence to draw international attention. It also proposes some conceptual approaches to tackling the identified challenges.

7.2 Overview of Digital Evidence Lifecycle in the ICC Investigation

In this section, the ICC's organizational structure, legal basis, and the lifecycle of digital evidence will be explored to provide a better understanding in which context digital forensic investigation is conducted. Since the scope of this chapter is limited to the identification of challenges and finding potential solutions, the discussion will focus on the outstanding features and peculiarity of the ICC investigation practice and procedure rather than try to explore the whole aspect.

7.2.1 ICC Organizational Structure and Legal Basis

7.2.1.1 ICC Structure and Roles of Each Organ

The Rome Statute[1] ("Statute"), the founding treaty of the ICC, establishes the Court's functions, jurisdiction, structure and the legal basis of the procedure. Based on the Statute, the ICC is composed of four primary organs: The Presidency, the Judicial Divisions, the Office of the Prosecutor, and the Registry. Among the four organs, the Office of the Prosecutor ("OTP") has the power to investigate on the territory of a State.[2] The OTP's responsibility includes preliminary analysis of referrals and information on crimes that it receives to determine if they meet the jurisdictional requirements needed to merit an investigation. If the OTP determines that the situation meets the jurisdictional requirements, then it investigates the situation. The judiciary of the Court, consists of 18 judges, and is composed of three Divisions: the Pre-Trial Division, the Trial Division, and the Appeals Division. Each division is responsible for conducting the proceedings of the Court on specific situations and cases at different stages of the judicial procedure. The Registry provides judicial and administrative support to all organs of the Court and carries out its specific responsibilities in the areas of defense, victims and witnesses, outreach and detention.

[1]Rome Statute of the International Criminal Court, U.N. Doc. A/CONF.183/9, 2187 U.N.T.S. 90 (17 July 1998).

[2]Ibid., Article 54.

7.2.1.2 Legal Basis

Pursuant to the Statute, diverse legal instruments are applied by the ICC.[3] The applicable laws and principles are as follows: firstly, (a) the Statute, Elements of Crimes (International Criminal Court, 2011) and Rules of Procedure and Evidence (International Criminal Court, 2013); secondly (b) applicable treaties, principles and rules of international law. Failing those first two sources, the following are applied: (c) general principles of law derived by the Court from national laws of legal systems of the world including appropriate national laws of States, provided that those principles are consistent with the Statute and with international law and internationally recognized norms and standards, and lastly (d) rules of law as interpreted in the Court's previous decisions. Among the above listed legal instruments, the Rome Statute, Elements of Crimes, and Rules of Procedure and Evidence provide the fundamental legal basis for the ICC's investigations and prosecutions. The general rules and principles of evidence are applied to all evidence, including digital evidence. Despite of the unique features of digital evidence, so far there has been no particular article or provision specifically established for digital evidence.

7.2.2 Digital Evidence Lifecycle in the ICC

7.2.2.1 Preservation and Collection

In national criminal investigations, preservation and collection of digital evidences may require legal authority such as the consent of a person, judicial orders, or search and seizure warrants. Execution of compulsory measures, once legally authorized, would be relatively direct and expeditious. For instance, access to crime scenes, digital evidence collection and preservation may be conducted by police or other competent law-enforcement authorities with a minimum delay to limit the window of loss for digital evidence. At the ICC, as previously mentioned, the OTP has the power to investigate, which includes the powers to (a) collect and examine evidence; (b) request the presence of and question persons being investigated, victims and witnesses; (c) seek the cooperation of any State or intergovernmental organization or arrangement in accordance with its respective competence and/or mandate; (d) take necessary measures, or request that necessary measures be taken, to ensure confidentiality of information, the protection of any person or the preservation of evidence.[4] In terms of the measures to execute the power of investigation, the Statue indicates two avenues. One is based on the international cooperation and judicial assistance, and the other is based on the Pre-Trial Chamber's authorization.[5]

---

[3]Ibid., Article 21 paras. 1–2.

[4]The Statute, supra note 1, Article 54 para. 3.

[5]Ibid., Article 54 para. 2.

Requests based on non-compulsory measure, such as taking evidence from a person on a voluntary basis can be executed directly on the territory of a State.[6] When it comes to compulsory measures, these are executed through the cooperation of State Parties. Requests for cooperation are transmitted through diplomatic channels or other appropriate channel as designated by each State Party.[7] States that are not party to the Statute are not bound to cooperate with the OTP in collecting evidence, although the Statue provides some measures.[8] Avenues for the Prosecutor to take compulsory measures without the cooperation of a State Party are quite limited. Firstly, an investigation is authorized when the Pre-Trial Chamber has determined that the State is clearly unable to execute a request for cooperation because of the unavailability of any authority or any component of its judicial system competent enough to execute the request for cooperation.[9] Secondly, an investigation is also possible based on a unique investigative opportunity where the Prosecutor considers an investigation to examine, collect or test evidence may not be available subsequently for the trial.[10] In this case, the Pre-Trial Chamber, upon request of the Prosecutor, can authorize the OTP to take such measures as may be necessary to ensure the efficiency and integrity of the proceedings and particularly to protect the rights of the defense. Despite of above mentioned possibilities, in a practical sense, it is likely that execution of compulsory measures without cooperation of a State Party would be used in very exceptionally circumstances (Guariglia, 1999). Consequently, ICC investigations widely rely on State Parties' cooperation in various forms.[11] In addition to this procedural peculiarity, in an ICC investigation, the scope of

[6]Ibid., Article 99 para. 4.

[7]Ibid., Article 87 para. 1(a).

[8]Ibid., Article 87 para. 5 states (a) The Court may invite any State not party to this Statue to provide assistance under this Part based on an ad hoc arrangement, an agreement with such State or any other appropriate basis; (b) Where a State not party to this Statute, which has entered into an ad hoc arrangement or an agreement with the Court, fails to cooperate with requests pursuant to any such arrangement or agreement, the Court may so inform the Assembly of State Parties or, where the Security Council referred the matter to the Court, the Security Council.

[9]Ibid., Article 57 para. 3(d).

[10]Ibid., Article 56 para. 1(a).

[11]The Statute, supra note 1, Article 93(1) provides the forms of cooperation. (a) The identification and whereabouts of persons or the location of items; (b) The taking of evidence, including testimony under oath, and the production of evidence, including expert opinions and reports necessary to the Court; (c) The questioning of any person being investigated or prosecuted; (d) The service of documents, including judicial documents; (e) Facilitating the voluntary appearance of persons as witnesses or experts before the Court; (f) The temporary transfer of persons; (g) The examination of places or sites, including the exhumation and examination of grave sites; (h) The execution of searches and seizures; (i) The provision of records and documents, including official records and documents; (j) The protection of victims and witnesses and the preservation of evidence; (k) The identification, tracing and freezing or seizure of proceeds, property and assets and instrumentalities of crimes for eventual forfeiture, without prejudice to the rights of bona fide third parties; and (l) Any other type of assistance that is not prohibited by the law of the requested State, with a view to facilitating the investigation and prosecution of crimes within the jurisdiction of the Court.

evidence collection and preservation is also notable. The ICC Prosecutor has a duty to investigate incriminating and exonerating circumstances equally. To fulfill this duty and establish the truth, the extent of the investigation must cover all facts and relevant evidence.[12]

7.2.2.2 Analysis

Once collected by the ICC's investigation, digital evidence is registered into the internal management system and analyzed by digital forensic examiners. All ICC investigations try to best utilize digital evidences in a scientific way. Trained and qualified digital forensic examiners play a key role in the examination to identify relevant information, accurately interpret the data and produce a scientific report.

7.2.2.3 Disclosure

The duty of the ICC prosecution to disclose information to the defense is broad. The Prosecutor discloses any tangible objects in the possession or control of the Prosecutor to the defense, which are material to the preparation of the defense or are intended for use by the Prosecutor as evidence in the confirmation hearing or at trial, as the case may be, or were obtained from or belonged to the person (International Criminal Court, 2013). The assessment of whether information is material to the preparation of the defense pursuant to Rule 77 should be made on a prima facie basis. Information that is material to the preparation of the defense may ultimately not be used as evidence at the trial or may not turn out relevant to it and yet the Defense is still entitled to this information based on a prima facie assessment.[13] The disclosure obligations of the Prosecution and the Defense differ significantly. The Prosecution bears the burden of proof and must investigate both incriminating and exonerating circumstances pursuant to Article 54(1)(a) of the Statute, the role of the Defense is largely reactive to the Prosecution's presentation of evidence.[14]

7.2.2.4 Presentation in Proceedings

The judicial proceedings at the ICC are managed through an electronic system pursuant to the Regulations of the Court ("the Regulations").[15] In a proceeding

[12]Ibid., Article 54 para. 1(a).

[13]Prosecutor v. Abdallah Banda Abakaer Nourain and Saleh Mohammed Jerbo Jamus, ICC-02/05-03/09-501, 28 August 2013, para. 42.

[14]Prosecutor v. Germain Katanga and Mathieu Ngudjolo Chui, ICC-01/04-01/07-2388, 14 September 2010, para. 36.

[15]See International Criminal Court (2004), Regulation 26, para. 1.

before the Court, evidence other than live testimony is presented in electronic form whenever possible.[16] The ICC created an 'E-court' protocol for this purpose.[17] This Protocol defines the standards according to which the participants should prepare and provide evidence, potential evidence and material in electronic form with the Court. The standards include format requirement, imaging and data standards, numbering regime, provision of metadata information relating to evidence and material in electronic form. In accordance with these standards, material collected in physical form (documents or tangible objects) is converted into a 'Standard Image Format' by scanning or other digitization. Material collected in an electronic form is provided in its original electronic format.

7.3 Challenges

With the understanding provided from the previously discussed context of an investigation conducted by the ICC, this section presents some operational challenges in digital forensics and evidence handling in an international criminal investigation.

7.3.1 Challenges in Investigations Based on Cooperation

As discussed, ICC investigations widely rely on cooperation from State Parties. The Prosecution can execute a compulsory process without the cooperation of the State only if strict conditions are satisfied. This limitation is in keeping with the complementarity principle of the Rome Statute, which allows the ICC's involvement only if the State's national jurisdiction has failed to investigate, prosecute and try individuals who committed international crimes. National justice systems retain primary responsibility to address the international crimes (Fife, 1999). The initiation of an ICC investigation does not immediately follow after the crimes. An investigation is opened after a preliminary examination process has decided if the ICC has jurisdiction over the crimes, which can be a lengthy process. Timely evidence collection and preservation is important to the ICC's cases, similar in any criminal investigation. Naturally, States have better access to the crime scenes, persons and evidences, until and even after the ICC officially opens investigations in their territory. Therefore, theoretically, investigations based on the cooperation of the States may work efficiently when various conditions are met, however, in reality,

[16] Ibid., para. 4.

[17] International Criminal Court (2015) Unified Technical protocol ("Ecourt Protocol") for the provision of evidence, witness and victims information in electronic form. ICC-01/12-01/15-11-25-Anx, para. 1.

the conditions required for the efficient or effective collection and preservation of digital evidence are often hard to be fully met for various reasons.

7.3.1.1 Jurisdiction on the Data in Cloud

To send a request for cooperation on digital evidence preservation and collection, firstly the recipient of the request must be decided. Identifying an appropriate jurisdiction or a State may not always be easy. It is often not obvious to know the whereabouts of the data that is sought because of delocalization. Many technology giants, including Google, Microsoft, Apple, Facebook, and Amazon, host and process their data abroad. This requires multiple geo-locations or jurisdictions to be involved in the hosting, processing, and archiving of user data. The headquarters of a service provider may be based in a State's jurisdiction, but its regional office may be based in another State, and furthermore, the data may be stored in several other jurisdictions with distributed data warehouses. This implies that there could be jurisdictional conflicts between entities contest their right to investigate and prosecute a criminal case. With this regard, there is no standard across the countries on the jurisdiction in case there is a compulsory process initiated against a user's data. For instance, national legal systems have different approaches on the acceptance of remotely accessing data that has been saved outside a State's territory for compliance purposes. Research that studied on this subject demonstrates the differences between countries (Maxwell and Wolf, 2012; Wolf and Cohen, 2014). It found that 12, out of the 17 examined countries, allow law enforcement to remotely access data stored in the cloud located on servers in another country, while the laws of five countries do not permit the government to systematically demand data stored in the cloud extraterritorially without the cooperation of the foreign government where the data is stored. In addition, even in the same country, the interpretation of relevant laws and legal positions could be inconsistent between courts.[18] Moreover, adding an additional layer of complexity to the situation, data and privacy legislations are actively evolving worldwide.[19]

[18] See Microsoft Corp. v. United States, 14-2985-cv (2nd Cir. 2016). The view of Second Circuit was diametrically opposed to United States District Court in the matter of a warrant to search a certain Mail account controlled and maintained by Microsoft servers outside the United States.

[19] CBPR (Cross Border Privacy Rules, http://www.cbprs.org/GeneralPages/About.aspx), a voluntary accountability-based system to facilitate privacy-respecting data flows among APEC economies, was endorsed by APEC Leaders in 2011; EU GDPR (General Data Protection Regulation, http://www.eugdpr.org/eugdpr.org.html), designed to harmonize data privacy laws and reshape the way organizations across the EU approach data, will take effect on 25 May 2018 replacing the Data Protection Directive 95/46/EU (http://ec.europa.eu/justice/policies/privacy/docs/95-46-ce/dir1995-46_part1_en.pdf); Russia Federal Law No. 242-FZ, which regulates data operators to process and store Russian citizens' personal data using databases located within the territory of Russia, was enacted on 31 December 2014; China Cybersecurity Law (http://www.npc.gov.cn/npc/xinwen/2016-11/07/content_2001605.htm), which contains requirements of comprehensive privacy and security for the cyberspace, will come into force on 1 June 2017.

7.3.1.2 Delay and Data Loss

Even after the location of the data is identified, it takes time before the digital evidence can be accessed and collected as requests need to go through appropriate diplomatic channels and legal processes of the States involved. Every step of iteration adds a certain amount of time to the overall process. The duration ranges from a few days to a year depending on the situation. Furthermore, in worse cases, complexities of the political situation often create serious delays in the whole procedure, including decision making on the timing of requests. Throughout this, time sensitive information tends to be destroyed.

7.3.1.3 Reliability

The issue of the reliability of the evidence may arise when the knowledge and expertise of persons involved in the collection and preservation of evidence is not sufficient. In a situation where the crime scene is still preserved and digital evidence collection is required, the Court may be able to send trained staffs to ensure the digital evidence is handled properly until the evidence arrives at the Court.[20] However, unfortunately, accessing an intact crime scene is not guaranteed for the ICC investigations. The ICC usually investigates crimes committed many years ago, with occasions where more than 10 years have passed. It is therefore natural for the ICC to face situations where evidence has already been collected by various organizations (e.g. local police, military, intelligence service of the State) during or after the crimes. When this occurs, the already collected evidence is handed over to the ICC upon request. The issue is that the received evidences keep different level of reliability depending on the criminal procedure and level of digital forensics awareness in each of the States. Digital evidence, without proper documentation on the chain of custody or guaranteed integrity, will not be considered to have the same level of reliability during an investigation and trial. Concerns about the evidence before its arrival to the ICC prosecution are certainly not easy to cope with or to prevent. Although, in general, the level of expertise in digital forensics is increasing worldwide, the reality is that there are many countries in which digital forensic procedures, technologies and trained human resources are not yet established.

7.3.1.4 Non-cooperation

It is difficult, if not impossible, to collect evidence located in or controlled in non-member States' territories, unless there is a voluntary basis cooperation. This particular issue often arises when digital data saved through web-based services

[20]The Statute, Article 99 provides that the Court can specify the procedure or to send specific persons to be present at and assist in the execution of the request for cooperation.

and cloud computing are found in a third jurisdiction that are non-member States. Service providers may not be allowed, under domestic legislation, to disclose the data sought. Even when there are domestic laws that allow access to the data, not all the service providers may be willing to cooperate because of their societies' controversy surrounding a service provider supplying user data to law enforcement agencies.[21]

7.3.2 Technical Challenges

7.3.2.1 Device Diversity

Device diversity is one of the problems the digital forensic community faces. ICC investigations are also severely confronted with this issue. The severity of this challenge is more apparent at the ICC because of the variety of countries under investigation. Presently, there are ten situations involving nine countries that are under investigation by the ICC. The diversity of digital devices collected from these countries is remarkable. The range vastly extends from far outdated old model electronic devices to the latest models, which include genuine brand-made devices to counterfeits, and industry standard technology based devices to self-developed non-standard devices. The diversity of devices frequently results in obstacles during forensic image acquisition, data extraction and analysis. It commonly occurs that questioned devices are found to not be supported by commercial forensic tools. It is feasible that no commercial or non-commercial digital forensic tool exists that covers all devices that exist in the world. The tendency for forensic researchers and commercial forensic companies is to invest their resources in developing digital forensic technologies for widely used devices, programs, and data formats, rather than rarely used or unknown ones. Consequently, there remains quite big terra incognita in terms of digital forensic technology.

7.3.2.2 Anti-forensics and Data Protection

The development of anti-forensic technologies and information security technologies provides a further challenge. Because of the prevalence of information security and privacy technology, new devices are frequently equipped with strong security measures. This is not a new concern, but is an ever-growing one. In the ICC investigations the various layers of technologies, such as device locks, data encryption, trail obfuscation, anonymization, and artifact deletion are creating difficulties in digital forensic data acquisition and examination.

[21]See supra note 18.

7.3.2.3 Language Diversity

The linguistic diversity in digital evidence also creates challenges. Jargons, special vocabularies used by particular groups or abbreviations are an issue faced in any criminal investigation, including cases under national jurisdiction. The linguistic diversity issue is, however, a more noticeable characteristic in ICC investigations. In addition to the most commonly used languages and characters (e.g. English, French, Arabic, Russian, etc.), minority languages and local dialects are also found during digital forensic examination. The knowledge of the examiner in these instances is an issue. In addition, texts are perceived as problematic when they were not written in ordinary terminologies. For instance, texts found in some digital evidence are written in Latin characters with representation of the sounds of spoken language. Because many spoken language contexts are characterized as more oral than written, written forms have often not yet been standardized. In such cases, because of the lack of standardized format of writing, text indexing and keyword searching applied during digital forensic examination is substantially impacted decreasing analysis speed and efficiency. In the FF POIROT European project, formal and shareable knowledge repositories (i.e. ontologies) and ontology-based applications have been developed at the aim of the detection of securities fraud (Kerremans et al., 2005). In the EVIDENCE European project a thesaurus (see Chap. 9) has been developed as a first step to devise an ontology in the forensics area but no linguistic issues have been addressed.

7.3.2.4 Open Source Data: Volume and Processing

Open source data retains a high importance to the ICC's investigations and can include: media articles, broad cast audio and videos, governmental reports, commercial analytic reports, intergovernmental project reports, personal blogs, social media website posts, and academic research. Although reliability issues must be solved, open source materials are considered valuable, particularly at the initial stage of investigations. They sometimes serve as leads to prompt the direction of an investigation. At a trial phase they are sometimes presented as circumstantial evidence in corroboration with other forms of evidence such as witness testimony, medical examination reports and forensic analysis reports.[22] As the nature of crimes investigated by the ICC is often violent, political, and high profiled, there is an abundance of material obtainable from publicly available sources especially on the internet. The challenging aspect is how to best utilize these sources in an investigation. There is a requirement to develop technologies that process, filter and extract the most relevant material from the overwhelming volume of data whilst providing credible and useful information to the investigation. It is not simple as it is necessary to handle two conflicting needs at the same time. While sufficiently

[22] Prosecutor v. Jean-Pierre Bemba Combo, ICC-01/05-01/08-2981, 23 June 2016, paras. 56, 64.

utilizing the already collected investigative information, the technology should not expose any confidential information when searching and collecting data from an open source. Finding a balance will be the key to success.

7.3.3 Legal Challenges: Evidentiary Value of Digital Evidence

Unlike in some national legal systems where the admissibility of evidence is strictly scrutinized under complex standards, the Rome Statute provides quite a simple framework for the admission of evidence.[23] The Chamber of the ICC considers the admissibility of evidence in accordance with the three-part test of relevance, probative value, and potential prejudice.[24] For the exclusion of admissibility, the Statue prescribes that "evidence obtained by means of a violation of this Statute or internationally recognized human rights shall not be admissible if: (a) the violation casts substantial doubt on the reliability of the evidence; or (b) the admission of the evidence would be antithetical to and would seriously damage the integrity of the proceedings". Once admitted, the test on digital evidence goes to the matter of evidentiary weight. As the evidentiary weight of each piece of digital evidence is not expressively described in decisions, and the reasoning behind it may vary from case to case, it is important to conduct cumulative analytics to set up a guideline for investigation. The usefulness could be further if analysis could be detailed per type of digital evidence. This would eventually work as a tool towards making decisions on how to best prioritize the allocation of resources during investigation and prosecution. In national legal systems where digital evidence has been widely introduced and tested by various courts, legal researchers and practitioners have been making efforts to create guidelines on digital evidence based on accumulated case data (Frieden et al., 2011; Givens, 2003; Goode, 2009; Grimm and Bergstrom, 2012; Jablon, 1996; Kurzban, 1994). The ICC, as a relatively young court with less than 20 years history, has not yet accumulated enough cases, at least to cover major types of digital evidence. Consequently, it is not avoidable that digital evidence is introduced with uncertainty in their status to some extent in trials.

7.4 What is Required to Tackle the Challenges

Given the previously identified challenges, the discussion in this section sets forth some requirements and conceptual approaches to resolve them.

---

[23]The Rome Statute, supra note 1, Article 69 para. 4, prescribes that "The Court may rule on the relevance or admissibility of any evidence, taking into account, inter alia, the probative value of the evidence and any prejudice that such evidence may cause to a fair trial or to a fair evaluation of the testimony of a witness, in accordance with the Rules of Procedure and Evidence".

[24]Prosecutor v. Jean-Pierre Bemba Combo, ICC-01/05-01/08-2981, 23 June 2016, paras. 15.

7.4.1 Building a Knowledge Base

Widespread utilization of the cloud by service providers has become a growing jurisdictional concern and is also a challenge to law enforcements as it has broken traditional geographical boundaries and the notion of jurisdiction. The complexity and uncertainty of the jurisdiction impacts law enforcements' investigative activities by creating delays and additional coordination. In this regard, it is highly relevant to closely follow up the regulations and laws on privacy, data localization and data sovereignty issue. In compliance with these regulations and laws, companies are establishing new policies and technical solutions leading to a changing landscape of data location and legal implications. They are creating systems to locate data and control cross-border data flow while processing, transferring, storing and backing-up. To correctly and efficiently request for cooperation to the relevant State and acquire data from companies, understanding the global and local regulations and companies' implementation is crucial. As the same challenges would be encountered by all the organizations worldwide that are seeking international cooperation for criminal investigations, developing and sharing a corpus of relevant information would be useful. The implementation of such as a knowledge base might contain each country's relevant laws, judicial decisions, contact list of major service providers, data localization, data protection, and data sovereignty compliance status. Furthermore, if consensus is created, building and connecting an international cooperation request management system would be beneficial. As a prerequisite, strong technical measures must be installed to authenticate, protect and control the information in the system.

7.4.2 Digital Evidence Container Standard Setup

In an international investigation where digital evidence is received from many sources in a variety of formats, eventually the received evidence must be preserved and managed in a certain way. This management does not only mean securely archiving the evidence, but it also includes creating and maintaining some relevant metadata (e.g. data source, owner, collector's identity, organization, collected time, collected location, data integrity verification information, and a relevant legal basis), together with the evidence itself. The transmission and archiving of data could be facilitated if there is a standardized digital evidence exchange format implemented. In the digital forensic field, there has been some significant research on this topic (Casey et al., 2015; Garfinkel et al., 2006; Garfinkel, 2012; Levine, 2009; Richard et al., 2007; Woods et al., 2011), although none of them could reach a de facto standard for the forensic community, regardless of the perceived advantages of the proposed approaches. It would not be easy to form a global consensus on the requirement of standards and format specification, however once settled and commonly acknowledged, this could play an extremely positive role. The standard may effectively contribute to the convenience of managing the collected digital evidence, and ensure the proper data collection and transmission procedure establishment by guiding participants of the digital evidence handling procedure to collect and maintain important information. It may eventually contribute to the reliability of the collected evidence and admission at a trial.

7.4.3 Provision of Trainings and Raising Awareness

Authentication, integrity verification and chain of custody documentation are crucial in digital evidence handling. Evidence collected or transmitted without these measures may eventually be challenged in the trial and the admissibility of the evidence could be seriously impacted. Despite its importance, in international investigations that rely on multi-lateral cooperation, it is often difficult for requesters to predict or prevent these issues as evidence collection happens to be conducted out of their control. Therefore, it is required that the persons involved in the digital data preservation or collection be trained or at least be aware of the appropriate procedure. Unfortunately, not all organizations or law enforcement agencies have enough budget or resource to train and equip with technologies. In this regard, universal efforts to raise general awareness and provide relevant trainings for practical staffs would be needed. International level capacity building programs between forensic practitioners could be highly contributive if knowledge and expertise can be shared as a reciprocal interest in the global context.[25] In addition to the technical knowledge sharing, this kind of training creates interpersonal connections that can facilitate cooperation when there are investigations requiring the involvement of different organizations.

7.4.4 Technology Sharing and Joint Development

In an international investigation, technical diversity and complexity provides a challenge when handling and analyzing digital evidence. Each country is in a different IT development phase and results in distinctive technologies. For instance, the most frequently used office programs, messenger programs, email services, web browsers, audios/video compression formats, accounting programs, and encryption tools differ depending on the country. This is also true for the most used mobiles and platforms. International investigations that deal with evidence collected from diverse countries pose big challenges in digital forensic data acquisition and

[25]For instance, INTERPOL provides international trainings for examiners, investigators and other first responders to ensure they possess the latest knowledge of cybercrime trends, and the use of digital forensic tools and techniques.

analysis. Since globally used digital forensic tools are not able to address all the technical issues caused by these diversity, the local law enforcements tend to develop special digital forensic technologies that are specific to them. It frequently requires a large budget and takes a considerable duration to develop solutions, and hence sharing information on the existing technologies would be extremely useful. The scope of sharable information does not have to necessarily be detailed. Categorized and summarized information might be useful for the parties who are seeking already existing solutions for immediate application in their forensic examination during an investigation. Another more proactive approach would be creating joint projects between organizations and institutions. It is obvious that most of the countries and organizations are facing common problems to progress with the ever-changing technology innovation. Law enforcement agencies usually suffer from persistent digital forensic technology development when there is a misalignment between the limited resources (e.g. budget, human resource) and growing demand. Hence, seeking coordination and collaboration among diverse parties with common interests might be very positive. Inter-governmental or inter-institutional joint development projects may enable many organizations to solve or reduce technological and budgetary issues of research and development.

7.5 Conclusion

Digital evidence is enhancing the credibility and providing more opportunities to the investigations conducted by the ICC. The benefits also bring enormous challenges with different layers in each step of the life-cycle of digital evidence from the collection phase through to the trial phase. Difficulties in international cooperation, technological complexity and uncertainty of legal standards are the main concerns faced by the ICC investigations and must be addressed. As previously emphasized, the challenges are not easy to solve without a global collaborative approach requiring a consensus on the establishment of standards, cooperation reinforcement, and an organized effort to find technical solutions. The partnership and engagement between various parties to instate an agreement and aligned efforts are of the highest importance. These efforts will serve to greatly improve the international exchange of digital evidence, and to ultimately achieve the ICC's mission of ending the impunity of the most serious crimes against human rights.

References

Case: Microsoft Corp. v. United States, 14-2985-cv (2nd Cir. 2016)
Case: Prosecutor v. Abdallah Banda Abakaer Nourain and Sale Mohammed Jerbo Jamus, ICC-02/05-03/09-501
Case: Prosecutor v. Germain Katanga and Mathieu Ngudjolo Chui, ICC-01/04-01/07-2388

Case: Prosecutor v. Jean-Pierre Bemba Combo, ICC-01/05-01/08-2981
Casey E, Back G, Barnum S (2015) Leveraging CybOX™ to standardize representation and exchange of digital forensic information. Digit Investig 12:S102–S110
Fife RE (1999) PENALTIES. In: Lee RS (ed) The international criminal court: the making of the Rome statute, issues, negotiations, results. Kluwer Law International, The Hague, pp 319–345
Frieden JD, Murray LM (2011) The admissibility of electronic evidence under the federal rules of evidence. Richmond J Law Technol 17:5–16
Garfinkel S (2012) Digital forensics XML and the DFXML toolset. Digit Investig 8(3):161–174
Garfinkel S, Malan D, Dubec KA, Stevens C, Pham C (2006) Advanced forensic format: an open extensible format for disk imaging. In: IFIP international conference on digital forensics. Springer, New York, pp 13–27
Givens JS (2003) The admissibility of electronic evidence at trial: courtroom admissibility standards. Cumberland Law Rev 34:95
Goode S (2009) The admissibility of electronic evidence. Rev Litig 29:1
Grimm PW, Bergstrom LY, O'Toole-Loureiro MM (2012) Authentication of social media evidence. Am J Trial Advocacy 36:433
Guariglia F (1999) Investigation and prosecution. In: Lee SK (ed) The international criminal court: the making of the Rome statute, issues, negotiations, results. Kluwer Law International, The Hague, pp 227–238
International Criminal Court (2004) Regulations of the court. https://www.icc-cpi.int/NR/rdonlyres/B920AD62-DF49-4010-8907-E0D8CC61EBA4/277527/Regulations_of_the_Court_170604EN.pdf
International Criminal Court (2011) Elements of crimes. https://www.icc-cpi.int/NR/rdonlyres/336923D8-A6AD-40EC-AD7B-45BF9DE73D56/0/ElementsOfCrimesEng.pdf
International Criminal Court (2013) Rules of procedure and evidence. https://www.icc-cpi.int/iccdocs/PIDS/legal-texts/RulesProcedureEvidenceEng.pdf
Jablon A (1996) God mail: authentication and admissibility of electronic mail in federal courts. Am Crim Law Rev 34:1387
Kerremans K, Desmeytere I, Temmerman R, Wille P (2005) Application-oriented terminography in financial forensics. In: Ibekwe-SanJuan F, Condamines A, Teresa Cabré Castellví M (eds) Application-driven terminology engineering. John Benjamins, Amsterdam, 2005, pp 83–106
Kurzban SA (1994) Authentication of computer-generated evidence in the United States Federal courts. Idea 35:437
Levine BN, Liberatore M (2009) DEX: digital evidence provenance supporting reproducibility and comparison. Digit Investig 6:S48–S56
Maxwell W, Wolf C (2012) A global reality: governmental access to data in the cloud, White paper, Hogan Lovells, London, p 18
Richard GG, Roussev V, Marziale L (2007) Forensic discovery auditing of digital evidence containers. Digit Investig 4(2):88–97
Wolf C, Cohen B (2014) Pan-American governmental access to data in the cloud. Hogan Lovells, London
Woods K, Lee CA, Garfinkel S (2011) Extending digital repository architectures to support disk image preservation and access. In: Proceedings of the 11th annual international ACM/IEEE joint conference on digital libraries. ACM, New York, pp 57–66

Chapter 8
The Online Environment as a Challenge for Privacy and the Suppression of Crime

Daniel Drewer and Jan Ellermann

Abstract Anonymity and encryption offered by the Internet represent huge resources for cybercriminals: ransomware and spyware are just two examples of cyber threats that in the past years caused serious damage, not only via desktop computers, but via mobile devices as well.

By its own nature, cybercrime has an outreach which goes well beyond national level. This leads to great difficulties in detecting it, and raises questions over how Law Enforcement can effectively fight it without violating any fundamental rights, including rights on data protection. Europol is the most controlled agency in the world of Law Enforcement and manages to provide high standards of internal and external accountability, as demonstrated by the supervision activity of the DPO, EDPS, and the growing control by the EU Parliament via the JPSG. Europol is a clear example that enhancing both Freedom and Security is possible in the fight against serious and organised crime.

8.1 Data is the New Oil

Collection and processing of huge amounts of personal data are nowadays an everyday activity. Google and other companies offering "free" online services keep emphasising how much they are committed to making knowledge available to more people, no matter where they may be, no matter what language they speak. However, for these "free" services, people are "paying" with their personal data.

The increasing value of information has lead Shivon Zilis, a partner with the venture capital firm Bloomberg Beta to describe data as "the new oil".[1] It is not

[1]See http://fortune.com/2016/07/11/data-oil-brainstorm-tech, last accessed on 20/03/2017.

D. Drewer (✉) · J. Ellermann
Europol, Data Protection Office, The Hague, The Netherlands
e-mail: daniel.drewer@europol.europa.eu; jan.ellermann@europol.europa.eu

M. A. Biasiotti et al. (eds.), *Handling and Exchanging Electronic Evidence Across Europe*, Law, Governance and Technology Series 39,
https://doi.org/10.1007/978-3-319-74872-6_8

a secret that *criminals are also* aware of that. Data has become a key commodity for organised crime: increasing internet connectivity by citizens, businesses and the public sector, along with the exponentially growing number of connected devices and sensors as part of the Internet of Things will create new opportunities for criminals.[2]

Data is no longer just procured for immediate financial gain. Increasingly it is acquired for the furtherance of more complex fraud, encrypted for ransom, or used directly for extortion. When considering intellectual property, the illegal acquisition of this data can reflect the loss of years of research and substantial investment by the victim.[3] Europol's business is hence *increasingly* focussed on handling and exchanging electronic evidence, as well as criminal intelligence across Europe.

8.2 Challenges for Law Enforcement

A growing number of criminals are exploiting the anonymity offered by the Internet to commit a range of criminal activities.[4] They know no borders and earn huge illicit profits. Some EU Member States already report that the number of cyber-crime offences may have surpassed those associated with traditional crimes.[5] It is of particular concern how an expanding cyber-criminal community has been able to exploit our increasing dependence on technology and the Internet.

8.2.1 An Unfortunate Example: Ransomware

Ransomware has become the most prominent malware threat, overshadowing data stealing malware and banking Trojans. Ransomware is a malware locking computers, for instance, by clicking on a malicious link. All personal data on a

[2]Europol's Serious and Organised Crime Threat Assessment 2017, p. 30, https://www.europol.europa.eu/activities-services/main-reports/european-union-serious-and-organised-crime-threat-assessment-2017, last accessed on 21/03/17.

[3]Europol's Internet Organised Crime Threat Assessment 2016, p. 11, https://www.europol.europa.eu/activities-services/main-reports/internet-organised-crime-threat-assessment-iocta-2016, last accessed 20/03/2017.

[4]"*The anonymisation techniques used in parts of the Internet, known as Darknets, allow users to communicate freely without the risk of being traced. These are perfectly legitimate tools for citizens to protect their privacy. However, the features of these privacy networks are also of primary interest to criminals that abuse such anonymity on a massive scale for illicit online trade in drugs, weapons, stolen goods, forged IDs and child sexual exploitation*" Europol's Internet Organised Crime Threat Assessment 2014, p. 9, https://www.europol.europa.eu/activities-services/main-reports/internet-organised-crime-threat-assessment-iocta-2014, last accessed 20/03/2017.

[5]Europol's Internet Organised Crime Threat Assessment 2016, p. 7, https://www.europol.europa.eu/activities-services/main-reports/internet-organised-crime-threat-assessment-iocta-2016, last accessed 20/03/2017.

machine become unavailable to the user. The cybercriminals ask on average 1 Bitcoin of ransom to unlock the computer. Bitcoins is the most prominent cyber-currency *that is hardest* to trace back. *As of this writing*, 1 Bitcoin has a value of a little more than EUR 900.[6] Already if the locked computer is full of family photographs with no backup anywhere else, the user may be willing to pay that Bitcoin. Things get way more serious if this is not just about family photographs but about the IT infrastructure of a hospital holding the health data of hundreds of patients. People may die if access is not immediately regained. Earlier in 2016 a hospital in Los Angeles in the US paid $17,000 to regain access to their data[7]—the initial demand has reportedly been north of $3 Million. The hospital obviously was lucky to have *an exceptional* negotiator at their disposal.

Europol and a coalition of industry partners have reacted to this phenomenon and have created a website called 'No More Ransom'.[8] This is an awareness raising tool but also a hands-on attempt to help victims decrypting their machines without paying ransom. The website meanwhile has a consolidated average of 0.4 Million clicks per day. This probably gives a very good flavour of the magnitude of the issue. Help was offered to at least more than 6000 individuals to decrypt their machines without paying anything to the criminals.[9]

8.2.2 Not Only Big Brother is Watching You: Spyware

Another cyber issue *that* has huge privacy implications is "spyware".[10] While the Snowden revelations[11] have triggered a public debate suggesting that intelligence agencies in many countries use such software, it often goes unnoticed that *cyber criminals also* take advantage of related vulnerabilities. Furthermore, malware, which was previously only a threat for desktop computers, is increasingly an issue for smartphones. *Particularly*, Android phones are affected.[12] Again, it can be enough to click on one link, which looks perfectly legitimate. Now the intruder can remotely turn on the phone's camera, microphone and take screenshots—even when the user is just reading end-to-end encrypted messages. The little recording sign of the mobile device camera will most likely not start blinking this time. But there are

[6]http://preev.com/btc/eur, last accessed 20/03/2017.

[7]http://www.dailymail.co.uk/news/article-3452178/Los-Angeles-hospital-paid-17-000-ransom-hackers-regain-control-computers.html, last accessed 20/03/2017.

[8]https://www.nomoreransom.org/ransomware-qa.html, last accessed 20/03/2017.

[9]https://www.europol.europa.eu/newsroom/news/no-more-ransom-new-partners-new-decryption-tools-new-languages-to-better-fight-ransomware, last accessed on 21/03/2017.

[10]http://dictionary.cambridge.org/dictionary/english/spyware, last accessed on 21/03/2017.

[11]http://www.bbc.com/news/world-us-canada-23123964, last accessed on 21/03/2017.

[12]http://www.dailymail.co.uk/sciencetech/article-3189613/Millions-Android-phones-risk-software-installed-handset-makers-Certifi-gate-flaw-let-hackers-listen-conversations-steal-data.html, last accessed on 22/03/2017.

also law enforcement challenges in the sense that the criminal just operating the camera may be sitting on another continent.

8.2.3 The Infamous Encryption Debate

While the above examples have shown in how far criminals are threatening our privacy, law enforcement operations in the digital age certainly *also* entail data protection implications. This is probably best illustrated by the meanwhile infamous encryption debate.

It is widely acknowledged that strong encryption is highly important to e-commerce and other cyberspace activity[13]—and key tool to safeguard privacy. But adequate security also depends on law enforcement to have the ability to investigate criminal activity. A huge challenge for law enforcement in the context of collecting e-evidence and criminal intelligence is the growing misuse of legitimate anonymity and encryption services and tools for illegal purposes. This poses a serious impediment to the detection, investigation and prosecution of crime.

In May 2016 Europol has hosted a conference on 'Privacy in the Digital Age of Encryption and Anonymity Online'[14] to discuss this conflict of values with relevant stakeholders from all parts of the society. The heads of Europol and the EU's Network Security Agency ENISA issued a joint statement sending the clear message that backdoors are not an option. They will weaken online security and can hence not be the solution. Alternative solutions to decryption must be offered.[15]

Life data forensics fall into this category. *Further*, the "hacking-back" debate came up once again—with all its data protection and ethical implications, notably with the FBI–Apple encryption dispute.[16] It is also interesting to note that some countries have so called "key disclosure legislation" in place whereby suspects can be forced to reveal their passwords; otherwise, the person denying to give away his/her password might end up in prison—just for not revealing it. UK and Australia are probably the most prominent examples of this practice (Holt et al., 2015). Other jurisdictions including some EU Member States are discussing such options or have partly implemented them in law under certain conditions. However, there is another challenge for the law enforcement authorities since modern software offers the installation of hidden encrypted containers and even if suspects are caught

[13]Europol's Internet Organised Crime Threat Assessment 2016, p. 8, https://www.europol.europa.eu/activities-services/main-reports/internet-organised-crime-threat-assessment-iocta-2016, last accessed on 21/03/2017.

[14]https://www.europol.europa.eu/events/privacy-in-digital-age-of-encryption-anonymity-online, last accessed on 21/03/2017.

[15]https://www.enisa.europa.eu/publications/enisa-position-papers-and-opinions/on-lawful-criminal-investigation-that-respects-21st-century-data-protection, last accessed 20/03/2017.

[16]https://www.cnet.com/news/apple-versus-the-fbi-why-the-lowest-priced-iphone-has-the-us-in-a-tizzy-faq, last accessed 20/03/2017.

and forced to reveal their password, they will only open the container with some trivial content. Law enforcement currently has no possibility to establish that yet another container even exists—which the criminal will certainly NOT reveal to law enforcement.

Law enforcement will only be provided with appropriate tools if citizens have trust that these will be used in full respect of their fundamental rights including the right to data protection.

8.3 Data Protection in the Fight Against Cybercrime

Full compliance with data protection principles is an asset towards effectively preventing and combating cybercrime (Drewer and Ellermann, 2012). It forms the basis for the trust of Member States, which provide related intelligence to Europol. *Further*, citizens expect Europol's Cyber Crime Centre (EC3) to tackle the issue of cybercrime in a way *that* fully respects fundamental rights including the right of protection of privacy and personal data protection. Europol has a comprehensive, robust and tested regime in place *that* is widely recognised as safeguarding and ensuring the highest standards of data protection in the law enforcement world. It aims at ensuring the protection of privacy of the persons whose data are processed in Europol's systems. At the same time it serves the needs of operational units in preventing and combating organised crime, terrorism and other forms of serious crime affecting two or more Member States. Since its launch in 2013, the boundaries of EC3 operations were determined by the Europol Council Decision and its implementing rules. However, since May 2017 a new legal regime, the Europol Regulation (ER) applies.[17]

8.3.1 New Europol Regulation, More Personal Data Protection

A central element of this new legal framework is the introduction of an Integrated Data Management Concept (IDMC). The idea is to move away from specifically described systems towards defined purposes of processing operations. These can be implemented in a tech-neutral manner. The concept is based on general data protection principles and specifically defined safeguards such as time-limits for storage of information, prior consultation, as well as logging and documentation

[17]Regulation (EU) 2016/794 of the European Parliament and of the Council of 11 May 2016 on the European Union Agency for Law Enforcement Cooperation (Europol) and replacing and repealing Council Decisions 2009/371/JHA, 2009/934/JHA, 2009/935/JHA, 2009/936/JHA and 2009/968/JHA (ER).

requirements.[18] The application of data protection rules by Europol is supervised on various levels and throughout the entire information cycle. Contributions from national level to Europol are scrutinised by national competent data protection authorities *based on* applicable national law. Once the information is processed at Europol, the Data Protection Officer (DPO) has the task to ensure, in an independent manner, lawfulness and compliance with the Europol Regulation and its implementing rules. The DPO *must* be a member of staff and an integral part of the organisation.[19] Being an internal function is essential for the role of the DPO as it facilitates the building of trust amongst Europol staff, ensures compliance from the inside and enables the provision of advice or intervention at an early stage when potential risks for data subjects can be mitigated. Established procedures ensure the use of Privacy Enhancing Technologies (PETs) following a privacy-by-design approach for any new technical infrastructures.

8.3.2 Supervision

Europol is often referred to as "the most controlled police agency in the world".[20] In the past supervision was carried out by the Joint Supervisory Body (JSB),[21] an entity comprising experts of all 28 national DPAs.

The Europol Regulation entails a further reinforcement of Europol's external data protection supervision—even including a "right to pull-the-plug" of any Europol system.[22] This is allocated to the European Data Protection Supervisor (EDPS)[23] acting in close cooperation with national supervisory authorities. The same applies to parliamentary scrutiny of Europol's activities by the European Parliament together with national parliaments who will constitute a specialised Joint Parliamentary Scrutiny Group (JPSG) with the task of politically monitoring Europol's activities in fulfilling its mission, including as regards the impact of those activities on the fundamental rights and freedoms of natural persons,[24] including the right to data protection.

The JPSG can subpoena the Chairperson of the Management Board, the Executive Director or their Deputies to appear before the Group at its request to discuss matters relating to Europol activities, including the budgetary aspects of such activities, the structural organisation of Europol and the potential establishment of new units and specialised centres, *considering* the obligations of discretion

[18]See Chapter VI of the Europol Regulation.

[19]Article 41 ER.

[20]Fijnaut, quoted as per Groenleer (2009), p. 282.

[21]http://www.europoljsb.europa.eu/about.aspx, last accessed 21/03/2017.

[22]Article 43(3)(f) ER.

[23]https://secure.edps.europa.eu/EDPSWEB/edps/EDPS, last accessed 21/03/2017.

[24]Articles 51(1) and (2) ER.

and confidentiality. The Group may decide to invite to its meetings other relevant persons, where appropriate.[25] This may include the DPO whenever Europol's internal supervision of data processing operations is concerned. The particular relevance of data protection in the JPSG context is further underpinned by the fact that the EDPS shall appear before the JPSG at its request, and at least once a year, to discuss general matters relating to the protection of fundamental rights and freedoms of natural persons, and *particularly* the protection of personal data, with regard to Europol's activities, *considering* the obligations of discretion and confidentiality.[26]

The JSPG is to be provided by Europol with certain strategic documents enabling it to exercise its political monitoring function. Furthermore, it can use the instrument of a public access request to request any additional information it deems relevant.[27]

The European Parliament is being granted even more far reaching powers, namely the explicit right to access sensitive non-classified, as well as classified information subject to the appropriate proceedings.[28]

This shall not be perceived as a burden but as a successfully established data protection culture, which recognises the value of fundamental rights observance.

8.4 Conclusion

It is crucial to tackle the challenges of handling and exchanging electronic evidence, as well as criminal intelligence across Europe, in a way *that* fully respects fundamental rights including the right to data protection. The DPO can in this context play an important role acting as an internal but independent adviser with the aim to provide guidance and best practice on how to implement the toolkit available to Europol's cyber analysts in a data protection compliant manner.

But external accountability and supervisory mechanisms *also* play a key role in this regard. The Europol Regulation entails a clear reinforcement of Europol's external data protection supervision—even including a "right to pull-the-plug" of any Europol system—which will be allocated to the European Data Protection Supervisor acting in close cooperation with national supervisory authorities. *Further*, the parliamentary scrutiny by both the European Parliament *and* national parliaments acting through the Joint Parliamentary Scrutiny Group will significantly strengthen oversight over Europol which is—already now—often referred to as the "most controlled police agency".

In that endeavour terminology suggesting that freedom *must* be balanced versus security *must* be avoided. A balancing exercise always entails a logic that freedom *must be sacrificed* to increase security—and vice versa. On many occasions security

[25]Article 51(2)(a) ER.

[26]Article 51(2)(b) ER.

[27]Article 51(3) and (4) ER.

[28]Article 52 ER.

can step up without giving up our freedoms. 'Data protection by design and by default' are the buzzwords in this context. Europol *also has a record of* implementing these principles in practice.

References

Drewer D, Ellermann J (2012) Europol's data protection framework as an asset in the fight against cybercrime, 2012. ERA Forum 13:381–395. https://doi.org/10.1007/s12027-012-0268-6

Groenleer M (2009) The autonomy of European union agencies. A comparative study of institutional development. Eburon Academic Publishers, Delft, p 282

Holt TJ, Bossler AM, Seigfried-Spellar KC (2015) Cybercrime and digital forensics: an introduction, Routledge, p 500

Chapter 9
Electronic Evidence in Criminal Trials: The Use of PowerPoint Presentations by Prosecutors and Attorneys in the Courtroom

Xavier Tracol

Abstract Organising training courses on electronic evidence in criminal trials at EU level would contribute to create a common legal and judicial culture among judges, prosecutors, attorneys, experts as well as police and military police officers. The content of such courses may include the use of PowerPoint presentations by prosecutors and attorneys to support their oral submissions in criminal trials. These presentations especially assist litigators in making factual arguments during hearings.

9.1 Introduction

EU law does not provide any definition of electronic evidence. Its determination falls within the discretion of Member States, which may define it in their domestic law. This comment equally applies to the admissibility of electronic evidence in criminal trials. In addition, available domestic law of Member States is inconsistent on both the definition of electronic evidence and its admissibility in criminal trials (Biasotti, 2017).

Senior Legal Officer at Eurojust. The views expressed herein are those of the author in his personal capacity and do not necessarily reflect those of EUROJUST or the EU in general.

The author has been working as an attorney at the Bar of Paris and as an Appeals Counsel with the Office of the Prosecutor of the United Nations International Criminal Tribunal for the former Yugoslavia in The Hague. This publication is based on the presentation made by the author in Rome on 11 December 2015 during the workshop on Obstacles and Facilitating Factors towards the Digitalisation of Justice: the Specific Issue of Electronic Evidence in Criminal Trials.

X. Tracol (✉)
Eurojust, The Hague, The Netherlands
e-mail: xtracol@eurojust.europa.eu

M. A. Biasiotti et al. (eds.), *Handling and Exchanging Electronic Evidence Across Europe*, Law, Governance and Technology Series 39,
https://doi.org/10.1007/978-3-319-74872-6_9

In this context, it is necessary for both prosecutors and attorneys to always be able to show the source of electronic evidence, i.e. establish the identity of the author with certainty, and to establish that the electronic evidence may not be altered so that the judge can admit it into evidence, assess its reliability and determine its legal value in criminal trials. Domestic courts of Member States exercise discretion in assessing both the probative value and weight of electronic evidence.

However, the use of electronic evidence in criminal courts requires the adequate equipment of courtrooms with computers and monitors (both e-Registry and e-Court), as well as the basic familiarity, interest and technological knowledge of judges. It may not be safely assumed that such is always the case in all Member States. The organisation of training courses on electronic evidence in criminal trials may therefore be a welcome initiative.

9.2 Training Courses on Electronic Evidence in Criminal Trials

It is quite striking to see that no training course on electronic evidence in criminal trials is currently available in any Member State. Organising such a training course at EU level would be a good idea to create a common legal and judicial culture.

The target group of this training could include judges, prosecutors and attorneys. It could also include experts, police and military police officers who may be called to testify as witnesses before criminal courts of Member States.

The European Judicial Training Network, the European Centre for Judges and Lawyers, which is part of the European Institute of Public Administration in Luxembourg, the Academy of European Law (Europäische Rechtsakademie—ERA) in Trier or the Max Planck Institute for Procedural Law in Luxembourg may be interested in organising it. They may learn from the experience and best practices of the National Institute for Trial Advocacy (NITA) in the US. In the longer term, the organisation of this training course may lead and aim to establish an equivalent to NITA in the EU. The content of such course may cover the use of PowerPoint presentations by prosecutors and attorneys in criminal trials.

9.3 The Use of PowerPoint Presentations by Prosecutors and Attorneys in the Courtroom

Prosecutors and attorneys may request to make PowerPoint presentations in support of their oral submissions before criminal courts of Member States. They should then also request the admission of both the electronic and paper versions of such presentations into evidence. If not formally admitted into evidence, PowerPoint presentations may not be considered part of the (electronic) evidence of the case. PowerPoint presentations may assist prosecutors and attorneys in making mainly factual arguments but also legal arguments in the courtroom.

Prosecutors and attorneys may use PowerPoint presentations for **underlining, pointing at and highlighting** relevant elements of exhibits such as names and dates. These functions may also be used to show links and connect the dots between relevant elements of exhibits.

Prosecutors and attorneys may also use **call-outs and blow-ups** to present electronic evidence in criminal trials (see Figs. 9.1, 9.2, 9.3, 9.4, 9.5, and 9.6). The following slides provide examples that mention fictitious personal data and ethnic origin.

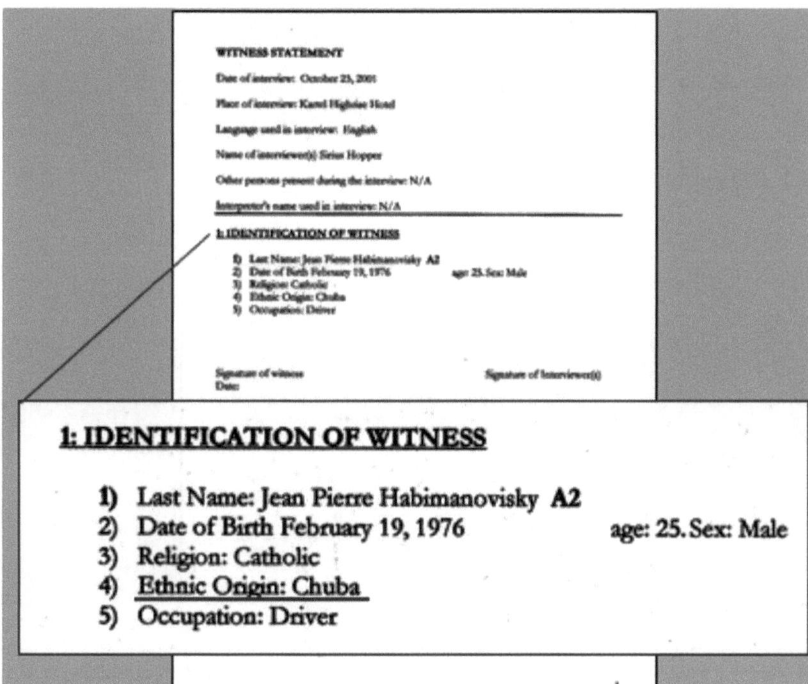

Fig. 9.1 Call-out, blow-up and underline

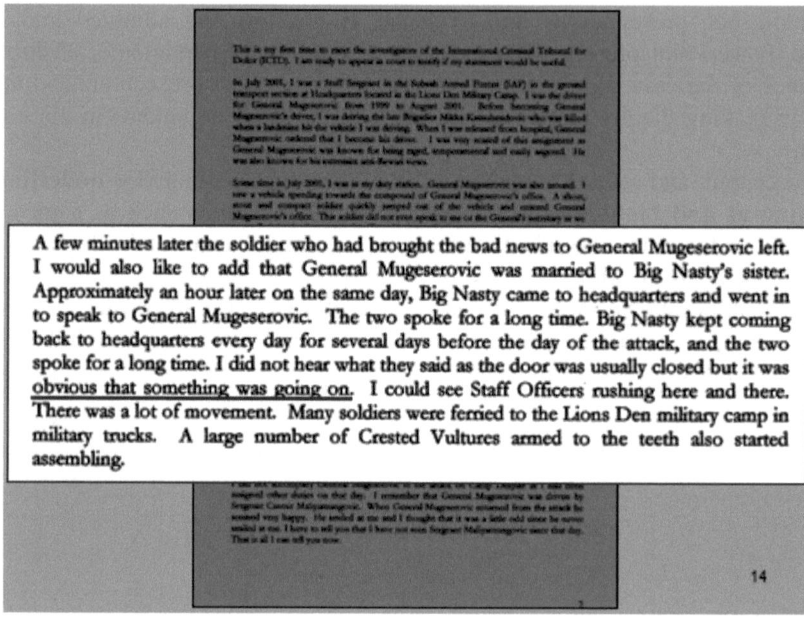

Fig. 9.2 Call-out, blow-up and underline

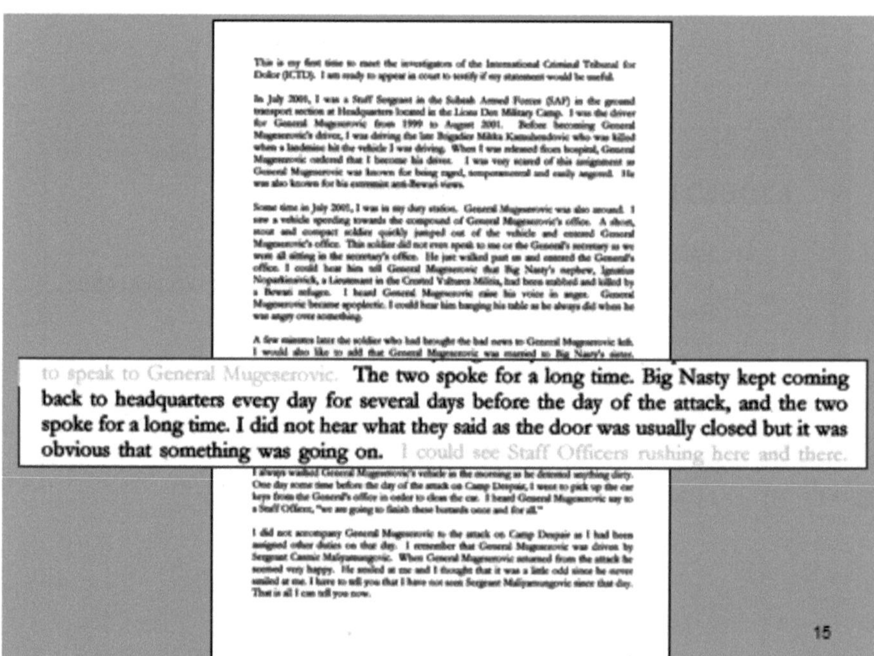

Fig. 9.3 Call-out and blow-up

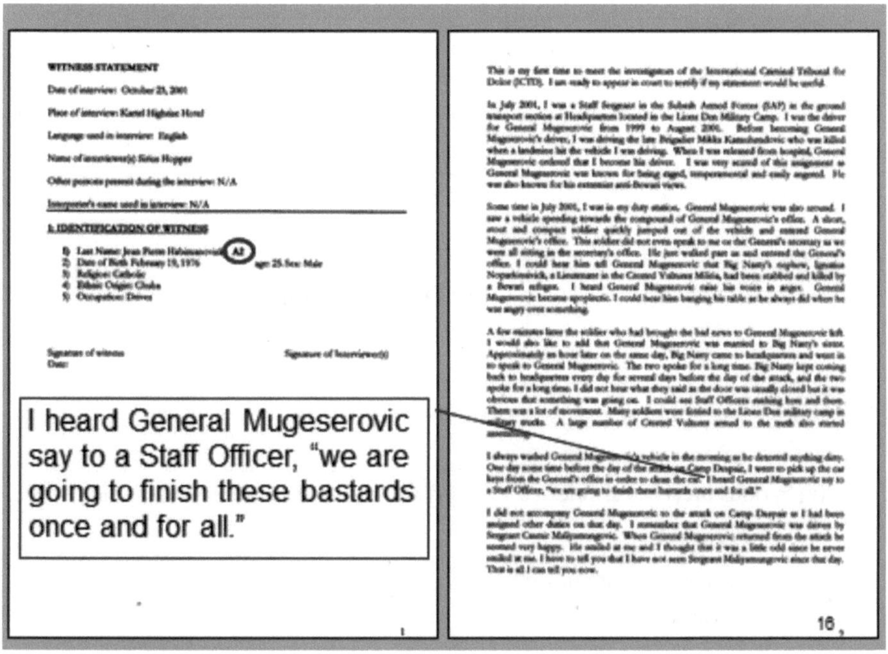

Fig. 9.4 Call-out and blow-up

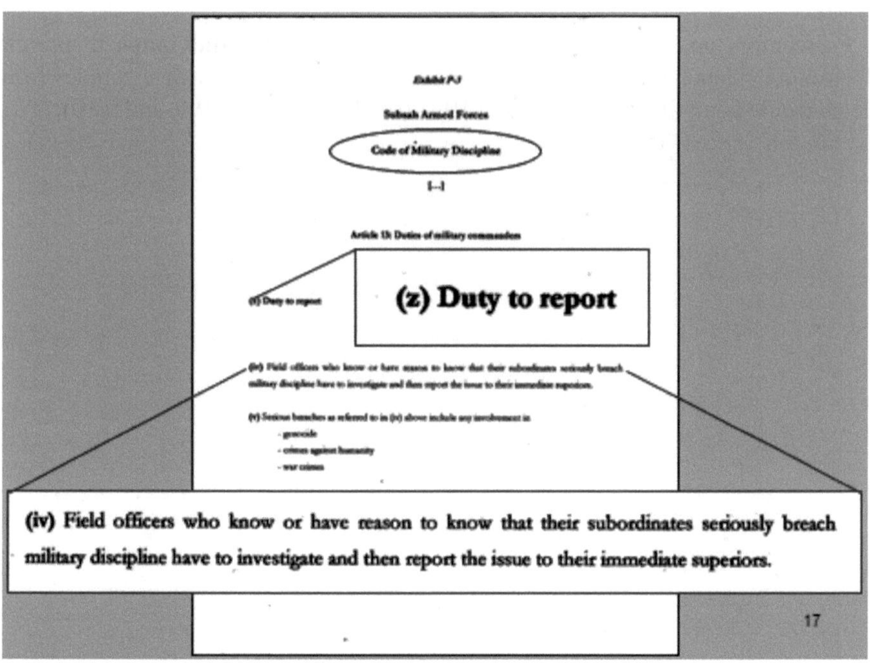

Fig. 9.5 Call-out and blow-up

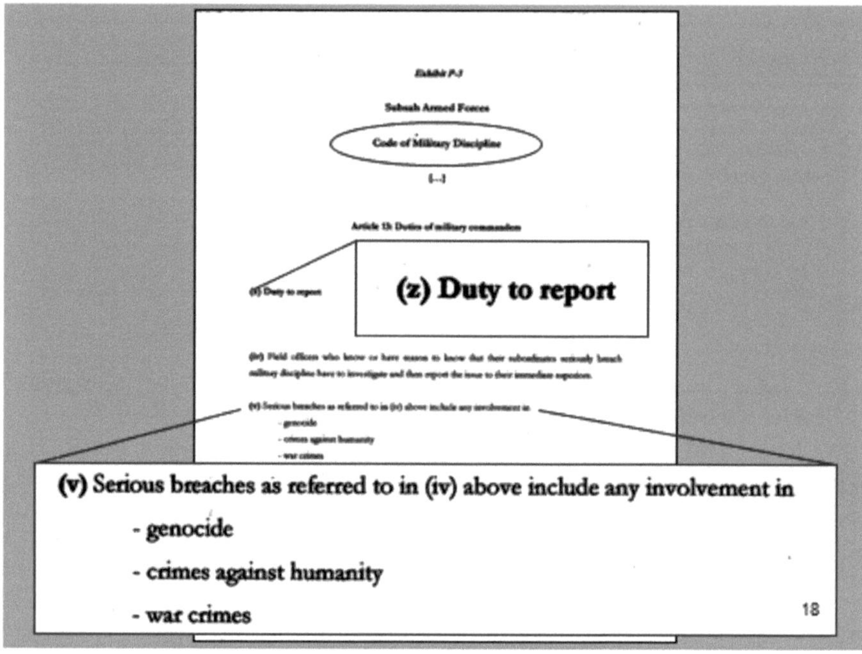

Fig. 9.6 Call-out and blow-up

Prosecutors and attorneys may also use **photographs and maps** to present electronic evidence in criminal trials. The following slides provide examples from the genocide committed in Rwanda in 1994 (see Figs. 9.7, 9.8, 9.9, and 9.10).

Fig. 9.7 Photograph of a massacre committed in a church

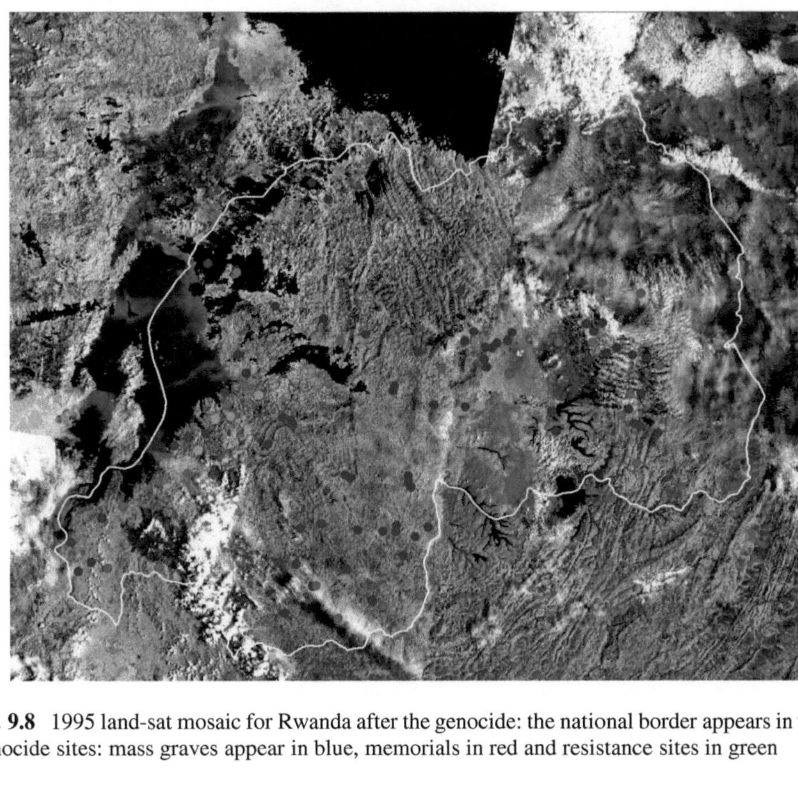

Fig. 9.8 1995 land-sat mosaic for Rwanda after the genocide: the national border appears in white. Genocide sites: mass graves appear in blue, memorials in red and resistance sites in green

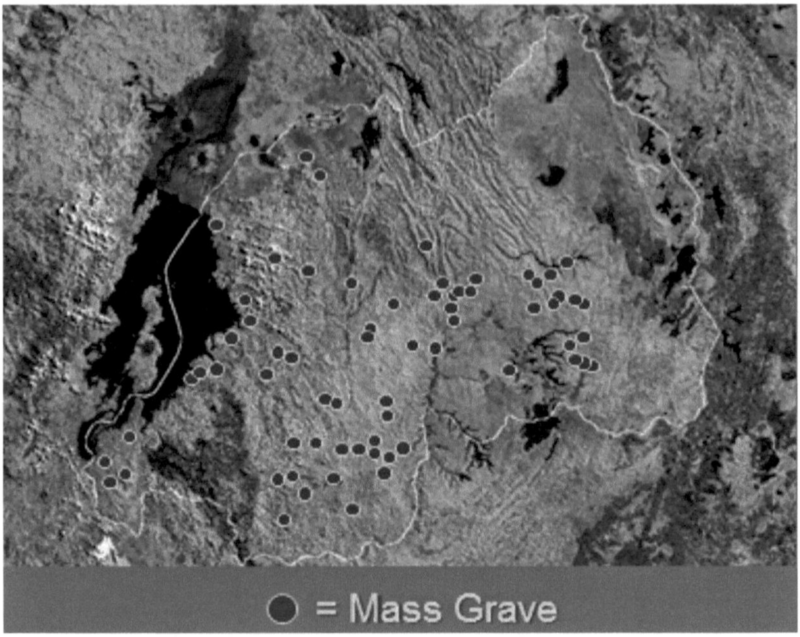

Fig. 9.9 Rwanda after the genocide

Fig. 9.10 RPF camps located in Uganda and Tanzania across the borders of Rwanda

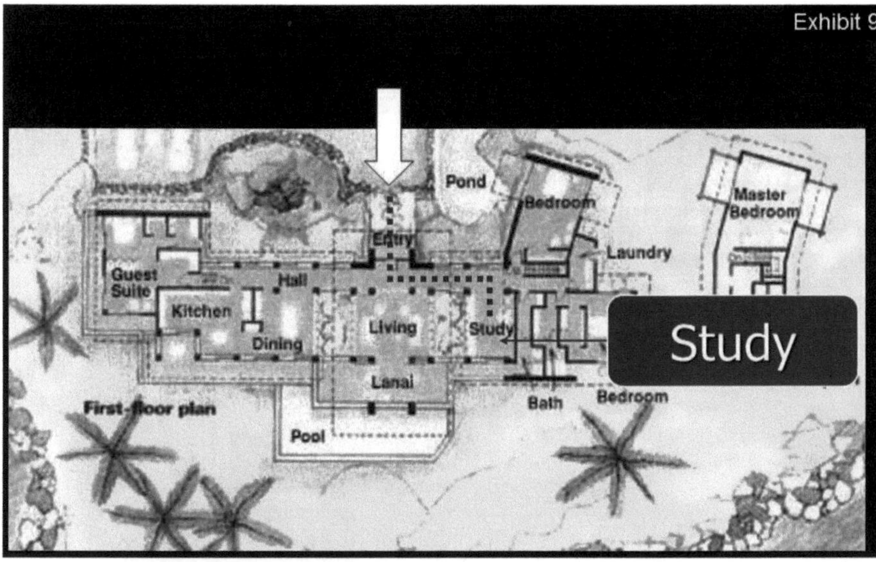

Fig. 9.11 Whereabouts of a person involved in a criminal case

	Witness 1	Witness 2	Witness 3
Colour of car	Dark	Blue	Greenish
Speed of car	50-55	at least 130	90

Fig. 9.12 Tables comparing inconsistent testimonies of witnesses

Prosecutors and attorneys may also use **overviews of facts and chronologies of events** to present electronic evidence in criminal trials. The following slide provides an example from a fictitious domestic case. The term "exhibit" clearly appears in the right hand corner of Fig. 9.11, thereby showing that it has been admitted into (electronic) evidence.

Prosecutors and attorneys may also use **tables comparing inconsistent testimonies of witnesses** (see Figs. 9.12, 9.13, and 9.14) to present electronic evidence.

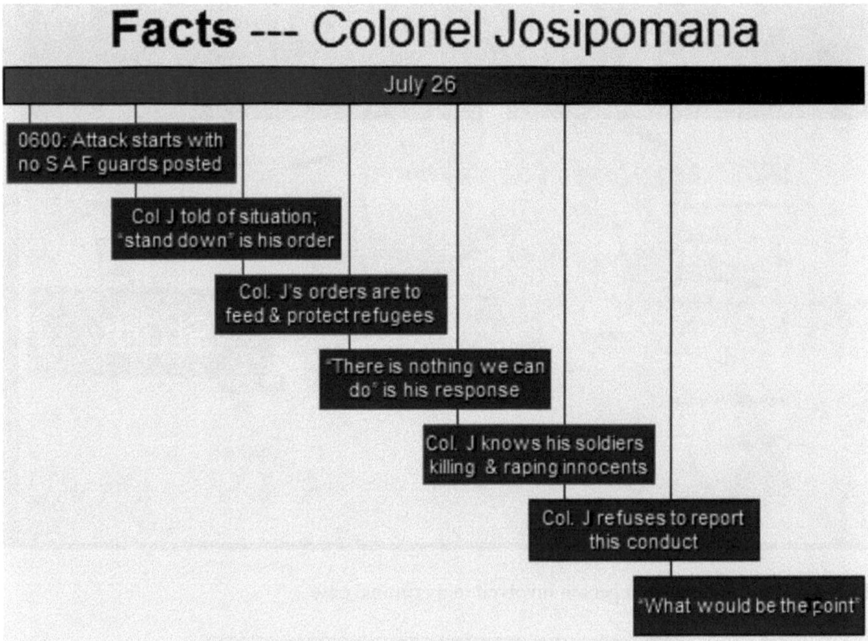

Fig. 9.13 Example of a timeline

Fig. 9.14 Example of a timeline

Last, prosecutors and attorneys may use **timelines** to present electronic evidence in criminal trials. The two following slides provide examples that mention fictitious personal data and facts.

9.4 Conclusion

In addition to criminal courts, prosecutors and attorneys may use PowerPoint presentations before military and civil including commercial courts of Member States. Beyond Member States, lawyers may also use PowerPoint presentations to litigate in the context of the EU.

In three cases, the General Court has for instance already granted requests of applicants to make PowerPoint presentations at hearings and requested them to submit paper versions.[1] The General Court found both the electronic and paper versions admissible.[2] Similarly, PowerPoint presentations may assist lawyers in making mainly factual arguments in hearings before Boards of Appeal of EU organisations[3] and Disciplinary Boards established pursuant to Article 9 of the Staff Regulations and Articles 3 and 5 of Annex IX thereto.

References

Biasotti MA (2017) A proposed electronic evidence exchange across the European Union. Digit Evid Electron Signature Law Rev 14:1–12

Bolzonello L (2016) Independent administrative review within the structure of remedies under the treaties: the case of the board of appeal of the European Chemicals Agency. Eur Public Law 22(3):565–577

Case law of the General Court: Cases T-74/12, T-75/12 and T-76/12, judgments of 18 November 2015, Mecafer SA v. Commission, Nu Air Polska sp z.o.o. v. Commission and Nu Air Compressors and Tools SpA v. Commission

Chirulli P, de Lucia L (2015) Specialised adjudication in EU administrative law: the boards of appeal of EU agencies. Eur Law Rev 40(6):832–857

[1]Cases T-74/12, T-75/12 and T-76/12, judgments of 18 November 2015, Mecafer SA v. Commission, Nu Air Polska sp z.o.o. v. Commission and Nu Air Compressors and Tools SpA v. Commission, paras 34 and 35.

[2]Ibidem, paras 36 to 38.

[3]Regarding Boards of Appeal of EU organisations, see Bolzonello (2016) and Chirulli and de Lucia (2015).

Part IV
Evidence Project Perspective

Chapter 10
The Conceptual Representation of the "Electronic Evidence" Domain

Sveva Avveduto, Sara Conti, Daniela Luzi, and Lucio Pisacane

Abstract The conceptual representation of the "Electronic Evidence" domain presented in this chapter aims at building a common language to identifying, connecting and aligning all relevant concepts for the systematic and uniform application of new technologies in the collection, use and exchange of evidence. For setting the domain boundaries, a literature review is presented along with the current standards used to define and handle Electronic Evidence. These sources of information allowed to identify a first set of terms and definitions used in the top-down extraction of relevant concepts to be considered the basis for the development of the full categorization exercise. In parallel, the gathered documentation was used to apply a bottom-up strategy that foresees a semi-automatic extraction of lemmas and syntagms, using a natural language processing technique. The results of this activity allowed the identification of further terms and concepts to enrich the top-down extraction. The research team identified eight classes to represent the Electronic Evidence domain: Crime, Source of Evidence, Process, Electronic Evidence, Requirement, Stakeholder, Rule, and Digital Forensics. These main classes have been hierarchically structured in sub-classes that may be easily updated and maintained. A SKOS structure, Simple Knowledge Organization System, was chosen to represent the domain. Finally considering that one of the main focuses of the EVIDENCE Project concerns the development of a framework for data exchange between judicial actors and LEAs, the study has taken into account the exchange of both digital-born evidence and of not digital-born one.

S. Avveduto · D. Luzi · L. Pisacane (✉)
CNR, Institute for Research on Population and Social Policies, Rome, Italy
e-mail: sveva.avveduto@irpps.cnr.it; daniela.luzi@irpps.cnr.it; lucio.pisacane@irpps.cnr.it

S. Conti
CNR, Institute of Legal Information Theory and Techniques, Florence, Italy
e-mail: sara.conti@ittig.cnr.it

M. A. Biasiotti et al. (eds.), *Handling and Exchanging Electronic Evidence Across Europe*, Law, Governance and Technology Series 39,
https://doi.org/10.1007/978-3-319-74872-6_10

10.1 Introduction

All legal proceedings rely on the production of evidence to take place. According to the Council of Europe[1]:

> Electronic Evidence is no different from traditional evidence in that is necessary for the party introducing it into legal proceedings, to be able to demonstrate that it is no more and no less than it was, when it came into their possession. In other words, no changes, deletions, additions or other alterations have taken place. The very nature of data and information held in electronic form makes it easier to manipulate than traditional forms of data.

When acquired and exchanged the integrity of information must be maintained and proved. Legislations on criminal procedures in many European countries were enacted before these technologies appeared, thus not considering them. Therefore, the Electronic Evidence treatment, as well as exchange among EU Member States jurisdictions, are based on different criteria and uncertain, not harmonized procedures. What is missing is a Common European Framework to guide policy makers, Law Enforcement Agencies (LEAs) and legal authorities when dealing with Electronic Evidence treatment and exchange.

The developments in information technologies, the process of digitization and the continuing globalization of computers networks have basically changed society and the occurred advancements have given rise to fundamental social changes. This revolution has also had a negative impact: the emergence of new types of crime, the commission of traditional crimes by means of new technologies, as well as new types of evidence that needed additional and specific ways of handling. The introduction and the extensive use of ICT has additionally generated new forms of crimes or new ways of perpetrating them, as well as a new type of evidences. This different setting implies that, although all kinds of evidences must be handled according to criminal law and procedures, the 'new' types of evidences need additional and specific ways of handling.

The use of Electronic Evidence has become therefore a necessary element to consider when solving a crime and conducting a fair trial. The electronic and digital evidence management and exchange is an emerging field with relevant connections with different scientific disciplines. The rapid changes in this landscape require a common background for all actors involved in the Electronic Evidence lifecycle (policy makers, LEAs, judges, lawyers, forensic scientist and investigators). Those are the emerging scientific and social aspects at the base that required the implementation of a knowledge systematization in the electronic evidence domain. The proposed categorization offers a common terminology base for the vast domain bearing into account the twofold challenges to be considered according to the Electronic Evidence lifecycle:

- the treatment of evidence/data/information by means of ICT in the context of criminal law, considering the entire evidence lifecycle from the incident on, passing through the investigative phase;

---

[1]See Council of Europe (2013), p. 6.

- the exchange of evidence/data/information by means of ICT complying with the issues related to specific requirements and shared procedures.

10.2 A Snapshot of Electronic Evidence and Its Exchange

The following sequence of illustrations[2]—from Figs. 10.1 to 10.2—provides an example of the activities regarding the identification, investigation and presentation before a Court of Electronic Evidence, showing the different actors involved. It is a simplified view that does not consider possible loops and interactions that may occur during the process. The last illustration, Exchanging Electronic Evidences in Europe shows the possible evolution of the exchange process after the achievement of the Project objectives: contribute to the constructions of the missing Common European Framework for the systematic and uniform collection, use and exchange of Electronic Evidence.

10.3 Electronic Evidence Across Disciplines

According to Ćosić and Ćosić (2011), Talib and Alomary (2015) the difficulty of providing a conceptual representation of the electronic evidence domain depends on the need to consider the different aspects of a highly multidisciplinary sector. An ontology or a categorization of the domain would require the knowledge organization of both the technical aspects and the legal ones, considering the procedural implications of evidence presentation in court. This multidisciplinary approach is evident when considering two relevant disciplines, the digital forensics and diplomatic, that contribute to the development of research and methodologies in this area.

Forensic sciences deal with the application of scientific methods and techniques of investigation of criminal offenses and, particularly, of the acquisition, storage, analysis and presentation of evidences that are placed in an increasing number of electronic and digital devices. This multiplicity of sources of evidence is creating, as shown by Daniel and Daniel (2011), a specialization in sub-disciplines (from the cell forensics to GPS forensics to Social network and cloud forensics) that best identify appropriate techniques and tools to manage the various types of electronic evidence.

On the other hand, the idea of conceptualizing the source of evidence and to outline the transition from general evidence into electronic evidence, and to establish rules and methods to ensure its authenticity over time, have become important topics even in diplomatics. The science of diplomacy has its origins in the seventeenth century to establish the authenticity and, indirectly, the reliability of the archival

[2]Credits: illustrations by Gaia Soldatini. www.gaiasoldatini.com

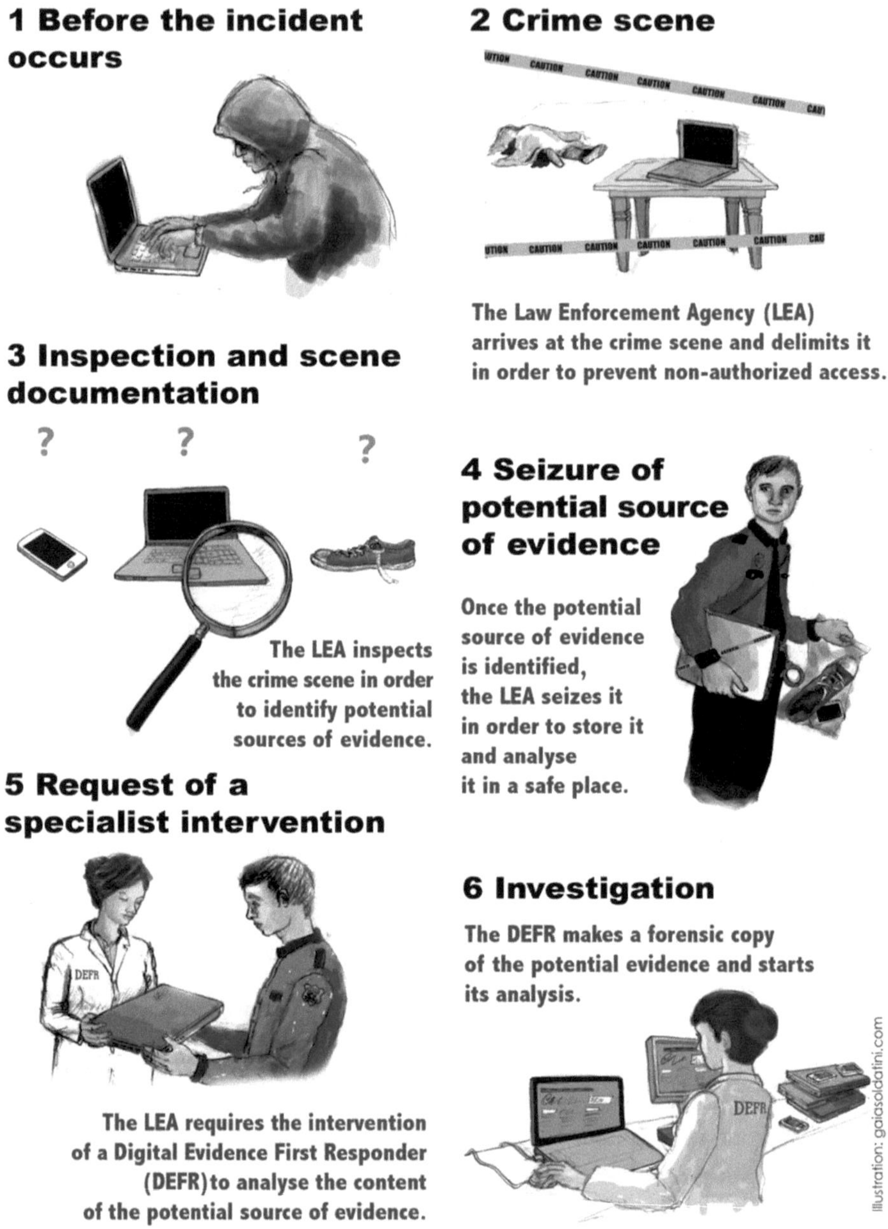

Fig. 10.1 A snapshot of Electronic Evidence and its exchange, steps 1–6

documents to determine the rights of people and to identify and eliminate false documents. It studies the origins, forms, and transmission of documents and the relationships of the various records associated with actions, persons, and legal consequences.

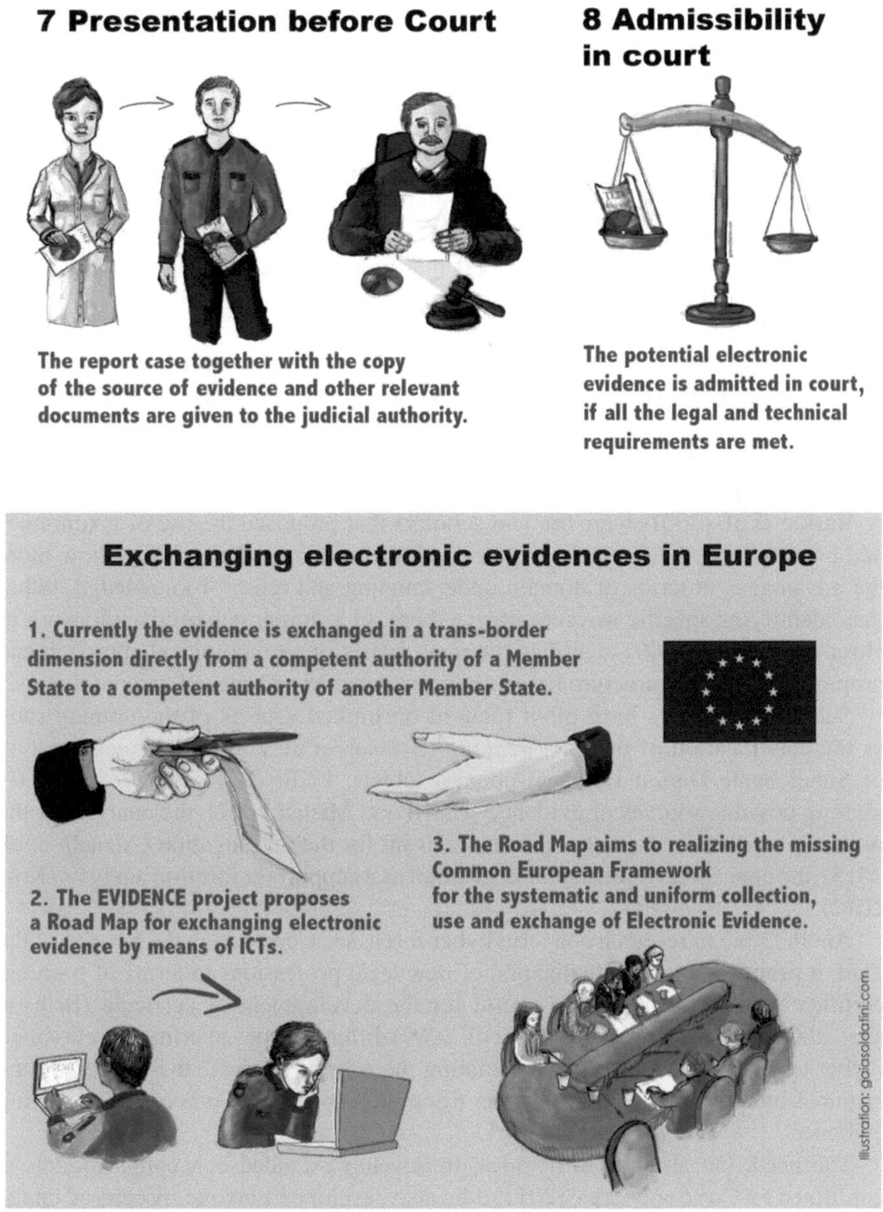

Fig. 10.2 A snapshot of Electronic Evidence and its exchange, steps 7–8

Digital diplomatics has recently developed a framework for evaluating the authenticity of digital documents and can offer a powerful method for analysing them. This field is making an important contribution, stating the principle of "record trustworthiness" (Duranti 1995, 2009). This principle has two quality dimensions: reliability and authenticity. The record should then be able to ensure the reliability of the facts to which it is related, and at the same time his own authenticity: the record is what it declares to be. The concept of reliability of the records as an evidence has been of particular interest in the EVIDENCE project, where the electronic evidence is reliable if it is the result of a process that monitors and evaluates its reliability, authenticity and trustworthiness.

Those disciplines provide the framework for the management of electronic evidence by identifying a series of fundamental principles and methods. It is worth mentioning also the studies aimed at providing a conceptual representation of the domain, actually not many because of the already mentioned difficulties to represent a multidisciplinary field continuously evolving. However, they represented useful insights closely related to our categorization work.

Raskin et al. (2001) were the first scholars that proposed the use of taxonomies and ontologies in the field of computer and information security. They show more the advantages in terms of domain understanding and reuse of knowledge, rather than identifying specific ways to achieve them. In a similar perspective the work of Hoss and Carver (2009) identifies the main issues of an ontological approach and proposes an abstract structure based on interconnected and specialized ontologies.

Subsequent studies have often focused on limited aspects of the domain such as the classification of the data tracking (Brinson et al. 2006), the categorization of Small Scale Digital Devices (phones, tablets, USB, etc.) useful for properly treating possible sources of evidence (Harril and Mislan 2007), the analysis of the information contained in smartphones relevant for the investigation (Alzaabi et al. 2015), the conceptual representation of email as a support for forensic analysis (Kota 2012).

Another line of research concerns cyber forensics. Considering the novelty of the field, it proposes a conceptualization of new legal professions in terms of training, certification and specialization useful for the development of curricula (Brinson et al. 2006). In another paper (Park et al. 2009) different types of crime are classified (cyber terrorism, hacking, etc.) associating them with "objects" that can prove the criminal intent, however, limiting the discussion to just the process of acquiring evidence.

The need, but also the difficulties, to develop extended conceptual models is confirmed by Ćosić and Ćosić (2011) who also developed a taxonomy centred on the "chain of custody" to help experts to identify standard procedures for the treatment of electronic evidence (Ćosić and Ćosić 2011, 2012). Moreover, the debate on the possibility of building sufficiently large ontologies to understand all the concepts of interest for forensic investigation is still open (Huang et al. 2010). However recent works (Karie and Venter 2014; Talib and Alomary 2015) have undertaken the first steps in this direction.

10.4 Electronic Evidence Legal and Technical Scenario

European Member States in Europe have fundamentally different criminal legal systems and different tradition in the sources of criminal law. That is, there is a lack of uniformity within Member States criminal legislations and most of them adopted their rules on evidence long before the coming of the digital era, continuing to apply traditional ones to electronic evidence (Koops and Robinson 2011). Solutions to the raised problems tried to be addressed by International and European Union law, through the adoption of legal and technical measures.

The Council of Europe and the European Union are, in this respect, two supranational entities that have influenced and are influencing, with their activities and with their measures, national legislation on cybercrime and consequently in the field of collection, storage and exchange of Electronic Evidence related to a particular offense. Their action aims to create a common legal substrate at European level and represents a challenge to the implementation of legislative harmonization between the various EU countries and with third States.

Specifically, the Council of Europe aims to protect societies worldwide from the threat of cybercrime through the provisions of the Convention on Cybercrime.[3]

This is an international instrument signed as a response to the different legal computer crime initiatives taken in Europe and it might be an ongoing instrument of interaction between national and international initiatives to keep the national legal cybercrime framework up to date (Marion 2010).

The aim of the Convention is to "harmonize the domestic criminal substantive law elements of offences and connected provisions in the area of cybercrime, providing for domestic criminal procedural law powers necessary for the investigation and prosecution of such offences, as well as other offences, committed by means of a computer system, with due respect to human rights in the new Information Society" (Ciurea 2010; Clough 2014; Gatt 2002).

The Convention serves as a guideline against Cybercrime for Member States of the Council of Europe and the other signatory States and establishes principles for international cooperation between State Parties to the treaty itself (Weber 2003). The Convention is divided in four parts, concerning: the use of terms (chapter I), measures to be taken at domestic level (chapter II), international cooperation (chapter III), final clause (chapter IV). Section 1 of Chapter II (substantive law issues) has been relevant to our point of view.[4] More specifically, this section refers to the definition of offences, grouped in four different categories (offences against the confidentiality, integrity and availability of computer data and system; computer-related offences; content-related offences, finally offences related to infringements

[3]Convention on Cybercrime, Budapest 23 Nov 2011, see http://www.coe.int/en/web/conventions/full-list/-/conventions/treaty/185.

[4]Explanatory Report to the Convention on Cybercrime, https://www.coe.int/en/web/conventions/full-list/-/conventions/treaty/185.

of copyright and related rights) dealing with the use of computer networks and Internet.

Moreover, for each of the mentioned categories, specific offences are defined and described: such as, illegal access, illegal interception, data interference, system interference, misuse of devices, computer-related forgery, computer-related fraud, offences related to child pornography and offences related to copyright and related rights. The purpose of Section 1 of the Convention (Articles 2–13) is to improve the means to prevent and repress computer- or computer—related crime, by establishing a common minimum standard of relevant offences.

The conceptual representation of the Electronic Evidence domain based on these distinctions: the different offences have represented a starting point to build up our categorization, as the basis for the development of the "legal" classes and subclasses of the categorization itself (particularly, class Crime and subclass Cybercrime, finally the class Rule). Another important point of reference for the "legal classes" have been several initiatives, at EU level, addressed to create a common framework to combat crime in general, and cybercrime, by establishing a cooperation between Member States.

Within this scenario, the Convention on mutual assistance in criminal matters[5] aims to facilitate mutual judicial assistance, between the authorities of the Member States to improve the speed and efficiency of judicial cooperation. Even if the Convention does not refer explicitly to electronic evidence, and to evidence in general, it has been essential to Electronic Evidence categorization, because of its value to combat crimes, which are committed across borders, and to create a common framework in criminal proceedings.

Worth mentioning is the European Evidence Warrant (EEW), which may be used to obtain any objects, documents and data for use in criminal proceedings for which it may be issued. For example, this encompasses "documents or data from a third party, from a search of premises including the private premises of the suspect, historical data on the use of any services including financial transactions, historical records of statements, interviews and hearings, and other records, including the results of special investigative techniques".[6]

The European Evidence Warrant may be a key element of the criminal justice cooperation within the EU Member States. The EEW found its legal basis on the principle of mutual recognition, which is the cornerstone for mutual legal assistance in criminal matters within the Union. As the Convention on mutual assistance in criminal matters, the EEW aims to facilitate speedier cooperation between Member States in criminal proceedings, but specifically in the transfer of evidence (Murphy 2011).

[5]Council Act of 29 May 2000, establishing in accordance with Article 34 of the Treaty on European Union the Convention on Mutual Assistance in Criminal Matters between the Member States of the European Union.

[6]Council Framework Decision 2008/978/of 18 December 2008 on the European evidence warrant for obtaining objects, documents and data for use in proceedings in criminal matters.

A significant role for the "legal classes" of the Electronic Evidence categorization has been also played by the Directive 2013/40/EU of the European Parliament and of the Council of 12 August 2013, on "Attacks against information systems",[7] and by the Directive 2014/41 of the Parliament and of the Council of 3 April 2014, on the "European Investigation Order"[8] (EIO).

The purpose of the first one is to create a common framework in the attacks against information systems, by establishing "minimum rules concerning the definition of criminal offences and sanctions" in that field. Particularly, the Directive aims to tackle large-scale cyber-attacks by requiring Member States to strengthen national cybercrime legislation and to introduce strict criminal sanctions. The Directive provides for common definitions in the attacks against information systems: these definitions comprise offences of illegal access to an information system, illegal system interference, illegal data interference and illegal interception.

An in-deep analyzes of the EIO has been carried out because of its relation to other legal instruments at EU level: the Directive 2014/41 will replace, as from 22 May 2017, the corresponding provisions of the EU Convention on mutual assistance in criminal matters and the Framework Decision 2008/978. Based on the principle of mutual recognition of judgments and judicial decisions and on the necessity of immediate mutual recognition of orders to prevent the destruction, transformation, moving, transfer or disposal of evidence, the EIO is to be issued to have one or several specific investigative measure(s) carried out in the State executing the order ("the executing State"). This order should apply to all investigative measures aimed at gathering evidence and it will foster the gradual increase of a comprehensive system for obtaining evidence, in cases with a cross-border dimension.

All these instruments at International and European level demonstrate and strengthen the importance of a common effort in preventing and combating crimes, and especially cybercrime, trying to create a strict cooperation between States. But all these instruments show a fragmentary and incomplete regime: there is no comprehensive harmonization and common procedures in the field of criminal proceedings and, above all, when dealing with Electronic Evidence treatment and exchange. Developing a common and shared language on the Electronic Evidence domain has properly been the aim of the categorization, as a starting point for providing a legal framework for the systematic and uniform application of new technologies in the collection, use and exchange of electronic evidence in the criminal field.

According to this point of view, to make it possible, it is necessary to build the "legal" classes and subclasses of our categorization considering the definitions of the Convention on cybercrime, and in general with a specific view to all the EU criminal legislation, as to have a common minimum standard of offences and terms within

[7]Directive 2013/40/EU of the European Parliament and of the Council of 12 August 2013 on attacks against information systems and replacing Council Framework Decision 2005/222/JH.

[8]Directive 2014/41/EU of the European Parliament and of the Council of 3 April 2014 regarding the European Investigation Order in criminal matters.

the Electronic Evidence domain. This approach of creating a common minimum basis in the field of Electronic Evidence categorization has also been carried out when studying another group of important sources: the ISO International Digital Forensics Standards (ISO/IEC 27037 2012), which aim at promoting good practices in forensic investigation involving Electronic Evidence.

The ISO 27037 (ISO/IEC 27037 2012) was mainly relevant for the categorization: in fact, the standard aims at providing guidance on the identification, collection and/or acquisition, marking, storage, transport and preservation of electronic evidence, especially to maintain its integrity. The processes described by this standard are associated with legal principles and technical requisites that must be satisfied to make Electronic Evidence admissible in Court. The choice to consider ISO 27037 was made considering both the authoritative nature of the standard and the detailed description of all the activities that need to be carried out to fulfill the principle of relevance, reliability and sufficiency of any Electronic Evidence.

Because of this feature, the processes and the terms identified by the ISO 27037 have been used to develop the classes and subclasses of the categorization (particularly, the class "Process" and the class "Rule") to achieve an acceptable and qualified methodology that may assist in the facilitation of electronic evidence exchange between different jurisdictions.

10.5 Methodology

The Evidence Project developed a model for the categorization of the domain "Electronic Evidence" with a dual function. The first was to map a universe characterized by strong ambiguity in the definitions and the relations among concepts. This objective has been addressed to create a common language for the project partners, to count on shared definitions of the main classes of the domain and to build the common research activities. Secondly the categorization has identified the main relationships between the classes of concepts and was therefore used with purely research purposes to guide the detailed work towards concepts identified according to a relationship logic.

The first goal was to determine the domain boundaries. To achieve this purpose a threefold action was taken: the examination of the relevant literature, the consultation with various internal partners and external stakeholders identified by the Project.

We analyzed and collected in full text 128 sources that include, in addition to scholarly articles and books, guidelines and standards used by major agencies to define and manage electronic evidence, and specific reports. These sources of information have allowed us to identify a first set of terms and definitions to be used for the top-down extraction of the relevant concepts to be considered as a basis for the development of categorization. In parallel, the documentation collected was used to apply a bottom-up approach that allowed the semi-automatic extraction of terms and phrases, using a natural language processing technique. This allowed us to verify, on the one hand, the validity of the concepts collected manually and on the other, to identify additional terms and concepts to be included in the categorization also based on the number of occurrences and the context in which they appeared.

Starting from the results of this dual strategy we identified the concepts on which it was possible to build the first level of classes that were then associated to sub-classes that represent instances of the conceptual model.

To represent the categorization, it was decided to use the SKOS system, Simple Knowledge Organization System, which allows a graphical display and a semantic description of the categorization items, as well as a structuring into classes and subclasses. This tool was selected also for its user friendliness considering that the EVIDENCE partners may not have the necessary background to deal with ontological structures. Moreover, SKOS modular and flexible features facilitate the representation of the main concepts expressed in a structured controlled vocabulary as the basis for an agreed terminology by the project partners that can be gradually updated and improved. Exploiting SKOS labelling and documentation properties, we defined and then correlated these concepts building also relations between classes and subclasses based on the type of relationship and association that bind the different concepts. The definitions have been specified in a separate tab (Definition, Scope Notes, Related Terms, etc.) then merged in SKOS: all entries can be viewed online at http://www.evidenceproject.eu/categorization. The Categorization can be viewed on line in dynamic mode, including the "explosion" function of the classes, thus facilitating the users' scrolling between the various classes, concepts and subclasses.

10.6 Defining Digital and Electronic Evidence

The analysis of the most significant sources of information demonstrated that there is no uniform use of the terms that identify this domain: electronic evidence or digital evidence. Indeed, both terms are accepted and used by the scientific community. We can refer to two relevant documents to show this feature. The International Standard Document, ISO/IEC 27037 prefers the term digital evidence, because it refers to data that is already in a digital format and does not cover the conversion from analogical data into digital one. On the other hand, the authoritative source such as the Council of Europe, has opted for the term Electronic Evidence in its Guide. Preferences may derive from a major focus given to the growing number of digital tools and devices that store, elaborate and transmit data of probative values.

Moreover, there are many different definitions of "Electronic/Digital Evidence", each of them highlighting some essential features. The followings are the main definitions, emphasized in italics, we have analyzed so far.

One of the first definition available in this domain, nowadays far too old, is the one suggested by the research activities promoted by the Scientific Working Group on Digital Evidence (SWGDE)—FBI that in 1998 defined Digital Evidence as:

> Digital Evidence is any information of probative value that is either stored or transmitted in a digital form (SWGDE 2000).

A few years later the International Organization of Computer Evidence defined Electronic Evidence as:

> Electronic Evidence is any information stored or transmitted in binary form that may be relied upon in court.[9]

Casey (2011) comments that these definitions "focus on proof in court and neglect data that can make an investigation advance further". He also adds that the term "binary" is "inexact describing just one of many common representations of computer data" (Casey 2011). This term is currently not used anymore and SWGDE changed the term "binary" with "digital" to include digital audio, video, etc. (Whitcomb 2002).

The scholar Brian Carrier proposed a general definition:

> Digital Evidence is any digital data that support or refute a hypothesis about digital events or the state of digital data (Carrier 2006).

Recently, Casey proposed a new definition

> Digital Evidence is any data stored or transmitted using a computer that support or refute a theory of how an offense occurred or that address critical elements of the offense such as intent or alibi (Casey 2011).

This definition does not refer directly to the acceptance in courts and therefore includes information produced during the investigative activities. Mason and Schafer criticized the emphasis on criminal investigation as not being general enough to explicitly include relevant and admissible evidence, as well as the parties (both practitioners and lawyers) involved in a trial. Moreover, as Mason and Schafer noted, it can be assumed that the word "computer" is "to be understood in its widest possible sense", incorporating "any form of device that store, manipulates and transmits data" (Schafer and Mason 2012).

A similar focus on the device is contained in the broad ranging definition developed by the ACPO—UK (Association of Chief Police Officers) in 2012 that reports that:

> Digital Evidence is any information and data of investigative value that are stored on or transmitted by a computer (Association of Chief Police Officers UK).

The already cited Guide by the Council of Europe (2013), used the term Electronic Evidence to include all possible devices that generate and/or store potential Electronic Evidence. This standpoint has been adopted also by the EVIDENCE

[9]The International Organization of Computer Evidence is no longer active. The definition was adopted by IOCE in 2000 as a working definition.

project as explained hereafter. The Council of Europe Guide defines Electronic Evidence as:

> Electronic Evidence is any information generated, stored or transmitted using electronic devices that may be relied upon in court. To guarantee that the evidence is accepted in court, it is necessary to obtain the information following very well defined processes using specialised personnel and operating within an adequate legal framework (Council of Europe 2013).

The scholars Schafer and Mason also opted for the term Electronic Evidence that is defined as follows:

> Electronic Evidence is data (comprising the output of analogue devices or data in digital format) that is manipulated, stored or communicated by any man-made device, computer or computer system or transmitted over a communication system, that has the potential to make the factual account of either party more probable or less probable than it would be without the evidence (Schafer and Mason 2012).

This definition, as Schafer and Mason explain, is based on three elements:

a. it includes all forms of evidence;
b. it also includes the various form of devices by which data can be stored or transmitted;
c. it emphasizes the aspect of relevance (being admissibility a criteria that the adjudicator evaluates based on different principles) and "restrict the definition of Electronic Evidence to those items offered by the parties as part of the fact-finding process".

However, none of the definitions mentioned above were considered satisfactory for the needs of the project, which has adopted its own one as the basis of the categorization exercise that can, in our view, capture all the different aspects as it is based on a general level of abstraction. The project has therefore chosen to use the term electronic evidence including in it both the digital born evidence and those that during their lifecycle are transformed, stored or exchanged in an electronic form. The following is the definition adopted by the EVIDENCE Project: "*Electronic Evidence is any information of potential or tangible probative value that is generated through, stored on or transmitted by any electronic device*"

10.7 From the "Electronic Evidence" Domain Analysis to the Class Categorization

The Categorization development is based on the extraction of concepts from the relevant literature and on the identification and classification of the building blocks modelled on the lifecycle of Electronic Evidence.

Figure 10.3 shows a simplified view of the Electronic Evidence lifecycle: from the evidence origin (liked to a specific crime) till the presentation as admissible evidence in a Court for a civil or penal proceeding.

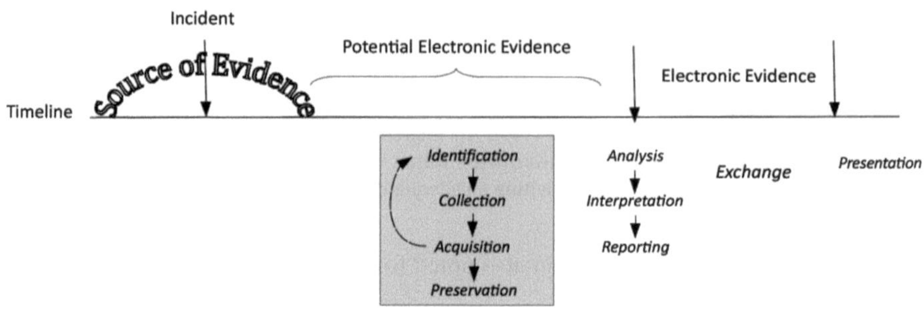

Fig. 10.3 Electronic Evidence processes and lifecycle

The very first milestone starts with an incident, defined as an unlawful criminal, civil or commercial act, and sets the scene for the Electronic Evidence lifecycle scenario. Indeed, an artefact or a data enters into the forensic process only if an incident forces it to do so. Otherwise, for all its natural lifespan the artefact or data will remain outside the forensic process and thus forensically irrelevant—although it may continue to be relevant to its user or owner. Figure 10.1 represents a simplified view of the whole process involved in the evidence lifecycle, for example it does not consider many other sub-processes, such as obtaining authorization, chain of custody, documenting that are all essential for making the potential evidence admissible before a Court. However, it highlights the main processes of the investigation phase in which a potential Electronic Evidence is identified, collected, and acquired (this may be repeated over time) and then safely preserved. The following step includes the phases of analysis, interpretation and reporting that are related to the transition from a potential to an Electronic Evidence. In this time span the exchange of Electronic Evidence may occur between judicial actors. Then Electronic Evidence is presented in courts. Evidence presented in court can be further analyzed by other parties involved in the trials.

The categorization is organized in eight main classes: Crime, Source of Electronic Evidence, Process, Electronic Evidence, Requirement, Stakeholder, Rule, Digital Forensics. Figure 10.4 shows the conceptual model that underpins the classes of the categorization illustrating the main relationships at a high level of detail. The core of the categorization is the class Electronic Evidence that relates all the other classes. The Electronic Evidence class is related with the class Source of Evidence (through the relation) is "contained in" and is "managed" following specific Processes and is "validated" according to legal and technical Requirements, generally studied in the different disciplines of Digital Forensics and it "concerns with" different types of Crimes. Finally, different types of Stakeholders are concerned with the Electronic Evidence, who apply specific Rules, such as standards, soft and hard laws to examine it.

In the figure arrows represent the relationship direction. This allows to visualize, in addition to relationship among Classes, the polarity of relationship among them.

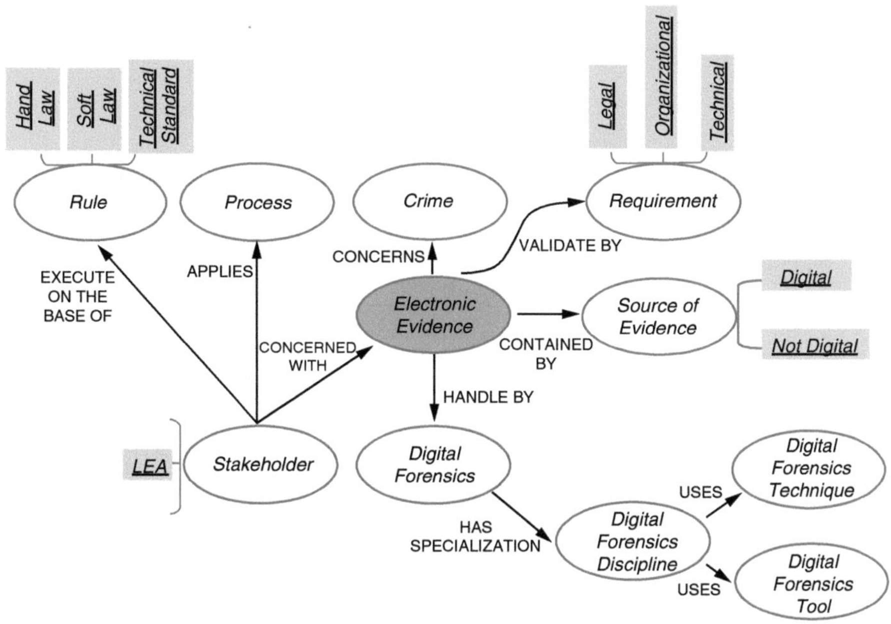

Fig. 10.4 Categorization relationships at high level

The Classes have been described in detail in EVIDENCE project report[10] and therefore, we illustrate here a brief explanation of their structure. The Classes together with their description are presented thought a tree structure that included the different subclasses and their instances with the relative concepts and scope notes. In the specific case of the Stakeholder Class we expand the description to main definition of the class, the sub classes and the relative concepts and scope notes. For the remaining Classes the main concept definitions and structure are presented. All the Classes, subclasses and concepts included in the Categorization have univocal definition to shape a common language in the domain.

10.8 The Categorization Classes

The Class Stakeholder, whose hierarchical view is shown in Fig. 10.5, comprises actors or organizations having a concern in or playing a specific role in the Electronic Evidence lifecycle. This Class encompasses both private and public actors: experts involved in the Electronic Evidence and all the professional working

[10]See the deliverable D2.1—EVIDENCE Semantic Structure at http://s.evidenceproject.eu/p/e/v/evidence-ga-608185-d2-1-410.pdf.

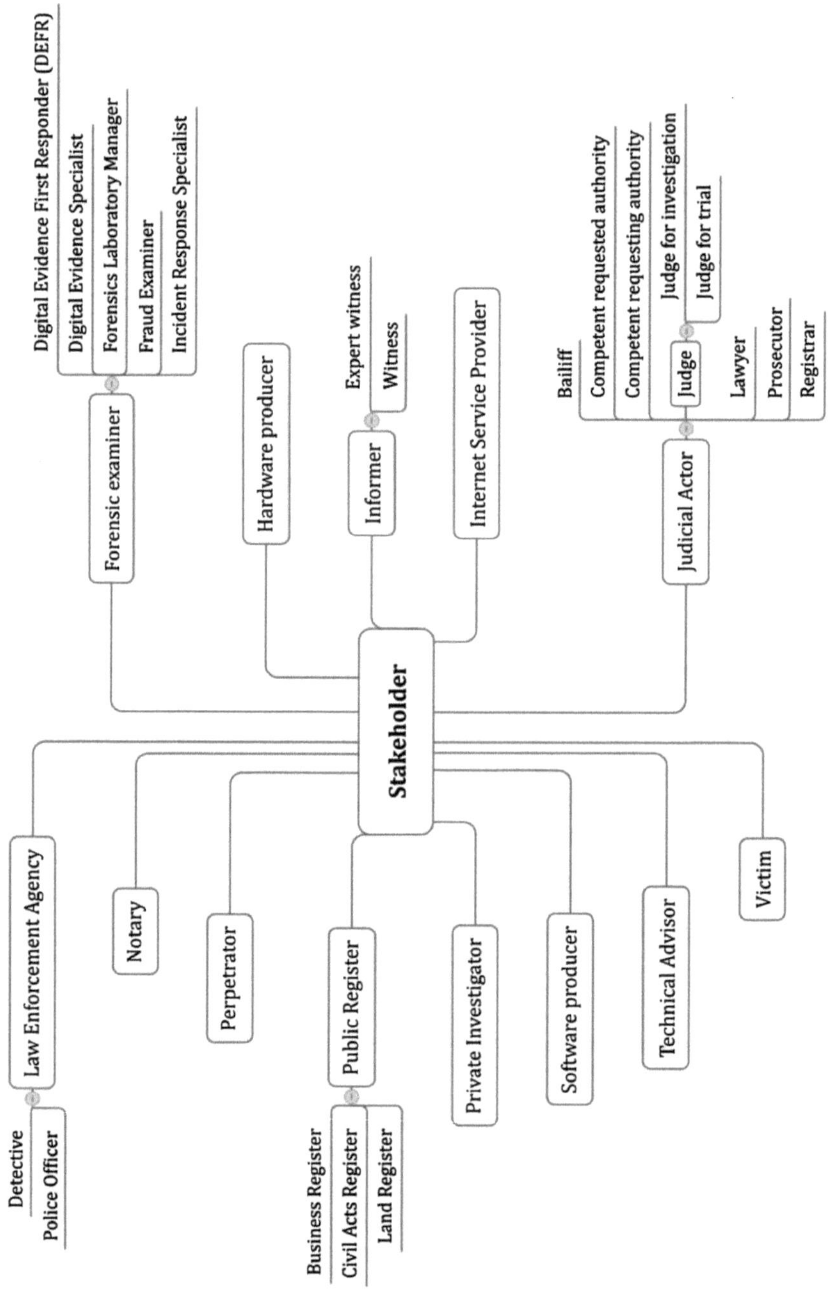

Fig. 10.5 Hierarchical view of Stakeholder Class

in a Court. Public Institution such as Police Agency and Law Enforcement Agencies (LEAs) are included as main entitled actors to face crime and to use and exchange Electronic Evidence. In addition, private actors engaged in tackling crime (investigators and experts) are included. An additional subclass "Public register" has been introduced to include stakeholders that preserve other types of evidence, including civil act, land proprieties—increasingly in digital form—that could be exchanged and used by European Courts. Moreover, the Forensic examiner subclass is particularly important because computer forensics as a discipline demands specially trained personnel, support from management, and the necessary funding to keep a unit operating. Finally this Class includes victims or perpetrators of crime as the relevant stakeholders involved in Electronic Evidence.

Each subclasses showed in Fig. 10.5 have specific instances that are defined in the Categorization and enclosed with a *Scope Note*. In addition, each subclass is associated with specific relationship both within the same Class or to other Classes. Table 10.1 shows as an example the Scope Note for the subclass Law Enforcement Agency with corresponding definition, the reference its source and RT Relations.

The Categorization adopted language is English. A linguistic alignment of concepts in different languages would require not only a translation of terms, but also the compliance with specific legal and judicial systems, as well as with the specific context in which those concepts are used (legislation, case law, European, domestic, etc.).

The class Crime (Fig. 10.6) comprises an act, default or conduct prejudicial to the community for which the person responsible may, by law, be punished by fine or imprisonment. Considering the specific focus of the Categorization, the subclass Cyber-crime has been structured according to EU legal Framework referring to crimes identified by the Budapest Convention, as well as to those specifically described by EU law (Directive 2013/40/EU of the European Parliament and of the Council of 12 August 2013 on attacks against information systems and replacing Council Framework Decision 2005/222/JHA).

Table 10.1 Scope note example: Law enforcement agencies

Law enforcement agencies (LEAs)
Definition
A government agency responsible for the enforcement of laws
Editorial note
Definition based on Oxford dictionary
RT Relation
LEAs—*enforce* Hard law
LEAs—*suggest* Soft law
LEAs—*struggle against*—cyber-crime
LEAs—*struggles against*—Act against the security of the state
LEAs—*struggles against*—Act against peace
LEAs—*struggles against*—Act against the environment
LEAs—*struggles against*—Act against individual
LEAs—*struggles against*—Act against property

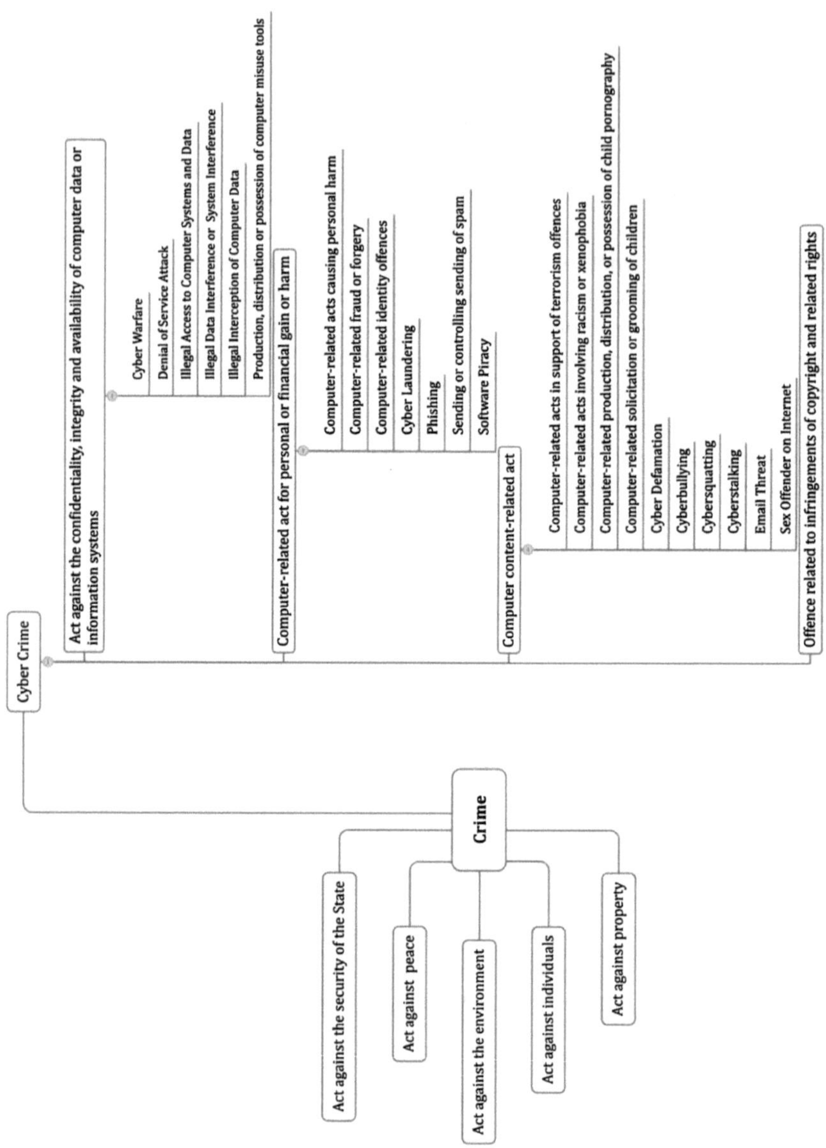

Fig. 10.6 Hierarchical view of Crime Class

The Source of Electronic Evidence is defined as any physical, analogical and digital device (computer or computer like device) capable of creating information that may have a probative value in courts. This definition allows to distinguish between tangible devices (computers, cameras, etc.) and data and information contained in these devices. Tangible devices may be inspected to find data and information (evidence) that may have probative value in courts and provide a link between a crime and its victim or a crime and its perpetrator. To distinguish between different sources of potential evidence, the class Source of Electronic Evidence (Fig. 10.7) is divided into two sub-classes: "Digital Source" meant to group those sources of evidences connected to computer or computer like devices and the "not Digital Source" subclass grouping those sources recognized as analogical or physical one.

The class Process, whose hierarchical view is shown in Fig. 10.8, encompasses the set of sub-processes/activities carried out on potential Electronic Evidence to maintain its integrity, demonstrate its relevance, reliability and sufficiency, as well as to make it admissible in court. This class is divided into three main sub-classes to distinguish between the activities carried out when dealing with a digital-born evidence and the cases when evidence—both not electronic and/or analogical—must be digitized. This choice was made considering both the authoritative nature of ISO standards and the detailed description of all the activities that need to be carried out to fulfill the principle of relevance, reliability and sufficiency of any electronic evidence. Moreover, a specific class Exchange between courts has been introduced to represent the activities carried out by Courts.

The Class Electronic Evidence, whose hierarchical view is shown in Fig. 10.9, encompasses the different forms that Electronic Evidence may assume. As already pointed out he concepts Electronic Evidence and Source of Electronic Evidence are strictly connected, as the first represents the logical form, while the second one represents the physical form from which the Evidence may be detected. Electronic Evidence is any information that may have probative value in Courts generated by or kept in an electronic device. This Class was foreseen to include the various forms that Electronic Evidence may have. This Class is potentially unlimited, both for the continuing ICT developments and because of the progressive acceptance of different forms of Electronic Evidence by Courts. The first (Human Generated) refers to the Evidence that may be produced intentionally by human interaction with an electronic device. The second (Automatic Generated) groups traces that electronic devices produce automatically: this sub-class comprises various automatically produced information ranging from automated telephone records, ISP logs, and automatic teller records. The human/automatic classification was proposed for the first time by Casey (2011).

The Class requirements (Fig. 10.10) represent criteria and principles related both to legal rules and handling procedures to make a potential Electronic Evidence admissible in court. Moreover, procedures and best practices applied in investigations are based on managerial aspects that pertain the organization supporting the investigation, the so-called Forensics Readiness. To represent these concepts, we

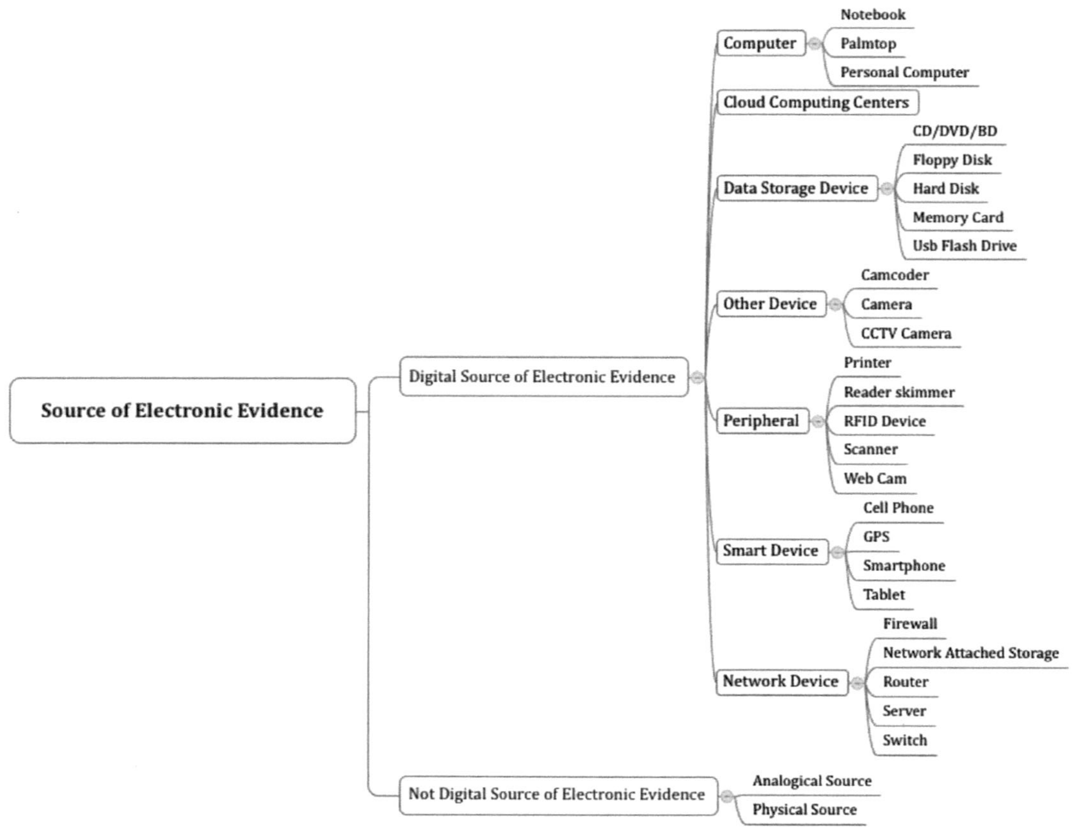

Fig. 10.7 Hierarchical view of Source of Electronic Evidence Class

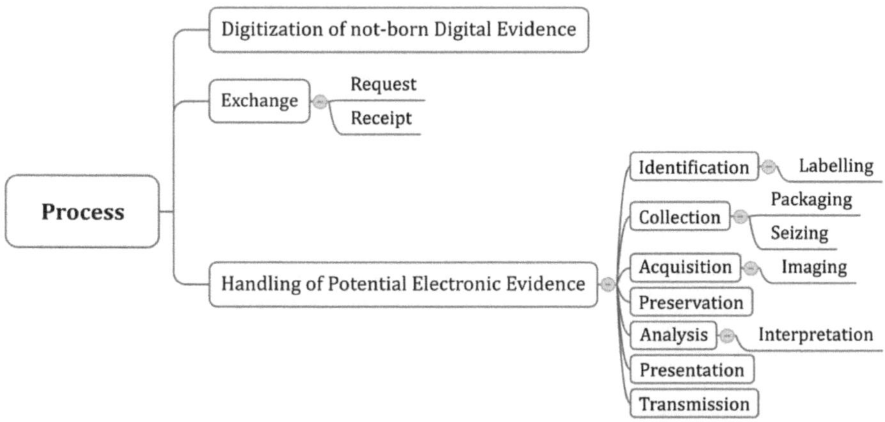

Fig. 10.8 Hierarchical view of Process Class

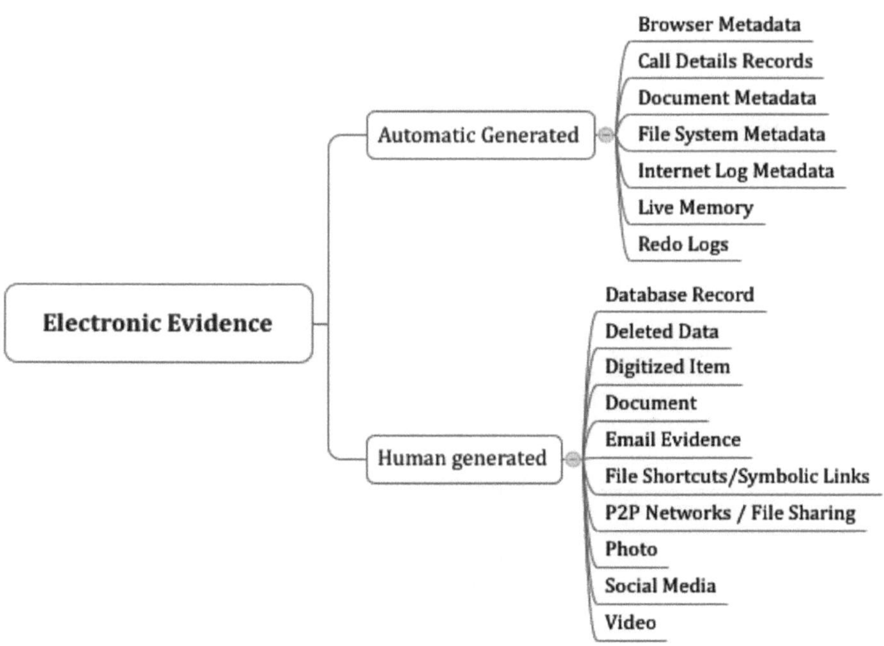

Fig. 10.9 Hierarchical view of Electronic Evidence Class

identified the class Requirement, whose hierarchical view is shown in Fig. 10.10 that gathers these criteria and principles, specifying them into two main subclasses.

The Class Rule, shown in Fig. 10.11, groups three different sources of regulation related to the handling of Electronic Evidence with a special focus on the exchange of Electronic Evidence between competent Authorities. The Class is divided into three sub classes: Hard Law, Soft Law and Technical Standards. In the hard law subclass relevant measures relating to cooperation between courts are included, as

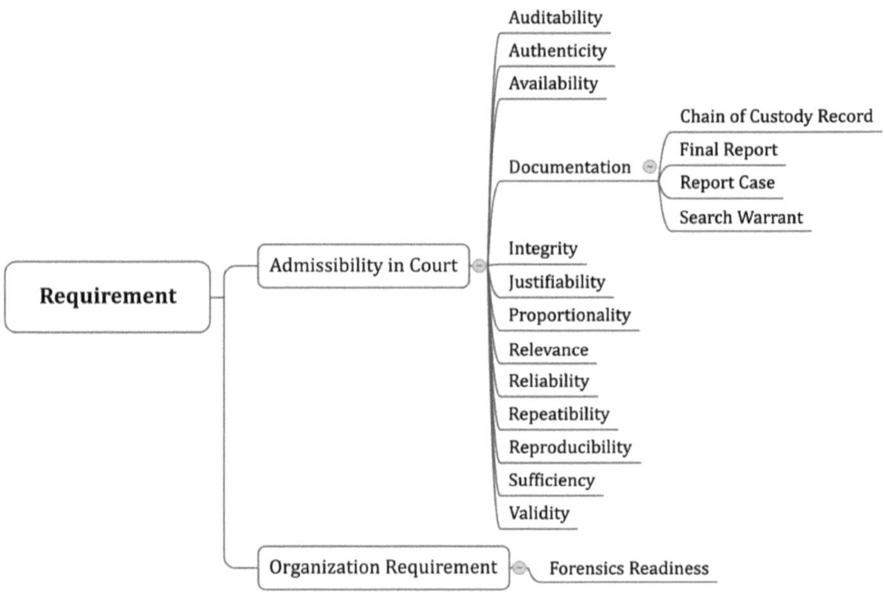

Fig. 10.10 Hierarchical view of Requirement Class

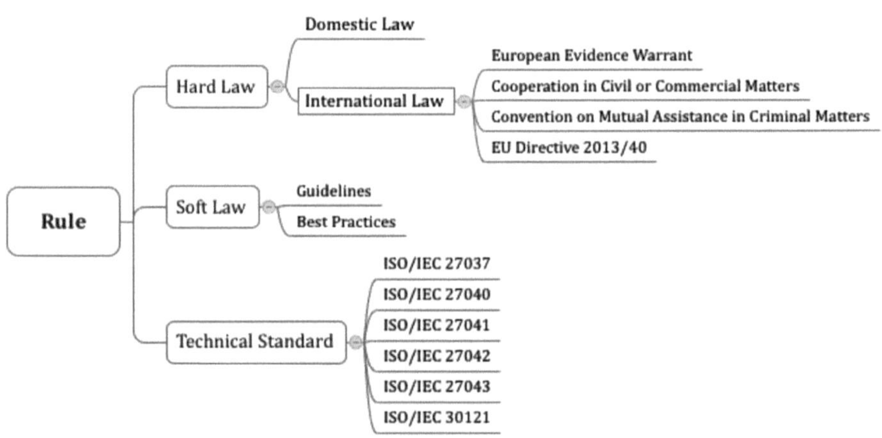

Fig. 10.11 Hierarchical view of Rule Class

well as domestic legislation Technical Standards included into the relative sub-Class are those elaborated by the ISO-International Standard Organization relevant to the handling and the exchange of Electronic Evidence. Soft Law Class lists rules of conduct, which in principle, have no legally binding force but which nevertheless may have practical effect in the process of exchanging/transmission of Electronic Evidence.

Finally, the Digital Forensic Class (Fig. 10.12) refers to digital forensic as the application of scientific methods and techniques used to the investigation of crime,

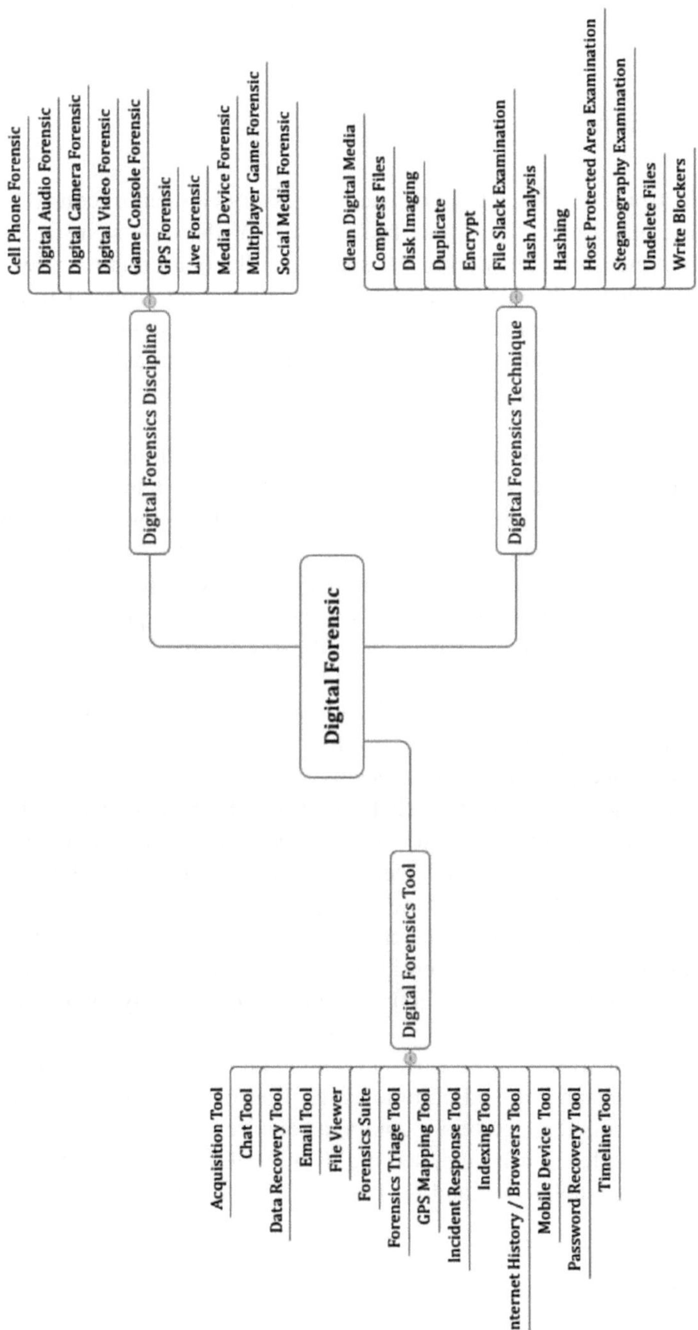

Fig. 10.12 Hierarchical view of Digital Forensic Class

with a focus on informatics. The Class has been dividend n three subclasses: Digital forensics discipline, Digital forensic technique and Digital forensics tool.

10.9 Conclusion

The use of Electronic Evidence has become a necessary element to consider when solving a crime and conducting a fair trial. This is of the utmost importance in a cross-border dimension considering the specific collaboration among European Union Member States related to criminal investigations and criminal trials. The challenges and problems surrounding the use and the exchange of Electronic Evidence in the legal systems are therefore crucial elements to achieve a common and shared understanding of what Electronic Evidence is and how it should be treated.

This article reported the activities carried out toward a tailor-made categorization of relevant concepts, that could allow a common and shared knowledge in this domain. The categorization provides a starting analysis for the exchange of Electronic Evidence and data between judicial actors and LEAs, with a specific focus on issues of the criminal field and criminal procedures. Moreover, consideration is devoted to the impact of harmonized procedures on how police, prosecutors and lawyers in criminal cases, and parties in civil cases, handle Electronic Evidence to preserve its integrity.

The choice of SKOS (Simple Knowledge Organization System) as the standard way to represent and support the categorization activities ensures the advantage of expressing knowledge organization systems in a machine-understandable way within the framework of the semantic web. In addition, SKOS guarantees that further developments of the conceptual structure may be updated and adapted in the future.

To organize the knowledge of the electronic and digital evidence domain eight main classes have been identified: Crime, Source of Electronic Evidence, Process, Electronic Evidence, Requirement, Stakeholder, Rule, Digital Forensics. The main relationships among classes have been identified, as well as relationships among sub-classes that associate and conceptually link them, identifying the type of relations.

The categorization results allow a better comparability of different contents and assures mutual understanding and common use of terms and concepts within the domain. It also answers to a need for a common background for all actors involved in the Electronic Evidence lifecycle, serving as a baseline to design standardized procedures in the use, collection and exchange of Electronic Evidence across EU Member States.

Acknowledgements We would like to thank Cristiana Crescimbene for her invaluable technical support.

References

Alzaabi M, Martin T, Taha K, Jones (2015) The use of ontologies in forensic analysis of smartphone content. J Digit Forensic Secur Law 10(4). https://doi.org/10.15394/jdfsl.2015.1215

Association of Chief Police Officers (UK) (2012) Good practice guide for computer-based electronic evidence. http://library.college.police.uk/docs/acpo/digital-evidence-2012.pdf

Brinson A, Robinson A, Rogers M (2006) A cyber forensics ontology: creating a new approach to studying cyber forensics. Digit Investig J 3S:S37–S43

Carrier B (2006) Hypothesis-based approach to digital forensic investigations. Center for Education and Research in Information Assurance and Security, Purdue University

Casey E (2011) Digital evidence and computer crime. forensic science, computers, and the internet, 3rd edn. Elsevier, Amsterdam

Ciurea A (2010) Legal implications of accessing and using information technology. Legislation in Romania and in the EU. In: ICCOMP'10 Proceedings of the 14th WSEAS lmputers: part of the 14th WSEAS CSCC multiconference, vol I, p 258

Clough J (2014) A world of difference: the Budapest convention on cybercrime and the challenges of harmonization. Monash University Law Rev 40(3):698–736

Ćosić J, Ćosić Z (2011) An ontological approach to study and manage digital chain of custody of digital evidence. J Inf Organ Sci 35(1):1–13

Ćosić J, Ćosić Z (2012) The necessity of developing a digital evidence ontology. In: Proceedings of the 23rd central European conference on information and intelligent systems, University of Zagreb, pp 325–230

Council of Europe (2013) Electronic evidence guide. A basic guide for police officers, prosecutors and judges

Daniel L, Daniel L (2011) Digital forensics for legal professionals. Understanding digital evidence from the warrant to the courtroom. Syngress, Boston, p 368

Duranti L (1995) Reliability and authenticity: the concepts and their implications. Archivaria 39:5–10

Duranti L (2009) From digital diplomatics to digital records forensics. Archivaria J Assoc Can Arch

Gatt GG (2002) The misuse of computers in Maltese criminal legislation, University of Malta, p 9

Harril DC, Mislan RP (2007) A small scale digital device forensics ontology. Small Scale Digit Device Forensics J 1(1):1–7

Hoss A, Carver D (2009) Weaving ontologies to support digital forensic analysis. In: Intelligence and security informatics, ISI'09, pp 203–205

Huang J, Yasinsac A, Hayes PJ (2010) Knowledge sharing and reuse in digital forensics. In: Digital investigation, pp 1–6

ISO/IEC 27037 (2012) Guidelines for identification, collection, acquisition, and preservation of digital evidence

Karie NM, Venter HS (2014) Toward a general ontology for digital forensic disciplines. J Forensic Sci 59(5):1231–1241

Koops B-J, Robinson T (2011) Cybercrime: a European perspective. In: Casey E (ed) Digital evidence and computer crime, 3rd edn. Elsevier, Amsterdam, pp 123–183

Kota VK (2012) An ontological approach for digital evidence search. Int J Sci Res Publ 2(12):1–5

Marion NE (2010) The Council of Europe's cyber crime treaty: an exercise in symbolic legislation. Int J Cyber Criminol 4(1–2):699–712

Murphy CC (2011) The European evidence warrant: mutual recognition. In: Konstadinides E (ed.) Crime within the area of freedom security and justice. A European public order. Cambridge University Press, Cambridge

Park H, Cho S, Kwon HC (2009) Cyber forensics ontology for cyber criminal investigation. In: Forensics in telecommunications, information and multimedia. Springer, Berlin, pp 160–165

Raskin V, Hempelmann CF, Triezenberg KE, Nirenburg S (2001) Ontology in information security: a useful theoretical foundation and methodological tool. In: Proceedings of the 2001 workshop on new security paradigms. ACM, New York, pp 53–59
Schafer B, Mason S (2012) The characteristics of digital evidence. In: Mason S (ed.) Electronic evidence. LexisNexis Butterworths, London, p 25
SWGDE (2000) Digital evidence: standards and principles. Forensic Sci Commun 2(2):2
Talib AM, Alomary FO (2015) Toward a comprehensive ontology based-investigation for digital forensics cybercrime. Int J Commun Antenna Propag 5(5):263–268
Weber AM (2003) The council of Europe's convention on cybercrime. Berkeley Technol Law J 18(1):425–446
Whitcomb CM (2002) An historical perspective of digital evidence: a forensic scientist's view. Int J Digital Evid 1(1):1–9

Chapter 11
The European Legal Framework on Electronic Evidence: Complex and in Need of Reform

Jeanne Pia Mifsud Bonnici, Melania Tudorica, and Joseph A. Cannataci

Abstract More and more, "electronic evidence", defined as "any of potential probative value that is manipulated, generated through, stored on or communicated by any electronic device", plays an important role in criminal trials. This is not surprising given that most of the activities we take part in daily are captured in an electronic way, for example, our electricity consumption is registered electronically by smart meters, our smart mobile phones store information on our calls, messaging, Internet behavior, lifestyle choices, etc., all of which may have some potential probative value in a criminal trial. Apart from, or because of, its particular nature, electronic evidence is not necessarily linked to the same territorial jurisdiction as where an alleged crime would have taken place or is being investigated. This paper focuses on three aspects of this cross-border nature: (a) where it may be due to the information provider "recording" the information; (b) where the actual digital information is stored; (c) where the crime itself has a cross-border nature. This paper reflects on these three effects of this "cross-border" nature of electronic evidence when regulating electronic evidence in the criminal law process. This paper shows how current national and international legal frameworks are insufficient to meet with the current needs. Further it is argued that solving the current shortcomings is not merely a matter of introducing new agreements but is more complex, needing new theoretical frameworks and the collaboration of a large variety of actors.

11.1 Introduction

With most of our lives organised online and by using the latest technologies we rely on Information and Communications Technology (ICT) and use it in our daily lives to interact with our friends, families, colleagues, even with the government, we use it to share and store information, conduct our business, etc. The systems

J. P. Mifsud Bonnici (✉) · M. Tudorica · J. A. Cannataci
University of Groningen, Security, Technology and e-Privacy (STeP), Groningen, The Netherlands
e-mail: g.p.mifsud.bonnici@step-rug.nl; m.tudorica@step-rug.nl; j.a.cannataci@step-rug.nl

M. A. Biasiotti et al. (eds.), *Handling and Exchanging Electronic Evidence Across Europe*, Law, Governance and Technology Series 39,
https://doi.org/10.1007/978-3-319-74872-6_11

keep our economies running. Consequently, we leave digital traces everywhere. Therefore, the evidence we may need to bring to Court is increasingly in electronic form. This is especially the case in criminal matters. Evidence in criminal cases is how the facts are established to prove an individual's guilt or innocence. This evidence may be traditional (physical evidence, a murder weapon for example). However, increasingly, evidence nowadays are in electronic form (for example mobile mast records showing the location of a suspect at the time of the murder). This is not surprising given that most of the activities we take part in daily are captured in an electronic way, for example our electricity consumption is registered electronically by smart meters, our smart mobile phones store information on our calls, messaging, internet behaviour, life-style choices etc., all of which may have some potential probative value in a criminal trial. Apart from, or because of, its particular nature, electronic evidence is not necessarily linked to the same territorial jurisdiction as where an alleged crime would have taken place or is being investigated. Data may for example be stored in a cloud service that is located in another jurisdiction. Moreover, criminal activities are also increasingly conducted using ICT and perpetrators rely on digital technologies to perform their activities (for example cybercrimes). All this evidence in criminal cases needs to be collected by enforcement authorities, preserved, used in criminal proceedings and possibly transferred or exchanged (cross-border) between authorities.

Evidence may come in different forms. As described in other parts of this Volume, there are various definitions of electronic evidence and in some cases the term is used interchangeably with the term 'digital evidence'. However, we use the term *electronic evidence*, which is defined as "any information (comprising the output of analogue devices or data in digital format) of potential probative value that is manipulated, generated through, stored on or communicated by any electronic device".[1] We therefore take a wide approach to electronic evidence to include: physical or traditional (not electronic) evidence such as a murder weapon or the bloodstain of the victim, which may be digitised for example by taking a digital photo of the murder weapon; evidence born in an analogue format (videotape or vinyl), which may be digitised and entered into a digitisation process acquiring digital status; and evidence originally born digital as created by any digital device (computer or computer like-device). All these types of evidences are considered as 'electronic evidences' considering that at the end of the process they can be labelled as electronic regardless of their origin.

Because of the very nature of it, modern technologies and growing globalisation, electronic evidence may be located or stored anywhere in the world. This is especially the case in cybercrime cases, as cybercrime is a global problem that does not stop at our countries' borders, but also increasingly in crimes in general and terrorism cases. It is therefore not sufficient to say that electronic evidence is only relevant to cybercrime cases. Electronic evidence may be used in any criminal case. In criminal matters all types of electronic evidence need to be collected and handled

[1] Definition used in the EVIDENCE Project—Deliverable 2.1—EVIDENCE Semantic Structure, p. 18.

by enforcement authorities and prosecutors before they can be presented and used in Court. In investigating criminal matters, enforcement authorities need a variety of powers to collect, preserve and exchange (electronic) evidence. They might need traditional powers (interview, surveillance, etc.) but also cyber-specific powers, such as search and seizure of stored computer data, real-time collection of traffic data and interception of content data as evidence may come in the form of computer files, logs, transmissions, metadata, computer data, etc. This evidence then needs to be preserved and handled, possibly by digital forensic experts, to be presented and used in Court. To be presented and used in Court the electronic evidence needs to comply with all necessary rules, if any, including rules on admissibility. For example, in many legal systems the (electronic) evidence needs to be legally obtained, i.e. by Court order, for the evidence to be admissible in Court. As electronic evidence can be easily modified, overwritten or deleted, the authenticity of the evidence may also be questioned in Court. Like physical evidence, electronic evidence needs to be authenticated and verified.[2] A clear chain of custody is therefore of the essence.

This chapter reviews the current legal framework for electronic evidence in Europe. It first looks at the international level, examining frameworks coming from the Council of Europe and the European Union (EU). It then moves to review the position at a national level (within Europe). The review shows a complex patchwork of legislation and practices relating to electronic evidence and one that needs reform to meet the demands of the increasing use of electronic evidence in the criminal process.

It is important at this stage, before moving on with the review to discuss the use of some of the terms used in this chapter. Processing evidence in criminal matters refers to collecting, preserving, using and exchanging evidence, i.e. the chain of custody of evidence in criminal proceedings. By collection of electronic evidence, we mean the process of gathering items that contain potential electronic evidence in the widest sense, meaning search, seizure, interception and any other forms of gathering evidence by Law Enforcement Agencies (LEAs), but also capture of evidence by the private sector and any other forms of gathering potential electronic evidence. Once the evidence is collected, it needs to be preserved before it can be used during the criminal trial. Preservation is the process of maintaining and safeguarding the integrity and/or original condition of the potential electronic evidence, meaning that it needs to be stored in a secure way to safeguard against alterations, that the chain of custody needs to be logged and that access to the evidence needs to be restricted to persons authorised to process the evidence. Before the criminal trial starts the electronic evidence needs to be to be analysed, for example by digital forensic experts, and the final document or report needs to be produced before it can be used and presented in court. At any point during the electronic evidence lifecycle the evidence may thus be interchanged between various competent authorities including LEAs, digital forensic experts, courts, etc. To distinguish between the interchange

[2]United Nations Office on Drugs and Crime, Comprehensive Study on Cybercrime, draft February 2013, p. 158.

within a country and cross border interchange, we refer to the first as *transfer* and to the latter as *exchange*. Transfer may occur between different national legal actors and LEAs in the same country. Exchange may take place between competent national authorities of different countries (cross-border exchange) in the field of cooperation in criminal matters. All the actions from collection to eventually using the evidence in court require a legal basis.

11.2 International and European Legislation and Practices

When describing whether and how electronic evidence is perceived and regulated in the EU legal framework it is important to realise that criminal law is based on national laws and traditions that differ per Member State. However, these national laws may be inspired by international instruments or may even have implemented international instruments such as EU and Council of Europe legal instruments and best practices. When describing the European legal scenario, it is therefore relevant to look at these instruments before going into the scenarios at national level.

There is no comprehensive international or European legal framework relating to (electronic) evidence. Parties involved rely on national law when it comes to the collection, preservation, use and exchange of (electronic) evidence. These national criminal laws have been written ages ago, long before there was such a thing as the internet and modern technologies that could generate electronic evidence. While it is true that some countries have adapted their legislation to include such developments, others rely on traditional criminal laws and apply them to electronic evidence as well. There are thus big differences in national legislation and approach, which makes handling transnational electronic evidence difficult. According to the United Nations (UN) Study on Cybercrime,[3] evidence rules vary considerably even amongst countries with similar legal traditions.[4] In certain countries traditional investigative powers might be general enough to apply to electronic evidence, while in other countries traditional procedural laws might not cover specific issues regarding electronic evidence, making it necessary to have additional legislation. In certain countries there are defined rules as to admissibility of evidence in Court while in other countries admissibility is flexible. In all cases legislation requires a clear scope of application of powers and sufficient legal authority for actions by the authorities involved.[5] While there is no comprehensive international or European legal framework relating to electronic evidence, few international and European

[3]United Nations Office on Drugs and Crime, Comprehensive Study on Cybercrime, draft February 2013.

[4]United Nations Office on Drugs and Crime, Comprehensive Study on Cybercrime, draft February 2013, p. 158.

[5]United Nations Office on Drugs and Crime, Comprehensive Study on Cybercrime, draft February 2013, p. 122, 123.

legal instruments and policy documents are relevant to electronic evidence. These instruments and documents may inspire national laws and practices or may even be implemented into national law. Apart from these international and European instruments and documents it is furthermore worth mentioning that Member States may also rely on bilateral and multilateral agreements between them, particularly when it comes to cross-border exchange of (electronic) evidence. We will not go into these agreements. However, it is relevant to know that these agreements may exist between countries.

The two main international legal regimes that influence national laws are the EU legal framework and Council of Europe legal instruments. The EU cannot adopt general EU criminal law, however, with the entry into force of the Lisbon Treaty and the creation of an Area of Freedom, Security and Justice (AFSJ), the EU can add important value to existing national criminal laws within the limits of its competence. However, there is no comprehensive EU legal framework regarding criminal law and none whatsoever regarding electronic evidence. There are only few EU instruments that may be directly or indirectly relevant to the collection, preservation, use and exchange of electronic evidence. The Council of Europe is highly relevant in this respect as all Member States of the EU are States Parties to the Council of Europe as well and the Council of Europe has produced several international treaties relevant to electronic evidence. The Council of Europe Convention on Cybercrime[6] (Cybercrime Convention) remains the main (and only) international treaty that defines the procedural provisions for investigating and pursuing cybercrime. Although electronic evidence may not necessarily flow from cybercrime but may also be processed in proceedings of traditional crimes, the electronic evidence may be collected, preserved, used and exchanged in the same manner in criminal investigations of both cybercrimes and traditional crimes. The EU and Council of Europe legal frameworks will be discussed in the following paragraph. It is important to note in advance the patchwork of legal instruments that authorities, particularly law enforcement, are left to operate with. This highly uncertain and politically sensitive landscape filled with legal lacunae makes cross-border cases and international cooperation difficult.

11.2.1 European Union Legal Instruments

With the adoption and entering into force of the Lisbon Treaty[7] a supranational regime for EU criminal law was introduced. Title V of the Treaty on the Functioning of the European Union[8] (TFEU) provides for the AFSJ within the EU. Based on

[6]Convention on Cybercrime [2001] ETS 185.

[7]Treaty of Lisbon amending the Treaty on European Union and the Treaty Establishing the European Community [2007] OJ C 306/01.

[8]Consolidated version of the Treaty on the Functioning of the European Union [2012] OJ C 326/47.

Article 67 (3) TFEU, with this area the EU will endeavour to ensure a high level of security through measures to prevent and combat crime, through police and judicial coordination and cooperation, through mutual recognition of judgements in criminal matters and if necessary through harmonisation of criminal laws. The AFSJ thus includes EU criminal law and police cooperation, which is further developed in Chapters 4 (judicial cooperation in criminal matters) and 5 (police cooperation) of Title V TFEU. Although it is thus true that there has been progress on the EU legal framework front, the realities are somewhat different. Judicial and police cooperation are subject to Article 4 (2) of the Treaty on the European Union[9] (TEU), which states that national security is the sole responsibility of each Member State, interpreted in the sense that the provisions regarding judicial and police cooperation are on stringent terms with sovereignty regarding national security. Even more so considering that sensitive matters can be referred to the European Council. Instruments adopted prior to the Lisbon Treaty furthermore retain their earlier status, the United Kingdom (UK) and Ireland can opt out of any of the instruments and Denmark is only bound by its commitments under the Schengen Convention.[10] Having said that, the regime has been a step forward, as judicial and police cooperation is of utmost importance regarding the collection, preservation, use and exchange of (electronic) evidence and judicial authorities and police forces across Europe tend to work together in preventing and solving cross-border

According to Article 82 (1) TFEU judicial cooperation in the EU is based on the principle of mutual recognition of judgements and judicial decisions and includes approximation of laws and regulations of the Member States in several areas including mutual admissibility of evidence between Member States (Article 82 (2, a) TFEU) and in some number areas of serious crimes including terrorism, organised crime and cybercrime (Article 83 (1) TFEU). According to Article 87 TFEU police cooperation in the EU is established involving the competent authorities of the Member States and the EU. Based on these provisions the EU may issue Directives and other measures to the extent necessary to facilitate judicial and police cooperation within the EU. The EU has adopted few Directives and other measures regarding criminal law. This includes the EU 2000 Convention on mutual assistance in criminal matters,[11] which was adopted by the Council in 2000 in accordance with Article 34 TEU and entered into force on 23 August 2005 to facilitate mutual judicial assistance between the authorities of the Member States (police, customs and courts) to improve the speed and efficiency of judicial cooperation. The EU 2000 Convention encourages and facilitates mutual assistance between judicial, police and customs authorities on criminal matters that complements and adds to the

[9]Consolidated version of the Treaty on European Union [2012] OJ C 326/13.

[10]See Chalmers et al. (2010), p. 582.

[11]Council Act of 29 May 2000 establishing in accordance with Article 34 of the Treaty on European Union the Convention on Mutual Assistance in Criminal Matters between the Member States of the European Union (2000/C 197/01) [2000] OJ C 197/1.

Council of Europe Convention on Mutual Assistance in Criminal Matters.[12] Based on the EU 2000 Convention Member States may request other Member States for mutual assistance. Requests might also include requests for (electronic) evidence. However, the downside with such procedures for mutual assistance is that they are time consuming as requests for mutual assistance generally take a long time to be processed, which cannot be afforded, particularly when it comes to electronic evidence that is easily altered or even deleted. In 2008, the European Evidence Warrant (EEW) Decision[13] replaced the system of mutual assistance in criminal matters between Member States for obtaining objects, documents and data for use in criminal proceedings (Article 1 (1) EEW Decision) and established the procedures and safeguards for Member States whereby EEWs are to be issued and executed. The EEW Decision was adopted to apply the principle of mutual recognition in obtaining objects, documents and data for use in proceedings in criminal matters. However, the EEW is only applicable to evidence that already exists and covers therefore a limited spectrum of judicial cooperation in criminal matters with respect to evidence. Because of its limited scope, competent authorities have been free to use the regime of Directive 2014/41/EU, the European Investigation Order (EIO) Directive,[14] when it was issued in 2014 or to use mutual legal assistance procedures that remain applicable to evidence falling outside of the scope of the EEW.[15] The EIO Directive sets up a comprehensive new system that allows EU Member States to obtain evidence in other Member States in criminal cases that involve more than one Member State. This Directive thus aims to simplify and speed up cross border criminal investigations in the EU. It introduces the EIO, which enables judicial authorities in one Member State (the issuing state) to request that evidence be collected in and transferred from another Member State (the executing state). It replaces the existing EU mutual legal assistance schemes, notably the EU 2000 Convention and EEW Decision. It needs remain to be seen how this will work given that it has only come into force on 22 May 2017.

Based on Article 1 of the EIO Directive, the EIO is a judicial decision that has been issued or validated by a judicial authority of the issuing State to have one or several specific investigative measure(s) carried out in the executing State to obtain evidence or to obtain evidence that is already in the possession of the competent authorities of the executing State. Member States are obliged to act swiftly and to execute the EIO based on the principle of mutual recognition. The EIO covers any investigative measure except for the setting up of a Joint Investigation Team

[12]European Convention on Mutual Assistance in Criminal Matters [1959] CETS 030; Additional Protocol to the European Convention on Mutual Assistance in Criminal Matters [1978] CETS 099.

[13]Council Framework Decision 2008/978/JHA of 18 December 2008 on the European evidence warrant for obtaining objects, documents and data for use in proceedings in criminal matters [2008] OJ L 350/72.

[14]Directive 2014/41/EU of the European Parliament and of the Council of 3 April 2014 regarding the European Investigation Order in criminal matters [2014] OJ L 130/1.

[15]Directive 2014/41/EU of the European Parliament and of the Council of 3 April 2014 regarding the European Investigation Order in criminal matters [2014] OJ L 130/1, Recital 4.

(JIT) and the gathering of evidence within such a team as provided in Article 13 of the EU 2000 Convention. The EIO improves on existing EU laws covering this field by setting strict deadlines for gathering the evidence requested and by limiting the grounds for refusing such requests. It also reduces paperwork by introducing a single standard form for authorities to request help when seeking evidence. The EIO may be issued in writing if it is necessary and proportionate for the proceedings and if the investigative measure(s) indicated in the EIO could have been ordered under the same conditions in a similar domestic case (Article 6 (1,b) EIO Directive). The Directive does not mention electronic evidence as such. However, it refers to 'data', which indicates that evidence may indeed be in electronic form. Article 13 of the EIO Directive arranges for the exchange of evidence and stipulates that the executing authority transfers the evidence obtained or already in the possession of the competent authorities to the issuing State. However, it does not stipulate how the evidence should be transferred, nor does the Directive determine how evidence should be collected and preserved. This is left to the Member States, meaning that this may vary considerably between Member States.

Other EU police cooperation schemes include the Schengen acquis, the European Arrest Warrant (EAW) and JITs. The Schengen acquis facilitates, amongst other things, police cooperation within the Schengen Area. The Schengen Area is an area without internal borders, an area within which people can freely circulate without being subjected to border control. By abolishing the internal borders, Schengen States made rules to ensure the security of those living or travelling in the Schengen Area, including tightened controls at their common external border and enhancing police cooperation. The Schengen acquis is the body of law regulating the Schengen Area. It includes the Schengen Implementing Convention and other legal instruments.[16] Title III of the Schengen Implementing Convention is devoted to police and security. To facilitate the Schengen Area and police cooperation the Schengen States introduced the Schengen Information System (SIS). SIS enables competent authorities to enter and consult alerts on certain categories of wanted or missing persons and objects. It is the largest and highly secure and protected EU database that is exclusively accessible to the authorised users within competent authorities, such as national border control, police, customs, judicial, visa and vehicle registration authorities. The EAW based on Framework Decision

[16]The Schengen acquis—Convention implementing the Schengen Agreement of 14 June 1985 between the Governments of the States of the Benelux Economic Union, the Federal Republic of Germany and the French Republic on the gradual abolition of checks at their common borders [2000] OJ L 239/19. See also: Regulation (EC) no 1987/2006 of the European Parliament and of the Council of 20 December 2006 on the establishment, operation and use of the second generation Schengen Information System (SIS II) [2006] OJ L 381/4; Council Decision 2007/533/JHA of 12 June 2007 on the establishment, operation and use of the second generation Schengen Information System (SIS II) [2007] OJ L 205/63; Regulation (EC) No 1986/2006 of the European Parliament and of the Council of 20 December 2006 regarding access to the Second Generation Schengen Information System (SIS II) by the services in the Member States responsible for issuing vehicle registration certificates [2006] OJ L 381/1.

2002/584/JHA[17] is a judicial decision issued by a Member State for the arrest and surrender by another Member State of a requested person in conducting a criminal prosecution or executing a custodial sentence or detention order (Article 1 (1) EAW Decision). The Decision simplifies and speeds up procedures whereby EU citizens who have committed a serious crime in another Member State can be returned to that country to face justice. Like all the other EU instruments in this regard the EAW is executed based on the principle of mutual recognition.[18] Finally, and possibly most importantly, European police cooperation may include JITs, which find their legal basis in Council Framework Decision 2002/465/JHA.[19] Member States meeting in Tampere in 1999 called for JITs to be set up without delay with a view to combating trafficking in drugs and human beings, as well as terrorism. The EU 2000 Convention had already provided for the setting-up of JITs, however, in view of slow progress towards ratification of the EU 2000 Convention, the Council adopted Decision 2002/465/JHA to carry out criminal investigations in Member States that necessitate coordinated and concerted action.[20] JITs may be set up by at least two Member States for a specific purpose and a limited period based on an agreement of all the parties involved. Representatives of Europol, OLAF and of third countries may take part in the team's activities. Increasingly, this is one of the most relevant instruments for Europol to share its expertise in collection, preservation and facilitation of exchange of electronic evidence, particularly in the context of cybercrimes.

11.2.2 Council of Europe Legal Instruments

Apart from the above-mentioned EU legal instruments, there are few instruments by the Council of Europe that are relevant to electronic evidence. In fact, the Council of Europe instruments and documents are generally more authoritative than the international and EU ones. Regarding international organisations, the Council of Europe has more members than the EU and all EU Member States are States Parties to the Council of Europe as well, particularly concerning cybercrime, the Council of

[17]Council Framework Decision of 13 June 2002 on the European arrest warrant and the surrender procedures between Member States (2002/584/JHA) [2002] OJ L 190/1.

[18]The EAW Decision has been criticised enormously, in fact it has prompted more challenges before constitutional Courts of the Member States than any other EU law. The most important concern in this regard is related to trust, trust in the prosecutorial and judicial process of the issuing state, mainly in that there might be insufficient guarantees that the surrendered person will receive a fair trial in the issuing state. See Chalmers et al. (2010), p. 599.

[19]Council Framework Decision of 13 June 2002 on joint investigation teams (2002/465/JHA) [2002] OJ L 162/1.

[20]On the relevance of JITs, see: Communication from the Commission to the European Parliament, the Council, the European Economic and Social Committee and the Committee of the Regions *The European Agenda on Security* COM(2015) 185 final, p. 9.

Europe provides a binding international treaty that affords an effective framework for the adoption of national legislation and a basis for international cooperation in this field.[21] In several pieces of EU legislation and policy documents it is reiterated that the Council of Europe's instruments are the legal framework of reference for combating cybercrime and that the EU legislation and policies build on those of the Council of Europe. As far as electronic evidence is concerned, several Council of Europe instruments are highly relevant. Firstly, the European Convention for the Protection of Human Rights and Fundamental Freedoms[22] (ECHR) particularly when it comes to the protection of the right to privacy. Secondly, the Council of Europe Convention on Mutual Assistance in Criminal Matters[23] and its 1978 Protocol.[24] This Convention entered into force on 12 June 1962 and has 50 States Parties, which includes all Member States of the EU. It does not have specific provisions on electronic evidence but is the widest measure of mutual assistance with a view to collecting evidence, hearing witnesses, experts and prosecuted persons, etc. in cross-border criminal cases. The Convention sets out rules for the enforcement of letters rogatory by the authorities of a State Party that aim to procure evidence or to communicate the evidence in criminal proceedings undertaken by the judicial authorities of another State Party and specifies the requirements for such proceedings. However, considering the year 1959 when it was adopted, the Convention on Mutual Assistance in Criminal Matters does not consider the modern technologies we are faced with today, making it a too slow a process for today's fast modern world. Finally, and most importantly, the third Council of Europe relevant instrument within the context of electronic evidence is the Council of Europe Convention on Cybercrime[25] (Cybercrime Convention). This Convention remains the main (and only) international treaty that defines the substantive elements that lead to some cyber activities to be classified as crimes and has procedural provisions that allow for the prevention, detection and prosecution of these activities. Although electronic evidence may not necessarily result from cybercrime, this is the main framework for reference in this area, which offers many provisions to enhance investigations where electronic evidence is involved.

The European Committee on Crime Problems (CDPC), which was set up in 1958 by the Council of Europe and is responsible for overseeing and coordinating

[21] Joint communication to the European Parliament, the Council, the European Economic and Social Committee and the Committee of Regions Cybersecurity Strategy of the European Union: An Open, Safe and Secure Cyberspace [2013] JOIN(2013) 1 final, p. 9, 15; See also Directive 2013/40/EU of the European Parliament and of the Council of 12 August 2013 on attacks against information systems and replacing Council Framework Decision 2005/222/JHA [2013] OJ L 218, Recital 15.

[22] Convention for the Protection of Human Rights and Fundamental Freedoms [1950] as amended by Protocols No. 11 and No. 14 [2010] CETS No. 194.

[23] European Convention on Mutual Assistance in Criminal Matters [1959] CETS 030.

[24] Additional Protocol to the European Convention on Mutual Assistance in Criminal Matters [1978] CETS 099.

[25] Convention on Cybercrime [2001] ETS 185.

the Council of Europe's activities in the field of crime prevention, decided in November 1996 to set up a committee of experts to deal with cybercrime because of the fast developments in technology. Following that decision, the Council's Committee of Ministers set up the Committee of Experts on Crime in Cyberspace (PC-CY), which started working on a draft international convention on cybercrime. The final draft of the Cybercrime Convention was approved by the CDPC in June 2001 and submitted to the Committee of Ministers for adoption and opening for signature.[26] The Cybercrime Convention was adopted on 8 November 2001 and opened for signature in Budapest on 23 November 2001. The Cybercrime Convention entered into force on the first of July 2004 and currently[27] has 53 ratifications and 4 signatures not yet followed by ratification (including few EU Member States[28]). The Cybercrime Convention goes beyond Europe as it includes several ratifications and signatories, which are non-members of the Council of Europe, such as the United States of America (USA), Japan and Australia.[29] The aim of the Cybercrime Convention is to harmonise domestic criminal substantive law elements of offences and connected provisions in the area of cybercrime, to provide for domestic criminal procedural law powers necessary for the investigation and prosecution of such offences, as well as other offences committed by means of a computer system, or evidence in relation to which is in electronic form and to set up a fast and effective regime of international cooperation.[30] The investigative powers and procedures enshrined in the Cybercrime Convention also apply to the collection of evidence in electronic form of a criminal offence (Article 14 (2,c) Cybercrime Convention). Because of the very nature of cybercrime, the evidence in cybercrime cases is mostly in electronic form. Such evidence can easily be altered, meaning that the admissibility of the evidence may be at stake. Therefore, when collecting and handling electronic evidence, the integrity, authenticity and continuity of such evidence must be guaranteed during the entire chain of custody—from seizure until trial. Given the importance of electronic evidence particularly during the criminal process (in the prosecution of crimes), there is increasingly more attention to the setting of common standards for the acquisition, collection, custody and exchange of electronic evidence. While some states still apply traditional evidential rules to electronic evidence, some states already have special rules for electronic evidence.[31]

[26]Council of Europe, "Explanatory report to the Convention of Cybercrime" (ETS No 185), p. 1–4.

[27]Latest update: 20 March 2017.

[28]Ireland and Sweden have signed but not yet ratified the Cybercrime Convention.

[29]See also Deliverable 3.2 of the E-CRIME project (Grant Agreement Number 607775): E-CRIME Deliverable 3.2 final report on countermeasure including policy and enforcement responses, March 2015 for more information on cybercrimes and the Cybercrime Convention.

[30]Council of Europe, "Explanatory report to the Convention of Cybercrime" (ETS No 185), p. 4.

[31]United Nations Office on Drugs and Crime, Comprehensive Study on Cybercrime, draft February 2013, p. 55. See more in Part II of this deliverable.

11.2.2.1 Investigative Powers

Effective investigation and prosecution is not possible without the proper powers for law enforcement. The Cybercrime Convention provides that the States Parties to the Convention shall adopt legislation and measures to establish powers and procedures for criminal investigations and proceedings to be applied to the offences referred to in the Convention, other criminal offences committed by means of a computer system and to the collection of electronic evidence (Article 14 of the Convention). These powers and procedures thus apply to electronic evidence in relation to any offence for law enforcement to secure electronic evidence. For investigations in criminal cases, law enforcement requires investigative powers to collect (electronic) evidence. In certain cases, traditional powers (interview, surveillance, etc.) might be sufficient, however, when it comes to electronic evidence, specific powers may be necessary to collect the evidence. Such powers may include search and seizure of stored computer data, real-time collection of traffic data and interception of content data considering that evidence may come in the form of computer files, logs, transmissions, metadata, computer data, etc. The Cybercrime Convention focusses on cybercrimes, but when it comes to handling electronic evidence the same techniques may be necessary and the same investigative powers may apply. However, there are big differences in national enforcement legislation and approach. In certain countries traditional investigative powers might be general enough to apply to cybercrime cases while in other countries traditional procedural laws might not cover cyber specific issues, making it necessary to have additional cyber specific legislation. In both cases legislation requires a clear scope of application of powers and sufficient legal authority for actions. According to the UN study, the main gaps in investigative powers include the lack of power to enter electronic networks to search for evidence and the lack of power to preserve computer data to support existing search powers. The same study also shows that Europe scores highest in the sufficiency of national law for cybercrime investigations, approximately 70% of responding European countries reported that investigative powers were sufficient. The remaining 30% responded that investigative powers were sufficient in part (25%) and not sufficient (5%). When investigating an (alleged) offence under the substantive law provision of the Cybercrime Convention, national law should at least provide some investigative powers including expedited preservation of stored computer data, expedited preservation and partial disclosure of traffic data, production order, search and seizure, real-time collection of traffic data and interception of content data (Article 16–21 Cybercrime Convention). The Cybercrime Convention thus provides for powers for investigation and prosecution, which are specialised to investigations in an electronic environment, that can be highly intrusive. For this reason, the Convention stipulates that all investigative powers are subject to the conditions and safeguards under Article 15 of the Convention, meaning that they are to be executed with regard for human rights and the principle of proportionality.

11.2.2.2 Jurisdiction

When exercising investigative powers, particularly where electronic evidence is concerned, law enforcement may stumble upon evidence that is stored or located in another country so that jurisdiction may be problematic. For example, in cybercrime cases or when electronic evidence is stored in a cloud, the evidence may be located in another jurisdiction than the one investigating the crime. When it comes to cybercrime between 50 and 100% of cybercrime acts involve a transnational element.[32] Jurisdiction in such cases thus requires both executive and judicial jurisdiction to be effective.[33] Executive jurisdiction meaning the capacity of a state to act within the borders of another state and judicial jurisdiction meaning the power of a Court to try cases in which a foreign factor is present.[34] International law permits states to exercise jurisdiction on some principles.[35] The Cybercrime Convention relies on the territoriality and nationality principles to establish jurisdiction. According to Article 22 of the Cybercrime Convention, States Parties to the Convention are required to adopt legislative and other measures necessary to establish jurisdiction over the offences mentioned in the Cybercrime Convention when the offence is committed in its territory, on board a ship flying the flag of that Party, on board an aircraft registered under the laws of that Party or when the offence is committed by one of the nationals of a State Party, if the offence is punishable under criminal law where it was committed or if the offence is committed outside the territorial jurisdiction of any State.

11.2.2.3 International Cooperation

If a state investigating a criminal offence does not have jurisdiction to collect evidence, which is stored or located in another country, international cooperation comes into play. Chapter 3 of the Cybercrime Convention regulates international cooperation. The chapter consists of two sections: general principles and specific provisions. The first section on general principles consists of general principles relating to international cooperation, principles related to extradition, general principles related to mutual assistance and procedures pertaining to mutual assistance requests in absence of applicable international agreements. In accordance with Article 23 of the Cybercrime Convention, the general principles relating to international cooperation, the States Parties to the Convention shall cooperate with each other, in accordance with the principles of the Convention, and through the application of relevant international instruments on international cooperation in

[32]United Nations Office on Drugs and Crime, Comprehensive Study on Cybercrime, draft February 2013, p. 55.

[33]United Nations Office on Drugs and Crime, Comprehensive Study on Cybercrime, draft February 2013, p. 55.

[34]See Shaw (2008), pp. 650, 651.

[35]See Shaw (2008), pp. 652–673. See also Brenner and Koops (2004).

criminal matters, arrangements agreed based on uniform or reciprocal legislation, and national laws, to the widest extent possible for investigations or proceedings concerning criminal offences related to computer systems and data, or for the collection of evidence in electronic form of a criminal offence. The principles based on which the Convention requires the States Parties to cooperate include extradition and mutual assistance. Apart from these principles, states may also be part of a broader network of multilateral and bilateral agreements relating to cooperation in criminal matters.

11.2.2.4 Mutual Assistance

Mutual assistance is the most important means of international cooperation and one of the most important aspects regulated by the Cybercrime Convention considering the cross-border nature of cybercrime. One of the main aims of mutual assistance is to obtain evidence for use in criminal proceedings and trials. Evidence collected abroad by the requested state and under its own procedures will need to meet the evidentiary rules of the requesting state. According to Article 25 (1) of the Cybercrime Convention States Parties to the Convention shall afford one another mutual assistance to the widest extent possible for investigations or proceedings concerning criminal offences related to computer systems and data, or for the collection of evidence in electronic form of a criminal offence. Thus, mutual assistance is to be extensive and impediments strictly limited and is to be applied to both criminal offences related to computer systems and data and to the collection of electronic evidence of a criminal offence. The obligation to cooperate is thus a broad one, however, Article 34 and 35 permit States Parties to provide for a different scope of application of these measures. The obligation to provide mutual assistance is generally to be carried out pursuant to the terms of applicable mutual legal assistance treaties, laws and arrangements including bilateral or multilateral agreements. States Parties to the Convention are required to have a legal basis to carry out the specific forms of cooperation described in the remainder of the chapter, if its treaties, laws and arrangements do not already contain such provisions (Article 25 (2) Convention). The availability of such mechanisms, particularly those in Article 29–35, is vital for effective cooperation in computer related criminal matters. Mutual assistance typically requires lengthy verification of the validity of the request. In practice, this formal mutual assistance is often complemented by informal police-to-police or agency-to-agency communication in law enforcement investigations, which can be used prior to a formal mutual legal assistance request. In such informal communication the assistance of international LEAs such as Interpol or Europol may prove useful.

11.2.2.5 Gaps in the Investigative Framework

An effective enforcement scheme is required to have an effective international scheme for the collection, preservation and, in particular, exchange of electronic evidence. However, there are big differences in national enforcement legislation and approach and practices and readiness may vary significantly on the different levels of law enforcement (local, regional, national). Although international cooperation has proven successful, there are few realities that need to be faced as coordination is costly and difficult to carry out for trivial matters such as time zone differences and nuances of local laws and customs in the jurisdictions involved. One of the main challenges is the need for law enforcement to cooperate with third parties such as industry. Another main challenge is that technologies are developing rapidly and that policing technologies will need to be revolutionised with it. However, the UN cybercrime study shows that the capacities and resources of the police forces vary dramatically, especially at local level. The average police officer may lack the knowledge about new technologies and the average police unit may not have the right resources to handle electronic evidence. While some local police forces may have some sort of cyber unit, others barely have trained officers. Specifically, cybercrime offenders are highly equipped and skilled and enforcement cannot lag behind. This is especially important considering the growing importance of electronic evidence. Not all police forces are equipped to handle such evidence. It is therefore important to revolutionise policing technologies, capacities and knowledge. The critical elements of consistent and effective law enforcement should thus include an effective legal framework, access to investigative tools and techniques, training and technical capabilities and best practices policies that ensure proportionality between the protection of privacy and infringements for legitimate crime prevention and control.[36] The third main challenge is jurisdiction since electronic evidence may not consider national borders that leads to another main challenge when the investigating jurisdiction is required to ask for mutual assistance, which is a time-consuming procedure. The issue of when the investigating jurisdiction is permitted to unilaterally access computer data stored in another jurisdiction without seeking mutual assistance was a question that the drafters of the Cybercrime Convention discussed at length. Because of lack of experience and the understanding that it often depends on the circumstances of the case it was ultimately determined that it was not yet possible to prepare a comprehensive, legally binding regime regulating this area. Article 32 was the ultimate outcome. Thus, when faced with a cross-border case, law enforcers in most cases will have to ask for mutual assistance or pass on information to their counterparts across the border that is time consuming and, especially in the financial sector, often arrives too late. This has instigated an interesting discussion on hacking back or strikeback, meaning electronic countermeasures to track down hackers' computers and disable

[36] United Nations Office on Drugs and Crime, Comprehensive Study on Cybercrime, draft February 2013, p. 118.

them, which has been a growing sentiment in the financial sector. However, hacking back or striking back in itself is most likely an illegal act. These challenges in current legislation have not yet been addressed.[37]

One major criticism raised in literature (and by practitioners) is that the notion of territorial jurisdiction, particularly as the notion governing investigative powers is rather limiting and problematic in today's world where electronic information is processed, shared and stored across several territorial jurisdictions and spaces. What is being argued by Svantesson,[38] is that it is time to separate judicial and enforcement jurisdiction from investigative jurisdiction. While territorial scope of judicial and enforcement jurisdictions is logical and understandable; the territorial scope of investigative jurisdiction is unnecessarily limiting the access to cross-border data (and electronic evidence). The argument here is that in the case of an investigation, the investigative jurisdiction should extend to any space where the data required for the investigation is located.

While from a law enforcement access to cross-border data this development of 'investigative jurisdiction' may make sense in some cases, in others the current problems may still not be overcome. One scenario where the notion of 'investigative jurisdiction' may work is when a law enforcement agent is following a trail in real-time: the investigation should not stop because the suspect or suspected information shifts servers and is on a server outside the territorial reach of the law enforcement agent. Having an 'investigative jurisdiction' would allow the agent to follow the trail irrespective of territorial concerns. One scenario where this notion of 'investigative jurisdiction' may be less useful is when requiring information directly from a private actor: which rules would the private actor be expected to follow (of location or of the investigating party) is not immediately clear and would still be dependent on some form of legal agreement. Furthermore, as Svantsson notes "it should be acknowledged that some (coercive) investigate measures may fall within a grey zone between investigative jurisdiction and enforcement jurisdiction. This is an area requiring further work."[39] Within the EU, Council Framework Decision 2002/465/JHA regulates the setting up of JITs. To carry out criminal investigations in Member States, which necessitate coordinated and concerted action, at least two Member States may set up a JIT. To that end, the competent authorities of the

---

[37] See Guidance note adopted by T-CY on Article 32 issued in December 2014: http://www.coe.int/t/dghl/cooperation/economiccrime/Source/Cybercrime/TCY/2014/T-CY%282013%297REV_GN3_transborder_V12adopted.pdf; the work of the T-CY Cloud evidence group: http://www.coe.int/t/dghl/cooperation/economiccrime/cybercrime/T-CY/Transborder%20Access/TCY_Transborder_EN.asp; Discussion paper prepared by the T-CY Cloud Evidence Group Criminal justice access to data in the cloud: challenges 2015 https://rm.coe.int/CoERMPublicCommonSearchServices/DisplayDCTMContent?documentId=0900001680304b59; Communication from the Commission to the European Parliament, the Council, the European Economic and Social Committee and the Committee of the Regions, The European Agenda on Security, http://ec.europa.eu/dgs/home-affairs/e-library/documents/basic-documents/docs/eu_agenda_on_security_en.pdf and Koops and Goodwin (2014).

[38] See Svantesson (2016) and Jerker et al. (2016), pp. 671–682.

[39] See Svantesson (2016), p. 8.

relevant Member States enter into an agreement determining the procedures to be followed by the team. The JIT must be set up for a specific purpose; and a limited period (which may be renewed with the agreement of all the parties involved). The Member States that set up the team decide on its composition, purpose and duration. They may also allow representatives of Europol and OLAF and representatives of third countries take part in the team's activities. Members of the JIT from Member States other than the Member State in which the team operates are referred to as being "seconded" to the team. They may carry out tasks in accordance with the law of the Member State where the team is operating. With respect to offences committed by them or against them, officials from a Member State other than the Member State of operation are to be regarded as officials of the Member State of operation.[40] Increasingly, this is being acknowledged as one of the most relevant instruments for LEAs to overcome territorial limitations in investigation of cross-border crimes and for sharing of cross-border electronic evidence.

11.2.3 Guidelines and Best Practices

Apart from the various existing international legal instruments there are also international guidelines and best practices, for example those provided by the EU and the Council of Europe that complement the legal instruments and provide practical guidance for handling electronic evidence. Given the importance of electronic evidence, particularly during the criminal process (in the prosecution of crimes), there is increasingly more attention to the setting of common standards for the acquisition, collection, custody and exchange of electronic evidence. While some states still apply traditional evidential rules to electronic evidence, some states already have special rules for electronic evidence.[41] Common standards include guidelines and best practices by the European Union Agency for Network and Information Security (ENISA) and by the Council of Europe. ENISA assists the EU and the Member States and cooperates with the private sector to help them meet the requirements of network and information security, it provides guidance, advice and assistance within its objectives.[42] To this end ENISA drafted a handbook[43] and a guide[44] to bridge the gap between Computer Emergency Response Teams (CERTs)—teams responsible for handling cyber incidents and risks—and law enforcement. According to ENISA

---

[40]See http://eur-lex.europa.eu/legal-content/EN/TXT/?uri=URISERV:l33172.

[41]United Nations Office on Drugs and Crime, Comprehensive Study on Cybercrime, draft February 2013, p. 55.

[42]Article 1 Regulation (EC) No 460/2004 of the European Parliament and of the Council of 10 March 2004 establishing the European Network and Information Security Agency [2004] OJ L 77.

[43]ENISA, Identification and handling of electronic evidence—Handbook, document for teachers [2013] September 2013.

[44]ENISA, Electronic evidence—a basic guide for First Responders Good practice material for CERT first responders [2014].

effective cooperation on all levels is required when it comes to cyber incidents as they do not respect organisational and territorial boundaries. While collecting and preserving electronic evidence is ultimately a task and responsibility of law enforcement, CERTs may aid law enforcement in preserving it when they detect an incident.[45] ENISA's electronic evidence guide provides guidance for CERTs on how to deal with evidence and evidence collection. According to this guide there are five internationally accepted practical principles that are considered a good basic guideline; data integrity, audit trail, specialist support, appropriate training and legality.[46] The handbook divides the collection of electronic evidence in few phases, namely: preparation, on-site, seizure, examination, evaluation and presentation.[47] The ENISA handbook and guide lack information regarding the exchange of electronic evidence. It focusses mainly on collecting evidence and a little bit on preserving and presenting (using) the evidence. It furthermore does not mention anything regarding data protection or secure systems used to exchange the data. Furthermore, from discussions with LEAs, it appears that they often consider the ENISA guidelines as more tailored towards private companies rather than LEAs. Another set of common standards is provided by the Council of Europe. The Council of Europe developed the Electronic Evidence Guide[48] (EEG) intended for use by law enforcement and judicial authorities.[49] The purpose of the guide is to provide support and guidance in the identification and handling of electronic evidence, i.e. developing responses to cybercrime and establishing rules and protocols to deal with electronic evidence. The guide may particularly be useful for training and self-training as it was developed for a wider audience including law enforcement, judges, prosecutors, private investigators, lawyers, notaries, etc. The EEG identifies the possible sources of electronic evidence and uses the same principles, as a basis that

[45]ENISA, Electronic evidence—a basic guide for First Responders Good practice material for CERT first responders [2014], p. iv.

[46]ENISA, Electronic evidence—a basic guide for First Responders Good practice material for CERT first responders [2014], p. 5–8. These principles are discussed in more detail in the handbook: ENISA, Identification and handling of electronic evidence—Handbook, document for teachers [2013] September 2013. The principles used by ENISA are the same principles used by the Council of Europe in its Electronic Evidence Guide: Council of Europe Data Protection and Cybercrime Division, Electronic Evidence Guide A basic guide for police officers, prosecutors and judges Version 1.0, Strasbourg France 18 March 2013, available via: http://www.coe.int/t/dghl/cooperation/economiccrime/cybercrime/Documents/Electronic%20Evidence%20Guide/default_en.asp.

[47]ENISA, Electronic evidence—a basic guide for First Responders Good practice material for CERT first responders [2014], p. 9–19. See also ENISA, Identification and handling of electronic evidence—Handbook, document for teachers [2013] September 2013.

[48]Council of Europe Data Protection and Cybercrime Division, Electronic Evidence Guide A basic guide for police officers, prosecutors and judges version 1.0, Strasbourg, France, 18 March 2013.

[49]Council of Europe Data Protection and Cybercrime Division, Electronic Evidence Guide A basic guide for police officers, prosecutors and judges Version 1.0, Strasbourg France 18 March 2013, available at: http://www.coe.int/t/dghl/cooperation/economiccrime/cybercrime/Documents/Electronic%20Evidence%20Guide/default_en.asp.

justifies all dealings with electronic evidence, as the ENISA handbook and guide (data integrity, audit trail, specialist support, appropriate training, legality).[50] When it comes to the collection of electronic evidence the EEG provides detailed guidance on how to search and seize onsite, how to capture evidence from the internet and how to collect evidence from third parties. The EEG furthermore provides guidance on the analysis of electronic evidence and how to prepare and present (use) the evidence in Court. Considering the complexity of cross-border crimes and dealing with electronic evidence the EEG furthermore devotes a chapter on jurisdiction and roles of the various actors. The EEG does not go into detail on the exchange of electronic evidence, but refers to the mutual legal assistance provisions in the Cybercrime Convention.[51]

11.2.4 Actors

As pointed out in chapter *The Operational Scenario* of this Volume, on a national level the actors involved in the collection, preservation, use and exchange of electronic evidence include law enforcement authorities including police forces on local, regional and national level, cybercrime units and specialised forces, prosecution and the judiciary. There are thus a massive number of actors involved. These national authorities are supported by various international and European agencies and bodies that assist Member States in preventing, detecting, investigating and prosecuting cross-border crimes. This is highly relevant when it comes to electronic evidence as these agencies and bodies may assist in international cooperation, collection and facilitate the exchange of electronic evidence. These authorities include Interpol and various EU agencies and bodies, such as Eurojust, Europol (EC3) and ENISA.

Interpol is an organisation under international law and the world's largest international police organisation with 192-member countries, which enables police around the world to work together. Interpol is a global coordinating body that ensures and promotes the widest possible mutual assistance between all criminal police authorities and establishes and develops institutions likely to contribute

[50]Council of Europe Data Protection and Cybercrime Division, Electronic Evidence Guide A basic guide for police officers, prosecutors and judges Version 1.0, Strasbourg France 18 March 2013, available via: http://www.coe.int/t/dghl/cooperation/economiccrime/cybercrime/Documents/Electronic%20Evidence%20Guide/default_en.asp, p. 14–15. See also ENISA, Electronic evidence—a basic guide for First Responders Good practice material for CERT first responders [2014], p. 5–8; ENISA, Identification and handling of electronic evidence—Handbook, document for teachers [2013] September 2013.

[51]Council of Europe Data Protection and Cybercrime Division, Electronic Evidence Guide A basic guide for police officers, prosecutors and judges Version 1.0, Strasbourg France 18 March 2013, available via: http://www.coe.int/t/dghl/cooperation/economiccrime/cybercrime/Documents/Electronic%20Evidence%20Guide/default_en.asp, p. 14–15. See also ENISA, Electronic evidence—a basic guide for First Responders Good practice material for CERT first responders [2014], p. 152.

effectively to the prevention and suppression of crimes.[52] This global coordination pays off. Operations coordinated by Interpol, Europol and/or Ameripol[53] with the support of LEAs from all over the globe has led to numerous arrests in multiple jurisdictions.[54] Interpol has a high-tech infrastructure of technical and operational support and ensures that police around the world have access to the tools and services necessary to do their jobs effectively. Interpol furthermore provides targeted training, expert investigative support, relevant data and secure communications channels and facilitates international police cooperation. Concerning cybercrime, Interpol has a new cutting-edge research and development facility, the Global Complex for Innovation (IGCI) that includes a Digital Crime Centre. This centre provides proactive research into new areas and latest training techniques, and coordinates operations in the field. The initiative about cybercrime focusses mainly on harmonisation (encouraging the creation of cybercrime investigation units and updating legal frameworks), capacity building (training courses) and operational and forensic support (Cyber Fusion Centre providing assistance during investigations, Digital Forensics lab providing practical forensic support and Working Groups Working Groups facilitating the development of regional strategies, technologies and information on the latest crime trends and methods).[55]

Interpol's European counterpart is the European Police Office (Europol), which is the EU's law enforcement agency whose main goal is to help achieve a safer Europe for the benefit of all EU citizens by assisting Member States in their fight against serious international crime and terrorism. The establishment of Europol was agreed in the Maastricht Treaty[56] and regulated in the Europol Convention,[57] which was replaced in 2010 by Council Decision 2009/371/JHA[58] and in 2016 by the Europol Regulation.[59] The new Regulation extends Europol's role and responsibilities in coordinating crime investigations and constitutes the legal basis of a new framework for Europol including a new opt-in decision that is required by Member States. This Regulation particularly names the development of the European Cybercrime Centre (EC3) as one of its key objectives. Europol supports and strengthens action by the competent authorities of the Member States and their mutual cooperation in preventing and combating organised crime, terrorism and other forms of serious

[52]Interpol Office of legal affairs, Constitution of the ICPO-INTERPOL, I/CONS/GA/1956(2008).

[53]The Police community of the Americas.

[54]See: <http://www.interpol.int/News-and-media/News>.

[55]See: http://www.interpol.int/Crime-areas/Cybercrime/Cybercrime.

[56]Treaty on European Union of 7 February 1992.

[57]Convention based on Article K.3 of the Treaty on European Union, on the establishment of a European Police Office [1995] OJ C 316/2.

[58]Council Decision of 6 April 2009 establishing the European Police Office (Europol) (2009/371/JHA) [2009] OJ L 121/37.

[59]Regulation (EU) 2016/794 of the European Parliament and of the Council of 11 May 2016 on the European Union Agency for Law Enforcement Cooperation (Europol) and Replacing and Repealing Council Decisions 2009/371/JHA, 2009/934/JHA, 2009/935/JHA, 2009/936/JHA and 2009/968/JHA [2016] OJ L 135/53.

crime. Europol staff may furthermore participate in supporting capacity in JITs. Europol's tasks include, amongst other things, to collect, store, process, analyse and exchange information and intelligence and to aid investigations in the Member States and developing specialist knowledge of investigative procedures. Each Member State has a Europol national unit, which is the liaison body between Europol and the competent authorities of the Member States. Each national unit has at least one liaison officer at the Europol headquarters in their own liaison bureau as part of the organisation mentioned before. These officers represent the interests of their national unit at Europol in accordance with the national law of their Member State. Apart from the liaison officers of the Member States Europol also hosts liaison officers from 10 non-EU countries and organisations that work together with Europol based on cooperation agreements including Interpol and several USA LEAs. In return Europol also has liaison officers in Washington DC and Interpol. This network is supported by secure channels of communication provided by Europol. Europol does not have an explicit mandate to handle electronic evidence. However, Europol's secure system "Siena" is frequently used to transfer documents. These documents may come from a competent authority in a Member State and may be sent from the national unit in that Member State to Europol and via Europol to one or more national units in other Member States, which in its turn send it to the competent authorities. The Sienna system is used between all the members of the network mentioned before. This means that the transfer from the national units to the competent authorities in the Member States need to be secured by the Member States and that the Sienna system does not provide security from end point to end point. This might provide security problems. With specific regard to cybercrime Europol has a European Cybercrime Centre (EC3) and a Joint Cybercrime Action Taskforce (J-CAT). EC3 is part of the operations department and its main task includes providing support to Member States concerning cybercrime. J-CAT further strengthens the fight against cybercrime in the EU and beyond.[60] J-CAT is a pilot hosted at the EC3 that coordinates international investigations with partners from all over the world including the UK's National Crime Agency (NCA), EC3, Eurojust, EU Cybercrime Taskforce, the Federal Bureau of Investigation (FBI) and other USA agencies NCA's with cyber liaison officers from countries including Austria, Canada, Germany, France, Italy, the Netherlands, Spain, the UK, etc. J-CAT already booked some successes, for example in taking down dark markets on the TOR network.[61]

Apart from Europol, the EU also set up Eurojust, a unit composed of national prosecutors, magistrates, or police officers of equivalent competence, detached from each Member State according to their own legal systems. Eurojust was formally established as a judicial coordination unit in 2002 by Council Decision

[60]See: https://www.europol.europa.eu/content/expert-international-cybercrime-taskforce-launched-tackle-online-crime.

[61]See: https://www.europol.europa.eu/content/global-action-against-dark-markets-tor-network.

2002/187/JHA[62] following the 9/11 attacks in the USA. The Decision was amended in 2003 by Council Decision 2003/659/JHA and in 2008 by Council Decision 2009/426/JHA. A consolidated version of the Decisions was published in 2009.[63] Eurojust is composed of 28 national members seconded by each Member State in accordance with its legal system, who is a prosecutor, judge or police officer of equivalent competence. The national officers have their regular place of work at the Eurojust seat in The Hague and are assisted by a deputy and an assistant. The national members, deputies and assistants are subject to the national law of their Member State regarding their status.[64] All 28 national members form the College of Eurojust, which is responsible for the organisation and operation of Eurojust. The College of Eurojust is supported by an administration and secretariat and is supervised by an independent joint supervisory body and a data protection office. Eurojust assists the competent authorities of Member States when dealing with cross border criminal matters. It stimulates and improves cooperation and coordination of investigations and prosecutions between the competent authorities in Member States, particularly organised crimes and crimes and offences in respect of which Europol is competent.[65] It does so for example by facilitating the execution of international mutual legal assistance and the implementation of extradition requests. It supports the competent authorities to make their investigations and prosecutions more effective in cross border cases and may, at the request of a Member State, assist in investigations and prosecutions concerning that particular Member State and a non-Member State if a cooperation agreement has been concluded or if an essential interest in providing such assistance is demonstrated.[66] Eurojust has a facilitating role in the sense that it makes requests rather than give orders, it provides advice (for example regarding jurisdiction), builds relationships with different stakeholders across Europe and hosts coordination meetings (for example when search and seizure on multiple locations in Europe take place on the same day). The competent authorities and Eurojust exchange any information necessary for the performance of its objectives and tasks.[67] Although not explicitly mentioned as such, this may include electronic evidence. Based on the Decision data security is provided for. Eurojust uses a system to communicate with home authorities that is fit for purpose.

[62]Council Decision of 28 February 2002 setting up Eurojust with a view to reinforcing the fight against serious crime (2002/187/JHA) [2002] OJ L 63/1.

[63]Council of the European Union, Consolidated version of Council decisions 2002/187/JHA, 2003/659/JHA and 2009/426/JHA, Brussels 15 July 2009, 5347/3/09 REV 3.

[64]Article 2 Council of the European Union, Consolidated version of Council decisions 2002/187/JHA, 2003/659/JHA and 2009/426/JHA, Brussels 15 July 2009, 5347/3/09 REV 3.

[65]Article 3 and 4 Council of the European Union, Consolidated version of Council decisions 2002/187/JHA, 2003/659/JHA and 2009/426/JHA, Brussels 15 July 2009, 5347/3/09 REV 3.

[66]See: http://www.eurojust.europa.eu/about/background/Pages/mission-tasks.aspx.

[67]Article 13 and 13a Council of the European Union, Consolidated version of Council decisions 2002/187/JHA, 2003/659/JHA and 2009/426/JHA, Brussels 15 July 2009, 5347/3/09 REV 3.

11.3 National Legislation and Practices

While the use of new technologies in the commission of old and new crimes (cybercrimes), contribute to make the collection and exchange of electronic evidence increasingly relevant in criminal justice, this evolution and gradual digitisation of the means necessary to collect and analyse electronic evidence has not been accompanied by a consistent and uniform evolution of the legal frameworks across Europe. Different rules and practices regarding the collection, preservation, use and exchange of electronic evidence exist in the European countries. Given the increasing use of digital devices in daily activities the attention for electronic evidence in the European and national legislation is expected to increase. While there is a certain amount of EU competence to harmonise some aspects of criminal procedural laws and to facilitate cooperation among states (e.g. providing minimum rules on mutual recognition of judgements and judicial cooperation), the competence to legislate in the field of criminal matters was left to the Member States. Most criminal laws in the European countries have a long historical background and were written long before the digital age. Legal traditions and approach thus vary per country, even per countries with similar legal traditions. Moreover, electronic evidence particularly is hardly regulated at all and a specific legal definition of electronic evidence does not exist in the European countries. The common trend among the legal frameworks is to apply general principles and rules regarding traditional evidence (on collection, exchange and probative value) also to cases involving electronic evidence. In the last years there was a slow but gradual interpretative evolution of the national criminal laws regarding the treatment of evidence, which allowed the competent actors (judges, prosecutors, lawyers, LEAs) to apply, to some extent, existing norms to cases involving electronic evidence. In other cases, some amendments to existing norms of criminal law (substantial and procedural) were necessary to make them applicable to the new technological scenarios and yet in other cases, the amendments have been considerable, comprising the replacement of, for instance, entire articles or even sections of the national criminal procedural law or the introduction of new articles also because of the implementation of a supranational legislation (e.g. the Cybercrime Convention). These laws and regulation need to be applied and interpreted accordingly by the actors involved. Although the specific knowledge and expertise of the main actors involved in the handling of electronic evidence seems to increase and best practices are gradually developing, there is, in general, a lack of knowledge by some of the main actors, as well as a lack of specific standards on the procedures and modalities to follow in the phase of collection, preservation and especially in the exchange of electronic evidence. Even when best practices do exist, they are rarely mentioned in the national laws but more often contained in non-binding texts.

The EVIDENCE project researched the need for legislative measures at the European level and created a roadmap for a uniform and efficient application of digital technologies in the collection, use and exchange of evidence. To be able to assess the need for legislative measures at European level it was necessary to research the status quo of the European legal frameworks covering the electronic evidence and to offer a picture of the existing laws and practices related to the electronic evidence. An in-depth study of thirteen EU Member States,[68] representative of different legal traditions and areas of Europe and a high level overview of the remaining Member States was carried out. The remainder of this chapter offers an extract of the results of the research carried out in this regard.

11.3.1 Differences and Similarities Between Member States

Differences in the national legal systems or the system of protection of fundamental rights may have an impact on the practices governing the handling of electronic evidence. This may have an impact on, for example, admissibility in Court in cross-border cases. To collect electronic evidence, different measures can be taken. Some Member States for example make a distinction between preventive and investigative or repressive measures. Preventive measures (including collecting electronic information, such as preventive interception of communications) are aimed at impeding, preventing the commission of crimes and at ensuring the public order in situations or in relation to individuals deemed by the competent authorities to be dangerous for society. Preventative measures are in general a competence of national bodies dependent on the Ministry of Interior and may be adopted by LEAs, police and other bodies competent to safeguard national security and may also fall within the general competences of national Security and Intelligence Services (SIS). Investigative or repressive measures are usually a competence of LEAs and police forces and presuppose the commission of a fact that might be deemed as a crime and therefore, they are aimed at investigating and collecting information on committed crimes. Transfer of information or actionable intelligence between SIS and LEAs and vice-versa is often not regulated. The distinction in legal treatment (and application of laws) to LEAs and SIS is not always clear. In most cases, the prime function of SIS is to produce actionable intelligence, which is passed on to the LEAs to act, whether it is to further monitor, follow, detain, arrest or prosecute a person or group of persons. However, there is a general lack of rules in the transfer and exchange of information or actionable intelligence and whether this information can be admitted as evidence in a criminal trial. Rules in this regard are necessary to establish whether the information or actionable intelligence can be admitted as evidence in a criminal trial. If the origin of the data is unknown or if the data was collected by SIS, the legitimacy of the source and transfer might be put in question as a clear chain of custody and documentation thereof is missing. In countries where a clear distinction between preventive and investigative measures exists the information collected for preventive purposes usually could generally not be legally used afterwards as evidence in Court. Data collected in the context of a preventive measure can however often be used as a

[68]Belgium, Bulgaria, Croatia, Denmark, Finland, Germany, Hungary, Italy, The Netherlands, Poland, Spain, Sweden and The United Kingdom.

starting point for an investigation. The functional distinction between preventive and investigative measures does not necessarily correspond to a distinction of the actors involved, i.e. both type of measures may well fall within the competence of several authorities, who may act sometimes for preventive and other times for investigative purposes and in collaboration with each other.[69] Preventive measures, such as covert surveillance on communications aimed at acquiring information necessary to ensure national public security, may be executed by SIS that generally do not have executive powers (such as arrest, search or seizure of data). These powers are exercised by LEAs and police forces based on the information transmitted by SIS.[70] These powers need to be executed regarding privacy, data protection and related rights within the system of fundamental rights. Where specific safeguards apply for the protection of fundamental rights, this may have an impact on the lawfulness and consequences of investigative measures aimed at collecting, preserving or exchanging electronic evidence. There are slight differences between Member States regarding whether and how the national legal systems provide for fundamental rights, such as data protection, telecommunications privacy, integrity of IT systems or other fundamental rights that can be affected by the collection and use of electronic evidence. Beside the different historical-cultural conceptions of these rights and the constitutional traditions of the Member States, this varied landscape is attributable to the slightly different implementation of related European legislation (e.g. in the field of data protection) and to the interpretation of these rights by the Courts of each country, particularly as it comes to deciding limits and safeguards in relation to other national rules, such as rules of criminal justice that are traditionally a competence of national Member States.[71]

11.3.1.1 Applicable Law

All legal frameworks require a legal basis for the adoption of investigative measures, such as search and seizure and any other measures in the collection, preservation, use and exchange of electronic evidence. As a general consideration it can be said that national law(s) in evidence and criminal proceedings have hardly been adjusted

[69] Italy for example has different forces, including Polizia, Guardia di Finanza and Carabinieri.

[70] In Italy and Germany for example, SIS are entitled only to gather information conducting researches and coordinating activities; this can happen through measures technically similar to those taken by the police (e.g. wire-tapping), although the adoption of these measures need to be laid down in distinct provisions defining the related conditions and purposes. From the gathered intelligence, the services can notify the police where appropriate. In northern countries such as Sweden, Finland, Denmark and Poland this distinction does not have so much relevance or it is not well-defined.

[71] Moreover, concerning the Members States' obligations on human rights as derived by international treaties, it should be recalled here that, for instance, in the application of the European Convention of Human Rights (that includes the right to privacy and other fundamental rights), the ratifying States gain a *margin of appreciation* on *how* to ensure certain rights enshrined in the Convention.

to the increasing use of new technologies, as well as on the limitations they provide in electronic evidence, including in case of collection of data by or through third parties, such as Internet Service Providers (ISPs). With a few exceptions, Member States in general do not have separate, specific rules in electronic evidence and apply general, traditional evidence rules to electronic evidence. It is striking that, with the exception of Croatia,[72] none of the Member States, which were considered for the EVIDENCE project, provides for a definition of electronic evidence. The general trend is to apply a general definition of evidence, as well as general principles of evidence also to electronic evidence. Having said that, the common factor of all Member States is that they have ratified the Cybercrime Convention and have thus introduced some rules applicable to electronic evidence into their legal frameworks. National legal frameworks applicable to electronic evidence are quite limited and fragmented, but it is possible to identify substantial and procedural norms in national legislation that are, subject to judicial interpretation, applicable to the cases that involve electronic evidence. Moreover, in some countries, specific norms have been introduced to criminal law and criminal procedural law to adapt the legal framework to the growing use of digital technologies which distinguish between physical and electronic evidence and which provide indications concerning the procedure to be followed for collecting, preserving and lawfully exchanging electronic evidence. Most of these changes to the national legal frameworks have been introduced as implementation of supranational treaties, such as the Cybercrime Convention or European legislation in related fields.

Considering that Member States in general do not have specific rules in electronic evidence the question arises whether national legislations pose any restrictions to the collection, use and admissibility of electronic evidence in Court. The answer to this question becomes clear only in 'digital documents', which are generally considered admissible in Courts and used in practice, although the conditions for their admissibility may vary according to the legal system. Some guidelines exist, although these are mainly aimed at preserving the security of (electronic) evidence during and after the trial, such as for example in England and Wales. Methods and systems to preserve (electronic) evidence vary per country and it is striking that in this digital age the digital filing systems used are often still limited in that they are generally non-interoperable systems and for internal use only. However, some countries have a more advanced digitalisation of documents where digital filing systems are used also for the exchange of data between authorities or files sent to Court electronically. For example, in Poland digitalisation of documents is encouraged and the digital filing systems are used also for the exchange of data between authorities and in Sweden the file (dossier or book of evidence) is sent to the Court electronically when charges are brought against an individual. In many cases however, digital documents are still printed out and deposited at the Courts on a physical carrier. It is furthermore striking that there is a general lack of standards

[72]Croatian Law CPC Article 202 (32) determines that *electronic (digital) evidence means data that was collected as evidence in the electronic (digital) form pursuant to this Act.*

or uniform application of digital technologies in collecting, preserving, using and exchanging evidence. Beside the existence of ISO international standards, most Member States use non-binding guidelines or procedures that include technical procedures such as chain of custody or specific forensic-technical norms. Among the conditions and procedural requirements established by law for the collection, preservation, use and exchange of electronic evidence, mention should be made of those requirements aimed at safeguarding individuals against violation of data protection rights, as well as against 'function creep', i.e. e-evidence collected for a certain purpose may end up being used for a different purpose. In this respect, the concept of 'surplus information' that can be found for example in Finland and Denmark is very interesting. Surplus information is information obtained by telecommunications interception, traffic data monitoring, obtaining base station data and technical surveillance that is not related to an offence or averting a danger, or that concerns an offence other than the one for the prevention of which the authorisation has been granted or the decision made. Only in some countries can the evidence collected for a certain case be used in different proceedings under specific safeguards.

11.3.1.2 New Technologies and Investigative Measures

In this digital age where technologies keep evolving, so do crimes. Criminals may use advanced technologies and law enforcement cannot lag behind. New technologies have influenced the different techniques of investigation that law enforcement and prosecution use in criminal proceedings. Most legal frameworks include rules covering the legal and technical procedures that need to be followed in the collection of electronic evidence in criminal investigations. These procedures primarily aim at ensuring a minimum set of legal safeguards (e.g. judicial oversight) and, secondly, at ensuring the integrity, reliability and preservation of the evidence itself. However, these existing rules remain quite general and imprecise for the technical measures to be adopted. As general rules regarding the collection of traditional evidence (e.g. inspection and seizure) usually apply, the evidence is considered admissible in Court if it has been collected in accordance with the law. Its probative value is usually deemed to be the same as of the traditional evidence, although the (level of) authenticity and reliability of the electronic evidence may play a relevant role on this regard. There is a general consensus regarding the effectiveness of using digital technologies in the collection of evidence; technologies make copying and transferring data easier and facilitates exchange, it enables investigative bodies to collect a much wider spectrum of information, improves the speed and accuracy of investigation as it allows access to information about a suspect's activities for a long period, it ensures the collection of sturdy and precise information about a committed crime, allows the collection of evidence that was previously unavailable and safeguards the integrity, reliability and preservation of electronic evidence.

11.3.1.3 Lawful Interception

Electronic evidence can be collected in different ways, including by way of lawful interception. Within the legal frameworks across Europe the following interceptions are distinguished:

- Lawful interception of digital data in a network (e.g. internet);
- Direct access to a terminal device;
- Computer assisted search and;
- Seizure of digital data.

While in some countries certain specific provisions have been introduced in the national criminal system to cover at least some of the new kinds of interceptions of digital communications, in other countries these provisions do not exist and general rules on interceptions may apply. The common trend is that, in general, interceptions are considered exceptional, admitted only in relation to serious crimes (although the definition of serious crimes varies per country) and are subject to legal procedures (e.g. judicial warrant). However, it is not always clear what legal regime would apply in case of interceptions of digital devices by certain modalities, such as covert monitoring of computer devices, as in some countries this would fall within the special investigative measures, permitted only under 'national security' investigations. This means that the legal safeguards that these legal procedures seek to ensure may be jeopardised by the absence of a clear legal framework that is worrisome considering the development of digital technologies and the ease for LEAs and SIS to access large amounts of data, especially on the internet. In this regard it is also important to mention that, because of the Court of Justice of the European Union (CJEU) ruling which invalidated the Data Retention Directive,[73] some national legal frameworks across Europe were subject to constitutional review before the respective Constitutional Courts and declared unconstitutional. For example, Germany invalidated its national Data Retention law as unconstitutional and does not require ISPs and telecom companies to retain their clients' traffic data while other countries do. In other countries the corresponding law is still in force or new legislation was put in place.[74] These issues are further developed and discussed in Chap. 13 of this Volume.

11.3.1.4 Preservation and Use

Electronic evidence is volatile, it can be quite easily altered or deleted. It is therefore very important to have rules in place regarding chain of custody, preservation

[73]CJEU, C-293/12 Digital Rights Ireland, ECLI: EU: C104:238.

[74]In CJEU, C-203-15 Tele2 Sverige, ECLI:EU:C2016:970 the CJEU also held that national laws providing for the retention of traffic data need to be in line with Article 7 and 8 of the Charter of Fundamental Rights of the European Union.

and access control. Most legal frameworks do not determine explicitly who is authorised to process electronic evidence. Processing electronic evidence, particularly search and seizure of computer data and information systems, requires expertise and knowledge. In general, national Courts appoint a consultant or judicial expert to process the evidence. However, there is a general lack of binding rules regarding professional requirements. With a few exceptions where norms have been introduced, to consider preservation of seized computer data and information systems, in most cases general rules of preservation of evidence also applies to electronic evidence. Where norms have been introduced, these are binding only in the results ('suitable measures to preserve the authenticity, integrity and reliability of data'), not in technical methods to be adopted. Generally, operating procedures for the preservation of electronic evidence exist in secondary legislation or internal rules. Increasingly, electronic evidence nowadays is held by the private sector. In this regard there is a general lack of rules and procedures for LEAs to comply with when accessing data held by the private sector. In general, LEAs need to obtain authorisation by a Court to access this data. There is a consensus that digital technologies make processing and preserving evidence more effective. Digital technologies can offer advantages when handling large amounts of data. Considering that electronic evidence can be copied, a larger amount of people and even several competent authorities can work simultaneously on the same case to investigate the large amount of data. Preserving electronic evidence furthermore does not require much physical space compared to physical evidence and it is easier and more cost efficient to preserve electronic evidence over a longer timeframe while protecting its integrity, reliability and keep it from being altered. However, this requires secure storage. From a prosecution perspective, the use of computers and electronically accessible files by prosecutors during trial opens possibilities for the use of more pedagogical methods to explain a complex case in a way that gives full effect to the value of the evidence. However, as much as technology aids to acquire and process large amounts of data, if the evidence is preserved for long amount of time, from a technical perspective, the hardware and/or software used may become obsolete and the authenticity and trustworthiness of the electronic evidence could be put in question. Records or electronic evidence management systems should be build, organised and preserved by trained professionals in modern archival procedures of digital preservation.

11.3.1.5 Admissibility and Probative Value

The evidence collected in criminal investigations will eventually need to be used in Court. In cross-border cases, when the evidence was collected under the rules of a different legal regime, the question rises whether the evidence is admissible in Court. While some countries have specific best practices and practical guidelines (including technical procedures) that are used in practice in the collection, preservation and exchange of electronic evidence,[75] others countries do not have any publicly available information on operational guidelines or on specific codes of conduct. Technical or automated means, which are possibly used by LEAs in investigations, are defined broadly. The only explicit legal limitation to the use of digital technologies in the collection, preservation and exchange that may affect the admissibility of electronic evidence are those arising from general rules on the collection of evidence. This includes rules that require the evidence to be collected in respect of certain procedural requirements and in a lawful manner, i.e. legal safeguards to avoid breach of fundamental rights.[76] Courts will generally decide on admissibility of evidence on a case by case basis and if the evidence is collected contrary to legal safeguards it may be declared inadmissible. For instance, the issue of admissibility may arise when evidence is illegally obtained because the conditions for applying the measures that led to the collection of evidence were not fulfilled. However, since these measures are in general under the control of the Court, in most of the cases admissibility issues are avoided. As for the probative value of electronic evidence, rules that count are usually those aimed at ensuring the authenticity, integrity and reliability of the evidence (e.g. irregularities may affect the trustworthiness of evidence).[77] In practice, although the national legal systems do not have explicit regulations on the probative value of electronic evidence and no standards exist, it is generally recognised as very important to duly document the data acquisition procedure, for instance, the interception techniques used and how the evidence has been preserved, according to the chain of custody. Therefore, the electronic nature of evidence, while it does not seem to affect its admissibility, it may have impact on its probative value (quality), depending on the evidence and how it was obtained. The problem seems to be more ‘how’ to interpret the conclusions that one can draw from the (forensic) findings resulting from a digital evidence. For those reasons, in most of the countries, Courts refer to (forensic) experts to examine the electronic evidence (including the procedure used in individual cases to collect it) and to provide their assessment and evaluation. Forensic experts seem to play an important role as expert witnesses, to explain and thereby give reliability to the electronic evidence. Therefore, judges usually base their decision on experts’ analysis, although they remain free to decide differently, if they motivate their judgements. This also means that it is essential that the judge can truly understand how the evidence has been handled and is able to determine its authenticity. However, the level of knowledge of the judiciary still lags behind

[75]See Mason (2012).

[76]See e.g., rules safeguarding the right to due process or fundamental right, including, in certain cases, data protection: the compliance with the latter, although cannot be considered as general ‘conditio sine qua non’ for the admissibility of electronic evidence, may affect the admissibility of evidence in certain countries.

[77]For instance in Germany, the general legal conditions of §9 BDSG obliges law enforcement agencies as public authorities to secure their systems and digital technology-based investigative measures through technical and organisational measures.

dramatically considering that there is a general lack of training and education in this regard.

11.3.1.6 Cross-Border Scenarios

Considering that electronic evidence is not necessarily linked to the same territorial jurisdiction as where an alleged crime would have taken place or is being investigated, cross-border scenarios are an important aspect when dealing with electronic evidence. There are three aspects of this cross-border nature of electronic evidence: (1) where the evidence may be located because of the information provider recording the information[78]; (2) where the actual digital information is stored[79]; and (3) where the crime itself has a cross-border nature.[80] These three effects of the cross-border nature of electronic evidence are very important when regulating electronic evidence in the criminal law process. Cross-border scenarios and exchanging electronic evidence between the competent authorities of the countries involved are thus an important part of legislation in electronic evidence considering the very nature of electronic evidence and that it can be stored or located globally. However, current national and international legal frameworks are insufficient to meet with the current needs and current shortcomings are not merely a matter of introducing new agreements but are more complex, needing new theoretical frameworks and the collaboration of a large variety of actors. As mentioned before, the Cybercrime Convention (as well as the other international and European legal instruments) is the common factor between Member States and the leading legal instrument in Europe and beyond to exchange electronic evidence. International laws are implemented in the national legal systems of Member States and impact on investigations of national prosecution authorities that exceed national borders. Most Member States have national legislation covering cases of requests for exchange of evidence in general or exchange evidence pursuant to bilateral or multilateral agreements (e.g. European Convention on Mutual Assistance in Criminal Matters). Legislation mostly refers to evidence in general and does not specifically mention electronic evidence. In cross-border scenarios, cloud services

---

[78]*Location of (private) information provider*: Many forms of electronic evidence originates from private sources e.g. internet services providers have access/possess useful electronic information that can at times be used as electronic evidence in a trial. Many of the key private actors involved are not registered or located in the same country where a particular crime is being investigated and prosecuted.

[79]*Location and storage of electronic evidence*: Because of the very nature of it, modern technologies and growing globalisation, electronic evidence may be located or stored anywhere in the world. This is especially the case in cybercrime cases, as cybercrime is a global problem that does not stop at our countries' borders, but also increasingly in crimes in general.

[80]*Cross-border nature of the alleged crime*: In some crimes e.g. cybercrimes, the crime often takes place across different jurisdictions, making the collection, preservation and use of information for evidentiary purposes more difficult and reliant on pre-existing agreements between states (where these exist) for the exchange of electronic evidence.

for data storage have become an increasingly interesting area that is hardly covered by legislation. Legally speaking, this cloud services are particularly interesting considering that the cloud service provider, the data centres and the 'suspect' may be located in different countries. Various legal challenges pop up in this regard, including investigative issues and questions of jurisdiction. This is a relatively new area, meaning that the academic and public debate on these issues are still ongoing and that there is hardly any research in this field, let alone legislation covering the collection or exchange of electronic evidence that is stored in the cloud. Considering that there is hardly any specific legislation covering this topic, the Cybercrime Convention and general evidentiary rules on evidence apply and are left to the discretion of the national judicial authorities. For example, in cases where the cloud service provider or the suspect are located in a known foreign country, the general rules for the collection of other evidences apply. In cases where the physical storage location is unknown, the legal scenario becomes more problematic. This impacts investigation of evidence located in cloud services. Considering the very nature of electronic evidence and that it can be stored or located anywhere in the world, the exchange of electronic evidence between competent authorities in cross-border scenarios is a very important aspect when dealing with electronic evidence. While there is international legislation in this regard as elaborated in the first part of this chapter, there is a general lack of regulation in national legislation concerning the exchange of electronic evidence. Member States hardly provide for specific rules, guidelines or procedures on the exchange of electronic evidence and apply general rules and guidelines that are applicable to traditional evidence.

What national laws seem to ignore is the overwhelmingly cross-border nature of electronic evidence. The presence of electronic evidence is often not linked to the same territorial jurisdiction as where an alleged crime would have taken place or is being investigated. Given that predominantly territorial nature of judicial (or adjudicative) and enforcement jurisdiction of most crimes, any cross-border element to a crime or evidence of a crime is primarily regulated through international agreements concluded for this purpose between states. The same applies to the cross-border nature of electronic evidence. However, there is no comprehensive international or European legal framework relating to (electronic) evidence. What is present is a patchwork of international and European legal instruments and policy documents as mentioned before, as well as bilateral and multilateral agreements, which govern some of the issues often in an unsatisfactory manner. For example, when obtaining (electronic) evidence from a different country, within the EU, the EIO Directive[81] sets up a comprehensive new system that allows EU Member States to obtain evidence in other Member States in criminal cases that involve more than one Member State. The EIO covers any investigative measure except for the setting up of a JIT and the collection of evidence within such a team as provided in Article 13 of the Convention on Mutual Assistance in Criminal Matters. Within

[81]Directive 2014/41/EU of the European Parliament and of the Council of 3 April 2014 regarding the European Investigation Order in criminal matters [2014] OJ L 130/1.

all of Europe, the Council of Europe Convention on Mutual Assistance in Criminal Matters also applies which sets out rules for the enforcement of letters rogatory by the authorities of a Party that aim to procure evidence or to communicate the evidence in criminal proceedings undertaken by the judicial authorities of another Party and specifies the requirements for such proceedings. These general rules and guidelines were of course introduced with traditional evidence in mind. Most states have extended their application also to electronic evidence. While this is the most used method to obtain evidence from other countries, the process is slow, bureaucratic and time consuming and does not match the volatile and fast-moving nature of electronic evidence.

Perhaps the strongest drawback is that it is primarily aimed at states and not private actors considering that in many instances electronic information is under the control of private actors such as the larger ISPs, including Google, Facebook, Yahoo, etc. From yearly disclosure reports of some of these companies[82] several hundreds of thousands of requests for information go out every year from European states to major USA providers. Each of these requests need to be accompanied by a mutual legal assistance request for the information to be considered admissible as evidence by the courts of the requesting state. These mutual legal assistance requests go from the requesting state authority to the requested state then the requested state must transmit that request (subject to few legal requirements) to the private company. It is important to keep in mind that this cumbersome process needs to be followed for evidence that may be easily deleted, moved or changed to another format (e.g. encrypted) and where speed of capture or seizing the evidence is crucial. The further issue with being so reliant on private actors in the collection and preservation of potential electronic evidence is ascertaining the reliability of the evidence. In traditional crimes, the investigation of a crime and handling of potential evidence is carried out by law enforcement agents who follow pre-determined protocols to ensure the integrity of evidence collected. One criticism levelled against private actors is that they are unprepared to ensure the same levels of integrity that is expected for a legal process. There is no legal framework so far that determines what level of 'forensic readiness' private actors should be expected to follow. As has been documented,[83] using mutual legal assistance to obtain information or electronic evidence from private actors is often very challenging for LEAs. Several issues have been identified: (1) mutual legal assistance requests are not specific and precise enough to enable companies to reply rapidly and efficiently; (2) services on mobile devices, based on apps; (3) data retention; and (4) difficulties with obtaining evidence on certain types of technologies, such as blockchains and virtual currencies.

[82]See for example the Google Transparency Report, available at https://www.google.com/transparencyreport/ and the Vodafone Law Enforcement Disclosure report, available at https://www.vodafone.com/content/sustainabilityreport/2014/index/operating_responsibly/privacy_and_security/law_enforcement.html?.

[83]See for example James and Gladyshev (2016), p. 23–32.

Apart from the EIO Directive and the Council of Europe Convention on Mutual Assistance in Criminal Matters, the Cybercrime Convention applies in cases where the crimes involved are cybercrimes. One of the weaknesses of the Convention is that it does not clearly provide for the real-time collection and/or interception of traffic and content data when the alleged content is outside the jurisdiction of the state investigating a particular crime. According to the Convention, competent authorities are empowered to collect or record traffic data transmitted by a computer system by technical means in real-time (Article 20 Convention). The competent authority may also compel a service provider to collect or record or to cooperate and assist the competent authorities in the collection or recording of traffic data. The collection or recording should be related to specified communications and within the territory of the state where the competent authority is located. If general principles of domestic law prevent the State Party to do so, it shall take other measures necessary to ensure the real-time collection or recording of traffic data. If a service provider is asked for assistance, the service provider is obliged to keep the execution of this power confidential. Cybercrime does not consider national borders, meaning that the data involved in cybercrime and the crime itself or the perpetrator are found extraterritorially to the investigating jurisdiction. In certain cases, the investigating jurisdiction may access the data regardless of the geographical location of the data without authorisation of the other jurisdiction based on Article 32 of the Cybercrime Convention. In all other cases, the investigating party is required to ask for mutual assistance, which is a time-consuming procedure.

Based on the international and European legal instruments and agreements, the extent to which states have tailored these general rules to the collection and sharing of electronic evidence varies greatly. In Italy, for example, in accordance with supranational agreements, Italian legislation explicitly covers cases in which national authorities are requested to collect or transfer evidence to another country (Article 723–726 ter CPC) and vice-versa (Article 727–729 CPC). These are general rules on evidence, but no specific rule exists on the cross-border exchange of electronic evidence. As for the Cybercrime Convention, Italy implemented this Convention with the Law 48/2008, which has not only introduced new types of crimes in the Criminal Code (CC) and has amended the Criminal Procedure Code (CPC) providing for new provisions on the use of new technologies (e.g. Article 254 bis CPC), but has also modified the existent provisions in the CPC and the CC to regulate cases in which electronic evidence is involved.[84] However, the provisions of the Criminal Procedure Code seem to contain less detailed or specific measures than the Cybercrime Convention. A similar situation can be found in Bulgaria where the general rules on international cooperation in criminal matters cover the collection of evidence. However, they do not provide for detailed rules. Apart from the obligations originating from the Cybercrime Convention, there are no specific national rules about requests and obligation to collect and/or

[84]For example Article 615 quinquies, 635 bis CC; Article 244 co. 2, 247 co. 1-bis, 254, 352 co.1-bis, 354 co. 2 of the Italian CPC.

transfer electronic evidence to authorities of another country. It can be said that Cybercrime Convention has been fully implemented into national law in Bulgaria.[85] As for similar constitutional traditions, the international treaties in Bulgaria, which have been ratified in accordance with the constitutional procedure, are part of the legislation of the state. The related norms have primacy over any conflicting provision of domestic legislation, i.e. the provisions of the Convention prevail in case of conflict with national provisions, including the rules on procedural law. Germany has also ratified and implemented the main international and European agreements, such as the Act on international cooperation in criminal matters[86]; Act on bilateral treaty between Germany and the USA about mutual assistance in criminal matters.[87] and the Convention on Mutual Assistance in Criminal Matters between the Member States of the European Union.[88] As for the Cybercrime Convention, it can be said that it has been implemented only partially in Germany, at least as far as the procedural law is concerned.

11.3.2 Challenges and Shortcomings

Based on the status quo of national and international legislation in the collection, preservation, use and exchange of electronic evidence, the challenges and shortcomings of the legal frameworks within the EU become apparent. These challenges and shortcomings include legal and data protection issues, problems with law enforcement particularly cross-border cases when evidence needs to be exchanged and technical issues in training and technical capabilities.

While criminal law is regulated at national level, it is inevitable to have some overarching international regulations and agreements. Not only considering globalisation and modern technologies and because crimes—both 'regular' crimes

[85]The relevant provisions include Article 125, 159, and 163 of the Bulgarian Criminal Procedure Code; Article 73, Chapter 15 on security and confidentiality of electronic communications networks and services, confidentiality of communications and data protection and Chapter 19 on ensuring conditions for interception of electronic communications related to national security and public order of the Electronic Communications Act; Special Intelligence Means Act and Article 90 of the Ministry of Interior Act.

[86]See: Gesetz über die internationale Rechtshilfe in Strafsachen (IRG).

[87]Available at: http://www.bgbl.de/banzxaver/bgbl/stArticlexav?start=//*[@attr_id=%27bgbl207034.pdf%27]#__bgbl__%2F%2F*[%40attr_id%3D%27bgbl207034.pdf%27]__1409231444625.

[88]See: Gesetz zu dem Übereinkommen vom 29 Mai 2000 über die Rechtshilfe in Strafsachen zwischen den Mitgliedstaaten der Europäischen Union. If there is no bilateral treaty that governs the legal assistance between the Federal Republic of Germany and the partner country, the IRG applies subsidiarily to countries outside the EU (§38 IRG and §39 IRG) and to Member States of the EU (§88 ff: Confiscation and Deprivation, §94 IRG: Request for sequestration, §97 IRG: Requests for passing on of evidence). Available at http://www.gesetze-im-internet.de/englisch_irg/index.html.

and cybercrimes may be committed across borders, but also considering the very nature of electronic evidence, particularly cybercrimes, and that it may be found anywhere in the world. The fact that criminal law is regulated at national level makes this problematic as all countries have different rules, procedures and approach. In certain countries traditional investigative powers might be general enough to apply to cases involving electronic evidence while in other countries traditional procedural laws might not cover such issues, making it necessary to have additional specific legislation. In both cases legislation requires a clear scope of application of powers and sufficient legal authority for actions.[89] Although Europe scores reasonably high on the sufficiency of national law for investigations, the main gaps in investigative powers include the lack of power to enter electronic networks to search for evidence and the lack of power to preserve computer data to support existing search powers.[90] There is thus a lack of harmonisation in substantive and procedural provisions, different approach to jurisdictional coverage of substantive and investigative provisions and there are different powers of investigation and enforcement. This makes it particularly difficult when the crime is committed in or has effects in several jurisdictions.

While a crime may be reported locally, the offence may have been initiated outside national boundaries or have some cross-border dimension, meaning that evidence may be found across borders, particularly cybercrime. Cybercrime is a global problem, meaning that law enforcement must adopt a coordinated and collaborative cross border approach to respond to this growing threat.[91] Enforcement can thus go from a local to a global level and back to local level (e.g. where the start of an investigation starts at a local level following a report by a victim in the state where the law enforcement agency is placed, then ask for evidence to be collected and retained by a foreign agency and then using that evidence in the prosecution of a crime in the Courts of the requesting state). This local-global-local process requires an effective legal framework that allows this process to happen. An effective enforcement scheme is required to prevent, detect and investigate crimes. However, the differences in national legislation and approach are problematic for law enforcement particularly concerning successful international cooperation. Although international cooperation has proven successful, there are few realities that need to be faced as coordination is costly and difficult to carry out for trivial matters such as time zone differences and nuances of local laws and customs in the jurisdictions involved.[92] Furthermore, technologies are developing rapidly and policing technologies need to be revolutionised with it, especially

[89] United Nations Office on Drugs and Crime, Comprehensive Study on Cybercrime, draft February 2013, p. 122, 123.

[90] United Nations Office on Drugs and Crime, Comprehensive Study on Cybercrime, draft February 2013, p. 124.

[91] Joint communication to the European Parliament, the Council, the European Economic and Social Committee and the Committee of Regions Cybersecurity Strategy of the European Union: An Open, Safe and Secure Cyberspace [2013] JOIN(2013) 1 final, p. 9.

[92] See Gragido et al. (2013), p. 137.

considering the growing importance of electronic evidence. However, not all police forces may be equipped to handle such evidence. Finally, and probably most importantly, because of this local-global-local dimension of international crimes there are different levels of law enforcement involved and international cooperation and the exchange of evidence usually takes place via international actors such as Interpol or Europol. There is generally no direct contact between the local law enforcement authorities making the process slow and more difficult.

While there have been certain initiatives to bridge the gaps, including by the EU and Council of Europe, limitations remain. While certain of the international instruments attempt to provide for a basic level of harmonisation and standards for international cooperation there are still several limitations. Not all countries over the world are part of European initiatives, certain international instruments allow for reservations, diminishing their effect, difficulties with electronic evidence, jurisdiction, enforcement procedures, difficulties in enforcement, possible infringements of fundamental rights, etc. Existing legislative and enforcement frameworks and the concepts enshrined therein, as well as data protection concepts, precede the creation of the internet as we know today and do not satisfactorily deal with the realities of technological developments. Certain crimes do not consider national borders, the (electronic) evidence involved and the crime itself or the perpetrator may be found extraterritorially. This requires international cooperation, which may prove difficult in some cases because of differences in national enforcement legislation and approach. This is further difficult considering that electronic evidence is increasingly held by the private sector and that there is a general lack of legislation and uniform procedures to collect this evidence. Cybercrimes for example are rarely only EU-based as in many cases they involve third countries' companies (e.g. from the USA). Given that third countries do not seem to be very cooperative with European LEAs when asked to provide information or evidence on a crime and the European Convention on Mutual Assistance in Criminal Matters might not be invoked, a way out may be identified in making sure that LEAs are trained so that specific and precise (legal or technical) questions to third countries' companies can be asked and that companies may be able to reply more rapidly and efficiently. A better cooperation with ISPs and standard procedures or format to facilitate investigations in the collection of electronic evidence from the private sector is necessary. In many cases companies provide access to data but they deliver it as printouts of thousands of documents that require further investigation and efforts. It would therefore be useful to establish a common regulation at EU level on how companies are obligated to deliver their data in particular standard format. The formats would depend in the type of data (text, audio, video, etc.). Criminal investigations are too much in the hands of the willingness of a particular provider to provide the investigation with crucial information on traffic data, on subscription information or the personal data that may reveal an individual's doings on the internet. A further problem of obtaining electronic evidence from ISPs is represented by the growing world of services on mobile devices, based on apps. While before it was quite simple to identify the ISP to ask information nowadays, every app producer, in theory, can become a service provider but at the same time not be viewed as a service provider in legal terms. It may be unclear, for each mobile service, what the internal structure of the database is or how the data is distributed and copied. The problem with this kind of entities not being recognised as service providers is in the non-applicability of the corresponding legal duties. ISPs have particular obligations, e.g. when it comes to providing data to LEA authorities as defined by (some) national data retention laws. All this electronic evidence needs to be preserved in terms of implementation of adequate archival procedures of (long-term) preservation of electronic records that might one day become evidence and proactive preservation of collected electronic evidence during the prosecution period. There is a general lack of standards in this regard and data retention periods vary across Europe, which is a main challenge that requires more harmonisation.

After the evidence is collected it will eventually need to be used in Court. One of the major challenges in this regard is lack of knowledge within the judiciary. Judicial actors need to be trained so that a minimal knowledge on electronic evidence and on its use in the judicial system is guaranteed, which would reduce the waste of time and resources in, for instance, translating investigation results from LEA to other judicial actors. It would be useful to clarify how the use of offensive technologies by LEAs to acquire data is compatible with the rules of law, notably, to clarify what lawful interceptions are (if we consider the use of sophisticated technologies). To investigate efficiently an alleged criminal, it may be necessary for LEAs to act in an offensive manner by performing intrusion on criminals' systems or internet networks used by criminals or find other ways to intercept message and data exchanged to and from criminals' system. Without a clear definition at the EU level of what is allowed for LEA, sometimes an investigation cannot take place. In the virtual world, investigations cannot follow the same model as in real physical world, for instance, because there is the possibility of making identical copies. While in the physical world when an object is seized it can be returned to the owner after the judicial process in the same state, virtual things (e.g. virtual currencies) could change over time. Currently, there is no legislation on acquiring virtual currencies that may evolve over time. For example, a bitcoin may completely change in value during the investigation and the question is who is responsible for the loss or benefits.

11.3.3 Criteria for Uniform Regulation

Solving the current shortcomings is not merely a matter of introducing new agreements or a better harmonisation of rules on electronic evidence. The situation is arguably more complex, needing new theoretical frameworks and the collaboration of a large variety of actors. When identifying the challenges and shortcoming concerning the collection, preservation, use and exchange of electronic evidence the question arises whether the EU should move towards a uniform set of rules that facilitate the exchange of electronic evidence across borders; "What should be harmonised, if at all?". To answer this question reflections on the current rules on collection, preservation and use of electronic evidence around Europe; and existing rules on transfer and exchange are necessary.

Before embarking on answering this question it is important to remember that all Member States have at least one important basis in common: protection of fundamental rights. The collection, preservation, use and exchange of electronic evidence can only be sound and effective if it is based on fundamental rights and freedoms and individuals' rights cannot be secured without safe networks and systems. Law enforcement, prosecution and the judiciary should execute investigative powers and procedures with regard for human rights and liberties. Protecting fundamental rights, freedom of expression, personal data and privacy are of utmost importance. Therefore, security, investigative and procedural measures need to be proportionate and guided by core values such as human dignity, freedom, democracy, equality, the rule of law and the respect for fundamental rights. Fundamental rights, democracy and the rule of law need to be protected in cyberspace while protecting against incidents, malicious activities and misuse. These rights and freedoms also include the right to a fair trial, particularly when preparing a defence case where electronic evidence forms part of the evidence. All Member States provide for the codification of fundamental rights. Any common European framework for the systematic and uniform application of new technologies in the collection, use and exchange of electronic evidence should be based on the protection of fundamental rights and freedoms, including proper restrictions and safeguards. The basis for this already exists in the Member States of the EU through the ratification of the ECHR and through constitutional provisions and traditions in the different Member States.

11.3.3.1 Should the Prevailing Rules on Collection, Preservation and Use of Electronic Evidence in Europe be Harmonised?

Legal Basis and Uniform Definitions, Concepts and Standards

The collection, preservation, use and exchange of electronic evidence should be based on clear and precise legislative provisions. This is currently embedded within the national laws of the Member States. All Member States provide a legal basis for investigative measures, be it traditional or specialised laws, and all Member States allow applying general rules of (traditional) evidence to electronic evidence. However, there is no uniform regulation, no standardisation and use of definitions.

So far there is no evidence that a lack of a common definition of what is electronic evidence has kept Member States from working together on the collection, preservation and use of electronic evidence. Neither is there evidence that the lack of a definition of what constitutes 'evidence' in the European Convention on Mutual Assistance in Criminal Matters, has been an impediment for the mutual assistance between European countries. While, in theory, having a uniform definition of electronic evidence may be of assistance to facilitate the process of exchange of electronic evidence, this is dispensable for the collaboration between Member States. The definition developed and used in the EVIDENCE project mentioned at the beginning of this chapter may be a useful point of departure: *electronic evidence* is defined as "any information (comprising the output of analogue devices or data in digital format) of potential probative value that is manipulated, generated through, stored on or communicated by any electronic device".[93]

Common and Specific Rules, Definitions, Standards and Procedures of Collection

While some Member States may have certain specialised technical provisions in the collection of electronic evidence, all Member States (also) apply the rules, concepts and procedures for traditional evidence apply to electronic evidence. These rules, concepts and procedures in many cases may however be outdated and not equipped for electronic evidence, which leads to enforcement issues and possibly to admissibility issues, particularly cross-border cases. A common European framework for the systematic and uniform application of new technologies in the collection, use and exchange of electronic evidence should be based on clear and specific rules for the collection of electronic evidence, common definitions and standards and approximation of legal procedures.

It can also be argued that what is needed is not uniform legal rules for collection (as a legal basis for collection exists already in all Member States) but rather operational guidelines or rules on the actual handling of electronic evidence. While all Member States have within their country certain specific agencies or units, particularly forensic institutes, specialised in the collection, examination and preservation of evidence, there are limited guidelines or procedures for the use of digital technologies in criminal proceedings. A common European framework for the systematic and uniform application of new technologies in the collection, use and exchange of electronic evidence should include a plan for the development of common guidelines and procedures.

Collection of evidence by private sector actors and the passage of electronic evidence from the private sector and LEAs also needs to be addressed. It is increasingly evident that a large part of electronic evidence originates from private sector actors, e.g. ISPs providing traffic data of internet transactions, telecommunications providers providing information on mobile communications, etc. There is currently no national framework that clearly regulates this relationship and the origin, collection and use of electronic evidence from the private sector. This is a gap that a common European framework for the systematic and uniform application of new technologies in the collection, use and exchange of electronic evidence can address.

Guidelines for Preservation and Use

Apart from the provisions in the Cybercrime Convention (and as implemented by the States Party to the Cybercrime Convention) on expedited preservation of data stored on a computer and of traffic data, there is a general lack of specialised regulation across Europe concerning preservation methods and use, including standards or

---

[93]Definition used in the EVIDENCE Project—Deliverable 2.1—EVIDENCE Semantic Structure, p. 18.

guidelines on who is authorised to process the electronic evidence in what stage of the criminal proceeding and access restrictions, specifications on how the evidence must be preserved and how to handle evidence obtained from private companies. In line with the suggested position for rules on the collection of electronic evidence a common European framework for the systematic and uniform application of new technologies in the collection, use and exchange of electronic evidence need to include legislative and other measures, including guidelines on the preservation of electronic evidence, and including rules on access restrictions, authorisation, method and duration of preservation, data protection, and other rules. Furthermore, where any of the tasks of preservation and examination of electronic evidence is to be carried out by private sector actors, additional safeguards are to be put into place to ensure the proper preservation and retention of electronic evidence.

Specific Investigative Measures

Not all Member States cover certain interception and search and seizure methods (that lead to electronic evidence) within their national legal frameworks. Where rules exist these follow from the provisions of the Cybercrime Convention and apply mostly to the investigation of cybercrimes. Most of the Member States extend the application of traditional investigative methods to electronic evidence. While in some cases this might work, generally these methods do not sufficiently cover the specific nature of electronic evidence collection. A more specific legal basis is necessary to obtain electronic evidence, particularly to avoid admissibility issues in cross-border cases. A common European framework for the systematic and uniform application of new technologies in the collection, use and exchange of electronic evidence should thus include specific, clear and precise investigative measures in the collection of electronic evidence.

Admissibility Based on Mutual Trust

Admissibility of electronic evidence is generally not an issue and electronic evidence is generally admissible if it has been legally obtained and is assessed on a case by case basis by the Court. However, given that the requirement of 'legally obtained' is not a uniform requirement (e.g. in Sweden the principle of free evaluation of evidence, meaning that evidence is not refused on the ground of how it was collected, prevails), the non-uniform approach may be a barrier for the use of electronic evidence obtained from another jurisdiction. It is thus important to set common standards in this regard. While the probative value of the evidence is not diminished because of the electronic nature of the evidence and collection, preservation, use and exchange of electronic evidence in criminal proceeding is generally not restricted or prohibited by law, the very nature of electronic evidence makes it volatile and easy to manipulate. Common standards for maintaining the integrity of the electronic evidence are therefore necessary while at the same time electronic evidence obtained in one Member State should not have any difficulties with admissibility in another Member State.

There may be two approaches here: either the drafting of common rules on that admissibility of evidence (in the cross-border context) or an agreement that the law of the requested state (that is the law of the state providing the evidence to a requesting state) prevails in the context of cross-border situations. It is then still up to the Court of the requesting state to decide whether to admit the evidence to the proceedings or not. This concept of following the law of the requesting state is a concept familiar to both the Cybercrime Convention and to the European Convention on Mutual Assistance in criminal matters.

Regulation of Cloud Computing
There is hardly any regulation across Europe concerning cloud computing and electronic evidence that is stored or located in the cloud. Considering the growing importance of cloud services, a common European framework should include specific provisions in the collection of electronic evidence out of a cloud service. This rule should go further than the search and seizure rules (for electronic evidence) that exist in the Cybercrime Convention, as the current rules are bound to the territorial jurisdiction of the state where the investigation is taking place. Rules on the obtaining of evidence from the cloud need to go beyond the current limitations of territorial jurisdiction. One possible way is to agree on a 'universal jurisdiction' approach in the investigation of serious crimes.

11.3.3.2 Should the Prevailing Rules on the Transfer and Exchange of Electronic Evidence in Europe be Harmonised?

Transfer of Electronic Evidence
It is remarkable how little regulation there is concerning the transfer and exchange of electronic evidence within domestic boundaries and internationally. One would expect that states would have clear rules on transfer considering the volatile nature of electronic evidence and the large potential of tampering with the evidence during the electronic evidence's lifecycle that could lead to the inadmissibility of the evidence and/or could impact the fundamental rights of suspects and/or victims. This is clearly not the case. Most Member States rely on, where available, rules for the transfer of evidence between actors in the evidence chain of custody. Most of the rules that exist, where they exist have been prepared by some of the prominent actors themselves, e.g. most national forensic institutes have rules on the receipt and transfer of electronic evidence to be examined by them.

Provisions to Regulate the Role of Private Sector Actors
Furthermore, the lack of rules on exchange of electronic evidence is even more critical in the transfer of electronic evidence to or from private actors. Increasingly, as already noted, electronic evidence originates from private sector actors, and increasingly digital forensics expertise is more common in the private sector than in the public sector. This creates dependence in many states of LEAs on private actors for the collection, examination and preservation of electronic evidence. There are at least three main reasons that militate in favour of harmonised rules on the transfer of electronic evidence within a domestic space and further internationally:

1. An increased reliance on electronic evidence as primary or main source of evidence for crimes previously having no link with an electronic reality. There is an exponential increase of the collection, use and preservation of electronic evidence in trials or criminal law proceedings where previously electronic evidence may not have been thought of (e.g. there is hardly any murder trial where for example evidence from a mobile phone does not play some part in the collection of evidence and building up of the case by the prosecution). This increased reliance requires a recalibration of resources within a LEA to meet with the demand and a better legal certainty on the legal processes for collection, transfer, exchange, use, examination and preservation.
2. Increase in use of electronic evidence collected by the private sector. As already pointed out, most of electronic evidence originates within a private sector context. It is important for LEAs to have clear rules of what categories of data can be obtained from the private and what procedures need to be followed. Requests by LEAs to the private actors generally take a long time to be answered or acted upon, if at all. A common framework may include, inter alia, a list of 'open' information across Europe and ways LEAs can access this information, rules on uniformity to access telecommunications information and/or highly demanded categories of information, rules on how LEAs in one Member State can directly ask a telecom company in another Member State for specific categories of information and rules on how the transactions between the private companies and LEAs are carried out, including audit trails.
3. Increase in use of private sector expertise for the analysis and examination of electronic evidence. With the increase in use of electronic evidence, national forensic institutes (if they exist at all within Member States) cannot meet all the demands or requests for the analysis of electronic evidence. This creates a demand for private sector experts to carry out the analysis and to give expert testimony before Courts. So far there are no rules in Member States on the transfer of the electronic evidence to the private sector experts nor on the responsibilities of experts. Traditional domestic rules on expert witness have often been extended to cover expertise on electronic evidence. A common framework needs to include rules on the engagement of private sector experts and on the way the electronic evidence is transferred to and from private sector experts.

Transfer of Actionable Intelligence from Intelligence Agencies and LEAs and Vice-Versa

So far, the transfer of information or actionable intelligence between SIS and LEAs and vice-versa, where this happens, is often not regulated. Few states, amongst which Germany, have clear rules on the transfer of information between the two. Especially following the Snowden revelations there seems to be an on-going debate questioning the previously 'water-tight' distinction in legal treatment (and application of laws) to law enforcement and security services/ intelligence agencies. It becomes increasingly obvious that the distinction is less water-tight then has been portrayed so far (and which is furiously fought over especially by security services/intelligence agencies). As Cannataci argues in "Defying the logic, forgetting the facts: the new European proposal for data protection in the police sector", "In many states SIS do not have executive powers, although there do exist a few exceptions especially in the case of anti-terrorist activities. However, in most cases the prime function of the SIS is to produce "actionable intelligence", which is then passed on to the LEAs to act about whether it is to further monitor, follow, detain, arrest or prosecute a person or group of persons." Given this context, it may be opportune to include in a common European framework for electronic evidence rules on the transfer and exchange of information/actionable intelligence and whether this information can be admitted as evidence in a criminal trial.

Effective Cross-Border Regulation
The whole process of exchange of evidence between states in Europe is based on mutual legal assistance bilateral agreements, the European Convention on Mutual Legal Assistance in Criminal Law Matters, the EU 2000 Convention, which was recently replaced by the EIO Directive and for evidence related to cybercrimes, the provisions of the Cybercrime Convention. All these legal frameworks have been used for the exchange of electronic evidence. However, it is increasingly evident that (apart from the provision of the Cybercrime Convention) the procedures offered in these frameworks are too slow for the volatile and fast-moving nature of electronic evidence. The provisions and procedures in the Cybercrime Convention are better suited for electronic evidence but States have often not extended their application beyond the scope of the Cybercrime Convention when ratifying the Convention. A common European framework for the systematic and uniform application of new technologies in the collection, use and exchange of electronic evidence can build on the existing provisions and procedures in the Cybercrime Convention. Furthermore, a common European framework could take up and build on the current efforts of the Council of Europe to create an electronic version of the mutual legal assistance request form.

Joint Investigation Teams
Under the auspices of Europol and Eurojust, several JITs have been set up during investigations. These joint investigations allow for an efficient way of collecting and sharing of electronic evidence pertinent in an investigation. A common European framework may need to increase the legal certainty needed for such joint investigations to be carried out in a smoother and more efficient manner.

11.4 Conclusion

Over time, the European legal scenario regulating the life cycle of electronic evidence has evolved in a complex patchwork of rules. As to the setting up of rules on collection and preservation of electronic evidence, the Cybercrime Convention has been the most influential and progressive framework for electronic evidence in Europe. Many national frameworks are a combination of national criminal law provisions developed in the off-line context and provisions that were introduced through the ratification of the Cybercrime Convention. While this combination brings some degree of uniformity, the national criminal law approaches remain the primary source for the rules on admissibility and probative value of electronic evidence.

The most evident deficiency in the current patchwork is the inability of current national and international legal frameworks to meet the needs that come from the 'cross-border' nature of electronic evidence. As this chapter has discussed, the current prevalent notions of jurisdiction, particularly as the notion governing investigative powers is rather limiting and problematic in today's world where electronic information is processed, shared and stored across several territorial jurisdictions and spaces. Here new theoretical frameworks, such as the notion of 'investigative jurisdiction', are being proposed in literature but are still not in practice.

One scenario where this notion of 'investigative jurisdiction' may be less useful is when requiring information directly from a private actor: which rules would the private actor be expected to follow (of location or of the investigating party) is not immediately clear and would still be dependent on some form of legal agreement.

One other aspect that needs to be rethought in the context of (cross-border) electronic evidence is the notion of admissibility of evidence. Admissibility of electronic evidence is generally not an issue and electronic evidence is generally admissible if it has been legally obtained and is assessed on a case by case basis by the Court. However, given that the requirement of 'legally obtained' is not a uniform requirement the non-uniform approach may be a barrier for the use of electronic evidence obtained from another jurisdiction.

What needs further reflection is the role of private actors in the electronic evidence life cycle. While literature is replete with recommendations that a better cooperation with the service providers is desirable, there are no clear recommendations on how this cooperation should be developed. Improving mutual legal assistance requests and the way the requests reach the private actors is important and increasingly urgent. The legal framework for legal assistance requests while unsatisfactory for today's requirements, shows that establishing a clear legal process is very important in cross-border relations between states in criminal matters. Learning from this principle and corroborated by the findings of the EVIDENCE project, one can clearly establish that there is a need for electronic information/evidence exchange protocols and standards. These protocols need to have a legal basis, ideally internationally agreed and accompanied by a technical protocol for the fast transfer of the requested information exchange. Given further that these protocols and standards need to work not only between states but also between law enforcement agencies and several private actors, different stakeholders (including digital forensic experts) are involved in the process of setting up these protocols and standards.

In conclusion, while the current frameworks provide an important basis upon which law enforcement and prosecutors work, solving the current shortcomings is not merely a matter of introducing new agreements but is more complex, needing new theoretical frameworks and the collaboration of a large variety of actors.

References

Brenner SW, Koops BJ (2004) Approaches to cybercrime jurisdiction. J High Technol Law 4(1):46
Chalmers D, Davies G, Monti G (2010) European Union law. Cambridge University Press, Cambridge, p 582
Gragido W, Molina D, Pirc J, Selby N (2013) Blackhatonomics - an inside look at the economics of cybercrime. Syngress (Elsevier), Waltham
James JI, Gladyshev P (2016) A survey of mutual legal assistance involving digital evidence. Digit Investig 18:23–32
Jerker D, Svantesson D, van Zwieten L (2016) Law enforcement access to evidence via direct contact with cloud providers - identifying the contours of a solution. Comput Law Secur Rev 32:671–682
Koops BJ, Goodwin M (2014) Cyberspace, the cloud, and cross-border criminal investigation. The limits and possibilities of international law, December 2014. https://www.wodc.nl/onderzoeksdatabase/2326-de-gevolgen-van-cloudcomputing-voor-de-opsporing-en-vervolging.aspx?cp=44&cs=6796
Mason S (2012) Electronic evidence, 3rd edn. LexisNexis Butterworths, London
Shaw MN (2008) International law. Cambridge University Press, Cambridge
Svantesson D (2016) Law enforcement cross-border access to data, Preliminary Report, November 2016

Chapter 12
Digital Forensic Tools Catalogue, a Reference Point for the Forensic Community

Mattia Epifani and Fabrizio Turchi

Abstract In the digital forensics community, there is no a general agreement on how to classify forensic tools related to the acquisition and analysis phases. The Digital Forensic Tools Catalogue has been developed flowing a bottom-up approach. Each tool has been distinguished on the basis of its own features and later it has been structured and classified in a coherent and sensible way. At the moment, the Catalogue, available on the web, includes about 1500 tools divided into two main branches: tools for the acquisition and tools for the analysis activities.

12.1 Introduction

The Evidence Project[1] aims at providing a Road Map (guidelines, recommendations, and technical standards) for realizing the missing Common European Framework for the systematic and uniform application of new technologies in the collection, use and exchange of evidence. This road map incorporating standardized solutions aims at enabling all involved stakeholders to rely on an efficient regulation, handling and exchanging of digital evidence, according to common standards and rules.

One of the main goals of the project consisted of creating an overview of the standards related to the handling and exchanging of electronic evidence across EU Member States. This overview of practices and procedures for gathering electronic

[1] *European Informatics Data Exchange Framework for Court and Evidence*, www.evidenceproject.eu.

M. Epifani · F. Turchi (✉)
CNR, Institute of Legal Information Theory and Techniques, Florence, Italy
e-mail: mattia.epifani@ittig.cnr.it; fabrizio.turchi@ittig.cnr.it

M. A. Biasiotti et al. (eds.), *Handling and Exchanging Electronic Evidence Across Europe*, Law, Governance and Technology Series 39,
https://doi.org/10.1007/978-3-319-74872-6_12

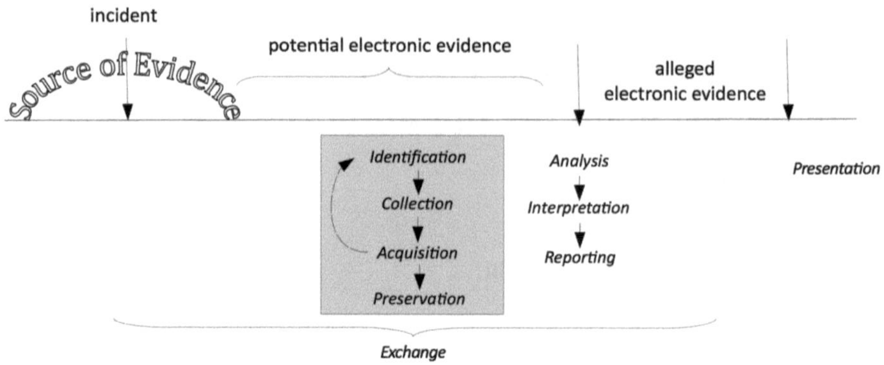

Fig. 12.1 Electronic evidence life cycle

evidence, has been organized according to the Electronic Evidence life-cycle (see Fig. 12.1) and depicted in Fig. 12.2.[2]

The mentioned life-cycle has been further developed according to survey findings and operational feedback. The digital evidence management timeline is the result as represented in Fig. 12.2. Eight main different phases have been distinguished, regarding the handling of digital evidence, starting from the incident event:

- Case Preparation: this is the first step of the digital evidence management timeline and it comprises organizational, technical and investigative aspects and includes:
  - Case Assessment: the identification of all available information and the evaluation of data to be searched.
  - Human resources identification: the evaluation of the human resources needed to carry out the investigation activity.
  - Tools Checklist: the preparation of a tools checklist whereby all the authorized people check the available tools and their appropriateness regarding the investigation to be carried out.
  - Media destination: the preparation of media destination where data will be forensically copied to
- Evidence Identification: this is the step consisting of examining/studying the crime scene to preserve, as much as possible, the original state of the digital/electronic devices that are going to be acquired.

[2]Figure 12.2 represents a simplified view of the overall processes involved in a digital evidence handling , because it is not a sequential flow but it may be circular in some points, for example during the Analysis process, it may be possible to realize that some pieces of evidence have been disregarded, so it is necessary to come back to the Acquisition phase to perform a new acquisition activity.

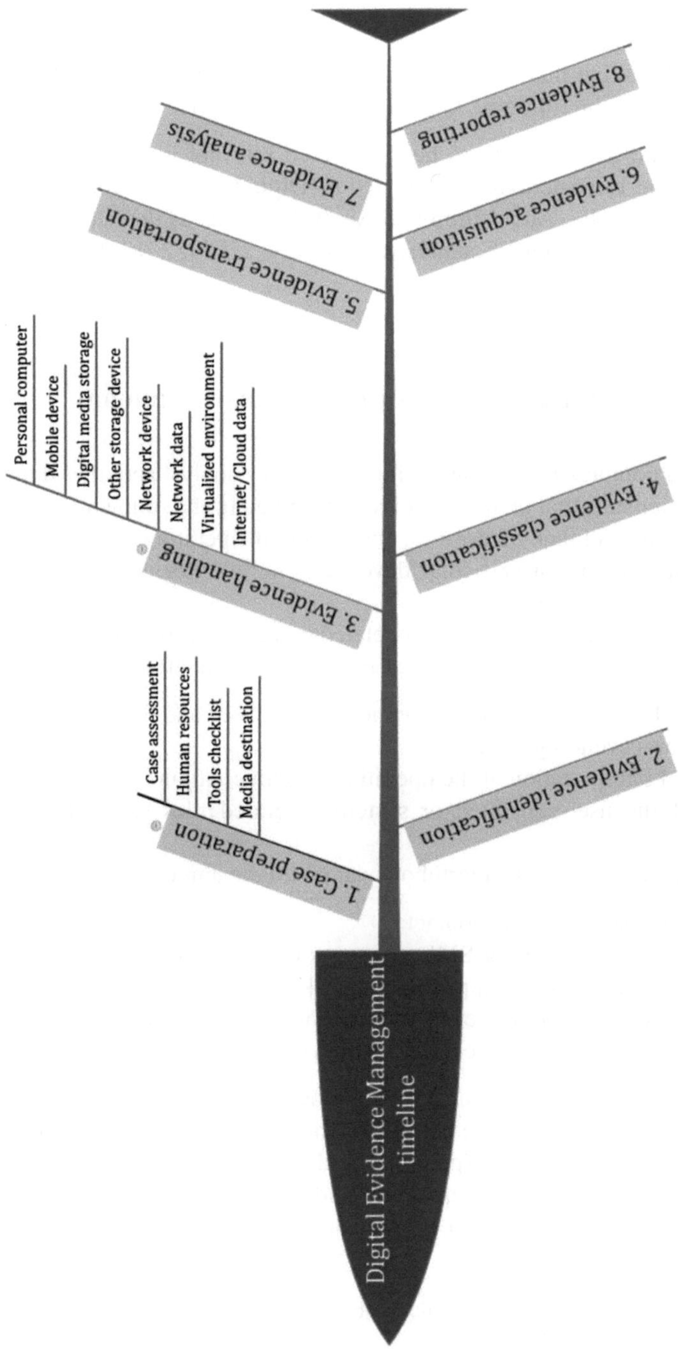

Fig. 12.2 Electronic evidence management timeline

- Evidence Classification: this is the step consisting of identifying the main features and the status of the device, taking notes about Case ID, Evidence ID, Seizure place/date/made by/ Evidence type, picture, status, etc.
- Evidence Handling: this is the step where it is defined which specific standard procedures are to be followed, based on the kind of device is being handled.

In drafting the overview, it has been gathered relevant information on a huge number of digital forensic tools and created a "Digital Forensic Tools Catalogue", concerning tools for the Acquisition and Analysis phases as described at different levels of details by the ISO/IEC standards (ISO/IEC 27037, 2012; ISO/IEC 27042, 2015; ISO/IEC 27043, 2015).

12.2 The Need for a Digital Forensic Tools Catalogue

The increasing complexity of today's digital forensics analyst activities depends on a multiple of elements that include, but are not limited to the following:

The increasing number of devices; the different operating systems; the huge number of applications, in particular devoted to mobile devices the different file formats to interpret and process.

For instance, a forensic investigation related to a cyber intrusion to the detriment of a corporate server, a rather common case, may involve the following activities:

- analysis of the log files related to the network devices and the operating system (e.g. Windows event register)
- analysis and interpretation of the operating system configurations;
- analysis of the user-generated or system-generated files (e.g. LNK files[3] or JumpList[4]);
- acquisition and analysis of smartphone data with the aim of:
  - identifying each personal contact;
  - selecting and interpreting SMS messages or chats through different kind of applications (e.g. WhatsApp, Telegram, Skype, etc.);
  - selecting and interpreting each activity carried out through the use of social network platform (e.g. Facebook, Twitter, etc.).

The effectiveness of a forensic investigation depends mainly on the forensic analyst's expertise and experience but also on the availability of forensic tools being able to extract and interpret data (potential evidence) quickly.

Until recently the forensics acquisition and analysis have been carried out by using all-inclusive software tools (i.e. Forensic Toolkits) because they cover a wide

[3]LNK files, known as link files, allow to quickly access to files stored in different locations. They assume the features of the file they point to.

[4]JumpList, part of the Windows systems starting with version 7, allow to swiftly access to the most used folders.

range of forensics processing and to accomplish an almost comprehensive analysis of a device.

Nowadays these forensics toolkit while still playing a fundamental role in investigative activities, may not cope with particular cases because they may not be appropriate for interpreting/deciphering a specific artifact[5] or a given file format. For example in case of email box analysis, locally stored, there are many formats only readable and understandable by specific tools.

Under the outlined considerations, the availability of a digital forensic tools Catalogue, organized into various categories including the supported features for each product, allow the forensic analyst to identify the most suitable tool for their investigative case. Furthermore when the forensic expert already knows/owns a tool for carry out a forensic analysis, the Catalogue can be used to pinpoint/identify similar/comparable tools and therefore conduct a significant cross-checking results with them. This use of the Catalogue is particularly relevant in cases where is of utmost importance correctly interpret data without mistakes to avoid or significantly moderate the risk of wrongful conviction, and prevent effective investigation and/or delay justice for victims.

12.3 Digital Forensic Tools Catalogue

Currently the Digital Forensic Tools Catalogue (form now on Catalogue) comprises information on the most significant digital forensic tools related to:

1. Acquisition: 461 tools
2. Analysis: 1031 tools

The total number of software tools considered so far is 1492.[6]

The whole collection has been organized using a specific categorization briefly represented by Fig. 12.3 (Analysis) and Fig. 12.4 (Acquisition):

The classes of the *Analysis* classification have the following meaning:

1. *Computer Forensics*: tools for the analysis of File System, Operating System and Applications as follows:
    (a) File System: tools for the analysis of File System metadata (e.g. FAT, NTFS, HFS+, etc.)
    (b) Operating System, broken down into:
        i. Windows: tools for the analysis of Windows OS artifacts (e.g. Registry, Events, Prefetch, JumpList, Recycle Bin, Thumbnails, etc.)

[5]*Artifact* includes all the information stored in the registry of the system, related to users or system activities, In Windows system examples of artifact are: file download, file opening/creation, programs. execution, USB or Drive usages, Account usage, Browser usage, etc.

[6]The total number does not correspond to the algebraic sum of the acquisition and analysis tools, because some tools belong to both branches.

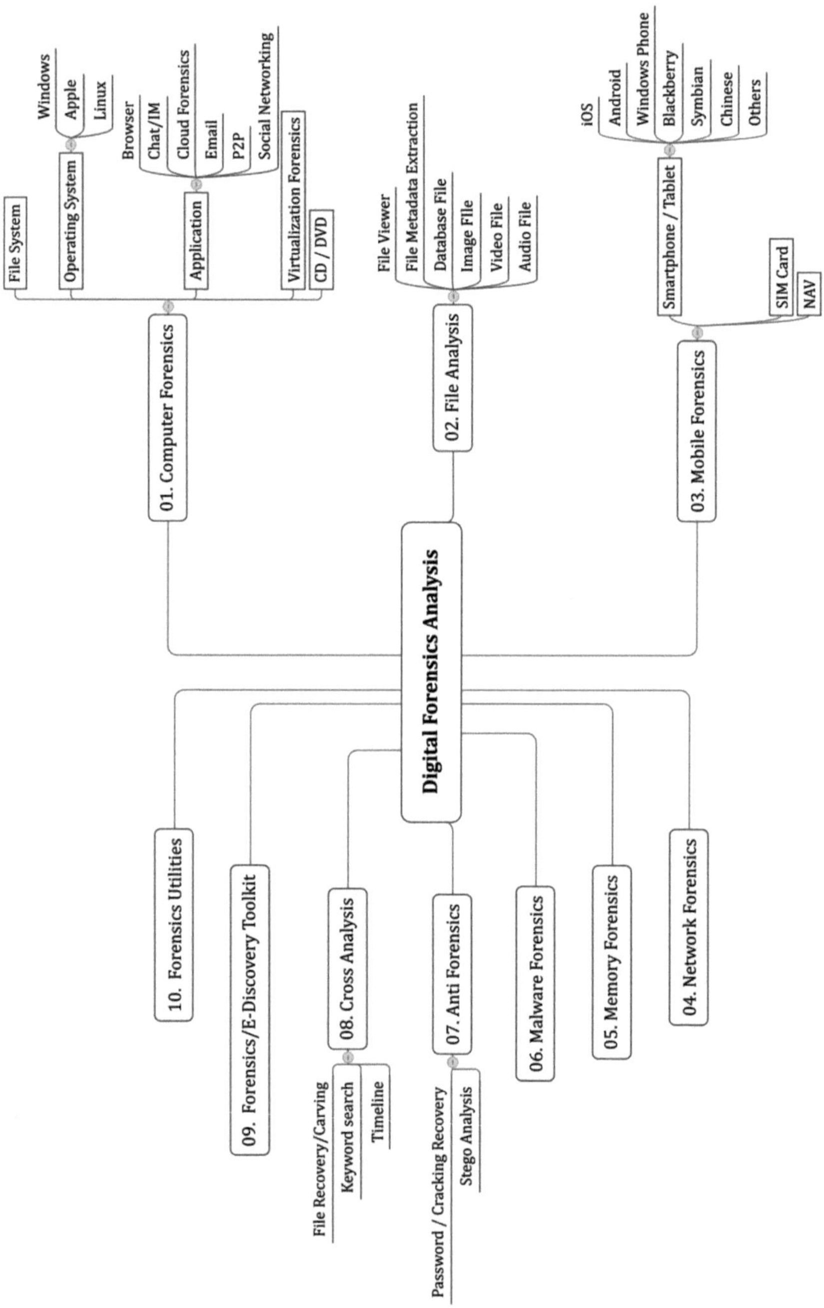

Fig. 12.3 Analysis branch classification

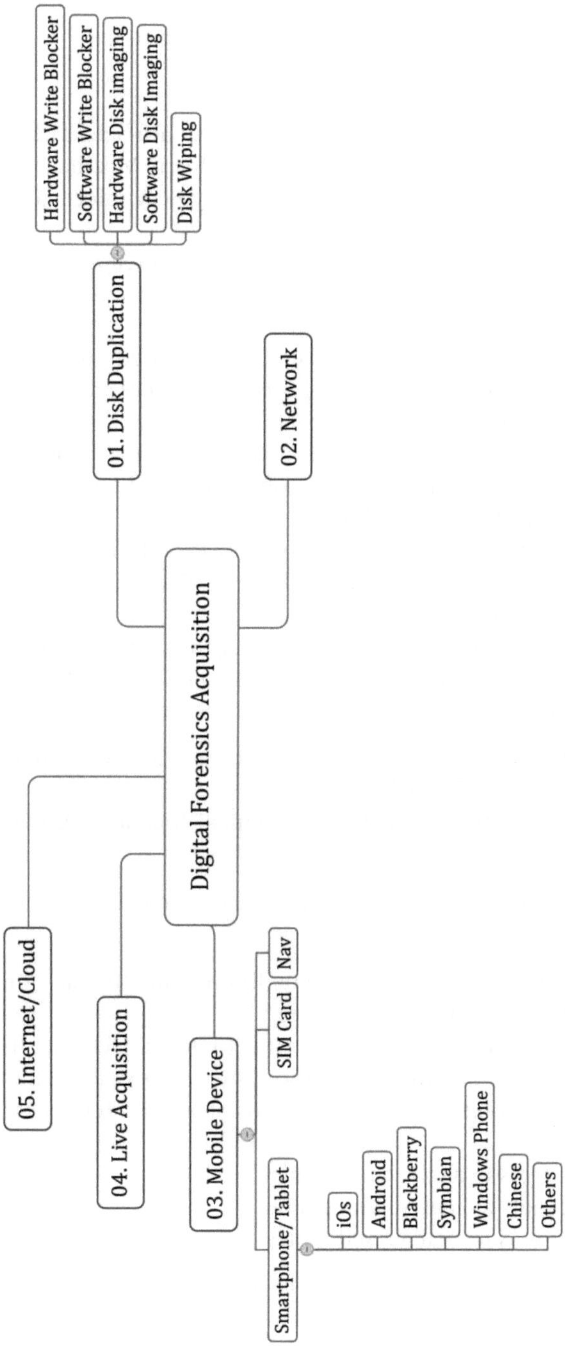

Fig. 12.4 Acquisition branch classification

ii. Mac/Apple: Tools for the analysis of Apple OS artifacts (e.g. Plist configuration file, Fsevents, log file, etc.)
iii. Linux: Tools for the analysis of Linux OS artifacts

(c) Application

i. Browser: tools for the analysis of Browser artifacts. The most common browsers are considered (Internet Explorer, Mozilla Firefox, Google Chrome, Apple Safari, Opera) with typical information of interest (History, Cache, Cookies, Downloads, etc.)
ii. Chat: tools for the analysis of Chat configuration and logs. The most common Chat applications are categorized (Skype, Facebook Messenger, Yahoo Messenger, etc.)
iii. Cloud Storage: tools for the analysis of Cloud Storage configuration files. The most common Cloud Storage services are categorized (Dropbox, Google Drive, OneDrive, etc.)
iv. Email: tools for the analysis of Email archive. The most common Email archive format (Microsoft Outlook, Lotus Notes, Microsoft Exchange, Thunderbird, etc.)
v. Peer To Peer: tools for the analysis of Peer To Peer configuration and data files. The most common Peer To Peer services are categorized (eMule, Torrent, LimeWire, etc.)
vi. Social Networking: tools for the analysis of Social Network configuration and data files. The most common Social Network services are categorized (Facebook, Linkedin, Twitter, etc.)

(d) Virtualization: tools for the analysis of Virtualization environment, like VMware, vSphere, VirtualBox, etc.
(e) CD/DVD: tools for the analysis of Optical Media (CD, DVD, BlueRay, etc.)

2. *File Analysis*: tools for the analysis of a file (content view, metadata view, specific file format analysis)

(a) File Viewer: tools for viewing many different file formats (Images,Audio, Video, Office, PDF, Compressed, etc.)
(b) File Metadata Extraction: tools to extract internal metadata from the most common file formats (Images, Audio, Video, Office, PDF, etc.)
(c) Database file: tools to parse various database file format (SQLite, ESE, MySql, etc.)
(d) Image file: tools to analyze image files
(e) Video file: tools to analyse video files
(f) Audio file: tools to analyse audio files

3. *Mobile Forensics*: tools for the analysis of Mobile Devices (Smartphone/Tablet, SIM Card, Sat Nav, etc.)

   (a) Smartphone/Tablet, classified based on the native and third-party apps supported:

      i. iOS: tools for the analysis of iOS devices
      ii. Android: tools for the analysis of Android devices
      iii. Windows Phone: tools for the analysis of Windows Phone devices
      iv. Blackberry: tools for the analysis of Blackberry devices
      v. Symbian: tools for the analysis of Symbian devices
      vi. Chinese: tools for the analysis of Chinese brand devices.
      vii. Others: tools for the analysis of other operating system (both feature phones and smartphones)

   (b) SIM Card: tools for the analysis of SIM card
   (c) Nav: tools for the analysis of Sat Nav devices

4. *Network Forensics*: tools for the analysis of Network Traffic (NetFlow, PCAP), Network log files. Proxy Server and WiFi network
5. *Memory/Live Forensics*: tools for the analysis of RAM Memory Dump or Hibernation files
6. *Malware Forensics*: tools for the analysis of Malware specimen. Tools are categorized in respect to the analysis type (e.g. Automated, Behavioural, Code, Sandbox, etc.)
7. *Anti Forensics*: tools useful to defeat anti-forensics techniques.; two distinct categories are considered: Password Cracking tools and Stego Analysis tools:

   (a) Password Cracking/Recovery: tools for password cracking and recovery of files, encrypted containers, operating system, and so on
   (b) Stego Analysis tools for discovering hidden text merged into images through the steganography technique.

8. *Cross Analysis*: ttools useful to perform analysis in more than one areas. Three sub-categories are present: File Carving, Keyword Search and Timeline:

   (a) File Recovery/Carving: tools for deleted file recovery and carving
   (b) Keyword Search: tools for searching specific keywords
   (c) Timeline: tools for creating usage timelines[7]

9. *Forensics/E-Discovery Toolkit*: comprehensive tools for in depth analysis of multiple artifacts (e.g. Operating System, Applications, Memory) and with a lot of specific features (e.g. File Carving, Timeline, Password Cracking, etc.)
10. Forensics Utilities: various forensic utilities (hashing, evidence mover, time converter, hex-decimal editor, and so on).

[7]The chronological representation of the events occurred in a given time frame, rebuilt through digital traces left on a digital device.

The classes of the *Acquisition* classification have the following meaning:

1. *Disk duplication*: hardware and software tools to acquire storage devices (e.g. Hard Disk, Pen Drive, Memory Card, etc.)
   (a) Hardware Write Blocker: hardware devices to prevent writing on storage devices. They are characterized by the supported interfaces (e.g. SATA, PATA, USB, Firewire, etc.)
   (b) Software Write Blocker: software tools to prevent writing on storage devices
   (c) Hardware Disk Imaging: hardware devices to create forensics images. They are characterized by the supported interfaces, both in input and output (e.g. SATA, PATA, USB, Firewire, etc.)
   (d) Software Disk Imaging: software tools to create forensics images, both standalone live distribution and installed software
   (e) Disk wiping: tool for cleaning storage devices to be used for forensics copies. The cleaning process is carried out through a low level formatting.
2. *Network*: tools to acquire network traffic both on cabled and wireless network
3. *Mobile device*: tools for the acquisition of Mobile Devices (Smartphone/Tablet, SIM Card, Sat Nav, etc.)
   (a) Smartphone/Tablet, classified in respect to the specific type of supported acquisition (Physical, File System, Logical, Backup, Cloud, etc.):
      i. tools for the acquisition of iOS devices.
      ii. Android: tools for the acquisition of Android devices.
      iii. Blackberry tools for the acquisition of Blackberry devices
      iv. Symbian: tools for the acquisition of Symbian devices.
      v. Windows Phone: tools for the acquisition of Window Phone devices.
      vi. Chinese: tools for the acquisition of Chinese brand devices.
      vii. Others: tools for the acquisition of Other operating system.
   (b) SIM Card: tools for the acquisition of SIM card
   (c) Nav: tools for the acquisition of Sat Nav devices
4. *Live acquisition*: tools to acquire data from a live computer (RAM capture, process activities, network connections, incident response/forensics toolkit, opened files, etc.).
5. *Internet/Cloud*: tools to acquire data from remote services (e.g. Web Site/Page, Email Accounts, Social Network, Cloud Storage, etc.).

12.4 Tools Data

Each tool is represented by the following data:

- *Tool Name*: it represents the name of the tool assigned to it by its producer or reseller or developer

- *Tool Description*: it contains a short description of the tools, taken from its official web site, the whole description is available on mouse hover in a similar manner to a tooltip feature
- *License type*: it may assume values like Open Source, Freeware, Commercial, Multi (when the tool has more than one single value)
- *Category*: it represents the hierarchical view of the different kind of forensics tools. Each tool may assume more than one single category: in this case the multiple occurrences of the same tool are separately considered and therefore are considered as two distinguished tools
- *Operating System*: it may assume values like: Windows, Mac, Linux, Standalone, Online, Hardware, Multi. Its value represents the operating system on which the tool run.
- *Developer*: it is the author of the development of the tool and it may be a person, an organization or a community
- *Test report*: it is the official web address where a well-known organization has tested the software and put the results of the operation on the web
- *Useful references*: it contains a list of web resources related to the tool, such as documentation, manual, unofficial tests and others
- *Features*: each Category is connected to a single or multiple features, although in some cases, it may not have any features at all. Each Feature may assume a single or multiple values. Three distinct cases are possible:
  - Categories without Features: for example Computer Forensics (01.); File Analysis (02.); File Recovery / Carving (08.02), Forensics Toolkit (08.03)
  - Categories with Single Feature: for example Computer Forensics -> File System (01.01.), Feature = File System Supported
  - Category with Multiple Features: for example Browser Forensics (01.03.01.), Features = Internet Explorer, Firefox, Google Chrome, Safari, Opera

  Each Feature may assume multiple values, getting data from a default list of values.

12.5 Catalogue Browsing

The Catalogue's main page[8] has been broken down into two frames:

- the left frame or Search Frame, is dedicated to query preparation;
- the right frame or Results Frame, shows the result of a query.

At the beginning, the right frame shows the Categories in a tag cloud style, where the importance of each tag is emphasized using different font sizes and colours on the base of the number of tools belonging to each category (tooltip). From this

[8] See wp4.evidenceproject.eu.

view, it is possible to run a query activating the hyperlink provided on the single classification item, allowing the extraction of all the tools belonging to the selected category.

On the left frame, it is possible to set the field for the query. The starting point is the radio button that allows the selection of one of the main branches of the Catalogue: Analysis or Acquisition.

Every time a branch is selected, some elements of the page change in a coherent way, for example:

- the total number of available tools;
- the hierarchical structure of the Category field;
- the link related to Mind Map: it represent the mind map of the chosen;
- the link related to Tag Clouds: it shows a tag cloud representation of the Categories, within the selected branch, based on the number of tool belonging to the related Category.

It is possible to prepare a query based on the fields: Tool name, License type, Category, Operating System, Developer, and Features/Values. The Category combo box represents one of the main user interface elements for preparing a query. This is illustrated in the following two examples.

12.5.1 Tools Retrieval: Example 1

The first example pertains to the selection of the item Computer Forensics→Operating System→Windows. After the selection the application shows the values in the Features Panel as depicted in Fig. 12.5:

If I press the Search button I will retrieve all the current 126 tools belonging to the selected Category, but the Feature Panel values allow to prepare a specific query for extracting only and exactly the tools useful for one's forensic activity (analysis or acquisition). For example, if there is a need to detect tools being able to carry out an analysis on the Prefetch artifact for Windows 10, it's possible to select the appropriate check box and get the sought-after tools, as shown in Fig. 12.6:

12.5.2 Tools Retrieval: Example 2

A second example concerns the Mobile Forensics Category. Selecting the Mobile Forensics→Smartphone/Tablet→iOS, the Featured Panel will show a rich set of values, as partially shown in Fig. 12.7.

When pressing the Search button, the application will retrieve all the current 42 tools belonging to the selected Category. To extract the analysis tools for the Chat Viber, for instance, this can be accomplish rather straightforward by relying on the

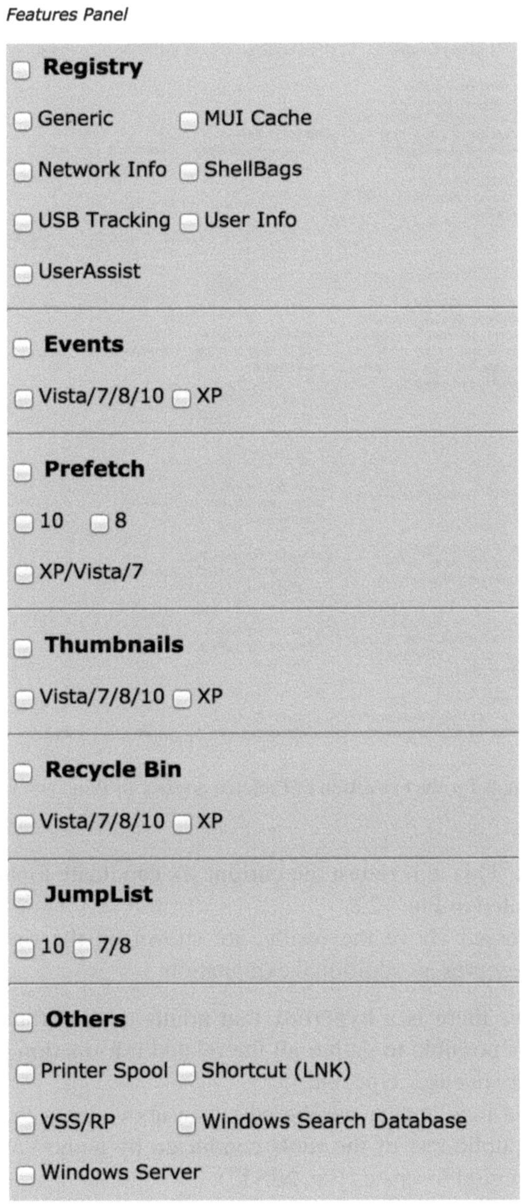

Fig. 12.5 Feature Panel values for ComputerForensics→OperatingSystem→Windows

EVIDENCE project: results - Found tools: 6

Tool (Developer)	Description	Category	License	O.S.	Features / Values
Cold Disk Quick Response (Alan Orlikoski)	The Cold Disk Quick Response (CDQR) tool is a fast and easy to use forensic artifact parsing tool that works on disk images, mounted drives and extracted artifacts from Windows, Linux and MacOS devices.	Computer Forensics >Operating System >Windows	Opensource	Multi	**Registry** *Generic, MUI Cache, Network Info, ShellBags, USB Tracking, User Info, UserAssist* **Events** *Vista/7/8/10, XP* **Prefetch** *10, 8, XP/Vista/7*
Internet Evidence Finder (Magnet Forensics)	Magnet IEF is a digital forensics software solution that you can use to discover, analyze and report on digital evidence from various types of drives and devices. ... more	Computer Forensics >Operating System >Windows	Commercial	Windows	**Registry** *Generic, MUI Cache, Network Info, ShellBags, USB Tracking, User Info, UserAssist* **Events** *Vista/7/8/10, XP* **Prefetch** *10, 8, XP/Vista/7* **Thumbnails** *Vista/7/8/10, XP* **Others** *Shortcut (LNK), Volume Shadow Copies* **Recycle Bin** *Vista/7/8/10, XP* **JumpList** *10, 7/8*
PECmd (Eric Zimmerman)	Prefetch Explorer command line.	Computer Forensics >Operating System >Windows	Freeware	Windows	**Prefetch** *10, 8, XP/Vista/7*
Windows 10 Prefetch Parser (505Forensics)	This is a simple script that can be utilized to parse Windows 10 Prefetch files. ... more	Computer Forensics >Operating System >Windows	Opensource	Windows	**Prefetch** *10*
Windows Prefetch Parser	Python script created to parse Windows Prefetch files: Supports XP - Windows 10 Prefetch files.	Computer Forensics >Operating System >Windows	Opensource	Multi	**Prefetch** *10, 8, XP/Vista/7*
WinPrefetchView (Nirsoft)	WinPrefetchView is a small utility that reads the Prefetch files stored in your system	Computer Forensics >Operating System	Freeware	Windows	**Prefetch** *10, 8, XP/Vista/7*

Fig. 12.6 Forensic tools for the extraction of Prefetch artefact in Windows 10

specific checkbox. This will return the current six candidate tools for the analysis, as partially illustrated in Fig. 12.8.

As already stressed above the results are shown on the right frame, but the following fields deserves an additional explanation:

- above the *Name* there is a hyperlink that points to the official website of the tool, where it is possible to gather all the related information (e.g. descriptions, versioning, tests, licenses type, etc.);
- under the *Name* may appear numbered icons: above them there is a hyperlink that points to public test of the tools conducted by authoritative organizations specialized in digital forensics (i.e. NIST[9]).
- *Description* briefly explains the tool's functionalities, if the text is long it will be shown only a portion of the whole field, and when the mouse pointer hovers above it the complete text is shown in a separated frame (see Fig. 12.9);

[9]Il *National Institute of Standards and Technology*. NIST is a government agency of the USA that deals with technologies.

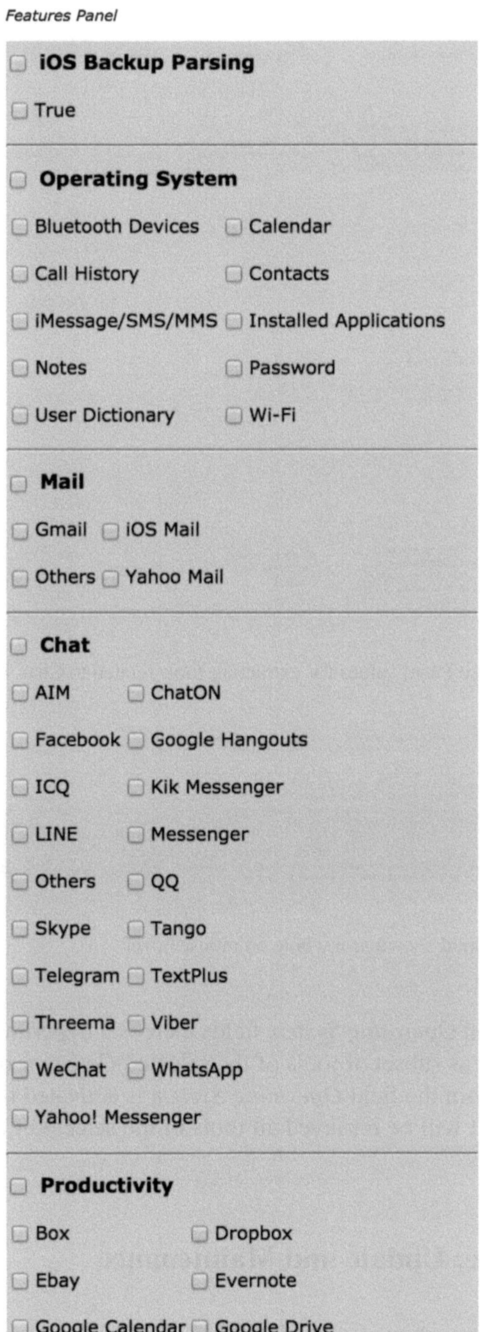

Fig. 12.7 Feature Panel values for Mobile Forensics→Smartphone/Tablet→iOS

EVIDENCE project: results - Found tools: 6

Tool (Developer)	Description	Category	License	O.S.	Features / Values
Belkasoft Evidence Center (Belkasoft)	Belkasoft Evidence Center makes it easy for an investigator to search, analyze, store and share digital evidence found inside computer and mobile devices. ... more	Mobile Forensics >Smartphone/Tablet >iOS	Commercial	Windows	**iOS Backup Parsing** *True* **Operating System** *Calendar, Call History, Contacts, iMessage/SMS/MMS, Installed Applications, Notes* **Chat** *ChatON, ICQ, Kik Messenger, LINE, Others, Skype, Tango, Viber, WeChat, WhatsApp, Yahoo! Messenger* **Social Network** *Grindr, Tinder* **Browser** *Apple Safari, Google Chrome*
Internet Evidence Finder (Magnet Forensics)	Magnet IEF is a digital forensics software solution that you can use to discover, analyze and report on digital evidence from various types of drives and devices. ... more	Mobile Forensics >Smartphone/Tablet >iOS	Commercial	Windows	**iOS Backup Parsing** *True* **Operating System** *Bluetooth Devices, Calendar, Call History, Contacts, iMessage/SMS/MMS, Installed Applications, Notes, User Dictionary, Wi-Fi* **Mail** *iOS Mail* **Chat** *AIM, Google Hangouts, Kik Messenger, LINE, Others, QQ, Skype, Telegram, TextPlus, Viber, WeChat, WhatsApp* **Productivity** *Dropbox* **Social Network** *Facebook, Foursquare, Grindr, Instagram, Tinder, Twitter* **Navigation** *Apple Maps, Google Maps* **Browser** *Apple Safari, Google Chrome*
iPhone Backup Analyzer (Mario Piccinelli)	This python tool is a browser to explore and understand the contents of an iPhone backup directory, as created by iTunes.	Mobile Forensics >Smartphone/Tablet >iOS	Opensource	Multi	**iOS Backup Parsing** *True* **Operating System** *Call History, Contacts, iMessage/SMS/MMS, Notes, Wi-Fi* **Chat** *Skype, Viber, WhatsApp* **Browser** *Apple Safari*

Fig. 12.8 Use of Feature Panel values for extracting tools related to Chat Viber for iOS

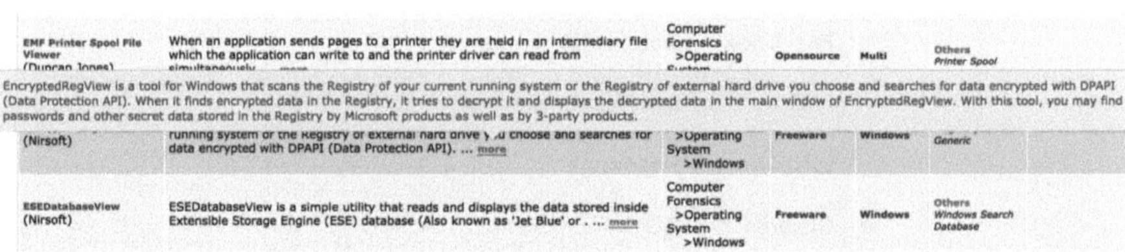

Fig. 12.9 Description field shown as a whole on mouse hover

- above *License* and *Operating System* fields there is a hyperlink that allows to run a query selecting as subset of tools of the selected *Category* of the related value. For instance if from the field *Operating System* is activated the hyperlink on the *Windows* value, it will be retrieved all tools of the selected *Category* that run on Windows systems;

12.6 Catalogue: Update and Maintenance

Based on the huge number of tools included in the Catalogue, the updating and the extension of its content can be ensured only leveraging a network of forensics experts, who can give their contribution in a collaborative manner so that the Catalogue becomes a reference pint in the digital forensics community.

To keep the Catalogue updated, a maintaining plan has been developed. It consists of two actions:

- collecting feedback from the digital forensics community;
- creating a trusted restricted group of experts to allow them to directly intervene in the Catalogue contents.

12.6.1 Digital Forensics Experts Group Network

It has been requested help from a selected group of Digital Forensics Experts to receive feedback. It has recently been prepared a questionnaire and asked the experts to take the time to fill it out.

At this aim it has been prepared a trusted list, about 35 members of Digital Forensics Experts, belonging to different organizations:

- LEA (Belgium, France, Greece, Italy, USA)
- Digital Evidence Specialists (France, Italy, Norway, Spain, USA)
- Organizations (Netherland Forensics Institute, CCIS—Norway, SANS, IISFA, ONIF, ...)

The questionnaire is available via the following URL: *http://wp4.evidenceproject.eu/Q.html* and contains the following questions:

1. Do you think it is of use to the digital forensic community?
    - Absolutely agree
    - Pretty much agree
    - Neutral
    - Disagree
    - Strongly disagree
2. Would you give us suggestions/recommendations/proposals for improving the Catalogue?
3. Would you agree with the Category classes (Computer Forensics, Mobile Forensics, etc.)?
4. Would you propose additional/alternative Category items/sub-items?
5. At the moment the Catalogue comprises about 1500 tools. Would you suggest others relevant tools, missing from it?
6. Would you recommend any authoritative organization that makes available forensic tools tests in addition to the NIST? (the Catalogue already includes some tool tests from this organization)
7. Which of these features would it be important to include? (1 = not important, ..., 5 = of utmost importance)
    - Develop a version of the Catalogue for mobile devices, updating on demand.
    - Develop a desktop version of the Catalogue, working also without Internet connection and updating on demand.

- Implement an automatic weekly/monthly newsletter that gives the user an update of added/modified tools and new versioning.
- Export all/part of the Catalogue in JSON o XML/XSL o CSV o PDF formats.
- Provide graphic representations on the use of tools: their popularity, general satisfaction based on direct experience.
- Add a "Versioning" field to keep track of the latest version of a specific tool.

The answers gathered are available via the following url: https://wp4.evidenceproject.eu/Q.answers.pdf.

12.6.2 Catalogue Web Editor

It has been also developed an Editor, as a web application, for the Catalogue for making easier its updating and its extension in line with the sustainability/maintaining plan.

The Catalogue Editor, based on web interface, allows to directly intervene in the content of the Catalogue for updating and extending it. The Editor is available, through a login process, to a trusted list of digital forensics experts that have declared their willingness in evaluating/integrating/improving/keeping update the content. It has been decided to develop this new software for a variety of reasons:

- for allowing users to directly intervene in the content of the Catalogue
- for maintaining the Catalogue and leveraging a trusted list of forensics expert in participating to the update and extension of the Catalogue
- for the sustainability of the Catalogue as the Reviewers pointed out in their Review Report and I'll be explaining this in the next slide.

Figure 12.10 illustrates the architecture of the Catalogue Editor.

Before giving a brief description of the Editor functioning, it is important to underline that the whole application is provided under HTTPS the web protocol for secure communication to protect the privacy and integrity of the exchanged data (login user/password).

The entry point of the Editor is the Login page where a user can:

- provide her/his credentials if they have already registered
- follow the Password Reset way/branch in case they have forgotten their credentials
- register to the Catalogue Editor

In case of a new user who wants to make a registration, this enrolling is not automatic: it will be evaluated and approved by the Catalogue Editor Administrators. Actually each registration request triggers a notification, by email, to the Administrator who will approve/refuse that request.

After the approval the new user will receive a notification by email and from that time on, they could be enter the system and work on the content of the Catalogue. Once the user has accessed to the system it's possible to update the content or to

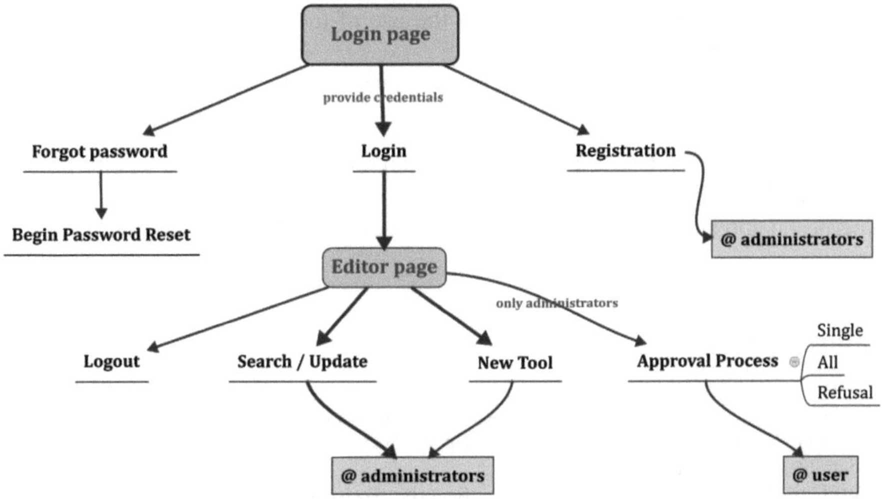

Fig. 12.10 Catalogue editor: architecture overview

add a new tool. The updating is preceded by a search in a similar manner as in the Catalogue browsing.

The editing process can be carried out in two ways:

1. search a tool in the same way as in the Catalogue browsing and next change each field of the retrieved tool;
2. add a new tool.

Each modification/insertion is put into a pending state until the administrators, who receive the related notification, approve them. The approval/refusal process triggers a notification, sent by email, to the user responsible of the proposed change.

12.7 Prospective Future

Some of the new features already planned include, but are not limited to the following:

- Developing a version of the Catalogue for mobile devices, updating via Web, on demand.
- Developing a desktop version of the Catalogue, working also without Internet connection and updating via Web on demand.
- Implementing an automatic weekly/monthly newsletter that gives the user an update of added/modified tools and new versioning.
- Exporting all/part of the Catalogue in JSON o XML/XSL o CSV o PDF formats.

- Providing graphic representations on the use of tools: their popularity, general satisfaction based on direct experience.
- Adding a "Versioning" field to keep track of the latest version of a specific tool.

The Catalogue has the potentialities to become a reference point in the digital forensics community. In witness of the attention raised by this initiative, Interpol has expressed the willingness to support the Catalogue maintaining through its forensics experts and spreading its use in all locations of the 190 Member States.

References

ISO/IEC 27037: Information technology – Security techniques – Guidelines for Identification, Collection, Acquisition and Preservation of Digital Evidence. http://www.iso.org/iso/catalogue_detail?csnumber=44381 (2012)

ISO/IEC 27042: Information Technology – Security Techniques – Guidelines for the Analysis and Interpretation of Digital Evidence. http://www.iso.org/iso/iso_catalogue/catalogue_tc/catalogue_detail.htm?csnumber=44406 (2015)

ISO/IEC 27043: Information Technology – Security Techniques – Incident Investigation Principles and Processes. http://www.iso.org/iso/catalogue_detail.htm?csnumber=44407 (2015)

Chapter 13
Privacy Protection in Exchanging Electronic Evidence in Europe

Nikolaus Forgó, Christian Hawellek, Friederike Knoke, and Jonathan Stoklas

Abstract This chapter provides an overview of the legal framework addressing the exchange of electronic evidence and the implications related to privacy and data protection. While in Chap. 11 of this Volume, the current legal situation *in general* is reviewed, this chapter focuses specifically on privacy and data protection. Whereas many sources of law are subject to examination in both chapters—to a certain extent, this is in the nature of things, as they both deal with legal aspects—this review looks at the sources from a particular point of view. This chapter therefore follows a particular train of thoughts: after introducing the background and relevance of the protection of privacy in the collection and exchange of electronic evidence, and presenting the methodology used, the current European legal framework is examined about existing and applicable rules on data protection regarding electronic evidence, concluding with a final summary and recommendations for a future implementation of data protection standards.

13.1 Introduction

13.1.1 Criminal Investigation and Fundamental Rights to Privacy

Not only regarding privacy do criminal investigation and criminal trial create a high impact on the fundamental/constitutional rights of those being subject to any of such measures (not only the suspect, but also any affected third-party in the focus of investigators). Also, to effectively prosecute a crime, authorities such as public

N. Forgó (✉) · C. Hawellek · F. Knoke · J. Stoklas
Leibniz Universität Hannover, Institute for Legal Informatics, Hannover, Germany
e-mail: nikolaus.forgo@iri.uni-hannover.de; christian.hawellek@iri.uni-hannover.de; friederike.knoke@iri.uni-hannover.de; jonathan.stoklas@iri.uni-hannover.de

M. A. Biasiotti et al. (eds.), *Handling and Exchanging Electronic Evidence Across Europe*, Law, Governance and Technology Series 39,
https://doi.org/10.1007/978-3-319-74872-6_13

state prosecution, the police and any other authority entrusted with investigation, need to seek information (and finally evidence) while an offender will seek to hide it, which makes all measures of collecting evidence of any kind 'intrusive measures' by nature.

Because of the digital transition, both 'conventional' crimes can be committed by electronic means in virtual environments (defamation, fraud, etc.) and entirely genuine forms of criminal activity referred to as 'cyber-crime' have emerged. Moreover, 'conventional crimes' not committed in virtual environments at all, e.g. a straight-forward murder case, today almost always produce electronic evidence of significant importance as well, simply because daily lives are connected to various kinds of digital data to such a degree that many actions in the 'physical' world leave some form of digital trace.

For this reason, 'digital forensics' have developed as sub-branch of forensics, and digital means of investigation increasingly gain relevance.

However, laws and jurisprudence and the principles to guarantee proportionality date back to an era in which digital means to investigate crimes were basically unknown. Therefore, it cannot be easily assumed that data protection safeguards adequate for the physical world remain adequate for measures being taken in the digital world; it is also not guaranteed that the relevant fundamental rights such as the fundamental right to data protection or informational self-determination are fully respected *per se*.

This becomes apparent when considering an example of seizure. Formerly, seizure always concerned physical objects as such, but—prior to the existence of data carriers—in most cases did not concern any information stored on that particular physical carrier.[1] If, e.g., a knife of which it is assumed that it was used in an assault, were seized by investigators, such seizure would have an impact on the fundamental right to property of the owner (only). Furthermore, it can be observed that the temporary loss will most likely not significantly influence the daily life of the owner, nor will it be difficult and/or costly to replace that knife. The assessment changes radically when considering the seizure of data carriers, particularly mobile devices. Such a carrier of digital data (*smart phone or personal computer*), if seized, will contain immense amounts of personal data not only of the owner, but also of their peers. In that case, not only the fundamental right to property, but also the fundamental rights to privacy and most likely telecommunications privacy would be affected. Analysing the data stored on such a device is likely to give comprehensive insights in various spheres of both the professional and the private life of the owner (and their peers), while large amounts of the data retrieved and thereby becoming accessible to prosecutors are likely to be irrelevant for the case (which cannot be avoided when physically seizing the entire device as such and thereby

[1]Except some particular cases, in which (paper) files would be seized, e.g. in cases of tax crimes. Even in these cases, however, these files, other than modern smart phones or other mobile devices, typically would not contain comprehensive personal data repositories of the owner and all their peers.

all data contained). Moreover, the loss of such device is likely to have significant consequences on both the private life and the work life of the owner (loss of messages, contact numbers/addresses, files, etc.), which cannot be overcome easily as the data—other than the physical object carrying it—will be highly individual and, unless professionally backupped, not easily recoverable (which constitutes the second important difference to seizure of (most) physical objects).

It appears therefore at least debatable whether the seizure of objects which are carrying vast amounts of personal data (and/or telecommunications data) can be easily based upon the general legal basis for seizure, which was introduced for the seizure of physical objects only and which therefore does not provide for the safeguards needed to accompany the privacy risks involved. Although seizure of paper files was common before the digital age, these were usually very particular cases of tax and/or economic crimes, and the seized files would be likely to carry crime relevant information only (and not necessarily personal data at all), as opposed to the unequally more extensive sets of personal data available e.g. on a smart phone. Conversely: even if in this particular case seizure of a folder with tax relevant bills already prior to the digital transition did not only impact the fundamental right to property, but possibly also the fundamental right to privacy, and even if such bills in certain cases may have given insights in the personal life of the owner to some extent, they would not allow tracing the entire social network of the owner or give access to all their private correspondence (and similar). As a result, it appears debatable whether the implemented safeguards for seizure remain sufficient for the threats to privacy imposed through seizure of data carriers. Moreover, in countries following a strong positivist tradition it might be needed to re-think whether formally a legal basis introduced to seize objects solely can be used to seize non-physical data at all.

13.1.2 Electronic Evidence and Data Protection

Gathering and exchanging electronic evidence therefore holds a potential to impact data protection rights in two different ways.

Firstly, electronic evidence—as opposed to physical evidence—typically must be considered ‘data’ in the sense of data protection rights, which means that the general principles of data protection need to be considered. These are the well-known principles such as the principles of lawfulness, proportionality and purpose limitation, the data subject’s rights to blocking, erasure and rectification, as well as information and access, storing time limits, particular protection of the special categories of personal data, limitations on automated decision-making, data quality checks for transferred data, limitation of transfer to private parties, security of processing, legal remedies, prior consultation of data protection authorities, and similar. These are general principles of data protection law and not particular to electronic evidence. They have been widely discussed over the past three decades, and have been implemented in the existing European legal frameworks governing e.g. the exchange of data between law enforcement authorities (see Chap. 11 of this Volume for further information on international cooperation and mutual legal assistance). The initial desktop research[2] carried out to analyse the status-quo of the legal debate surrounding the collection and exchange of digital evidence for this chapter has not shown that this debate would particularly focus on this field of data protection.

Secondly, however, the availability of new technologies to gather electronic evidence and the digital transition have created new and genuine data protection risks (particularly regarding online environments, cloud storage and telecommunications), which—it appears—mostly, and different to the more classic aspects of data protection outlined above, have not yet been addressed by the legislator at all. This chapter therefore gives particular attention to this second field of privacy risks.

The example given above (seizure of a knife vs. seizure of mobile telecommunications and data device) shows that already on a relatively general level the digital transition has imposed new challenges to the existing codes of criminal procedure, both formally and substantively.

This issue becomes more apparent, when the methods of collecting and analysing electronic evidence are further examined:

- Traditionally, gathering evidence required accessing the crime-scene physically—an overt process, which additionally faces certain limitations (traces on a crime-scene tend to fade, the crime scene as such including all of yet undiscovered evidence cannot be 'frozen' and stored). Analysing the retrieved evidence requires human resources, and—as these typically refer to specially trained experts of a particular department—imposed significant limitations of capacitive nature.
- Gathering digital evidence, on the contrary, particularly over IP-based networks such as the internet, can be done covertly (theoretically not leaving any traces at all), remotely (without any access to the device, the crime-scene and/or the suspect), and allows applying powerful automated means of analysing vast amounts of data without necessarily binding any human resources.

Consequently, balancing the need to guarantee efficient criminal prosecution and likewise guaranteeing sufficient protection of everyone's fundamental right to privacy requires safeguards of a different nature than those required for conventional investigations. Conversely: what may have been adequate safeguards in the physical world are not necessarily adequate safeguards in the digital world.

Not only do technically different methods of gathering evidence (e.g. telephone bug in the PSTN vs. Trojan horse software in an IP-network) require different safeguards, but also will the different degrees of the data subject's exposure need to be considered in any proportionality analysis. Given the fact that digital collection and exchange of evidence does not face the traditional limits of space and time (e.g. intercepting an email does not require physical access to any of the correspondents,

[2]See Sect. 13.2.

their mail boxes or the service provider and their establishment), and that technically digital evidence can be made available without any delay anywhere in the world by any authority in multiple loss-less copies of the original piece of evidence, that these conditions may require more focused legal safeguards. Such safeguards will need to be designed in such a manner that they do not create unwanted obstacles to (transnational) investigation, while simultaneously remaining proportionate under all conditions.

An expert meeting held in Lyon at INTERPOL in December 2014 as part of the EVIDENCE project has underpinned that electronic evidence causes a variety of practical challenges for law enforcement agencies, particularly concerning data protection: In practice, anonymisation and encryption tools are used to disguise criminal activity and legitimate actions likewise. Therefore, when considering providing law enforcement agencies with extended investigative powers or more powerful tools to meet this altered threat environment, these tools and powers will necessarily have to include proper privacy safeguards ensuring compliance with fundamental rights.

Moreover, storing data in foreign countries by using cloud services and other web services has become quite habitual, which results in law enforcement agencies facing legal obstacles in accessing such data. This leads to legal uncertainties[3] which will need to be addressed both to ensure effective law enforcement and adequate privacy protection.

The methodology used to further analyse and examine the data protection issues outlined above will be described in the following. The content of this chapter is based upon the research carried out in work package 8 of the EVIDENCE project. The related research activities took place between 2014 and 2015 primarily. For the publication of this work updates have been incorporated regarding the European legal framework to reflect the situation as of early 2017, particularly regarding the European data protection reform package that meanwhile came into force.

13.2 Methodology

13.2.1 General Objectives

The overall objective of the Evidence Project has been to create a roadmap "for realizing the missing Common European Framework for the systematic and uniform application of new technologies in the collection, use and exchange of evidence."[4] Therefore, the research underlying this chapter aimed at providing input to this

[3]For example the practice of using a seized device to access data that may be stored in a cloud storage outside the jurisdiction in which operates the LEA accessing that data, results in questions regarding territorial competence, which have not yet found a unanimous answer.

[4]608185 EVIDENCE Description of Work—Part A—Page 4 of 6.

roadmap by outlining legal requirements for privacy and data protection framing a possible future European legal framework on collection and use of digital evidence.

Consequently, there were three major questions, which needed to be addressed through this work:

- What can be harmonised? (Legal competence of the European Union)
- What needs to be harmonised? (Principle of subsidiarity)
- What can be learned from existing domestic legislation? (Good practice/'model law' character of existing provisions/set of rules).

13.2.2 The Methodological Outset

A first step was to conduct a desktop research to analyse the *status quo* of the legal debate surrounding electronic evidence concerning data protection. The objective of this first step was to identify the most important data protection issues related to the collection and exchange of electronic evidence to be able to set foci for the following activities. This analysis has shown that the data protection issues related to electronic evidence that are most intensely discussed are to be found less in the field of the well-known "classic" data protection principles[5] and their implementation into law (which has been achieved through European legislation such as 2008/977/JHA and 2008/978/JHA). Instead, intensely discussed data protection issues related to the collection of electronic evidence identified are:

- Innovative technologies to collect electronic evidence:
  - Hidden software used to monitor telecommunications on devices prior to encryption (lawful interception through direct access to a terminal device)
  - Lawful interception of data in networks (internet)
  - Innovative forms of access to data with probative value:
    * Computer-assisted search
    * Seizure of data
    * Data retention

  and
- Innovative services used by data subjects, e.g. cloud services.

To provide respective input to the EVIDENCE project's roadmap, these issues were in the focus of the further work underlying this chapter.

[5]Such as the principles of lawfulness, proportionality and purpose, the data subject's rights to blocking, erasure and rectification, as well as information and access, storing time limits, particular protection of the special categories of personal data, limitations on automated decisions, data quality checks for transferred data, limitation of transfer to private parties, security of processing, legal remedies, prior consultation of data protection authorities, and similar.

13.2.3 The Technological Outset and Its Privacy Impact

The technological advance and corresponding changes in criminal prosecution that have followed may have led to a situation in which the existing legal framework may not entirely be suitable anymore to provide for the investigative instruments needed or to cover the use of new tools of investigation becoming available. Innovative technologies, however, tend to provide powerful means of collecting electronic evidence and thereby give rise to the potential for privacy infringement, if not balanced with appropriate safeguards. For these reasons, lacunae in this field are likely to have a direct impact on the data protection assessment.

If, however, potential data protection issues arise from lacunae that appear when new technologies for collecting evidence become available while not (yet) being clearly covered by the law, the resulting question must be: how does the respective legal system handle this situation? Will it allow extending the scope of the existing legal provisions to the application of the new technologies (new measures)? Can therefore, for example, a legal provision legitimating lawful interception of phone calls be used to legitimate intercepting skype chat protocols? Or would that require an amendment of the legal framework? And if so, should this amendment be coordinated by European law to create a harmonised legal framework, or would it be better to leave the drafting fully in the hands of the national legislator?

The answers to these questions become very relevant wherever the original legal basis for a measure does not provide for adequate data protection safeguards, while the measure itself impacts data protection. If seizure of objects containing personal data is legitimated by a legal provision that was designed to serve as a legal basis for seizing objects, which back then would not contain any personal data, the legal provision consequently will not contain any safeguards tailored to preserve privacy and to balance it with the public interest in effective prosecution. As a result, applying the provision for the seizure of data storages or any kind of device giving access to data storages (smart phone, key card, etc.) will cause a privacy issue. This might cause a conflict with European fundamental rights (Articles 7 and 8 CFR[6]; Article 8 ECHR[7]) as well as with domestic fundamental rights (which are not necessarily entirely congruent with the European fundamental rights, mainly because of the divergent constitutional frameworks and long histories of autonomous constitutional jurisprudence in the Member States).

[6]Charter of Fundamental Rights of the European Union (2010/C 83/02): http://eur-lex.europa.eu/legal-content/EN/TXT/PDF/?uri=CELEX:12010P&from=DE.

[7]Convention for the Protection of Human Rights and Fundamental Freedoms, http://www.echr.coe.int/Documents/Convention_ENG.pdf.

13.2.4 Addressing the Privacy Impact

If the use of new technologies for collecting electronic evidence has a potential impact on privacy through possible conflicts with both European and domestic fundamental rights, any (European or domestic) legal framework for future statutory law regulating the collecting and use of digital evidence will need to consider these conflicts.

There are several factors to be considered to address this:

- The influence of both European and domestic (privacy related) fundamental rights on statutory criminal procedure law in the Member States;
- The particular setup of the domestic (privacy related) fundamental rights in the respective Member State;
- The setup of (the resulting) privacy safeguards in statutory criminal procedure law.

The roadmap provided by the EVIDENCE project, into which fed the research reproduced in this chapter, can be considered a pre-stage to making suggestions for a common European legal framework on electronic evidence, and, as such, that roadmap is not (yet) aiming at proposing legal regulations in full granularity, but rather at outlining the legal requirements for such common framework on a strategic level. Consequently, the data protection analysis described in this chapter remains on a strategic level as well.

A future EU framework is likely to be influenced by at least three factors:

- The extent of the competence of the European Union to harmonise criminal procedure law (Article 82 II TFEU[8]);
- The existing European data protection framework in the law enforcement sector and beyond;
- Possible limitations created by the domestic constitutions wherever European fundamental rights do not provide a comparable level of protection (e.g. if there is no corresponding fundamental right on the European level) (Article 82 III TFEU);
- Existing safeguards that may serve as models.

Out of the comprehensive work undertaken to analyse these four aspects of the legal framework governing the collection and use of electronic evidence, this chapter is going to focus on the first two aspects, to provide an overview on the existing European legal framework and its significant impact on future European legislation concerning privacy and data protection. For an examination of existing European legal framework, please see Chap. 11 of this Volume.

[8]Consolidated versions of the Treaty on European Union and the Treaty on the Functioning of the European Union 2012/C 326/01; http://eur-lex.europa.eu/legal-content/EN/TXT/?uri=CELEX:12012E/TXT.

13.3 European Legal Framework and International Law

It has been one of the EVIDENCE project's premises that there is no common European legal framework for gathering (and exchanging) electronic evidence; and, additionally, that such framework should be created.[9]

13.3.1 Competences of the European Union

A harmonisation of criminal procedure law to harmonise collecting and exchanging electronic evidence—and the related privacy safeguards—requires a corresponding competence of the European Union. This competence is laid down in Article 82 of the Treaty on the Functioning of the European Union,[10] for in depth study see Chap. 11 of this Volume.

13.3.2 European Fundamental Rights to Privacy and Data Protection

A fundamental right to privacy is laid down by Article 8 Council of Europe Convention for the Protection of Human Rights and Fundamental Freedoms (4/11/1950).[11] Fundamental rights to privacy, (tele-)communications privacy and data protection are laid down jointly in Articles 7 and 8 Charter of Fundamental Rights of the European Union 2010/C 83/02.[12]

These are binding for both the European Union itself and its Member States (when implementing EU law, Article 51 (I) Charter of the Fundamental Rights of the European Union), and thereby affect all legislative acts on privacy matters of collecting electronic evidence both on a European and on a domestic level (when transposing EU law).

[9]608185 EVIDENCE Description of Work—Part A—Page 4 of 6.

[10]Consolidated versions of the Treaty on European Union and the Treaty on the Functioning of the European Union 2012/C 326/01; http://eur-lex.europa.eu/legal-content/EN/TXT/?uri=CELEX:12012E/TXT.

[11]Convention for the Protection of Human Rights and Fundamental Freedoms, http://www.echr.coe.int/Documents/Convention_ENG.pdf.

[12]Charter of Fundamental Rights of the European Union (2010/C 83/02): http://eur-lex.europa.eu/legal-content/EN/TXT/PDF/?uri=CELEX:12010P&from=DE.

13.3.3 *European Secondary Data Protection Law*

It appears that as of now (January 2017) no (comprehensive and common) rules on data protection regarding the collecting of electronic evidence have been implemented on a European level.

13.3.3.1 Directive 95/46/EC

The data protection Directive 95/46/EC[13] excludes applicability in activities of the state in criminal matters.

> Article 3
> Scope
> [...]
>
> 2. This Directive shall not apply to the processing of personal data:
>
> – in the course of an activity which falls outside the scope of Community law, such as those provided for by Titles V and VI of the Treaty on European Union and in any case to processing operations concerning public security, defence, State security (including the economic well-being of the State when the processing operation relates to State security matters) and the activities of the State in areas of criminal law,
>
> [...]

A similar limitation can be found in recital 13:

> (13) Whereas the activities referred to in Titles V and VI of the Treaty on European Union regarding public safety, defence, State security or the activities of the State in the area of criminal laws fall outside the scope of Community law, without prejudice to the obligations incumbent upon Member States under Article 56 (2), Article 57 or Article 100a of the Treaty establishing the European Community; whereas the processing of personal data that is necessary to safeguard the economic well-being of the State does not fall within the scope of this Directive where such processing relates to State security matters;

[13]Directive 95/46/EC of the European Parliament and of the Council of 24 October 1995 on the protection of individuals regarding the processing of personal data and on the free movement of such data, http://eur-lex.europa.eu/LexUriServ/LexUriServ.do?uri=CELEX:31995L0046:en:HTML.

The relation of Directive 95/46/EC and domestic criminal procedure law, however, is not entirely clear as likewise the directive explicitly contains a few rules on data related to criminal matters:

> Article 8
> [...]
>
> 5. Processing of data relating to offences, criminal convictions or security measures may be carried out only under the control of official authority, or if suitable specific safeguards are provided under national law, subject to derogations which may be granted by the Member State under national provisions providing suitable specific safeguards. However, a complete register of criminal convictions may be kept only under the control of official authority.
>
> [...]

> Article 13
> Exemptions and restrictions
>
> 1. Member States may adopt legislative measures to restrict the scope of the obligations and rights provided for in Articles 6 (1), 10, 11 (1), 12 and 21 when such a restriction constitutes a necessary measures to safeguard:
>
> [...]
>
> (d) the prevention, investigation, detection and prosecution of criminal offences, or of breaches of ethics for regulated professions;
>
> [...]

Similarly, the explicit exclusion in recital 16 for audio and video files related to state activities relating to criminal law indicates that other file types might be within the scope.

> (16) Whereas the processing of sound and image data, such as in cases of video surveillance, does not come within the scope of this Directive if it is carried out for the purposes of public security, defence, national security or in the course of State activities relating to the area of criminal law or of other activities which do not come within the scope of Community law;

13.3.3.2 Directive 2002/58/EC

The non-applicability on issues of law enforcement and criminal prosecution becomes slightly clearer through Directive 2002/58/EC,[14] which states in recital 11:

> (11) Like Directive 95/46/EC, this Directive does not address issues of protection of fundamental rights and freedoms related to activities which are not governed by Community law. Therefore, it does not alter the existing balance between the individual's right to privacy and the possibility for Member States to take the measures referred to in Article 15(1) of this Directive, necessary for the protection of public security, defence, State security (including the economic well-being of the State when the activities relate to State security matters) and the enforcement of criminal law. Consequently, this Directive does not affect the ability of Member States to carry out lawful interception of electronic communications, or take other measures, if necessary for any of these purposes and in accordance with the European Convention for the Protection of Human Rights and Fundamental Freedoms, as interpreted by the rulings of the European Court of Human Rights. Such measures must be appropriate, strictly proportionate to the intended purpose and necessary within a democratic society and should be subject to adequate safeguards in accordance with the European Convention for the Protection of Human Rights and Fundamental Freedoms.

Consequently, the scope of Directive 2002/58/EC is limited similarly to the scope of Directive 95/46/EC:

> Article 1 (directive 2002/58/EC)
> Scope and aim
> [...]
>
> 3. This Directive shall not apply to activities which fall outside the scope of the Treaty establishing the European Community, such as those covered by Titles V and VI of the Treaty on European Union, and in any case to activities concerning public security, defence, State security (including the economic well-being of the State when the activities relate to State security matters) and the activities of the State in areas of criminal law.

[14] Directive 2002/58/EC of the European Parliament and of the Council of 12 July 2002 concerning the processing of personal data and the protection of privacy in the electronic communications sector (Directive on privacy and electronic communications), http://eur-lex.europa.eu/LexUriServ/LexUriServ.do?uri=CELEX:32002L0058:en:HTML.

13.3.3.3 Directive 2006/24/EC

Directive 2002/58/EC was amended by the Directive 2006/24/EC.[15] This latter directive, also referred to as data retention directive, actually at least indirectly contained rules on the collection of electronic evidence as it obliged telecommunication service providers to store certain traffic data for a period of 6–24 months, making them available on demand of i.e. prosecution authorities. However, the directive was declared invalid by the CJEU in 2014[16] for lack of proportionality in the light of the European fundamental rights. In 2016, the CJEU ruled that laws allowing for the blanket collection and retention of telecommunication data violate EU law.[17] According to the court, "[n]ational legislation such as that at issue in the main proceedings therefore exceeds the limits of what is strictly necessary and cannot be considered to be justified, within a democratic society, as required by Article 15(1) of Directive 2002/58, read in the light of Articles 7, 8 and 11 and Article 52(1) of the Charter."[18]

13.3.3.4 2008/977/JHA

Council Framework Decision 2008/977/JHA1 contains rules on the protection of personal data processed in the framework of police and judicial cooperation in criminal matters. While this framework decision implements a relatively diversified set of data protection rules, it applies to the exchange of evidence only, but not on the collection. Moreover, 2008/977/JHA does not address electronic evidence at all, but the exchange of personal data on a more general level.

---

[15] Directive 2006/24/EC of the European Parliament and of the Council of 15 March 2006 on the retention of data generated or processed in connection with the provision of publicly available electronic communications services or of public communications networks and amending Directive 2002/58/EC, http://eur-lex.europa.eu/LexUriServ/LexUriServ.do?uri=OJ:L:2006:105:0054:0063:EN:PDF.

[16] Judgment of the Court (Grand Chamber) of 8 April 2014 (requests for a preliminary ruling from the High Court of Ireland (Ireland) and the Verfassungsgerichtshof (Austria))—Digital Rights Ireland Ltd (C-293/12) v Minister for Communications, Marine and Natural Resources, Minister for Justice, Equality and Law Reform, The Commissioner of the Garda Síochána, Ireland and the Attorney General, and Kärntner Landesregierung, Michael Seitlinger, Christof Tschohl and Others (C-594/12), http://curia.europa.eu/juris/document/document.jsf;jsessionid=9ea7d2dc30dd27b7f477581446fabc2a85b30309ef55.e34KaxiLc3qMb40Rch0SaxuPc3v0?text=&docid=153045&pageIndex=0&doclang=EN&mode=req&dir=&occ=first&part=1&cid=610451.

[17] CJEU, Joined Cases C203/15 and C698/15, http://curia.europa.eu/juris/document/document.jsf?text=&docid=186492&pageIndex=0&doclang=EN&mode=req&dir=&occ=first&part=1.

[18] See margin no. 107 of the judgement.

However, 2008/977/JHA has well implemented the classic principles of data protection law and corresponding rights of the data subject on a European level with particular focus on the exchange of personal data between law enforcement authorities. These are:

- Article 3—Principles of lawfulness, proportionality and purpose
- Article 4—(Data subject's right to) rectification, erasure and blocking
- Article 5—Establishment of time limits for erasure and review (of need to keep personal data)
- Article 6—(Limitations on) processing of special categories of data
- Article 7—(Limitations on) automated individual decisions
- Article 8—Verification of quality of data that are transmitted or made available
- Article 10—Logging and documentation (of transmissions)
- Article 13—(Rules and limitations on) transfer to competent authorities in third States or to international bodies
- Article 14—(Rules and Limitations on) transmission to private parties in Member States
- Article 16—Information for the data subject
- Article 17—(Data subject's) right of access
- Article 18—(Data subject's) right to rectification, erasure or blocking
- Article 19—Right to compensation
- Article 20—Judicial remedies
- Article 21—Confidentiality of processing
- Article 22—Security of processing
- Article 23—Prior consultation (of data protection authorities).

While 2008/977/JHA therefore broadly implements the classic instruments, principles and rights of data protection law regarding the exchange of personal data (and thus electronic evidence) between law enforcement authorities in the Member States, it does not cover the field of innovative methods of gathering electronic evidence (such as installing hidden software on a mobile device to capture transmissions before encryption, or retrieving data from cloud services and so forth). 2008/977/JHA accordingly does not provide for the necessary data protection safeguards either.

In May 2018, 2008/977/JHA will be replaced by Directive 2016/680/EU.

13.3.3.5 2008/978/JHA

Another framework governing the exchange of electronic evidence between EU Member States is the council framework decision on European evidence warrant (EEW).[19] The EEW contains regulations designed explicitly for electronic data (evidence), such as Article 2 paragraph (b) or Article 4, Section 2, paragraph (e).

[19] http://eur-lex.europa.eu/LexUriServ/LexUriServ.do?uri=OJ:L:2008:350:0072:0092:en:PDF.

According to Article 15, Section 5, "the executing State shall without undue delay transfer the objects, documents or data obtained under the EEW to the issuing State". The procedure for requesting data under the EEW is described in the annex of the council framework decision.[20] Recital 13 states that the "executing authority should be obliged to execute the EEW for electronic data not located in the executing State only to the extent possible under its law".

The requirements for issuing the EEW are codified in Articles 5 and 7 of the framework decision. Concerning criminal proceedings, the EEW may be issued in respect of a criminal offence under the national law of the issuing state, even for offences or infringements for which a legal person may be held liable or punished in the issuing State.[21] According to Article 7 paragraph (a) EEW, obtaining the objects, documents or data sought must be necessary and proportionate for the aforementioned purposes. It is, however, required, that the possibility to obtain objects, documents or data under the law of the issuing state would be given in a comparable case if they were available on the territory of the issuing state, although different procedural measures might be used.[22] The technical procedure for transferring and securing the data is not codified in the EEW. 2008/978/JHA does not cover innovative means and methods of gathering electronic evidence, and therefore accordingly does not provide for the necessary data protection safeguards either. Subsequent regulation to 2008/978/JHA is the Directive 2014/41/EU (European Investigations Order), which is to be implemented by the Member States by 22 May 2017.[23]

13.3.4 EU and CoE Conventions

13.3.4.1 Convention on Mutual Legal Assistance in the European Union

Concerning privacy intrusive measures, Articles 19 and 20 of the Convention on Mutual Legal Assistance in the European Union[24] contain a rule that entitle the competent authorities of one Member State to directly intercept telecommunications in another Member State. Given the fact that most telecommunications nowadays happen in IP-based networks (namely the internet), and therefore are electronic

[20] See http://eur-lex.europa.eu/LexUriServ/LexUriServ.do?uri=OJ:L:2008:350:0072:0092:en:PDF.

[21] Article 5 EEW.

[22] Article 7 paragraph (b) EEW.

[23] For more details see chapter XX "The European Legal Scenario, p. XX.

[24] Council Act of 29 May 2000 establishing in accordance with Article 34 of the Treaty on European Union the Convention on Mutual Assistance in Criminal Matters between the Member States of the European Union (2000/C 197/01); http://eur-lex.europa.eu/LexUriServ/LexUriServ.do?uri=OJ:C:2000:197:0001:0023:EN:PDF.

telecommunications, gathering evidence through intercepting telecommunications is a form of collecting digital evidence.

Article 19
Interceptions of telecommunications on national territory by the use of service providers

1. Member States shall ensure that systems of telecommunications services operated via a gateway on their territory, which for the lawful interception of the communications of a subject present in another Member State are not directly accessible on the territory of the latter, may be made directly accessible for the lawful interception by that Member State through the intermediary of a designated service provider present on its territory.
2. In the case referred to in paragraph 1, the competent authorities of a Member State shall be entitled, for the purposes of a criminal investigation and in accordance with applicable national law and provided that the subject of the interception is present in that Member State, to carry out the interception through the intermediary of a designated service provider present on its territory without involving the Member State on whose territory the gateway is located.

[...]

Article 19 applies to cases, in which the subject of interception (the suspect) is located on the territory of the intercepting Member State, while the gateway used to intercept is located abroad. The provision *entitles* the intercepting Member State to intercept (through an intermediary) on foreign territory, under the preconditions that such interception is legal under domestic law and that the subject of interception is located on the territory of the intercepting state. Conversely, the routing of traffic through foreign territories shall not hinder interception on foreign territory as long as interception would have been legal if the traffic had been routed domestically only. This is one of the few legal provisions on European level regulating the collection of electronic evidence; albeit it does so only in dependency on national law (Article 19 does not constitute an autonomous legal basis for lawful interception, but only provides for the legitimacy of lawful interception already regulated under national law in certain cross-border cases).

Article 20, oppositely, applies on cases in which the subject of interception is located abroad. In these cases, the foreign Member State needs to be notified and has a right to intervene, should interception violate national law.

Article 20
Interception of telecommunications without the technical assistance of another Member State
[...]

2. Where for the purpose of a criminal investigation, the interception of telecommunications is authorised by the competent authority of one Member State (the 'intercepting Member State'), and the telecommunication address of the subject specified in the interception order is being used on the territory of another Member State (the 'notified Member State') from which no technical assistance is needed to carry out the interception, the intercepting Member State shall inform the notified Member State of the interception:

   [...]

4. The following shall apply where a Member State is notified pursuant to paragraphs 2 and 3:

   (a) Upon receipt of the information provided under paragraph 3 the competent authority of the notified Member State shall, without delay, and at the latest within 96 h, reply to the intercepting Member State, with a view to:

      (i) allowing the interception to be carried out or to be continued. The notified Member State may make its consent subject to any conditions which would have to be observed in a similar national case;
      (ii) requiring the interception not to be carried out or to be terminated where the interception would not be permissible pursuant to the national law of the notified Member State, or for the reasons specified in Article 2 of the European Mutual Assistance Convention. Where the notified Member State imposes such a requirement, it shall give reasons for its decision in writing;
      (iii) in cases referred to in point (ii), requiring that any material already intercepted while the subject was on its territory may not be used, or may only be used under conditions which it shall specify. The notified Member State shall inform the intercepting Member State of the reasons justifying the said conditions;

   [...]

Article 20, too, regulates the collection of electronic evidence to the extent to which telecommunications are carried out electronically, but even less than Article 19 does so in a genuine way (in terms of actually allowing for the collection of electronic evidence), but only through setting-up a few additional pre-conditions for cross-border cases, which mainly lead to national law of the Member State, in which the suspect is located, remaining applicable. Conversely, the provision ensures that the national (privacy) safeguards remain in force and cannot be circumvented. It must be noted that the provision does not refer to the location where the interception is carried out, but to the location of "use of the communication address". Consequently, this provision applies also to cases, in which the interception is carried out by the intercepting Member State on its home territory, while the suspect is abroad (e.g. sending home emails from another Member State).

Moreover, data protection rules are laid down in Article 23 of the convention:

Article 23
Personal data protection

1. Personal data communicated under this Convention may be used by the Member State to which they have been transferred:
   (a) for the purpose of proceedings to which this Convention applies;
   (b) for other judicial and administrative proceedings directly related to proceedings referred to under point (a);
   (c) for preventing an immediate and serious threat to public security;
   (d) for any other purpose, only with the prior consent of the communicating Member State, unless the Member State concerned has obtained the consent of the data subject.
2. This Article shall also apply to personal data not communicated but obtained otherwise under this Convention.
3. In the circumstances of the particular case, the communicating Member State may require the Member State to which the personal data have been transferred to give information on the use made of the data.
4. Where conditions on the use of personal data have been imposed pursuant to Articles 7(2), 18(5)(b), 18(6) or 20(4), these conditions shall prevail. Where no such conditions have been imposed, this Article shall apply.

   [...]

6. This Article does not apply to personal data obtained by a Member State under this Convention and originating from that Member State.

   [...]

These data protection rules remain on a relatively general level, and additionally—according to paragraph 6—apply only in cross-border cases. They do not consider any particular privacy risks related to the collection of electronic evidence as such and on a solely national level.

13.3.4.2 European Convention on Mutual Assistance in Criminal Matters (CoE)

Another tool for exchanging evidence as outlined in Chap. 11 of this Volume, is the European Convention on Mutual Assistance in Criminal Matters.[25] As it was signed in 1959, it does not aim specifically at electronic evidence and related privacy issues. Moreover, the convention addresses the exchange, not the collection of evidence. Its objective was to allow law enforcement agencies of the Member States to approach each other directly instead of using diplomatic channels. It therefore does not cover the particular data protection issues arising from innovative methods and technologies to gather electronic evidence. This convention, however, has been supplemented for the EU Member States by Council Act of 29 May 2000 establishing in accordance with Article 34 of the Treaty on European Union the Convention on Mutual Assistance in Criminal Matters between the Member States of the European Union,[26] which has been described in Sect. 13.3.4.1.

13.3.4.3 Cybercrime Convention (CoE)

Concerning the collection and exchange of electronic evidence, another important tool as outlined in Chap. 11 of this Volume, is the Cybercrime Convention.[27] It contains several provisions on collecting electronic evidence in “Section II—Procedural Law”. These are:

Article 16—Expedited preservation of stored computer data
Article 17—Expedited preservation and partial disclosure of traffic data
Article 18—Production order
Article 19—Search and seizure of stored computer data
Article 20—Real-time collection of traffic data
Article 21—Interception of content data

These articles outline certain procedural measures to collect electronic evidence, while allowing signatories to achieve the objectives through other measures should their domestic legal principles require so. However, these articles do not contain (privacy) safeguards. The latter are outlined in Article 15:

[25] http://conventions.coe.int/Treaty/Commun/ChercheSig.asp?NT=030&CM=&DF=&CL=ENG.

[26] See Article 1 (1) a of the Convention established by the Council in accordance with Article 34 of the Treaty on European Union, on Mutual Assistance in Criminal Matters between the Member States of the European Union.

[27] Convention on Cybercrime; http://conventions.coe.int/Treaty/en/Treaties/Html/185.htm.

Article 15—Conditions and safeguards

1. Each Party shall ensure that the establishment, implementation and application of the powers and procedures provided for in this section are subject to conditions and safeguards provided for under its domestic law, which shall provide for the adequate protection of human rights and liberties, including rights arising pursuant to obligations it has undertaken under the 1950 Council of Europe Convention for the Protection of Human Rights and Fundamental Freedoms, the 1966 United Nations International Covenant on Civil and Political Rights, and other applicable international human rights instruments, and which shall incorporate the principle of proportionality.
2. Such conditions and safeguards shall, as appropriate in view of the nature of the procedure or power concerned, *inter alia*, include judicial or other independent supervision, grounds justifying application, and limitation of the scope and the duration of such power or procedure.
3. To the extent that it is consistent with the public interest, in particular the sound administration of justice, each Party shall consider the impact of the powers and procedures in this section upon the rights, responsibilities and legitimate interests of third parties.

Albeit these safeguards remain relatively general and do not consider the particular risks involved with certain measures, they are, however, the only (privacy) safeguards in relation to collecting electronic evidence on a European level. While leaving quite some leeway to the CoE Member States, there are three mandatory safeguards:

- Judicial or other independent supervision
- Grounds justifying application and
- Limitation of the scope and the duration.

13.3.5 CoE Recommendation 87 (15)

Recommendation 87 (15)[28] contains several principles both on the collection and on the transfer of personal data in the police sector (and therefore including electronic evidence). While dating back to 1987, Recommendation 87 (15) has proven to be quite visionary in many regards and thus been influential to many subsequent legal acts (including council framework decision 2008/977/JHA). Consequently, some

[28]Recommendation 87 (15) of the Committee of Ministers to Member States Regulating the Use of Personal Data in the Police Sector, https://wcd.coe.int/com.instranet.InstraServlet?.

of the principals and rules recommended in Recommendation 87 (15) have been adopted and diversified in later EU legislation since (i.e. the various data subject's right laid down in 2008/977/JHA). Still, several principles are exceeding those laid down in 2008/977/JHA and are formulated in an abstract way, and since have not lost any of their significance. The following list is supposed to give an overview over those principles, which in the view of the authors should be particularly considered regarding any future European legislation on electronic evidence.

Principle 1—Control and notification

[...]

1.2. New technical means for data processing may only be introduced if all reasonable measures have been taken to ensure that their use complies with the spirit of existing data protection legislation.
1.3. The responsible body should consult the supervisory authority in advance in any case where the introduction of automatic processing methods raises questions about the application of this recommendation.

[...]

Principle 2—Collection of data

2.1. The collection of personal data for police purposes should be limited to such as is necessary for the prevention of a real danger or the suppression of a specific criminal offence. Any exception to this provision should be the subject of specific national legislation.

[...]

2.3. The collection of data by technical surveillance or other automated means should be provided for in specific provisions.
2.4. The collection of data on individuals solely on the basis that they have a particular racial origin, particular religious convictions, sexual behaviour or political opinions or belong to particular movements or organisations which are not proscribed by law should be prohibited. The collection of data concerning these factors may only be carried out if absolutely necessary for the purposes of a particular inquiry.

Principle 3—Storage of data

[...]

3.2. As far as possible, the different categories of data stored should be distinguished in accordance with their degree of accuracy or reliability and, in particular, data based on facts should be distinguished from data based on opinions or personal assessments.

(continued)

3.3. Where data which have been collected for administrative purposes are to be stored permanently, they should be stored in a separate file. In any case, measures should be taken so that administrative data are not subject to rules applicable to police data.

[...]

5.5.i. *Requests for communication*

[...]

5.5.ii. *Conditions for communication* As far as possible, the quality of data should be verified at the latest at the time of their communication. As far as possible, in all communications of data, judicial decisions, as well as decisions not to prosecute, should be indicated and data based on opinions or personal assessments checked at source before being communicated and their degree of accuracy or reliability indicated.

If it is discovered that the data are no longer accurate and up to date, they should not be communicated. If data which are no longer accurate or up to date have been communicated, the communicating body should inform as far as possible all the recipients of the data of their non-conformity.

5.5.iii. *Safeguards for communication*

The data communicated to other public bodies, private parties and foreign authorities should not be used for purposes other than those specified in the request for communication. Use of the data for other purposes should, without prejudice to paragraphs 5.2 to 5.4 of this principle, be made subject to the agreement of the communicating body.

5.6. *Interconnection of files and on-fine access to files*

The interconnection of files with files held for different purposes is subject to either of the following conditions:

a. the grant of an authorisation by the supervisory body for the purposes of an inquiry into a particular offence, or
b. in compliance with a clear legal provision.

Direct access/on-line access to a file should only be allowed if it is in accordance with domestic legislation, which should take account of Principles 3 to 6 of this recommendation.

13.3.6 Europol Rules on the Collaboration Between Member States LEAs and Their Data Protection Rules

Through coordinating the collaboration of national police authorities, Europol plays an important role regarding the exchange of electronic evidence.[29]

About data protection, according to Article 10 of the Europol decision,[30] Europol can process information—including personal data—as it is necessary to achieve Europol's objectives. Processing data can be, for instance, done through the "Europol Information System" as further described in Article 12. The Europol information system may contain personal data about suspects, particularly the name, date and place of birth, nationality, sex, place of residence, profession and whereabouts, social security numbers, driving licenses, identification documents, and password data.

Europol may also store, modify, and use data concerning criminal offences in respect of which it is competent in analysis work files for the performance of its tasks. Article 14 paragraph 1 contains a regulation permitting the processing of sensitive data such as racial or ethnic origin, political opinions, religious or philosophical beliefs or trade union membership and the processing of data concerning health or sex life unless strictly necessary for the file. A list of personal data that can be stored in an analysis work file can be found in Article 6 paragraph 2 of council decision 2009/936/JHA implementing rules for Europol analysis work files.[31]

Further rules on the use of personal data through Europol can be found in Article 19 of the Europol decision, stating that personal data retrieved from any of Europol's data processing files or communicated by any other appropriate means shall be transmitted or used only by the competent authorities of the Member States to prevent and combat crimes in respect of which Europol is competent. Europol shall use the data only for the performance of its tasks. Restrictions for the usage of personal data shall be complied with by the user of the data. The usage of the personal data for other purposes or by authorities other than the national competent authorities shall be possible only after consultation of the Member State that transmitted the data.

According to Article 20, the Europol shall hold data in data files only for as long as is necessary for the performance of its tasks.

In respect of automated data processing at Europol, each Member State and Europol must ensure a proper level of data security. Article 35 contains provisions

[29]See section 10, chapter 2.4 for general information on the role of Europol in the overall legal system.

[30]Council Decision 2009/371/JHA, https://www.europol.europa.eu/sites/default/files/council_decision.pdf.

[31]https://www.europol.europa.eu/sites/default/files/rules_applicable_to_europol_analysis_files.pdf.

regarding data security to be implemented by each Member State and Europol. Those measures shall be designed to:

- Deny unauthorised persons access to data-processing equipment (equipment access control);
- Prevent the unauthorised reading, copying, modification or removal of data media (data media control);
- Prevent the unauthorised input of data and the unauthorised inspection, modification or deletion of stored personal data (storage control);
- Prevent the use of automated data-processing systems by unauthorised persons using data-communication equipment (user control);
- Ensure that persons authorised to use an automated data processing system have access only to the data covered by their access authorisation (data access control);
- Ensure that it is possible to verify and establish to which bodies personal data may be or have been transmitted using data communication equipment (communication control);
- Ensure that it is possible to verify and establish which personal data have been input into automated data processing systems and when and by whom the data were input (input control);
- Prevent the unauthorised reading, copying, modification or deletion of personal data during transfers of personal data or during the transportation of data media (transport control);
- Ensure that installed systems may, in the event of interruption, be restored immediately (recovery);
- Ensure that the functions of the system perform without fault that the appearance of faults in the functions is immediately reported (reliability) and that stored data cannot be corrupted by system malfunctions (integrity).

Rules governing Europol's relations with partners, including the exchange of personal data and classified information have been implemented with council decision 2009/934/JHA.[32] The transmission of information through Europol is limited to certain conditions laid down in Article 9. Accordingly, information shall only be transmitted if

- There is an agreement or working arrangement between Europol and the EU body or third party (Article 9 no. 1);
- If the information was transmitted by a Member State, Europol shall transmit this information only with the Member State's consent (Article 9 no. 2);
- Information transmitted by Europol may not obstruct the proper performance of the tasks in respect of which a Member State is competent or jeopardise the security or public order of a Member State or otherwise prejudice its general welfare (Article 9 no. 3).

---

[32] https://www.europol.europa.eu/sites/default/files/rules_governing_europols_relations_with_partners.pdf.

Article 9 no. 4 contains provisions under which the transmission of personal data is permissible:

> Article 9—Conditions for the transmission of information to EU bodies and third parties
>
> [...]
>
> 4. The transmission of personal data to third parties shall only be permissible where:
>
>   (a) it is necessary in individual cases for the purposes of preventing or combating criminal offences in respect of which Europol is competent; and
>
>   (b) Europol has concluded an operational agreement with the third parties concerned which permits the transmission of such data on the basis of an assessment confirming an adequate level of data protection ensured by those third parties in accordance with Article 5(4).

E contrario this means that the transfer of personal data to third parties is prohibited as long as the requirements of Article 9 no. 4 are not met.

The transfer of personal information—to third parties, as well as to EU bodies—is further limited in Article 15:

> Article 15—Purposes for which personal data are transmitted 1. Personal data requested without any indication as to the purpose of, and reason for, the request shall not be transmitted.
>
> 2. The transmission of personal data revealing racial or ethnic origin, political opinions, religious or philosophical beliefs or trade union membership and the transmission of data concerning a person's health or sex life shall not be permitted unless strictly necessary.

While those safeguards require the indication of a purpose and a reason, further requirements on the nature of such purpose or considerations of proportionality are not explicitly mentioned. However, according to Article 10, the usage of the data must be limited to the purpose for which it was transmitted.

Europol also has several cooperation initiatives with Member States, EU institutions and agencies, non-EU-states and international institutions such as INTERPOL.[33] Those cooperations may in some cases also include provisions regarding

[33] See https://www.europol.europa.eu/content/page/europol-eu-121 and https://www.europol.europa.eu/content/page/external-cooperation-31.

the transfer and exchange of information while the exchange of personal data is excluded explicitly in other cases (e.g. with Russia).

13.3.7 Eurojust Rules on Data Protection

Another entity established in the European law enforcement system is Eurojust.[34] The rules of procedure on the processing and protection of personal data at Eurojust were adopted unanimously by the college of Eurojust during the meeting of 21 October 2004 and approved by the Council on 24 February 2005.[35] Article 4 of the rules on data protection state that Eurojust shall act in full respect of the human rights and fundamental freedoms of individuals (as further described in Sect. 13.3.2) and particularly their right to privacy regarding the processing of their personal data, regardless of nationality or place of residence. General principles are laid down in Article 5:

> Article 5—Principles of lawfulness and fairness, proportionality and necessity of processing
>
> 1. Personal data must be processed fairly and lawfully.
> 2. Eurojust shall only process personal data that are necessary, adequate, relevant and not excessive in relation to the purposes for which they are collected or further processed.
> 3. Eurojust shall define its processing operations and systems in accordance with the aim of collecting or further processing only personal data that are necessary as defined in paragraph 2. In particular, use is to be made of the possibilities for aliasing and rendering data anonymous, in so far as this is possible, taking into account the purpose of the processing and that the effort involved is reasonable.

The fairness and lawfulness of processing data is further described in Article 14 for case-related processing operations and Article 30 for non-case-related processing operations. Purpose limitations can be found in Articles 15 and 31, accordingly. Provisions regarding data security can be found in Article 7 of the data protection rules, as well as in Article 22 of the Eurojust decision.[36] According

[34]For further information, see section 10, chapter 2.4.

[35]See Official Journal of the European Union 2005/C 68/01, http://eurojust.europa.eu/doclibrary/Eurojust-framework/dataprotection/Eurojust%20Data%20Protection%20Rules/Eurojust-Data-Protection-Rules-2005-02-24-EN.pdf.

[36]http://www.eurojust.europa.eu/doclibrary/Eurojust-framework/ejdecision/Consolidated%20version%20of%20the%20Eurojust%20Council%20Decision/Eurojust-Council-Decision-2009Consolidated-EN.pdf.

to Article 7 paragraph 1 of the data protection rules, Eurojust "shall put in place the necessary technical measures and organisational arrangements to protect personal data against accidental or unlawful destruction, accidental loss or unauthorised disclosure, alteration, access or any unauthorised form of processing". Additionally, Eurojust shall develop a comprehensive security policy in accordance with Article 22 paragraph 2 of the Eurojust decision to satisfy the need of avoiding data breaches.

Article 22—Data security

1. Eurojust and, insofar as it is concerned by data transmitted from Eurojust, each Member State, shall, as regards the processing of personal data within the framework of this Decision, protect personal data against accidental or unlawful destruction, accidental loss or unauthorised disclosure, alteration and access or any other unauthorised form of processing.
2. The rules of procedure shall contain the technical measures and the organisational arrangements needed to implement this Decision with regard to data security and in particular measures designed to:
   (a) deny unauthorised persons access to data processing equipment used for processing personal data;
   (b) prevent the unauthorised reading, copying, modification or removal of data media;
   (c) prevent the unauthorised input of data and the unauthorised inspection, modification or deletion of stored personal data;
   (d) prevent the use of automated data processing systems by unauthorised persons using data communication equipment;
   (e) ensure that persons authorised to use an automated data processing system only have access to the data covered by their access authorisation;
   (f) ensure that it is possible to verify and establish to which bodies personal data are transmitted when data are communicated;
   (g) ensure that it is subsequently possible to verify and establish which personal data have been input into automated data processing systems and when and by whom the data were input;
   (h) prevent unauthorised reading, copying, modification or deletion of personal data during transfers of personal data or during transportation of data media.

Further data security aspects are addressed in chapter III. of the Eurojust data protection rules. Among these, special attention is paid to the automated case management system, temporary work files and index, log files and audit trails and the access to data. In addition to that, Eurojust shall take appropriate technical and organisational measures to safeguard the secure use of the telecommunications networks and terminal equipment such as computers, servers, hardware and software (Article 39).

According to Article 18 of the Eurojust decision, the access to personal data is restricted to national members, their deputies and their assistants, as well as national correspondents for the Eurojust national cooperation system and authorised Eurojust staff.

Finally, the rights of data subjects are stipulated in Articles 8, 9 and 18–22 of the data protection rules.

To ensure that the data protection regulations are satisfied, Eurojust shall have a specially appointed data protection officer, Article 17 of the Eurojust decision. The Data Protection Officer shall

- Ensure in an independent manner the lawfulness and compliance with the provisions of the Eurojust decision concerning the processing of personal data,
- Ensure that a written record of the transmission and receipt of personal data is kept in accordance with the provisions to be laid down in the rules of procedure and
- Ensure that data subjects are informed of their rights under the Eurojust decision at their request.

13.3.8 Data Protection Reform Package

Since the beginning of 2012 the reformation process of European data protection law is taking place,[37] notably the legislative process for the General Data Protection Regulation[38] and for the data protection directive in the law enforcement

[37] http://www.europarl.europa.eu/oeil/popups/ficheprocedure.do?lang=en&reference=2012/0011%28COD%29.

[38] Regulation (EU) 2016/679 OF THE EUROPEAN PARLIAMENT AND OF THE COUNCIL of 27 April 2016 on the protection of natural persons with regard to the processing of personal data and on the free movement of such data, and repealing Directive 95/46/EC (General Data Protection Regulation), http://eur-lex.europa.eu/legal-content/EN/TXT/HTML/?uri=CELEX:32016R0679; http://www.europarl.europa.eu/registre/docs_autres_institution/commission_europeenne/com/2012/0011/COM_COM%282012%290011_EN.pdf.

sector,[39] both of which are in force in since May 25, 2016. The General Data Protection Regulation will be directly applicable from May 25, 2018 onwards (Art 99 paragraph 2 GDPR); the directive will need to be transposed (with very few exceptions[40]) until May 6 2018 by provisions applicable from this date onwards (Article 63 paragrapah 1 2016/680/EU).

Article 2 paragraph 2. lit (d) of the General Data Protection Regulation states that the regulation shall not be applicable to the processing of personal data "by competent authorities for the purposes of the prevention, investigation, detection or prosecution of criminal offences or the execution of criminal penalties, including the safeguarding against and the prevention of threats to public security". The General Data Protection Regulation therefore is not applicable to the collection and exchange of electronic evidence.

These are covered by the directive, as is laid down in Article 2 paragraph 1 jointly with Article 1 paragraph 1. The general principles are laid down in Article 4.

Article 6 for the first time, as it appears, introduces different categories of data subjects (such as "suspects" and "convicted persons"), Article 7 introduces different degrees of accuracy and reliability of data. Article 8 lays down the principle of lawfulness of processing.

Article 10 sets limitations to the processing of special categories of personal data (which is prohibited safe for few exemptions) and Article 11 sets rules on profiling and automated processing. Chapter III contains the rules on the rights of data subjects (information, access, rectification, erasure) and the related to exercising modalities. Chapter IV contains the rules on controllers and processors, notably their general obligations, their data security obligations and the obligation to establish a data protection officer. Chapter V contains rules on transfer of data to third countries or international organisations.

The directive refers generally to "processing", which is defined in Article 3 paragraph 3 and contains "collection". However, the directive does not contain any specific rules on surveillance (as was recommended by CoE Recommendation 87 (15)), and any rules on innovative methods and technologies of gathering electronic evidence (such as retrieving data from cloud storages, interception of communications prior to encryption through hidden software on terminal devices, and so forth). As a result, the directive does not provide for adequate safeguards in this particular field.

[39]Directive (EU) 2016/680 of the European Parliament and of the Council of 27 April 2016 on the protection of natural persons with regard to the processing of personal data by competent authorities for the purposes of the prevention, investigation, detection or prosecution of criminal offences or the execution of criminal penalties, and on the free movement of such data, and repealing Council Framework Decision 2008/977/JHA; http://eur-lex.europa.eu/legal-content/EN/TXT/HTML/?uri=CELEX:32016L0680; http://www.europarl.europa.eu/oeil/popups/ficheprocedure.do?lang=en&reference=2012/0010%28COD%29.

[40]Article 63 paragraph 2. and 3. 2016/680/EU.

13.3.9 The ePrivacy Reform Package

In early 2017, the Commission published its proposal[41] for a new ePrivacy Regulation concerning the protection of personal data in electronic communications to replace Directive 2002/58/EC, to modernise telecommunications privacy law and to adjust the framework to the GDPR. According to Article 1 (3), the provisions of this Regulation will particularise and complement the GDPR by laying down specific rules for the purposes mentioned in paragraphs 1 and 2. The relation to Directive 2016/680/EU, hence to the data protection framework in the law enforcement sector, as such is not mentioned specifically. However, the reference to the GDPR includes the reference to its recital (19):

> Recital (19) 2016/679/EU:
> "The protection of natural persons with regard to the processing of personal data by competent authorities for the purposes of the prevention, investigation, detection or prosecution of criminal offences or the execution of criminal penalties, including the safeguarding against and the prevention of threats to public security and the free movement of such data, is the subject of a specific Union legal act. This Regulation should not, therefore, apply to processing activities for those purposes. However, personal data processed by public authorities under this Regulation should, when used for those purposes, be governed by a more specific Union legal act, namely Directive (EU) 2016/680 of the European Parliament and of the Council".

This consideration is reflected in Articles 1 and 2 (1) of Directive 2016/680/EU, according to which the material scope of this directive is limited to "processing by competent authorities" for the listed purposes. A "competent authority" can be a private entity as well (Article 3 (7) b) 2016/680/EU), but only if exercising public authority on a Member State's behalf. Conversely: any collection or storing of electronic evidence stemming from telecommunications networks by the service provider or any private entity, will not fall under Directive 2016/680/EU, for service providers are not entrusted with public powers. It will fall under the new ePrivacy regulation (this concerns e.g. any future data retention).

If, however, LEAs become active themselves, the situation becomes more complex. According to CJEU in reference of Directive 2002/58/EC, the access to telecommunications data by public authorities, too, falls into the scope of the

[41] 2017/0003 (COD), Proposal for a REGULATION OF THE EUROPEAN PARLIAMENT AND OF THE COUNCIL concerning the respect for private life and the protection of personal data in electronic communications and repealing Directive 2002/58/EC (Regulation on Privacy and Electronic Communications), http://ec.europa.eu/newsroom/dae/document.cfm?doc_id=41241.

ePrivacy directive[42] when this data was collected by private entities in compliance with a law aiming at the use of such data for criminal investigation. However, the key argument of CJEU is that access to such data by public authorities concerns the processing by telecommunications providers, and (only) therefore falls into the scope of the directive.[43]

The situation, therefore, is different, if LEAs lawfully intercept telecommunications data themselves. Accordingly, the material scope of the Draft ePrivacy Regulation explicitly excludes “activities of competent authorities for the purposes of the prevention, investigation, detection or prosecution of criminal offences or the execution of criminal penalties, including the safeguarding against and the prevention of threats to public security” (Article 2 paragraph 2 lit. d)), therefore leaving Directive 2016/680/EU solely applicable for all cases, in which electronic evidence is collected by competent authorities from telecommunications networks.

13.4 Summary and Recommendation

It appears there is no European legal framework comprehensively addressing data protection issues related to the collection of electronic evidence through innovative measures and technologies (particularly online environments). The major reason for this is supposedly the fact that, except Directive 2016/680, all EU legislative acts predate the Treaty of Lisbon, and accordingly are implemented under limited legislative competences of the European Union. Consequently, Directive 95/46/EC and 2002/58/EC explicitly exclude application on state activities in criminal investigations. Directive 2006/24/EC only had an indirect impact on the collection of electronic evidence, but was declared invalid by CJEU in 2014.

Council framework decision 2008/977/JHA contains data protection rules on the exchange of personal data (also) in criminal matters, but this framework decision does not apply on the collection of electronic evidence. This, however, has changed with Directive 2016/680 that replaces this council decision. The new directive, nevertheless, still does not contain any tailored rules on innovative methods of collection of electronic evidence—such as covert remote access to a suspect’s IT system—and, as a result, cannot provide for the necessary safeguards, which need to exceed that general safeguards to give justice to the specific nature of such intrusive measures.[44] The future ePrivacy Regulation (and not Directive 2016/680/EU) will

[42]CJEU, 21.12.2016, Joined Cases C203/15 and C698/15, Marginal Numbers 76 et seq, http://curia.europa.eu/juris/document/document.jsf?text=&docid=186492&pageIndex=0&doclang=EN&mode=lst&dir=&occ=first&part=1&cid=1380714.

[43]Ibid, Marginal Number 78.

[44]Lawful “hacking” of IT systems, if legal under a given domestic legal framework, should e.g. require subsequent undoing of all alterations applied to the infiltrated system and be governed by specific rules on how to prevent third parties from exploiting potential vulnerabilities created during the infiltration process.

apply if telecommunications providers collect electronic evidence without excercising public powers. In all other cases, especially in cases of lawful interception by LEAs themselves, Directive 2016/680/EU solely is applicable.

Meanwhile, the European Union has gained legal competences for certain aspects of criminal procedure law, stipulated by Article 82 paragraph 2 TFEU, including the collection and admissibility of electronic evidence. This competence seeks minimum harmonisation and is limited by the right of Member States to suspend the legislative procedure should fundamental legal principles of that Member State be at stake (Article 82 paragraph 3 TFEU). This competence, however, as it seems, as of early 2017 has not yet been used.

The European Union may seek to implement minimum data protection standards for the collection of electronic evidence to ensure a harmonised minimum level of data protection in accordance with the European fundamental rights throughout the European Union. The existing domestic regulations on privacy in criminal procedure, particularly those with explicit reference to measures that typically result in collecting electronic evidence (such as lawful interception), may serve to some extent as models and examples. This appears desirable, as the harmonisation should consider the existing fundamental legal principles in the Member States to the extent possible (due to Article 82 paragraph 3 TFEU and to avoid implementation issues because of conflicts with domestic constitutional law). It can be recommended to consider the safeguards already implemented by the Cybercrime Convention, to the extent to which this is not yet foreseen in the draft data protection directive, which are:

- Judicial or other independent supervision
- Grounds justifying application and
- Limitation of the scope and the duration.

References

CJEU: Joined Cases C203/15 and C698/15, http://curia.europa.eu/juris/document/document.jsf?text=&docid=186492&pageIndex=0&doclang=EN&mode=req&dir=&occ=first&part=1

Charter of Fundamental Rights of the European Union (2010/C 83/02) (2010). http://eur-lex.europa.eu/legal-content/EN/TXT/PDF/?uri=CELEX:12010P&from=DE

Consolidated Versions of the Treaty on European Union and the Treaty on the Funkctioning of the European Union (2012/C 326/01) (2012). http://eur-lex.europa.eu/legal-content/EN/TXT/?uri=CELEX:12012E/TXT

Convention for the Protection of Human Rights and Fundamental Freedoms (1950). http://www.echr.coe.int/Documents/Convention_ENG.pdf

Convention on Cybercrime, CoE ETS. No. 185 (2001). http://conventions.coe.int/Treaty/en/Treaties/Html/185.htm

Council Act of 29 May 2000 establishing in accordance with Article 34 of the Treaty on European Union the Convention on Mutual Assistance in Criminal Matters between the Member States of the European Union (2000). http://www.bgbl.de/banzxaver/bgbl/start.xav?start=//*%5B@attr_id=%27bgbl205016.pdf%27%5D#__bgbl__%2F%2F*%5B%40attr_id%3D'bgbl205016.pdf'%5D__1409154081805

Council Act of 29 May 2000 establishing in accordance with Article 34 of the Treaty on European Union the Convention on Mutual Assistance in Criminal Matters between the Member States of the European Union (2000). http://eur-lex.europa.eu/LexUriServ/LexUriServ.do?uri=OJ:C:2000:197:0001:0023:EN:PDF

Council Decision 2009/371/JHA (2009). https://www.europol.europa.eu/sites/default/files/council_decision.pdf

Council Framework Decision 2008/977/JHA of 27 November 2008 on the protection of personal data processed in the framework of police and judicial cooperation in criminal matters (2008). http://eur-lex.europa.eu/legal-content/EN/TXT/HTML/?uri=CELEX:32008F0977&from=EN

Directive 95/46/EC of the European Parliament and of the Council of 24 October 1995 on the protection of individuals regarding the processing of personal data and on the free movement of such data (1995). http://eur-lex.europa.eu/LexUriServ/LexUriServ.do?uri=CELEX:31995L0046:en:HTML

Directive 2002/58/EC of the European Parliament and of the Council of 12 July 2002 concerning the processing of personal data and the protection of privacy in the electronic communications sector (Directive on privacy and electronic communications) (2002). http://eur-lex.europa.eu/LexUriServ/LexUriServ.do?uri=CELEX:32002L0058:en:HTML

Directive 2006/24/EC of the European Parliament and of the Council of 15 March 2006 on the retention of data generated or processed in connection with the provision of publicly available electronic communications services or of public communications networks and amending Directive 2002/58/EC (2006). http://eur-lex.europa.eu/LexUriServ/LexUriServ.do?uri=OJ:L:2006:105:0054:0063:EN:PDF

Directive (EU) 2016/680 of the European Parliament and of the Council of 27 April 2016 on the protection of natural persons regarding the processing of personal data by competent authorities for the prevention, investigation, detection or prosecution of criminal offences or the execution of criminal penalties, and on the free movement of such data, and repealing Council Framework Decision 2008/977/JHA (2016). http://eur-lex.europa.eu/legal-content/EN/TXT/HTML/?uri=CELEX:32016L0680

Eurojust data protection rules (2005). http://eurojust.europa.eu/doclibrary/Eurojust-framework/dataprotection/Eurojust%20Data%20Protection%20Rules/Eurojust-Data-Protection-Rules-2005-02-24-EN.pdf

Eurojust Decision (2009). http://www.eurojust.europa.eu/doclibrary/Eurojust-framework/ejdecision/Consolidated%20version%20of%20the%20Eurojust%20Council%20Decision/Eurojust-Council-Decision-2009Consolidated-EN.pdf

European Convention on Mutual Assistance in Criminal Matters CETS No. 030 (1962). http://conventions.coe.int/Treaty/Commun/ChercheSig.asp?NT=030&CM=&DF=&CL=ENG

European Court of Justice: Judgment of the court (Grand Chamber) of 8 April 2014, joined cases C-293/12 and C-594/12 (2014). http://curia.europa.eu/juris/document/document.jsf?docid=150642&mode=req&pageIndex=1&dir=&occ=first&part=1&text=&doclang=EN&cid=361892

Europol cooperations with EU entities (2013). https://www.europol.europa.eu/content/page/europol-eu-121

Europol rules for analysis files (2009). https://www.europol.europa.eu/sites/default/files/rules_applicable_to_europol_analysis_files.pdf

Europol rules governing Europol's relations with partners (2009). https://www.europol.europa.eu/sites/default/files/rules_governing_europols_relations_with_partners.pdf

608185 EVIDENCE Description of Work – Part A (2014)

Proposal for a Regulation of the European Parliament and of the Council concerning the respect for private life and the protection of personal data in electronic communications and repealing Directive 2002/58/EC (Regulation on Privacy and Electronic Communications (2002). http://ec.europa.eu/newsroom/dae/document.cfm?doc_id=41241

Recommendation 87 (15) of the Committee of Ministers to Member States Regulating the Use of Personal Data in the Police Sector. https://wcd.coe.int/com.instranet.InstraServlet?command=com.instranet.CmdBlobGet&InstranetImage=2196553&SecMode=1&DocId=694350&Usage=2 (1987)

Regulation (EU) 2016/679 of the European Parliament and of the Council of 27 April 2016 on the protection of natural persons regarding the processing of personal data and on the free movement of such data, and repealing Directive 95/46/EC (General Data Protection Regulation) (1997) http://eur-lex.europa.eu/legal-content/EN/TXT/HTML/?uri=CELEX:32016R0679; http://www.europarl.europa.eu/registre/docs_autres_institutions/commission_europeenne/com/2012/0011/COM_COM%282012%290011_EN.pdf (2016)

Chapter 14
Some Societal Factors Impacting on the Potentialities of Electronic Evidence

Daniele Mezzana

Abstract Electronic evidence is an important area of innovation, and inasmuch is characterized by strong and profound social dynamics. These dynamics can generate both opportunities and risks (if not managed or poorly managed), in terms of the functioning of the institutions of justice, the proper administration of justice for citizens and their rights, the representation of justice in public opinion, and so on. The aim of this paper is to present a panorama of some initial theoretical and empirical insights on this issue, from a sociological point of view. Our research tried to identify the types of actors that play a role in electronic evidence and its presence in judicial systems, as well as the obstacles and facilitating factors for the introduction of electronic evidence in courts.

14.1 Electronic Evidence as Innovation

The introduction of electronic evidence in courts can effectively be considered a major innovation[1] in the sphere of justice. In fact, as the justice system becomes increasingly digitized, many see the use of electronic evidence as a means of simplification, facilitation, acceleration, and rationalization, depending on the circumstances, compared to the use of paper-based texts, providing a better service to citizens.

[1]Nowotny (2006) and Etzkowitz and Leydesdorff (1997).

D. Mezzana (✉)
Laboratorio di Scienze della Cittadinanza, Rome, Italy
e-mail: daniele.mezzana@scienzecittadinanza.org

M. A. Biasiotti et al. (eds.), *Handling and Exchanging Electronic Evidence Across Europe*, Law, Governance and Technology Series 39,
https://doi.org/10.1007/978-3-319-74872-6_14

This innovation may result in changes at legal, technological, and social levels. Moreover, the dynamics of these changes are complex, so they are neither predictable nor automatic. The aim of this paper, based on specific research activities undertaken under the EVIDENCE project,[2] is to present a panorama of some initial theoretical and empirical insights on this issue, using a sociological approach and within a multi-disciplinary context, in accordance with the aforementioned project. This sociological approach can perhaps help grasp some of the dynamics of interest to us here, which are usually not considered.

Here, the sociological approach is based on several premises of a general nature, which are particularly important when studying the relationship between science, technology and society (in our case, between information and communication technologies and society).[3] Some of these premises, which are particularly pertinent to this study, relate to the following aspects:

- the co-evolution of technology and society, in the sense that society and technology develop as part of a single process (each social phenomenon involves the need for a set of technologies, and, at the same time, each technological development refers to social phenomena)[4];
- the importance of the actions taken by concrete and specific human actors (as individuals or collectively) in technological processes;
- societal factors having the same weight as economic aspects in orienting scientific and technological research and managing its results;
- the specific weight of cognitive factors (ideas, representations of reality, prejudices, expectations, intentions, etc.) in the process of the development, management, acceptance, and adaptation of technologies

As we shall see below, these premises led first to a study of the actors directly or indirectly involved in the introduction of electronic evidence in courts of law, especially, although not exclusively, about the criminal sphere. In addition, these premises led to an examination of several "structural" social factors, i.e. those that can impede or facilitate this introduction of electronic evidence.

The approach adopted here also had a further implication, more specific and related to the sociology of knowledge. In fact, the research carried out was based on the recognition, promotion and validation of the expertise already available in studies on electronic evidence. This has been reflected, as will be seen, in the production of specific phenomena "maps".

[2]The studies described in this paper were developed by LSC, represented by the writer, as part of the work package "Market Size" within the EVIDENCE project, in the years 2014–2015.

[3] For an analytical discussion of these aspects, see: d'Andrea et al. (2005). See also: Bijker and d'Andrea (2009), Mezzana (2011).

[4]Bijker (1995).

14.2 The "Social Arena" of Electronic Evidence and Types of Actors Involved

14.2.1 A Map Describing the "Social Arena" of Electronic Evidence

Using the approach briefly described above, our research first explored the "social arena" of electronic evidence. Here we use the notion of "social arena"[5] in a broad sense, to denote a set of actors who, through their choices, actions and power relations, can affect the configuration of rules and processes in a specific sphere of social life (in our case, that of electronic evidence), possibly influencing political decisions regarding the governance of this sphere. Particularly, our research tried to identify the types of actors that play a role in electronic evidence and its presence in judicial systems (as said, especially, but not exclusively, in the criminal field) and, generally, in the social, political, and economic life of our societies.

Here, were considered both:

- the types of actors having a direct "interest" in electronic evidence, that is those public and private actors involved in handling the electronic evidence, and those providing technical solution and assistance in this field; in this sense, many of these actors can also be considered part of the specific dynamics of the electronic evidence market, in that, depending on situations and needs, they are actors that make up the "demand" for technologies and services, or the "supply" of the same;
- the types of actors that play an indirect role, since they are part of a broader political, social, economic context influencing the introduction and the use of electronic evidence in courts, in general terms.

The first were described as electronic evidence "process" actors, while the second were described as electronic evidence "context" actors, acting on a national, European, or global scale, depending on the case.

These types of actors were mapped using a specific documentary and qualitative procedure based on the sociology of knowledge.[6] The first step was to create, as our starting point, an "ideal typological map" of these actors, based on: an initial analysis of the literature and documentation concerned with electronic evidence, together with the reports produced by other EVIDENCE partners; some discussions and exchanges with EVIDENCE partners, academics and experts; a first draft of

[5]Bourdieu (1993), Kitschelt and Offe (1980), Renn (1992, pp. 179-196).

[6]For this study, we used a theoretical and methodological approach to mapping based on the sociology of knowledge, used by LSC for many years in various areas. This includes, by way of example, the RESPECT project map on social costs linked to socio-technical surveillance systems (http://respectproject.eu; Colonnello (2014)), and the map underlying the Obstacles for Civil Society in Serbia, see: Mezzana (2008).

the map and a "Track for information gathering"İfor its validation. This "ideal typological map" was then validated by the EVIDENCE partners and advisors, as well as by external experts (thirteen in all, most of whom were European), making it a "real" typological map. The use of the term "real", related to the map, indicates a shift from a typology based on documentation to a typology based also on the knowledge and experience of a range of interlocutors such as those consulted that we considered informed about the reality of electronic evidence in Europe.

At the end of this work, a "typological map" was produced,[7] divided into:

- Nine typological areas of "process" actors (see Table 14.1, Part I), in turn comprising a total of 40 types of actors;
- Ten typological areas of "context" actors (see Table 14.1, Part II), in turn containing 26 types of actors (a number which, given the limited nature of the information provided in this regard, is to be considered partial in all respects, and requiring completion)

This typological map is a kind of general photograph of the "social arena" of electronic evidence, representing, of course, only a first step in the knowledge acquisition process. More information can be gained, as will be seen in the next section, from an examination of the roles played by the different types of actors.

14.2.2 The Roles of the Different Types of Actors: A Complex Picture

Different actor types (and, of course, the individual actors) play diverse roles within the electronic evidence social arena, and each, in their own way, produces or will produce important events in societal terms.

The role of different "process" actors seems more intuitive in this respect. Depending on the circumstances, they play a role in the collection, evaluation, storage, management and/or acceptance of this type of evidence, or are involved in the development of hardware, software and services that are vital to ensure that the operations mentioned above are carried out in a way that is as correct and effective as possible. In any event, in carrying out these roles, the actors may have a greater or lesser agency[8] as regards the introduction of electronic evidence, driving change or putting up resistance; they may or may not seek alliances and promote regulation

[7]EVIDENCE (2014). In this report, for each typological area, and, possibly, for each type of actor, beside their definitions, general information, data, examples of the roles played in the electronic and evidence field were provided.

[8]In general terms, agency can be defined as the orientation of actors towards changing or influencing dominant "structures", i.e. societal patterns, which may be cognitive (values, beliefs, etc.), relational (models of behavior, procedures, etc.) or political-institutional (laws, power relations, areas of expertise, etc.). Purely by way of example, see Giddens (1984).

Table 14.1 Typological areas of "process" and "context" actors

1. Actors involved in the electronic evidence "process"	
Typological area	*Actors*
A Public law enforcement and Intelligence agencies	• Law enforcement officers • Detectives • Intelligence agencies
B Actors of legal criminal trial	• Judges • Prosecutors • Lawyers • Registrars • Bailiffs and Court officials • Court administrative staff • Court interpreters • International Courts • Central authorities for mutual legal assistance • Victims and Third parties
C Notaries	• Notaries
D Public register actors	• Business register actors • Civil acts register actors • Land register actors • Embassies/Consular services • Local residents' registration office/registers • Automobile record sections
E Forensic examiners	• Fraud examiner • Forensic laboratory staff member • Digital Evidence First Responder (DEFR) • Digital Evidence Specialist (DES) • Incident Response Specialist • Other IT specialists • Expert witnesses • Chief Information Officers
F Private investigators	• Private investigators
G Hardware producers	• Hardware producers for Computer Forensics • Hardware producers for Mobile Forensics • Hardware producers for Network Forensics
H Technology/software producers	• Software houses that produce complete commercial toolkits for forensic analyses • Software houses that make software for specific commercial analyses • Software houses that produce commercial software for mobile forensic • Software houses that produce commercial software for network forensic • Software house, communities or individual developers who make freeware/opensource software
I Service providers	• Major consulting firms • Medium and small consultancy firms • Associated professional studios • Freelance consultants

(continued)

Table 14.1 (continued)

2. Actors in the electronic evidence "context"	
Typological area	*Actors*
J Specialized International Organizations	• UN agencies concerned with justice and technological innovation • Police coordination bodies • Internet governance bodies • Other international organizations
K Law making bodies	• European transnational organizations • National governments
L Technological innovation actors linked to the Internet	• Internet service providers • Cloud technology providers
M Legal and forensic associations and networks	• General legal and forensic associations and networks (international and national) • Associations and networks concerned with issues linked to new technologies
N Research bodies, associations and networks	• Organizations and associations concerned with Internet and ICT • Academic institutions concerned with ICT • Digital forensics research organizations and networks • Academic institutions concerned with digital forensics
O Actors involved in the field of human rights	• Civil rights organizations • Hackers associations • Consumer associations • Privacy protection organizations
P The media	• Traditional media • Media linked to web 2.0 • Social media
Q Enterprises interested in the proper functioning of justice	• Individual firms • Business associations
R Transnational projects	• Digital forensics research projects and training
S Other actors collecting evidence	• Private actors that collect data/potential evidence • Public actors that collect data/potential evidence

and governance; they may or may not meet obstacles or facilitating factors of various kinds (as will be seen in the next section), and so on.[9]

[9]Our research showed that no specific studies have been undertaken on the sphere of justice (particularly criminal justice) in terms of an electronic evidence market. An effort was, therefore, made to provide, first, some statistical data as a first approach to the analysis of this issue. By way of example, in the 28 European Union countries there are a total of 1,019,684 lawyers and legal advisors, 81,879 professional judges and 35,330 technical judicial experts (analysis based on CEPEJ data); see: CEPEJ (2014).

Perhaps less evident, but still important, is the role of those who fit into the category of "context" actors. Unlike "process" actors, they are not directly concerned with electronic evidence, but they have an important role in framing the social context of digital evidence, because of the actions they take in fields such as decision-making, governance, technology, entrepreneurship, communication, collective action, etc. For example, the roles of governance and regulation are played by international organizations such as the Economic and Social Council of the United Nations (ECOSOC), the United Nations Office on Drugs and Crime (UNODC) and the International Telecommunication Union (ITU). In policing, a coordinating role is played by organizations such as INTERPOL. In addition, Internet service providers are crucial innovation actors which hold crucial and increasingly strategic information (political, economic, and legal) about the users of their services: their orientations and actions are therefore deeply relevant in terms of collaboration, or non-collaboration, with authorities in charge of criminal investigations.

It is worth noting that, at the theoretical level, a major driving force in the sphere of training, information and awareness is also played by actors such as national and international bar associations, research institutions, organizations for human rights and the defense of privacy (some of which specialize in issues related to computerization, like the European Digital Rights[10]), as well as transnational research and training projects in the field of digital forensics. Naturally, what was said about "process" actors is also true for "context" actors: agency can be exercised in either one direction or the other, in collaboration or in conflict with other actors, encountering obstacles and facilitating factors of various kinds.

Within this framework, we should also note the emergence of new professions, new ad hoc university courses, new interdisciplinary and inter-professional exchange networks, not counting, of course, the emergence and spread of new types of businesses and services in this field (companies, consultants, initiatives like Forensic Europe Expo, online shops, etc.). With the digitalization of justice, however unevenly it may be proceeding (at least in Europe[11]), the global digital forensics market had revenues of around $1.4bn in 2013 and is expected to grow at a compound annual growth rate of 10.5% between now and 2018.[12]

From all this there emerges a comprehensive framework, characterized by the presence and action of numerous actors, with specific orientations and strategies about the introduction and use of electronic evidence. These actors (as perhaps will be made clearer in the next section) were not always in agreement nor did they always coordinate with each other, in a context of rapid change which, however, requires more interaction, and common rules and standards. It is clear, therefore, that policies in support of the introduction of electronic evidence in courts cannot disregard this complexity.

[10]For more details, see: Cannataci et al. (2016).

[11]Bear in mind that only two of the 28 EU countries showed a decrease in computer facilities in 2012–2014 (Croatia and Cyprus); in most, it remained stable or even showed an increase (in about half the cases) (analysis based on CEPEJ data); see: CEPEJ (2014).

[12]IndustryARC (2013).

14.3 Obstacles and Facilitating Factors for the Introduction of Electronic Evidence in Courts

14.3.1 Study of "Structural" Factors

The next step in our research involved an exploration of the "structural" factors of this technological transformation in the field of justice.

As we have seen, this transformation involves a wide range of actors operating in different ways, a first type having been illustrated in the previous paragraph. Considering the above, it may be presumed, that, in the introduction of electronic evidence in courts, these actors either have their own agency, making use of a specific culture, a capacity to use power and resources to control their own environment, and a capacity to promote certain actions that affect, directly or indirectly, the institutional system of justice.[13] These actors operate in a "social structure" (see footnote 8), in which they can encounter (or produce) resistance and opportunities of various kinds concerning the innovation of which we are speaking. We consider these resistances (or obstacles) and opportunities (or facilitating factors) as important structural factors to be examined specifically here.

For the specific purposes of this study, an "obstacle" is an impediment to the introduction of electronic evidence in courts. On the other hand, by "facilitating factors" we mean factual elements (choices, rules, equipment, organizational solutions, policies, etc.) which have already been proven to promote the use of electronic evidence.

Here, we are mainly interested in all obstacles and facilitating factors of an organizational, cultural or regulatory (i.e. linked to governance) nature which risk jeopardizing the implementation of any decision at the legal or technical level. Legal, institutional, and strictly technical issues are, therefore, largely taken for granted and here discussed in general terms.

To identify the obstacles and facilitating factors, an approach typical of the sociology of knowledge has been adopted, like the one used for the actor typology map (see previous paragraph), aimed at enhancing, during research on a particular subject, the knowledge already produced by other scientific research actors.

14.3.2 The Construction of a Map of the Obstacles and Facilitating Factors

Thus, a specific map was also produced for these obstacles and facilitating factors. The construction of this second map[14] involved, first, the production of an "ideal

---

[13] D'Andrea and Quaranta (1996).

[14] EVIDENCE (2015).

map", in the sense that it was a map based on an initial collection of information on the obstacles and facilitating factors for the use of electronic evidence in courts, as can be found in scientific literature and existing documentation. This "ideal map" was then transformed into a "real map" when the list contained in the "ideal map" were assessed, through a questionnaire, by a set (which certainly did not have the pretension to be a statistical sample) of 30 key informants (particularly, judges, lawyers, senior management of justice ministries and other public bodies[15]), scholars and experts in 16 European countries, as well as EVIDENCE partners and advisors, who could also propose changes to the title given a phenomenon and its description, and assess its importance (expressing its degree of importance, 1–5). By convention, it was decided to consider each type of obstacle or facilitating factor as valid when it was awarded a score of 3, 4 or 5 by at least half of all respondents (including those who did not respond or responded "I don't know"). In-depth interviews and discussions were then carried out with a small number of European and international experts.

Under the procedure described, a final map of 40 obstacles and 21 facilitating factors was drafted. Below is a basic outline of the structure of the map, which is composed by eight areas of obstacles and three areas of facilitating factors.[16]

14.3.3 Obstacles

A. Mistrust

Some impediments to the use of electronic evidence are tied to a sense of mistrust, suspicion, or even fear by operators towards this type of evidence, as opposed to conventional types. These impediments, which are strictly "cognitive" in nature, may be because of the technical characteristics of electronic evidence, poor knowledge of the subject, or an insufficient formalization of rules and standards in this field.[17]

1. Fear of manipulation;
2. fears of the vulnerability;
3. misunderstanding (of the nature and characteristics of electronic evidence).

---

[15]Representatives of law enforcement agencies were not consulted, as they were the main focus of other activities of the EVIDENCE project.

[16]The maps produced as part of this work (especially as regards the obstacles and facilitating factors) also formed the basis for a discussion in the workshop held in Rome on 10–11 December 2015, organized by LSC within the framework of EVIDENCE project, and entitled "Obstacles and facilitating factors towards the digitalization of Justice: the specific issue of electronic evidence in criminal trials". The workshop was attended by 36 people, representing organizations based in eight European countries (Austria, Bulgaria, Germany, Italy, Malta, the Netherlands, Spain, the United Kingdom) and some international bodies (INTERPOL, Eurojust, Council of Europe Cloud Evidence Group).

[17]Insa (2006), CYBEX (2006), Boddington et al. (2008), Evidence (2013), and Mason (2013).

B. Issues Relating to Competences and Professions

Another kind of obstacles found concerns the availability of knowledge, technical expertise, assistance and consultancy services for judges and lawyers who have to handle electronic evidence, concerning both the definition and the recognition of specific skills in this field. At the heart of this obstacle, therefore, are crucial issues such as the professionalism, public recognition of it and training.[18]

4. Operators (in the legal profession) lacking experience;
5. lack of training courses;
6. lack of specific competences in the local police;
7. difficulties in presenting evidence at court in a way that is comprehensible;
8. few experts;
9. vagueness of digital forensic profession[19];
10. inadequate remuneration of digital forensic experts.

C. Security Issues

A specific problem area concerns the capacity of electronic evidence management systems to defend themselves from attack and from various types of manipulation. The particular nature of electronic evidence, including its "volatility", creates great challenges for justice systems.[20]

11. Data volatility[21];
12. difficulty of proving the existence of possible manipulation;
13. difficulty in proving the authenticity, reliability and origin of data.

D. Fragmentation

Another category of obstacles concerns the fragmentation of the institutional system that uses and manages electronic evidence, because of lack of operational coordination and understanding between the actors and organizations involved and their different levels of intervention. This fragmentation has a strong impact on the possibility of introducing and make operational the use of electronic evidence in courts.[22]

14. Dissimilarities in the definition of "electronic evidence";
15. differences in capacities within the same national context;
16. lack of standards for information exchange;
17. poor communication among the different actors in this field;
18. difficulties in sharing information among different offices and organizations.

[18]CYBEX (2006); Costabile and Attanasio (2012); UNODC (2013).

[19]Digital forensics has yet to produce a defined, recognized and stable professionalism.

[20]Caloyannides (2004); Boddington et al. (2008); Yuan (2011); Evidence (2013).

[21]Being on an electronic medium, data can disappear easily.

[22]Cohen (2010a); Kahvedzic (2013a); (Cohen et al., 2011, pp. 3–21).

E. Cultural and Personal Opposition

Some impediments to the adoption of electronic evidence in courts are connected to the existence of cultural resistance or personal opposition, which may be because of age, work experience, approach to information and communication technologies. This opposition may show itself in various ways, such as explicit resistance to organizational or social change or otherwise associated with the adoption of electronic evidence, or through unconscious behaviors and attitudes.[23]

19. Sense of confusion before the technical complexity of electronic evidence;
20. difficulties in following technological changes in the field of electronic evidence;
21. failure to consider the specificity of electronic evidence.

F. Isolation of Technological Processes

Particular types of obstacles, such as those included in this area, are because of a certain degree of isolation or disconnection between the technological processes for the management of electronic evidence and the justice system as a whole and the broader social and political context.[24]

22. Differences in view among the various actors working in justice;
23. distortions because of media use of electronic evidence[25];
24. insufficient government attention to cybercrime.

G. Lack of Governance

A series of obstacles regards the absence of a proper governance of the system that should preside over the introduction and use of electronic evidence in courts. This can be seen, for example, in the difficulties of establishing an agenda to discuss and resolve some crucial issues, both at national and transnational level.[26]

25. Lack of certification models;
26. lack of specialized judicial services;
27. high cost of examining and interpreting information;
28. assignment of cases to judges who are not experts in the field;
29. difficulties in the relation between law enforcement agencies and international server providers;
30. difficulties related to the non-binding nature of international cooperation in this area;
31. difficulties because of lack of jurisdiction;
32. lack or insufficient involvement of justice operators in implementation of software.

---

[23]Mason (2012); Cohen (2010b); UNODC (2013).

[24]Cottim (2010); CYBEX (2006).

[25]Often the media make a hasty, superficial and distorted use of litigation material, including electronic evidence such phone records or wire-tapping, the probative value of which the media are unaware or insufficiently informed.

[26]UNODC (2013); ECOSOC-UN (2010); Cottim (2010).

H. Difficulties of a Functional Nature
The last group of obstacles focuses on impediments because of the malfunctioning of the electronic evidence management system, aspects that concern infrastructure, monitoring and operational procedures, including the lack of shared standards and guidelines for the handling of electronic evidence.[27]

33. Lack of procedures or guidelines for obtaining, preserving and presenting electronic evidence;
34. lack of tools and procedures for the validation of electronic evidence;
35. lack of a shared methodologies for e-evidence analysis;
36. lack of technical infrastructure;
37. lack of forensic tools[28];
38. overwhelming quantity of data requiring analysis;
39. excessive use of data encryption;
40. length of time needed to obtain and interpret electronic evidence.

14.3.4 Facilitating Factors

A. Creating a Favorable Technological and Professional Environment
This area includes facilitating factors (suitable infrastructure, existence of specialized service organizations, opportunities for training, etc.) that encourage operators to accept fully the transformation brought about by information technology, which is now becoming established in the judicial world. It is a wide-ranging technological transformation, which, once started, can increase the chances of effectively introducing electronic evidence in courts. As can be seen, both in this area and others, in some cases these facilitating factors are, in a sense, the positive "response" to some obstacles presented in the previous part.[29]

1. Court infrastructure;
2. existence of specialized service organizations;
3. existence of specific research and training organizations;
4. opportunities for the training of experts and technicians;
5. consolidation of digital forensics in the academic syllabus;
6. attractiveness of digital forensic professions;
7. containment of prices for digital forensic tools.

B. Activities Aimed at Promoting the Introduction and Management of Electronic Evidence
Another area includes a range of activities, experiences and situations, implemented in specific national or local circumstances, which may foster the consolidation of digital forensics and, specifically, the introduction and management of electronic

[27] Carrier and Spafford (2003); Piccini and Vaciago (2008); Cohen (2010a,b).

[28] It means lack of digital forensic hardware and software, which also affects electronic evidence collection and management.

[29] Allied Market Research (2014); Cohen (2010a,b); UNODC (2013).

evidence in courts. These facilitating factors range from the formalization of procedures to support actions and various kinds of networking.[30]

8. Standardization of procedures;
9. production and dissemination of guidelines;
10. existence of technology consulting services;
11. creation of partnerships;
12. existence of opportunities for meetings and exchanges;
13. existence of professional networks;
14. proactive role of professional associations.

C. Support Policies

A third area of facilitating factors includes policies of various kinds that can promote the introduction of electronic evidence in courts. They regard specific policies for governance, standardization, and partnerships. Broader policies aimed at the digitalization of justice were not mentioned here, since they were taken for granted, as they are a prerequisite for any program aimed at introducing electronic evidences in courts.[31]

15. Standardization of electronic document certification;
16. enhancement and coordination of expertise;
17. transnational exchange of information and expertise;
18. involvement of Internet governance bodies;
19. coordination of law enforcement agencies;
20. dissemination and mainstreaming practices;
21. promotion of the role of private enterprises.[32]

The validation procedure adopted enabled us not only to select the obstacles and facilitating factors validated and omit the ones that were not, but also to distinguish, within the group of those validated (40 obstacles and 21 facilitating factors), the ones which, conventionally, may be considered to be very important and those that were quite important.

To the first category belong the obstacles and facilitating factors for which at least half of all respondents expressed values of importance of either 4 or 5. The remaining obstacles and facilitating factors were, therefore, considered only "quite" important.

In the next two sections, dedicated respectively to obstacles and facilitating factors, the "very important" phenomena, classified within the areas mentioned above, are presented first, and then the same factors are presented in order of importance. For the ranking (see Tables 14.2 and 14.3), the criterion was used of the average score obtained from each obstacle and facilitating factor, considering only the "valid" answers, that is, those that provided a value of 1–5.

---

[30]Casey (2013); Adams (2012); Brezinski and Killalea (2002); Albert and Greenfield (2002); Mason (2013); Hickok (2014); Grundy (2004).

[31]ITU (2013); UNODC (2013); Kahvedzic (2013b).

[32]Private companies can play a significant role in the target area, especially in the development and dissemination of technological solutions in the field of cybercrime (e.g. against online pedophilia).

14.3.5 Obstacles (Rated as Very Important)

A. *Mistrust*

- Misunderstanding (of the nature and characteristics of electronic evidence).

B. *Issues relating to competences and professions*

- Operators (in the legal profession) lacking experience;
- lack of training courses;
- lack of specific competences in the local police;
- difficulties in presenting evidence at court in a way that is comprehensible;
- few experts;
- vagueness of digital forensic profession.

C. *Cultural and personal opposition*

- Difficulties in following technological changes in the field of electronic evidence;
- failure to consider the specificity of electronic evidence.

Table 14.2 Obstacles ranking

Ranking and score			
Ranking	Obstacle	Area	Score
1	Lack of training courses	B	4.05
2	Operators lacking experience	B	4.00
3	Difficulties related to the non-binding nature of international cooperation in this area	G	3.90
4	Difficulties in the relation between law enforcement agencies and international server providers	G	3.75
4	Overwhelming quantity of data requiring analysis	H	3.75
6	Difficulties in following technological changes in the field of electronic evidence	E	3.67
7	Failure to consider the specificity of electronic evidence	E	3.61
8	Few experts	B	3.60
9	Lack of procedures or guidelines for obtaining, preserving and presenting electronic evidence	H	3.58
9	Difficulties in presenting evidence at court in a way that is comprehensible	B	3.58
11	Misunderstanding	A	3.47
12	Lack of specific competences in the local police	B	3.45
13	Difficulties because of to lack of jurisdiction	G	3.40
14	Lack of specialized judicial services	G	3.39
15	Assignment of cases to judges who are not experts in the field	G	3.37
16	Vagueness of digital forensic profession	B	3.32

D. *Lack of governance*

- Lack of specialized judicial services;
- assignment of cases to judges who are not experts in the field;
- difficulties in the relation between law enforcement agencies and international server providers;
- difficulties related to the non-binding nature of international cooperation in this area;
- difficulties because of lack of jurisdiction.

E. *Difficulties of a functional nature*

- Lack of procedures or guidelines for obtaining, preserving and presenting electronic evidence;
- overwhelming quantity of data requiring analysis.

Table 14.3 Facilitating factors ranking

Ranking and score			
Ranking	Facilitating factor	Area	Score
1	Court infrastructure	A	4.63
2	Coordination of law enforcement agencies	C	4.05
3	Standardization of procedures	B	4.00
4	Existence of specific research and training organizations	A	3.95
5	Production and dissemination of guidelines	B	3.90
6	Opportunities for the training of experts and technicians	A	3.89
6	Consolidation of digital forensics in the academic syllabus	A	3.89
8	Dissemination and mainstreaming practices	C	3.84
9	Transnational exchange of information and expertise	C	3.83
10	Enhancement and coordination of expertise	C	3.78
11	Standardization of electronic document certification	C	3.76
12	Proactive role of professional associations	B	3.72
13	Existence of specialized service organizations	A	3.71
14	Existence of professional networks	B	3.68
15	Creation of partnerships	B	3.63
16	Existence of opportunities for meetings and exchanges	B	3.53
17	Involvement of Internet governance bodies	C	3.50

14.3.6 Facilitating Factors (Rated as Very Important)

A. *Creating a favorable technological and professional environment*

- Court infrastructure;
- existence of specialized service organizations;
- existence of specific research and training organizations;
- opportunities for the training of experts and technicians;
- consolidation of digital forensics in the academic syllabus.

B. *Activities aimed at promoting the introduction and management of electronic evidence*

- Standardization of procedures;
- production and dissemination of guidelines;
- creation of partnerships;
- existence of opportunities for meetings and exchanges;
- existence of professional networks;
- proactive role of professional associations.

C. *Support policies*

- Standardization of electronic document certification;
- enhancement and coordination of expertise;
- transnational exchange of information and expertise;
- involvement of Internet governance bodies;
- coordination of law enforcement agencies;
- dissemination and mainstreaming practices.

14.3.7 Some Remarks About Obstacles and Facilitating Factors

The findings, which are briefly described here, lead to the following considerations. First, among those classed as "very important" there is a preponderance of obstacles regarding the areas of competence and professionalism (for instance, Lack of training courses, Difficulties in presenting evidence at court in a way that is comprehensible, Vagueness of digital forensic profession), as well as those related to the governance of innovations underlying the introduction of electronic evidence in courts (for instance, Lack of specialized judicial services, Assignment of cases to judges who are not experts in the field, Difficulties in the relation between law enforcement agencies and international server providers, Difficulties because of lack of jurisdiction). Moreover, the list includes both "operational" obstacles (related to powers, constraints, resources, availability) and "cognitive" obstacles (related to the representations that the actors have of reality, their culture, their mentality, their attitudes, their abilities and skills). It is important to keep this in mind in view of future strategies and regulations in this field, to supplement the necessary measures to be taken in the infrastructural, technical and organizational fields, with actions in the areas of training, awareness raising, information, and exchange of experiences.

A further consideration (which applies to all the obstacles found) is that the obstacles are most likely connected to one another, either strengthening each other or in conflict, thus producing complex dynamics. For example, it may be supposed that problems related to competences and professionalism (obstacle area B) or those concerning security (area C) can only lead to an increase in mistrust (area A); fragmentation (D) tends to strengthen lack of governance (G); the isolation of technological processes (F) accentuates functional problems (H). In general, the uncertainty that may occur in this field creates the premises for conflicts between actors and strengthens various forms of cultural resistance or personal opposition (E).

It may also be supposed that a problem exists vis-à-vis an awareness of the presence and weight of these factors. For example, fragmentation (D) means that each actor believes they have the key to the innovation of justice (at least in the specific context of electronic evidence): new technology for the technologist; new legal procedures for lawyers; new investigative practices for the police. All this creates the serious risk of producing a lack of overall understanding of ongoing phenomena and processes, as well as a lack of operational coordination.

An overview of facilitating factors tends to confirm some of the above observations about the obstacles: the respondents, in fact, reported both the "operational" and "cognitive" aspects of the problem of electronic evidence as being particularly important. The "operational" practices assessed as very important (and therefore to be supported in future) include those relating to the provision of infrastructure, operational cross-border coordination, and determination of procedural standards. While the "cognitive" practices include those relating to training, the provision of services, and the dissemination of experiences. It should be noted that the facilitating factors are not only related to policies. Often support policies (C), as also the other two facilitating factor categories, emerge from the autonomous behavior of individual actors and their agency, before being transformed into institutional interventions, when they are. Clearly, these facilitating factors can also interact with each other, creating complex configurations, as well as with obstacles, working against them and creating even more complex dynamics. Consideration should also be given to a probable dynamic formed by the relationships between the global and local dimensions. Because of the results of the validation process conducted in 16 countries, and considering the fact that European and international experts were interviewed, it is indisputable that the factors analyzed are global in nature, or at least cross-national. Nevertheless, it is also true that their mix can vary greatly depending on the context, even from one court to another. This variability should certainly be managed by trans-national regulation to channel policies and actions towards some preferential forms of action. However, it is also illusory to think that the same solutions can be used everywhere. The awareness of the presence of all these dynamics should warn us against the development of solutions exclusively focused on one aspect of the situation, i.e. only at the technological, legal or, institutional level, or in sectoral terms only (although this may be unavoidable).

What seems to be missing today is a sort of socio-technical closure,[33] i.e. a shared and diffuse agreement on the interpretive standards and operational solutions to be adopted for the overall management of the complicated process of the introduction of electronic evidence in courts. In the absence of this closure, and operational strategies that could ensue, there is a risk of taking partial and ineffective action, which can create additional problems.

14.4 The Social Fabric of Electronic Evidence: From Interpretation to Decision-Making

As may be supposed from what has so far been set forth, albeit in outline form only, electronic evidence is an important area of innovation, and inasmuch is characterized by strong and profound social dynamics. Specifically, it may be supposed that the introduction of electronic evidence in courts, in the broader context of the digitization of justice, is exerting strong "technological evolutionary pressure" on the institutional system of justice itself. This evolutionary pressure gives rise to a situation of social and cultural "stress" that has probably yet to be adequately managed, or has been managed only partially, or in sectoral terms and in a limited fashion.

It is important to be aware that these dynamics of change can of course generate opportunities but also great risks (if not managed or poorly managed), in terms of the functioning of the institutions of justice, the proper administration of justice for citizens and their rights, the representation of justice in public opinion, and so on. If this is true, the development and fine-tuning of technologies, as well as the production of legislation, must include an analysis of societal dynamics in which technology and legislation are themselves involved. It is for this reason that we believe that it is important to speak of the "social fabric" of electronic evidence, not only from an interpretative point of view but also from an operational point of view and in terms of policies.

As we have seen, the "social fabric" of electronic evidence is manifested in various ways and in explicit forms, which are not linear, concordant, or unidirectional. For example, as stated above, several actors have been identified in this field who have very different education and cultural orientations, agency, powers, resources and modes of operation, some of which are not always stated or discernible. We also saw that these actors come up against structural forces (in our case, obstacles and facilitating factors) of different kinds and intensities, both material and immaterial, both operational and cognitive. Moreover, structural factors can push in opposite or contrasting directions, thus either facilitating the introduction of electronic evidence in courts or making its acceptance more difficult, and even leading to rejection.

[33] Pinch and Bijker (1990).

The "social fabric" of electronic evidence is also made up of the specific institutional and organizational contexts in which this innovation is introduced (different courts, various branches of law enforcement agencies, etc.), each with its own history, with its own rules of operation (and inertias), leadership, professionalism, expertise, material and human resources. Furthermore, as regards the introduction of this innovation, the time factor can also have a weight and a specificity of a societal nature, such as the time needed to produce profound changes within a given organization or the vast legal apparatus of the justice system; or the different lengths of time required for the development, understanding and acceptance of new technologies which may have actors with a different education or professional background, like digital forensic experts or judges.

Given all this, a need emerges to develop the capacity for broad spectrum governance, one which includes the development and management of technology, the production of legislation, as well as the interpretation and guidance of societal factors; one that can orient processes, coordinate actors, manage situations and resources, in such a way as to properly introduce electronic evidence in courts, and act in depth and continuously at various levels.

In fact, based on what was said earlier about the obstacles and facilitating factors, we can say that the existence of an electronic evidence "social fabric" would leads us to suppose that the only sensible policies are those that take note of the risks associated with the choices to be made in this field, and consider the numerous actors present so that they may interact explicitly and in a regulated fashion, to find shared solutions compatible with the new emerging ways of developing and implementing shared public policies. This involves dialogue, guided experimentation, and public engagement, which, however, are still in short supply.

Knowledge of the obstacles and facilitating factors for the introduction of electronic evidence in courts should also enable us to dose the type of policy to be implemented. For example, certain obstacles (like the functional ones of area H) primarily require a mix of technological, legal and organizational solutions; some (for example, those associated with skills and professions—see area B) mostly require educational input; others (such as those related to mistrust—Area A—and fragmentation—area D) chiefly require raising awareness or relational actions.

An additional aspect to consider in governance is the speed of technological change. This speed also implies a need to anticipate as far as possible the future prospects of electronic evidence, perhaps by developing specific technological and social forecasting policies.

It will be crucial to act also in the sphere of research to deepen the emerging issues in this field (including those illustrated here), bringing into play different disciplinary perspectives, including of course a sociological approach. It will also be important to promote more targeted and thorough studies, both at European level and in different countries, on issues such as the obstacles and facilitating factors to the introduction of electronic evidence in courts, in interpretative and operational terms.

This broad-spectrum governance has yet to be built, and we believe that the research carried out has at least provided some ideas in this regard, to be further developed in the future.

Acknowledgements This work has been encouraged and supported by my colleagues Federico Marta and Luciano d'Andrea through ideas and suggestions in the revision phase of this contribution.

References

Adams R (2012) The Advanced Data Acquisition Model (ADAM): a process model for digital forensic practice. http://researchrepository.murdoch.edu.au/14422/2/02Whole.pdf
Albert MJ, Greenfield RS (2002) Cyber forensics—a field manual for collecting, examining, and preserving evidence of computer crimes. CRC Press, Boca Raton
Allied Market Research (2014) Global Forensic Technologies Market (Service, Products and Geography)—Size, Share, Global Trends, Company Profiles, Demand, Insights, Analysis, Research, Report, Opportunities, Segmentation and Forecast, 2012–2020
Bijker W (1995) Of Bicycles, bakelites, and bulbs: toward a theory of sociotechnical change. MIT Press, Cambridge, MA
Bijker W, d'Andrea L (eds) (2009) Handbook on the socialisation of scientific and technological research. Social Sciences and European Research Capacities (SS-ERC) Project. European Commission, Rome. http://www.scienzecittadinanza.org/public/SSERChandbook.pdf
Boddington R, Hobbs V, Mann G (2008) Validating digital evidence for legal argument. ECU, Perth. www.ro.ecu.edu.au/cgi/viewcontent.cgi?article=1041&context=adf
Bourdieu P (1993) The field of cultural production. Polity Press, Cambridge
Brezinski D, Killalea T (2002) Best current practice—guidelines for evidence collection and archiving, IEEE RFC 3227
Caloyannides MA (2004), Privacy protection and computer forensics. Artech House, London
Cannataci JA, Zhao B, Torres VG, Monteleone S, Mifsud Bonnici J, Moyakine E (2016) Privacy, free expression and transparency: redefining their new boundaries in the digital age. UNESCO series on internet freedom.United Nations Educational, Scientific and Cultural Organization, Paris
Carrier B, Spafford E (2003) Getting physical with the digital investigation process. Int J Digit Evid 2, Fall 2003, pp 1–20
Casey E (ed) (2013) Handbook of digital forensics and investigation. Elsevier, London
CEPEJ (2014) Report on "European judicial systems—edition 2014 (2012 data): efficiency and quality of justice". http://www.coe.int/t/dghl/cooperation/cepej/evaluation/2014/Rapport_2014_en.pdf
Cohen F (2010a) Toward a science of digital forensic evidence examination. In: Advances in digital forensics VI. IFIP advances in information and communication technology, vol 337. Springer, Berlin
Cohen F (2010b) Digital forensic evidence examination, 2nd edn. ASP Press, Livermore, CA
Cohen F, Lowrie J, Preston C (2011) The state of the science of digital evidence examination. In: IFIP advances in information and communication technology, vol 361. Springer, Berlin, pp 3–21
Colonnello C (2014) Map of the present and incipient social dangers related to the development and spreading of surveillance socio-technical systems. RESPECT Project, Deliverable D13.1
Costabile G, Attanasio A (2012) IISFA memberbook 2012. Digital forensic, Forlì, Experta
Cottim A (2010) Cybercrime, cyberterrorism and jurisdiction: an analysis of article 22 of the COE convention on cybercrime. Eur J Leg Stud, 2(3). http://cadmus.eui.eu/handle/1814/15118

CYBEX (2006) The admissibility of electronic evidence in courts. www.itu.int/osg/csd/cybersecurity/WSIS/3rd_meeting_docs/contributions/libro_aeec_en.pdf
d'Andrea L, Quaranta G (1996) Civil society and risk. Contribution for a general theory, Workshop CERFE-Amsterdam School of Social Research, Amsterdam, 26 February 1996
d'Andrea L, Quaranta G, Quinti G (2005) Manuale sui processi di socializzazione della ricerca scientifica e tecnologica. CERFE, Rome
ECOSOC-UN (2010) Digital evidence certification recommendation, recommendation no. 37, 19 February 2010
Etzkowitz H, Leydesdorff L (eds) (1997) Universities in the global economy: a triple helix of university-industry-government relations. Cassell Academic, London
Evidence (2013) Description of Work (DOW), 18 September 2013
EVIDENCE (2014) Deliverable D7.1—report on prima facie size of the market. Laboratorio di Scienze della Cittadinanza (LSC), 31/12/2014
EVIDENCE (2015) Deliverable D7.2—map of obstacles and facilitating factors before validation. Laboratorio di Scienze della Cittadinanza (LSC), 30/9/2015
Giddens A (1984) The constitution of society: outline of the theory of structuration. Polity Press, Cambridge
Grundy BJ (2004) Computer crimes division the law enforcement and forensic examiner introduction to linux—a beginner's guide. NASA Office of Inspector General
Hickok G (2014) Digital forensic global trendsİ, GRC-daily. http://www.grc-daily.com/dsp_getFeaturesDetails.cfm?CID=3875
IndustryARC (2013) Global digital forensics market—global trends, market analysis, competitive landscape, recent developments, value market, forecasts to 2018. IndustryARC
Insa F (2006) The Admissibility of Electronic Evidence in Court (A.E.E.C.): fighting against high-tech crime-results of a European study. J Digit Forensic Pract 1(4):285–289. Also in http://doi.org/10.1080/15567280701418049
ITU (2013) Establishment of harmonized policies for the ICT market in the ACP countries, electronic evidence. Assessment report, HIPCAR, harmonization of ICT policies, legislation and regulatory procedures in the Caribbean, ITU. www.itu.int/en/ITU-D/Projects/ITU-EC-ACP/HIPCAR/Documents/FINAL%20DOCUMENTS/ENGLISH%20DOCS/e-evidence_assessment.pdf
Kahvedzic D (2013a) Planning and justifying the search and seizure of electronic evidence in criminal proceedings before presenting it to court. Academy of European Law, Trier
Kahvedzic D (2013b) The impact of emerging technologies (mobile and cloud computing) on the preservation and management of electronic evidence. Academy of European Law, Trier
Kitschelt H, Offe C (1980) Kernenergiepolitik Arena eines gesellschaftllichen Konflikts. Campus, Frankfurt [am Main] and New York
Mason S (ed) (2012) Electronic evidence, 3rd edn. LexisNexis Butterworths, London
Mason S (2013) The fundamentals of electronic evidence. In: Relazione presentata al seminario "Introduction to the Use of Electronic Evidence in Criminal Proceedings"
Mezzana D (2008) Guidelines on the management of juridical and non-juridical obstacles for civil society. Ministero degli Affari Esteri, CERFE, Rome. http://www.cerfe.org/public/PRAVOKLG.pdf
Mezzana D (ed) (2011) Technological responsibility. Guidelines for a shared governance of the processes of socialization of scientific research and innovation, within an interconnected world, SET-DEV, 7th Framework Programme for Technological Research and Development of the European Commission, Roma, Consiglio Nazionale delle Ricerche. http://www.scienzecittadinanza.org/public/SetDevGuidelines.pdf
Nowotny H (ed) (2006) Cultures of technology and the quest for innovation. Berghahn Books, New York
Piccini ML, Vaciago G (2008) Computer crimes, milano, moretti honneger
Pinch T, Bijker W (1990) The social construction of facts and artifacts. Or how the sociology of science and the sociology of technology might benefit each other. In: Bijker et al. (eds) The social construction of technological systems. MIT Press, Cambridge

Renn O (1992) The social arena concept of risk debates. In: Krimsky S, Golding D (eds) Social theories of risk. Praeger, Westport, CT, pp 179–196

UNODC (2013) Comprehensive study on cybercrime, Draft February 2013. http://www.unodc.org/documents/organized-crime/UNODC_CCPCJ_EG.4_2013/CYBERCRIME_STUDY_210213.pdf

Yuan P (2011) L'admission de la preuve électronique dans le droit français et le droit chinois. m2bde.u-paris10.fr/content/ladmission-de-la-preuve-électronique-dans-le-droit-français-et-le-droit-chinois-par-peihao-y

Chapter 15
Standard for the Electronic Evidence Exchange

Mattia Epifani and Fabrizio Turchi

Abstract Within the activities of the Evidence Project, it has been proposed a standard for the representation of the data and metadata involved in the electronic evidence exchange process. The main aim is to consider the widest range of forensic information and processing results including legal requirements. The standard consists of a set of data and metadata for describing all actions (i.e., tasks), actors (e.g., subjects, victims, authorities, examiners, etc.), tools (i.e., digital tools for carrying out different forensic processes), digital and physical objects involved in the investigative case (e.g., hard disk, smartphone, memory dump, etc.) and objects relationships (e.g., contains, extracted from, etc.); formal languages for representing in a standard way all the elements above cited; a platform for implementing the exchange process in terms of functionalities along with a recommendation for an integration with existing platforms already in place and run by European/international public bodies.

15.1 Introduction

One of the main aims of the Evidence project[1] consisted in defining functional specifications for the exchanging of digital evidence. This has been accomplished identifying the main meta data involved in the exchange process based on the following activities:

- identifying and proposing a standard for the representation of data and metadata involved in the digital evidence exchange process;

[1]Evidence Project—"European Informatics Data Exchange Framework for Courts and Evidence", www.evidenceproject.eu.

M. Epifani · F. Turchi (✉)
CNR, Institute of Legal Information Theory and Techniques, Florence, Italy
e-mail: mattia.epifani@ittig.cnr.it; fabrizio.turchi@ittig.cnr.it

M. A. Biasiotti et al. (eds.), *Handling and Exchanging Electronic Evidence Across Europe*, Law, Governance and Technology Series 39,
https://doi.org/10.1007/978-3-319-74872-6_15

- addressing issues related to provenance[2];
- highlighting the lack of standards for the representation of the forensic tools results;
- proposing an integration/extension toward existing platforms already in place (Siena led by Europol, e-Testa led by Eurojust, I-24/7 led by Interpol, etc.), including e-CODEX, for digital evidence exchanging within EU Member States.

Based on the information gathered through questionnaires/interviews and meetings/workshops with expert groups both in the legal and technical fields, it has been drawn that, currently, in cross-borders criminal cases, cooperation is mostly based upon international agreement or letter rogatory to the foreign Court. Independently from the legal framework identified by the EU Member States, the cooperation is mostly human based when the electronic evidence is exchanged between judicial stakeholders from a judicial authority (requesting) to another (requested) judicial authority within the EU Member States. This approach is similar across countries and, at first glance, the Exchange does not appear based on any electronic means at all.

In most cases the forensic copy of the original source of evidence is exchanged: a judicial/police authority from an EU Member State A (requesting authority) requests an EU Member State B (requested authority) to generate a forensic copy, based on mutual trust between the two competent authorities. Later the exchange of the forensic copy will be attained on human based: the authority from country A appoints someone who will take the copy or alternatively the copy is delivered by a secure courier to the requesting authority. In any case, it must be emphasized that no electronic means is involved in the exchange process.

In examining the exchange process, a group of questions are to be born in mind:

1. What information should be exchanged?
2. When may the exchange take place?
3. How can the information be exchanged, taking into consideration security/privacy issues?
4. When the amount of electronic evidence is huge, how should it be dealt with?
5. Which stakeholders are involved?

Additionally, there is no standard concerning the Electronic Evidence Exchange, in contrasts to the Acquisition and Analysis processes (ISO/IEC, 2012, 2015), and the scenario is rather diversified, so it might occur that the exchange is carried out differently based on the kind of evidence.

Presently, the regular international procedures for mutual legal assistance in criminal matters represent, the only way for the evidence exchange, but these

[2]In the forensics community there is no a general agreement on the exact meaning of the evidence provenance, although all experts unanimously consider the great importance of the provenance in digital forensics investigation. Some experts see the provenance as chain of custody documentation (Turner, 2005a), other interpret the provenance as the "the set of tools and transformations that led from acquired raw data to the final findings" (Levine and Liberatore, 2009).

procedures are time-consuming, unpredictable and not suitable to deal with the electronic evidence. Moreover, in cross-borders criminal cases, cooperation is mostly human based.[3]

The present situation raises the following issues:

- exchange evidence procedures may be slow. This aspect must be especially born in mind in investigative cases where time is crucial for fighting against serious cross-border and organized crime;
- evidence exchange procedures may involve big expenses, such in case of travelling abroad to take the original/copy source of evidence to be handled;
- Judicial and Police authorities must invest large amounts of money to keep up with the development of forensics technology;
- exchanging trusted procedures are of utmost importance.

There are already existing platforms devoted to the information exchange.[4]

Nevertheless, these platforms do not use a detailed structure related to digital forensic information for exchanging data so a deeper study has been conducted to find a better solution for streamlining the exchange process.

The proposal for the representation of data and metadata involved in an electronic evidence exchange consists of:

1. A set of data and metadata for describing all actions (i.e. tasks), participants (e.g. subjects, victims, authorities, examiners, etc.), tools (i.e. digital tools for carrying out different forensic processes), digital and physical objects involved in the investigative case (e.g. hard disk, smartphone, memory dump, etc.) and objects relationships (e.g. Contains, Extracted From, etc.).
2. Formal languages for representing all the elements above cited in a standard way.
3. A platform for implementing the exchange process in terms of functionalities, together with a recommendation for an integration with existing platforms already in place and run by an European or an International public body.

This proposal may be adopted by the forensics community and the other important agencies and authorities involved, if, at least, two essential aspects will be considered:

- the platform should be led by an European/International public body to guarantee security and spread trust among all the public/private subjects involved;

[3]Public Prosecutor speech during a 2 days meeting held in Florence, on 8–9 April 2015.

[4]The main important system in the evidence exchange is SIENA, that stands for Secure Information Exchange Network Application. It is a secure communication system managed by EUROPOL and dedicated to the EU law enforcement community. The storage and exchange of information through SIENA is properly governed by legal framework, observing strong data protection regime. SIENA is used for exchanging personal information related to the crime areas within the mandate of EUROPOL, including EU restricted information. Basically, the SIENA application is a tool used for exchanging case relevant information (operational information).

- the participation of the main software companies in digital forensics arena, is of utmost importance to this initiative. The big actors in the forensic tools development field should extend their tools for making them fully complied with the metadata structure represented with the formal languages above mentioned. On the other hand, these companies will be willing to collaborate to the action, if the standard will be adopted at European/International level. In that case they will be eager to accustom their tools knowing that their efforts could foster their business and gain market share, contributing, at the same time, to the adoption of the standard at EU Member States level.

15.1.1 Existing Formal Language

The requirement upon a standard language to represent a broad range of forensic information and processing results has become an increasing need within the forensics community. For the electronic evidence exchange, a similar need must be addressed although the aim of the exchange may address different problems, for example malware analysis, relevant artifacts exchange, tools result comparison. Research activities conducted in this field have been used to develop and propose many languages including those presented in Table 15.1.

The description of some of these languages/formalisms requirements according to the different parameters (e.g. digital evidence life cycle, metadata involved, stakeholders, etc.) will be in-depth described in the next paragraphs.

15.1.2 The Digital Forensics XML

The Digital Forensics XML (DFXML) language was proposed since 2007, by Garfinkel (2012a). The author defined the language during his first presentation, in the following way:

> Digital Forensics XML (DFXML) is an XML language designed to represent a wide range of forensic information and forensic processing results. By matching its abstractions to the needs of forensic tools and analysts, DFXML allows the sharing of structured information between independent tools and organizations.

From a digital forensics expert/specialist perspective, this type of language tries to address two different issues:

- comparing and validating results produced by different forensic tools;
- representing and exchanging, in a standard format, forensics analysis findings.

Table 15.1 Standard formal languages

- DEB (Turner 2005a, pp. 45–49, 2005b, pp. 223–228, 2006, pp. 59–64)
- XIRAF (Alink et al. 2006, pp. 50–58, Bhoedjang et al. 2012, pp. 96–108)
- RDF (Schatz 2007)
- IODEF (Danyliw 2007)
- DEX (Levine and Liberatore 2009, pp. 48–56)
- AFF4 (Cohen et al. 2009, pp. 57–68)
- MILE (Inacio 2012)
- NIEM—*National Information Exchange Model* (NIEM) is a standard that provides an understanding of data grounded in a consensus-based vocabulary, and enables organizations to move information across organizational boundaries to interoperate and act as one while maintaining authority of their own existing systems. (www.niem.gov)
- UMF—*Universal Message Format* (UMF) is a standard, represented in XML format, or agreement on what the structure of the most important law enforcement concepts when they are exchanged across borders should be.(tools.ietf.org/html/draft-cordell-mmusic-umf-00). It contains tags for representing identities, relationships, and activities. It is used by Europol for their information system *Siena*
- STIX (*Structured Threat Information Expression*)[a] a structured language for cyber threat intelligence that enables organizations to share intelligence in a consistent, machine-readable way. STIX lets you anticipate computer-based attacks and respond faster and more effectively. STIX is part of OASIS,[b] a nonprofit consortium that drives the development, convergence and adoption of open standards for the global information society
- DFXML (Garfinkel 2006, pp. 71–81, 2009, 2012b, pp. 161–174)
- CybOX (Barnum et al. 2012)—Open-source standardized representation of digital observables represent digital actions and objects along with their context, and cover digital forensic information. Developed with extensibility in mind: new object types can be added to CybOX without altering the core schema
- DFAX (Casey et al. 2015)—*Digital Forensic Analysis eXpression* (DFAX) leverages CybOX for representing the purely technical information (github.com/DFAX/dfax)
- UCO (Casey et al. 2015)—It expresses constructs that are common across the cyber and the forensics domain (github.com/ucoproject)
- ORD2i (Chabot et al. 2015, pp. 83–100)

[a]https://stixproject.github.io.
[b]https://www.oasis-open.org/org.

One of the most common issue concerns the possibility to verify findings extracted/generated by forensics analysis tools. This need is becoming even clearer considering the ever-increasing speed of innovation involving digital devices and the consequences on forensic tools (i.e. operating system, data storage strategies, etc.). Software tools, currently used by the forensic community, encompass:

- forensics toolkits,[5] monolithic software that include many features to carry out different forensics analysis;
- lighter tools aim at specific/limited forensics analysis activities[6];
- small, slender tools or scripts devised for carrying out peculiar tasks.

[5]See section *Forensic Toolkit* in the Digital Forensic Tools Catalogue at wp4.evidenceproject.eu.

[6]See, for example, the File Carving or Application Forensics categories in the Digital Forensic Tools Catalogue.

Each tool operates in a similar way: it takes, as input, the output of a forensics acquisition (e.g. forensic image, file set, network dump, memory dump, etc.) and generates, as output, a set of files or an analysis report.

The lack of a standardized format for representing the output of forensics analysis software makes difficult comparing results produced by different tools with similar features/functionalities. On the other hand, the use of a common standard language would offer many advantages:

- it would allow comparing results produced by different versions of the same forensic tool to evaluate the progress in terms of information extraction and interpretation;
- it would speed the automatic search activity avoiding analyzing the same information already processed by previous versions of the same tool; it would foster the data and information exchange between different organizations and different actors involved in the investigation.

In some cases, it could be enough exchanging only the metadata expressed in a XML format, rather than the original input data (i.e. forensics copy), making the process extremely quicker (i.e. smaller data size) and allowing a smoother management of the data privacy. In the authors' proposal, the DFXML language aims at representing specific kind of data for achieving the purposes mentioned before, particularly metadata describing the object provided as input to the analysis tool, such as:

- disk image
- file container
- single file
- network dump
- memory dump
- others

Examples of common metadata are:

- file name, hash values, etc.
- information about the tool used for carrying out the forensics process: tool name, version, etc.
- how the executable program has been created, the libraries involved, etc.
- state of the computer on which the forensics processing has been conducted: name, operating system, date of the execution process, etc.
- extracted information: extraction methods, physical position, file system metadata, MAC times,[7] etc.
- hash values of extracted data;
- specific information about the operating system, useful during a forensics analysis

[7]MAC times are pieces of file system metadata that record when certain events pertaining to a computer file occurred most recently. M stands for Modify, A for Access and C for Change or Create.

Moreover, the use of an XML-like language has a further advantage: it is very easy to export data in other common format such as JSON, ProtoBufs, and others.

15.1.3 CybOX Language

In the field of information exchange regarding malware activities, many standard languages have been proposed and exploited, even considering that the use of common standards is important for the exchange of any kind of information. CybOX (Cyber Observable eXpression) was previously one of the most important languages that has been proposed. It has been devised along with other related languages, by Mitre,[8] such as:

- CAPEC[9] (Common Attack Pattern Enumeration and Classification)
- MAEC[10] (Malware Attribute Enumeration and Characterization)
- STIX[11] (Structured Threat Information eXpression)
- TAXII[12] (Threat Automated eXchange of Indicator Information)

The use of standard languages for the information exchange has been dealt in recent scientific contributions, published in 2014, by the European Union Agency for Network and Information Security[13] (ENISA) and particularly, Actionable information for Security Incident Response[14] and in Standards and tools for exchange and processing of actionable information.[15]

CybOX (Casey et al., 2015) is an open standard language for representing cyber objects along with their relationships that are very suitable for storing and sharing digital forensic information. It has been devised by E. Casey and S. Barnum at MITRE and its main features are:

- it's an open-source standardized representation of digital observables;
- it represents digital actions and objects along with their context, and covers digital forensic information;
- it has been developed with extensibility in mind: new object types can be added to CybOX without altering the core schema.

[8]The MITRE Corporation is a not-for-profit company that operates multiple federally funded research and development centers (FFRDCs), https://www.mitre.org.

[9]http://capec.mitre.org.

[10]http://maec.mitre.org.

[11]http://stix.mitre.org.

[12]http://taxii.mitre.org.

[13]https://www.enisa.europa.eu.

[14]https://www.enisa.europa.eu/activities/cert/support/actionable-information/actionable-information-for-security.

[15]https://www.enisa.europa.eu/activities/cert/support/actionable-information/standards-and-tools-for-exchange-and-processing-of-actionable-information.

A CybOX observable is a dynamic event or a static property. Examples of CybOX observable are:

- a registry key is generated (dynamic event);
- a file is deleted (dynamic event);
- a file has a specific MD5 hash value (static property);
- the value of a specific registry key (static property).

The CybOX language can express many different digital objects and their associated characteristics, examples of cyber objects envisaged by CybOX include, but are not limited to the following:

- Device
- Disk and Disk Partition
- Email Message
- File
- HTTP Session
- PDF File
- Pipe
- Port
- URI
- Volume
- Win Event Log, Win Executable File, Win File, Win Handle, Win Process, Win Registry Key

Each single object is represented by a XML Schema,[16] for instance the Email File Object is outlined in Fig. 15.1.

Moreover, the CybOX schemas contain a huge number of items (i.e. elements and attributes) but the bulk of them are optional so the formalism is very flexible and prone to its extension. CybOX also defines some Object to Object relationships that comprise a well-supplied definition, a list of potential involved Objects, and their inverse (if existing), are shown in Table 15.2.[17]

15.1.4 DFAX Language

DFAX is a standard language for representing the processes involving in handling digital evidence with the aim to foster the interoperability among forensic tools and the exchanging of forensic information. It incorporates its own structure to represent the more procedural aspects of the digital forensics domain, including those for chain of custody, case management, forensic processing. This initiative for

[16]For the current list of objects, see https://cyboxproject.github.io/documentation/objects.

[17]For a complete list see https://cyboxproject.github.io/documentation/object-relationships.

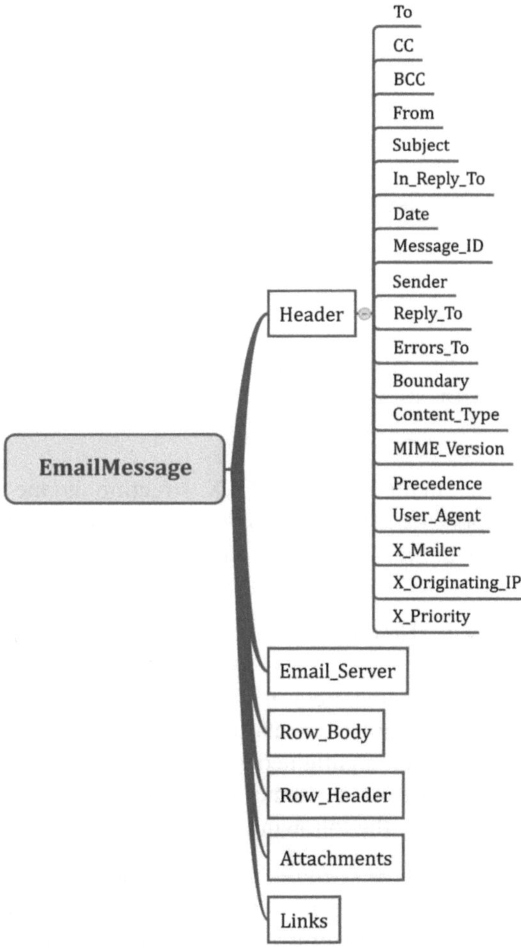

Fig. 15.1 CybOX, Email Message Object

a standard language evolved into the development of Cyber-investigation Analysis Standard Expression (CASE).

DFAX uses CybOX (Cyber Observable eXpression) language, for representing digital actions and objects along with their context. It has been developed with extensibility in mind: new object types can be added to CybOX without altering the core schema. DFAX (Digital Forensic Analysis eXpression) leverages CybOX for representing the purely technical information.

Another independent part, used by DFAX, is the Unified Cyber Ontology (UCO) that provides an abstract layer and express constructs that are common across the cyber domain (e.g. Action Lifecycle) and represents the actors/stakeholders, or Identities, involved in a case, such as: Attorney, Investigator, Examiner, Subject, Victim. Each Identity is described through an XML schema.

Table 15.2 CybOX objects relationships

Name	Inverse	Applicable objects (source)	Applicable objects (related)
Created	Deleted, Killed	Archive File, Process	File, Process, Mutex, Win Registry Key, Win Service, Win Thread
Downloaded_By	Uploaded_By	File	Process
Contains	N/A	File, Archive File, Email Message, URI, DNS Record, ARP Cache, URL History, Win Registry Key	File, Link, Domain Name, Address, URI, Win Registry Key
Parent_Of	Child_Of	Process	Process, Win Thread
Child_Of	Parent_Of	Process, Win Thread	Process

The main item of DFAX structure is the *DFAXPackageType* element that comprises 14 different complex elements, including three reference elements, as shown in Fig. 15.2. Each complex element includes further sub elements.

15.1.4.1 Element *Case*

The fundamental item of the *DFAXPackage* is the *Case* element, composed by the following main elements and shown in Fig. 15.3, where the items of the UCO ontology are highlighted in blue and the items defined as *ref:attribute* defined in other part of the same or different document are highlighted in red. The sub-elements are the following:

- *Title* and *Description*: they are related to the case.
- *External_ID*: it ia a unique identifier for the case.
- *Suspected_Offense*: it represents the kind of offense, whose values come from a controlled vocabulary.
- *Investigator*, *Examiner*, *Attorney*, *Subject*, *Victim*: they represent the different Actors/Identities involved in the case.
- *Authorization*: it contains all authorization needed for carrying out actions during the life cycle of the evidence.
- *Forensic_Action*: it includes all possible forensics actions performed (e.g. seize, acquisition, preservation, an, etc.).
- *Provenance_Record*: it is the potential evidence as input or output of forensics actions (e.g. a seized smartphone, a forensic copy, etc.). This element is fundamental for proving the admissibility of an evidence and its reproducibility as well.

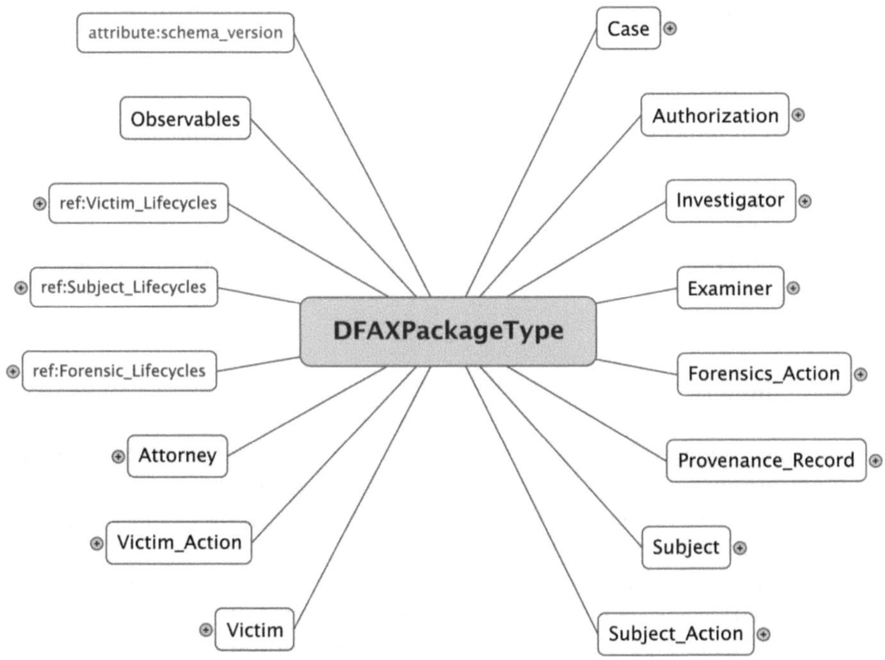

Fig. 15.2 DFAX, DFAXPackageType element

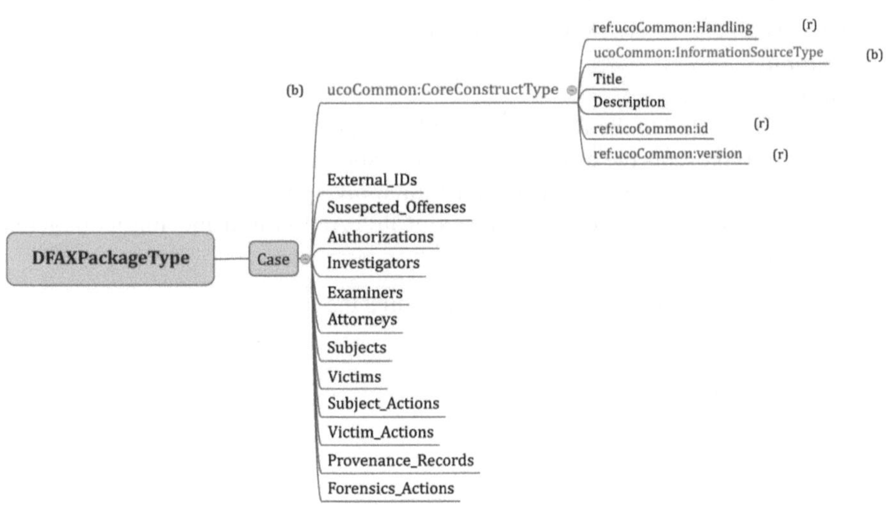

Fig. 15.3 DFAX, Case element

15.1.4.2 Authorization

An authorization is identified by the following elements:

- *Authority*: it is an object defined as an *ucoCommon:IdentityType* element used to express identity information for both individuals and organizations, and basically composed of a Name and a unique identifier within the case.
- *Warrant_Identifier*: it is a string representing the warrant identifier
- *Related_Athorizations*: it contains a reference to other authorizations connected with the current one.

15.1.4.3 Subjects

Each of the elements *Investigator*, *Examiner*, and *Attorney* are in turn defined as an extension of the *ucoCommon:IdentityConstructType* object and comprises the *ucoCommon:CoreConstructType* already seen in the above element Case and *ucoCommon:IdentityType* that includes *Name*.

Subject and *Victim* elements contain the item *Related_Actions* because the actions carried out by *Subjects* or *Victims* are represented by an extension of the *ucoCommon:ActionType* element that includes the following base and complex elements:

- *Type*: it is a field that specifies the type of this Action, whose value are picked up from a controlled vocabulary
- *Objective*: it characterizes the objective of this Action
- *Location*
- *DateTime*
- *Phase*: it is related to the forensic action life cycle
- *Impact*: it represents the estimated impact of applying this Action
- *Cost*: it characterizes the estimated cost for applying this Action.
- *Efficacy*: it represents the effectiveness of this Action in achieving its targeted Objective

Furthermore the *Subject* element also contains the items:

- *Provenance_Record*
- *Victim*
- *Activity_Lifecycle_Phases*

15.1.4.4 Forensic Action

Each *Forensic_Action* is characterized by elements related to *Authorizations*, *Examiners* and *Provenance_Record* elements as input and/or output, as shown in Fig. 15.4. All *Forensic_Action* elements compose the *Forensic_Lifecycle* element.

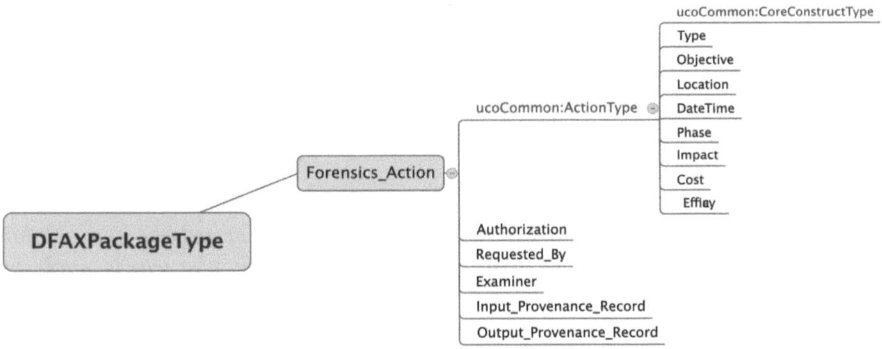

Fig. 15.4 DFAX, Forensic_Action element

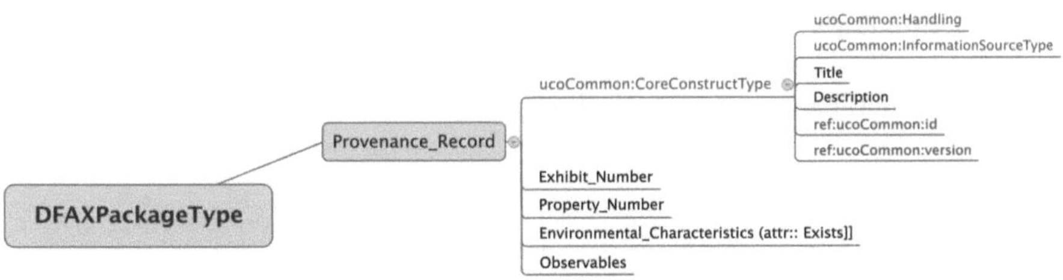

Fig. 15.5 DFAX, Provenance_Record element

15.1.4.5 Provenance Records

Each *Provenance_Record* element, at both Input and Output, depicted in Fig. 15.5, is identified by elements related to the *Information_Source* of evidence[18] and by the *Observables* elements associated with them.

15.1.5 Forensic Case

To provide a more in depth vision of the DFAX language, and better explain how this formalism can represent the metadata involved in an investigative case, it is worth examining a complex example[19] with the aim to put in evidence strengths and weaknesses of the language.

[18]The UCO element *ucoCommon:InformationSourceType* that details the source of a given data entry.

[19]A basic example, called *basic_example.xml* has been provided, by the DFAX developers, on the Github site—the well-known a web-based Git repository hosting service—via the github.com/DFAX/dfax/tree/master/examples.

This example is useful to describe a complete forensic investigation process involving a personal computer, an USB drive and a smartphone.

The process is described as the sequence of actions related to Identification, Acquisition and Analysis of the Forensics Life Cycle phases, and provides a DFAX/XML output file containing all the information related to the case.

The case is described as follows:

The CEO (Adam Smith) of a private company (EarlyBird Corporation) is suspected of trade secrets infringement and disclosure of private information to another company (NightOwl Corporation), the forensic lifecycle is made by Identification, Acquisition, Analysis and Report.

The outline of the case is represented in Fig. 15.6.

The involved information are:

- the Subject: Adam Smith
- the Victim: EarlyBird Corporation
- the Judge: Tom Softy
- the Examiner: the investigator Ian Law

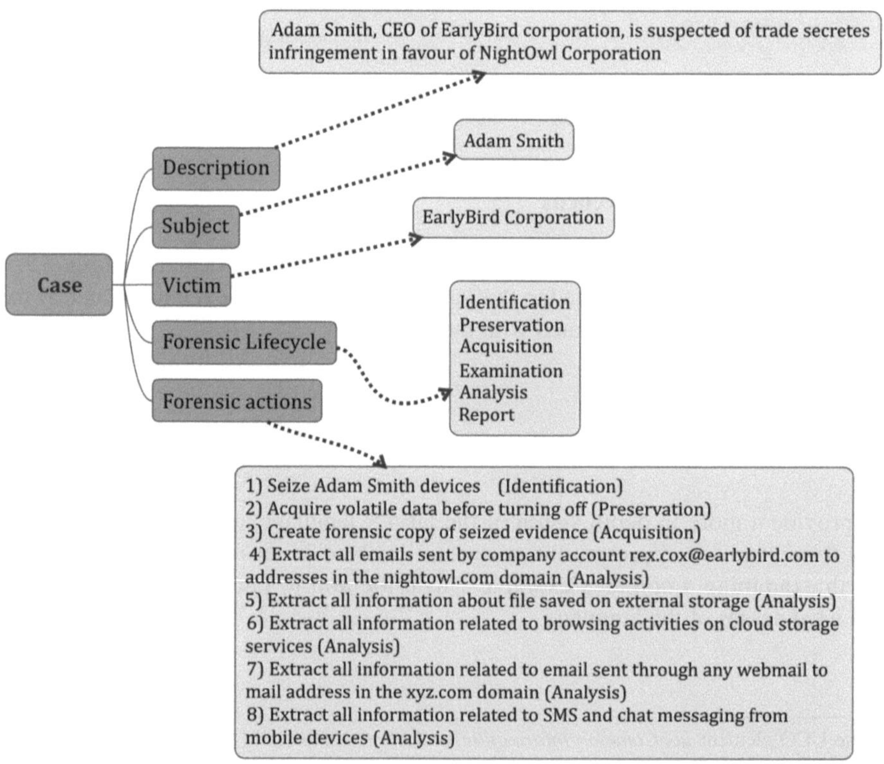

Fig. 15.6 A representation in CybOX/DFAX of trade secrets infringement and disclosure of private information case

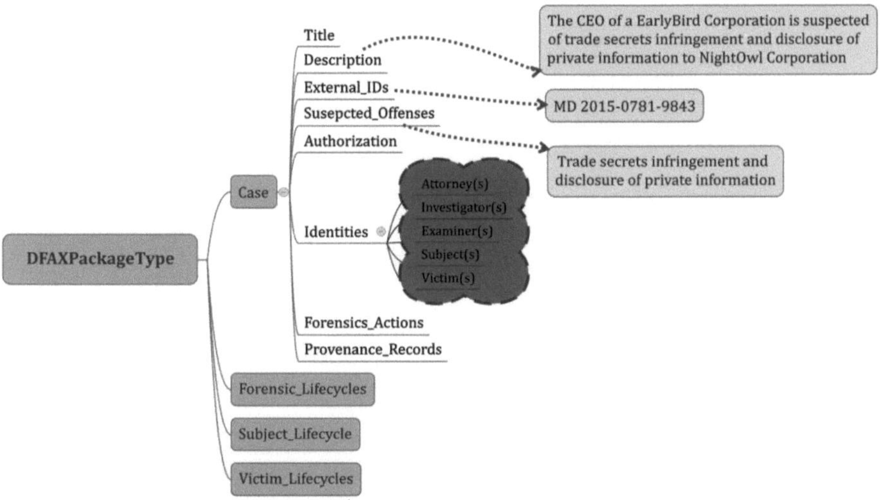

Fig. 15.7 DFAX, Trade secrets infringements case, Identities elements

- Actions:
  - Seize suspect's personal computer, USB pen and a smartphone
  - Make forensic image of suspect's devices (hard disk, USB and smartphone)
  - Analysis of source of evidence
  - Report
- Find communications (emails) subject and the NightOwl Corporation

  The DFAX Package element is composed of:

- Identities element: Description, External_ID, Suspected_Offense, as shown in Fig. 15.7 in the round rectangle.
- Authorization elements: Authority, Warrant_Identifier, as shown in Fig. 15.8 in the green round rectangles.
- Investigator/Examiner: in this case the roles are played by the same person, sometimes they may be different.
- Subject (suspect) and Victim

The forensics investigative phases are represented by the Forensic_Lifecycles element, and composed of:

- Identifier: a unique alphanumeric-code,
- Name: a description of the forensic action
- Ordinality: a time sequence within the investigation process model, that is loaded from an external source letting each organization to choose their own model.

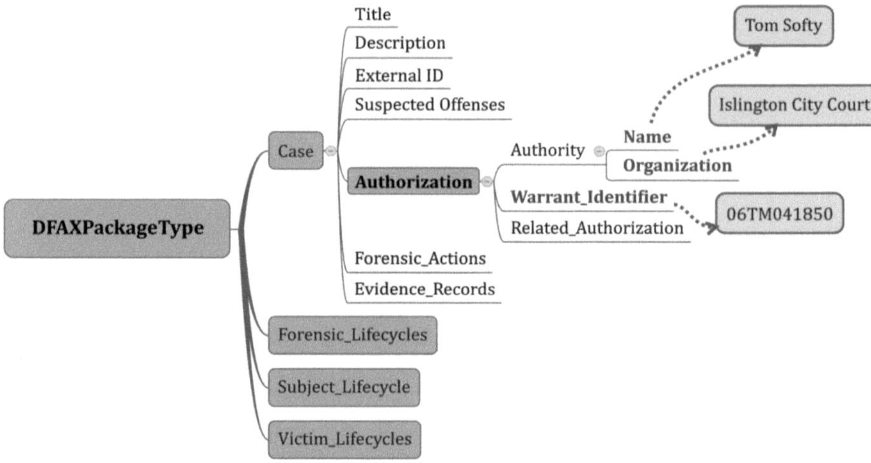

Fig. 15.8 DFAX, Trade secrets infringements case, Authorization elements

Each Identifier, related to a Forensic_Action element, describes forensics actions like:

- Survey
- Preservation
- Acquisition
- Examination
- Analysis
- Report

In the example, the Forensics_Actions consist of:

- Seize suspect's computer, USB and smartphone
- Create a memory dump while the computer is still switched on
- Make forensic copy of the hard disk
- Make forensic copy of the USB
- Acquiring the content of the smartphone
- Analysis
  - Find emails sent by computer from private/corporate subject's address to the NightOwl domain,
  - Access to cloud storage services by computer,
  - Find trade secrets files stored on the USB Drive,
  - Find messages exchanged with the NightOwl Corporation CEO by subject's smartphone

The first Actions of the Search and Seizure phase, is described as a *Forensic_Action* performed by an examiner, in a specific location and at a specified date and time that has no *Provenance_Record* as input and produces three *Provenance_Record* as output. The Action is identified by the following fields:

- Id
- Objective
- Location
- Date and Time
- Phase
- Authorization
- Examiner
- Output_Provenance_Record

In Fig. 15.9 it is depicted one single *Provenance_Record*, as output, corresponding to the smartphone seizing.

The first Action related to the Acquisition phase is performed on the hard disk and produces, as output, a File, corresponding to the bit- by-bit image of the hard disk itself. The following metadata (Table 15.3) can be used to describe the File, that in terms of Observable it can be represented as a CybOX File Object, and the Tool used to get it.

In Fig. 15.10 is illustrated the Provenance_Record produced in output by this Action along with some properties of the CybOX File object.

The complete XML code, as a mind map diagram, describing a very similar case is available via the following address: https://wp4.evidenceproject.eu/dfax/advanced.example.pc.usb.smartphone.html.

15.2 Problems to Be Addressed in Exchange Languages

The combination of the last languages/formalisms, DFXML, CybOX, DFAX and the UCO, represents the most suitable standards to representing data and metadata related to an evidence exchange for a variety of reasons:

- they include many essential elements to representing digital forensic information despite they have been developed in the cyber security environment
- they allow describing technical, procedural and judicial information as well
- they have been developed with the extensibility in mind so they are adaptable to the fast-pace development of technology and they allow introducing new elements to include forensic information not envisaged yet;
- they leverage the UCO ontology that permits the description of Actions, Actors and their relationships
- they are open source
- they already contain a composed structure for representing a wide range of forensic information

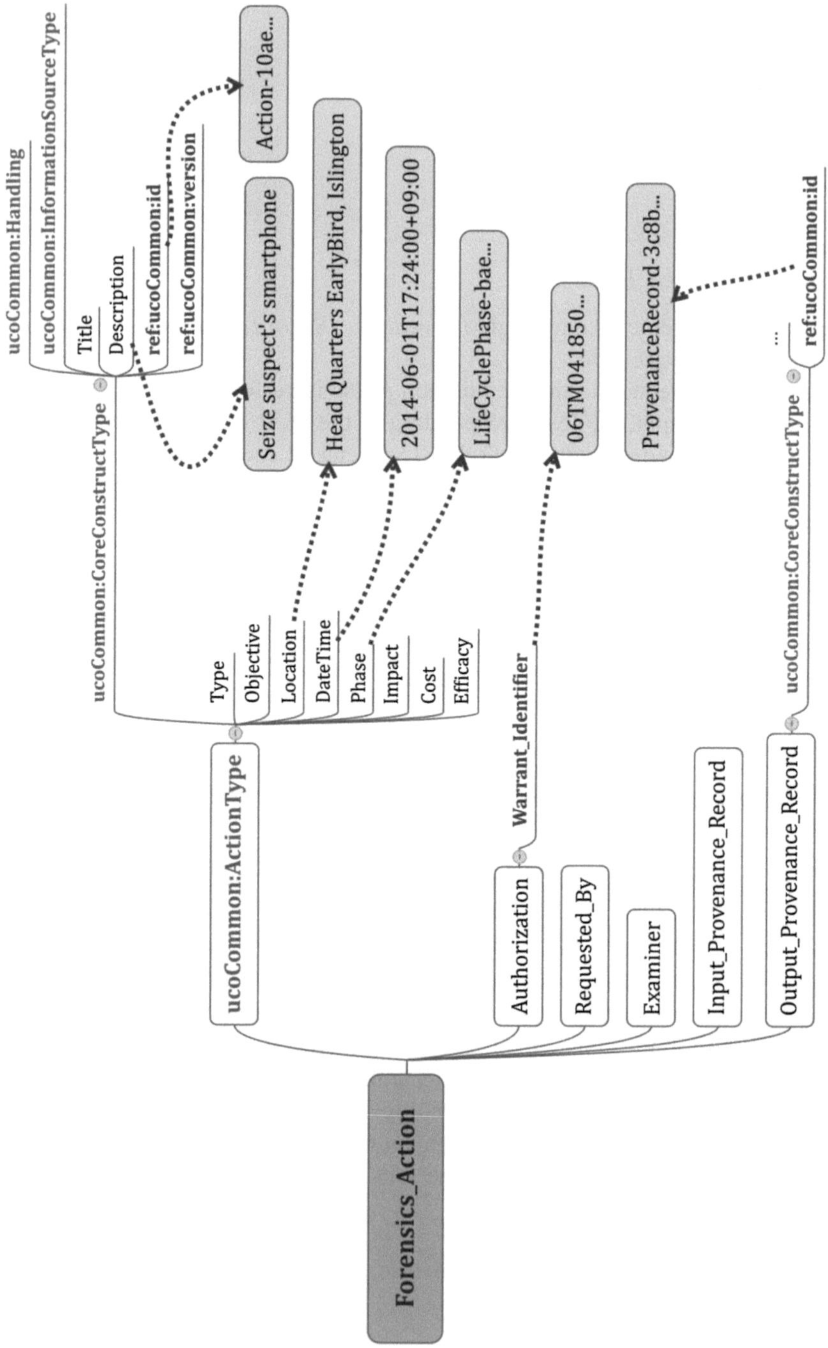

Fig. 15.9 DFAX, Trade secrets infringements case, Forensic_Action element

Table 15.3 Hard disk acquisition metadata

Description	EarlyBird CEO (Adam Smith) computer—forensics image
Exhibit number	EarlyBird_CTO_PC_DD
Property number	EarlyBird_CTO_PC_2_1
File name	EarlyBird_CTO_PC.DD
File size (bytes)	343597383680
File hash type	SHA1
File hash value	20EA3567BD6F4DD7002BBE2C1A5D339EE51AA308
Tool name	Forensic Falcon
Tool vendor	Logicube
Tool version	2.1.3

While DFAX has evolved into CASE, there are still issues that must be addressed, considering a typical scenario that investigators and analysts meet during real cases. Some points must be considered about the DFAX structure and its expansion:

(a) The Case Information part of the DFAX Package is structured with a strict Authority—Investigator—Victim—Subject paradigm. This fields must be discussed with legal experts for establishing if they fit into reality, also bearing in mind the different law systems existing among European countries and the rest of the World.
(b) The use of a specification such as CybOX is useful in a Digital Forensic context is necessary to define a list of common terms to be used for describing Objects. For example: a. Device object is commonly used to describe physical Source of Evidence and should contain a Description field. Examples of fixed Description values could be: Personal Computer, Notebook, SATA Hard Disk, USB Hard Disk, USB Pen Drive, CD, DVD, SD Memory Card, Smartphone, Tablet, etc. b. Some physical Objects may contain specific fields that must be defined. For example, in the case of a smartphone, it is more appropriate the use the IMEI rather than a Serial Number value.
(c) Using the concept of Provenance_Record as the Input/Output of every single action is in general a good choice. But there are cases where the description of the Provenance_Record in terms of Observable could be hard to do. For example, the acquisition of a hard disk carried out by splitting the output in fixed size file: to describe the Provenance_Record as output, it should be necessary to list as Observables all the single files produced by the acquisition tools.
(d) There is no easy way to describe deleted content that can be carved from the unallocated space or recovered through the file system of the disk. There is a shortage of Objects useful for describing elements that should be fruitful from a Digital Forensics point of view. This is especially true when we deal with Actions related to the Analysis stage. In Table 15.4 a list of such proper Objects, to be added to Cybox, is provided.

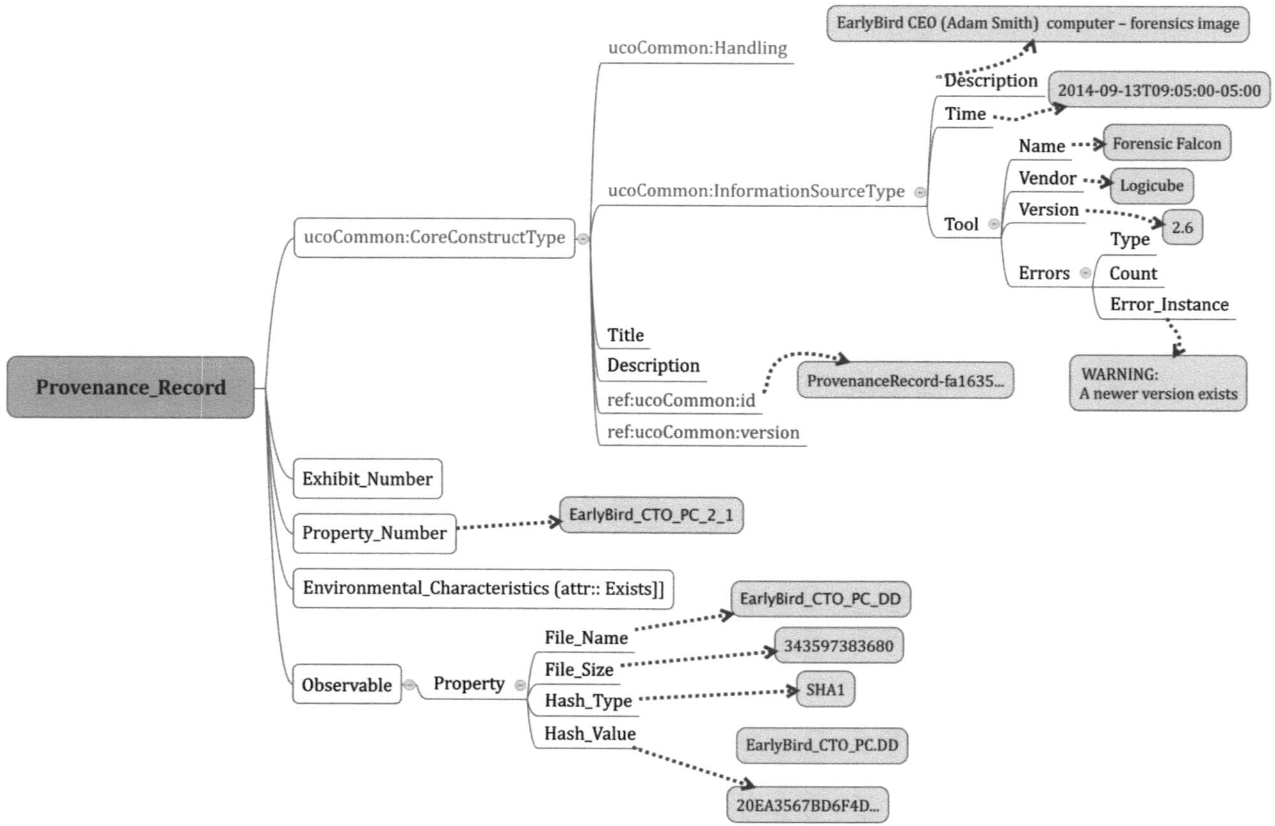

Fig. 15.10 DFAX, Trade secrets infringements case, Provenance_Record and the related Observable

Table 15.4 Objects to be added to DFAX standard

Object	References
Windows jumplist	Like shortcuts files it is commonly used to identify file access
Windows shortcuts	It is an artefact commonly used during forensic investigation to identify file access, device connection, network shares, and so on. It should be described by its specific fields
Windows prefetch	It is an already existing Object in Cybox but its structure has changed since Windows 8, so the object needs to be updated
Office document	Useful for describing Office Documents in terms of metadata
Image file	Already existing object in Cybox. It should be updated to describe typical image metadata
Audio file	Same concept as an Image file applied to an Audio
Video file	Same concept as an Image file applied to a Video
Database entry	Generic way to describe database entry in a table or the result of a SQLite query
Generic artefacts	Record/data contained inside a file in proprietary format. For example, an entry contained in a chat or P2P history file (i.e. MET files used by eMule software) or a plist file used in Apple OS for configuration and data
PCAP file	It should be useful to have a way to describe a Network Capture file with some metadata, for example those extracted by tools like capinfos; See the Catalogue at wp4.evidenceproject.eu)
Deleted files	There should be a way to describe deleted files

15.3 An Initiative to Promote the Adoption of the DFAX Standard

Before DFAX evolved into CASE, it has been developed *dfax2plaso* a tool being able to automatically produce CybOX objects from the timeline of a case to encourage the use of CybOX/DFAX standard formalism for representing data and meta-data involved in the Electronic Evidence Exchange process. The timeline that has been considered is the output of the Plaso[20] software, a very well-known tool in the forensics community.

To this aim, the following two repositories on GitHub, associated to the CNR-ITTIG organization account, have been created:

- plaso
- plaso2dfax

The first repository is a fork of Plaso that includes a DFAX extension; it allows to directly create a DFAX/CybOX xml, as output, starting from a proto buffer as

[20]Plaso is a Python-based backend engine for the tool log2timeline, developed and maintained by Google. log2timeline is a tool designed to extract timestamps from various files found on a typical computer system(s) and aggregate them.

Fig. 15.11 plaso2dfax tool architecture

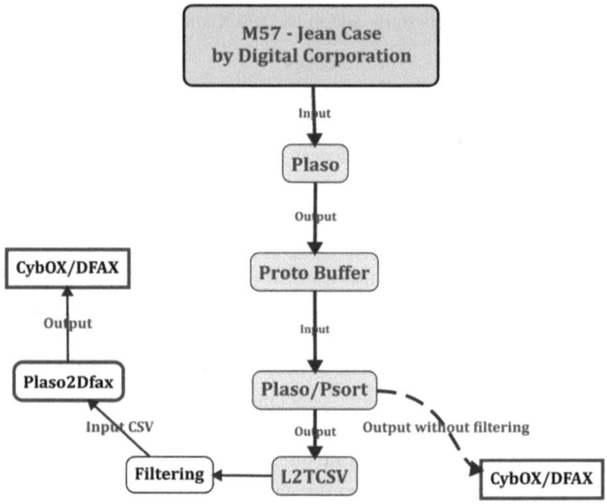

input of the psort[21] tool. This solution has not been considered the best one because the output produces a lot of noise (i.e. lots of rows that are not relevant for the case). In an academic case, an alternative solution has been proposed: starting from the *l2tcsv*[22] output produced by the *psort* tool, it is necessary to manually select a specify set of rows that are significant for the investigation because it's not always possible to extract/isolate them through the available filters provided by *psort*.

An attempt has been done to develop an alternative tool, having in mind the needs of a forensics analyst, which is to some extent an analyst centered application, with the aim to let an analyst produce their analysis in DFAX/CybOX language with the minimum effort (for the sake of the success of the formalism itself).

To achieve this goal, it has been devised and developed the *plaso2dfax* tool, that takes in input the *l2tcsv* produced by *psort* and turn it to CybOX Objects (see Fig. 15.11).

On a day-to-day basis, forensics analysts produce/write and examine/read reports on digital evidence finding. Despite of the professionalism and accuracy they were composed with, those reports are created based on personal experiences and guided by best practices, because there is no standard for their formal and functional structure.

In digital forensics context, the final report represents the most crucial phase where it is necessary to describe the conclusion of the analysis using a clear, not ambiguous and understandable language for both non-technical people (judges, magistrates, lawyers, etc.) and the counterparties analysts.

[21]psort is a command line tool to post-process plaso storage files. It allows you to filter, sort and run automatic analysis on the contents of plaso storage files.

[22]A format similar to the Comma Separated Value.

The aim of using a standard for the representation of the Evidence Exchange also comprises the introduction of a degree of objectivity in reports composition:

- digital evidences extracted are under the forensics analyst responsibility (i.e. what) and represent the Subjective analysis side
- how digital evidences are represented is the Objective analysis side and it can be automatically represented in a formal language

The *plaso2dfax*, outlined in Fig. 15.11 tool aims at representing the Objective side of a forensics analysis, emphasizing the advantages of the proposed standard.

15.4 Conclusions

The requirement upon a standard language to represent a wide range of forensic information and processing results is becoming an essential need within the forensics community.

It has been presented a standard proposal for representing data and metadata involved in Electronic Evidence Exchange and it has also been recommended the use of DFAX, that leverages CybOX and the Unified Cyber Ontology, for representing these metadata and describing in a detailed way all technical and legal information.

Presently, the DFAX and the related formalisms have been designed focusing on the extensibility and therefore adaptable for covering all possible information needs for representing forensics investigations.

It also has been emphasized the importance of the integration of the standard representation into existing platforms already up and running. All the platforms previously mentioned have already implemented security and privacy levels in accordance with standard ISO/IEC 27017, ISO/IEC 27002 and ISO/IEX 2704050 that guarantees a wide trust among all involved stakeholders.

The integration of the standard structure should be carried out, also extending the authorized users, to include private subjects such as the Internet Service Providers.

The use of such platform would bring many advantages:

- the platform would become a unique reference point for all evidence exchange processes, across the EU Member States. Furthermore, the platform would provide logging facilities (i.e. the action of keeping a single/multiple files for different events such as messages between different users in a communication process) and give the chance to trace the operation carried out by these private stakeholder, whilst now when judicial authorities receive the requested data there is no information about who was responsible for the job, because this service is provided by ISPs private web platforms;
- the platform would carry out the Exchange process including, when it is possible, also the data involved, not only the associated metadata. This would make the Exchange Evidence process much faster, strengthening the fight against serious

cross-border and organized crime especially in investigative case where time is crucial.;
- the platform would streamline the exchange procedures and avoid, except for special cases, traveling abroad to take the original source of evidence;
- a wider cooperation would be put in place optimizing costs and developing a stronger cooperation and trust among the involved competent authorities.

In addition to the advantages above mentioned, a standard for representing forensic information would also stimulate the research in forensics field, opening new scenarios in automatic handling forensic information, allowing, for instance:

- the development of new tools in machine learning field: relying on specific algorithms and given a set of data it is possible to infer information about the properties of the data making previsions about other data that might appear in the future;
- the gathering of big data for statistical processing or other automatic tasks relying on the standard structure.

References

Alink W, Bhoedjang R, Boncz P, de Vries A (2006) XIRAF - XML-based indexing and querying for digital forensics. Digit Invest 3(Suppl):50–58

Barnum S, Martin R, Worrell B, Kirillov I (2012) The CybOX language specification, Version 1.0. MITRE. https://cybox.mitre.org/language/specifications/CybOX_Language_Core_Specification_v1.0.pdf

Bhoedjang RAF, van Ballegooij AR, van Beek HMA et al (2012) Engineering an online computer forensic service. Digit Invest 9(2):96–108

Casey E, Back G, Barnum S (2015) Leveraging CybOX to standardize representation and exchange of digital forensic information. Digit Invest 12:102–110. https://www.sciencedirect.com/science/article/pii/S1742287615000158

Chabot Y, Bertaux A, Nicolle C, Kechadi T (2015) An ontology-based approach for the reconstruction and analysis of digital incidents timelines. Digit Investig 15:83–100. https://doi.org/10.1016/j.diin.2015.07.005

Cohen M, Schatz B, Garfinkel S (2009) Extending the advanced forensic format to accommodate multiple data sources, logical evidence, arbitrary information and forensic workflow. Digit Invest 6(Suppl):57–68

Danyliw (2007) tools.ietf.org/html/rfc5070

Garfinkel S (2006) Forensic feature extraction and cross-drive analysis. Digit Invest 3(Suppl):71–81

Garfinkel S (2009) Automating disk forensic processing with SleuthKit. In: XML and Python, Systematic approaches to digital forensics engineering (IEEE/SADFE 2009), Oakland

Garfinkel S (2012a) Digital forensics XML and the DFXML toolset. Digit Invest 8:161–174

Garfinkel S (2012b) Digital forensics XML and the DFXML toolset. Digit Invest 9(3–4):161–174

Inacio (2012) tools.ietf.org/html/draft-inacio-mile-forensics-00

ISO/IEC 27037:2012 (2012) Information technology—Security techniques—Guidelines for identification, collection, acquisition and preservation of digital evidence

ISO/IEC 27042:2015 (2015) Information technology—Security techniques—Guidelines for the analysis and interpretation of digital evidence

Levine BN, Liberatore M (2009) DEX: Digital evidence provenance supporting reproducibility and comparison. Digit Invest 6:48–56. github.com/umass-forensics/DEX-forensics

Schatz B (2007) Digital evidence: representation and assurance, PhD dissertation, Queensland University of Technology. eprints.qut.edu.au/16507/1/Bradley_Schatz_Thesis.pdf

Turner P (2005a) Digital provenance—interpretation, verification and corroboration. Digit Invest 2(1):45–49

Turner P (2005b) Unification of digital evidence from disparate sources (digital evidence bags). Digit Invest 2(3):223–228

Turner P (2006) Selective and intelligent imaging using digital evidence bags. Digit Invest 3(Suppl):59–64

Chapter 16
Connecting the Dots: A Tale of Giants and Dwarfs, or How to Manage, Disseminate, Network and Present Your Research

Alexandra Tsvetkova

Abstract The project EVIDENCE—European Informatics Data Exchange Framework for Courts and Evidence—was designed as a Coordinating and Support Action. As such, it mainly comprised activities of coordination and networking of projects, programmes and policies in the field of electronic evidence. This commentary presents the EVIDENCE best practices towards successful stakeholder awareness and engagement and recommendations about mind-set changes that can be used by other policy-oriented projects to improve their dissemination and communication strategies. Hence, emphasizing the process of connecting the dots within the project's ecosystem in such a way ensuring the project's recognition and sustainability by building on its strengths and openly acknowledging its weaknesses in a constant pursue of improvement and further development.

16.1 Introduction

The project EVIDENCE—'European Informatics Data Exchange Framework for Court and Evidence', was designed as a Coordinating and Support Action (CSA). As such, it mainly comprised activities of coordination and networking of projects, programmes and policies (European Communities, 2007) in the field of electronic evidence and research was left in a less prominent position. These coordinating and networking activities included a variety of actions. Some of them dealt with dissemination, awareness raising, communication, networking, coordination and support services. Others encouraged policy dialogues and mutual learning exercises and studies, including standardisation, design studies for new infrastructure and complementary activities of strategic planning. A third group of actions was

A. Tsvetkova (✉)
LIBRe Foundation, Sofia, Bulgaria
e-mail: alexandra.tsvetkova@libreresearchgroup.org

M. A. Biasiotti et al. (eds.), *Handling and Exchanging Electronic Evidence Across Europe*, Law, Governance and Technology Series 39,
https://doi.org/10.1007/978-3-319-74872-6_16

aimed at supporting networking and coordination between programmes in different countries (European Union, 2014; European Commission, 2016).

Dissemination and awareness raising are planned processes of providing information about the results of individual or collective work to key actors in a particular field. In the context of a project, these processes involve communication of the project's outcomes to build strong relations with stakeholders and to disseminate the project's results across the widest possible range of audiences. The main goal is to inform the target audiences about the project, to influence their organisations in the future and to raise the profile of both the project and the consortium implementing it. These activities are closely related to all other activities within the project and are implemented in a unifying way, which enables the future use and exploitation of the research results. To do that effectively, there should be a plan designed to serve the project from the very beginning to its end and beyond. This plan should seek to answer the most important questions of:

- what is the main purpose of dissemination, i.e. the objectives, goals and expected impact of the dissemination effort? (the 'why');
- what type of stakeholders does the project seek to reach in terms of professional field, level of expertise, level of influence, demographic characteristics, cultural background, language, and other psychographic characteristics etc., i.e. affected parties, parties interested in learning about the project's activities and findings, and the community at large? (the 'to whom');
- what is to be communicated to the audience, e.g. results, reports, recommendations etc.? (the 'what');
- what are the communication channels and tools that will be employed, i.e. what is the most effective way to reach each type of stakeholder and what kind of resources does each of the target groups need or typically access? (the 'how');
- when should the communication messages reach the audience? (the 'when');
- are there any specific locations, events, or any other geographically dispersed venues that the project seeks to reach out to? (the 'where').

The development of a dissemination plan is necessary for any project and it is one of the first steps to be implemented by analysing the target groups and linking the different audiences to the respective communication channels, tools and messages. A key element of this process is the analysis of the individual stakeholders or stakeholder groups, creating a taxonomy of stakeholders and identifying their internal motives (interests, needs, or drivers) to collaborate with the project's consortium. The results of this exercise form the basis for identifying the degree of importance of these groups, as well as the potential engaging activities (one-to-one discussions or presentations, group discussions or workshops, and/or other means) and/or resources they will need to effectively cooperate (e.g. analyses, findings, recommendations etc.) based on realistic stakeholder contexts and expectations.

To be effective, the dissemination plan must be oriented towards the needs of the audience with respect to using appropriate language and information means. It also should include various dissemination means such as, e.g. written text, tailored graphics and photos, paper- and web-based tools, and networking activities and presentations at community meetings and scientific conferences by fully leveraging existing resources, relationships, and networks.

The development of a matrix of Key Performance Indicators (KPI) or the establishment of criteria for measuring the impact of the dissemination processes and a timeline for the project's activities are also a *conditio sine qua non* for the proper implementation of these processes. Continuous measurement of the success achieved and adaptation to the environment in which the project exists is needed at every step within the project timeframe.

16.2 Status Quo

These key elements served as a baseline for the Dissemination and Communications Strategy of EVIDENCE. This strategy aimed to cover all dissemination processes throughout the project by identifying the respective target audience and by outlining the proper communication tools to reach it.

In addition to the general supporting measures, typical of CSA actions, the call for proposals (European Commission, 2013) required identification, definition, assessment and articulation of a complex set of coordinated developments by different actors at the legislative, standardisation, technological and law enforcement levels. These developments were aimed at elaborating a coherent framework of standards, guidelines and recommendations for the use, collection and exchange of electronic evidence. Therefore, the strategic goal of the EVIDENCE Dissemination and Communication Strategy was not only to raise awareness of the project activities to make EVIDENCE a successful and sustainable project, but also to support the achievement of its overall objective, namely "tracing a Road Map for the realization of a Common European Legal Framework for the application of new technologies in the collection, use and exchange of electronic evidence including a research agenda identifying issues, policies and actions to be undertaken in future programs and plans".

In accordance with the stakeholder theory of the business management sector, the project's team followed a four-step process to identify, classify, prioritise and integrate stakeholders (Freeman, 1984), defining thereby the EVIDENCE's primary and secondary (influencing) target audiences. The project had to take on board a wide range of individuals: policy makers regulating the use of electronic evidence in their national scenario; law enforcement officers gathering electronic evidence; judges and magistrates evaluating such electronic evidence in trials; prosecutors and lawyers relying on electronic evidence in conducting someone's defence; information and communication technology companies working in the field of security and digital forensics; critical infrastructure providers; academic researchers active in fields related to the collection, use and exchange of electronic evidence; and media and civil society following the latest news/case studies in the field.

As EVIDENCE strived to achieve policy and behavioural change, the strategic goal of the dissemination and stakeholder awareness activities were accordingly oriented towards obtaining support of the stakeholders and consensus among them about the project's issues and results. Soon after the beginning of the project, it became clear that while following a general approach towards dissemination and stakeholder awareness is practicable, it will not ensure the project's success or the audience's acceptance and recognition of its results.

The initially identified stakeholders turned out to be much more diverse. The project revealed a bewildering variety of stakeholders organised by sub-groups and sub-sub-groups of interests, goals, and level and depth of understanding of electronic evidence and related issues. Each of these 'new' target groups had a leader of its own who was recognised in the community and who had considerably more influence than the EVIDENCE Consortium itself.

The six different aspects of the project—legal, law enforcement, technical, standardisation, market size and data protection issues, necessitated six different methodologies of approaching the stakeholders with tangential messages and channels. Hence, the need of a new approach towards the development of a seventh, common way forward and getting all these aspects on board the same Road Map train.

The complex nature of electronic evidence also required a new approach of status quo analysis and a new interpretation of the existing taxonomies. To create a "common language" for all parties, a deep analysis and study of the electronic evidence domain was carried out along with a thorough review of existing literature, practices and standards (EVIDENCE, 2014–2016a). With the help of this semantic resource all project partners, regardless of their background and expertise, were able to 'speak' the same language referring in a unique way to concepts defined in accordance with the project's specific context. However, a new challenge arose—this new semantic structure had to be recognised and accepted by all other interested parties.

Each of the EVIDENCE streams also unveiled different needs in terms of complexity, interdependencies with other actors, processes and information, and intensity of communication with third parties.

16.3 The Way Forward

One of the most important findings concerned the special nature of the dissemination and stakeholder awareness activities within the EVIDENCE project with respect to their structure, dynamic nature and special need of attention and understanding.

To be successful in communicating the EVIDENCE results, one should appreciate the value of continuous engagement for dissemination and utilisation of project results; understand the value of 'structured' freedom in developing comprehensive dissemination sub-strategies as an integral part of the project's overall communication activities; and understand the importance of tailored dissemination tools, keeping in mind the different nature of the various target audiences. The dissemination activities require a specific set of skills and knowledge that is quite unique with respect to the other sector specific work streams. The distinctiveness of this skill set determines its different treatment compared to other research or research-related activities.

On one hand, the leading dissemination expert should be knowledgeable of the different elements of the marketing mix or of the different ways to design the set of marketing tools that the project uses to pursue its objectives in the target market (Kotler, 2000). One must fully understand the levels of marketing management decisions (also referred as the 8 Ps: product, price, promotion, place, process, people, physical environment, and performance) (McCarthy, 1964; Grönroos, 1994; Booms and Bitner, 1964; Kotler, 2012). Conversely, this should be a person with broad understanding of:

- the specifics of the different types of communication: one-to-many, many-to-one, one-to-one, and many-to-many, and how each type of communication refers to a different situation and time (both in terms of immediacy and longevity) (Doyle, 2011);
- the psychology of communication, or how the communication changes the audience's perception of the project and its decision-making processes (Ang, 2014);
- how the communication process works or how the information is shared with the intent that the receiver understands the message that the project intended to send (Business Dictionary, 2016);
- what the appropriate communication channels are, be they personal (face-to-face, person-to-person via distance, or social channels) or non-personal (print media, broadcast media, online media);
- the benefits and the downfalls of the different communication platforms and the related tools;
- the specifics of the different expertise required, i.e. digital and social communications, integrated marketing communications, creative design, event management etc.; and how to build a team based on the expertise required.

On the other hand, the leading dissemination expert should also understand the language and the specifics of the project's domain to better articulate the communication messages by tailoring the message, targeting the message to the specific audience, and using the narrative.

The leading dissemination expert is bound by the project's grant agreement in terms of both the description of activities and budget, and regardless of how the implementation process deviates, the basic activities and the finances will remain the same until the end of the project. At the same time, the leading dissemination expert should be able to provide their own internal evaluation to be able to adapt the actions taken with respect not only to the changes occurring within the project, but also with respect to the ever-changing political and stakeholders' environment.

Therefore, the EVIDENCE Consortium overthrew the general understanding of the traditional dissemination team and established a dissemination unit instead, consisting of:

- a leading dissemination expert with background in technology and law, supported by a graphic designer, a web developer and an event management expert;
- an expert knowledgeable in field of electronic evidence and related issues;
- a project management expert who is aware of the contractual and financial sides of the project and has the experience of balancing those with respect to the overall project management of budget and resources both on consortium and partner level; and
- a man-in-the-middle with specific knowledge of the political situation and the respective stakeholders influence, with the only task to bring the rest of the team back down to earth.

The main challenge was not only to organise these people to work together but, more importantly, to understand each other's specific needs of access to information, reaction time in case of an emergency, and workload and responsibilities they are carrying in the different stages of the project and with respect of the activities they are currently implementing.

The second major change was to give the separate EVIDENCE work streams a wider margin of freedom to make their own decisions on disseminating the results of their work on side events, via publications or in experts' discussions; adopting the notion of structured chaos to seek and foster constant change and innovation (Meyer and Heppard, 2000).

16.4 There Is No Persuasion Without Inspiration

In its early stages, the project adopted the understanding that the project's partners are part of its primary audience and treated them as such. Internal discussions, expressions of ideas and even feisty contradictions were encouraged to enable everyone to be able to express their own opinions and to reveal their expertise to its full potential. By creating specific communication tools available only to the project's partners and taking up on an informal and tolerant internal communication process, the consortium mastered a democratic project implementation where the individual was front and centre.

Further to this, a special sub-group of consortium members was established to form the Project Communication Team. Every partner in the consortium appointed a person from their team to serve as a Communications Representative in their country. Communication Representatives' duties and responsibilities included, among others: acting as a local direct dissemination contact point upon request; continuous identification and submission of interesting news/articles/respective links/information on the progress and/or recent development within the respective work stream/event information etc. suitable to be published on the EVIDENCE website and/or distributed via the EVIDENCE communication channels; participation and/or coordination of the other members of his/her team in project meetings and/or dissemination activities; etc. (EVIDENCE, 2014–2016b). Special Project Publicity Guidelines and Event Management Guidelines were developed to support the activities of the Communications Team and all partners' activities on national and international level.

Each team member was encouraged to express their passion and to entangle it in their activities and studies, thereby paying forward to external parties and stakeholders the inspiration driving the project. Throughout the project's implementation, it became evident that the personal attitude towards the project's activities had influence on how the stakeholders acknowledged the results of the respective group or individual's work and the level of stakeholder engagement was reciprocal to that of the group/expert involved.[1] Emotion emerged as the most important element of motivating an audience.

16.5 The Best Ambassadors of a Project Are the People, Not the Tools

In the beginning of the project, the consortium was focussed on the project implementation plan, the timely delivery of result and the quality of the project outputs. Thus, it created simple or more complex tools to foster the project implementation. The same applied to the dissemination and awareness activities: the development of a variety of tools as an initial project dissemination package was based on the strategy developed and recognised as best practice. However, later project stages proved that some of these tools are not as successful as previously expected, and in any case the tools are just that—tools. What was important were the people using them.

It was also recognised that the different project stakeholder groups required a variety of tools the development of which was estimated as much higher in terms of costs and efforts than the project could have afforded. Therefore, to keep the overall objectives of the dissemination activities (EVIDENCE, 2014–2016b) the same, i.e.:

- to keep policy makers informed about the project results in a way that enables them to realise an efficient regulation, treatment and exchange of digital evidence,

[1]Third parties' experts were involved in the actual development on the project results under WP2 'Overview and Categorization of Electronic Evidence', WP4 'Standard Issue', WP5 'Technical Issues' and WP7 'Market Size', and contributed to the WP9 'Preparing a Road Map for a Common European Framework' development. External experts also participated in the project Technical Standards Workshops, Validation and Categorization Workshops, and single-WP-dedicated events (i.e. 2-days expert meeting with Italian LEA and judicial authorities, Florence, April 2015; 2-day expert meeting on electronic evidence exchange at national and international level, Florence, July 2015, etc.).

- to inform stakeholders on the project development and encourage interactions between them,
- to establish and maintain mechanisms for effective and timely communication between partners, and
- to stimulate a debate on the specific project issues and exchange of information among stakeholders,

the EVIDENCE team utilised the most effective and universal 'tool' in their possession—the EVIDENCE experts. At the same time, the common dissemination tools such as website, visual online or print materials, events, etc. were redirected with a supporting role in the overall Dissemination and Communications Strategy, thus achieving a unique value-for-money ratio minimising the costs for what is considered 'disposable' materials.

The main resources were transferred to experts' appearances in electronic evidence related events, organisation of side-events workshops dedicated to project specific issues and organisation of experts' discussions to contribute to the main project activities towards the development of a common European framework on the collection, use and exchange of evidence.

16.6 Keep It Simple, Focused and Realistic

The EVIDENCE objectives are quite complex in their nature. They include:

- positively influencing the judges being the key actors in admitting electronic evidence and police experts holding the main position in gathering evidence;
- positively influencing the perceptions of security and reliability held by different agents by adjusting and creating national and supranational legislation;
- enhancing confidence in the experts related to the collection, analysis and conservation of electronic evidence;
- supporting training, knowledge and experience necessary and indispensable elements for experts;
- improving communication between the actors related to electronic evidence, at the national, European and international level;
- foreseeing future actions and plans to be undertaken by future policies, programs and plans, considering also the possible application, re-use and adaptation of the EVIDENCE Road Map to other legal domains different from the criminal one (civil justice, administrative justice, etc.).

The Road Map itself, being a set of guidelines, recommendations, technical standards, etc., was seen as the basis for realisation of the missing Common European Framework for the systematic, aligned and uniform application of new technologies in the collection, use and exchange of evidence.

The EVIDENCE context was so dense that the only possible solution for the consortium was to create communication messages, which are as simple as possible and contingent upon the following questions:

- What is the EVIDENCE project about?
- What is the aim of the EVIDENCE project?
- What are the major project outputs and accomplishments?
- What are the key milestones of the project?
- What would be the potential impact of the EVIDENCE Road Map?

The "keep it simple, stupid" (KISS[2]) principle is a design rule that states that most systems work best if they are kept simple rather than made complicated and that the simplicity should be a key goal when designing such a system, while the unnecessary complexity should be avoided (Dalzell, 1960; Partridge, 2007). Keeping the messages simple and focused impacts on the overall understanding of the project and its outcomes and how they are accepted by the different stakeholder groups.

Following the three main principles of communicating the EVIDENCE project (Wright and Cairns, 2011):

- communication processes must be clear and known to all Consortium partners;
- communication and dissemination of information must be purposeful and timely; and
- communication with stakeholders must be open and honest;

the project partners developed strong relationships on both personal and organisational level with different target organisations and individuals. This was achieved through persistent and focused communication aimed not just at disseminating the project's results, but also at establishing a network of professionals with a single purpose and common understanding of the problems ahead.

The messages were deliberately kept clear, simple and easy to understand with respect to the language of the target audience. The networking activities were divided between the work streams. This provided an opportunity to secure the right expert for each event: a legal, technical, law enforcement, forensics, sociological or data protection expert who is known to the specific stakeholder group and speaks their professional community's language.

Messages were tailored to the receiver. By checking the relevance and the timely manner of each message, as well as its importance to the specific group considering the narrative of the respective professional field, the speaker managed to narrow the EVIDENCE story down to the essential points that were truly significant to that group.

The effectiveness of the messages was always evaluated through the prism of expectations. It was important to create realistic understanding of the project stages

[2]For more information about the KISS principle and its origins, please refer to: http://people.apache.org/Thanik/kiss.html.

and its outputs, and not be afraid to ask for help when needed. The project's culture of honesty, openness and simplicity was greatly appreciated and particularly evident during the final project steps.

16.7 In Any Case, Stay Flexible

While the framework of a project always remains within the clauses of the contract, it is important for both the project's team and the project's supervisors to understand the specific needs as they occur. Sometimes a project activity needs more time, more resources or a change in its nature to produce the desired results or to adjust to the changes in the environment, be they legislative, technological or political.

The 'stay flexible' rule applies also to the smaller building blocks of what makes an event successful or a single news readable by the public. Adapting the situation to the project's needs and finding the best solution for each problem is a crisis management skill each project should master in time.

16.8 The Story Is More Important than the Words

Communications too often focus on finding the right words. Certainly, they are important, but what is more important is the story the project is trying to 'sell'. That is the most essential, and should always be the starting point for every project communication.

In EVIDENCE, each project presentation started with an overview of what the project is about and what it is aiming at. However, the team laid emphasis on the story, not the words themselves. Because of the complexity of the project and its goals, it was important for the audiences to understand the reasoning behind it, and the struggles it goes through; by putting a face next to each task, event, or report. Starting with clear rhetoric and adding arguments and anecdotes later on, thereby 'humanising' the project through the communication process, gave the project an advantage that was most visible in last year of its implementation, when all the efforts were building up towards the final conference and the presentation of the EVIDENCE Road Map.

16.9 Using the Narrative

Communication is always delivered in the form of a story, testimonial, or entertainment education. Each project event was organised around a problem or an idea instead of an agenda. Each participant had a pre-defined task to contribute to the overall purpose of the event itself. Using the 'structured' freedom strategy, each event session was organised by a different work stream following a framework of guidelines, thus giving the presenters and the audience a very clear message about the main point of the session and the result the group should be aiming at. Guided discussions organised as focus groups, games or informal gatherings were a common thread to all of the project meetings, be they official or informal and regardless of the size of the event.

16.10 The Competition Is Your Best Friend

The more people learn from others, who are better and smarter, the less fear and doubt will be able to prevent them from growing into a giant of their own. EVIDENCE started from nothing and irrespective of the enthusiasm and the energy, the project was far behind the established names and organisations in the field. Nevertheless, it managed to grow, and to grow big, by putting all pride aside. Teaming up with a competition organisation or a project requires time, specific knowledge and leverage, but also admitting weaknesses and sometimes taking a step backwards.

Engaging external organisations and experts in the EVIDENCE project was key to its development and further acknowledgement of its results. This was a priority from the very beginning and followed during the project implementation and beyond.

16.11 Empathy Is Key

Just knowing the project's audiences is not enough. What is essential to the communication process is an understanding of the stakeholder's interest, motivations and internal/external drivers to achieve effective dissemination and prioritisation of the information to be communicated. Stakeholders vary, they are heterogeneous, with different levels of power or interest in the project's outputs (Wright and Cairns, 2011). Although clear differences between the stakeholder categories could be identified, some stakeholder interests overlap as they are in relationship with one another. Overcoming the barriers between them or enhancing the level of integration require each member of the project's team to understand and know what the world looks like when they are in their audience's shoes. One of the reasons why EVIDENCE was so successful is because each of the project's members spoke a language that the audience understands, addressing the very same issues they are facing.

At the same time, they are not just abstract audiences, they are humans first and then experts in their field. Showing personal attitude towards the project stakeholders, especially to those that the consortium members interacts in person, is of key importance. Caring, understanding and giving back are of key importance but only if they are genuine and reflect the overall efforts of the team.

Empathy is key. Both personally and professionally. This is where one of the greatest secrets of EVIDENCE lies.

16.12 The EVIDENCE Story

EVIDENCE's main goal was to turn data into information, and information into insight; by providing a Road Map to enable policy makers to realise an efficient regulation, treatment and exchange of digital evidence; and law enforcement agencies, as well as judges/magistrates and prosecutors and lawyers practicing in the criminal field to have at their disposal as legal/technological background a Common European Framework allowing them to gather, use and exchange digital evidences according to common standards and rules.

EVIDENCE project's activities have enabled the establishment of a stable network of experts in digital forensics who communicate and exchange their opinions. The final project event, also being the first EVIDENCE annual conference, aimed to bring together different stakeholders in this network, including policy makers, law enforcement agencies, associations of judges/bars, prosecutors, lawyers, forensic experts and forensic associations, governmental organisations, civil society and academics. The ultimate goal was to encourage them to collectively share knowledge and experience, think together about issues, decision-making, and practices, and push forward recommended ways of dealing with the issues of digital evidence.

Well-aware of the fact that the field of digital evidence is ever-changing and that the technical possibilities are constantly developing, part of the EVIDENCE's task was to work on elaborating possible (legal) solutions to ensure that effective criminal investigation can take place and that European values and fundamental human rights are observed. Therefore, the main objective of this first EVIDENCE annual conference was the consultation of a Road Map outlining a desirable future technological, legal and institutional framework for the continuous development in the domain of digital evidence.

The various work streams of the EVIDENCE project studied the legal, standard, technical, law enforcement, and market and data protection status quo regarding the collection, preservation, use and exchange of electronic evidence and identified its challenges and shortcomings.

Based on the project's findings, and particularly on its challenges and shortcomings, the EVIDENCE team worked to produce a Road Map and identify the actions that must be taken for the introduction of a new technical standard on the legal, political, technical, ethical and social perspectives level. The actions include legal, political, technical, ethical and social actions, law enforcement actions and professionalisation in the field of digital forensics and further research. Based on these actions, the Road Map and an Implementation Plan were drafted to introduce and prioritise the actions required to enable a more efficient platform for the application of new technologies in the collection, preservation, use and exchange of electronic evidence.

The project's final event was organised not as a project sequel or a consecutive step of its implementation, but it represented the EVIDENCE story to the fullest. Summarising 32 months of work into 2 days and seven sessions of continuous discussions and sharing of information, the event helped audiences, which normally do not cooperate with each other, open up based on the EVIDENCE logic and findings. Even the ones hitherto unaware of the project's efforts or familiar with its outputs, managed to follow its development in time, leaping from session to session.

16.13 Conclusions

This commentary presented the EVIDENCE best practices towards successful stakeholder awareness and engagement and recommendations about mind-set changes that can be used by other policy-oriented projects to improve their dissemination and communication strategies.

The key takeaway is to always go beyond the project's framework, to look for and connect the dots within the project's ecosystem in a way that will ensure the project naturally continues its life long after its formal conclusion.

References

Ang L (2014) Principles of integrated marketing communications. Cambridge University Press, Cambridge

Booms BH, Bitner MJ (1964) Marketing strategies and organisation structures for service firms. Marketing of services. In: Donnelly J George WR (eds) Marketing of services. American Marketing Association, Chicago, IL, pp 47–51

Business Dictionary: Communication process (2016). http://www.businessdictionary.com/definition/communication-process.html. Accessed 4 Feb 2017

Dalzell T (1960) The Routledge dictionary of modern American slang and unconventional English. Based on U.S. Navy "Project KISS" of 1960, headed by Rear Admiral Paul D. Stroop, Chicago, Chicago Daily Tribune, p 43

Doyle C (2011) A dictionary of marketing. Oxford University Press, Oxford

European Communities: FP7 in Brief. How to Get Involved in the EU 7th Framework Programme for Research. Available via European Commission (2007). https://ec.europa.eu/research/fp7/pdf/fp7-inbrief_en.pdf. Accessed 4 Feb 2017

European Commission: FP7-SEC-2013-1, Topic SEC-2013.1.4-2 'Development of a Common European Framework for the application of new technologies in the collection and use of evidence'. http://ec.europa.eu/research/participants/data/ref/fp7/192060/k-wp-201302_en.pdf (2013). Accessed 4 Feb 2017

European Commission: Horizon 2020 – Work Programme 2016–2017, General Annexes. http://ec.europa.eu/research/participants/data/ref/h2020/other/wp/2016-2017/annexes/h2020-wp1617-annex-ga_en.pdf (2016). Accessed 4 Feb 2017

European Informatics Data Exchange Framework for Court and Evidence (EVIDENCE), GA. 608185 (2014–2016a). Deliverable D2.1 'EVIDENCE Semantic Structure Report'. http://www.evidenceproject.eu. Accessed 4 Feb 2017
European Informatics Data Exchange Framework for Court and Evidence (EVIDENCE): GA. 608185 (2014–2016b). Deliverable D1.2 'Dissemination and Communications Strategy'. http://www.evidenceproject.eu. Accessed 4 Feb 2017
European Union: Horizon 2020 in Brief (2014). The EU Framework Programme for Research & Innovation. Available via European Commission. https://ec.europa.eu/newsroom/horizon2020/document.cfm?doc_id=4752. https://doi.org/10.2777/3719. Accessed 4 Feb 2017
Freeman RE (1984) Strategic management: a stakeholder approach. Pitman Press, Boston
Grönroos C (1994) From marketing mix to relationship marketing: towards a paradigm shift in marketing. Manag Decis 32(2):4–20
Kotler P (1999) Marketing management: millennium edition. Custom Edition for University of Phoenix. Prentice Hall, London
Kotler P (2012) Marketing management. Pearson Education, Harlow, p 25
McCarthy JE (1964) Basic marketing. A managerial approach. Irwin, Homewood, IL (2000)
Meyer GD, Heppard KA (2000) Entrepreneurship as strategy: competing on the entrepreneurial edge. Sage Publication Inc., Thousand Oaks
Partridge E, et al (2007) The concise new partridge dictionary of slang. Psychology Press, New York, p 384
Wright G, Cairns G (2011) Scenario thinking: practical approaches to the future. Palgrave MacMillan, Basingstoke/Houndmills, p 92

Chapter 17
Systems for Electronic Evidence Handling and Exchange

Technical Issues and Findings Using a Proof of Concept Implementation

Nikolaos Matskanis, Jean-Christophe Deprez, Fabrice Estievenart, and Christophe Ponsard

Abstract The EVIDENCE project aims at providing a roadmap (guidelines, recommendations and technical standards) for realising the missing Common European Framework for the systematic and uniform application of new technologies in the collection, use and exchange of Electronic Evidence. This chapter provides insights and expert's recommendations for the roadmap regarding the software architecture design, the technologies, protocols and standards of software systems for digital evidence collection, handling and exchange. To this goal a software application and library prototypes have been developed that implement several of these protocols and have used the recommended representation language for applying a structure on the electronic evidence data, as well as metadata and for keeping the provenance of all steps of the digital forensic investigation lifecycle.

17.1 Introduction

With the growth in number and complexity of international crimes leaving trails of electronic and digital data extremely useful in building potential evidence, the judicial stakeholders are and will increasingly be challenged.

Already today, electronic and digital data trails of a single individual amount to Terabytes with a growing rate roughly doubling every 18 months. Furthermore, new technologies are developed at faster pace such as Cloud computing in remote data centres, Internet of Things with billions of sensors and connected objects deployed everywhere in the World in the next decades, 3D printing reaching laymen and

---

N. Matskanis (✉) · J.-C. Deprez · F. Estievenart · C. Ponsard
Centre of Excellence in Information and Communication Technologies, Charleroi, Belgium
e-mail: nikolaos.matskanis@cetic.be; jean-christophe.deprez@cetic.be; fabrice.estievenart@cetic.be; christophe.ponsard@cetic.be

M. A. Biasiotti et al. (eds.), *Handling and Exchanging Electronic Evidence Across Europe*, Law, Governance and Technology Series 39,
https://doi.org/10.1007/978-3-319-74872-6_17

nano-robots soon to be ingestible. Together data size and new technologies are heavily challenging the limit of the legal systems behind our democracies.

The overall process on the collection, the treatment and the exchange of electronic evidence and related information not only necessitate a harmonised legal framework but also technologies that will alleviate current tedious manual effort to follow this legal framework in transnational situation involving several types of stakeholders from LEA and judicial authorities.

This paper first provides a study of the aforementioned technological issues encountered in various European countries by exposing the overall rationale, the methods, protocols and systems used. Then it presents an analysis of the technical objectives and requirements capture for harmonising the exchange of data related to digital evidence across EU Countries. Finally, it describes the proof of concept system implementation, its technical analysis, and evaluation feedback from experts in the domain and their recommendations.

17.2 State of Practice on Systems for Electronic Evidence

As part of the Evidence project we have organised workshops and roundtable discussions dedicated to the technical issues of systems that handle electronic evidence. These events were at the premises of important European stakeholder organisations of the domain (Eurojust, Interpol, NFI) with invited experts from other European and international stakeholder organisation in digital evidence and digital forensics. In these workshops we have investigated the methodology, systems capabilities, protocols and standards used for digital evidence collection, analysis and exchange. In most cases we have found that there are systems already in place for the exchanging of digital evidence between organisations and handling metadata on the analysis of electronic evidence. These systems in most cases foresee some high-level structures for part of the investigation data and analysis but they use plain text to describe the actions of such processes and the chain of custody. Table 17.1 provides a summary of each system with the most relevant to our work technologies, features and functionality.

17.3 Analysis of Technical Objectives

The survey of the currently deployed systems described in the previous section helped us understand some of the user requirements, as well as the capabilities and shortcomings of the systems in place. The process of defining the technical objectives used the information collected from the survey as input and consisted of the analysis of the goals that the technical solution needed to satisfy for providing a digital evidence handling and exchange system. The approach followed was to use goal-oriented requirements engineering (GORE). GORE has been proven very

Table 17.1 Summary of evidence exchange and handling systems and their features and technologies used

Organisation	Tool/platform	Approach	Structuring method/standards	Transfer method/protocols	Security mechanisms/technologies
Netherlands Forensic Institute (NFI)	Hansken	Digital forensics as a service model; separation of investigation from administration	Structured document with general properties, metadata, tool output (depending on workflow used). PDF format	REST API (with web interface) service for querying the system; secure data uploading and storage service; in many cases EE storage media is brought in physically.	Data encryption at least one time, with keystore as close to the police domain as possible. Encryption for transfer and storage.
Eurojust	TESTA-NG (currently s-TESTA), EPOC IV	Dedicated network connection; cloud type of t services: public key infrastructure (PKI), video bridge, time-stamping, Secured FTP (SFTP), Secured email	EPOC IV standard: schema for structured data of judicial cases, based on NIEM schema, XML format	Secure e-mail, SFTP, secure cloud services	Dedicated network connection provided by EU with VPN, Secure email routing and package transfer, encryption of EPOC packages
Interpol	I-24/7, I-Link	Secure Interconnection of National Central Bureaus (NCBs), secure cloud services, InterPol maintained databases access	Database/application service specific	WISDM (INTERPOL Web Services for Data Management) for accessing the databases, services of the cloud and other application for exchanging information between INTERPOL and NCB	Secure network layer based on VPN tunnels over leased lines or the Internet using IPSec

(continued)

Table 17.1 (continued)

Organisation	Tool/platform	Approach	Structuring method/standards	Transfer method/protocols	Security mechanisms/technologies
Europol	SIENA, UMF	Secure Information Exchange Network Application—e-mail type of services with certain format and structure	Universal Message Format (UMF), XML based dialect for person identities, evidence item description, event description	SFTP based large file transfer, E-mail type messaging	Private, dedicated network, SIENA logs
NIEM project	National Information Exchange Model (NIEM)	Structured message exchange across all US government agencies	XML based, OGC, CAP, Codes		

effective at better understanding the scope of the problems that need to be solved, at identifying targeted goals that need to be satisfied by a new or extended solution and at structuring them in a clear and consistent way (van Lamsweerde, 2001).

The starting point or a goal-oriented analysis is to identify one or a few top-level goals that need to be achieved by a system. In this context, the term system is not restricted to being a machine or software but rather to an overall set of activities performed by various agents (or actors), which may be human stakeholders or mechanical or electronic automata. The high-level objectives targeted by the EVIDENCE project are as follows:

- Achieve a common and shared understanding on Electronic Evidence (EE).
- Achieve a common European Legal Scenario on EE.
- Achieve common perception and reliability on EE by stakeholders.
- Increase the efficiency in investigations of high-tech crimes involving EE.
- Define a criminal procedure and criminal investigation regulation (including EE) to face globalisation of crime.

A goal analysis proceeds through refinements: goals are refined into more concrete sub-goals until every leaf goal (requirement) can be assigned to a well-identified actor (or role). In this process, different alternatives can also be identified. This ability to explore different high-level design alternatives is very useful as the goal is not to attempt to provide a single rigid solution but rather various directions based on a common general technical approach. Providing a common base on which each stakeholder can build its solution seems especially appropriate to a European context where each Member State wants to keep sovereignty on how legal solutions are implemented in their jurisdiction.

Our analysis was carried out in close cooperation with the project consortium (composed of experts in IT, law both from universities, research and private sector) and several European actors such as LEA (Europol, Interpol), the EuroJust centre for judicial co-operation in criminal matters and international forensics experts like Eoghan Casey (Casey, 2011).

17.3.1 Goals Analysis

17.3.1.1 Top Level Goals

In the light of the EVIDENCE overall objectives including rationales, observations and constraints identified—represented in the top-level goals of Fig. 17.1 with an ellipse—the high-level goal is defined:

Main Goal of the Entire Investigative Process: G1 Maintain [**Efficient cooperation** *between stakeholders in transnational criminal cases involving electronic evidence to generate* **trusted** *information through the entire lifecycle of the of the judicial process*]

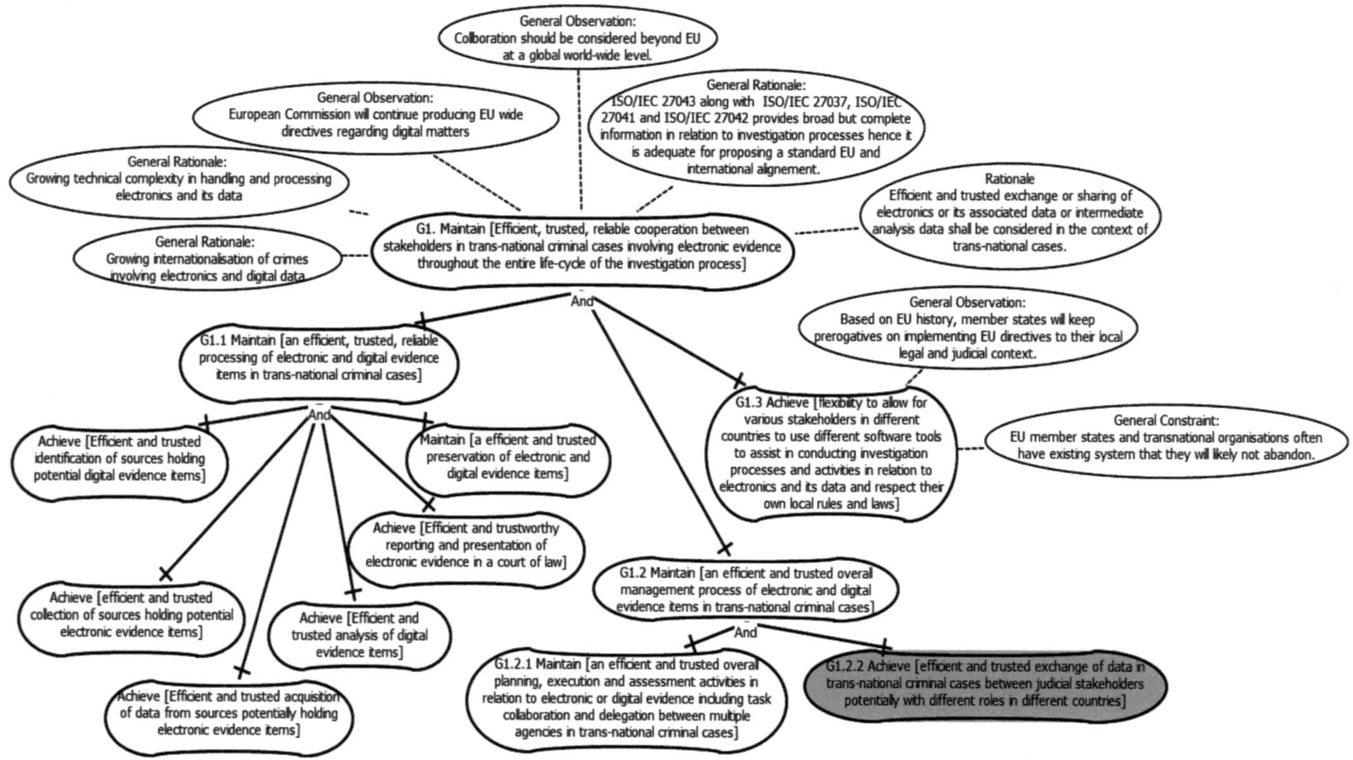

Fig. 17.1 Top level goals

As it is explained in detail in (Deprez et al. 2016), to breakdown this top-level goal, we note that maintaining an efficient collaboration between official judicial stakeholders on matters involving electronic evidence items through the entire lifecycle of the judicial process in a transnational criminal case means that:

- **It is worth leveraging existing ISO/IEC standards** on incident investigation processes and on the handling of electronic/digital evidence items, in particular (ISO/IEC (2012, 2015a,b,c,d)). Together these sets of standards provide a general but complete overview in terms of breadth on the various types of processes and activities in relation to electronic evidence. These standard processes are captured in requirement **G1.1** and its direct sub-goals.
- In parallel, **G1.3** emphasises that different systems already exist to help stakeholders to process electronic evidence. However, these systems have restricted access limited in terms of stakeholder types e.g. only for LEA officers or in term of geolocation e.g. only in a given country. These systems will continue being used and will keep their restrictive access control policies.
- In addition to each standard processes under G1.1, an effective cooperation will assume an overall efficient management process. Thus, **G1.2** indicates the need to maintain an overall efficient management process when processing electronic evidence.

Based on our review of these ISO standards and interactions with stakeholders, we have concluded that:

- G1.1 is satisfactory fulfilled by these existing ISO standards.
- The EVIDENCE project needs to focus its effort on requirement G1.2.2 Achieve [efficient and trusted exchange of data in transnational criminal cases between judicial stakeholders potentially with different roles in different countries]
- Each stakeholder consulted will not abandon existing systems in production since they satisfy many of their needs. A proposal of a globally shared EE system where all stakeholders would publish results of the investigative process is unrealistic because of lack of trust and willingness to share their systems and data.
- The alternate plausible approach to satisfy G1.2.2 together with G1.3 is to develop a means to import and export investigative data across existing systems. Stakeholders expressed efficiency and trust of the exchange process would greatly benefit if the series of actions they each performed on electronic evidence material is captured together with the investigative data.

Thus, the next section focuses on refining goal G1.2.2 on efficient and trusted exchange.

17.3.1.2 Efficient Data Exchange

The efficiency of data exchange relates to the amount of resources expended including time in relation to the accuracy and completeness with which users

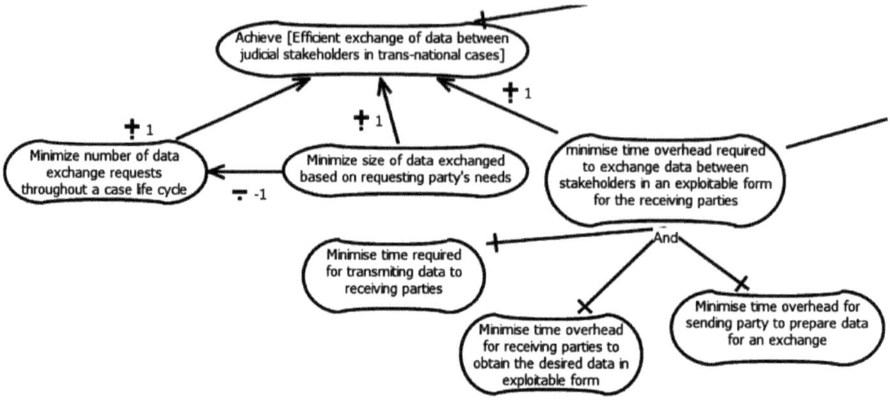

Fig. 17.2 Goal Refinement to achieve an efficient data exchange

exchange data holding or potentially holding electronic evidence. All goals related to the efficiency of the exchange and the contributing relationships are illustrated graphically in Fig. 17.2.

As depicted in the figure and described in (Deprez et al. 2016) the sub-goals of minimising the data exchanges and the dataset size that is being exchanged can reach an equilibrium of both being satisfied by performing:

- Coordination of the investigation effort from LEA and judicial actors in all countries involved. This is well addressed by Eurojust with their capability to organise coordination meetings between judicial authorities of Member States and by providing a mutual legal assistance service, named article 13. In addition, Eurojust often collaborates with Europol to perform some data forensic analysis or to invite relevant LEA agents from the EU Member States involved.
- Formulate accurately the data sought from an exchange with other actors. This is a requirement that is not fully addressed by systems in place.
- Reduce the overhead of exchange by preparing the data to exchange, while transmitting the packaged data and while unpacking the data into a form exploitable by a recipient.

17.3.1.3 Trusted Data Exchange

The trust of data exchange relates not only to the ability to guarantee a reliable data exchange means between well identified stakeholders with proper authorisation but also on the ability to obtain a complete provenance of data received from the authentic electronic source including the chain of custody and the tools used to collect, extract and analyse data up to the data received by a recipient of the exchange. A data exchange is deemed trusted if (see Fig. 17.3):

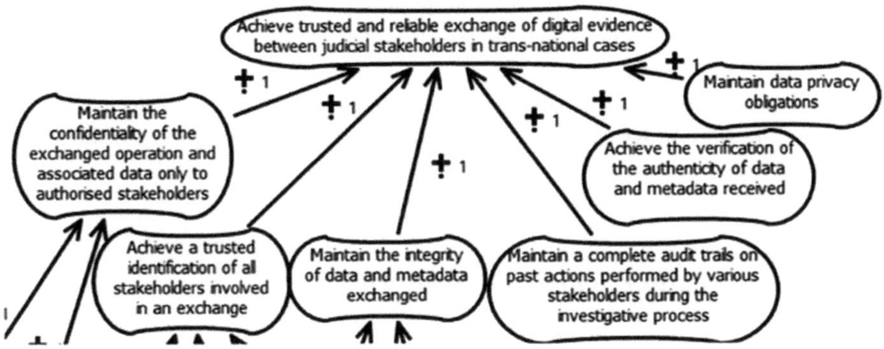

Fig. 17.3 Goal refinement to achieve a trusted data exchange

- Stakeholders are accurately identified to make sure that only trusted stakeholders can read the data
- The data exchange will only be considered reliable only if data integrity can be guaranteed when a dataset is exchanged between actors.
- There is a means to verify where the original authentic data may be found and who has access to it.
- Privacy regulations on the data exchanged are respected
- The actual exchange operation and the data exchanged must remain confidential only to authorised parties.
- Data associated to an exchange are fully auditable, in particular, a full audit trail of past investigative operations performed to obtain the data associated to an exchange is available.

While the TESTA-NG network of Eurojust and systems deployed on it, as well as SIENA network of Europol and i-Link of Interpol, meet many of the aforementioned conditions, (a) they only target one type of stakeholder, (b) lack in structure and formulation of data which has consequences in reliability and trust and (c) provide ways to verify authenticity and integrity of data. All these points are requirements for a system that is needed to provide the element of trust in exchanges between different authorities of Member States or organisations involved in the case.

17.4 Proof of Concept Application

The architecture design of the Proof of Concept (PoC) application follows the scope and objectives analysis as described in Sect. 17.3 and considers the results of the analysis of existing systems of important stakeholders (Eurojust and INTERPOL) as described in Sect. 17.2. Therefore, the PoC focuses on the metadata of the digital evidence exchange, the description and reproducibility of the analysis and the chain of custody. The aim was not to create yet another exchange or case management system, but try to fill the gaps of functional and data format heterogeneity of existing systems by using standard protocols and a semantically rich representation such as the DFAX and CybOX languages (Casey, 2015). The PoC application uses such protocols, data formats and technologies to help users produce, manage, export and import structured documents that describe the evidence exchange and handling/analysis actions.

17.4.1 Application Scope and Scenario

During our interactions with the experts at the workshops we have found useful to build and discuss a basic scenario of evidence exchange to identify what is already covered by existing systems, if there are any gaps, what tools would be nice to have for an evidence exchange scenario between authorities. We consider as basic the legal case where the requesting country sends a request to another country, which in turn acts on it and provides requested data (or devices) back to the requesting country. This scenario involves interactions and cooperation of law and law enforcement authorities from the two Member States. The basic scenario was produced based on the ISO standard procedures of evidence collection, extraction and analysis. These procedures, as well as the lifecycle phases of the Electronic Evidence investigation, are described in (ISO/IEC (2015d)). The main phases that we have used in the basic scenario are: Case preparation, Evidence collection, Evidence acquisition and Analysis. These phases are presented in Fig. 17.4 as collections of actions of actors involved in the use case with a different label for each lifecycle. The diagram below provides a use case of PoC based on the basic evidence exchange scenario.

17.4.2 Architecture

The PoC application is designed for deployment either to a distributed or centralised environment. The main benefit of a distributed architecture is the potential for broader compatibility with existing systems and platforms. The data integrity and finer control over accessing of data are the benefits of a centralised approach. In both cases the PoC is developed using web technologies, which will make it available in a variety of system environments, hardware platforms and end-user devices.

The diagram of Fig. 17.5 provides a component view of the services and interfaces of the Evidence PoC system. It also provides the type of interactions between the different components. The components Block Chain module, Document Oriented DB e-codex gateway driver and key repository, although part of the architectural design, are not implemented as part of the WP5 Proof of Concept Application and experiment. This experiment focuses on capturing the metadata of the extraction and analysis of digital evidence, as well as provides an example of

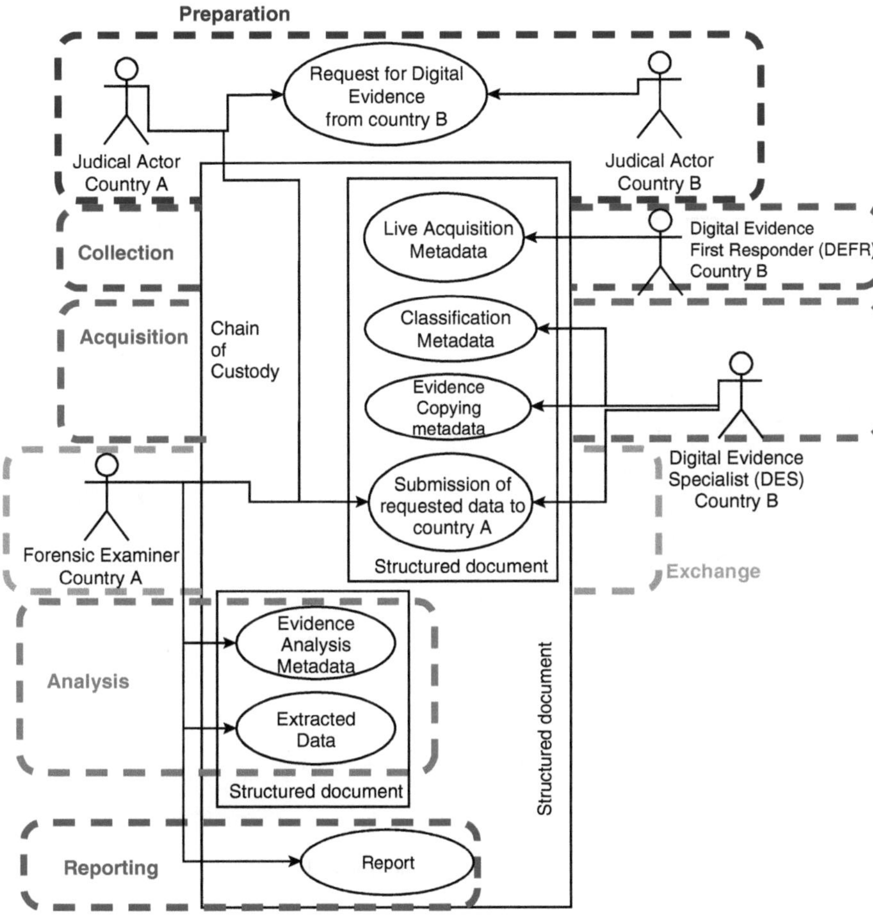

Fig. 17.4 UML use case diagram on the basic scenario with lifecycle phases

exchange and the chain of custody, but not on the distributed storage and encryption services.

The HTTP server provides the protocols for performing and receiving HTTP requests over TCP/IP. The TLS (or SSL as is better known by its previous name) component adds encryption to the messages allowing the implementation of the HTTPS protocol. The Basic Authentication component enables user password access to the system. The Web Frontend is a framework that constructs the application structure and views for the user browser and provides the interface for importing documents into the DFAX description. The user browsers connect to the services' REST API using HTTPS connections.

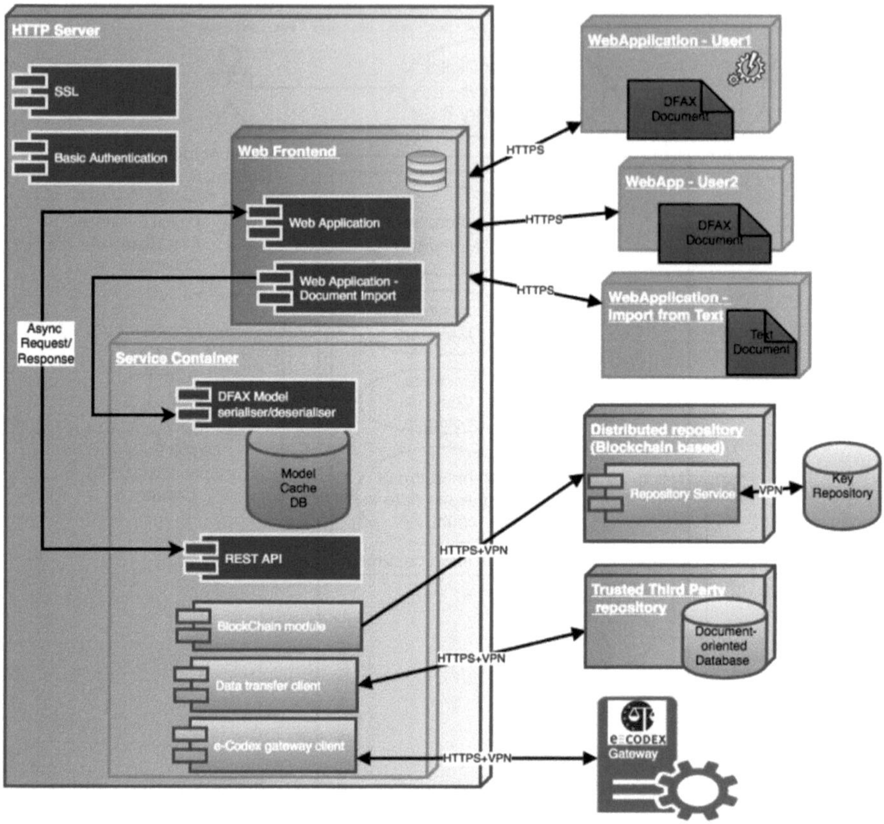

Fig. 17.5 Component diagram of the PoC services and frontend

The Service Container provides the REST API with all the services available to the user such as submit, retrieve or search for a document. The DFAX model serialiser/deserialiser component is the object representation of the DFAX XSD document and can produce XML or parse XML into objects. It validates the documents received by the users and stores them in its database for caching purposes. A component that is not in this diagram and can be part of the serialiser/deserialiser component is the DFAX Library. The library is a tool that has been developed independently (see Sect. 17.4.3.3) and will be used by the serialiser component or other open source systems. The aim of this tool is to convert output of popular forensic tools to DFAX XML format.

17.4.3 Implementation

17.4.3.1 Platform and Data Model

The Python-based MVC framework Django[1] has been chosen as the PoC Application development framework. Django is mature, very popular platform with support from a large community and is implemented using mainly the Python language. Django together with the Bootstrap framework[2] are targeting mobile first web frontends and provide compatibility to the PoC with most of operating systems, types of devices and platforms.

The persistence layer of the PoC Application is based on a relational database. The schema of this data model is provided by Fig. 17.6. The relational data model is made of tables, attributes and relations (between tables) represented by specific referential attributes called "Foreign Keys". The main concepts of the DFAX model are reflected in the structure of the underlying tables. The tables are organised hierarchically: a case is composed of several forensic actions, a forensic action is composed of several provenance records and, finally, a provenance record is composed of several observables. Case, forensic action, provenance record and observables are the four concepts that compose the backbone of the data model. They are linked together using foreign keys that are suitable to represent one-to-many (hierarchical) relationships. Because an observable can be the subject of multiple provenance records, the relation between provenance record and observable is particular and involves an extra table (evidence_record_has_observable) to represent the many-to-many relationship.

Besides those main concepts, the data model includes the notion of identity i.e. any person involved in (at least) one case and having a specific role (e.g. "examiner", "investigator", "victim" etc.). Finally, the table observable_type (resp. phase) allows the categorisation and the grouping of observables (resp. actions) according to their role in the investigation process. The data model is presented in further detail in the Annex 1 Data Model Specification section.

We choose the lightweight and simple SQLite as Database Management System of the Application PoC. However, thanks to the generic data access layer (Object Relational Mapping) implemented by the Django framework, we could easily switch to more scalable systems, such as MySQL or PostgreSQL and others[3] if needed, for performance reasons.

[1]Django Software Foundation, "Django Documentation Release 1.10.6.dev20170213221629" see https://media.readthedocs.org/pdf/django/1.10.x/django.pdf.

[2]Bootstrap front-end framework, see http://getbootstrap.com or alternatively https://en.wikipedia.org/wiki/Bootstrap_(front-end_framework).

[3]*Comparison of relational database management systems*, see https://en.wikipedia.org/wiki/Comparison_of_relational_database_management_systems.

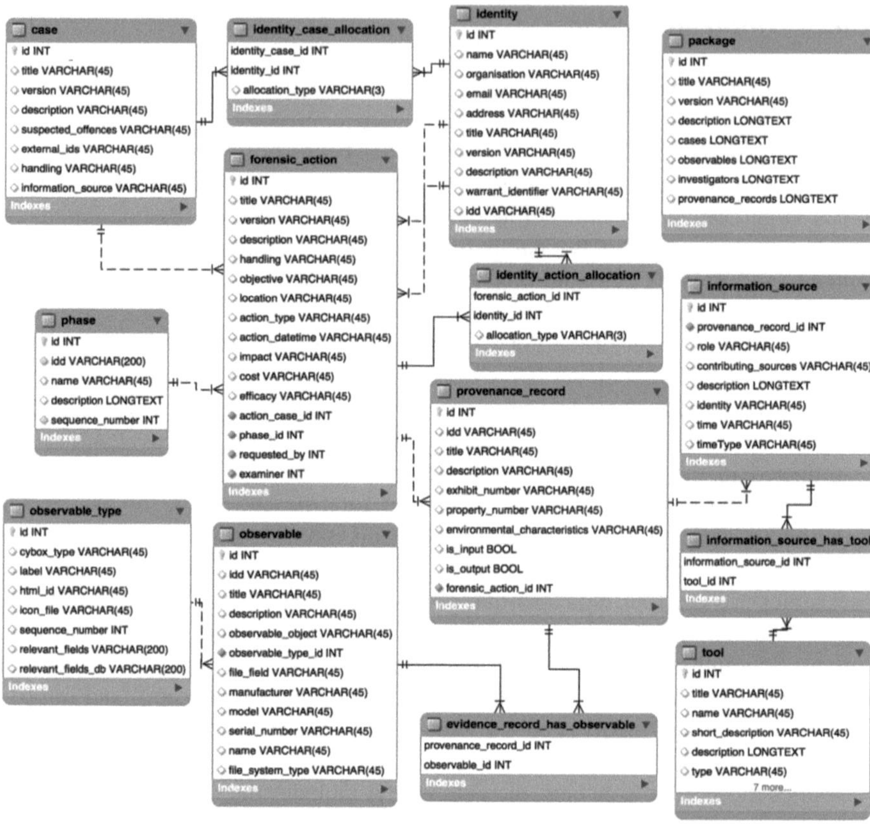

Fig. 17.6 A summary view of the data model

17.4.3.2 Application Functionality

The aim of this prototype application is to demonstrate the benefits of using standard protocols and representation language. Being such an application, its functionality is focused on features and capabilities that can be used in conjunction with or can be integrated with existing established forensic tools and case management systems.

Following the basic scenario use case that we have previously defined and illustrated in Fig. 17.4, we provide the user actions of this scenario and the respective application functionality in Table 17.2 and is illustrated at the following screen captures (Fig. 17.7).

Table 17.2 A list of the application functionalities

User action	Application functionality
Forensic examiner country A imports the case structured document with identities from case management	Importing of cases and case, identity editing operations
Forensic examiner imports output results of DES from country B	Import of forensic tool outputs in DFAX into the application
Creates further actions	Action management
Imports provenance records with observables produces by tools	Provenance record management, observables management, information source and tool management

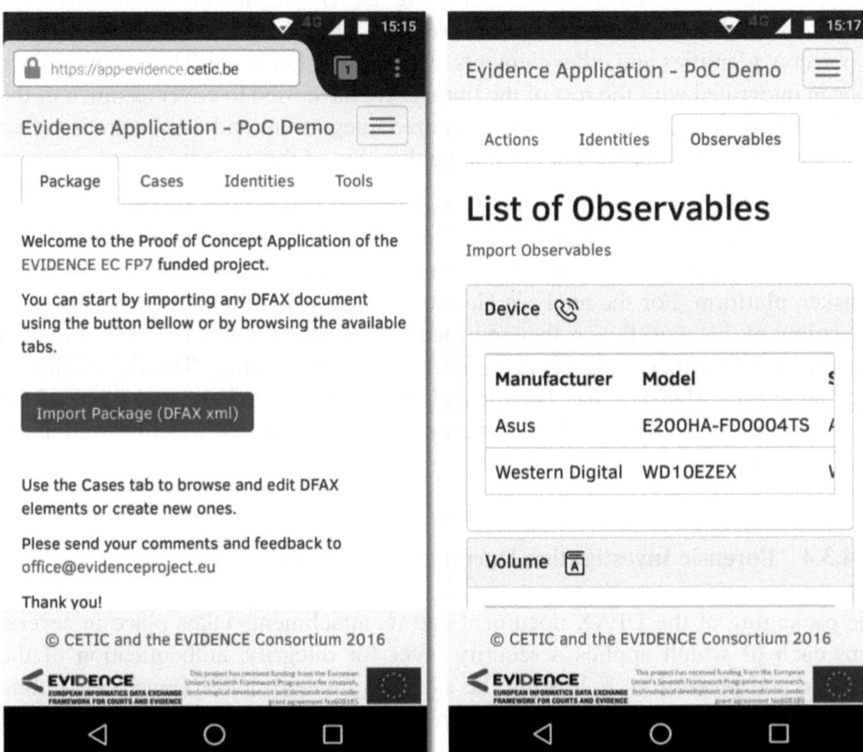

Fig. 17.7 Two views of the mobile version of the proof of concept application

17.4.3.3 DFAX Extension Library

The DFAX Library is an extension of the CybOX library[4] that was built using the python language. The aim of this library is to parse xml into python objects but most importantly to export a python object structure to DFAX xml. Both the CybOX and DFAX (Casey, 2015) libraries are designed to be integrated or be used together with other tools to generate DFAX document outputs that describe the actions and outputs of the tool users and the tool workflow and processes.

Following the CybOX library approach we have also developed the extensions using two levels of APIs:

- The DFAX binding extensions that is a low-level API that is auto-generated form the DFAX XSD schema and are used for parsing XML DFAX documents or serialising python objects to XML DFAX.
- The python "native classes" for building DFAX documents containing case elements, DFAX actions, provenance records, DFAX observables (with CybOX objects), identities and other elements of the DFAX language. These classes have been integrated with the rest of the library. We have tried to cover as much of the DFAX language as possible for the required integrations and demonstrations that we have organised or plan to hold in the duration of the project.

The DFAX library has been integrated with the Hansken system (van Baar et al., 2014) of NFI. Hansken is a platform that offers forensic tool services for digital investigation. Forensic investigators can submit their data for analysis at the Hansken platform. For the analysis Hansken is using its integrated forensic tools. The output of this workflow is then returned to the analysts and a report is compiled in a document form. This report is currently in the PDF format. The DFAX library integration with Hansken has been tested and demonstrated the exporting of the output results, as well as the documentation of the process that was followed in the DFAX language.

17.4.3.4 Forensic Investigation Document Packaging

The packaging of the DFAX document and its attachments takes place in several steps each of which applies a security layer for integrity, authentication of the message and protection. Following the standard method of the Enveloped Public Key Encryption[5] our implementation applies the following steps for securing the messages (see Fig. 17.8):

[4]https://github.com/CybOXProject/python-cybox.

[5]Enveloped Public Key Encryption in https://en.wikipedia.org/wiki/Public-key_cryptography.

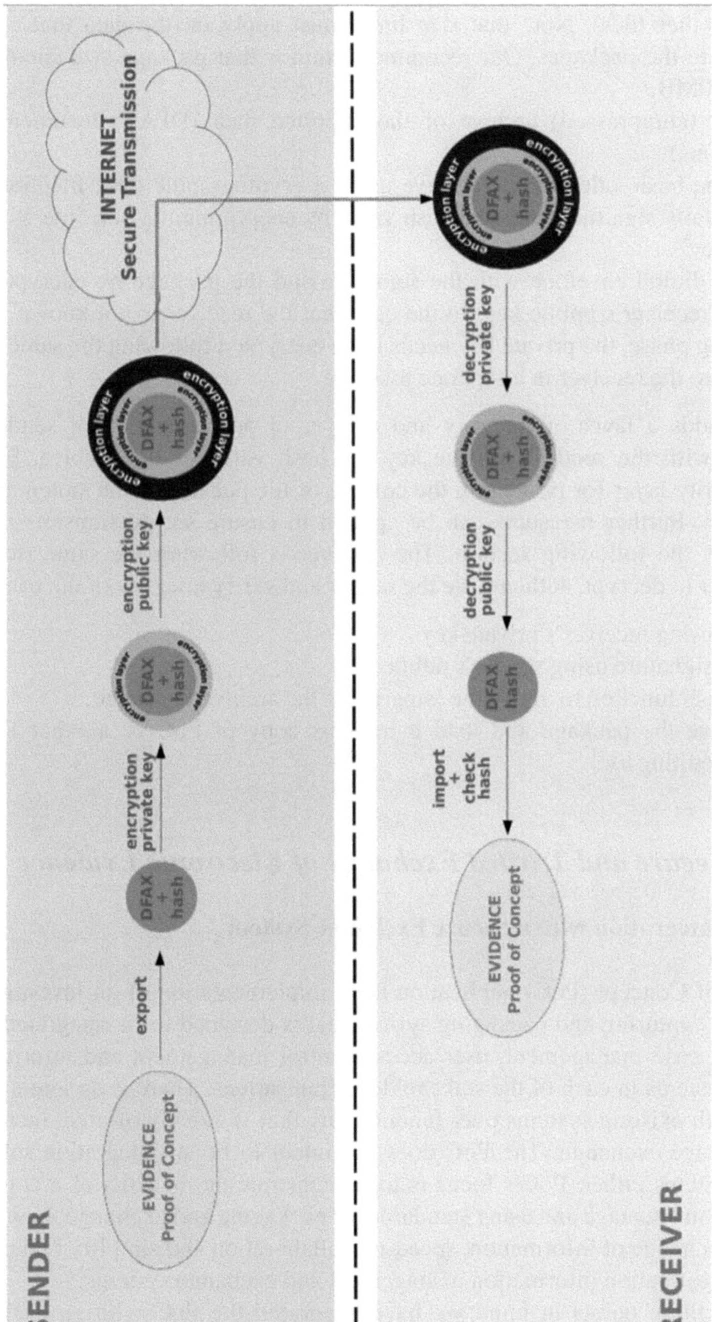

Fig. 17.8 The security layers (onion layers) of the DFAX package

- Export of the DFAX document in the XML format
- Export any imported investigation data as observable attachments (reports, images, other files). Note that size limit must apply on the data that can be attached to the packages. Our recommendation is that package size should not exceed 20MB.
- Create a (compressed) archive of the exported data (DFAX document and attachments)
- Create the hash value of the archive using a cryptographic hash function and then digitally sign the generated hash value by encrypting the outcome with the private key.
- Create a digital envelope with the signature and the package by encrypting it with the receiver's public key. In the case that the receiver is not known at the packaging phase, the private key needs to be encrypted following the same steps and sent to the receiver in a separate message.

Step 4 adds a layer of integrity and a layer of authentication of sender by encrypting with the sender's private key the hash value of the archive. Step 5 adds a security layer for protecting the content of the package to be stolen during transmission. Further measures can be applied to ensure secure transmission as explained in the following section. The receiver is following the same steps in reverse order to decrypt, authenticate the sender and verify integrity of the package:

- Decrypt using receiver's private key.
- Decrypt signature using sender's public key.
- Apply hash function to verify the integrity of the archived package.
- Un-archive the package and load it into his copy of PoC or another DFAX viewing/editing tool.

17.4.4 Secure and Trusted Exchange of Electronic Evidence

17.4.4.1 Integration with a Secure Exchange System

The Proof of Concept (PoC) application is an implementation of an investigation information capturing and packaging system that is designed to be integrated with the existing case management, user access control management and information exchange systems in each of the stakeholder organisations. There is no intention to compete with existing systems over functionality that is already offered, including secure package exchange. The PoC does not intent to be an integration solution for such systems either. PoC's focus is to demonstrate the benefits of a common representation language and using standards for packaging and exchange: how these assist the exchange of information, speed-up collaboration and simplify integration between investigation information management and exchange systems.

Keeping these points in mind we have integrated the PoC with an exchange solution for the demonstrations and Evidence project workshops. This implementation follows the trusted third- party approach and is based on a popular file

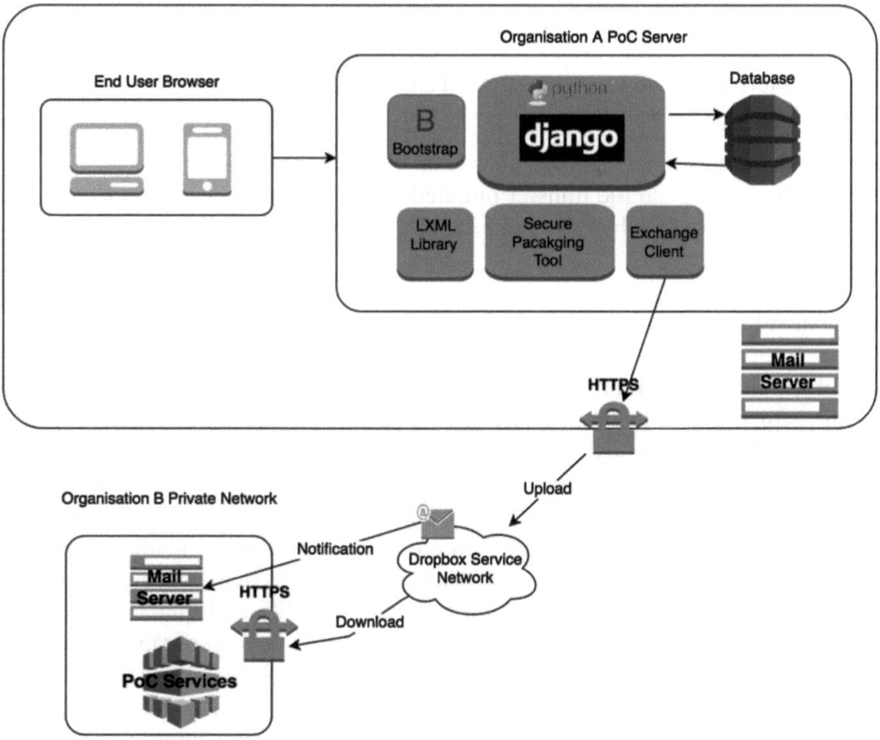

Fig. 17.9 Deployment configuration of all PoC components

sharing cloud service. The choice of this service was based on practical reasons: its popularity means that it is very likely that most of the stakeholders participating at the workshops would be familiar with it and it is a largely supported file exchange service with many tools and libraries available for using it. Figure 17.9 represents the deployment configuration of all PoC components for each side of the exchange of packages.

But using a cloud service for investigative data exchange is not the optimal solution neither particularly secure. In general, any kind of file transfer approach via an intermediate storage requires a service that is trusted, that complies with all—possibly conflicting—regulations of parties involved and can hold the data securely. As these requirements are quite difficult to implement for technical and mainly political reasons other alternatives have been examined and are described in the following section.

17.4.4.2 Alternative Exchange Approaches

The two alternatives we have investigated and discussed with experts in the domain from stakeholder organisations are

- the distributed storage approach based on block-chain algorithm[6];
- a synchronous, push file transfer initiated by the publisher of the package. Such approach is provided by the e-codex project (Pangalos et al., 2014).

Distributed Repository Approach Using Blockchain Technology

The block chain algorithm can be used between members of a group of organisations, which are collaborating in a case, to achieve distributed consensus of the DFAX based forensic analysis document and its chain of custody.

Blockchains are a new paradigm[7] that is by design allowing multiple parties to share and agree on a common view of data. They are effectively a distributed database that is tolerant to a wide range of failure, including malicious colluding actors. Blockchain, being a distributed exchange system leverages multiple machines connected by the Internet to provide reliability and quality of service: machines can be in different countries or dispersed over large geographical areas to provide failure tolerance. Many machines can assure the replication of the evidence without compromising their safety or without compromising privacy, thanks to cryptography. Cryptography allows data to be encrypted, preventing unauthorised people to read the data; encrypted data can be sent on unsecure channel (such as the internet) securely, and provide privacy and authenticity.

The decentralised nature of such exchange system removes the need for a central authority that you must trust. Because of this property, there is no possibility of censorship from one of the actor involved. Secret services of one country cannot tamper with the evidence of another country, nor censor them. Governance of the system is dictated by its members. The membership of the system can dynamically evolve and change following specific chosen rules that define how to involve a new member, or to revoke the access to the database to a current member. It is possible for one party to have multiple identities without compromising the security of the whole system: a forensic expert can be securely identified by a logical identity that cannot be linked to its real-world identity by a malicious party in the system, only when members that are given the authority to do so (e.g. a Judge) agree.

The **Sidechain** technology of blockchain allows ad-hoc creation of blockchains (see Fig. 17.10) per case between collaborating member organisations. The information in the per-case sidechain is only accessible to those members involved in the case but signatures that serve as proof of the exchanges that are taking place

[6]Blockchain distributed database system, see https://en.wikipedia.org/wiki/Blockchain.

[7]Ibidem.

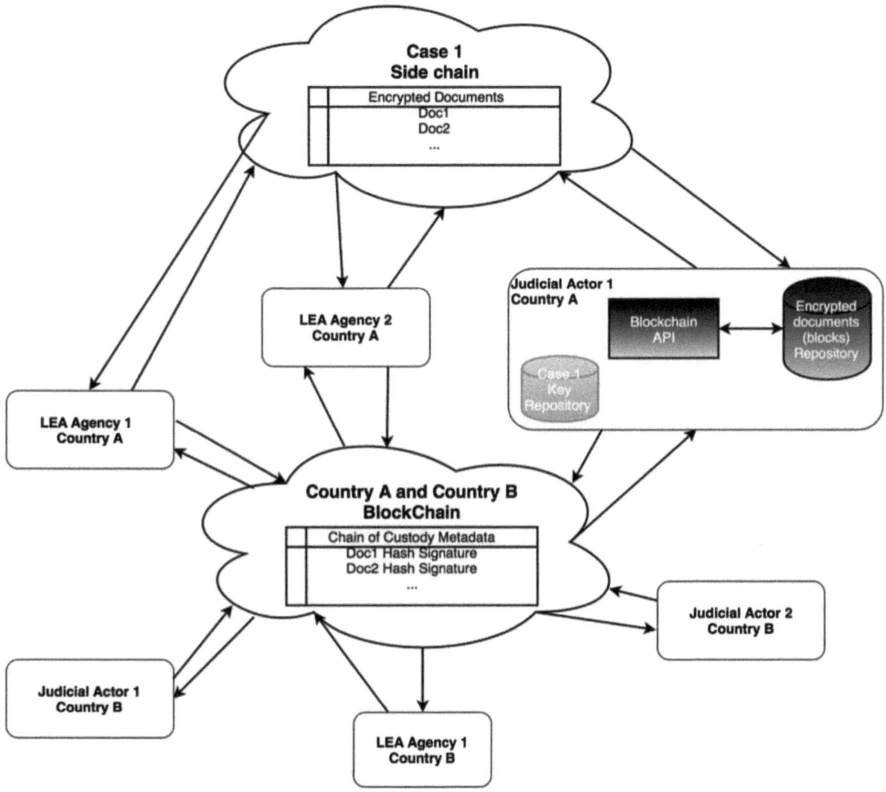

Fig. 17.10 Blockchain deployment example

in the sidechain are published in the main chain between all the collaborating organisations.

Push-Based File Transfer

A push transfer is a synchronous transfer between two peers, where the creator or owner of the data content initiates a communication channel and pushes the data to the other party of the communication. Such secure push-based net- work for collaboration between authorised organisation of EU Member States has been developed by the e-CODEX project (see (Pangalos et al. 2014)).

The e-CODEX EC-FP7 funded project has been completed in 2016. Its main goal was to improve the cross-border access of citizens and businesses to legal means in Europe, as well as to improve the interoperability between legal authorities within the EU. The e-CODEX has provided ready to use and tested solutions, which were built based on existing systems in Member States and made available for everyone without any charge. Every country can implement either all or just chosen modules and provide new functionalities for wide range of use cases (and not merely those piloted in the project). From a technological perspective e-CODEX is a multilateral, content agnostic, e-Delivery infrastructure that uses building blocks from previous large-scale projects to develop a single pan-European interoperability layer to support cross-border e-Justice services. The e-Delivery infrastructure consists of two main elements, which are the Gateway and the generic Connector framework handling the e-CODEX specific functionalities and components. Once the Gateways and National Connectors are up and running they provide the e-Delivery functionalities required to get pilots running (see (Pangalos et al. 2014)).

The Maintenance e-CODEX (Me-CODEX) (Me-CODEX, 2016) project is the follow-up of e-CODEX that aims to ensure a swift adoption and long-term sustainability of the e-CODEX platform. The main activities of Me-CODEX are:

- Outline the requirements and work of the future governance model. Manage political sensitivities.
- Offer technical support to countries adopting the platform and maintenance support to all platform users.
- Engage stakeholders and pursue awareness raising activities.
- Expand the business case around the sustainability by exploring e-justice use cases.
- Conduct regulatory checks for keeping an eye on the legislative horizon.

17.5 Conclusions and Future Work

The review of existing systems in the context and rationale of the Evidence project and the interactions with the end-users provided the necessary information to identify gaps and requirements in the exchange of evidence data. The goal-oriented analysis provided the scope and requirements of a prototype system for capturing, handling and exchanging data related to digital evidence. The main idea of developing such system was to complement existing ones deployed at stakeholder organisations and further facilitate investigation and data exchange.

The proof of concept application is designed to facilitate exactly this process as it provides a structure in documentation that guides the digital forensic investigators. Additionally—by using a structured representation language—the PoC enables serialisation of the investigation output and metadata, which makes packaging, sharing, reproducibility of results a straightforward process and in general it facilitates the exchange of digital evidence. A structure that has been approved by the forensics community helps the understanding of the package contents and speed up its processing both by users and machines. The standard representation format—an XSD schema defined XML—also facilitates the integration with the exchange mechanisms and systems in place and consequently speeds up the exchange process.

Another feature that existing systems can benefit from is the security in exchange and storage of digital investigation data. We have investigated and proposed a variety of solutions for the exchange of electronic evidence, including the use of a trusted third-party service, a distributed document repository approach, and a synchronous, push type of file transfer. These solutions have been investigated in depth and have been included in the design of the application's architecture but we have decided not to implement or strongly suggest one type of exchange solution in this experiment. We have only used the third-party approach for demonstration purposes. As each stakeholder organisation had a strong preference for its own deployed systems and would trust only known to them solutions, our position was limited to only suggest cross-organisation electronic evidence exchange alternatives and offer a demonstration of their benefits.

Our approach and solutions were demonstrated at the Proof of Concept Validation Workshop that was organised in the premises of CCBE in Brussels (September 6th, 2016) and the final Evidence project workshop that was organised in The Hague (September 29–30th, 2016). Participants of these workshops were various stakeholders and experts from the domain of digital forensics and legal domain, as well as experts of systems that collect, handle and exchange electronic evidence. The main feedback was the comments and approval of the architecture for managing and packaging electronic evidence using the representation language and the approval of the exchange mechanisms, protocols and standards that were researched and proposed by the Evidence project. Future versions of the Evidence Application will leverage on the outcome of the eCodex project, which uses Gateways for setting up push-based, synchronous communication between organisations of EU Member States participating in the platform. It will also explore how to best organise different circles of trusted partners (at different level of the hierarchy and different types of stake- holders). The Open source approach used by eCodex software in addition to the automated receipts and secure exchange, will make possible for any set of actors to establish their own circle of trust and make exchanges without any of the members of the circle needing to take the responsibility to centralise the data.

Finally, we intend to implement support of the evolving CASE standard which grew out of DFAX as described in Chap. 4 (https://github.com/CybOXProject/python-cybox)[8] and develop functionality that will support its new features, concepts and capabilities. The development efforts will also aim to increase/improve the maturity and robustness of the application and its security mechanisms for packaging and exchanging of documents.

[8]Cyber-investigation Analysis Standard Expression: https://casework.github.io/case.

References

Casey E (2011) Digital evidence and computer crime. In Forensic science, 3rd edn. Academic, London (2011)
Casey E (2015) Leveraging CybOXTM to standardize representation and exchange of digital forensic information. In: DFRWS 2015 Europe, 12, Supplement 1, pp S102–S110
Deprez JC, Ponsard C, Matskanis N (2016) A goal-oriented requirements analysis for the collection, use and exchange of electronic evidence across EU countries. In: iRENIC conference
ISO/IEC 27037:2012 (2012) Information technology – security techniques – guidelines for identification, collection, acquisition and preservation of digital evidence
ISO/IEC 27040:2015 (2015) Information technology – security techniques – storage security
ISO/IEC FDIS 27041 (2015) Information technology – security techniques – guidance on assuring suitability and adequacy of incident investigative method
ISO/IEC FDIS 27042 (2015) Information technology – security techniques – guidelines for the analysis and interpretation of digital evidence
ISO/IEC 27043:2015 (2015) Information technology – security techniques – incident investigation principles and processes
Me-CODEX: maintenance of e-justice communication via online data exchange, https://www.e-codex.eu/events/calendar/disclaimer-data-protection-and-copyright (2016)
Pangalos G, Salmatzidis I, Pagkalos I (2014) Using IT to provide easier access to cross-border legal procedures for citizens and legal professionals - implementation of a European payment order E-CODEX pilot. Int J Court Adm 6(2):43-52
van Baar RB, van Beek HMA, van Eijk EJ (2014) Digital forensics as a service: a game changer. In: Digital Investigation 11, Proceedings of the First Annual DFRWS Europe (2014), Supplement 1, pp S54–S62
van Lamsweerde A (2001) Goal-oriented requirements engineering: a guided tour. In: Invited Paper for RE'01 - 5th IEEE International Symposium on Requirements Engineering, Toronto, pp 249–263

Chapter 18
The Way Forward: A Roadmap for the European Union

Maria Angela Biasiotti, Joseph A. Cannataci, Jeanne Pia Mifsud Bonnici, and Melania Tudorica

Abstract The contributions describe the final Road Map for the realization of the harmonized framework on Electronic Evidence Treatment and Exchange. It is against a complex background that this "Roadmap" needs to be understood as it takes all challenges, including legal, operational, technical and data protection, forward and proposes ways to take action on a national and on a European level while taking into account various important aspects such as the actors involved. It is important to reiterate that no one action alone will solve the ensemble of challenges as regards the collection, preservation, use and exchange of electronic evidence. The actions need to be taken together for changes to be more effective. The Roadmap is aimed at showing the way forward for creating a Common European Framework for the systematic, aligned and uniform application of new technologies in the collection, preservation, use and exchange of evidence in criminal proceedings.

18.1 Introduction

It is against a complex background that this "Roadmap" needs to be understood as it takes all challenges, including legal, operational, technical and data protection, forward and proposes ways to act on a national and on a European level while considering various important aspects such as the actors involved. It is important to reiterate that no one action alone will solve the ensemble of challenges concerning the collection, preservation, use and exchange of electronic evidence. The actions must be taken together for changes to be more effective. The Roadmap is aimed

---

M. A. Biasiotti (✉)
CNR, Institute of Legal Information Theory and Techniques, Florence, Italy
e-mail: mariangela.biasiotti@ittig.cnr.it

J. A. Cannataci · J. P. Mifsud Bonnici · M. Tudorica
University of Groningen, Security, Technology and e-Privacy (STeP), Groningen, The Netherlands
e-mail: j.a.cannataci@step-rug.nl; g.p.mifsud.bonnici@step-rug.nl; m.tudorica@step-rug.nl

M. A. Biasiotti et al. (eds.), *Handling and Exchanging Electronic Evidence Across Europe*, Law, Governance and Technology Series 39,
https://doi.org/10.1007/978-3-319-74872-6_18

at showing the way forward for creating a Common European Framework for the systematic, aligned and uniform application of new technologies in the collection, preservation, use and exchange of evidence in criminal proceedings. The original Roadmap, as it was submitted to the European Commission,[1] was a policy brief aimed at policymakers that incorporates standardised solutions for a Common European Framework concerning the collection, preservation, use and exchange of electronic evidence to enable policymakers to define an efficient regulation for the treatment and exchange of electronic evidence. In this way Law Enforcement Agencies (LEAs), as well as the judiciary, prosecutors and lawyers practising in the criminal field may rely on a Common Framework that allows them to collect, preserve, use and exchange electronic evidence according to common standards and rules while fostering a sociological approach that is complementary to the legal, enforcement and technical approaches. The Roadmap furthermore provided a ground for further research considering that there still are areas that require further research considering that they are relatively 'young', such as virtual currencies. This chapter provides an extract of that Roadmap with an overview of the status quo of the most important challenges when dealing with electronic evidence, as well as suggestions for a way forward.

While there have been certain initiatives to bridge the gaps in the current framework of dealing with electronic evidence, including by the EU and Council of Europe, limitations remain that causes a variety of law enforcement challenges. Current national and international legal frameworks are insufficient to meet with the needs and solving the shortcomings is not merely a matter of introducing new agreements but is more complex, needing new theoretical frameworks and the collaboration of a large variety of actors. Considering the very nature of electronic evidence and rapidly evolving technologies and crimes it is important to act now and to address the challenges within the current system by realising a Common European Framework for the collection, preservation, use and exchange of electronic evidence. This framework should strike a balance between effective law enforcement on the one hand and proper protection of citizens' fundamental rights on the other hand considering that certain investigative measures that involve modern technologies can have a high impact on the suspect's fundamental rights Aulitano (2016). Especially the investigative measure that takes place in a digital environment can have a high impact on fundamental rights, as they allow for the gathering of a high volume of (personal) information through different channels.

Currently evidence is exchanged in a cross-border dimension directly from a competent authority of a Member State to a competent authority of another Member State or via international actors such as Interpol and Europol. However, there is a lack of specific rules regulating the collection, preservation, use and exchange of electronic evidence. The latter is of utmost importance considering the very nature of electronic evidence in that it may be stored or located anywhere in the world. Traditional means for international cooperation in crime prevention and

[1]EVIDENCE project, Deliverable 9.2—Roadmap.

prosecution are no longer sufficient, considering this nature of electronic evidence. There is furthermore an emerging need for a common language or terminology to be used in all relevant activities within Europe. Rules and cooperation for the management of electronic evidence are necessary to re-conceptualise evidence location including issues concerning direct access to extraterritorial data by law enforcement authorities as an increasing number of crimes involve geo-distributed electronic evidence, not only for cybercrime but for all crimes in general. Traditional means for international cooperation in crime prevention and prosecution are not sufficient for a timely response for obtaining volatile electronic evidence. When it comes to the exchange of electronic evidence, further cooperation is necessary. Considering the volatile nature of electronic evidence, broad security perspective and collaborative investigation activities between the different actors are necessary within the Common European Framework. Internationally agreed mechanisms for preservation, supply and exchange of electronic evidence in criminal matters must be strengthened and evidence management by means of ICT needs to comply with national laws for the evidence to remain authentic and trustworthy and to be admissible in national courts.

18.2 Status Quo

The collection, preservation, use and exchange of electronic evidence can be analysed from different perspectives, including legal, operational, technical, and data protection, while bearing in mind sociological and other relevant aspects. All perspectives taken together are necessary to improve the current way of handling electronic evidence in Europe and beyond. The EVIDENCE project analysed the status quo concerning the collection, preservation, use and exchange of electronic evidence and identified many complexities in the current system of handling electronic evidence. This includes legal gaps, realities and difficulties law enforcement is faced with, evolving crimes, evolving technologies and technical challenges, the enormous number of actors involved and trustworthiness, ethical issues, data protection issues, practical challenges such as authorisation, chain of custody and documentation, etc. The challenges in the current way of handling electronic evidence are addressed in the Roadmap.[2] An extract of the status quo analysis is provided in this paragraph.

18.2.1 Law and Policy

The introduction and extensive use of ICT has generated new forms of crimes or new ways of perpetrating them, as well as new types of evidence. Although all kinds

---

[2]EVIDENCE project, Deliverable 9.2—Roadmap.

of evidence must be handled according to criminal (procedural) laws, the 'new' types of evidence need additional and specific ways of handling to maintain the authenticity and integrity of the electronic evidence. The very nature of data and information held in electronic form makes it easier to manipulate than traditional forms of data. When acquired and exchanged the integrity of information must be maintained and proved, i.e. demonstrated that the electronic evidence has not been altered since the time it was created, stored or transmitted. Legislations on criminal procedures in many European countries were enacted before these technologies appeared, thus not considering them. Therefore, the handling of electronic evidence, as well as the exchange between EU Member States jurisdictions, are based on different criteria and uncertain, not harmonised procedures. What is missing is a Common European Framework to guide policy makers, LEAs and legal authorities when dealing with electronic evidence handling and exchange. There is a need for a common background for all actors (policy makers, LEAs, judges, lawyers) involved in the electronic evidence lifecycle, including a common legal framework and standardised procedures regulating the collection, preservation, use and exchange of electronic evidence.[3]

European legislation adds important value to the national legal systems, creating a common framework to prevent and ban crimes, considering that the most serious types of organised crime are committed across borders. It furthermore makes the fight against crime more efficient by adopting minimum standards in the criminal field, as well as in the cybercrime area. It thus strengthens the importance of a common effort in preventing and combating crime, especially cybercrime, by creating a common framework to foster and improve cooperation between states. Many guidelines and technical standards have been produced by LEAs, (European) institutions and (national) policy makers. These guidelines and standards are aimed at providing support and guidance in handling and examining electronic evidence. Many guidelines and best practices answer the need for LEA personnel to acquire necessary competencies and knowledge to fill the gap of standardised procedures across agencies, as well as the lack of specific legislation governing the collection, analysis, preservation, use and exchange of electronic evidence.[4] These legal instruments and guidelines are however a patchwork of documents and no comprehensive international or European legal framework relating to (electronic) evidence exists. Parties involved rely on national law when it comes to the collection, preservation, use and exchange of (electronic) evidence, which makes dealing with electronic evidence internationally difficult. Moreover, national criminal laws have been written ages ago, long before there was such a thing as the internet and modern technologies, which could provide electronic evidence. While it is true that some countries have adapted their legislation to address technological developments, others rely on traditional laws and apply them to electronic evidence as well. There are thus big differences in national legislation and approach. Evidence

[3]EVIDENCE D2.1 EVIDENCE semantic structure, pp. 11, 15.

[4]EVIDENCE D2.1 EVIDENCE semantic structure, p. 20.

rules vary considerably even amongst countries with similar legal traditions. In certain countries traditional investigative powers might be general enough to apply to electronic evidence while in other countries traditional procedural laws might not cover specific issues regarding electronic evidence, making it necessary to have additional legislation. In certain countries there are defined rules as to admissibility of evidence in Court while in other countries admissibility is flexible. In all cases legislation requires a clear scope of application of powers and sufficient legal authority for actions.

While there is no comprehensive international or European legal framework relating to electronic evidence, several international and European legal instruments and policy documents are relevant to electronic evidence. This includes the European Union (EU) legal framework and guidelines, but more importantly the legal instruments and documents by the Council of Europe. In cybercrime, the Council of Europe's instruments are the legal framework of reference for combating cybercrime. The Council of Europe Convention on Cybercrime[5] (Cybercrime Convention) remains the main (and only) international treaty that defines the substantive elements that lead to some cyber activities to be classified as crimes; and which has procedural provisions that allow for the prevention, detection and prosecution of these activities. Although electronic evidence may not necessarily result from cybercrime, this is the main framework for reference in this area that offers many provisions to enhance investigations where electronic evidence is involved. The development of new communication and information systems in criminal justice and their use in most of individuals' daily activities has transformed the processes of information and evidence exchange. The increasing production of electronic data because of this widespread use of ICTs, but also the use of new technologies in the commission of old and new crimes (cybercrimes), contribute to make the collection and exchange of electronic evidence increasingly relevant in national criminal justice. This evolution and the gradual digitisation of the means necessary to collect and analyse electronic evidence has not been accompanied by a consistent and uniform evolution of the legal frameworks across Europe. Different rules and practices regarding the collection, preservation, use and exchange of electronic evidence exist in the European countries.[6] Given the increasing use of digital devices in daily activities the attention for electronic evidence in the European and national legislation is expected to increase. To prevent more fragmentation and even more different rules and practices it is necessary to address the issue as soon as possible and to go for a more harmonised approach to facilitate international cooperation in cross-border crimes.

Major challenges and shortcomings of the legal frameworks within the EU Member States, which include legal and data protection issues, problems with law enforcement, particularly concerning cross-border cases when evidence needs to be collected abroad or exchanged with competent authorities from another jurisdiction, and technical issues concerning training and technical capabilities. Effective leg-

[5]Convention on Cybercrime [2001] ETS 185.

[6]See EVIDENCE Deliverable 3.1—Overview of existing legal framework in the EU Member States.

islation and law enforcement should include an effective legal framework, access to investigative tools and techniques, training and technical capabilities and best practices policies that ensure proportionality between the protection of privacy and infringements for legitimate crime prevention and control.[7]

18.2.2 Data Protection

In a digitalised world, the use of electronic evidence becomes increasingly important in criminal proceedings. To effectively prosecute a crime, LEAs must adapt to this situation by working with the electronic evidence generated by the ubiquity of these new technologies and by using digital technologies themselves to collect evidence. Those investigative measures can have a high impact on the suspect's fundamental rights, especially in a digital environment, which allows collecting (personal) information through different channels. Consequently, there must be a balance between effective law enforcement on the one hand and proper protection of citizens' fundamental rights on the other hand. A European legal framework comprehensively addressing data protection issues related to the collection of electronic evidence does not exist. There is a need to include specific safeguards in current legislative frameworks to address the shortcomings. A Common European Framework should set up a minimum standard of privacy safeguards to be established in relation to the use of certain means of collecting electronic evidence. It should furthermore include a definition of electronic evidence, which could act as a basis to regulate certain investigative measures that were identified to have an effect on privacy related fundamental rights and establish technical standards and non-binding guidelines for the use of electronic technologies, which could be developed by a future high-level expert group being set up by the EU. From a data protection perspective, a Common European Framework should also seek to set-up rules on minimum data protection standards that must be met during the life-cycle of electronic evidence. This applies to both privacy safeguards and data security safeguards, particularly safeguards against alteration of electronic evidence. Non-binding guidelines regarding privacy safeguards and data security rules on a practical level are necessary to assist achieve an adequate level of data protection.

18.2.3 Actors

Fragmentation does not only exist in the legal framework, but is also reflected by the vast number of actors involved. On an international level there are several actors

[7]For more information on the legal status quo see: EVIDENCE Deliverable 3.1—Overview of existing legal framework in the EU Member States and EVIDENCE Deliverable 3.2—Status quo assessment and analysis of primary challenges and shortcomings.

involved, such as Interpol, Eurojust, Europol and its EC3 cybercrime centre and Joint Cybercrime Action Taskforce (J-CAT), CEPOL and ENISA. However, when we look at national level the number of actors involved in one way or another becomes numerous. Certain public and private actors and actors providing technical solutions and assistance have a direct interest in electronic evidence. These are process actors who make up the supply and demand for technologies and services and context actors who play an indirect role in electronic evidence in a broader political, social or economic context. Process actors include LEAs, SIS, the judiciary, digital forensic experts, etc. Context actors include international organisations and legislative bodies, research organisations, human rights organisations, the media, etc. One of the challenges, considering this vast number of actors involved, is that actors are not always in agreement considering the different interests involved and that the actors do not always coordinate with each other. Research further shows that there is a general mistrust within the judiciary that generally comes from a lack of necessary knowledge and competencies and a lack of professionalisation concerning digital forensics. Because of the (potential) global nature of electronic evidence, cultural differences in dealing with electronic evidence may also provide a challenge for law enforcement. These challenges can be addressed by mandatory training and education, certification, building bridges between the private and public sector, raising awareness, validation of tools, investing in digital forensic tools, etc.[8]

18.2.4 Law Enforcement

The challenges law enforcement is faced with, which are plentiful, are mostly legal challenges considering that LEAs are left to operate in a field of patchwork solutions, particularly concerning cross-border access to data, data retention, etc. While industry continues to push boundaries, LEAs are left playing catch up and manoeuvering their way through a highly uncertain and politically sensitive landscape filled with legal lacunae. Among other things, in an increasingly globalised online environment, the collection and exchange of electronic evidence is hampered by outdated and lengthy mutual legal assistance practices no longer adapted to today's realities. Legal lacunae hamper international law enforcement cooperation. For example, the invalidation of the EU Data Retention Directive, as well as a lack of international consensus regarding cross-border access to data, has led to quite some uncertainty for law enforcement investigating crimes in the online environment. The need for modernisation efforts in the field of international police and judicial cooperation are therefore necessary. The legal lacunae mostly need to be addressed

[8]For more information on the 'market' (actors, obstacles, facilitating factors) see: EVIDENCE Deliverable 7.1—Report on prima facie size of the market; EVIDENCE Deliverable 7.2—Map on obstacles and facilitating factors before validation and EVIDENCE Deliverable 7.3—Workshop Mapping obstacles and facilitating factors after validation.

by legal solutions. However, apart from legal solutions, professionalisation in the field of digital forensics is necessary. Digital forensic practitioners have expressed an interest for their field of expertise to reach a similar level of professionalism and recognition as, for instance, the field of DNA analysis. This would, however, require a reassessment of the potential regulation of digital forensics professions to ensure that practitioners meet a certain standard. Furthermore, as these practitioners often rely on automated digital forensic tools for the acquisition and analysis of electronic evidence, these tools should ideally be subject to validation procedures to ensure that they are fit-for-purpose. Lastly, there are currently no universal standards particularly applicable to digital forensic labs. Thus, it is also worth considering the development of an accreditation procedure to ensure digital forensic labs meet certain pre-determined quality levels across Europe.

As law enforcement is not the sole actor within the electronic evidence domain, the importance of 'building bridges' between LEAs and other stakeholders, including the public, policymakers, the private sector and the judiciary cannot be understated. Therefore, collaboration between LEAs and these other stakeholders also needs to be addressed. Particularly towards the public, that entrusts LEAs with the powers and resources to fulfil their mandate, LEAs should continue to expand their efforts in increasing transparency and accountability regarding their activities and spending. By providing statistics and documented case examples of law enforcement activities and needs, LEAs can provide the evidence-basis for an informed public debate upon which policymakers can, in turn, base their decisions. Furthermore, LEAs are increasingly confronted with evidence that has been collected and analysed by others stakeholders, particularly private companies, other public sector entities and citizens. LEAs will need to continue developing best practices in recognition of the fact that trustful collaboration with other actors is of essence in this field. Finally, as the examined cases and the evidence collected by LEAs is aimed to be brought before court to prosecute wrongdoers, the technical competences of prosecutors and judges to understand the electronic evidence process are also key. LEAs should aim to further strengthen their communication channels with those in the justice system, as this can contribute to enhancing the understanding of digital evidence within the judiciary, thereby potentially also alleviating LEAs from unnecessarily burdensome analysis requests.[9]

[9]For more information on the law enforcement status quo see: EVIDENCE Deliverable 6.1—Overview of the existing mechanisms and procedures for collection, preservation and exchange of electronic evidence by law enforcement agencies within the European Union and beyond; EVIDENCE Deliverable 6.2—Status quo assessment and analysis of primary challenges and shortcomings and EVIDENCE Deliverable 6.3—Identification of best practices and guidelines to be integrated into a comprehensive European Framework.

18.2.5 Technical Standards

The EVIDENCE project provided an overview of existing standards for the treatment and exchange of electronic evidence, also considering tools that are thoroughly tested and generally accepted in the digital forensics field in the EU Member States context. In this regard the lifecycle of electronic evidence and the main processes of the investigation phase in which a potential electronic evidence is identified, collected, and acquired and then safely preserved were mapped. Based on this map, a Digital Forensic Tools Catalogue was developed, which can become a point of reference within the forensic community, that will allow forensics experts to determine the most suitable tool for their case and to identify a similar or comparable tool for conducting a dual-tool validation.

The EVIDENCE project furthermore provided an overview of existing procedures for exchanging electronic evidence at national and European levels and proposed a standard for representing data and metadata involved in the exchange process and formal languages for their representation and it introduced a cloud platform for implementing the exchange process, listing the main features that this platform should have and putting the focus for a desirable integration with other existing platforms already in place and managed by international or European public bodies.

The EVIDENCE project finally produced and implemented a Proof of Concept (PoC) application on the electronic evidence exchange, persistence and support for maintaining a detailed chain of custody. The proposed architecture follows the reasoning of the goal-oriented analysis and considers the results of the analysis of existing systems of important stakeholders (such as Eurojust, Europol and INTERPOL). The implementation of the PoC (application and library) is designed to fill the gap of capturing the investigation actions performed during the lifecycle of a judicial case. The PoC facilitates this process by providing a structure that guides the forensic investigators and a representation language that enables serialisation of the investigation metadata, which also means packaging, sharing, reproducibility of results and in general facilitating exchange of electronic evidence. Additionally, using a structure representation language that has been approved by the forensics community would facilitate the integration of this technology with electronic evidence exchange mechanisms and systems in place. The aim of the PoC is not to replace or attempt to compete with existing systems, but rather to fill the gaps of functional and data format heterogeneity of existing systems by using standard, semantically rich protocols such as the DFAX language.

One of the main challenges is that the electronic evidence exchange standards needs the involvement of the different stakeholders to be a success. From a strictly technical point of view, it is important to convince actors in forensic tools development to extend or adapt their software to this news standard.[10]

---

[10]For more information on the technical status quo see: EVIDENCE Deliverable 4.1—Overview of existing standard for treatment and exchange of electronic evidence; EVIDENCE Deliverable

18.3 Strategic Goals

Based on the challenges and shortcomings concerning the collection, preservation, use and exchange of electronic evidence as mentioned in the previous paragraph and in the previous chapters strategic goals can be drafted for realising a Common European Framework for the application of new technologies in the collection, preservation, use and exchange of electronic evidence. These strategic goals include further research, enhancing legislation, enhancing law enforcement and professionalising digital forensics, enhancing technical standards and enhancing trust among actors and stakeholders. These goals or objectives are reflected below and can be taken forward to identify actions to be taken for realising the Common European Framework within a Roadmap. Actions include regulatory action, non-legislative measures and challenges that require further reflection, which must be addressed by a variety of actors.

18.3.1 Enhancing Legislation

One of the major objectives of the Roadmap is to enhance the legal framework. An enhanced legal framework will not only provide a legal basis and thus more clarity, but it will also improve law enforcement considering that many of the law enforcement challenges must be addressed primarily through legal action. Research showed that there is no comprehensive legal framework, no legislative harmonisation, but instead, a patchwork of legislation implemented differently among Member States. Existing legislation does furthermore not address the specific aspects of electronic evidence, which is aggravated by rapidly developing technologies, leaving legislation lagging behind. Certain issues, such as investigations in the cloud, are not regulated at all or not sufficiently regulated. This may cause legal and practical uncertainty, but also problems with (international) cooperation and law enforcement. The application of general rules of evidence may not always be sufficient in the collection, preservation, use and exchange of electronic evidence because of the specific nature of electronic evidence. A legislative framework should include clear and precise legal basis, uniform definitions, concepts and standards, best practices policies that ensure proportionality between protection of privacy and infringements for legitimate crime prevention and control, and will facilitate a more efficient cooperation. Legislation requires a clear scope of application of powers and sufficient legal authority for actions. Legal action requires, primarily, political will and commitment, which is why most of the legal actions also require political

4.2—Status quo assessment and analysis of primary challenges and shortcomings; EVIDENCE Deliverable 5.1—Technical specification document and guidelines; EVIDENCE Deliverable 5.2—First evidence exchange application prototype; EVIDENCE Deliverable 5.3—Workshop results and final technical specification document and guidelines.

action. The Roadmap consists of recommendations to build, improve and strengthen existing legislation in the field of electronic evidence to enhance legislation.

18.3.2 Enhancing Law Enforcement and Professionalising Digital Forensics

The second major objective of Roadmap is to enhance law enforcement, including professionalisation in the field of digital forensics. While most of the law enforcement challenges, which are plentiful, would primarily find a solution through legislative action, there are several actions that must be taken within the LEA community and the digital forensics community. Law enforcement needs to, among other things, provide feedback and input, both quantitative and qualitative, for legislation and guidelines to mitigate the negative impact of legislation to make investigations more efficient and effective. Enhancing law enforcement also includes professionalising the sub-discipline of digital forensics to achieve a certain level of professionalism and recognition within this young field. Regarding digital forensics, there is a call for achieving a certain level of professionalism and recognition. While certain practitioners might fear that standardisation efforts may hamper innovation, there is a consensus that this is only the commencement phase of a lengthy standardisation process. Professionalising digital forensics requires a reassessment of the potential regulation of digital forensics professions to ensure that practitioners meet a certain standard. These practitioners often rely on automated digital forensic tools for acquisition and analysis of digital evidence. Therefore, these tools should be subject to validation procedures to ensure they are fit-for-purpose. Furthermore, there are no universal standards particularly applicable to digital forensic labs. The development of an accreditation procedure to ensure digital forensic labs meet certain pre-determined quality levels would aid in achieving a universal standard. The Roadmap consists of recommendations to build, improve and strengthen existing procedures and law enforcement to enhance law enforcement and professionalise digital forensics. Professionalisation of digital forensics includes regulation and certification of the profession and training, validation of digital forensic tools, accreditation of digital forensics labs and building bridges between different actors. Improving and strengthening law enforcement includes collaboration with the public, policymakers (increasing transparency and accountability), the private sector, the judiciary and eventually modernisation of international cooperation (coordinated operations and JITs, digitisation of MLA and modernisation of international law).

18.3.3 Enhancing Technical Standards

A Common European Framework for the application of new technologies in the collection, preservation, use and exchange of electronic evidence cannot be effective without enhancing technical standards. The Roadmap includes recommendations for a standard electronic exchange platform and language to represent a wide range of forensic information and processing results that is becoming an essential need in the forensics community. This includes a standard for representing data and metadata involved in the exchange process and formal languages for their representation. It also introduces a cloud platform for implementing the exchange process, which includes features such as cryptographic control and malware protection. The use of the standard DFAX, that leverages CybOX and the Unified Cyber Ontology, is recommended for representing metadata and describing in a detailed way all technical and legal forensic information. Presently, the DFAX and the related formalisms are not developed sufficiently, however, they have been designed for focusing on the extensibility and are therefore adaptable for covering all possible information needs for representing forensics investigations.

18.3.4 Enhancing Trust

Enhancing legislation and law enforcement cannot take place without support from all the actors involved. Challenges such as mistrust, security and cultural differences would stand in the way of implementation. The Roadmap therefore also includes supporting action from an ethical and social perspective to create awareness among actors, provide training of actors, etc. to enhance trust in and within the judiciary. The Roadmap consists of recommendations to build, improve and strengthen trust in and among judicial actors.

18.3.5 Further Research

Certain areas require further research before any action can be taken. More knowledge, for example, about (but not limited to) crypto-currencies, the Internet of Things and cloud computing is necessary before proper legislative and other measures can be taken in this regard. The final major objective of the Roadmap therefore is conducting further research and considering the results within a Common European Framework. Few areas have been identified by the EVIDENCE project as requiring further research. This includes constitutional limitations. Different constitutional traditions of the Member States lead to divergent implementation of international legislation and application of privacy and data protection principles. For better implementation of EU legislation, further insight in the constitutional traditions in the 28 Member States is required. Further research also needs to be conducted about data retention legislation in the Member States after the annulment of Directive 2006/24/EC by the Court of Justice of the EU (CJEU). Rules and procedures are mostly applied by LEAs. Input from this very important actor on how laws negatively impact investigation and prosecution, how severe this impact is and how frequently it occurs is therefore very important to improve investigative techniques procedures and rules. Once there is a better understanding of these issues, legislation and policies may be developed more fit-for-purpose. The Roadmap consists of recommendations for further research.

18.4 Roadmap

The original Roadmap can be seen as a policy brief to guide law- and policymakers, law enforcement and other stakeholders when dealing with electronic evidence. This paragraph provides an extract of this Roadmap for realising a Common European Framework for the collection, preservation, use and exchange of electronic evidence, which is of the utmost importance considering the growing variety of electronic evidence used in criminal trials across the globe. If we want to realise this Common European Framework certain strategic goals or objectives must be met, including, amongst other things, enhancing law enforcement and enhancing the legal framework as discussed in the previous paragraph. These objectives can be met by providing solutions or actions for addressing certain challenges on a short, medium or long term. The objectives are interconnected and can be reached by fulfilling a minimum set of requirements, which will provide output (legislation, guidelines, etc.) generated by certain actors. By interconnected, we mean that no one action alone will solve the ensemble of challenges concerning the collection, preservation, use and exchange of electronic evidence. The actions must be taken together for changes to be more effective. Furthermore, all actions, whether they are short, medium or long term, need to start simultaneously and feed into each other while certain actions are expected to finish sooner rather than others, meaning on a short, medium or a term. By addressing the challenges by taking the actions suggested in the Roadmap, the objectives will be met and the Common European Framework for the collection, preservation, use and exchange of electronic evidence will be realised. Figure 18.1 shows that the solutions provided on a short, medium and long term will feed into each other and together will form the Common European framework for electronic evidence.

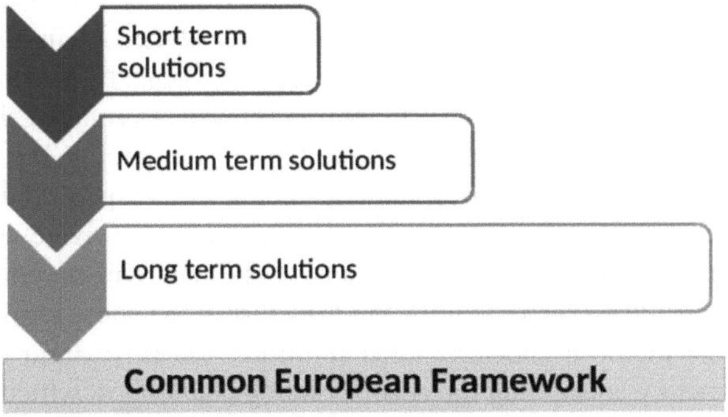

Fig. 18.1 Short, medium and long term solutions for the Common European Framework

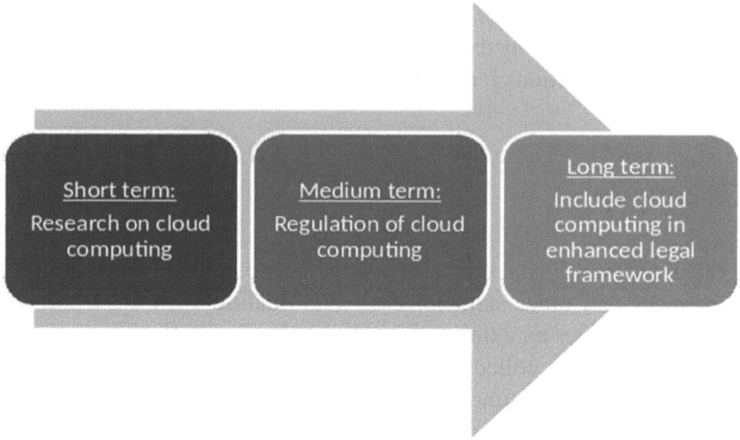

Fig. 18.2 Short, medium and long term solutions for addressing cloud computing issues

One might wonder why certain objectives and challenges are repeated on multiple levels, i.e. on a short, medium and long term. For example, 'enhancing law enforcement' is a short term, as well as a long-term objective. While the overall objective is indeed enhancing law enforcement, this may be achieved by a variety of solutions, some of which will take longer to achieve than others. Concerning challenges to reach the objectives, certain challenges need action on multiple levels. Figure 18.2 shows how one challenge, namely 'cloud computing', needs to be addressed on a short, medium and on a long term. On a short term, the subject needs to be further researched. The results of this research must be considered when regulating the subject before it can be included in the enhanced legal framework on the long term. The same goes for the MLA procedure, which will also be addressed on a short, medium and long term. On a short term, the challenge will be addressed by enhancing international cooperation and JITs, while on a medium term the MLA procedure will be digitised and on a long term the MLA procedure challenge will be addressed by modernising international law.

The Roadmap provides ten objectives for realising the Common European Framework for electronic evidence. Figure 18.3 shows the ten objectives and corresponding challenges, which are addressed in the Roadmap. Figure shows, again, the interconnected nature of the objectives and that only all actions taken together will realise the Common European Framework.

On a short term, the first steps in enhancing law enforcement will be taken by addressing three challenges; the MLA procedure, the realities of modern investigations and forensic readiness of the private sector. Moreover, on a short term, further research on many challenges will be conducted for the results to be considered on a medium and long term. The short-term solutions will thus feed into the medium and long-term solutions. On a medium term four objectives will be met by addressing the corresponding challenges, which will feed into the long-term

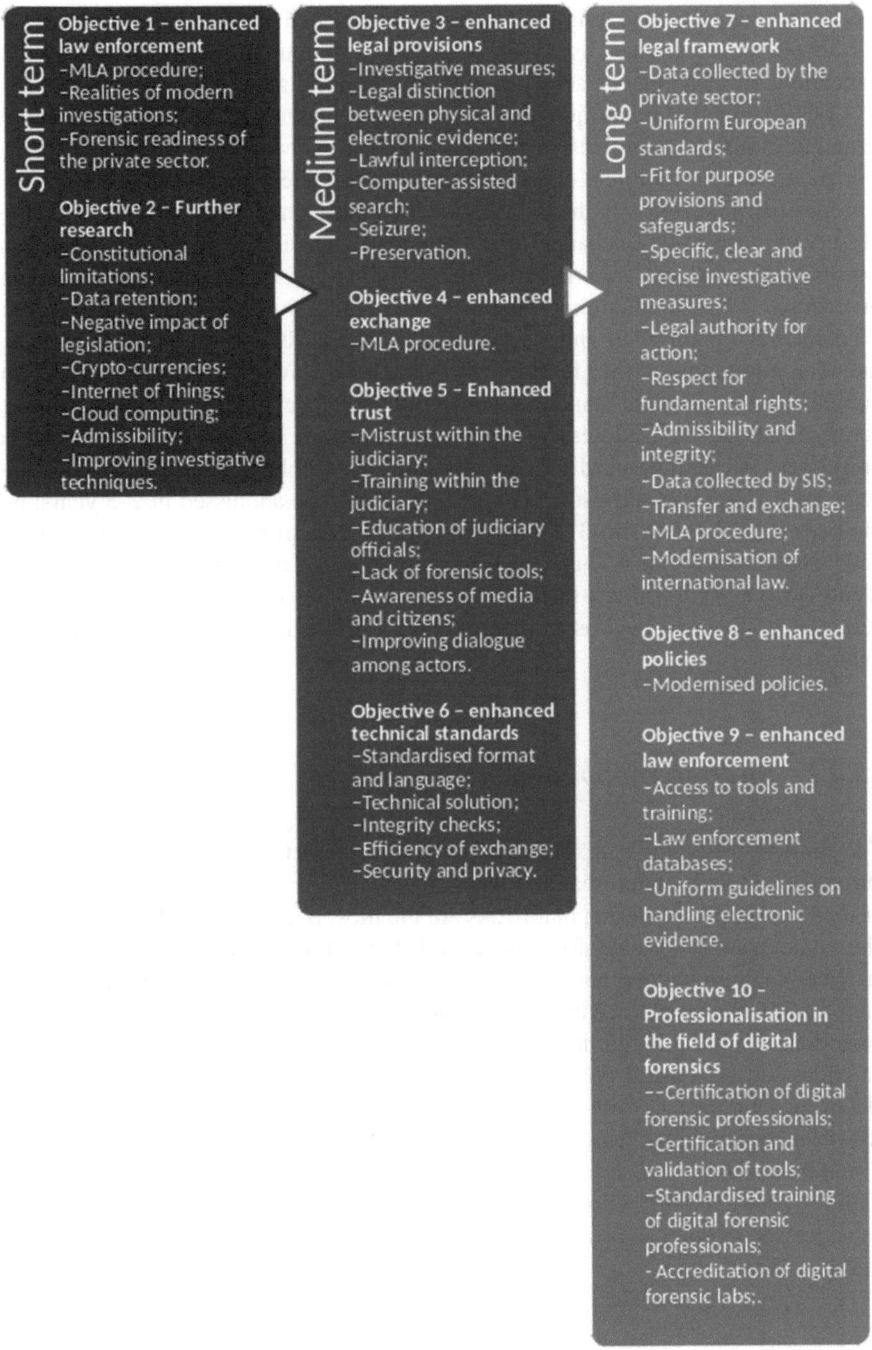

Fig. 18.3 The ten objectives and corresponding challenges which are addressed in the Roadmap

solutions where the final four objectives will be reached. As explained above, while certain objectives or challenges may be the same, the output or actions are different depending on what may be achieved within a certain timeframe.

Considering the status quo and the challenges found therein, as well as the strategic goals or objectives to improve the current way of handling electronic evidence, several solutions or actions may be provided for realising a Common European Framework for the application of new technologies in the collection, preservation, use and exchange of electronic evidence. The aim of the Common European Framework is to improve the efficiency of investigations and judicial procedures while maintaining adequate safeguards aimed at protecting relevant fundamental human rights and respecting clear standards of conduct. The objectives include conducting further research and enhancing law enforcement, legislation, policies, trust, technical standards and digital forensics and are divided in many actions that must be addressed on a short, medium or long term to reach the objectives. All actions need to start as soon as possible and preferably all at the same time. The short-term solutions are expected to be addressed in 2–3 years; the medium-term solutions in 3–4 years and the long-term solutions in 5–6 years. It needs to be noted that no one action alone will solve the ensemble of challenges identified. The actions must be taken together for changes to be more effective. All actions together will lead us to the Common European Framework for electronic evidence.

18.4.1 Short-Term Solutions

The short-term solutions are based on two major objectives, namely enhanced law enforcement and further research. Enhancing law enforcement is the major objective of the Roadmap considering that LEAs are the most important actors involved with electronic evidence. Law enforcement needs to work with the rules and procedures provided to them by law- and policymakers. Input from this very important actor is therefore of the essence. While most actions improving rules and procedures will be addressed on the longer term, certain actions to improve law enforcement must be addressed as soon as possible considering the urgency to address issues about electronic evidence, considering further the ever evolving technologies and crimes. However, certain areas require further research before they can be addressed in the Common European Framework as there are too many uncertainties regarding these topics. Conducting further research is therefore an important objective that needs to be addressed as soon as possible for the results to be included within the Common European Framework.

18.4.1.1 Objective: Enhanced Law Enforcement

Most of the law enforcement challenges, which are plentiful, would primarily find a solution through legislative and/ or policy action. However, there are several actions that must be taken within the LEA community and the digital forensics community. An enhanced enforcement scheme should include many elements to address the law enforcement challenges. A number of these elements can be addressed on the short term by LEAs and law- and policymakers such as national governments and European institutions (Europol and Eurojust). This includes finding an interim solution for the MLA procedure in increased international cooperation and JITs, drafting and using SOPs to fill the gap between law and reality until such time when the law can be changed, as well as preparing the private sector for forensic readiness by building bridges across sectors and enhancing communication and transparency.

The current enforcement scheme leaves LEAs to operate in a field of patchwork legal solutions with many challenges. One of the most important challenges law enforcement is faced with is Mutual Legal Assistance (MLA). MLA procedures are not adapted to the realities of today's crimes, which are increasingly global, complex and fleeting and heavily impact the potential for rapid and efficient transfers of electronic evidence. Improving the MLA procedure on several levels is necessary. On a short term and as a transitional and complementary solution international coordinated investigations and joint investigation teams (JITs) should be further realised to deal with global and complex crimes before the MLA procedure can be digitised and on international law can be modernised, which will take longer to realise. More legal certainty and guidelines on international coordinated investigations and JITs are necessary. Apart from addressing the MLA procedure, other legal provisions and policies may also negatively impact investigations, for example, privacy and data protection laws, which may prevent the collection of evidence, and varied data retention periods across jurisdictions may complicate investigations. Legislation may furthermore not sufficiently address the realities of modern investigations, especially when it comes to evolving new technologies. This negative impact and lack of transparency increases scrutiny by civil society and creates a gap between stakeholders. It is therefore necessary that (1) LEAs, digital forensics and prosecution keep clear records of investigation procedures, (2) Standard Operating Procedures (SOPs) are drafted to bridge the gap between reality and legislation[11] and (3) communication and transparency are enhanced and bridges are built across sectors and between different stakeholders. The final challenge law

[11]Existing guidelines and best practices, such as the ENISA handbook and guide (ENISA, Identification and handling of electronic evidence—Handbook, document for teachers [2013] September 2013; ENISA, Electronic evidence—a basic guide for First Responders Good practice material for CERT first responders [2014]) and Council of Europe Electronic Evidence Guide (Council of Europe Data Protection and Cybercrime Division, Electronic Evidence Guide A basic guide for police officers, prosecutors and judges Version 1.0, Strasbourg France 18 March 2013, available at: http://www.coe.int/t/dghl/cooperation/economiccrime/cybercrime/Documents/Electronic%20Evidence%20Guide/default_en.asp) may be used as a starting point to further

enforcement is faced with which may be solved on a short term is forensic readiness of the private sector. The importance of the private sector in criminal investigations is rapidly growing. The private sector has an impact on the development of new technologies, has more resources and electronic evidence may increasingly be held by the private sector (such as Internet Service Providers (ISPs)). To ensure correct handling of electronic evidence and enhance collaboration, the private sector should aim to reach an adequate level of 'forensic readiness' based on their activities and scale. This should be achieved by building bridges between the public and private sector and ultimately by clear legislation on a longer term. Preparing the private sector for 'forensic readiness' may be achieved by opening dialogue between stakeholders, by organising events and awareness raising campaigns across sectors on a European and international level.

18.4.1.2 Objective: Further Research

Many challenges to the current way of handling electronic evidence require further research before they can be included in the Common European Framework for electronic evidence. This includes some recent or modern developments, which have an impact on law enforcement and digital forensics in the collection and analysis of electronic evidence, such as crypto-currencies, Internet of Things and cloud computing. Developing research, techniques and software for the analysis of these developments is necessary to better understand the challenges and to provide clear and effective legal, policy, technical and other recommendations in this regard to include in the Common European Framework. It is furthermore necessary to identify how software technology can ease the capture of information to help verify admissibility criteria as the application of a technical solution can make electronic evidence become inadmissible and to improve investigative techniques, such as techniques for mobile devices and for data acquisition (including on mobile devices) before encryption, as well as possibilities for developing open source tools for specific acquisition. There is an abundance of best practices and guidelines concerning (electronic) evidence on a regional, national, European and international level. A lot of knowledge can be extracted from these best practices and guidelines to realise the Common European Framework in the best way possible.

Other challenges that would require further research are mainly legal challenges, such as constitutional limitations, data retention and the negative impact of legislation and policies on law enforcement. The systems of fundamental rights related to privacy and electronic data in the Member States are diverse resulting in constitutional limitations. Different constitutional traditions also lead to diverse implementation of international treaties such as the Cybercrime Convention. It is necessary to conduct an in-depth study to analyse the constitutional situation

build on. These SOPs should include record keeping and documentation by law enforcement, prosecution and digital forensics of the entire investigation process.

in the 28 Member States to allow for smooth implementation of the Common European Framework on the longer term. Data retention remains legal in some Member States despite the annulment of the data retention Directive by the Court of Justice of the European Union (CJEU). It is necessary to evaluate whether the remaining national provisions that had been implemented to transpose the annulled Directive and, which have not yet been removed, are possibly violating European fundamental rights and therefore must be annulled to evaluate which is the best way forward concerning data retention and safeguards thereof. Presently, data retention periods vary across jurisdictions. Harmonised legislation with appropriate safeguards in this regard is necessary. LEAs and prosecution should comment on the impact of data retention, the lack thereof in certain countries and the different periods applicable across countries from both a quantitative and qualitative perspective, as well as on other legislation and policies, which may negatively impact investigations. For example, privacy and data protection laws may prevent the collection of evidence and varied data retention periods across jurisdictions may complicate investigations. It is therefore necessary to collect feedback from LEAs and prosecution on the impact of certain laws, the severity of their impact and the frequency of their occurrence including the impact of data retention, the lack thereof in certain countries and the different periods applicable across countries from both a quantitative and qualitative perspective.

The areas for further research suggested in above have been selected based on the results of the EVIDENCE project and on what areas are most challenging for law enforcement and digital forensic specialists. However, there are more challenges that might be considered when realising the Common European Framework for electronic evidence, such as the dark net and malware. Concerning these topics, there is however already ample of research available and this was not seen as requiring most priority by the experts involved in the EVIDENCE project. The list of challenges and actions in this paragraph can therefore be seen as a non-exhaustive list of areas requiring further research or attention, notwithstanding any other relevant (technological) developments. It can furthermore be noted that, while further research in this document is indicated as a short-term solution, further research should always be an ongoing process, particularly considering the ever evolving technologies.

18.4.2 Medium-Term Solutions

Medium-term solutions address four objectives: enhanced legal provisions, enhanced exchange, enhanced trust and enhanced technical standards. Enhancing certain legal provisions that pose a challenge should be thought thoroughly and, as soon as possible, be addressed in the Common European Framework. To facilitate law enforcement and make investigations more efficient exchange should be enhanced as soon as possible. All actions cannot be addressed without the support of all actors and stakeholders involved. Trust issues should therefore be addressed and action taken to enhance trust among actors. Electronic evidence cannot exist and the process cannot be facilitated without enhanced technical standards.

18.4.2.1 Objective: Enhanced Legal Provisions

There is a general lack of specific investigative measures. Not all methods sufficiently cover the specific nature of electronic evidence collection. For example, lawful interception, computer assisted search and seizure of electronic evidence are hardly regulated in specific terms across Europe. It is necessary to clarify what lawful interceptions are and how the use of potentially intrusive technologies are compatible with the rule of law to provide a clear legal basis for lawful interception bearing in mind modern technologies and preventing admissibility issues. Covert and remote measures particularly highly affect fundamental rights. It is necessary to implement clear and precise legal provisions with clear authority for LEAs, which includes adequate privacy safeguards addressing the privacy risks related to computer-assisted search, particularly covert and remote measures. While seizure is mostly regulated across Member States, there is a lack of specific legal provisions in seizure of data and data storage as opposed to seizure of physical objects. Seizure of data should only be legal if adequate safeguards are implemented. A data specific legal provision, which considers that seizure of a data carrier involves serious privacy risks, should make a distinction between seizure of data and seizure of physical objects with respect to the potential impact on fundamental human rights. All these elements and other investigative measures specific to electronic evidence should be regulated including legal safeguards. A more specific legal basis to collect electronic evidence is necessary, particularly to avoid admissibility issues in cross-border cases. A common European framework for the systematic and uniform application of new technologies in the collection, use and exchange of electronic evidence should thus include specific, clear and precise investigative measures in the collection of electronic evidence. Security, investigative and procedural measures must be proportionate and guided by core values such as human dignity, freedom, democracy, equality, the rule of law and the respect for fundamental rights. These specific investigative measures must be addressed to provide more clarity, legal certainty and authority for LEAs in certain areas. These legal provisions may be drafted or amended on a medium term to provide a legal basis and can be included in the enhanced legal framework on the longer term. Legislation and policies may negatively impact investigations. Based on the feedback collected from LEAs and prosecution on the impact of certain laws amendments to certain investigative measures should be discussed and proposed on a European and on a national level. SOPs should furthermore be drafted and adopted to fill the legislative gap. In this regard, existing guidelines and best practices, such as the ENISA handbook and guide[12] and Council of Europe Electronic Evidence Guide[13] may be used as a starting point to further build on. This lack of a specific legal basis is furthermore challenging to the handling of electronic evidence considering that most Member States do not have a legal distinction between physical and electronic evidence. They apply traditional evidence rules to electronic evidence that, considering the specific nature of electronic evidence, may not be sufficient to cover electronic evidence. A distinction between physical and electronic evidence in legal provisions is recommended, or, where reasonable, the legal provisions should explicitly state that they apply to both physical and electronic evidence.

After the evidence has been collected, it needs to be preserved before it can be used in court. Preservation and storage of electronic evidence is of relevance, in terms of both implementation of adequate archival procedures of (long-term) preservation of electronic records that might one day become evidence, as well as proactive preservation of collected electronic evidence during the prosecution period (sometimes even a decade long). There is a general lack of legal provisions in the preservation of electronic evidence, including preservations methods and use, standards or guidelines on who is authorised to process the electronic evidence in what stage of the criminal proceeding, access restrictions, specifications on how the evidence must be preserved and stored and how to handle evidence obtained from private parties. It is necessary to introduce specific legal provisions concerning the preservation, storage and use of electronic evidence, including security measures and safeguards against alteration of data. Apart from legal provisions, it is advisable to draft operational guidelines, SOPs or similar in this regards. The Common European Framework needs to include legislative and other measures, including guidelines on the preservation and storage of electronic evidence, including rules on access restrictions, authorisation, method and duration of preservation, data protection, and other rules.

18.4.2.2 Objective: Enhanced Exchange

As previously stated, one of the most important challenges law enforcement is faced with is MLA considering that MLA procedures are not adapted to the realities of today's crimes, which are increasingly global, complex and fleeting and heavily impact the potential for rapid and efficient transfers of electronic evidence. Challenges in the MLA procedure must be addressed on multiple levels. After enhancing law enforcement by improving international cooperation and JITs on

[12]ENISA, Identification and handling of electronic evidence—Handbook, document for teachers [2013] September 2013; ENISA, Electronic evidence—a basic guide for First Responders Good practice material for CERT first responders [2014].

[13]Council of Europe Data Protection and Cybercrime Division, Electronic Evidence Guide A basic guide for police officers, prosecutors and judges Version 1.0, Strasbourg France 18 March 2013, available via: http://www.coe.int/t/dghl/cooperation/economiccrime/cybercrime/Documents/Electronic%20Evidence%20Guide/default_en.asp.

the short term this may be achieved in the second place and on a medium term by digitisation of the MLA procedure. Digitisation of requests and forwarding of evidence is necessary to address the challenge. e-MLA (Interpol), as well as solutions provided by the EVIDENCE project, are suggested as possible solutions in this regard.

18.4.2.3 Objective: Enhanced Trust

There is a general mistrust within the judiciary and other actors involved in the criminal trial, which includes fear of manipulation, vulnerability and misunderstanding concerning electronic evidence. Trust is necessary for all the other objectives to be successful. For the Common European Framework to be effective enhanced trust is necessary, particularly enhanced trust in the judiciary. It is not sufficient to enhance legislation, law enforcement and technical standards. Shared competencies and common values are necessary to support the ensemble of solutions proposed. Without cooperation of the actors involved the realisation of the Common European Framework will fail. The objectives and challenges proposed must be complemented by ethical and social action by addressing challenges such as mistrust, security, cultural differences, etc. to enhance trust among actors and trust in and within the judiciary. This can be achieved by (coordinated European) awareness raising activities, aimed at judiciary officials, magistrates and other actors involved in the criminal trial, as well as coordinated European meetings for actors in the field, to improve dialogue among actors to improve the general lack of communication, consensus and coordination between actors. Awareness raining campaigns should furthermore be aimed at the media and citizens. Media and citizens fail to understand the technical complexity and rapid technological developments and to consider the specificity of electronic evidence. Awareness raising activities and targeted training activities are required in this regard to improve cultural and personal oppositions and enhance trust.

Lack of trust also results from a lack of competences and professions. There is a general lack of technical knowledge, experience, education and training within the judiciary, as well as with prosecution and defence lawyers. It is a challenge to stay up to date with all the innovations and tools. It is desirable that every judicial actor is trained to guarantee minimum knowledge on electronic data and its use in the judicial system to reduce the waste of time and resources and to increase trust. This needs to be addressed by mandatory training (on technical issues, electronic evidence and digital forensics) of the judiciary in the field of electronic evidence. Coordinated European training programmes should be set up and carried out within the Member States to train judiciary officials within the field of electronic evidence. Compulsory education regarding these topics is furthermore necessary. These subjects should be added to the academic programme by consolidating them in the academic syllabus for legal studies to provide a basic knowledge of this by the judiciary. It is furthermore advisable to compile more information on the subject matter and develop a (cyber)crime repository including a repository of case law and lessons learnt.

Mistrust finally also results from a lack of competencies by certain (smaller) LEAs. Proper investigations require proper investigative tools. Mainly because of budgetary issues, not all LEAs possess proper investigative tools. This may impede trust in the evidence collected by (smaller) LEAs that do not have access to proper investigative tools. Investing in proper digital forensic tools is necessary. Particularly considering security challenges such as the volatile nature of data, difficulties to prove authenticity and possible manipulation, which make proper investigative tools a necessity for all LEAs.

18.4.2.4 Objective: Enhanced Technical Standards

An important part of the Common European Framework concerning the collection, preservation, use and exchange of electronic evidence includes enhancing technical standards. Technical action includes a proposed standard for representing data and metadata involved in the exchange process and formal languages for their representation. The EVIDENCE project provided a detailed overview on how to develop an electronic evidence exchange platform and introduced a cloud platform for implementing the exchange process, which includes features such as cryptographic control and malware protection and suggestions for the use of the evolving standards DFAX and CASE, that leverage the Unified Cyber Ontology. While some of the technical challenges may be addressed sooner than others, the general estimation is that enhancing technical standards will be addressed on a medium term.

One of the main technical challenges includes the lack of a standardised format and language, including the lack of a standardised format for representing the output of forensics analysis software, the lack of a standard format for information exchange, data and metadata processing, the use of a formal standard language for representing the wide range of digital forensic information and forensic processing results and a standard exchange method. The use of a common format and language (DFAX and its evolution called 'CASE' which is under development and should be considered) for exporting the metadata of the forensic investigation along with the associated findings will help transferring and comparing results between tools and thus assist verification of findings. A standard proposal for representing data and metadata involved in Electronic Evidence Exchange has been presented in Deliverable 4.1 of the EVIDENCE project that also recommends the use of DFAX, which later on ultimately evolved into CASE, for representing these metadata and describing in a detailed way all technical and legal forensic information. Previously, DFAX and the related formalisms were not mature enough, however, the design focuses on the extensibility and was therefore adaptable for covering all possible information needs for representing forensics investigations. The advantages of using such formalisms were clear:

- they have been developed in the cyber security environment but
- they include lots of essential elements to representing digital forensic information;

- they allow to describe technical, procedural and judicial information as well;
- they allow tools interoperability;
- they allow to compare results produced by different digital forensic tools;
- they leverage the UCO ontology that permits the description of Actions, Actors and their relationships within the Forensics Environment;
- they are open source;
- they already contain a composed structure for representing a wide range of forensic information.

The standard proposal chiefly consists of metadata and formalisms for their representation, so the platform on which these software layers may be implemented assumes less importance, while more relevant is the capacity/possibility to integrate this layers with an existing platform that is already up and running. All the platforms have already implemented security and privacy levels in accordance with standard ISO/IEC 27017, ISO/IEC 27002 and ISO/IEX 2704050 that guarantees a wide trust among all involved stakeholders.

The second technical challenge is due to the very nature of electronic evidence in that it is easier to copy or alter electronic evidence. Integrity checks when packaging and un-packaging the data and metadata using hash functions in this regard are necessary. These checks should be included in operational guidelines or SOPs. During the copying process, it is appropriate to carry out a hashing MD5 over the whole or parts of image to verify the integrity of the cloned data image. The most popular hashing function are those based on the MD5, SHA1 e SHA256 algorithms. It is crucial to have trustworthy data on which to carry out the analysis otherwise the analysis may have a limited or no value, since the evidence may be questioned during the trial. Each format allows to accomplish the acquisition task using a single file or splitting the copy into smaller pieces built up of many sequential files.

The acquisition can be accomplished using two distinct methods:

- dismounting the internal hard disk and then acquire the content using an external device (disk duplicator);
- using the personal computer itself, that contains the hard disk.

The first method is always recommended because it is less prone to making mistakes during the acquisition process, nevertheless there are cases where the second method is the only choice, such as in case of hard disks welded to the motherboard or computer hard to disassemble etc.

The acquisition based on the hard disk dismount is completed through the following steps:

- Usage of hardware duplicator or disk imaging tools;
- Usage of a forensics workstation with acquisition forensic tools using:
  - a write blocker hardware or;
  - a write blocker software.

Integrity checks when packaging and un-packaging data must be introduced and included in SOPs.

Mobile devices pose a particular challenge as acquisition entails various risks including tangling with the integrity of the original source of evidence. Evidence acquisition has some risks for the device state preservation. Unlike other storage device acquisition where the memory can be detached from the device and acquired afterwards using technologies described in previous sections, the mobile device acquisition requires the interaction with the device, the use of the installed operating system and the related communication protocols through a computer or directly loading an alternative operating system into the RAM (i.e. an injection technique). Special action should be taken to prevent from triggering security systems that might put the data integrity at risk. The Guidelines on Mobile Device Forensics (NIST Guidelines on mobile device forensics, 2014) should be used and constantly updated and delivered to LEAs in a concise format for facilitating their interventions/ tasks at least for the most common mobile devices. It would furthermore be desirable to develop a specific App for mobile devices as a first guide to carry out the initial forensic tasks. Based on the mobile device, model is necessary to take special care during the device interaction to prevent from trigging security systems that might put at risk the data integrity (i.e. erase all data on this iPhone after ten failed passcode attempts). Possibilities for this App should be investigated on the short term. Action includes using, constantly updating and delivering the guidelines on mobile device forensics (http://nvlpubs.nist.gov/nistpubs/SpecialPublications/NIST.SP.800-101r1.pdf) to LEAs in a concise format for facilitating interventions/ tasks for mobile devices and develop a specific application for mobile devices as a first guide to carry out the initial forensic tasks.

Exchange of electronic evidence is of the utmost importance, particularly in cross-border cases. The efficiency of data exchange relates to the amount of resources expended including time in relation to the accuracy and completeness with which users exchange data holding or potentially holding electronic evidence. A standard exchange method is necessary. Standard methodology, structure and formatting of evidence data analysis and exchange methods will help efficiency. The trust of data exchange relates not only to the ability to guarantee a reliable data exchange means between well identified stakeholders with proper authorisation but also on the ability to obtain a complete provenance of data received from the authentic electronic source including the chain of custody and the tools used to collect, extract and analyse data up to the data received by a recipient of the exchange. The EVIDENCE App and DFAX language implement these features by design. It is necessary to introduce a standard exchange method and language, the EVIDENCE application and DFAX and CASE language are recommended. An electronic evidence exchange system must furthermore reliably keep information confidential and respect data protection policies while, at the same time provide a means to verify the authentic origin of the data. Encryption of identities and sensitive private data of persons involved in the case or working on it is suggested, as well as security of investigation information by encryption of packages.[14] The EVIDENCE Application should be integrated with the user management system and deployed within a secure environment and privacy guidelines should be drafted in this regard. Policies and guidelines for information security should guarantee the protection of all assets involved in the exchange process information flow to create trust to all potential stakeholders/users. There is no uniform evidence exchange platform, it is recommended to establish an Evidence Exchange Platform. A general architecture of the cloud platform is necessary where there is a sender and a receiving authority who will be authenticated and authorised to upload/download data and meta data, relying on trusted mechanism, allowing to share data across different countries/jurisdictions and considering privacy/security issues. The platform should include:

- Access control;
- Physical and environment security;
- Backup;
- Malware protection;
- Cryptographic control;
- Communication security;
- Personal data and privacy protection.

Exchange of analysis results is sometimes difficult because it highly depends on the type of object to describe as Output. There are certain issues that must be addressed and extended in DFAX (standard)/CybOX formalism, including:

- The lack of Cybox objects to describe most of the common artefacts extracted from a source of evidence/ acquisition;
- Correlation between the extracted information and the tool used to recover/interpret it (e.g. specific tool used to recover internet history);
- Relationship between objects that share the same characteristics (e.g. two identical files, same MD5 hash, that are stored in two different Devices);
- There is no way to describe deleted contents (i.e. files or records within the unallocated space of a device);
- There is a need to describe general objects, such entry in a SQLite database.

Issues with the DFAX structure and its expansion in exchange languages include:

- The case information part of the DFAX Package is structured with a strict authority–investigator–victim–subject paradigm. This fields must be discussed with legal experts for establishing if they fit into reality, also bearing in mind the different law systems existing among European countries and the rest of the world.

[14]Data markings are an integral component of CASE (see Chap. 4), permitting information to be labeled as private or sensitive, and to be shared or protected appropriately at different levels of trust and classification. UCO provides for data markings that CASE can use to support proper handling of shared information (http://legacydirs.umiacs.umd.edu/~oard/desi7/papers/EC.pdf).

Table 18.1 Objects to be added to DFAX standard

Object	References
Windows Jumplist	Like shortcuts files it is commonly used to identify file access
Windows Shortcuts	It is an artefact commonly used during forensic investigation to identify file access, device connection, network shares, and so on. It should be described by its specific fields
Windows Prefetch	It is an already existing Object in Cybox but its structure has changed since Windows 8, so the object needs to be updated
Office Document	Useful for describing Office Documents in terms of metadata
Image File	Already existing object in Cybox. It should be updated to describe typical image metadata
Audio File	Same concept as an Image file applied to an Audio
Video File	Same concept as an Image file applied to a Video
Database Entry	Generic way to describe database entry in a table or the result of a SQLite query
Generic artefacts	Record/data contained inside a file in proprietary format. For example, an entry contained in a chat or P2P history file (i.e. MET files used by eMule software) or a plist file used in Apple OS for configuration and data
PCAP File	It should be useful to have a way to describe a Network Capture file with some metadata, for example those extracted by tools like capinfos; See the Catalogue at wp4.evidenceproject.eu)
Deleted Files	There should be a way to describe deleted files

- The use of a specification such as CybOX is useful in a Digital Forensic context is necessary to define a list of common terms to be used for describing objects. For example:
  - Device object is commonly used to describe physical source of evidence and should contain a description field. Examples of fixed description values could be: Personal Computer, Notebook, SATA Hard Disk, USB Hard Disk, USB Pen Drive, CD, DVD, SD Memory Card, Smartphone, Tablet, etc.;
  - Some physical objects may contain specific fields that must be defined. For example, in the case of a smartphone, it is more appropriate to use the IMEI rather than a serial number value.

It must be mentioned, however, that these issues and limitations were addressed when DFAX evolved into CASE, as discussed in Chap. 2.

Table 18.1 shows the changes that must be made to CybOX.

18.4.3 Long-Term Solutions

Long-term solutions address four objectives: enhanced legal framework, enhanced policies, enhanced law enforcement and professionalisation in the field of digital forensics. By addressing the actions in this paragraph all previous objectives will come together, will be finalised and the Common European Framework will be realised. Law and policies will be modernised and law enforcement facilitated.

18.4.3.1 Objective: Enhanced Legal Framework

There is a legislative gap concerning the collection, preservation, use and exchange of electronic evidence considering that there is no comprehensive legal framework and no legislative harmonisation. There is a patchwork of legislation, implemented differently among Member States causing legal and practical uncertainty. Existing legislative and enforcement frameworks and the concepts enshrined therein, as well as data protection concepts, precede the creation of the internet as we know today and do not satisfactory deal with the realities of technological developments and with the dynamic nature of modern investigations. There is no uniform definition of electronic evidence and a lack of a comprehensive European legal framework addressing data protection issues related to electronic evidence. The legislative gap leaves LEAs to operate in a field of patchwork solutions and playing catch up and manoeuvering their way through a highly uncertain and politically sensitive landscape filled with legal lacunae. Suggestions can be made for modernising and harmonising legislation and policy, including international law and treaties and for operational guidelines and SOPs as standards on the procedures and modalities to follow in the phase of collection, preservation and exchange of electronic evidence, which ensure proportionality between protection of privacy and infringements for legitimate crime prevention and control.

Legal challenges mostly originate from the fact that criminal law is mainly regulated at national level. This is challenging considering that all Member States have different rules, procedures and approach, making cross-border cooperation challenging in this modern society filled with evolving technologies. Uniform European standards would aid investigations in criminal cases and facilitate the process of exchange. A Common European Framework for the systematic and uniform application of new technologies in the collection, preservation, use and exchange of electronic evidence should be based on clear and specific rules for the collection of electronic evidence, common definitions and standards and approximation of legal procedures. There is a general lack of uniform European standards, particularly about:

- Uniform definitions;
- Uniform definition of electronic evidence;
- Standards for information exchange;
- Lack of communication/ agreement/ coordination between actors and difficulties in sharing information (between offices and organisations);
- Procedures and guidelines for the collection, preservation and use of electronic evidence;
- Procedures for the validation of electronic evidence;
- Methodologies for analysis;
- Technical infrastructure.

Lack of such standards causes difficulties on multiple levels including delays in obtaining and interpreting electronic evidence, admissibility, etc. This needs to be addressed on multiple levels to achieve the Common European Framework. Standardisation of procedures and drafting and disseminating guidelines is required. Practices should be disseminated and mainstreamed, partnership should be built (public, private, research, civil society) and coordinated European training and certification should be organised to improve the lack of uniform European standards from an ethical and social perspective to enhance trust. Trust should be enhanced by education, training and awareness raising campaigns, bridges should be built across sectors and technical solutions must be provided. While most of the uniform standards will be addressed from multiple angles, it is necessary to have a legal structure complemented by SOPs in the operational guidelines or rules on the actual handling of electronic evidence. While all Member States have within their country certain specific agencies or units, particularly forensic institutes, specialised in the collection, examination and preservation of evidence, there are limited guidelines or procedures for the use of digital technologies in criminal proceedings. A common European framework for the systematic and uniform application of new technologies in the collection, use and exchange of electronic evidence should thus include a plan for the development of common guidelines and procedures.

Legal challenges also originate from the fact that legislation lags behind rapidly developing technologies. Existing legislative and enforcement frameworks and data protection concepts do not satisfactory deal with the realities of technological developments. Legislation should be technology neutral and include new or adapted investigative measures. General laws may not provide solutions for today's digital society. Analogous argumentation of traditional legislation may not suffice and may not provide sufficient safeguards against potential privacy infringements. IoT, virtual currencies and other new developments and technologies present new challenges for LEAs, forensic analysts and the procedures, methods and tools they apply. Risks include disproportionate collection, misuse and transfer. Modernising and harmonising legislation and policy including authorisation for the collection of electronic evidence accompanied by specific safeguards to mitigate the impacts on fundamental rights and new/ adapted investigative measures is required. The legislative gap should be addressed by legislation that is fit-for-purpose with appropriate safeguards. From a EU perspective, existing legislation such as the European Investigations Order Directive[15] may be taken as a starting point to build further on and implement measures further to address the specificity of electronic evidence. Drafting and adopting fit-for-purpose legal provisions addressing the technological challenges while maintaining appropriate safeguards is of the utmost importance.

These fit-for-purpose legal provisions should include specific investigative measures considering that not all measures sufficiently cover the specific nature of

[15]Directive 2014/41/EU of the European Parliament and of the Council of 3 April 2014 regarding the European Investigation Order in criminal matters [2014] OJ L 130/1.

electronic evidence collection. Certain interception and search and seizure methods (that lead to electronic evidence) are not sufficiently covered legally. Where rules exist these follow from the provisions of the Cybercrime Convention and apply mostly to the investigation of cybercrimes. Most of the Member States extend the application of traditional investigative methods to electronic evidence. While in some cases this might work, generally, these methods do not sufficiently cover the specific nature of electronic evidence collection. A more specific legal basis is necessary to obtain electronic evidence, particularly to avoid admissibility issues in cross-border cases. A common European framework for the systematic and uniform application of new technologies in the collection, use and exchange of electronic evidence should thus include specific, clear and precise investigative measures in the collection of electronic evidence. One of the main gaps in investigative powers includes the lack of power to enter electronic networks to search for evidence and to preserve computer data to support existing search powers. Legislation requires a clear scope of application of powers and sufficient legal authority for action accompanied by specific safeguards. A more specific legal basis is necessary to obtain electronic evidence, particularly to avoid admissibility issues in cross-border cases. A common European framework for the systematic and uniform application of new technologies in the collection, preservation, use and exchange of electronic evidence should thus include specific, clear and precise investigative measures in the collection of electronic evidence. Security, investigative and procedural measures must be proportionate and guided by core values such as human dignity, freedom, democracy, equality, the rule of law and the respect for fundamental rights. One of the specific challenges in investigative measures is posed by cloud computing. There is a general lack of legal basis in Europe regarding investigation in the cloud. The Common European Framework should include specific provisions in the collection of electronic evidence out of a cloud service. This rule should go further than the search and seizure rules (for electronic evidence) that exist in the Cybercrime Convention, particularly as the current rules are bound to the territorial jurisdiction of the state where the investigation is taking place. Rules on the obtaining of evidence from the cloud need to go beyond the current limitations of territorial jurisdiction. One possible way is to agree on a 'universal jurisdiction' approach particularly in the investigation of serious crimes (here too however, the term 'serious crimes' may need to be defined further). Data is distributed to storage locations that in some occasions can be unknown, which may lead to jurisdiction issues such as overlapping jurisdiction. Another jurisdiction approach is an investigative jurisdiction based on a legitimate interest. Certain legal developments and studies should be considered while drafting the enhanced legal framework. A legal basis for investigations in the cloud is necessary including harmonised privacy safeguards for the collection of electronic evidence out of cloud storages. Based on the recommendations provided by further research in this regard investigations in the cloud should be regulated in the Common European Framework.

Considering modern technological developments, which have a changed impact on fundamental rights and the unchanged rules and safeguards to protect such rights, it is necessary for the Common European Framework for electronic evidence to consider the changed impact and to provide sufficient safeguards. All Member States have at least one important basis in common: protection of fundamental rights. The collection, preservation, use and exchange of electronic evidence can only be sound and effective if it is based on fundamental rights and freedoms and individuals' rights cannot be secured without safe networks and systems. Law enforcement, prosecution and the judiciary should execute investigative powers and procedures with regard for human rights and liberties. Protecting fundamental rights, freedom of expression, personal data and privacy are of utmost importance. Therefore, security, investigative and procedural measures must be proportionate and guided by core values such as human dignity, freedom, democracy, equality, the rule of law and the respect for fundamental rights. Fundamental rights, democracy and the rule of law must be protected in cyberspace while protecting against incidents, malicious activities and misuse. These rights and freedoms also include the right to a fair trial, particularly when preparing a defence case where electronic evidence forms part of the evidence. All respondent Member States provide for the codification of fundamental rights. Any common European framework for the systematic and uniform application of new technologies in the collection, use and exchange of electronic evidence should be based on the protection of fundamental rights and freedoms, including proper restrictions and safeguards. The basis for this already exists in the Member States of the EU through the ratification of the ECHR and through constitutional provisions and traditions in the different Member States. Data protection concepts precede the creation of the internet as we know today and do not satisfactory deal with the realities of technological developments. The enhanced legal framework should respect fundamental rights, include a minimum standard of data protection, privacy safeguards, security standards and should be accompanied by operational guidelines and rules on the handling of electronic evidence. Action includes drafting and adopting legal provisions, which respect fundamental rights, data protection standards, privacy safeguards and security and ensure that the entire Common European Framework respects such principles and values.

One of the major legal challenges to be addressed is data collected by the private sector. The importance of the private sector concerning criminal investigations is rapidly growing that creates a dependency of LEAs on the private sector for the collection, examination, preservation and transfer of electronic evidence. The private sector has an impact on the development of new technologies, has more resources, digital forensics expertise is more common in the private sector than in the public sector and electronic evidence is increasingly being captured and held by the private sector (ISPs). A large part of electronic evidence originates from private sector actors, e.g. ISPs providing traffic data of internet transactions, telecommunications providers providing information on mobile communications, etc. Legislation does not clearly regulate the relationship with the private sector. It is necessary to have clear rules of what categories of data can be obtained from the private sector and what procedures need to be followed, i.e. the origin, collection and use of electronic evidence from the private sector and transfer of evidence from the private sector to LEAs. Regulation in the transfer of electronic evidence between LEAs and the private sector including safeguards in the development stages of new technologies must be put in place. This should include a standard (secured) format for delivering data to LEAs from private sector is necessary to facilitate and speed up investigations. Challenges with connected devices and IoT include issues such as transfer of data from private to public sector, sensitive data and big data. A major problem of obtaining electronic evidence from ISPs is represented by the growing world of services on mobile devices, based on apps. In theory every app producer can be a service provider, but at the same time not be viewed legally as such, meaning that they do not have the corresponding legal duties making investigations challenging. Privacy by default and focus on the quality of the information (instead of data overload) are recommended in this regard. Clear rules in the transfer from the private to the public sector are necessary, as well as training the private sector for 'forensic readiness'. To ensure correct handling of electronic evidence and enhance collaboration, the private sector should aim to reach an adequate level of 'forensic readiness' based on their activities and scale. The Common European Framework needs to include rules on the engagement of private sector experts and on how electronic evidence is transferred to and from private sector experts.

The second major challenge is data collected by SIS or actionable intelligence. Transfer of information or actionable intelligence between intelligence agencies and LEAs and vice-versa is often not regulated. The distinction in legal treatment (and application of laws) to law enforcement and security services/ intelligence agencies is not always clear. In most cases, the prime function SIS is to produce actionable intelligence that is passed on to the LEAs to act, whether it is to further monitor, follow, detain, arrest or prosecute a person or group of persons. It is therefore necessary to include in a common European framework for electronic evidence rules on the transfer and exchange of information/actionable intelligence and whether this information can be admitted as evidence in a criminal trial. Rules in this regard are necessary to establish whether the information or actionable intelligence can be admitted as evidence in a criminal trial. If the origin of the data is unknown or if the data was collected by SIS, the legitimacy of the source and transfer might be put in question as a clear chain of custody and documentation thereof is missing. It is suggested to introduce a pseudonymisation process, to develop and establish internationally agreed standards with an interdisciplinary approach, to flag the unknown origin for transparency and to enable to use appropriate analysis techniques. Legal provisions about data collected by SIS must be drafted and adopted.

The final major challenge is exchange of electronic evidence. There is a general lack of regulation in the transfer and exchange of electronic evidence, within domestic boundaries and internationally. Most of the rules that exist nationally, if any, have been prepared by some of the prominent actors themselves, e.g. most national forensic institutes have rules on the receipt and transfer of electronic evidence to be examined by them. Considering the volatile nature of electronic evidence and the large potential of tampering with the evidence during electronic evidence's lifecycle, which could lead to the inadmissibility of the evidence and/ or affect the fundamental rights of suspects and/ or victims, clear rules in this regard are necessary. Internationally speaking, it is increasingly evident that (apart from the provision of the Cybercrime Convention) the procedures offered in existing legal frameworks are too slow for the volatile and fast-moving nature of electronic evidence. The provisions and procedures in the Cybercrime Convention are better suited for electronic evidence but States have often not extended their application beyond the scope of the Cybercrime Convention when ratifying the Convention. Clear rules in the transfer and exchange are necessary and can be built on the existing provisions and procedures in the Cybercrime Convention and on the current efforts of the Council of Europe to create an electronic version of the mutual legal assistance request form. Legal provisions concerning transfer and exchange of electronic evidence, particularly in cross-border cases, must be drafted and adopted. Considering that MLA procedures are not adapted to the realities of today's crimes that are increasingly global, complex and fleeting and that they heavily impact the potential for rapid and efficient transfers of electronic evidence it is necessary to increase international coordinated investigations. Under the auspices of Europol and Eurojust several JITs have been set up during investigations. These joint investigations allow for an efficient way of collecting and sharing of electronic evidence pertinent in an investigation. The common European framework should increase the legal certainty needed for such joint investigations to be carried out in a smoother and more efficient manner building on Council Framework Decision 2002/465/JHA.[16] Legal provisions increasing the legal certainty of JITs must be drafted and adopted. Considering that MLA procedures are not adapted to the realities of today's crimes that are increasingly global, complex and fleeting and that they heavily impact the potential for rapid and efficient transfers of electronic evidence it is necessary to digitise the MLA procedure and to provide a legal basis in this regard. Concerning the MLA procedure, it is furthermore necessary to eventually modernise international law. The legislative gap should be addressed by modernising and harmonising legislation and policy, including international law and treaties and adapting it to new technologies. A sound legal basis including uniform definitions (including a definition of electronic evidence), concepts and standards, access to investigative tools and techniques, training and technical capabilities, best practices policies that ensure proportionality between protection of privacy and infringements for legitimate crime prevention and control, and will facilitate a more efficient cooperation is required. Existing international law, such as the Cybercrime Convention[17] and the European Convention on mutual assistance in criminal matters[18] may be further build upon to address the challenges law enforcement is faced with when dealing with electronic evidence. Possibilities for modernising international law including draft amendments, new laws and recommendations

[16]Council Framework Decision of 13 June 2002 on joint investigation teams (2002/465/JHA) [2002] OJ L 162/1.

[17]Convention on Cybercrime [2001] ETS 185.

[18]European Convention on Mutual Assistance in Criminal Matters [1959] CETS 030; Additional Protocol to the European Convention on Mutual Assistance in Criminal Matters [1978] CETS 099.

should be discussed by the Council of Europe, the EU, LEAs, digital forensics, lawyers, private sector, national governments and European institutions.

18.4.3.2 Objective: Enhanced Policies

Challenges to the collection, preservation, use and exchange of electronic evidence cannot be addressed without clear policies reflecting the objectives to enhance legislation, law enforcement, trust and technical standards. Modernised policies should be aimed at enhancing legislation, investigation, prosecution, enforcement, trust and technical standards. These policies should support international cooperation, reflect the realities of new crimes, new technologies and new investigations and should ensure proportionality between protection of privacy and infringements for legitimate crime prevention and control and be guided by core values such as human dignity, freedom, democracy, equality, the rule of law and the respect for fundamental rights.

18.4.3.3 Objective: Enhanced Law Enforcement

LEAs are left to operate in a field of patchwork solutions and playing catch up and manoeuvering their way through a highly uncertain and politically sensitive landscape filled with legal lacunae. Most of the law enforcement challenges, which are plentiful, would primarily find a solution through legislative and/ or policy action. However, there are several actions that can be taken within the LEA community and the digital forensics community. An enhanced enforcement scheme should include many elements to address the law enforcement challenges. This includes investing in tools and training for LEAs. Modern crimes need modern solutions. LEAs cannot afford to lag behind innovations considering that criminals have access to modern tools and techniques. Enhanced enforcement requires access to investigative tools and techniques, training and technical capabilities. Access varies among LEAs, particularly mainly because of budget issues. For the system to be effective all LEAs should have similar access to tools, techniques, training and technical capabilities.

One of the law enforcement challenges is issues with law enforcement databases including purpose limitation, big data and interoperability. It is necessary to restrict the use to severe crime only and to introduce a life-cycle control of data, which is case independent. It is furthermore necessary to regulate and establish a gateway for interoperable standard interchange based upon open and existing standards and controls at EU level and international level. Preservation of electronic evidence is of relevance, in terms of both implementation of adequate archival procedures of (long-term) preservation of electronic records that might one day become evidence, as well as proactive preservation of collected electronic evidence during the prosecution period (sometimes even a decade long). There is a lack of standards for storage that should be addressed. It is necessary to introduce a case independent data life-cycle control and a gateway for interoperable standard interchange and draft guidelines for preservation and storage.

Considering the volatile nature of electronic evidence and to prevent admissibility issues it is necessary to follow uniform guidelines on the handling of electronic evidence, preservation thereof, methods and use, as well as access control and restrictions. Enhanced enforcement should include standards or guidelines on who is authorised to process the electronic evidence, in what stage of the criminal proceeding and should restrict access and provide specifications on how the evidence must be stored, preserved and should include guidelines on how to handle evidence obtained from private parties. Draft SOPs on handling electronic evidence are necessary. Existing guidelines and best practices, such as the ENISA handbook and guide[19] and Council of Europe Electronic Evidence Guide[20] may be used as a starting point to further build on.

18.4.3.4 Objective: Professionalisation in the Field of Digital Forensics

Most of the law enforcement challenges, which are plentiful, would primarily find a solution through policy and/ or legislative action. Part of these challenges may be addressed by professionalisation in the field of digital forensics. Professionalisation in the sub-discipline of digital forensics is necessary to achieve a certain level of professionalism and recognition within this young field. This requires standardisation efforts, reassessing potential regulation of digital forensics professions to ensure that practitioners meet a certain standard, validation of tool to ensure they are fit-for-purpose and accreditation for digital forensic labs to ensure that they meet certain pre-determined quality levels. Professionalisation in the field of digital forensics will complement law enforcement and includes regulation and certification of the profession and training, validation of digital forensic tools and accreditation of digital forensics labs.

The digital forensics profession is generally considered to be vague. There is a lack of certification models and specialised judicial services, high cost of examining and interpreting information, lack of expertise of the judiciary, difficulties related to the non-binding nature of international cooperation, jurisdiction issues and insufficient involvement of justice operators in the implementation of software. This can be addressed by recognition of the social and economic status of experts in the field of electronic evidence, introducing common certification, enhancement and coordination of expertise, involvement of internet governance bodies, coordination

[19]ENISA, Identification and handling of electronic evidence—Handbook, document for teachers [2013] September 2013; ENISA, Electronic evidence—a basic guide for First Responders Good practice material for CERT first responders [2014].

[20]Council of Europe Data Protection and Cybercrime Division, Electronic Evidence Guide A basic guide for police officers, prosecutors and judges Version 1.0, Strasbourg France 18 March 2013, available via: http://www.coe.int/t/dghl/cooperation/economiccrime/cybercrime/Documents/Electronic%20Evidence%20Guide/default_en.asp>.

of LEAs, overcoming difficulties between LEAs and service providers (by speeding up the process for accessing data in another jurisdiction, evaluating proportionality of requests, standardised electronic requests in agreement with providers, etc.). It is necessary to develop a system for coordinated European certification of digital forensic professionals and an official registry to provide for recognition of experts. To achieve a certain level of professionalisation degrees and certification for digital forensic professionals are necessary to ensure practitioners meet a certain standard (minimum degree and certification of digital forensic professionals by an independent certification board or organisation). A register of court experts at European level should be created that guarantees the quality of the contribution made by court experts to the legal process. It is essential to create a digital forensics experts register valid at European level. This would guarantee the quality of the professional advice, make the investigation faster, ensure the rights of the defence, foster the investigation of the public prosecutor and avoid questioning during the debate in front of the court.

There is an abundance of digital forensic tools, which vary in quality. LEAs and digital forensic professionals should work with the best available tools. Considering the large number of available tools on the market it is necessary to validate and certificate digital forensic tools, and/or validation of specific features of these tools to determine if a tool is legitimate to use during an investigation. Certification for tools is required to determine if a tool is legitimate to use during investigation. It is necessary to subject tools to validation procedures and to introduce certification. It is furthermore necessary to document what process was followed during the collection of electronic evidence, i.e. require proper documentation of what process was followed during the evidence gathering. Digital forensic tools require rigorous testing prior to use to catch bugs before they negatively impact a digital investigation. Some such datasets have been made available, including the Digital Forensic Tool Testing (DFTT) project, the NIST Computer Forensic Reference Data Sets (CFReDS) and the Digital Corpora project. Certification for tools is required to determine if a tool is legitimate to use during investigation or introduce a process certification, requiring proper documentation of what process was followed during the collection of electronic evidence. Each test must be accompanied by the following information:

- author of the test;
- date of the test;
- aim of the test;
- expected findings;
- equipment used to perform the test.

Test results must be repeatable and reproducible to be considered reliable from a scientific point of view. Digital forensics test results are repeatable when it is possible to get the same results using the same methods and starting from the same testing framework. Dual-method, or dual-tool, verification is the practice of using more than one method to verify data extracted. In doing so, a comparison is made between the two data sets to conclude the accuracy and precision of the data. While this practice may seem advantageous to determine the quality of evidence, there are also a few main limitations, as discussed in the following points. Dual-method, or dual-tool verification is not a substitute for method validation. It may allow further confidence in evidence obtained via either method, but only if they are known to operate independently of one another. Method validation on both tools should be conducted if possible. Validation and certification of digital forensic tools and process documentation during the collection of electronic evidence is necessary. The tools catalogue developed by the EVIDENCE project can be used as a system for the validation of tools.

There is a limited recognition for the digital forensics profession that includes a lack of standardised training. Professionalisation on international, national and regional level is required. Effective police and judicial cooperation requires broader, international and regional standardisation efforts. Therefore, the establishment of regional Forensic Science Regulators would be recommended, particularly a European Forensic Science Regulator. Standardisation should refrain from hampering innovation and advances and should involve all stakeholders. Training should include updated knowledge investigations of cloud environments and mobile devices. National Forensic Science Regulators and an overarching European Forensic Science Regulator to standardise training of digital forensic professionals should be established.

To achieve a certain level of professionalisation within the field of digital forensics it is necessary to provide for accreditation of digital forensics labs. Accreditation will address standardisation and professionalisation of current practices and ensure that labs and the processes they implement meet certain pre-determined quality levels. Furthermore, new standards that are more applicable to forensic science in general and/or convert existing ISO/IEC guidelines on digital forensics into standards are also suggested to further professionalise the field. Standards and procedures for accreditation of digital forensic labs should be established.

18.5 Conclusion

In the digitalised world we live in there is an increase in the use of electronic evidence in criminal proceedings. Evidence in criminal cases is collected by enforcement authorities, preserved and used in criminal proceedings and possibly exchanged (cross-border) between authorities. To effectively prosecute crimes, law enforcement authorities must adapt to rapidly developing technologies by working with electronic evidence generated by these new technologies and by using digital technologies themselves to collect evidence. There is no comprehensive EU legal framework regarding electronic evidence and law enforcement is left to operate in a patchwork of solutions. Existing legislative and enforcement frameworks and the concepts enshrined therein, as well as data protection concepts precede the creation of the internet as we know today and do not satisfactorily deal with the realities of technological developments. Considering the very nature of electronic evidence and rapidly evolving technologies and crimes it is important to act now and to address the challenges within the current system by realising a Common European Framework for the collection, preservation, use and exchange of electronic evidence to improve the efficiency of investigations and judicial procedures while maintaining adequate safeguards aimed at protecting relevant fundamental human rights and respecting clear standards of conduct.

These challenges must be addressed to reach the following objectives:

- **Objective 1: Enhanced law enforcement**;
- **Objective 2: Further research**;
- **Objective 3: Enhanced legal provisions**;
- **Objective 4: Enhanced exchange**;
- **Objective 5: Enhanced trust**;
- **Objective 6: Enhanced technical standards**;
- **Objective 7: Enhanced legal framework**;
- **Objective 8: Enhanced policies**;
- **Objective 9: Enhanced law enforcement**;
- **Objective 10: Professionalisation in the field of digital forensics**.

To reach these objectives, actions should be taken on a short, medium or long term that must be taken together for changes to the current system of handling electronic evidence to be more effective.

The **short-term solutions** address two objectives: enhanced law enforcement and further research. Enhancing law enforcement is the major objective of this Roadmap considering that LEAs are the most important actors involved with electronic evidence. Law enforcement needs to work with the rules and procedures provided to them by law- and policymakers. Most of the law enforcement challenges, which are plentiful, would primarily find a solution through legislative and/ or policy action. However, there are also other measures that can be taken to enhance law enforcement. This includes improving the MLA procedure on a short term by enhancing international coordinated investigations and joint investigation teams (JITs). It furthermore includes addressing the negative impact of legislation and lack of transparency by keeping clear records of investigation procedures, drafting SOPs which bridge the gap between reality and legislation and by building bridges across sectors, particularly between the public and private sector by achieving an adequate level of 'forensic readiness' of the private sector.

Certain areas require further research before they can be addressed in the Common European Framework as there are too many uncertainties regarding these topics. A better understanding of these challenges is necessary to provide clear and effective legal, policy, technical and other recommendations, which can be included in the Common European Framework. This includes research concerning constitutional limitations, data retention, the negative impact of legislation, crypto-currencies, the Internet of Things, cloud computing, technical solutions for admissibility, improving investigative techniques and best practices.

The **medium-term solutions** address four objectives: enhanced legal provisions, enhanced exchange, enhanced trust and enhanced technical standards. Enhancing certain legal provisions, particularly investigative measures, which pose a challenge, should be addressed as soon as possible for these legal provisions to be taken forward in the Common European Framework. There is a general lack of specific investigative measures and not all methods sufficiently cover the specific nature of electronic evidence collection. A more specific legal basis to collect electronic evidence is necessary, particularly to avoid admissibility issues in cross-border cases. A common European framework for the systematic and uniform application of new technologies in the collection, use and exchange of electronic evidence should thus include specific, clear and precise investigative measures in the collection of electronic evidence. This includes a legal distinction between physical and electronic evidence, lawful interception, computer-assisted search, seizure and preservation and storage. These specific investigative measures must be addressed to provide more clarity, legal certainty and authority for LEAs in certain areas. The provisions may be drafted or amended on a medium term to provide a legal basis and can be included in the enhanced legal framework on the longer term.

To facilitate law enforcement and make investigations more efficient exchange should be enhanced as soon as possible. MLA procedures are not adapted to the realities of today's crimes that are increasingly global, complex and fleeting and heavily impact the potential for rapid and efficient transfers of electronic evidence. Digitisation of the MLA procedure (request and forwarding of evidence) is necessary to address the challenge. Solutions provided by e-MLA, as well as the EVIDENCE project are recommended in this regard.

All actions cannot be addressed without the support of all actors and stakeholders involved. It is not sufficient to enhance legislation, law enforcement and technical standards. For the Common European Framework to be effective enhanced trust is necessary, particularly enhanced trust in the judiciary. Ethical and social issues should therefore be addressed and acted upon to enhance trust among actors, for example, by awareness raising aimed at the judiciary and aimed at the media and citizens and by improving dialogue among actors. This should be complemented by addressing the lack of technical knowledge, experience and training within the judiciary by coordinated European training programmes and improved education.

An important part of the Common European Framework includes enhancing technical standards. Technical action includes a proposed standard for representing data and metadata involved in the exchange process and formal languages for their representation, a Digital Forensic Tools Catalogue, introduction of a cloud platform for implementing the exchange process and a Proof of Concept application on the electronic evidence exchange, persistence and support for maintaining a detailed chain of custody. These technical solutions should address the technical challenges identified in this Roadmap to improve the efficiency of investigations and exchange.

The **long-term solutions** address four objectives: enhanced legal framework, enhanced policies, enhanced law enforcement and professionalisation in the field of digital forensics. By addressing the long-term solutions all previous objectives will come together and finalise the Common European Framework. Law and policies will be modernised and law enforcement facilitated.

The enhanced legal framework should address the legislative gap concerning the collection, preservation, use and exchange of electronic evidence. Existing legislative and enforcement frameworks and the concepts enshrined therein, as well as data protection concepts, precede the creation of the internet as we know today and do not satisfactory deal with the realities of technological developments and with the dynamic nature of modern investigations. The Roadmap provides actions for modernising and harmonising legislation and policy, including international law and treaties and for operational guidelines and SOPs as standards on the procedures and modalities to follow in the phase of collection, preservation and exchange of electronic evidence, which ensure proportionality between protection of privacy and infringements for legitimate crime prevention and control. This includes action as regards data collected by the private sector by further building on the forensic readiness of the private sector, building bridges and improving dialogue across sectors as well as drafting and adopting clear rules as regards transfer of data from the private sector and handling of electronic evidence by the private sector and regulation of a standard (secured) format for delivering data to LEAs from the private sector to enhance cooperation between the public and private sector. It also includes addressing the lack of uniform European standards to aid investigations in criminal cases and facilitate the process of exchange. A Common European Framework for the systematic and uniform application of new technologies in the collection, preservation, use and exchange of electronic evidence should be based on clear and specific rules for the collection of electronic evidence, common definitions and standards and approximation of legal procedures. The framework should furthermore be fit-for-purpose to keep up with rapidly developing technologies and to cover the specific nature of electronic evidence collection. Investigative measures can have a high impact on the suspect's fundamental rights, especially in a digital environment, which allows gathering (personal) information through different channels. Consequently, there must be a balance between effective law enforcement on the one hand and proper protection of citizens' fundamental rights on the other hand. While realising the Common European Framework the opportunity should be taken to address specific challenges such as cloud computing, admissibility, data collected by SIS (actionable intelligence), transfer and exchange, data retention and virtual currencies. All the actions proposed in the Roadmap should lead to modernisation and harmonisation of legislation and policy, including international law and treaties and adapting it to new technologies. The challenges identified in this Roadmap cannot be addressed without clear policies reflecting the objectives to enhance legislation, law enforcement, trust and technical standards.

LEAs are left to operate in a field of patchwork solutions and playing catch up and manoeuvering their way through a highly uncertain and politically sensitive landscape filled with legal lacunae. Most of the law enforcement challenges, which are plentiful, would primarily find a solution through legislative and/ or policy action. However, there are several actions that can be taken within the LEA community and the digital forensics community. An enhanced enforcement scheme should include many elements to address the law enforcement challenges, such as access to tools and training, solutions for law enforcement databases and uniform guidelines on handling electronic evidence. Improving law enforcement should furthermore be achieved by professionalisation in the field of digital forensics.

Professionalisation in the sub-discipline of digital forensics is necessary to achieve a certain level of professionalism and recognition within this young field. This requires standardisation efforts, reassessing potential regulation of digital forensics professions to ensure that practitioners meet a certain standard, validation of tool to ensure they are fit-for-purpose and accreditation for digital forensic labs to ensure that they meet certain pre-determined quality levels. Professionalisation in the field of digital forensics will complement law enforcement.

18.6 The EVIDENCE Road Map and the Future of Electronic Evidence in Europe

Table 18.2 shows the relationship between the objectives identified into the EVIDENCE Road map and the existing initiatives touching upon the electronic evidence domain. The matching of the EVIDENCE road map objectives with the goals of other Initiatives at EU level are described.

Because of this description, it is to be pointed out that some initiatives touch directly on the objectives of the EVIDENCE road map. It seems that time is enough mature for facing those issues related to enhancing exchange and legal provisions, as well as for taking care of LEAS operational issues. Also, trust and technical standards are considered by some initiatives. Certainly, these activities involve some future research work to produce further developments and achievements, while the focus on professionalisation in the field of digital forensics is still very low.

The important link of the EVIDENCE Roadmap with other complementary initiatives, such as e-Codex is now well established and formalised considering that the EVIDENCE2e-Codex Project and the EXEC- Electronic Xchange of e-Evidences with e-CODEX project, are now financed by EC (e-Justice Programme calls) and will kick off their activities in 2018. These two new initiatives will aim at bringing together and put into practise the EVIDENCE results and achievements as stated into the Road map by means of the e-Codex secured and trusted infrastructure to allow the implementation of the EIO and the exchange of evidence among different Member States.

A part from the various projects running in the EU contexts it is to be noted that the EVIDENCE Road Map is now formally linked also to the institutional activities carried out on electronic evidence by the European Commission and the Council.

The most important ones are the e-Evidence Project on the realisation of an online platform for the Exchange of EIO requests and evidence (e-Justice DG)[21] and

[21]See chapter *Present and future of the exchange of electronic evidence in Europe* by M. A. Biasiotti.

Table 18.2 Relationship between the objectives identified into the EVIDENCE Road map and the existing initiatives related to the electronic evidence domain

Project/initiative	Coordinated by	Topic	EVIDENCE RoadMap objectives
EVIDENCE	CNR-ITTIG, Institute of Legal Information Theory and Techniques of the National Research Council of Italy	Electronic evidence handling and exchange cross-border cooperation	All objectives
e-EVIDENCE	European Commission Directorate-General for Justice and Consumers	European Investigation Order (EIO), Electronic evidence exchange, Reference Implementation Portal	– Objective 2: Further research; – Objective 3: Enhanced legal provisions; – Objective 4: Enhanced exchange; – Objective 5: Enhanced trust; – Objective 6: Enhanced technical standards; – Objective 7: Enhanced legal framework; – Objective 8: Enhanced policies
EVIDENCE2e-CODEX	CNR-ITTIG, Institute of Legal Information Theory and Technicques of the National research Council of Italy	Electronic evidence exchange, EIO and MLA e-Codex Infrastructure	– Objective 1: Enhanced law enforcement; – Objective 2: Further research; – Objective 3: Enhanced legal provisions; – Objective 4: Enhanced exchange; – Objective 5: Enhanced trust; – Objective 6: Enhanced technical standards; – Objective 7: Enhanced legal framework; – Objective 8: Enhanced policies; – Objective 9: Enhanced law enforcement

(continued)

Table 18.2 (continued)

Project/initiative	Coordinated by	Topic	EVIDENCE RoadMap objectives
EXEC	Ministry of Justice of Austria	Exchange European Investigation Orders (EIO) and related e-Evidences fully electronically	– Objective 3: Enhanced legal provisions; – Objective 4: Enhanced exchange; – Objective 5: Enhanced trust; – Objective 6: Enhanced technical standards; – Objective 7: Enhanced legal framework; – Objective 8: Enhanced policies
me-CODEX	Ministry of Justice of North Rhine-Westphalia, Germany	Maintenance of the infrastructure realized by the e-Codex Project	– Objective 4: Enhanced exchange; – Objective 5: Enhanced trust
e-CODEX	Ministry of Justice of North Rhine-Westphalia, Germany	Cross-border e-Justice in Europe	– Objective 4: Enhanced exchange; – Objective 5: Enhanced trust
e-MLA	INTERPOL	Mutual Legal Assistance Requests Forms	– Objective 1: Enhanced law enforcement; – Objective 3: Enhanced legal provisions
MLA Tool	UNODOC	Mutual Legal Assistance Requests Forms drafting	– Objective 1: Enhanced law enforcement; – Objective 3: Enhanced legal provisions
Cybercrime Programme	Council of Europe	International Cooperation, Cybercrime, Electronic evidence treatment and exchange	– Objective 1: Enhanced law enforcement; – Objective 2: Further research; – Objective 3: Enhanced legal provisions; – Objective 4: Enhanced exchange; – Objective 7: Enhanced legal framework; – Objective 8: Enhanced policies

(continued)

Table 18.2 (continued)

Project/initiative	Coordinated by	Topic	EVIDENCE RoadMap objectives
ASGARD-ANALYSIS SYSTEM FOR GATHERED RAW DATA	Vicomtech-IK4 Visual Interaction and Communication Technologies	Tool set for the extraction, fusion, exchange and analysis of Big Data including cyber-offenses data for forensic investigation	– Objective 1: Enhanced law enforcement; – Objective 2: Further research; – Objective 4: Enhanced exchange; – Objective 6: Enhanced technical standards; – Objective 7: Enhanced legal framework; – Objective 9: Enhanced law enforcement; – Objective 10: Professionalisation in the field of digital forensics.
e-CRIME	TRILATERAL RESEARCH & CONSULTING LLP	Economic impacts of cyber crime	– Objective 1: Enhanced law enforcement; – Objective 2: Further research; – Objective 3: Enhanced legal provisions; – Objective 8: Enhanced policies
GIFT	Netherlands Forensic Institute	Forensic toolbox for CBRN incidents	– Objective 1: Enhanced law enforcement; – Objective 2: Further research; – Objective 10: Professionalisation in the field of digital forensics; – Objective 6: Enhanced technical standards
e-SENS	Ministry of Justice of North Rhine-Westphalia, Germany	Cross-border Public services, EU digital single market	– Objective 2: Further research; – Objective 3: Enhanced legal provisions; – Objective 4: Enhanced exchange; – Objective 5: Enhanced trust

(continued)

Table 18.2 (continued)

Project/initiative	Coordinated by	Topic	EVIDENCE RoadMap objectives
LASIE	Engineering – Ingegneria Informatica Spa	Forensic tools, data extraction, electronic evidence	– Objective 1: Enhanced law enforcement; – Objective 2: Further research; – Objective 3: Enhanced legal provisions; – Objective 4: Enhanced exchange; – Objective 10: Professionalisation in the field of digital forensics.
SIIP- Speaker Identification Integrated Project	VERINT	Suspect identification solution based on a novel Speaker Identification (SID) engine and Global Info Sharing Mechanism (GISM)	– Objective 1: Enhanced law enforcement; – Objective 2: Further research; – Objective 6: Enhanced technical standards; – Objective 8: Enhanced policies

the *Inception act Assessment*, for a legislative proposal on *Improving cross-border access to electronic evidence in criminal matters.*[22]

The latter initiative aims to address obstacles in cross-border access to electronic evidence in criminal investigations. Access should become more efficient and faster, while ensuring at the same time transparency and accountability, a high level of protection of fundamental rights including individuals' rights in criminal proceedings, data protection and privacy. It aims at the same time to ensure legal certainty by eliminating or at least reducing fragmentation and conflicts of law. It would also provide an alternative to data localisation requirements that could be imposed by Member States if data in other Member States is too difficult to access.

The impact assessment will develop various policy options based on further analysis, focusing particularly on the following possible measures at EU level.

1. A legal framework authorising authorities to directly request or compel a service provider in another Member State to disclose e-evidence processed in the Union, including appropriate safeguards and conditions. This framework can leave to the discretion of the service provider a decision on whether to provide a response ("production request") or can obligate service providers to respond ("production order"). This could also be considered with respect to service providers located

[22]Inception Impact Assessment (Ares(2017)3896097), available at https://ec.europa.eu/info/law/better-regulation/initiatives/ares-2017-3896097_en.

outside of the Union and/or data stored outside of the Union. This system could be complemented by an obligation for service providers established in third countries but offering services in the EU to designate a legal representative in the EU for cooperation based on production requests/orders.
2. A legal framework for law enforcement to access e-evidence pursuant to a set of safeguards and measures to mitigate cross-border effects, without cooperation of a service provider or the owner of the data, through a seized device or an information system. This could also be considered with respect to data whose storage place is not known or data that is stored outside of the Union.
3. A legal framework to provide for a common understanding of types of electronic evidence and service providers that fall within the scope of the measures proposed.
4. Initiating negotiations with key partner countries such as the U.S. to enable reciprocal cross-border access to electronic evidence, particularly on content data, and including appropriate safeguards.
5. Assessing the role of the EU towards the Council of Europe Budapest Convention on Cybercrime, in view of the negotiations on a second Additional Protocol to the Convention.

The above cited points of the Inception Impact Assessment are objectives that are common to what is stated into the EVIDENCE Road map.

Furthermore, in the Data collection paragraph of the *Inception Impact Assessment* the reference and link to the EVIDENCE project achievements and results is clearly stated whereas the document says "*…The Commission has conducted an expert consultation starting in July 2016 and issued in September 2016 a questionnaire to Member States. …Furthermore, many studies have been conducted on the problem of access to evidence across borders, including the recently concluded and EU-funded EVIDENCE project, which provides further data for the impact assessment*."

So, the EVIDENCE Project Roadmap is now formally linked to the European Commission Strategy on Security and in the EC initiatives on the electronic evidence domain and cross border access to electronic evidence. It is necessary now to concretely put in practise the exchange of electronic evidence in EU by putting together all the initiatives that are going on and aligning them to the unique and common final goal.

Reference

Aulitano S (2016) E-evidence in the European Union. In: De Zan T, Aulitano S (eds) EUnited Against Crime: Improving Criminal Justice in European Union Cyberspace, IAI Documents, 16–17 November 2016

MIX
Papier aus verantwortungsvollen Quellen
Paper from responsible sources
FSC® C105338

If you have any concerns about our products,
you can contact us on
ProductSafety@springernature.com

In case Publisher is established outside the EU,
the EU authorized representative is:
Springer Nature Customer Service Center GmbH
Europaplatz 3, 69115 Heidelberg, Germany

Printed by Libri Plureos GmbH
in Hamburg, Germany